Doll's Houses

Doll's Houses

Beryl Armstrong
Headley Holgate & Pamela Ruddock
Ellen Bedington

Grange Books

A QUANTUM BOOK

Published by Grange Books
an imprint of Grange Books Plc
The Grange
Kingsnorth Industrial Estate
Hoo, nr. Rochester
Kent ME3 9ND
www.grangebooks.co.uk

This edition printed 2001

1-84013-434-8

QUMMDH

This book is Produced by
Quantum Publishing Ltd
6 Blundell Street
London N7 9BH

Printed in Singapore by
Star Standard Industries (Pte) Ltd

Acknowledgments
Sincere thanks for the loan of their doll's houses are due to Barbara Herrington, Vivienne Kay, Clare Milligan, Anne Pollack and Stella Thomas. Thanks also to Valma and Paul Martin, who helped supply the building materials when needed. The publishers would also like to extend special thanks to Lionel Barnard of The Mulberry Bush, Brighton, Sussex, and Dijon Ltd, Heathfield, Sussex for the loan of the doll's house furniture used in the photographs in the Dolls section.

CONTENTS

DOLL'S HOUSES	**6**
Getting Started	8
Materials	20
Making a Box	24
Making the Framework	28
The Staircase	33
Adding the Room Dividers	38
Hanging the Doors	40
Wallpapering	45
Wiring your Doll's House	50
Windows	58
The Roof	64
The Front-Opening Doors	68
Finishing the Interior	74
Finishing the Outside	82
DOLL'S HOUSE FURNITURE	**93**
Kitchen Table	100
Kitchen Bench	105
Pine Corner Cupboard	108
Pine Hanging Shelves	112
Bed	117
Bedside Table	121
Chest of Drawers	124
Dressing Table	129
Doll's House	134
Cradle	136
Screens	138
Regency Dining Table	140
Chairs	146
Sideboard	151
Bookshelves	158
Desk	162
Occasional Table	168
Chesterfield Sofa	175
DOLL'S HOUSE DOLLS	**179**
A Shoulder-Plate Doll	182
A Flange-Neck Doll	190
Using a Mould	195
Modelling a Doll	205
Victorian Lady	210
Grandmother	216
Victorian Man	221
Victorian Girl	234
Sailor Boy	240
Cook	245
Pilot	251

DOLL'S HOUSES

Everyone makes mistakes when they are trying a new skill, and the best results are always achieved when we learn from each other.

Too often, though, experts seem to forget the multitude of problems that confront newcomers to a hobby, and making doll's houses is no exception. As a result, I learned mainly by trial and error. My book, therefore, assumes that you are creating your first doll's house and explains many of the initial problems that other books do not mention; at the same time it offers some useful tips and ideas for more experienced makers. Because there are always several ways to approach each step, the alternatives and the pros and cons of each are explained. It is for you to choose the method that best suits your temperament, ability and aims. The house can then truly be said to be your very own.

The brief underlying this book was to make a house that would have universal appeal. I decided that the completed house would be weather-boarded, a finish that is widely used and can cover many architectural styles – a hideaway cabin, a chalet, a country cottage, a town house, a Tudor manor or a wealthy merchant's residence.

My original plans were changed and updated frequently during the building as I developed more practical methods of achieving different effects or found ways of giving the house more aesthetic appeal. Do not be afraid to experiment or use your instinct for creation. This is your house, and I can only guide you through the building stages.

Specialist miniaturist suppliers are not always within easy reach, so, with few exceptions, I have used basic materials throughout. Someone, somewhere is no doubt selling every conceivable, ready-made item for use in building a doll's house, but if cost and self-satisfaction are important, no aspect is too difficult to undertake yourself, even if you are a newcomer to the hobby.

I am not a professional. I have made the same mistakes that you are likely to make. Most of the tools I use are basic do-it-yourself tools that are found in most houses, but home-made gadgets are cheap and invaluable. Problem solving while creating each building is part of the fun.

Before you embark on making your first doll's house, you should heed the warning: "Doll's houses become addictive!"

You may decide to make a doll's house because you remember the one you had as a child; because you have fond memories of granny's old home; because you want to design the home of your dreams; or because you have an urge to create. Whatever your reason, working with miniatures will stretch your imagination and tax your ingenuity. Modelmaking is a craft, but one that everyone can enjoy.

BERYL ARMSTRONG

OPPOSITE The completed doll's house that is built, stage by stage, in this book.

GETTING STARTED

The choice of style is almost infinite. You can make anything from a simple box room to a large mansion, and doll's houses can be built to represent every architectural period. Each country has its own architecture and history from which you can draw inspiration.

Most of the commercially made furnishings that used to be available were Victorian, but as the popularity of Tudor, Georgian and 1930s styles grew, manufacturers and suppliers have adapted to the new market. Someone, somewhere will be making whatever you need, either the items themselves in miniature perfection or the specialist materials needed to make them.

Study the craft magazines, explore the shops and attend as many of the doll's house exhibitions and fairs as you can. You will gradually find a path through the maze. If you have one nearby, join a club. The friendly, cooperative atmosphere in the doll's house world is wonderful, and clubs and workshops are becoming increasingly widespread, although some areas are less well served than others.

Study as many different architectural styles as you can until you find one that appeals to you. The real *aficionados* of the doll's house world choose a date and collect only the items that are authentic to that particular time. Most of us, however, are more likely to have a favourite style

RIGHT The imposing Queen Anne mansion was made from a basic kit.

ABOVE This house started life long ago as a child's toy, and what was a derelict building has been transformed into a Tudor hall.

RIGHT The San Francisco house was built with a rear opening because its frontage is so elaborate.

6
THE
LAURELS

OPPOSITE The original house has been extended, just as we add extensions to our modern homes.

of architecture, which we will furnish, as we do with our own houses, with whatever takes our fancy to give an overall pleasing effect.

Deciding on the size is important. The standard gauge for miniatures is 1:12 – i.e., 1 in (2.5 cm) to 1 ft (30 cm) – and when you come to furnish your doll's house and people it with dolls, you will find that commercially made items and kits are made to that scale. Do you want to make one

ABOVE The Bavarian chalet was created from a wooden wine box and was actually built in Bavaria.

LEFT The Victorian street scene was intended as one long building, but before assembly it was divided into a separate shop and a house for easy transport.

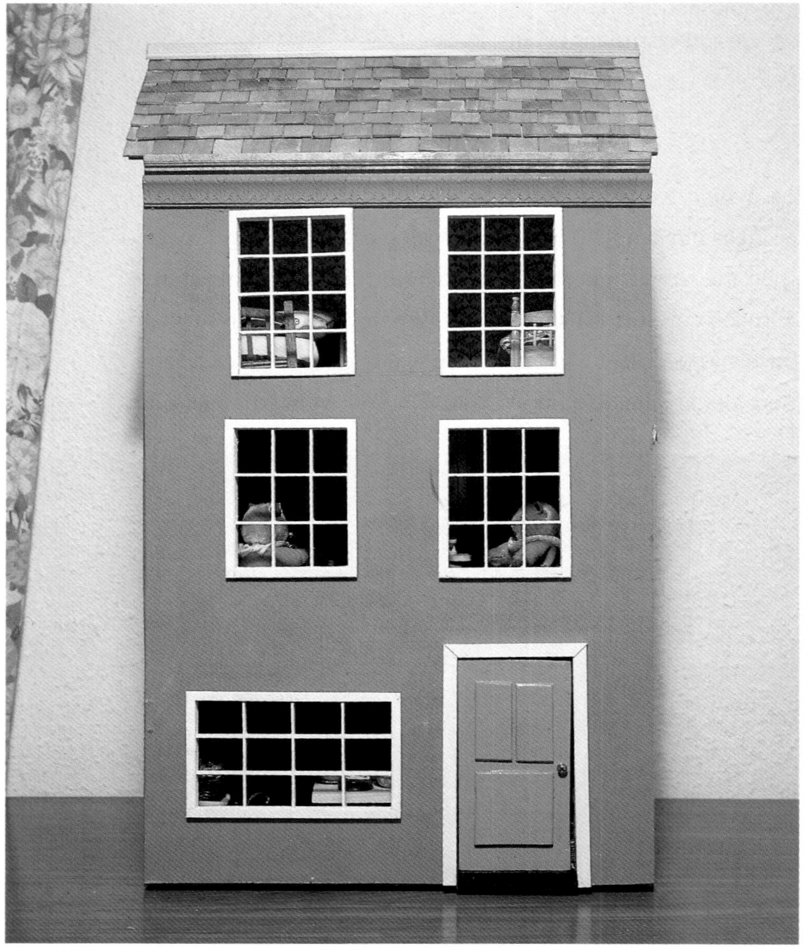

LEFT West Green Manor evolved from a plan for an eight-room house into a 15-room mansion during the building. No aspect of building a doll's house is too difficult, even for a newcomer to the hobby.

ABOVE All doll's houses are based on a simple box shape.

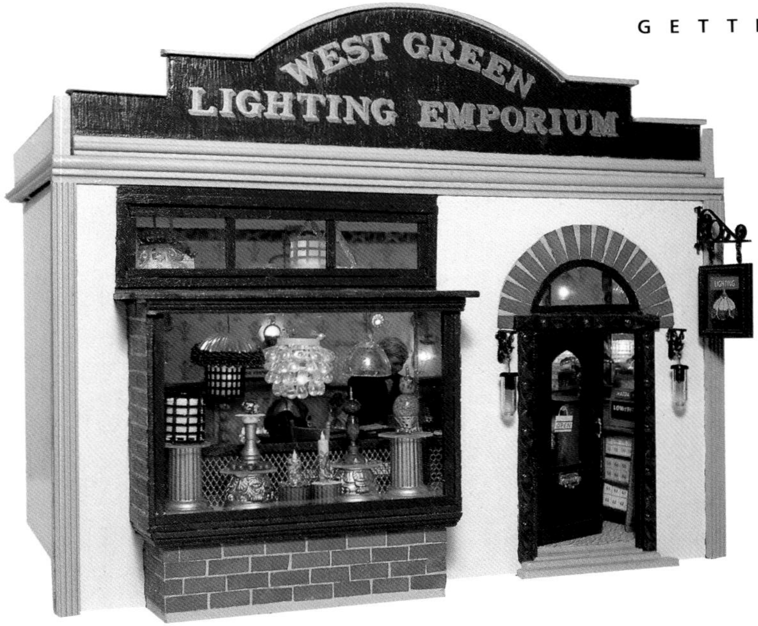

single room or a 20-room mansion? It is all very well allowing your original plans to evolve, as my first house, West Green Manor did, from eight rooms to 15, but you must think of the consequences. Do you have sufficient space to house such a large building? A doll's house as large as West Green Manor is likely to end up homeless if it is intended as a family heirloom.

If you live in a small house or flat, single box rooms or miniature shops and pubs are more practical, and they look most attractive when stored on shelves. Another consideration is that ambitiously large projects need more building space, whereas the construction of a single box can be undertaken on the kitchen table.

ABOVE AND RIGHT Shops and pubs have great creative potential.

ABOVE AND RIGHT Miniature scenes set in picture frames are perfect if your home is too small to accommodate a full-scale doll's house.

LEFT These models have been painted to accentuate the different styles of roofs. The shape you choose will govern the height of your tallest walls.

Do It Yourself

No kit or ready-built house will fully meet your expectations, and by the time you have re-designed much of the detail you will be left with little more than a basic box. Even if you have no experience whatsoever, doing everything yourself still seems to be the best solution. Several firms sell plans, but if you study enough doll's houses you will see that you can start with a simple box shape and elaborate on the basic design as you gain experience.

If the task seems daunting, it is worth bearing in mind that most doll's house additions such as window frames, doors, shutters, bricks and tiles, are all commercially available. If you have a strong image of your house in mind, you will probably find that to make it exactly right you will want to build all the details yourself.

Planning Ahead

Have you chosen the style and size of the house you wish to build? If you cannot find a printed picture of your ideal, draw a rough sketch of how you imagine it might look. Now draw this house to a conveniently reduced scale on a sheet of graph paper, remembering to draw it from all perspectives. The design will depend on whether you want gables and, if so, whether they are to be at either end, in the centre front or to one side. How many floors do you want to include? Do you want a flat roof, or one that is pitched or hipped, or would you prefer a mansard style? Will there be additional windows at the side or the back?

What size are the rooms to be and how many? Do not make them too small. Even the 12 × 12 in (30 × 30 cm) rooms in West Green Manor are not really large enough to give scope for exciting furnishings.

These five graphs show the dimensions of the house from all sides. You must draw a scale plan of your house on graph paper before you start building.

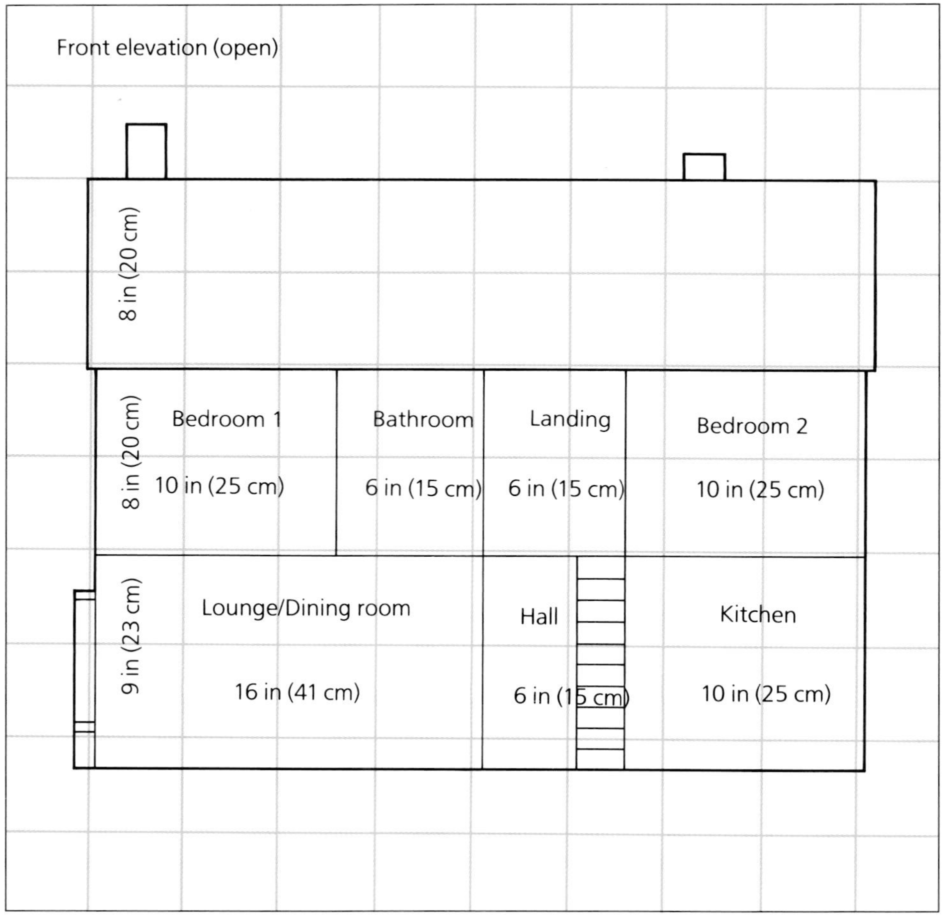

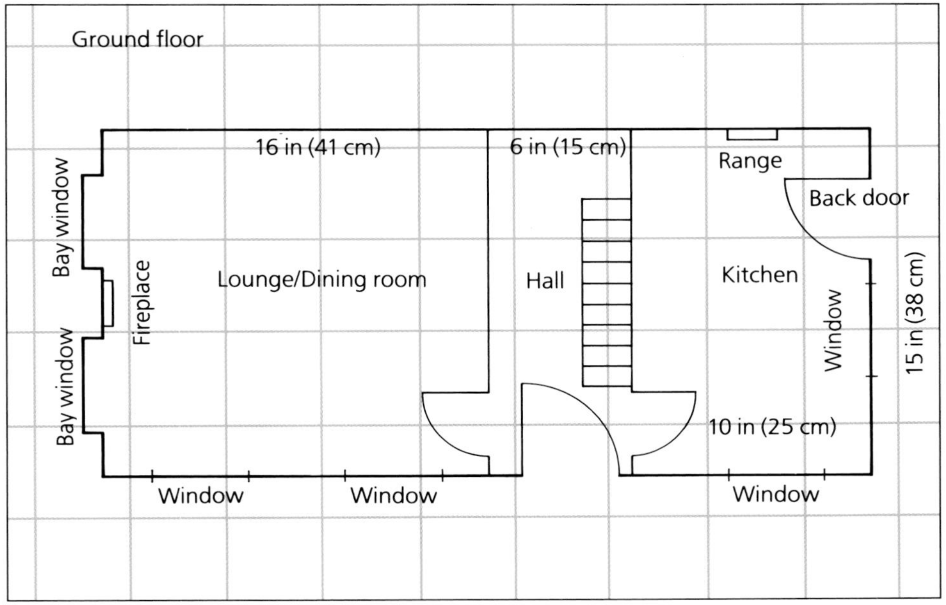
Ground floor
16 in (41 cm)
6 in (15 cm)
Range
Back door
Bay window
Bay window
Fireplace
Lounge/Dining room
Hall
Kitchen
Window
15 in (38 cm)
10 in (25 cm)
Window
Window
Window

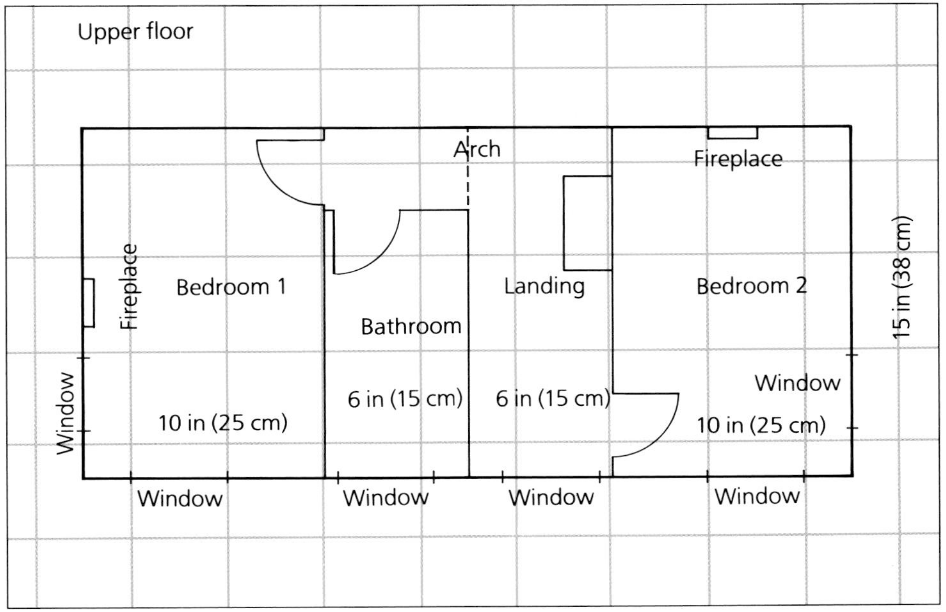
Upper floor
Arch
Fireplace
Fireplace
Bedroom 1
Landing
Bedroom 2
15 in (38 cm)
Bathroom
Window
Window
6 in (15 cm)
6 in (15 cm)
10 in (25 cm)
10 in (25 cm)
Window
Window
Window
Window

Left side wall
Right side wall

ABOVE Staggered stairs need an enlarged stairwell, which takes away half the usable floor space. However, twisted stairs are sometimes essential if the hall is tiny.

LEFT A small room offers less space for creative furnishings.

Another factor that you need to take into account when you are planning the overall dimensions is that a doll's house needs to be at least 15 in (38 cm) deep to accommodate a straight staircase with 3 in (7.5 cm) wide doors off the hall to the rooms. Entrance halls and upper landings can provide interesting areas to furnish without enlarging the overall size of the baseboard. If you want staggered stairs, you will lose half the floorspace so if this is your first doll's house, it is advisable to make a straight staircase – it won't be such a strain on your nervous system.

ABOVE You might consider placing the staircase in a large room if you need to reduce the overall width of your building. Be careful when planning the depth of rooms – if they are too deep they are difficult to reach into without knocking things.

The large rooms in the Sussex farmhouse are 13½ in (34.5 cm) wide and 18 in (46 cm) deep. If they are too deep, you will have problems reaching the back, so 14 × 15 in (35.5 × 36 cm) is a good compromise. This size gives you scope to divide a room – to create a small bathroom or night nursery, for example. The hallways need to be at least 7½ in (19 cm) wide if you have more than two floors, which requires double staircases, but 5½ in (14 cm) is sufficient for two-storey houses.

If space is really at a premium, you can sacrifice the landing room by having a half-flight, with the next flight doubling back. This will need a hallway that is only 5 in (12.5 cm) wide. In such circumstances you might decide not to have a hall or landing at all, but instead, to site the staircase in a living room so that you can keep a single flight of stairs.

The height of the rooms will range between 8 in (20 cm) and 10 in (25 cm). Remember that the main rooms will be larger and have higher ceilings than basements or attics.

Another question you must consider at the outset is how and where you want to guide your lighting wires. The wiring is probably something you do not even want to think about when you haven't started to build a house, but it is an aspect that you should consider at the outset. It is both easy and safe to install the lighting when you know the basics.

However anxious you are to make a start, do not skimp on the planning stages, because they will save you hours of unnecessary alterations and wasted wood. When I first started to make doll's houses I did not think far enough ahead, and it cost money and effort to solve problems that would not have arisen had I thought out all the stages before I began.

When you have designed your house, draw the three sides, and the ground and upper floors to full size on sheets of brown paper and cut them out. These paper patterns are only a guide so they do not have to be accurate, but they will indicate the amount of wood you will need. Forget the front at this stage because the shell is the most important part.

MATERIALS

WOOD

Your next questions will probably be the same as mine were initially: what kind of wood? How thick should it be? How much will I need?

Thin plywood can vary considerably in quality, and to prevent splintering it is worth paying extra. Plywood is light in weight and easy to cut with a fine-toothed, sharp saw. Always cut with the side that it going to show uppermost so that any splintering along the edges can usually be hidden. A good sanding smooths down the rough edges.

When thin plywood is held with the grain running vertically it bends sideways. This is a useful characteristic if you need curved surfaces. Wrap thin, flexible ply around a former, then stick other layers on top until you have a wall of the required strength.

Wood that is only about ⅛ in (2–4 mm) thick is liable to warp on the grain. You should avoid thin ply for fixtures to which items such as screw rings for curtain rods or door hinges are to be fixed. It is just not deep enough for a screw or panel pin to bite on.

Medium density fibreboard (MDF) comes in standard thicknesses up to about ¾ in (18 mm); 1⁄16 in (2 mm) is too thin, but you will find that ¼ in (6 mm) is useful. Unlike hardboard, MDF has two shiny surfaces and is dense all through. It is comparatively cheap and extremely easy to cut

RIGHT Medium density fibreboard (MDF) has its supporters and its uses.

FAR RIGHT Plywood is available in many thicknesses and qualities.

and shape. Its disadvantages are that it generates a lot of dust when it is cut and sanded. Because it is softer board, you can only screw into it once – there is no bite for a second try. Also, the surface is apt to peel off if you have stuck a feature to it that comes under a lot of pressure – a small shelf that is often knocked, for example, or hinges on opening doors.

MDF is ideal for small buildings, baseboards or roofs if you cover it with bricks or tiles. It is a matter of taste whether you use it throughout for a large house, but if cost is of the essence or ease of cutting is important, then take the practical view and use it. The weight is similar to that of wood.

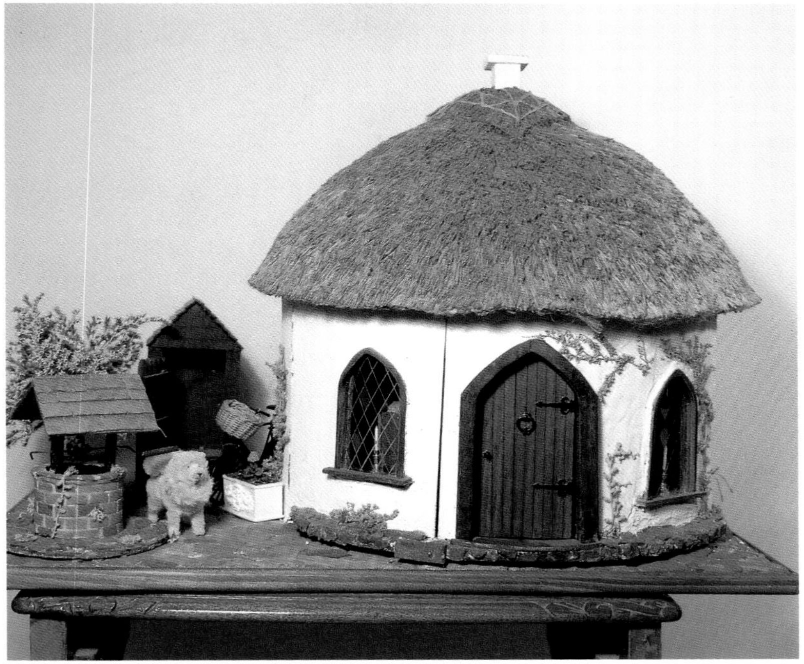

ABOVE Round houses are built by adding layers of thin, flexible plywood until the walls are strong.

LEFT Most doll's houses are built from woods like plywood and medium density fibreboard (MDF), which are widely available.

RIGHT Screws have many advantages over panel pins when it comes to holding a house in shape.

Birch ply is a quality wood, which is available in various standard thicknesses. It is smooth, makes good, strong doll's houses, rarely splinters and holds glue and screws firmly. Its only disadvantages are the price and the extra energy that is required for cutting. A good workable thickness is ¼ in (6 mm).

How much wood do you need? How big is your house? Ask your supplier what size sheets he stocks and which way the grain will lie. With string, mark out the sheet size on your house floor and lay the brown paper pattern inside this area to judge the quantity of wood you will need.

Screws

When I first started to make doll's houses, I was reluctant to glue any part permanently until I was 100 per cent certain that I wouldn't need to dismantle the house to add a feature that I had not foreseen. Even so, I had to resort to the mallet on several occasions to part a well-glued section.

While you are feeling your way in your first house you will no doubt screw and unscrew, trim, recut and rasp until you have a reasonable framework. This is tough on your hands and even more expensive in terms of screws.

The secret is to take two drill bits – one that is the thickness of the screw shank and the other, the pilot, a size smaller. Drill a full-depth hole with the thinner bit and a shallow hole, the length of the screw shank, with the other one. This will allow you to ease the screw in without tearing the wood and with less strain on your hands. It also enables you to remove and rescrew several times. If the hole becomes too big, a sliver of wood or matchstick will give an extra bite.

The recognized method of screwing into the end grain of wood, especially ply, is to insert a plug made of dowel on the flat side so that the screw is held in the strong side grain of the dowel. This is a useful tip to prevent hinges from tearing the plywood layers apart.

Brass screws are more expensive than steel ones and they are softer. Brass screws are not really suitable for door hinges because the heads can crumble under the constant strain, leaving you with an unsupported hinge.

Screws are expensive and you are bound to use more than you anticipate, so keep a good stock in various sizes. Thin screws are not so easy to find as those for normal household use.

Most experts suggest that you use panel pins. You may have problems though, as they are apt to bend over with the hammering or become so badly slanted that they come out of the side. When you are just starting, mistakes are bound to happen and it is more encouraging to know that the construction can be taken apart before the final gluing. Distorted walls caused by uneven cutting or warping can be forced into line and held in place with screws if they are not too far out of true.

Even after making many houses, I still find that screws are more practical than pins. It is easier to turn a screwdriver in confined spaces and in awkward corners than to raise a hammer.

General Tools

This list of tools may look formidable, but these items are really basic DIY tools similar to those used in the photographs. Even if you do not already have them around your home, they can be easily obtained from general hobby shops.

Expensive power tools, while useful, are definitely not essential. If you want to treat yourself, the vibratory fretsaw is probably the most versatile. Even the cheapest model is finger safe and has a long service life.

The 12-in (30-cm) frame, hand-held fretsaw is too unwieldy without a special table and, like the vibratory fretsaw, is too restrictive when it comes to cutting out windows. A frame around 6 in (15 cm) in size will involve fewer blade replacements and ensure a cooler temper! Even a small coping saw is adequate for many finer jobs.

Saws You will need the following saws to make the basic doll's house described here. A large saw for cutting sheets of wood; a small hobby saw for cutting trim – these usually come with replaceable blades; a small fretsaw or coping saw for carving shapes; and a keyhole or power jigsaw for cutting out areas too far inside the sheet for a fretsaw – for example, windows.

Knives A general-purpose craft knife can be used for many cutting and trimming tasks, while a hobby craft knife, which has a smaller blade, is useful for work in confined spaces. Both these knives have replaceable blades.

Drills A hand-turned or hobby power drill with all sizes of bits is needed for screw holes, especially for countersinking, and an Archimedes' drill for small pilot holes – for internal door hinges, for example – is invaluable.

LEFT A plug of dowel set into ply will hold screw hinges firmly and prevent them from tearing the plywood layers.

Files These are available in all shapes and sizes – flat, half-round, round, square, triangular and so on. Use whatever is available, but a large flat file and a set of small hobby files are the most useful.

Screwdrivers You will need a general selection of these in a range of sizes.

Extras You will also find that you will need the following at various stages: a bench vice, small clamps, tweezers, a mitre block, sandpaper, fine-grade steel wool, pencils, an accurate ruler and a wide steel ruler for a cutting edge.

Glues

The number of glues on the market has become bewildering, but if you buy three basic types you will cover most jobs: PVA white wood adhesive, which is water based; an all-purpose clear adhesive, which is spirit based; and a quick-drying contact adhesive – either general purpose or non-drip.

MAKING A BOX

Before you build a doll's house you should appreciate the principle of constructing a basic box. You may want to make a simple box room or a shop before you embark on a large building, which is, in effect, a series of boxes stacked together to form a house. The outside of a house is one large box divided into sections, called rooms.

The sides of your box should overlap the back, which should fit snugly between the two side walls but should be the same height. The base should fit between the walls and the back panel. This involves quite a tedious calculation, which needs time to master. Forget about the front-opening door for now.

Use ¼ in (6 mm) wood and no. 2 screws. The sides and back of the box need to be the same height; the side walls are ¼ in (6 mm) deeper than the baseboard, which is ½ in (12 mm) narrower than the roof and ¼ in (6 mm) less deep. The back panel is exactly the same width as the baseboard and the same height as the sides. The roof sits on top of the side walls and the back.

Because all ply is liable to warp, it is advisable to let the grain of the wood run vertically on upright sections and along the length of the longer, horizontal pieces. The direction of the grain is not as important with small, square sections.

Confused? Take heart, it isn't as complicated as it sounds. If you do not want a box room just yet, try making a small box to learn the basic principles, and keep it as a sample for future use.

You will probably find the diagram and illustrations clearer to follow than the written instructions.

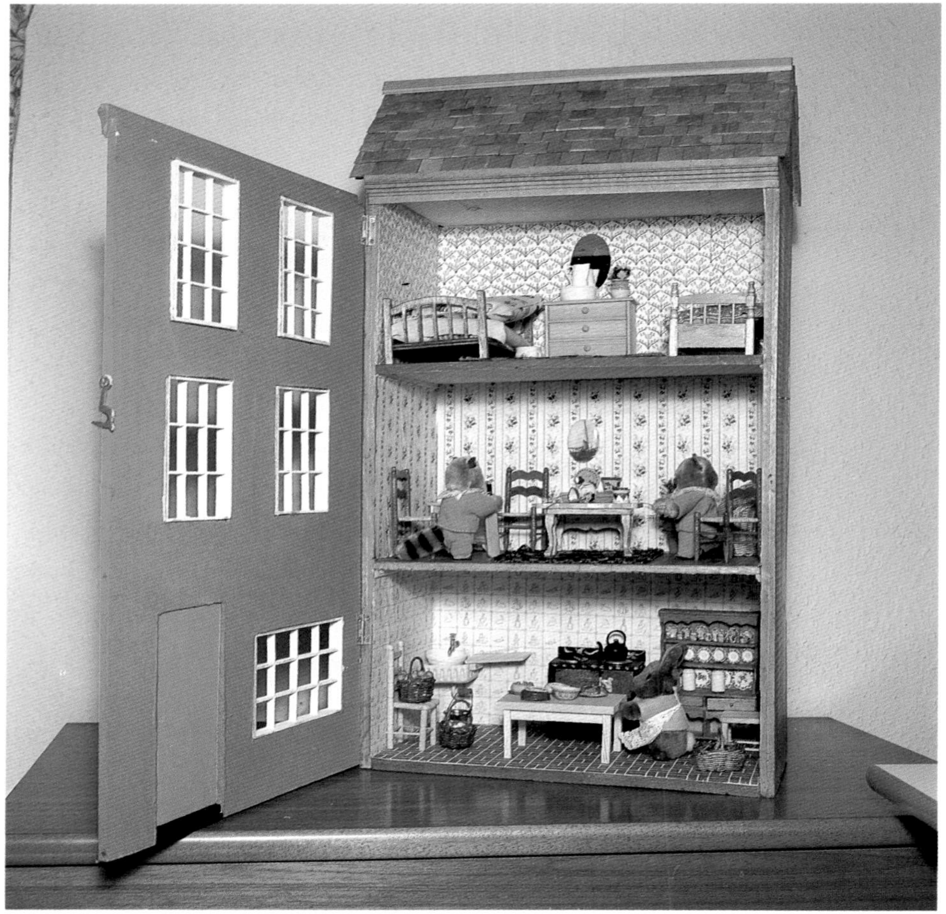

ABOVE All doll's houses are basically boxes divided into rooms. This example was built from an old wine box.

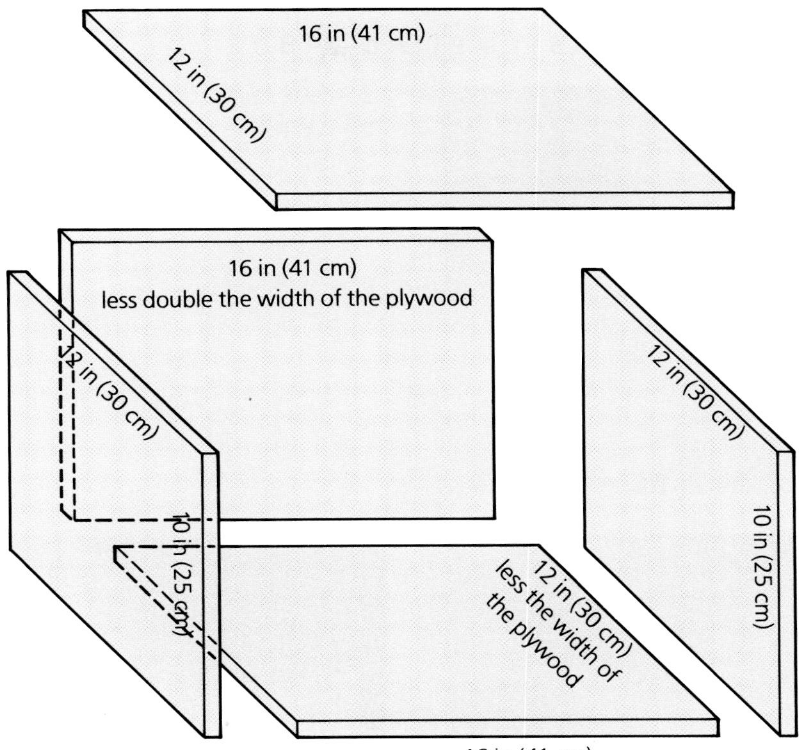

LEFT The external measurements of the finished box are 16 × 12 × 10 in (41 × 30 × 25 cm). The base sits between the sides and the back, while the back sits between the sides but not actually on the base. The roof rests on the sides and along the top edge of the back. All edges are flush at the front, so that a door may be added later if wished.

ASSEMBLY

When you have cut out the five pieces of wood, hold them together one at a time to check that you have measured them correctly.

Now lay one side flat on your working surface, butted against the baseboard. The side is ¼ in (6 mm) deeper, so push them both against another straight edge to make sure that the front edges are flush.

Use a ruler to draw short lines at intervals across the two pieces where you will need screws. Three or four screws on each side is quite adequate. Follow the pencil lines round to the edge of the baseboard. Double-check that the extended lines still marry up, and mark the centre point along the lines you have drawn. These pencil marks give you the position for drilling holes. Hold the base in a vice, and drill a hole with the thinner of the two drill bits (see page 26). Be careful that you keep the drill upright; if you do not, the hole will pierce the flat surface.

Draw a line ¼ in (6 mm) inside the edge of the side wall. Mark a ⅛ in (3 mm) centre point along each of the lines you drew to indicate the positions of the screws. Drill a hole right through with the thicker drill bit, then use the countersink bit to gouge the wood on the outer face so that the screw head will lie just slightly below the surface.

Assembling a Box

1 This box room is 16 in (41 cm) wide, 10 in (25 cm) high and 12 in (30 cm) deep. Before you assemble it, check that you have cut the component parts to the correct size.

1

2 Make sure that the front edges are level, then draw lines at intervals across both sections to indicate where the screws will marry up.

2

3 Start by assembling one wall and the base.

4 The rear wall is added next, followed by the second wall.

5 Finally, the roof is screwed into the top of the walls to complete the box.

3

4

5

Repeat this with all the sections that are to be joined together. When all the drill holes have been prepared, begin to assemble the pieces, starting with the baseboard and one side. Screw the rear panel into place, then the other side.

If all fits well you can move to the roof. If it does not, you should dismantle and start again by drilling fresh holes that marry up. When everything is correctly aligned, unscrew, run wood glue along the edges and rescrew. The basic box is ready for the roof.

Try the roof out for size and shave off any overlapping wood until it fits accurately. As before, allow for the ¼ in (6 mm) thickness, find a centre point and drill the wider hole and the countersink. Lay the panel on top of the walls. You can tape it in place to stop it from slipping. Drill

with the thinner bit into the upper edge of the side walls, using the roof holes as a guide. Again, when everything is correctly positioned, unscrew, glue, then rescrew.

Now you have made a box, you can go ahead and make a doll's house as complicated as you wish!

A front made as one removable section is usually best for box rooms. If you have a hinged door you can, if necessary, strengthen the front upright edges of the frame by gluing then screwing an extra piece of beading to take the thicker hinge screws.

It is best to use ¼ in (6 mm) birch ply for basic house building and approximately ⅛ in (4 mm) for roof sections and any smaller internal partitions that do not require hinges or screws. Some miniaturists use ⅓ in (9 mm) throughout, but these houses are extremely heavy and are not practical for most of us.

ABOVE AND RIGHT Identical boxes can be used in an almost infinite number of ways as these shops demonstrate. They were part of a 27-room shopping emporium.

MAKING THE FRAMEWORK

When you have successfully made a basic box, go back to your plan of the house and the paper patterns that you cut out. Lay these on the sheet of plywood and shuffle them around until you find the most economical arrangement. Remember, however, that laying one piece against the grain could be an expensive mistake if your wood warps either during assembly or if the doll's house sits in a damp room.

When you are satisfied, draw the sections accurately and directly onto the wood using a pencil, steel ruler and set square. Label each piece before you cut it out. The room dividers need to be fractionally taller than the space between the floors because you may later decide to gouge grooves for them to slot in place. Cut out all the sections. Do not be disheartened by your first effort: everyone complains that they cannot cut a straight line, even after they have made many houses. Most people do not possess or have the space to house a large saw bench with a guide, but the use of screws will enable you to rectify some mistakes. A long length of factory-cut beading or something similar can be used as a straight edge, and you can whittle down the bumps with a craft knife. Give everything a good finish with sandpaper.

By now you will be surrounded by a jigsaw puzzle of house building sections, each labelled in pencil. It is especially important to indicate which pieces are to be used to the left or right, at the front or back, and at the top or bottom. Be careful to draw in the exact positions of the floors in the same way you marked the position of screw holes in the box – lay the wood flat and draw a line over the two sections. All the drill holes must marry up along these lines.

ABOVE The basic framework. The floors fit between the end walls with the room partitions just slotted in place. They will be permanently fixed later.

Cutting Out The House Shapes

1

2

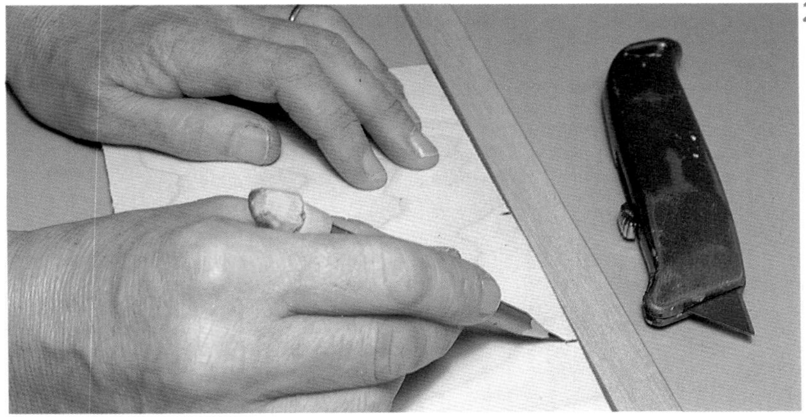

1 Draw the full-size measurements for all the sections of your house accurately onto the wood.

3

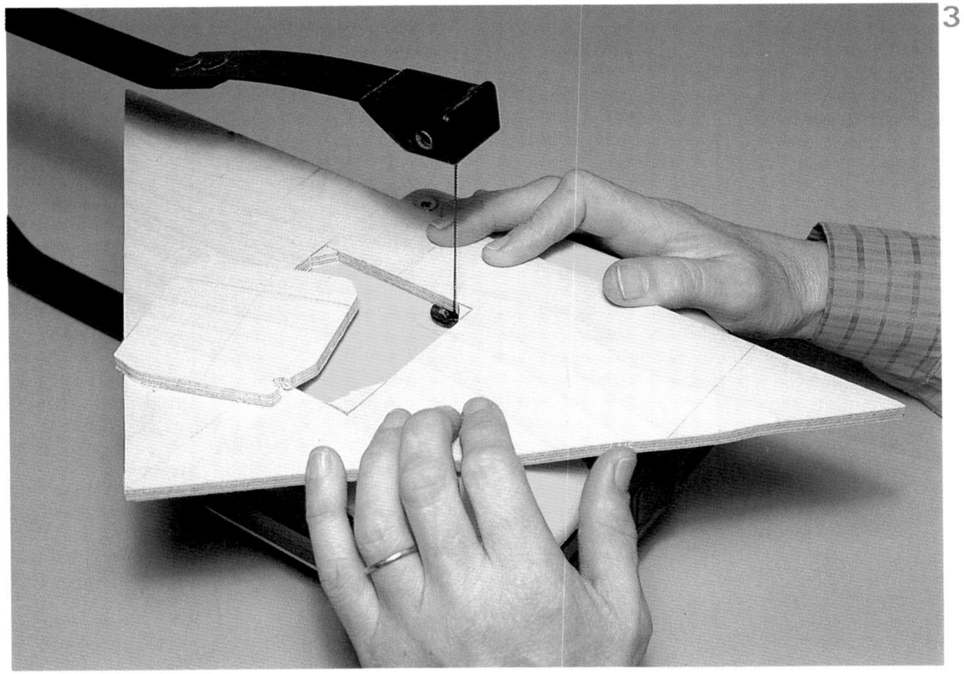

2 A piece of factory-cut beading makes a practical straight edge against which to check that your sides are straight. Mark the sections of uneven cutting that need whittling down with a craft knife.

3 In the sections that need holes for doors or windows, drill a hole in the area to be removed and thread the fretsaw blade through it. Cut away the waste by following straight lines and curving round the corners. Then cut neatly into each corner.

ASSEMBLING THE SHELL OF THE HOUSE

1

2

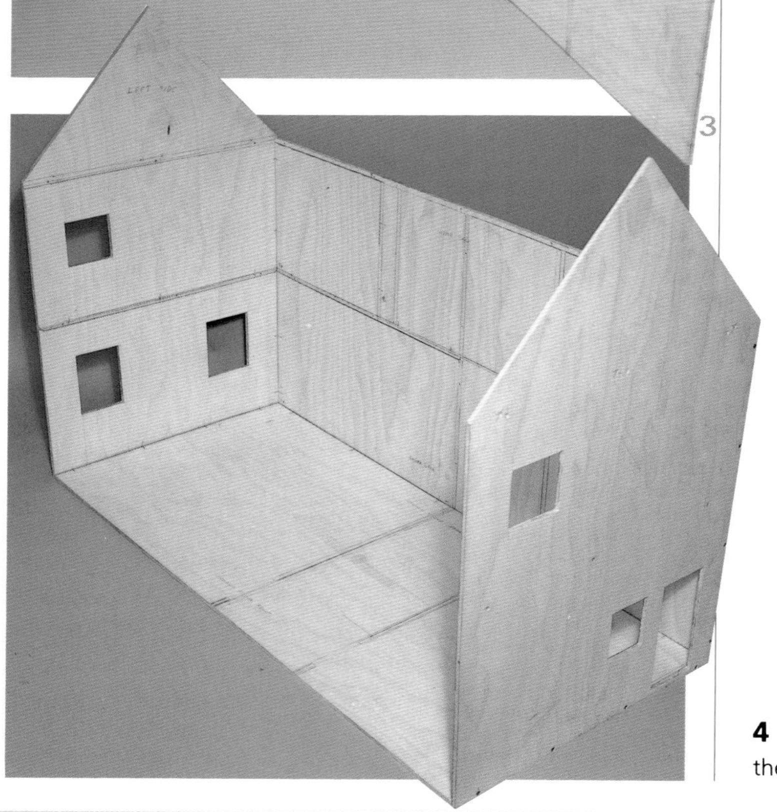

3

1 Assemble the shell of the house in the same order as you made the box. Start by attaching one side to the base.

2 Then add the rear wall.

3 Next comes the second side wall.

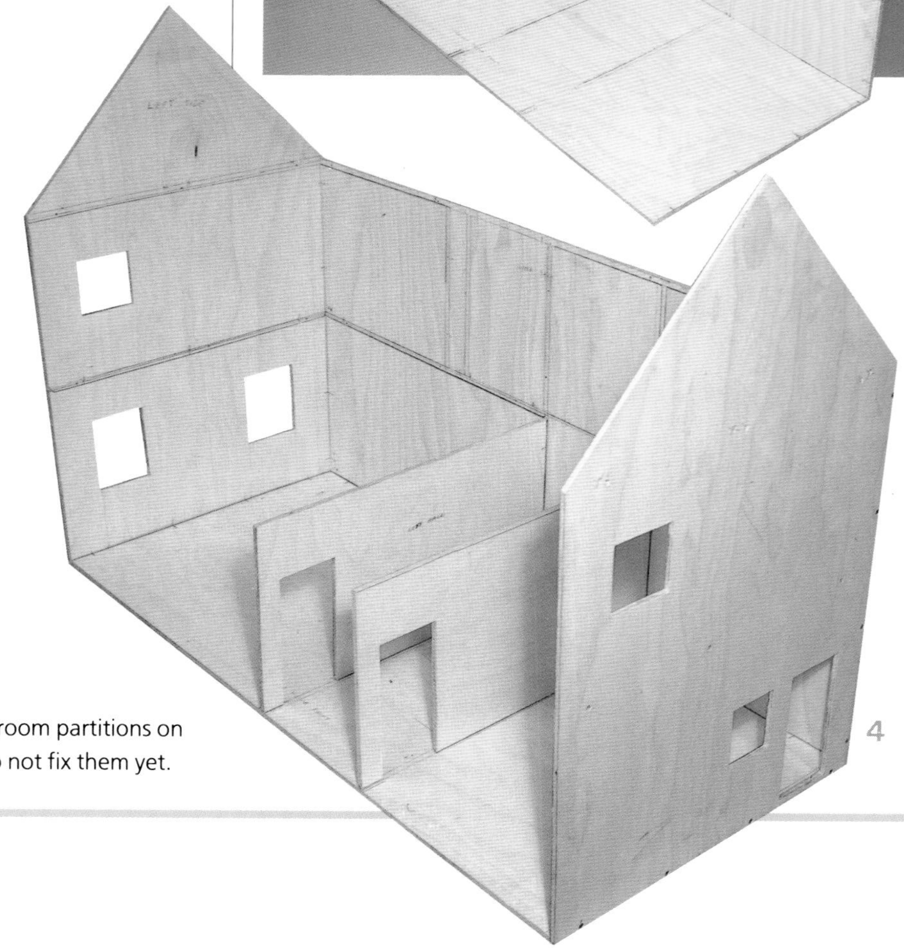

4

4 Finally, position the room partitions on the ground floor but do not fix them yet.

Up to now you have solid pieces of wood with no openings for doors, windows or fireplaces. Now that your walls are cut to size, you will find it easier to gauge exactly where you want these features and how many you want. The first house I made had 26 windows, nine internal doors and six open fireplaces. Making this number is not a problem but it is time-consuming.

If you are cutting openings in a sheet of wood and, say, the windows are too far in for the fretsaw, you will find an electric jigsaw useful, or for the faint-hearted, a simple keyhole saw. A vibratory fretsaw has many uses. You can thread the blade through inside spaces and it frees both hands for guiding the wood. The drawback is that is has a 14 in (37 cm) limit, so a single blade is needed for larger areas. Make the windows any size you wish, but around 3 × 4 in (7.5 × 10 cm) is average. When you are planning, do not forget to calculate the space needed for the window surrounds and curtains, especially if two windows are separated by an internal chimney breast.

Doorways must be a realistic 5½–6 in (14–15 cm) high, and you should allow a width of 3 in (7.5 cm), including the opening and its architraves.

Drill a hole in the area to be removed to give access for the fretsaw blade. Chisel three holes together to make a slot for the wider blades. Roughly cut away the waste by following the straight pencil lines but swerving round the corners until the centre block comes away. Now you can cut neatly into each corner, starting on a straight line and working from each direction.

If the window and door holes are not true to shape, use a set square, craft knife and sandpaper to give sharp right-angled corners. Do not worry if the holes vary in size by a fraction because the windows will be set individually. However, if you are buying ready-made door and window fittings, your holes will have to fit the manufacturer's specifications.

At this stage, too, you will have to decide if you are going to have internal chimney breasts for each fire or external flues up the outside walls, which involves cutting the fire holes before assembly.

The next job is to assemble the shell of the house in exactly the same way as you made the box, although it will be much bigger. It is less cumbersome if you work with the house lying on its back. You will have to insert all the floors in the same manner as you fitted the ground floor, because the top floor will be sitting between the gables, and the sloping roof will, in effect, be the box lid. Draw lines on each floor to indicate where you wish to divide these areas into rooms. At this stage you can screw in the upper ceiling, but do not glue anything. You should now have what looks rather like an open bookcase.

I hope you have done better than my first effort. I screwed and unscrewed, drilled and redrilled countless times. My shaky line cutting also meant that I had a lot of planing and rasping to do as well. In some pieces I had so many false holes, I had to circle the right holes with pencil so that I could be sure of putting the screws into their final resting places.

The main point at this stage is to make sure that the large back sheet fits accurately between the sides and against the floors. Do not worry about minor gaps. They can be plugged with a mix of fine sawdust and wood glue, which can be used like plastic wood. Never waste anything, not even your sawdust!

Spend some time studying the framework of your house because now is your last chance to change your mind and improve on your original design. Do you want to add an extension, such as a conservatory leading off the rear of the lounge? Or perhaps you would like a large bay window or a turret room. I chose to include an outside kitchen door and window because I may decide to add an extension here at some later date. Although this project is designed to demonstrate how to make a standard shape house, you can elaborate on it as you wish.

The Internal Floors and Walls

1

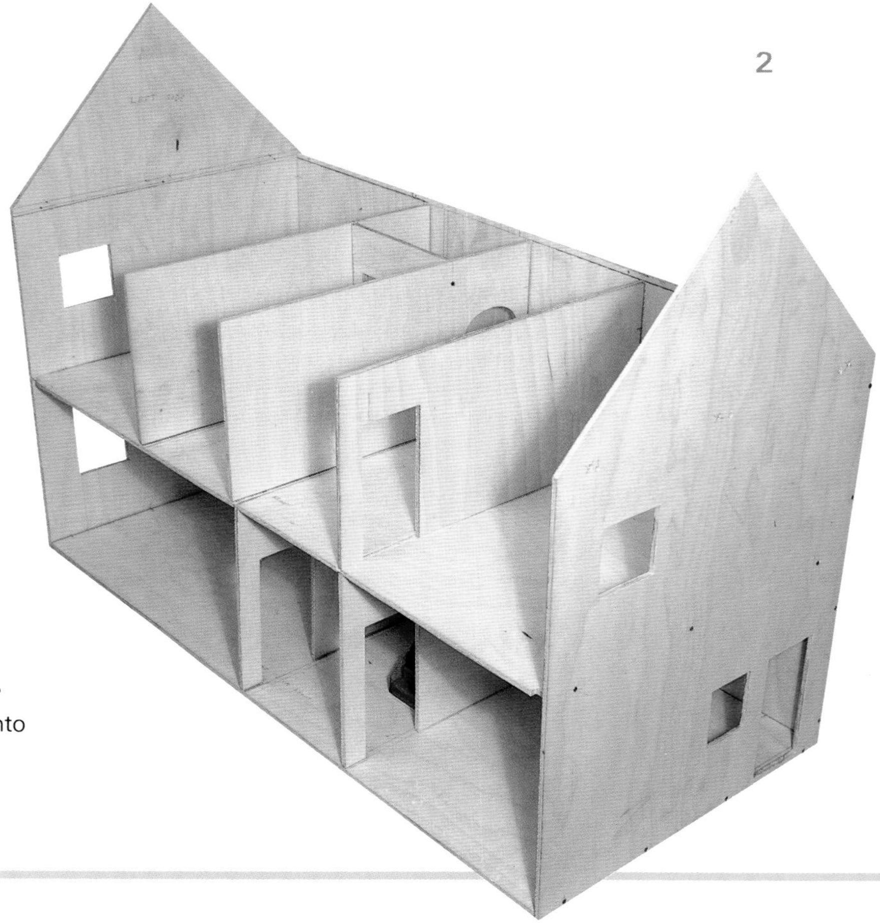

2

1 Once you have inserted the upper ceiling (screwed but not glued) and before you put in the room partitions, make the bathroom as a single unit, leaving a realistic corridor behind the room.

2 From this angle you can see how the bathroom fits in, with a door opening into the hall.

This is the point at which I redrew my original graph plans. The room dividers had to be moved to balance the rooms on the two floors. I also opted for windows on the sides of the bedrooms. All of these would have been extremely difficult to include if I had glued the framework first and demonstrates the benefit of using screws.

If a width of 3 ft (over 90 cm) is too large for your display table, you can scale the house down. You could eliminate the hallway and put the staircase in the lounge/dining room or against the rear wall of the kitchen.

Alternatively, you can reduce the width of the main room, although I would advise you to keep to the 15 in (38 cm) depth. Other options are to make the house taller by adding a third floor or to create rooms in the loft space. If you have already cut the wood to the measurements given here, all you need do now is to cut the same size strip from each of the floors and the back wall.

THE STAIRCASE

Now that you are satisfied with the basic framework, the next challenge is to make a staircase. Until this is made, you cannot cut out the exact position of the stairwell hole on the upper landings.

Making the stairs is comparatively easy. The hard part is adding the banisters and top rail and adjusting the height as they near the ceiling. This stage, however, can be left until you have decorated your house.

With the narrow hallway in this project, make a straight staircase fixed to one wall as this gives stability and more space for furniture.

For this size of house I would suggest you make the staircase around 2¼ in (5.5 cm) wide. You will need approximately 14 stairs cut from a strip of ¾ in (2 cm) triangle-shaped wood. Stick the wide bases close together on a length of 1⁄16 in (2 mm) ply, 14 in (35.5 cm) long and 2¼ in (5.5 cm) wide. Do not forget to stain the stairs before gluing if you do not intend using paint. Stain is not absorbed by glue, and you will be left with

RIGHT The simplest stairs are made by gluing strips of triangle beading to 1⁄16 in (2 mm) ply.

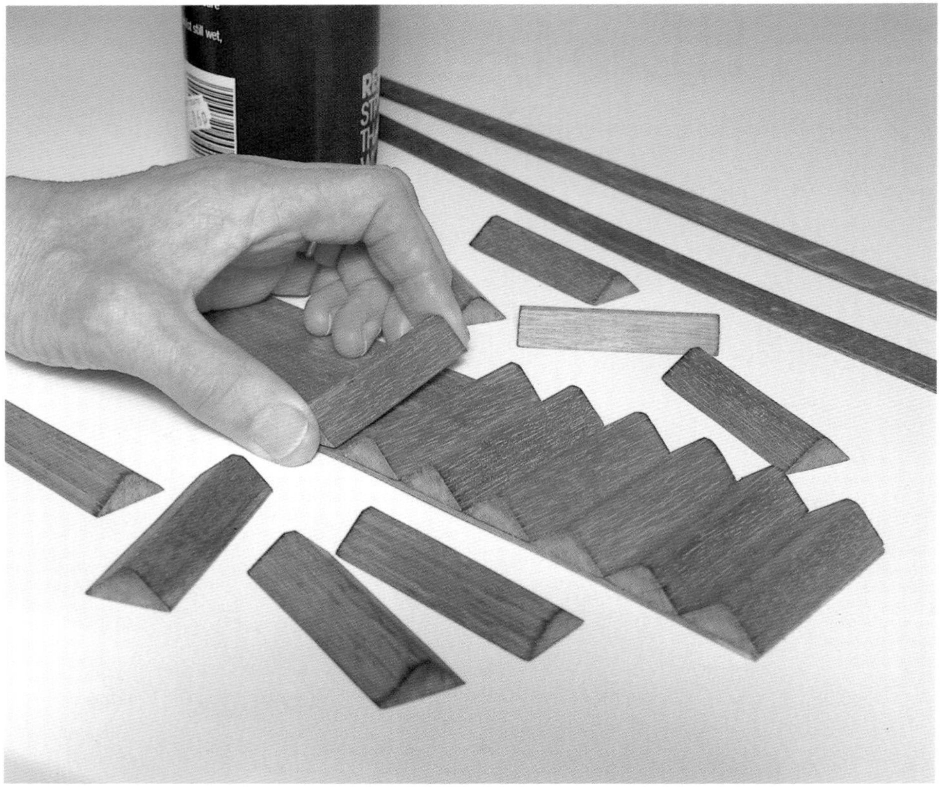

blotchy patches if you try to apply after gluing. Cover the rough sides of your stairs with strips of ply.

Another popular method is to stick solid blocks of wood on top of each other, each block set slightly back from the step beneath it.

A more sophisticated method for making a staircase is to use stringers, treads and risers as in real life. Cut out two stringers in 1⁄8 in (3 mm) thick wood using the full-size pattern. The stair treads should measure 7⁄8 in (22 mm) deep by 2¼ in (5.5 cm) wide, while the risers should be slightly smaller – 5⁄8 × 2⅛ in (16 mm × 5 cm). Cut them in 1⁄16 in (2 mm) wood. Mahogany is more attractive than ply.

You will find it easier if you make a jig from wood to support the two stringers and to keep them parallel. The outside faces of the stringers should be fractionally less than 2¼ in (5.5 cm) apart. Stick the risers on first so they sit neatly on the stringers. Butt the treads up against the risers so that they protrude just a little over the front and one side of the stringer. You can buy strips of stair nosing to finish off the front edges neatly.

If you have opted for the simple method of using triangle beading or solid blocks, your next step will be less complicated if you make yourself a mock hallway from, say, a stiff cardboard box. All you need are two

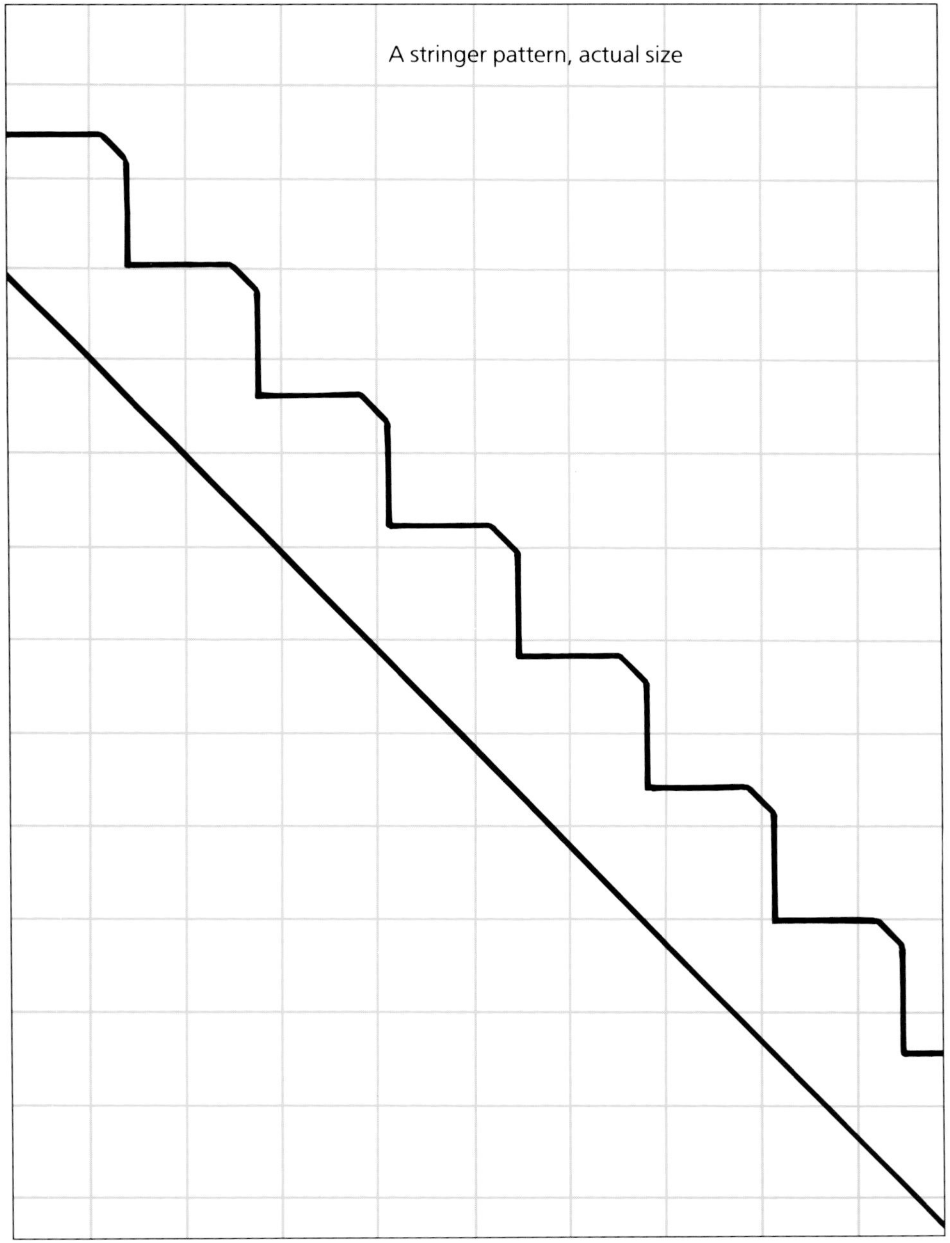

ABOVE Solid blocks are often used in a small hall with minimal depth because they can be adjusted to any height. Unfortunately, they may not look realistic. More sophisticated stairs are made with stringers, risers and treads.

RIGHT You can use this diagram of a full-size stringer as a pattern to cut out the two stringers for your staircase, if you choose this method.

RIGHT A mock hallway made from a cardboard box is invaluable during the construction of a staircase. It is particularly useful when you come to add the banisters and handrail.

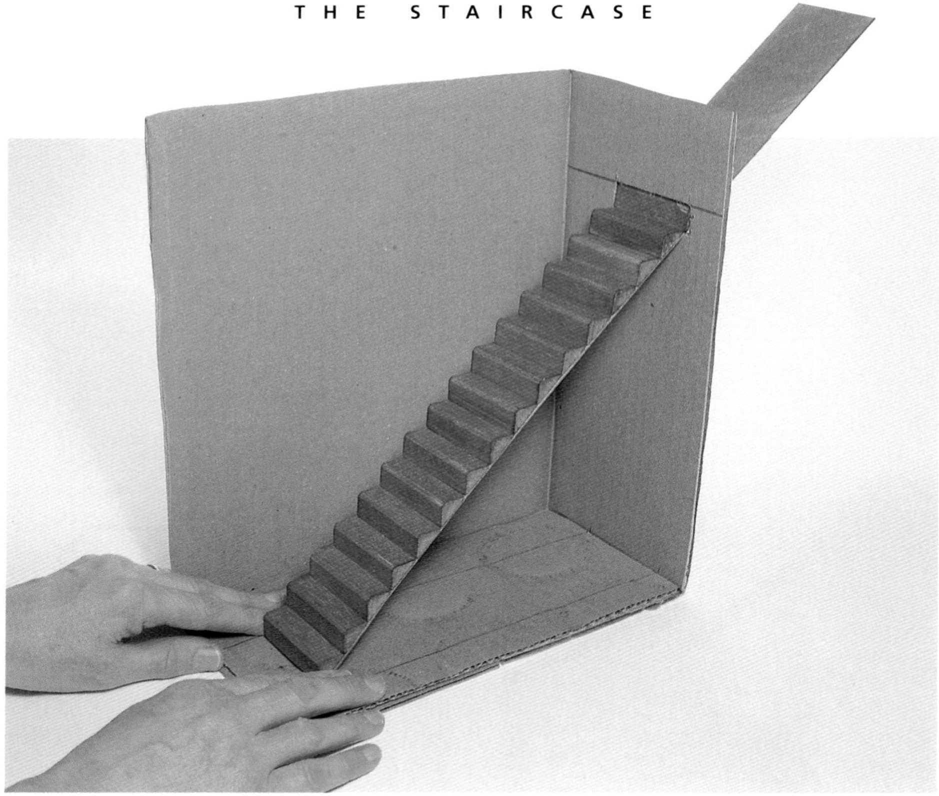

walls and a floor. Mark a line on the rear narrow wall that corresponds to your ceiling height. Cut a slit on and below the line so that you can slide the 1⁄16 in (2 mm) staircase ply and the top stair tread through it.

Move your stairs back and forth until the treads are horizontal, which will give an angle of around 45 degrees. The top tread will be stuck to the underside of your ceiling so, allowing for this, add an extra tread if necessary or take off one if you have too many. When you are satisfied that the staircase is level, make a line below the bottom tread.

Using your hall room divider as a guide, mark a line on the house floor to indicate where the stairs begin, beyond the inner doorway. Hold the top tread against the ceiling and pencil a line in front of this tread. The stairwell hole needs to be the width of your stairs and approximately 5½ in (14 cm) in front of your pencil line.

Do not place your stairway too far to the rear because you need an area where people can step off the stairs and turn to walk along the upper landing. The room doorway and staircase will take up around 12 in (30 cm) of your room, which is why you need a hallway that is at least 15 in (38 cm) deep. If you want to make a smaller house, you can, of course, save space by siting a door under the stairs.

Stairs to a third floor or to the roof space have to be set against the opposite landing wall and to rise in the reverse direction, so that, from the front, you will see the base rising to the ceiling. If you have more than two floors, your hallway needs to be 7½ in (19 cm) wide to take the double staircases.

Now dismantle your framework and cut out any areas where extensions are to be added and the hole for the stairwell.

LEFT If your house has more than two floors the hall must be wide enough to accommodate a double staircase and provide walking room for the occupants.

ADDING THE ROOM DIVIDERS

It is a good idea to gouge grooves for the upright room dividers. This is comparatively simple in theory if you are using birch ply.

Using a steel ruler and a sharp craft knife, make deep cuts into the floors, ceilings and back board along your pencilled lines. These should be ¼ in (6 mm) apart. Run a chisel between each pair of lines and the wood should come away to leave a smooth groove. The upright partition room walls can be trimmed to slide into the grooves, but should not be fixed at this stage. Merely slot them in and hold in place with tape if necessary. Grooving can be a somewhat hit and miss affair, so try it on a piece of scrap wood first. It is always easier to cut with the grain than across it. I managed to cut three grooves on this project before I gave up. Perhaps my chisel was not sharp enough or the wood was extra tough.

Only when you are satisfied with everything should you glue and screw the outer framework together. If your plans include unusual room features you could find it less difficult to work from above. If you decide to do this, do not glue the floors, but fully fit and decorate each level as if you are making a series of box rooms. You may prefer to paint or paper the ceiling and to drill lighting wire holes while it is on the work bench.

Always think one step ahead and sort out possible problems while you are doing a particular job. For example, if the hallway is deep and narrow, it is going to be difficult to decorate. Can you do it from above or by papering the partitions before you glue them into place? Do not forget to hang the internal doors and add doorknobs before decorating. Door and window architraves are added after papering.

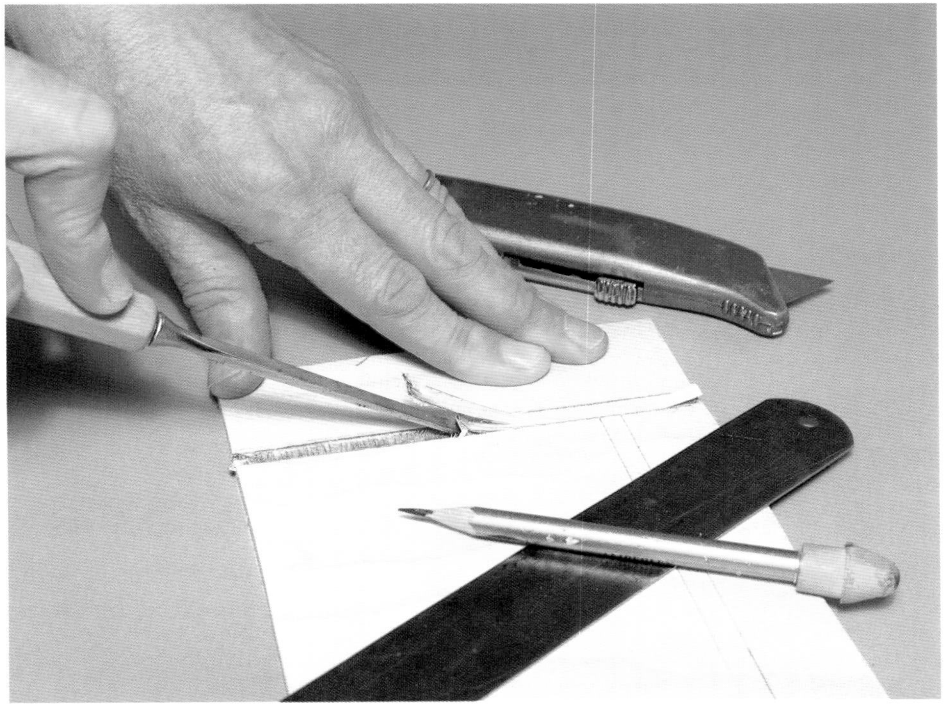

LEFT If you would prefer your room dividers to run in channels, practise on scrap wood to see if your particular ply lends itself to having grooves cut in it.

I know from experience that trying to screw rings above the windows for curtain rods, especially for the window behind a chimney breast, is difficult. You would be wise to glaze and dress this window before the ceiling is fixed. Glue each ceiling only when that floor is complete. (See the guide order later in the book.)

Before gluing the horizontal dividers, remember to cut the front corners to take a strip down each side to give added support to the long hinges when they are eventually fitted. Alternatively, you may decide to use dowel plugs instead or to rely on the extra support outside the house.

If you do not want to make slotting grooves, skirting boards and ceiling coving will add support to a glued wall after the house is decorated. There is no need to groove the upper central section in this house because the rear bathroom wall acts as a stabilizer. Another possibility is to screw the partitions to the lower and upper floors and/or to the rear wall.

Your house should be taking shape now, but it will look rather odd with all those holes for windows, doors and fireplaces. Nevertheless, remember what your vision of a dream house looks like and keep working towards it.

By this stage you will have discovered that making a doll's house is fraught with "chicken and egg" situations. You cannot do this before you do that, yet you cannot do that before you have done this. As with a real house, there are seemingly endless decisions to be made about the order in which each stage should be tackled. At least we do not need realistic plumbing.

HANGING THE DOORS

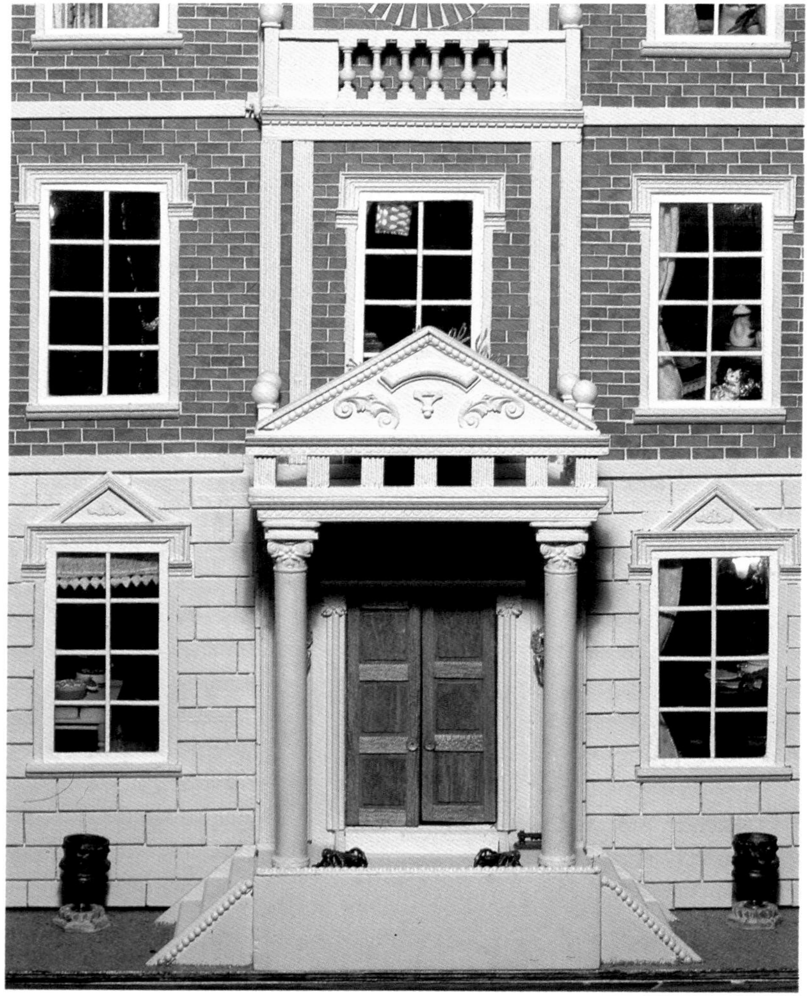

Before you glue the room partitions permanently into position, make and hang the doors while you can work at your bench.

The doors will vary according to the style and period of your chosen house. In the first houses I made I experimented with different types of wood and card – you will find that discarded doors make good bed bases!

Lay the room partition with the door opening on a piece of card and draw around it. This will give you a template, which will be necessary if your opening is not 100 per cent accurate. Use this card pattern to cut a piece of good quality ⅛ in (4 mm) grained wood. Try it for size, sanding it down where necessary until it fits the doorway, with a slight clearance at the sides and top and a little more at the bottom to allow for the floor covering you will fit later.

If you want a country-style door, you could gouge vertical grooves in ply to simulate planks. I have tried this method, but I found that unless I merely scratched the surface, the wood tended to roughen on the uneven grain. Using good quality wood, though, gave an acceptable result. The neatest way is to add strips of narrow beading with a tiny gap between each length. These must, of course, be stained first, unless you intend to paint the door. Repeat on the other side so that the ⅛ in (4 mm) ply is a sandwich. Sand all the edges smooth. When your door is complete, check that it fits your doorway space, then it is ready for hanging.

If you want to go up-market and have a panelled door, start with the basic ply as before and stain it if required. Now glue the strips in any

MAKING DOORS IN DIFFERENT STYLES

1

2

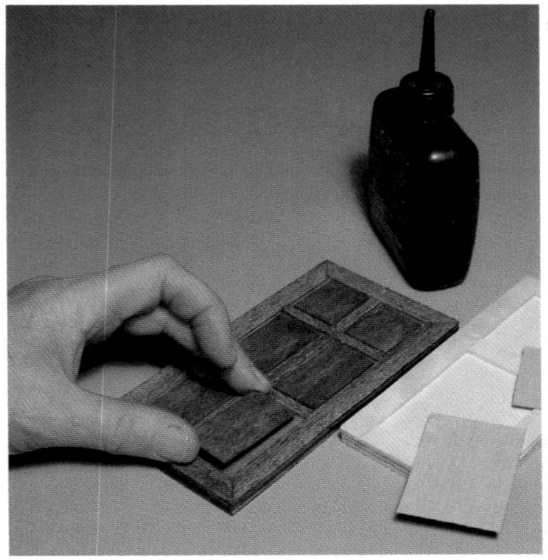

3

3 A panelled door looks effective and can be made in any style you choose.

4 There have been many door styles over the centuries, and you have a wide choice of designs.

4

1 Make card templates of your doors while the room partitions are on the workbench. Use these to cut out the pieces of ⅛ in (4 mm) ply to which you will add beading and/or panelling to both sides, in whatever style you choose.

2 For a country-style door you can groove planks in the door; some woods give better results than others.

pattern, according to the style you want to have. Start with the vertical edges and fit the cross bars in between. If you want a larger panel then cut a square of 1⁄32in (1mm) ply that fits in the space with a small gap all round to give the impression of stepped edge beading.

These are the simplest doors for a beginner to make, but as you gain experience you will be able to make something more elaborate. You can either paint your door or stain it.

Fitting Hidden Door Hinges

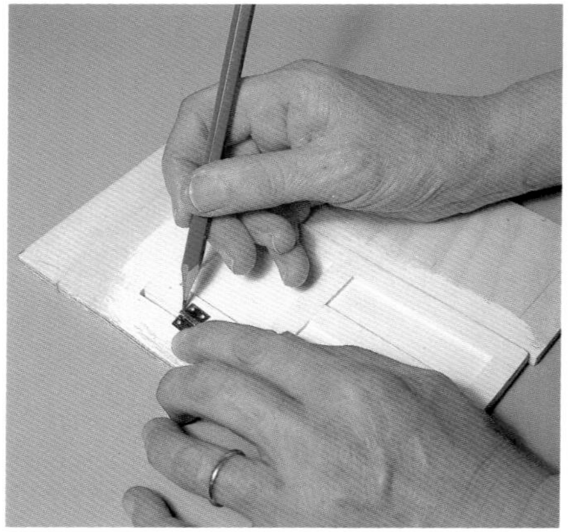

1

1 Mark the position of your hinge on the door with a pencil.

2 Hold the door firmly in a vice and gouge a seating for the hinge with a craft knife or chisel. Check the hinge fits, place the door in its frame again, mark the corresponding place for the hinge on the frame and gouge that out too.

2

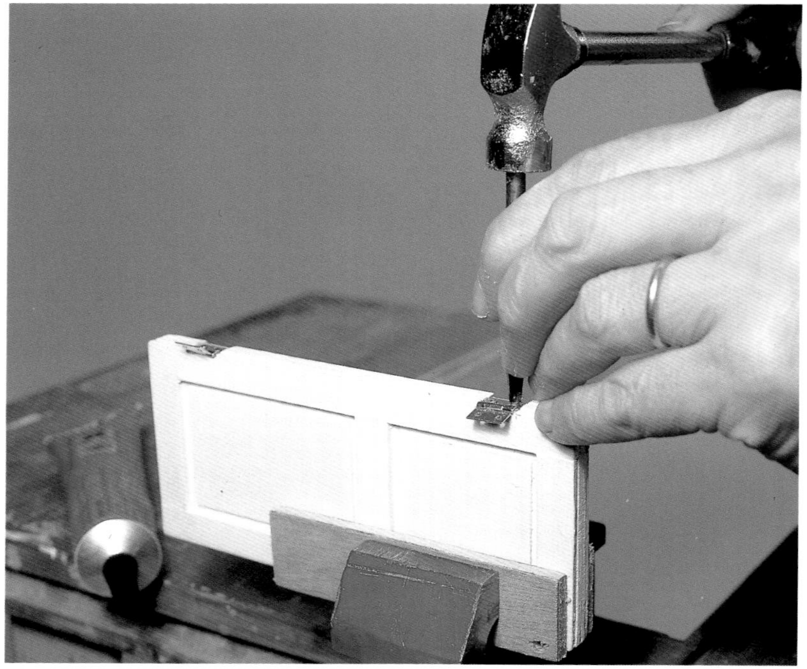

3

4

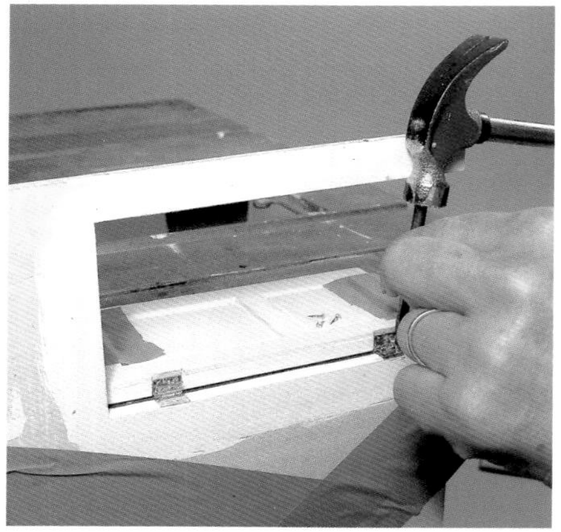

5

3 Put the folded hinge in position between the door and frame to check that it fits neatly. Then drill fine holes in the door to fix the hinges with brass pins. Add a little glue for extra strength before you fit the pins.

4 Pre-drill holes on the frame before tapping in the pins. An Archimedes' drill has many uses in building a doll's house.

5 Support the door at right angles to the frame before you tap the final pins into the frame.

HINGES

Adding hidden hinges to a door is one of those jobs that, even when you know the theory back to front and do everything according to the rules, usually comes out far from perfect.

Lay your door in the gap you have cut from the room divider. Open the hinges and lay them flat over the two pieces. Draw pencil lines above and below the hinges on the door only. Using a craft knife or chisel, carefully gouge out an area on the thin inner edge that is just deep enough to seat the hinge in the gap. When it fits, mark up the corresponding area on the door frame and gouge that in the same way.

You should be able to fold the hinge and fit it in the two gouged sections. If all looks well, put the door in a vice and drill fine holes; you will find an Archimedes' drill useful here. A dab of glue will give further

ABOVE Simple hinges can be used if you cut the door slightly larger all around than the frame. Lay the hinges flat on the door, pinning the other halves to a strip of wood that is the same thickness. Glue and pin the strip to the wall, and your door is in place.

ARCHITRAVES

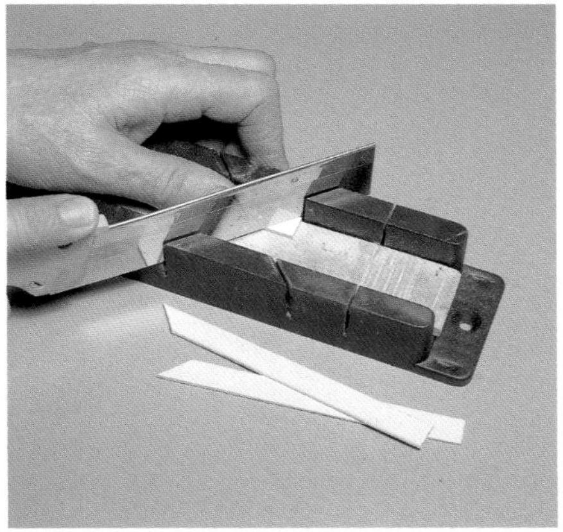

1 Door and window architraves are cut at an angle of 45 degrees, but they are not glued in place until after decorating.

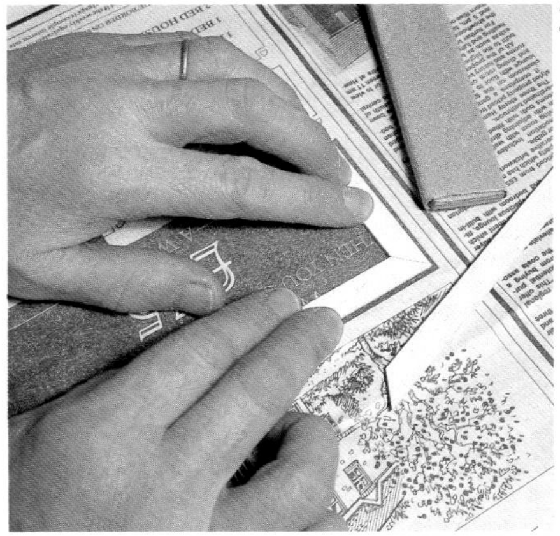

2 Newspaper column lines are useful guides for checking that mitred joints fit perfectly.

security for the hinges before you punch in brass pins. An impact adhesive is better than super glue because you can remove the hinge before it hardens if it is not quite right.

Fix both door hinges, top and bottom, before you attempt to glue and pin the other halves to the doorway. The door should swing freely and at least close. If it does not, you have probably not gouged out enough wood from the door or from the frame to allow for the protrusion of pin heads. If the groove is too deep, you will have to remove the hinges before the glue sets hard and pack out the recess.

If you feel you cannot cope with hidden hinges just yet, lay them flat across the front of the door and frame in the manner of a gate.

Another common method for hanging doors is to use dressmaker's steel pins. Drill a very fine hole in the top of the door as close to the corner as possible. Make a corresponding hole in the door frame. Press the pin hard into the door, cut off the head and poke the protruding pin up into the hole in the frame. Insert another pin into the bottom of the door and cut off the head. To hold it you will need to make a doorstep that will sit between the open frame. This means that the door needs to be slightly shorter than the frame.

If the door does not swing freely on its pin pivots, sand one long side edge to make it slightly rounded.

The architraves around the door frame are best added after you have wallpapered. The printed black rules in a newspaper or magazine are ideal for checking that your mitred corners are perfectly square.

Don't forget to add the doorknobs at this stage; it will be virtually impossible once the wall partitions are in place.

Hanging Doors using Dressmaker's Pins

1

1 Cut out a door that is slightly shorter than the frame. Drill a fine hole as near to the corner of the door as you can.

2

2 Drill a corresponding hole in the upper door frame.

3

3 Press dressmaker's steel pins into the top and bottom of the door and cut off the heads. Fit top pin into the upper hole in the frame.

4

4 The lower pin needs a step between the door jambs and the foot. Slightly round one long edge of the door so that it swings freely on its pivots.

WALLPAPERING

The whole question of decorating a doll's house raises additional questions about the sequence of individual steps. You will find it easier to decorate before the big front doors are added and will also probably encounter fewer problems if you decorate one floor at a time before you put the ceilings in place.

Are you considering introducing any permanent internal cupboards or fittings that would be less of a problem if you work from above? You may prefer to paint or paper the ceilings while they are flat on your workbench.

Always try to think one step ahead and anticipate possible problems. For example, the hallway and landing are deep and narrow, and they are going to be difficult to decorate. Can you do it from above or by papering the room partitions before you glue them in place? Remember, too, to hang and add doorknobs to your internal doors before you decorate.

Cut your paper to size before you actually stick it to the walls. Unless you have spare wallpaper, make templates first from scrap paper.

Start with the ceiling. Either paint it with a silk emulsion or use an embossed wallpaper to simulate plaster rendering. Never use gloss paint or heavy varnish on a doll's house, inside or outside, because it seems to break the illusion of a true-to-size miniature.

Cut the paper for the back wall slightly wider than the actual wall so that when you paste it in place it comes round the corner by about ½ in (12 mm). Put paste on the wooden walls, then on the paper.

The paper for the side walls should be cut to the exact size so that it fits right into the corner, overlapping the flap of back paper. This will

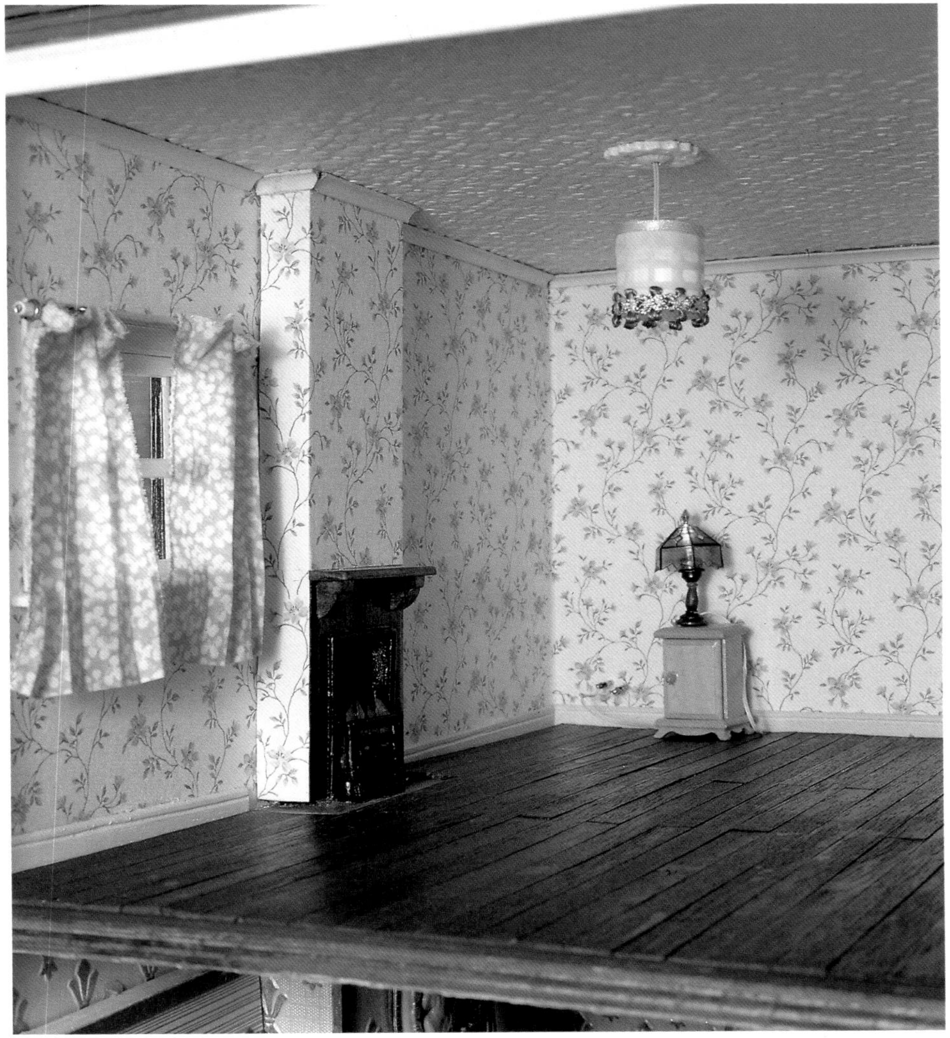

Papering Ceilings, and Back and Side Walls

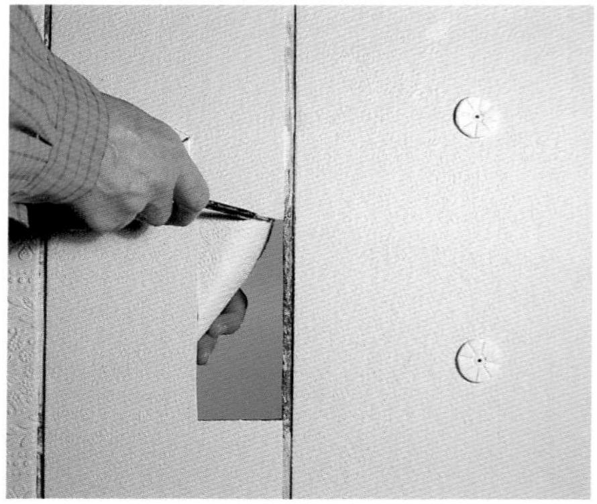

1

1 Paper and/or paint the ceiling first. Drill holes for the ceiling lights and glue on the roses. These can be made effectively from modelling clay or bought. Cut away the waste paper over the stairwell when the adhesive is dry.

2

2 Paper the back walls first, leaving the edges longer and unglued so that they can come around the corner onto the partition walls to hide the join.

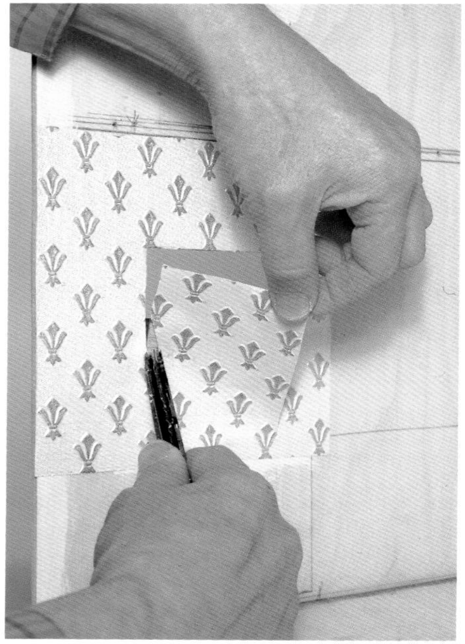

3

3 The wallpaper for the side walls should be cut to the right size and should overlap the back paper, which has turned the corner. Paper right over the window holes, then cut away the waste when the adhesive has dried. Then paper the partition walls.

ensure that the corner is well covered without a noticeable join. If you have rear or side windows, it is much simpler to paper right over the gaps and then cut out the window area with a craft knife when the paper has dried. It is a good idea to cut away a strip of paper all around the window opening so that the architrave has some wood to grip onto.

The choice of wallpaper for a doll's house is more important than for your own home. The whole house will be seen at once, so the colours should blend together to give an attractive overall appearance. Make sure that any patterns are small and in keeping with the 1:12 scale.

The way you decorate the large front doors is a matter of personal choice. Some people divide it up into sections with beading, then paper the appropriate divisions to match the individual rooms. Other people prefer to use a plain toning paper all over the inside.

Fit windows and their architraves when all the wallpapering is complete. Panelling is something that can be added at this stage if you wish. I always glaze the window behind a chimney breast before I add the ceiling. I also know from experience that trying to screw rings above the windows for curtain rods can be a problem.

Ceiling coving, skirting boards and the staircases are added after the house is finished.

Only one action can be explained at a time, but in practice they all dovetail into each other to become a single sequence. At the end of the book is an outline schedule for completing the downstairs decorating.

Finishing Internal Decoration

1 Trim any surplus paper from the wall partitions.

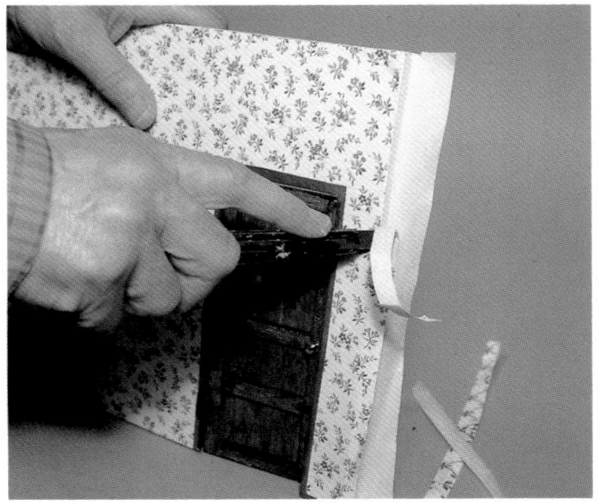

1

2

2 Add the architraves around the door when you have papered the partition.

3

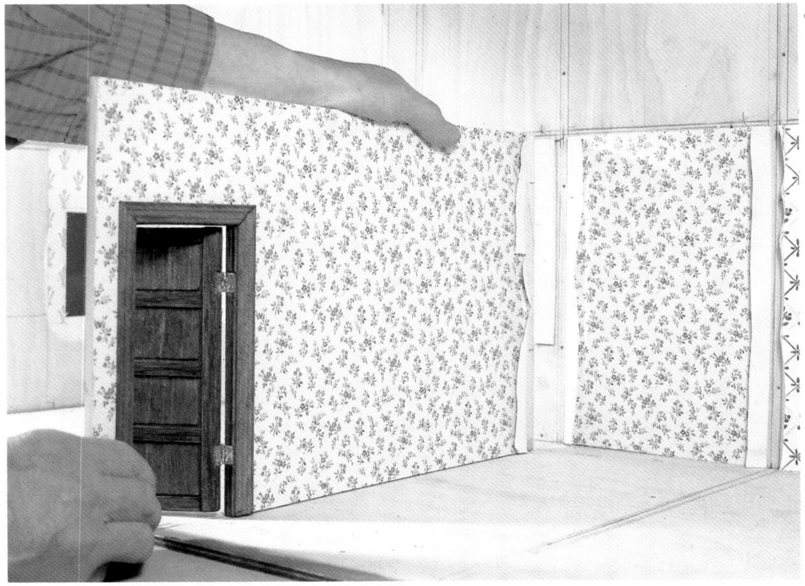

4

3 Run adhesive along the back and bottom edges of the partition.

4 Slide the partition into place and screw it to the back wall from the outside.

Finishing Internal Decoration

5 Paste the bare corner between the back wall and partition.

5

6 Add paste to the rear paper so that it comes around the corner and onto the side panel.

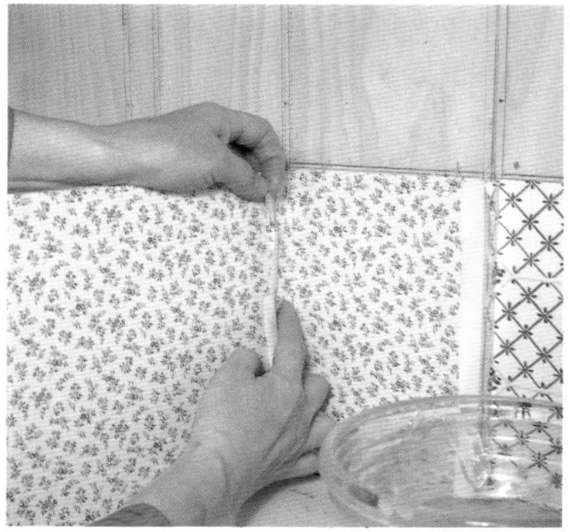

6

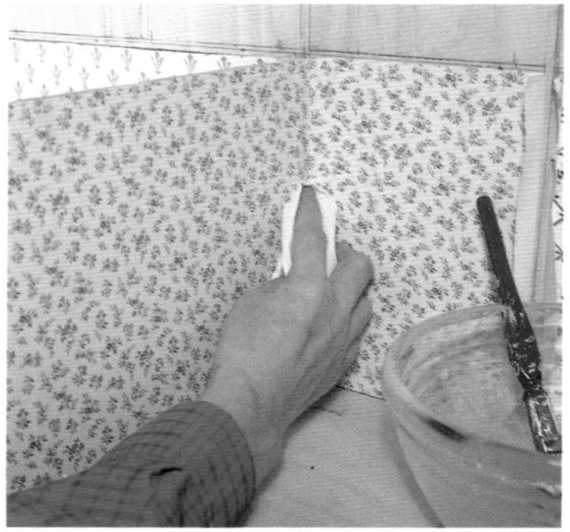

7

7 Stick the paper on the panel right into the corner.

8

8 Cut away a sliver of paper before adding the architraves to doors and windows.

9 Add the door and window architraves.

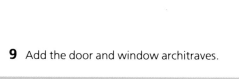

9

10 Wall panelling can be made by gluing three different widths of narrow beading to 1⁄16 in (2 mm) ply. Stain all wood before gluing.

10

11

11 Glue the rear panel first, then butt the side panels into the corners.

12

12 The front side panel under the window butts up against the chimney breast. (Making the fireplace, windows and curtains are covered later in the book.)

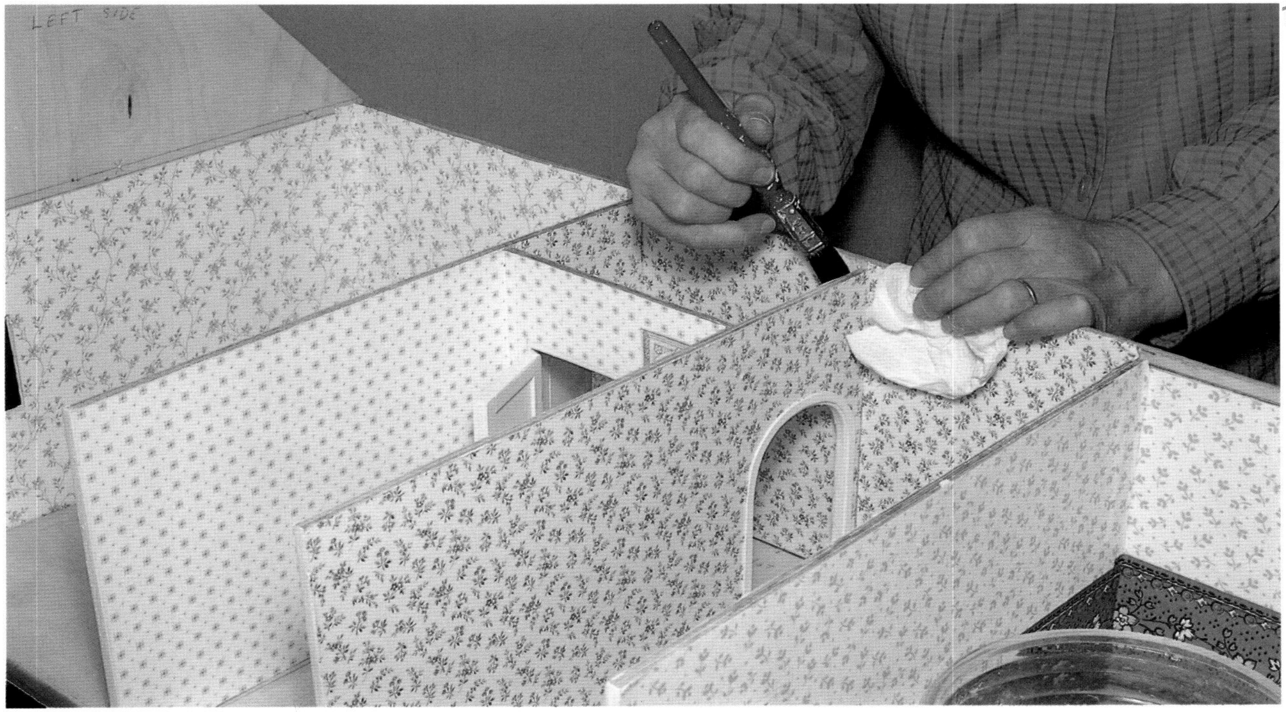
13

13 When all the decorating is finished you can screw and glue the ceiling of the first floor in place. The upstairs is decorated in the same way. Remember that the corridor behind the bathroom must be papered and the electrics and floor covering laid before the upper ceiling is fixed.

WIRING YOUR DOLL'S HOUSE

No two houses are the same, and each will need a different approach. The basic system is common to all buildings, and the explanation that follows will enable you to wire the doll's house described in this book.

Most professionals will tell you to hide the wiring behind the wallpaper. That is fine if you can guarantee that nothing will ever go wrong. I would strongly advise you to make your wiring concealed but accessible. The candle-shaped grain of wheat bulbs, for example, can be replaced only by removing their attached wires, and even if you use the larger pea bulbs, you need extra flex to give room for your fingers to unscrew a blown bulb from its holder. Bulbs also work loose and need screwing up. Remember you cannot wallpaper rooms with the lights in place.

When you are trying to decide how many lights you should install, think of your doll's house rooms as your own home and decide where and how many lights you would have in real life. Having decided this, you must have all the lights ready before you begin, because installing electrical wiring really is a chicken and egg problem.

Soldering is easy – you need only a few minutes to learn how to do it – but it opens up infinite possibilities and permutations for lighting. You will need to buy a reel of copper tape. Single strip will give you greater flexibility than the plastic-covered twin strip, and it is available from most hobby and craft shops. When it comes to the wire, the opposite is true – use a twin flex, which is neater than the single.

Think of your own home. You have a ring main circuit that starts and finishes at the fuse box. These wires are tapped at various places for

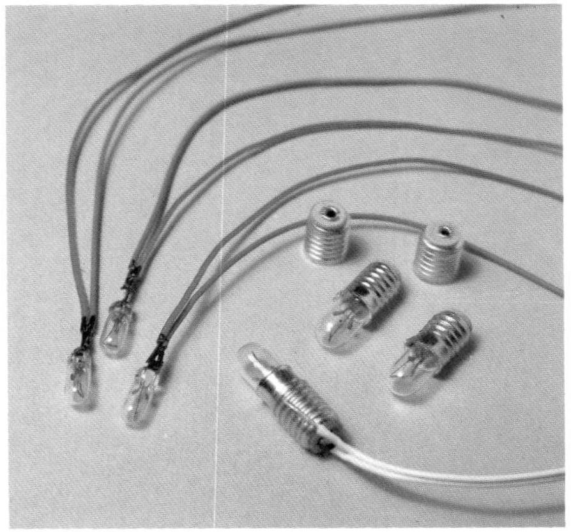

LEFT Grain of wheat bulbs (left) have the wires attached, and the whole unit has to be removed if the bulb blows. Pea bulbs (right) are more practical because you wire the holders and only the bulbs need changing. All bulbs are 12 volt.

BELOW There are dozens of everyday items that can be used for making miniature lamps.

WIRING INDIVIDUAL LIGHTS

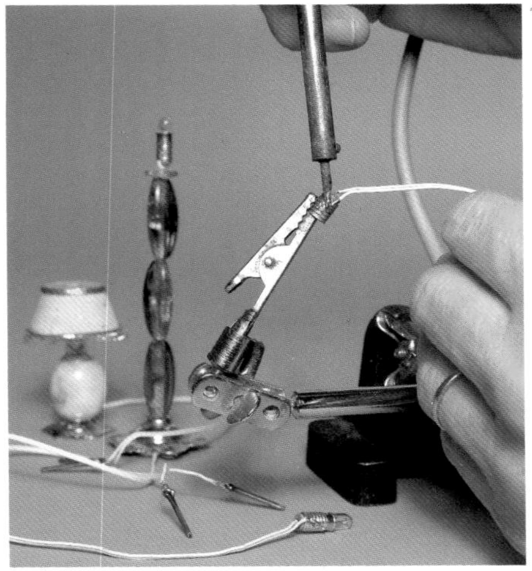

1 Solder one wire from the twin flex to the outside casing of the holder and the other to the centre rivet. Do not poke this wire through the rivet hole because it could cause a short if it touches the side of the bulb or inside the holder. A cheap gadget called "Helping Hand" (or "Third Hand") is extremely useful.

2 If you cannot obtain plugs and sockets, as a stop-gap you could try soldering the twin flex to slim, cut-down split pins, which can be pushed into brass tubing sockets so that they fit snugly.

lights or power points, each of which forms a secondary circuit. If one of them breaks and a light bulb or plug fuse blows, the ring main is not affected and all other lights and sockets remain operative. The wiring is said to be in parallel, and this is the system you should adopt in your doll's house.

Copper tape is your ring main and the transformer is your fuse box. All lights are then taken from as many points as you like on the circuit. Although it is called a circuit, you do not have to make a complete circle

RIGHT Two parallel strips of copper tape will be the equivalent to a household ring main, and you can take off it as many lights as you require. Nineteen ceiling lights were taken from one of the three circuits in the Lighting Shop.

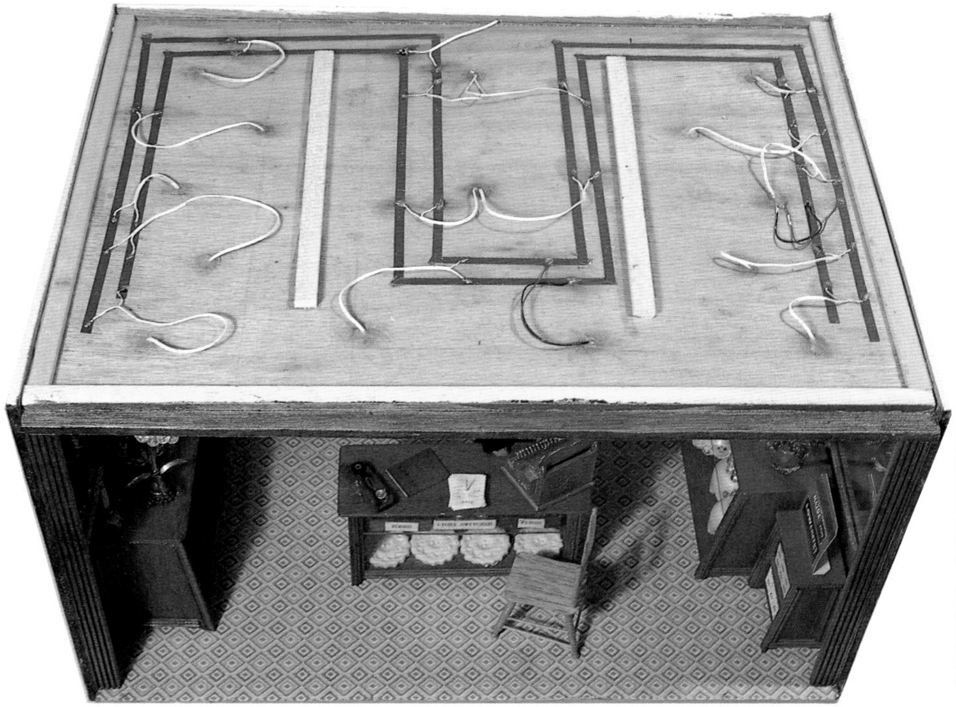

with each length of copper tape. Two parallel, open-ended strips of copper are all that you need. The circuit is completed when you wire a bulb onto these strips. You can have as many circuits as you like and feed any number of lights off each.

All the wires destined for the transformer will come together, preferably at the rear of your house, and then into a cheap plastic connector block, which will link one common exit wire to the transformer.

Laying a Circuit

The simplest method of installing a circuit is to lay all your wiring under a removable floor covering.

Drill holes in the floors at the points from which you want to hang ceiling lights in the room below. This is another job which could have been done before you assembled the house.

Lay two strips of copper tape across the floor area. You can just bend it around corners and press hard, but if you want to add twin strips directed at right angles, they have to be soldered, and if two strips cross you must cover the lower strip with insulating tape to avoid a short circuit. Some miniaturists use brass pins to join two pieces of tape, but while you are soldering other wires it is just as easy to use that.

Thread the light flex with its bulb and holder through the shade, through the ceiling rose and then through the drilled holes. Solder the ends to the nearest point on the copper circuit. Make sure that the wires are long enough for you to pull them down from below if you need to change a blown bulb or to raise the shade to grip the holder.

You can also solder the wires for plug sockets and red bulbs for the fires. Try to stagger all the connections so that the paired wires are not likely to touch and cause a short circuit.

LAYING CIRCUITS ON THE FIRST FLOOR

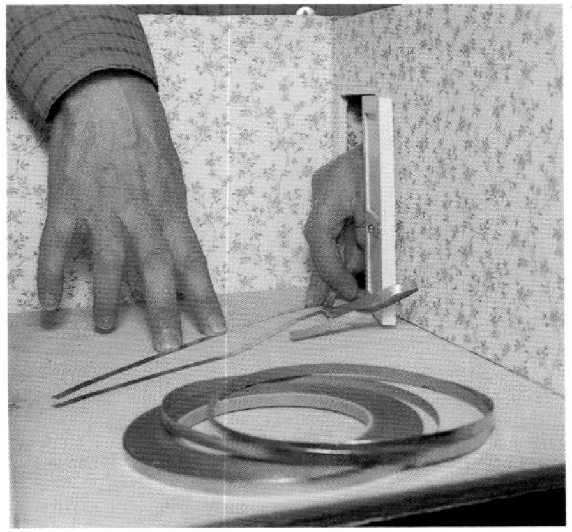

1

1 For the upstairs, lay two strips of copper tape across the room and guide them out into the corridor behind the bathroom.

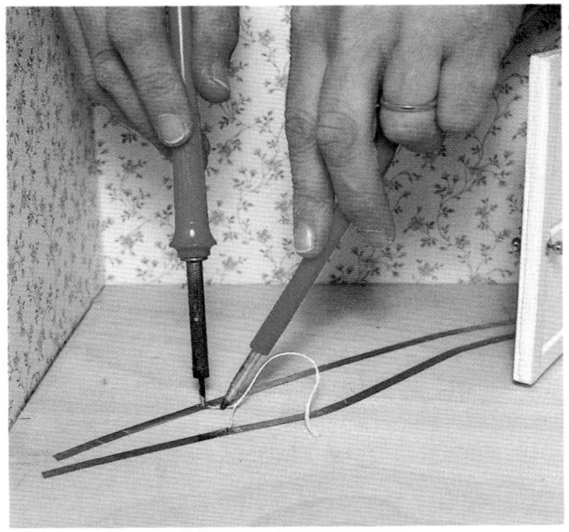

2

2 You will solder wires from one of the lounge ceiling lights and two fires and one bedside lamp onto this bedroom circuit.

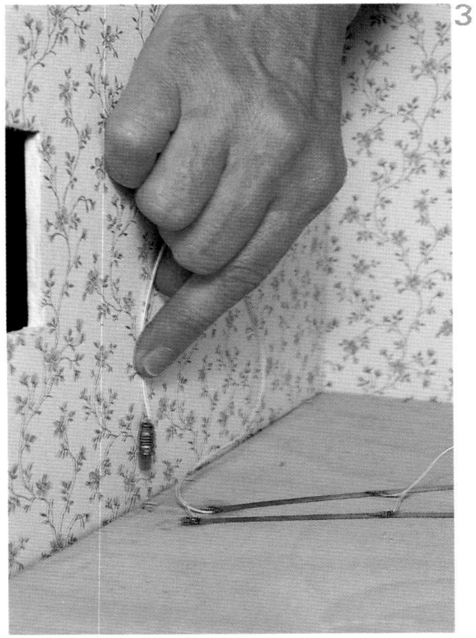

3

4

3 The lounge fire bulb has been dropped down the chimney to the open fire grate. The bedroom fire bulb shown here will be pushed through a hole on the far side of the chimney breast at floor level.

4 The completed bedroom fireplace.

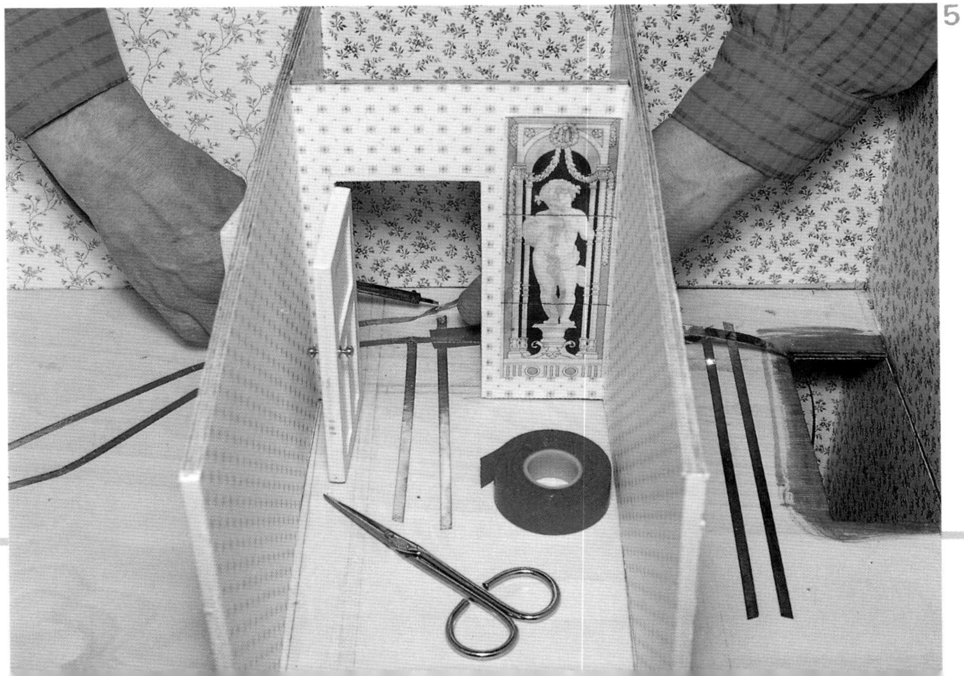

5

5 The landing circuit with a hall light from below, links up in the corridor with the bathroom, which takes the second lounge light. The flex leaves the house in the corner behind the stairwell. The right bedroom has its own circuit, with a wire leaving by the rear wall.

Downstairs Wiring

1 Drill two holes, one for each of the brass tubing plug sockets, near the floor in the lounge and bedroom above.

2 The two pairs of brass tubing protrude from the inside to the outside. Two copper strips link these, then run the full width of the house to the external chimney flue behind the kitchen.

Place insulating tape over the soldered joints to stop the ceiling lights dropping lower into the room and to prevent the wires snagging when the floor covering is laid into place.

Think carefully before you install any wall lights. You could bring the wires down the wall after papering and hide them behind some furniture; they would be linked into the circuit on that same floor. Another possibility is to drill holes in the side walls and direct the wires outside where they can be disguised by painting, or laid under the edges of wall trim or between brick courses, or brought down external chimney flues. The wires are so fine that they will not be too obtrusive. Whatever you choose to do, remember to make them accessible, especially as most commercial wall lights have grain of wheat bulbs.

Fire lights can be dropped down hollow chimney breasts but a more favoured method is to drill a hole in the far side of the fireplace at floor level and poke the bulb through. If you adopt this method of lighting you can always add or move lights around when the house is finished. For example, you might need to move a bedroom light to one side to accommodate a four-poster bed. You could even drill this extra hole right at the outset to give you greater freedom in the furnishing.

Because the bathroom in this house has no side doors, you cannot lay one copper circuit right across the house. Instead you will need two separate circuits – one for the lounge/dining room and hall and one for the kitchen. You can also solder wires for the upstairs and downstairs fires onto these circuits. If you cannot buy plug sockets for any reason, brass tubing can be used. Take it back through the rear wall and use split pins as plugs to fit into the tube holes. You may decide to use copper tape on the outside rear wall rather than have several long, trailing wires.

You will need a pair of wires from each of the two circuits to poke through holes drilled near the floor on the back wall together with holes for wires from the downstairs lamp and cooker.

UPSTAIRS LIGHTING

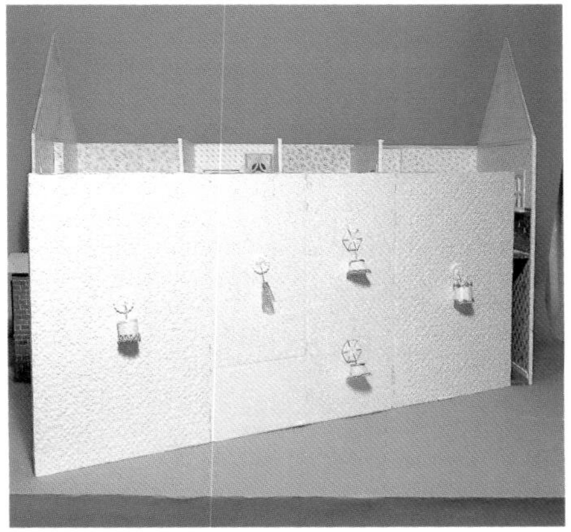

1

1 When the upper floor is complete prepare your lights and glue and screw in the ceiling.

2

2 Lay two strips of copper tape the full length of the roof floor. Solder onto these all the flex from the ceiling lights below.

3

3 The flex that is soldered to the ends of this loft circuit will drop down the outside rear wall.

4

4 A beam in the apex of each loft room rests on a pair of brackets. Wires from the three lights run along the top of the beams from room to room.

5

5 The three wires are held behind the chimney breast with doll's house wax and soldered onto the floor circuit.

For the upstairs lighting you can lay two strips of copper the full length of the roof space through the arched doorways. Wires from ceiling lights for the loft run along the top of beams in the apex. These beams rest on small brackets, but they are not fixed so they will always be removable. The three wires are guided down behind the chimney breast and soldered into the circuit on the floor.

To the Transformer

Now that the house is fully wired, the various circuits have to be connected to the mains through a transformer. Try to drill exit holes at the same point on each floor so that the wires can be hidden under one removable drain pipe or false flue.

Connector blocks come in plastic strips with pairs of screws along the length. Buy the smaller of the two sizes sold. They can be cut into multiples of four screws in a square, which for convenience I will refer to as one unit.

If you have no more than three pairs of wires leading from your circuits, the connection is simple. Separate the wires on each twin flex and, taking one wire from each, twist and solder them together. Do the same with the other three. Now you have two bundles of wire so you can screw them into the connector on one of the sides of a single unit. On the far side of the block, feed in another pair of wires a little thicker than the twin doll's house flex and only 3–4 in (7.5–10 cm) long.

This is soldered to the underside of a speaker terminal plate, which has red and black levers – these are obtainable from any good electronics or hi-fi shop. If you make a small box around the plate you can fix it to the back of your house with double-sided tape, Blu-tack or screws so that you can always take it off if necessary. All you have to do now is to flick the levers and pop in the two wires that lead from the transformer.

If you have more than three circuit wires from the doll's house you will need more than one connector unit, which is somewhat complicated to wire. Study the photograph carefully, but if you have any doubts, ask for professional advice.

Transformers

A transformer will reduce the high voltage household current to a safe 12 volts for your miniature circuit. This low voltage cannot harm you if you touch it. *The transformer is one piece of equipment on which you should not skimp on cost.* It has to be serviceable and, above all, reliable. Look for one that has a casing with a grill to disperse heat. The cheapest versions are enclosed and usually have thin wires and a minimum iron core, which becomes red hot after a short run. Remember, too, that 12 volt DC (direct current) is more reliable than AC (alternating current), which tends to fluctuate upwards. Some transformers have 12 volt DC and 16 volt AC, so be careful if you want long-life bulbs. Make sure, of course, that you have 12 volt bulbs.

You must be absolutely certain that the transformer has a cut-out button, which is a built-in fuse that will save your house from bursting into flames if things go wrong. I once used an old model railway transformer, in which, unknown to me, the cut-out failed when I accidentally had a crossed wire. In barely two seconds my lounge filled with smoke and I had to rewire all 36 bulbs in the doll's house. False economy can be dangerous and costly.

Look out for a transformer with a variable speed, which works on the same principle as a household dimmer switch. It will prolong bulb life and gives more realistic period lighting.

I use a large, 4 amp transformer because it is necessary for a modeller's power drill and also because I can plug three houses in a row into it. This project house has 20 bulbs, so I would suggest that you use a 1½ amp transformer as minimum.

CONNECTING WIRING TO A TRANSFORMER

1 All the various circuits are linked into the copper tape circuit on the rear wall. Take off a pair of wires to the speaker terminal plate with its red and black levers. You will attach your transformer wires into this.

1
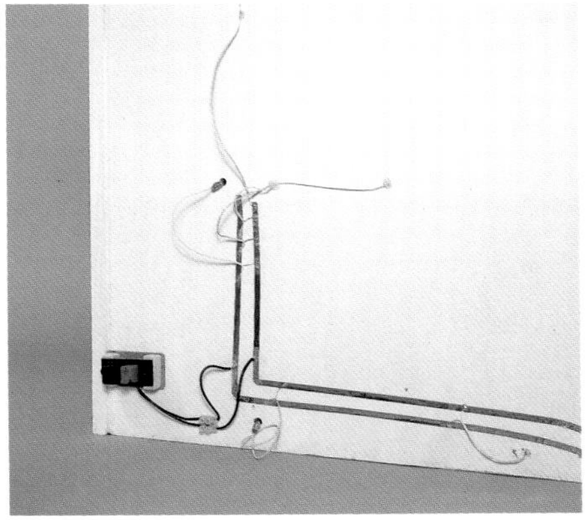

2
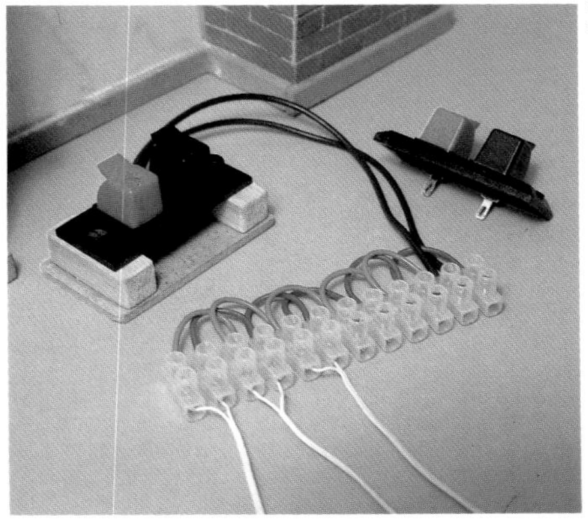

2 If you have many wires from a number of circuits you will need a long connector block, which should be wired as shown here.

3 An external chimney flue can be made from pieces of scrap wood because it will be either painted or bricked. It is a useful way to house the wiring.

4 The chimney flue can be attached to the wall with hooks and rings so that it is always possible to gain access to the lighting circuits.

3
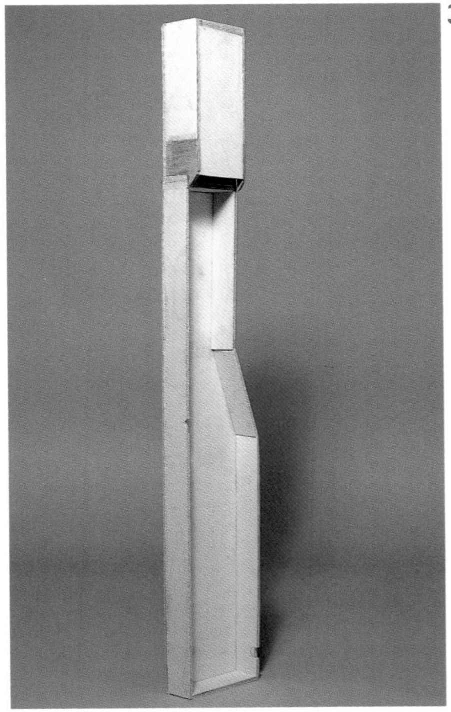

4
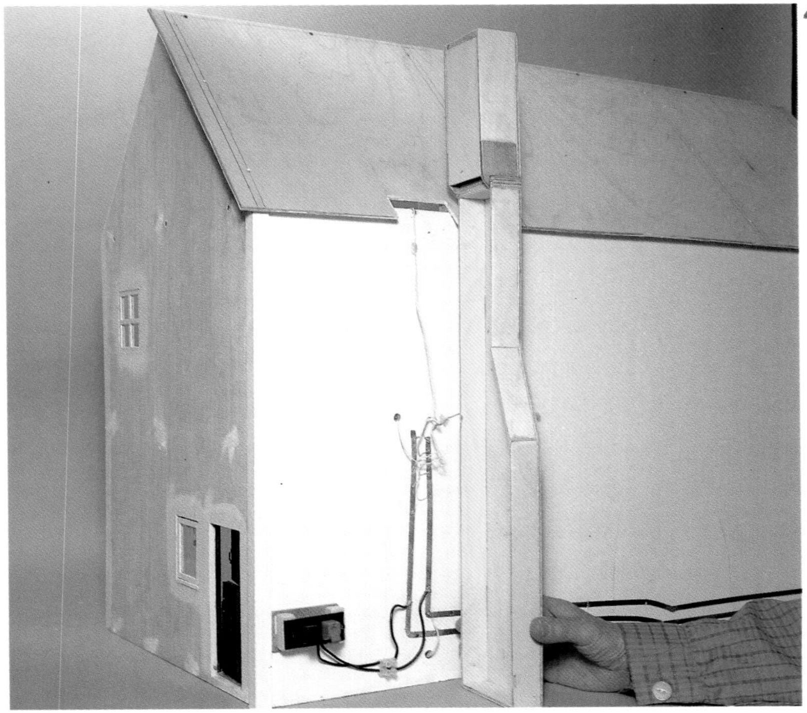

WINDOWS

Look around your town and out in the country and you will see a great variety of windows. Choose a style that suits the house you are building and study how the framework is built up. Notice especially which pieces of wood are longest and in which direction they are fixed. Windows usually resemble doors, with the long, vertical strips and the shorter cross-bars between. Look at the pattern of the glazing bars. Notice whether the windows are leaded or contain plain sheet glass.

Until you are an experienced woodworker you would be unwise to attempt sash windows. If you buy these ready made, remember that you cannot paint them because they are made so accurately that the sliding/opening movement has no spare room at all. You can of course, stain them. A casement window for the kitchen in this project house can be simply made using the pin method as described in the door section (see page 44).

If you decide to have non-opening windows, start by making an accurate template. Place a piece of card behind the hole, using a book or something similar to keep the card flat. Draw around the window hole and cut out this shape. This is yet another job that could have been done before you assembled your house and while the wood was lying flat on your workbench. Place this card on the acrylic sheet or perspex and draw around it. Cover the clear material with a piece of fine paper to prevent it from getting scratched, sticking it on with any washable paper glue.

Cut out the acrylic and test to see if it fits the hole reasonably accurately. Thin acrylic sheet can be cut with scissors or a knife. If you use perspex you will need either a fine-toothed saw or a sharp craft knife,

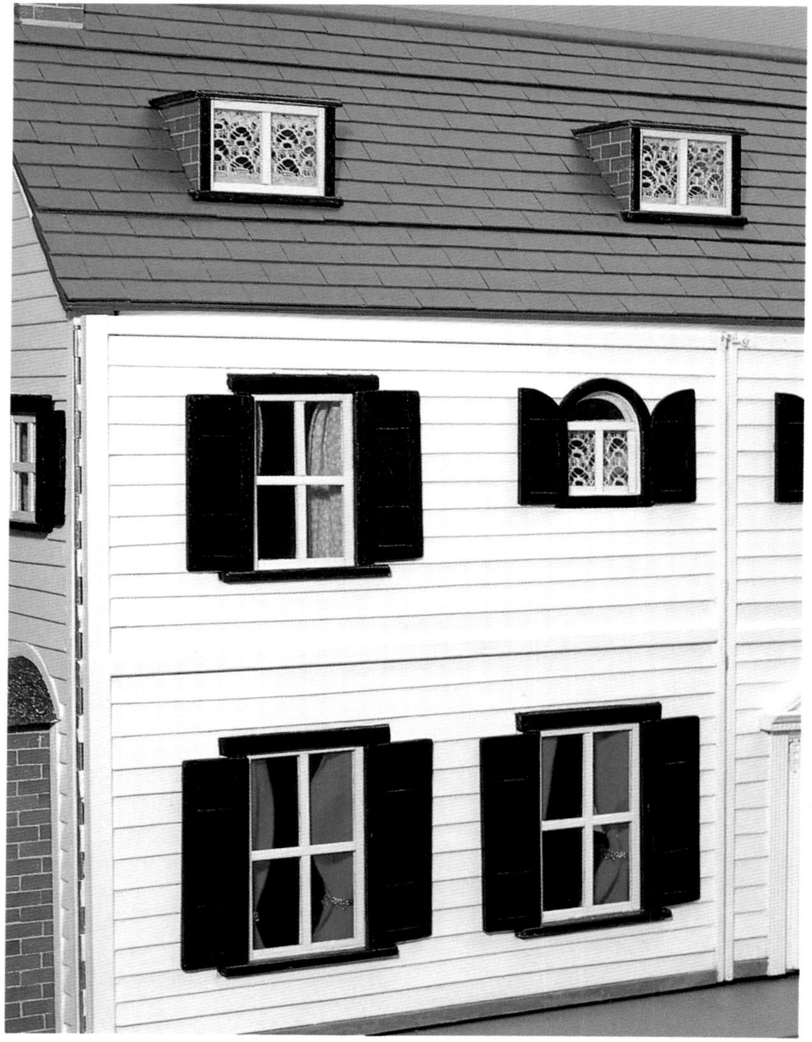

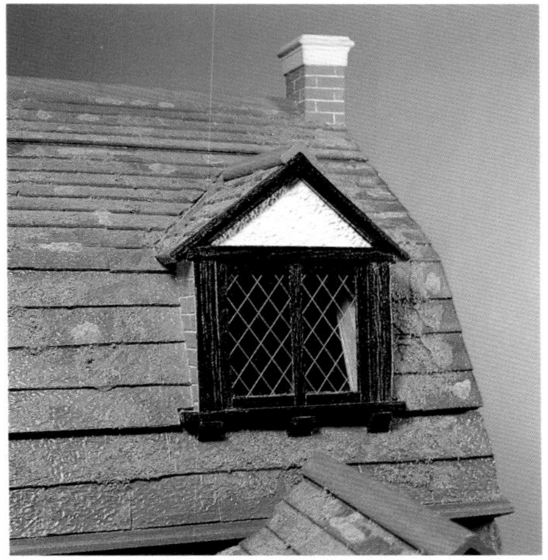

ABOVE An effective leaded window can be made by scoring the perspex with a sharp steel scriber.

ABOVE Windows of differing size and shape will need a template for each.

and it can be shaved down with coarse sandpaper or by scraping the knife along the edge.

For all your windows you will need many lengths of narrow, thin, well-sanded, strips of wood, which have to be painted or stained on both sides before they are cut. This is a time-consuming job, but it saves you getting splashes of paint on your windows. You may prefer to use white plastic strips.

Casement Windows

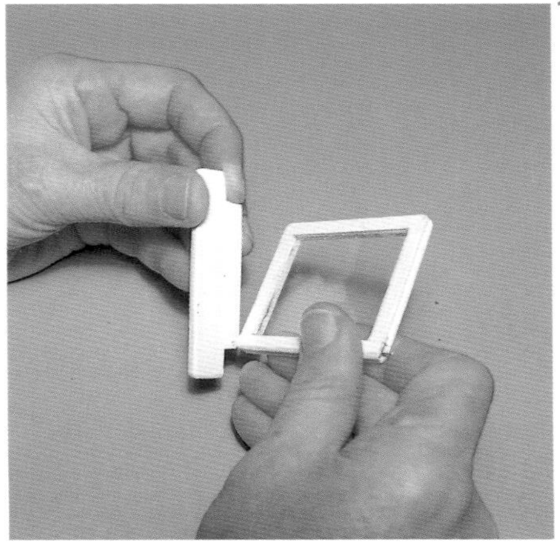

1 Make an opening casement window with pin hinges as described under the door section (see page 44).

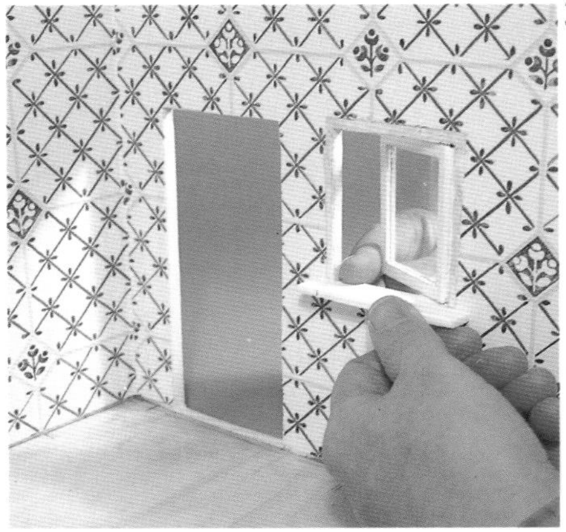

2 The upper pin is pushed into a hole in the top frame. The lower pin sits in a hole in the sill, which is glued to the frame.

MAKING A BAY WINDOW

1 These are the parts you will need to construct the bay window. The exact scale and size will depend on your personal taste and the size of your house.

2 It is basically a simple box shape.

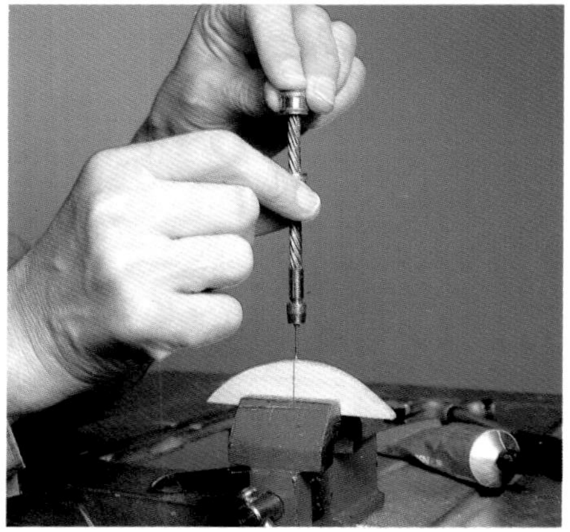

3 Pre-drill a small pin hole in the top centre of the curved section.

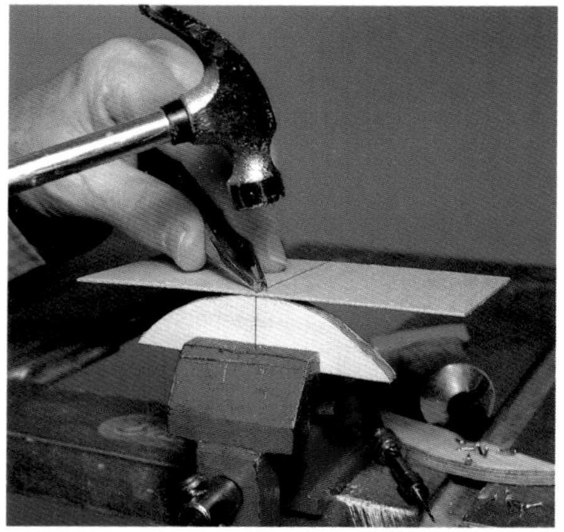

4 Pin a strip of 1⁄32 in (1 mm) ply into this hole.

5 Drill and pin the ply at intervals all round the curved top.

6

6 Glue it to the box frame.

7

7 Glue the perspex into the front of the window.

8 Make a wooden frame, inserting the vertical strips first, then the horizontal ones and finally the glazing bars.

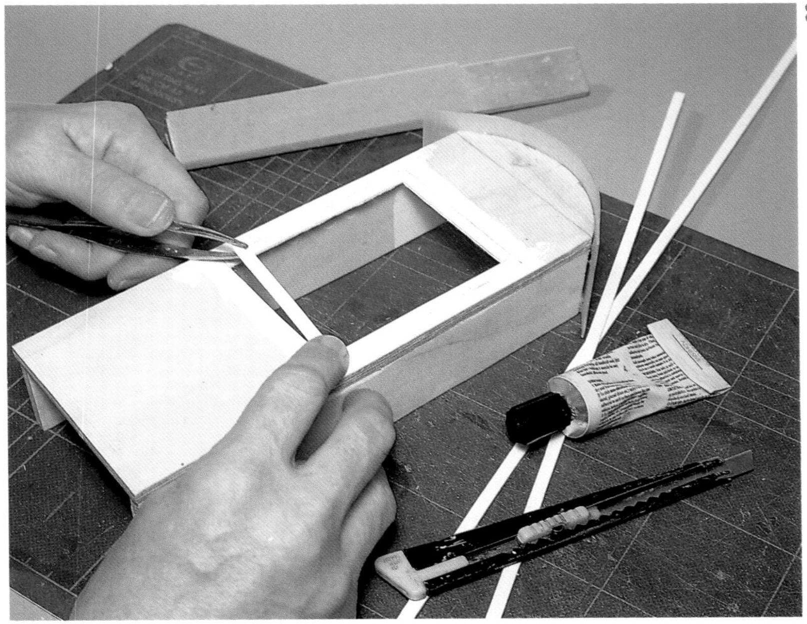
8

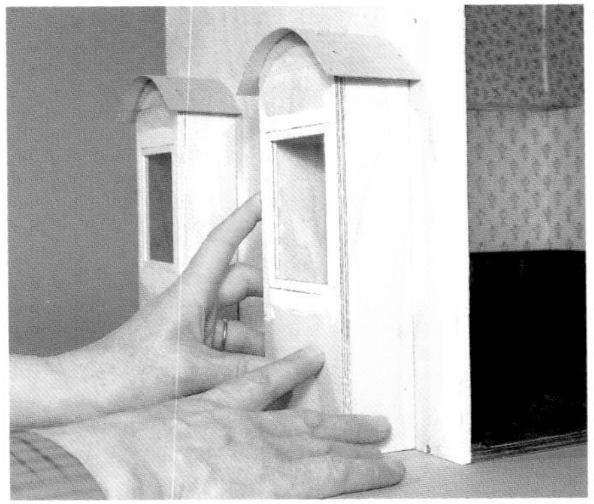
9

9 The whole bay unit is glued to the outer wall so that the inner ply edges are flush with the hole in the wall.

10

10 On the inside set in the windowsill, cut to fit.

11

11 The side walls should be put in place after the sill.

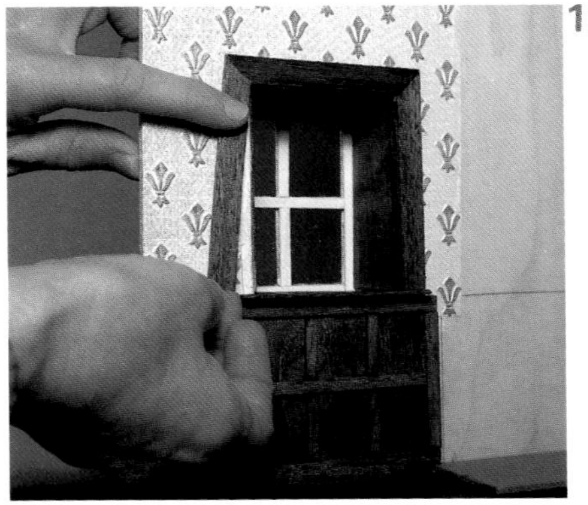
12

12 Finally, position the window architraves.

Because the acrylic sheet is thin and flexible, give the cut-out shape a border of strip wood, remembering to glue the vertical pieces first. Use a clear spirit-based glue. This is a messy job and needs careful application to avoid causing damaging smudges. Test that it fits tightly in the window hole and trim it down if necessary. Glue it in place. Add another frame to the inside, pressing it hard against the wood of the house so that any gaps on the outside will be filled in. Now you can add the glazing bars in your chosen pattern on both sides.

Perspex is thick enough to be glued directly in place, so you can add the frame while it is *in situ,* and the beading will fill in any gaps automatically.

Perspex can also be used to give the effect of a leaded window. A simple method is to make a diamond pattern on a sheet of paper and lay the perspex shape on top. Following the lines, score the surface with a sharp steel scriber on one side only. The reflection of the light in the grooves will give a good imitation of leading.

Unless you are a master-craftsman or have a die-cast machine, all your windows will vary slightly, and you will have to make a template for each individual one. The windows on each floor may be a different shape, varying from long or wide in the main rooms, to square near the top of the house.

Dormer Windows

Dormer windows may at first seem very complicated. However, once you have grasped the mathematics they will not seem quite such a problem.

The actual opening in the roof will probably be 3 × 3 in (7.5 × 7.5 cm), but this is not the size of the glass. Draw a line 3 in (7.5 cm) long on a piece of card and another at right angles from the centre of this line. The 3 in (7.5 cm) line is the base of your triangle. Now move the right-angled set square up and down the centre line until the sides touch the outer

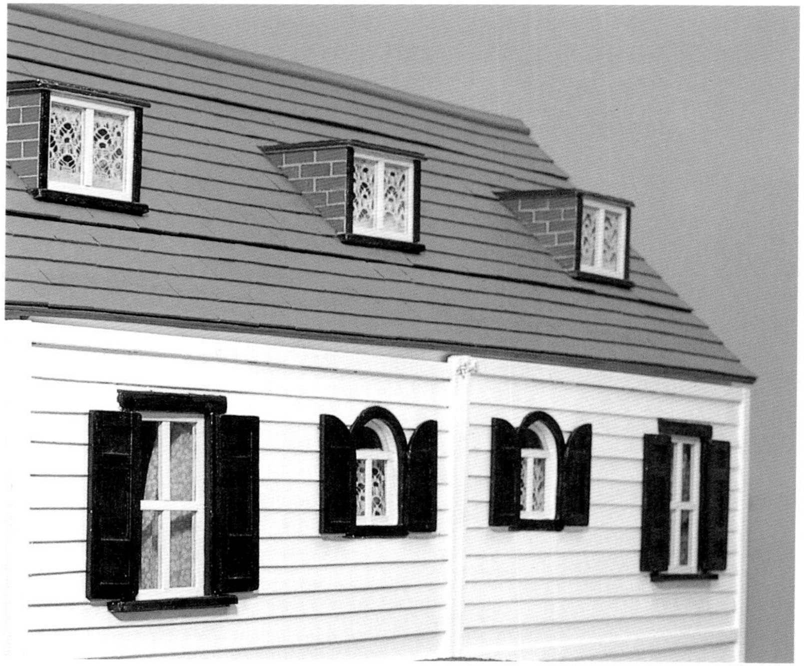

ABOVE Dormer windows add an interesting feature to a house.

points of the base line; draw around the right angle. This triangle of card forms a template for the sides of your dormer. When the longer base is held against the opening in the roof, the window will look upright at the front.

Cut two of these triangles in wood and add a roof that is the width of your required window. Draw a line around the inside and cut out this roof area so that the two walls can be glued to the wood, flush with the hole in the roof. The dormer is, in effect, another small box that is stuck to the roof. The flat lid of a dormer overhangs the walls. If the top is gabled, the lid must be flush so that the gables can overhang. Glaze the front as you would any other window.

Dormer Windows

1
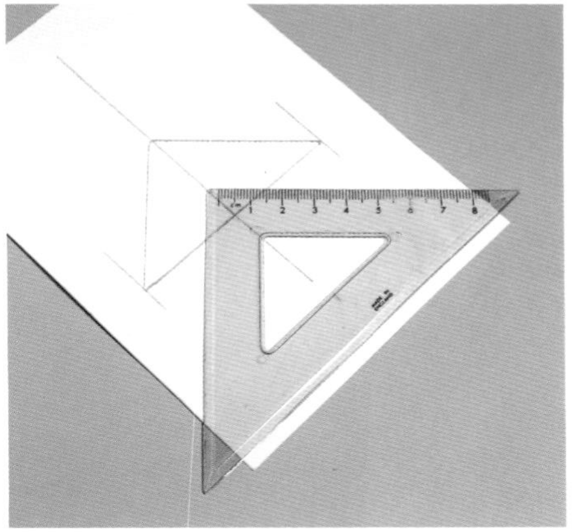

2

3
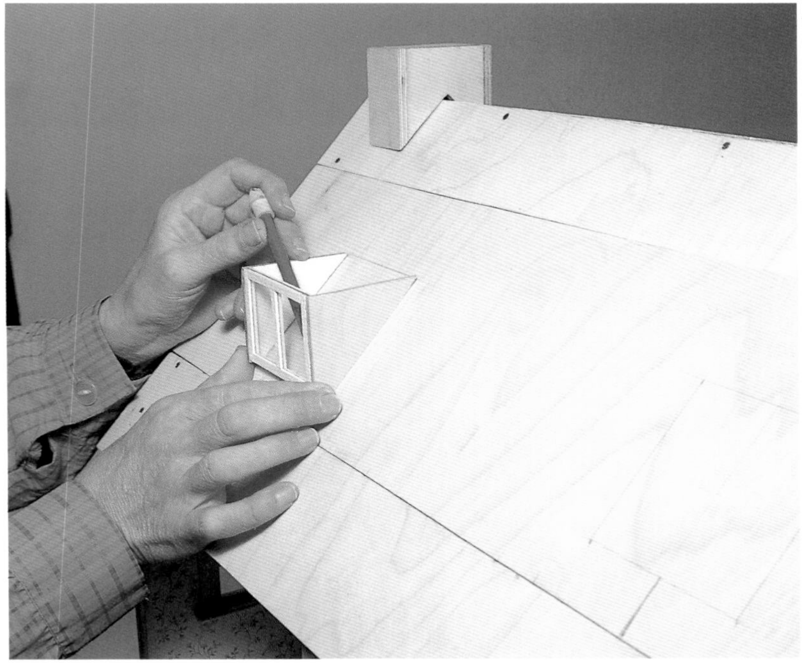

1 Take the width of the hole you require in the roof. Draw a line in the centre at right angles to it. Move a set square point up this line until the sides touch each end of the line. This is the template for the walls of your dormer window.

2 The component parts of the dormer window and the order of assembly.

3 Before you add the top of the window, draw around the inside to determine the area that is to be cut away in the roof.

4

5

4 The roofing material is added after the window is fixed. Here textured wallpaper has been used which will be painted with dark grey paint, to create the effect of a tarred roof.

5 The sides can then be bricked or painted and a windowsill added.

THE ROOF

The roof of your doll's house will be governed by the shape of your highest wall; in this case, the side panels are the highest. If you opt for attic rooms or merely loft storage space you will have direct access to the bedroom lighting. If you decide to have a sealed roof space, you can run the upstairs light flex along a groove in beams that are held against the ceiling with doll's house wax.

Because this project has attic rooms, the bedroom lighting circuit can run along the floor of the roof area. The attic ceiling light wires are laid across beams held in the apex of the roof on brackets (see page 55).

The wood used for the roof is ⅛ in (4 mm) because it will be strengthened with tiles, but it is a good idea to increase the width of the side walls on which it will be resting by adding another full section, which can be clamped tight against the original outer wall.

Cut a length of ½ in (12 mm) square strip beading to fit exactly between the two peaks, placing it with a corner edge uppermost. Glue and screw this ridgepole into place. Also glue strips of triangle wood along the floor on both edges of the roof. Before gluing the rear beading, cut out a section where your lighting wires will leave the house. If you

Fixing the Back of the Roof

1 Strengthen the gable ends with a lining. This also gives ½ in (12 mm) sloping walls to support the roof.

2 A strip of ½ in (12 mm) beading between the gable ends forms a ridgepole. Also add triangle beading between the gables at floor level. Remember to leave a gap for your exit wires which will drop down the outside rear wall. The rear slope of the roof is fixed first. Paper it if you want attic rooms. Room dividers help to support the panel.

1

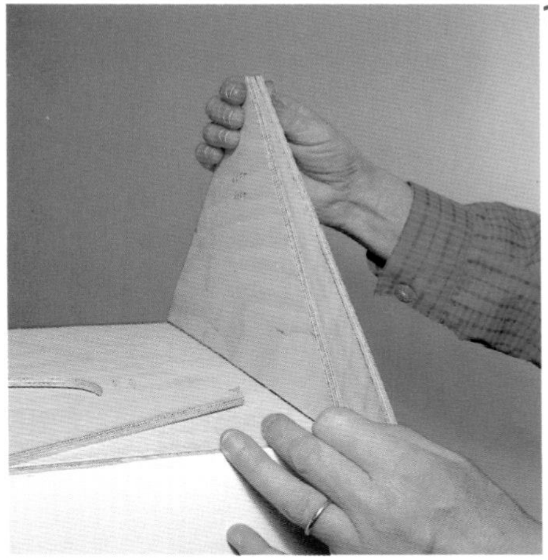

2

LEFT The opening front is often hinged to the ridgepole as in this house.

have an external chimney flue on the rear of the house, for example, position the gap so that the wires can run down the flue.

Because this project house is nearly 3 ft (90 cm) wide, the roof has been given additional support with two central dividers. If you are making rooms in the roof space, you may like to have doors in the partitions instead of arches.

The rear slope of the roof should be cut and fixed first so that it overlaps the back and side walls to form eaves.

Because the kitchen and the right bedroom windows are staggered,

MAKING A ROOF OPENING

1 One method is to fix two strips of wood to the top and bottom of the front area and to make a centre panel that rests in the opening like a box lid.

1

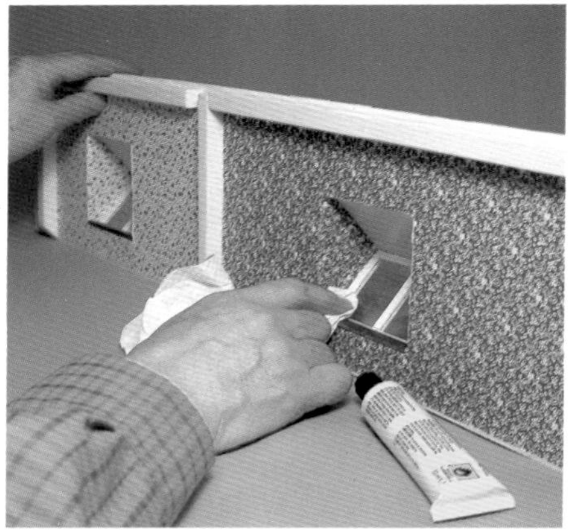

2

2 The inside beading to hold the centre panel of the roof in place need not be as thick as this – I could not buy small beading at the time. Fill in the gap behind the dormer window with a sill.

3 The attic will look more homely if you add walls to the front and back, to square off the rooms.

3

4 You could add a shelf to the front wall as an attractive feature. A false top to the stairs can be positioned in the roof over the corridor behind the bathroom.

4

room fires will have to be located on the rear wall. A chimney flue can be made to cover the main electrics and will therefore have to be removable (see page 57). It is again a basic box shape. Remember to cut out a section in the rear roof panel where the chimney flue will slot into the roof. Glue and screw the panel in place.

Before you fix the second roof section you have to consider the eaves, which will impede the main house opening. This problem can be overcome by adding a strip of wood outside the front edge of the house so that the opening doors clear the lower edge of the roof. Do not let your overhang be too deep.

If you were able to make the peak of the roof at an angle of 45 degrees the front half will sit neatly over the rear section. You would, of course, have to cut the front area ⅛ inch deeper than the rear section to allow for the overlap. Do not worry if the peak where the two halves of the roof meet is not perfect, because the join will be hidden by hollow triangle wooden ridge tiles. Use double-sided tape to hold the roof sections temporarily in place while you position the screw holes.

If your roof space is to open you have various options. First, you could hinge the front section along the ridgepole. Alternatively, you could glue and screw strips of beading around the underside of the roof in such a way that they sit snugly inside the house frame like a box top. Another possibility is to fix two chimneys to the upper edge so the slope is angled to hook over the ridge.

One of the easiest ways to make a roof opening is to add a strip of wood to the ridge area and another at the eaves – pieces around 2 inches deep will do. Fix some beading around the inside of the center section of the roof so that the front opening fits into the space like a box top. This removable section will need to be fitted with dormer windows if you are having attic rooms.

To make the attic space look like rooms, cut strips 2 inches wide to stand at the back from the floor to roof and two similar strips for the front. A shelf over the front pieces gives an added feature for ornaments. Cut out a piece from the rear mini wall for the wire to pass through to the outside. The hole can be hidden by furniture later. Remember the chimney breast, which runs up from the left wall fireplaces on the floors below. Dismantle the parts, and paper the rooms before you glue it in place. The last feature to add is the box, to act as a false top for the stairs. As long as you position it realistically over the hallway behind the bathroom, the viewer will imagine that you have an unseen spiral staircase leading up to the attic!

BELOW The attic rooms are complete apart from the floor covering.

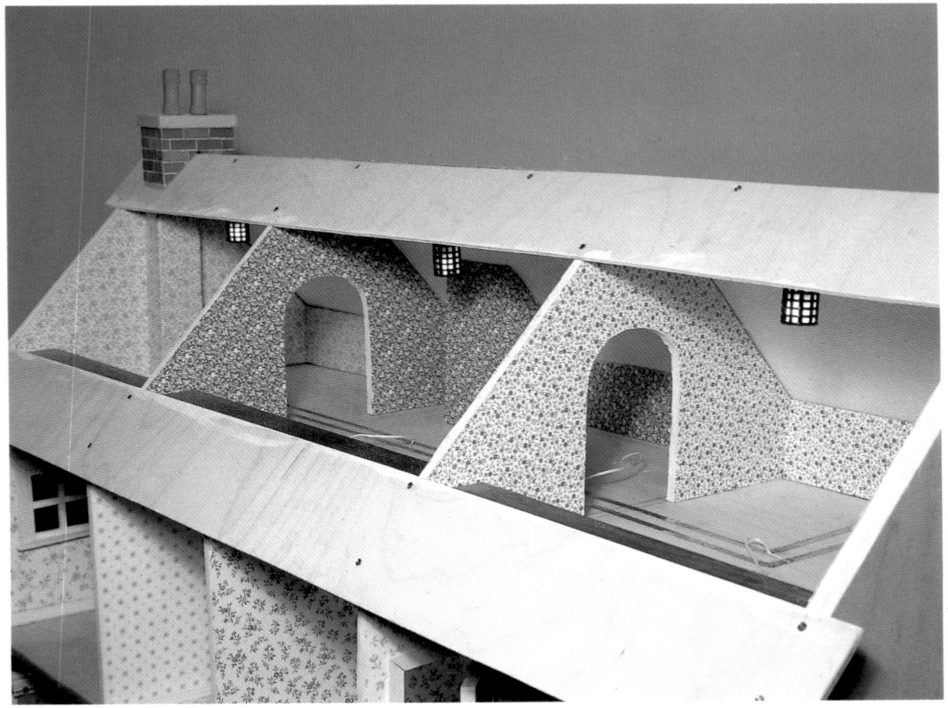

THE FRONT-OPENING DOORS

LEFT The English Tudor hall has a third door for the center section.

The front of your dollhouse is the feature that distinguishes it from every other.

There are a number of ways of tackling the opening. Do you want one complete, removable front or do you prefer two opening, hinged doors? Would you like to add an extension to one side like an extra room? Have you designed a high center gable or a gable to one side? Sliding doors are another option.

If you have opted for a long porch or any other elaborate feature that would be spoiled by cutting at any point, then one single, removable front is ideal. The drawback is that you always have to find somewhere to stand it when you open up the house. The front of the tythe barn, for example, is one piece.

Two long, opening, hinged doors are more traditional. The division between the two is usually made so that the hall/landing and one upstairs and one downstairs rooms are on one door while the remaining two rooms form a slimmer door. The center section will be attached to the

LEFT Two long opening doors are more traditional. In this manor the mansard roof and the front porch/garden are separate units.

half that has less weight or width. These long doors are practical, and they sweep the eye to the interior as they open.

If you want an L-shaped front extension, you can simply make a small house as you would make a box and attach it to the front, hinged to the outside wall edge. Because of the extra weight, you have to keep this as one separate door, and the hall would be linked to the other half. The farmhouse has such an extension, which increases the size of the rooms and also adds an interesting feature when the house is open.

You might like to extend the lower part of the flat half to come level with the room extension by adding a store front or an open porch. The popular Honeychurch Victorian dollhouse store has this kind of frontage.

A flat but high-sided gable would again form one of the doors on its own. Depending on its height, you would have to add a roof that fitted the slope of the main roof, which is not an easy job for a beginner. Practise with a dormer window in the roof to learn the principle.

If you choose sliding doors you will require a router to make a deep

ABOVE The weight of the L-shaped room extension means that it has to be made as a separate door.

RIGHT An open extension adds an interesting feature to a house.

ABOVE Both sides of the popular Honeychurch Victorian shop are extended at the front.

RIGHT This was an original, rather plain house front.

FAR RIGHT By turning it round and remaking the gable end into an opening door, then adding extensions on either side, a completely different aspect was achieved. The upper gable section is removable for access to the wiring only – that is, it is not a usable room. The arcade and kitchen at the sides are separate units, and the whole building can be transported in three easily disassembled sections. One day the lower half will have herringbone brick inlay.

RIGHT The front of the Queen Anne house is hinged on one side only but is divided into two halves horizontally.

ABOVE The San Francisco house front caused problems because of its complexity and so the house actually opens at the rear.

RIGHT An elaborate front of the kind on this tythe barn does not lend itself to two opening doors. It has to be removed in one piece.

If you choose sliding doors you will require a router to make a deep groove, or you can add channelling with plastic strip. Alternatively glue two pieces of strip wood to make a groove. The drawbacks are that all channelling is visible, gathers dust and eventually snaps. It also means you must have a perfectly flat front with no side extension on the eaves. Another major problem is that curtains and other features on the inside will jam the smooth running, and the little front door has to be hinged to open outwards if you want it to stay intact.

Whichever style you choose, cut the wood to size first then cut out the door and window openings. Do not use thin wood for this frontage, because it is weakened when the door opening is cut away. Even ¼ in (6 mm) is liable to warp, especially if you use a water-based glue, paint or wallpaper paste. You can overcome this by clamping the whole section to a flat bench and sizing it with either wallpaper paste or a water-based primer paint. Leave it clamped until the wood is thoroughly dry.

The small front door is made in a similar way to the internal room doors and in any style you choose. Add the hinges while you still have the big doors on the bench.

A door fitting that is often used for shops is also acceptable for some houses. Cut it slightly larger than the opening so that it sits behind the frame. Lay your hinges flat on the inside surface and across to a strip of the same wood. This strip is then glued and/or pinned to the inside wall.

The big hinges need a good grip with longer screws because of the extra wear and tear of the constant opening and knocking. Piano hinges are best because you do not need to recess the wood. Screw them to the doors first and mark up the position of screw holes on the front wall edges. If you feel it is necessary, insert plugs of dowel in the side walls as described on pages 22–3.

MAKING THE FRONT OPENING

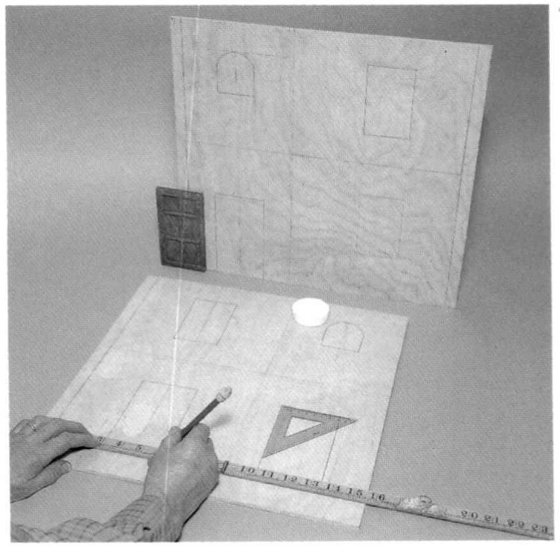

1 Cut out the large front doors and draw in the windows and front door.

2 Cut out the windows and door, then check that this style is your final choice.

3 Make the front door in the same way as the internal doors. Decide on the style of the surrounds and make them with whatever materials you can acquire.

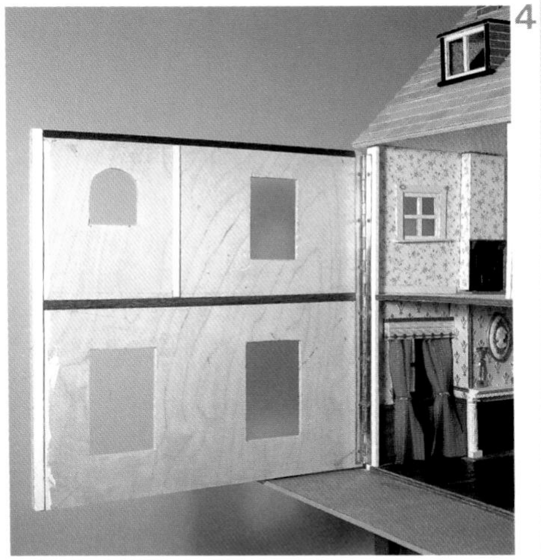

4 Piano hinges are by far the best type for the heavy front opening. Divide the inside with beading to correspond to the layout of the rooms.

5 Paper the inside to match the rooms or use a plain paper throughout.

6 Add the strip of beading under the eaves to fill the gap above the doors.

FINISHING THE INTERIOR

FLOOR COVERINGS

Because the wiring is on the floors, the floor covering has to be removable so that you have access to the electrics. You may perhaps select an all-over carpet, or possibly you might prefer patterned "lino" paper stuck to a piece of soft card. Whatever you use, it can usually be held down with double-sided tape, which can be stuck to the floors in the areas between the copper tape.

An effective method is to stain and polish strips of wood and, using plenty of white wood glue, stick them to a close-weave fabric such as curtain lining. You can roll up the floors as you would a roll-top desk so that they can be squeezed into the rooms and then spread out around the various fittings, such as fireplaces.

Cut the flooring to size after the skirting boards have been fitted.

ABOVE Suitably grained wallpaper can make an acceptable wooden floor when it is stained.

LEFT Vinyl floor tiles also have their uses. If the surface is too rough, fill it in with wall filler. Cut the tile into strips, then into tile or paving slabs. Pick them up at random and glue them to the floor.

A Flexible Wooden Floor

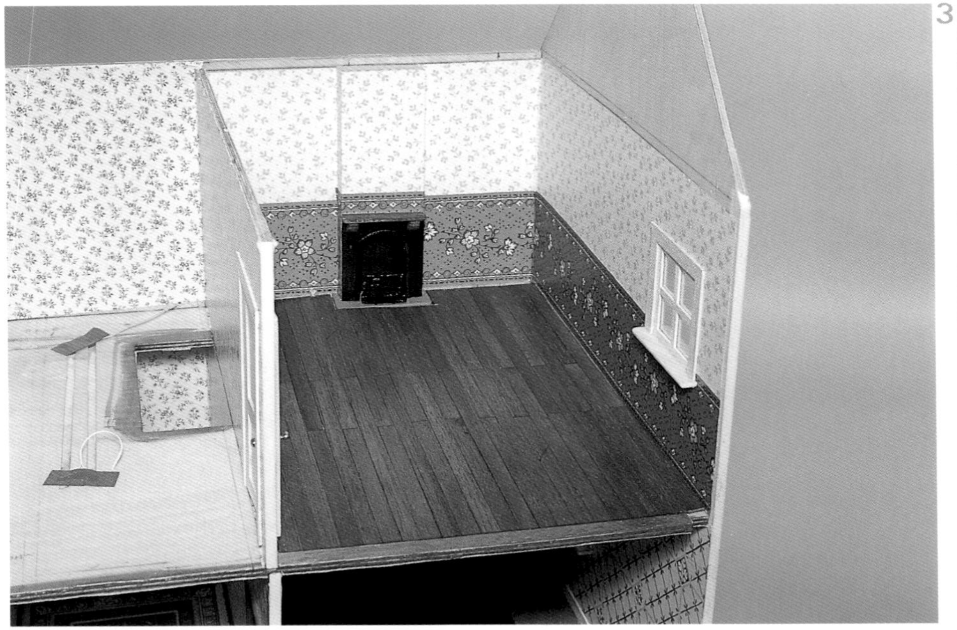

1 Glue strips of wood stained to your chosen colour to close-weave material to make a flexible boarded floor.

2 When it is cut to size, the floor can be rolled up, inserted into a room, then spread out neatly around fittings like fireplaces.

3 If the sheet is pressed down onto double-sided tape laid between the wiring, it can be removed if necessary.

FIREPLACES

When it comes to selecting a fireplace, your best plan is to study photographs and to see what materials you can acquire to build up the fire surround. If you have opted for external chimney flues, you will have to stick a box to the outside wall to cover the hole you cut away. Inside the room you will need only a fire surround. Fireplaces must be authentic, so take care that you do not position them under or over a window in another room. They must have a common flue right up the house.

Corner fireplaces take up less room, but recesses offer more opportunities for interesting furniture.

If you have an internal fire, you need to stick a wallpapered chimney breast to the room wall, with the fireplace and surround built into the lower one-third of the chimney breast. For both purposes $1/16$ in (2 mm) ply or balsa wood is light and practical.

When it comes to decorating the fire surround, you can use a variety of oddments, such as fans, bracelet links, plastic flowers and leaves, jewellery bits, fancy cord and ribbons. Almost anything can be used. When painted they look like plaster carvings.

LEFT Plastic fans have a wide variety of uses. The filigree carving can be cut and used almost anywhere including for the decoration of a fire surround. You could also use them for garden furniture and iron staircases.

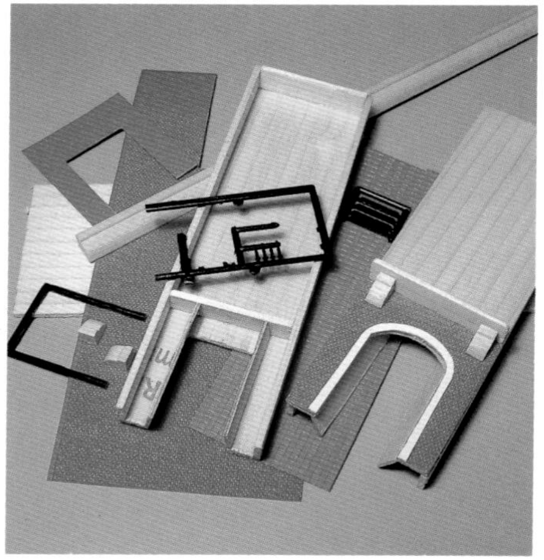

RIGHT The basic internal chimney breast can be made from any thin scrap wood. For the bedroom fires you could use model railway plastic brick sheets, the waste from model kits and shelf brackets cut from shaped strips of wood.

ABOVE An external firegrate is merely a thin ply box over a hole in the wall. The advantages are that the fire surround can be laid flat against the wall to save space in a small room and you have an exit line for wiring down the flue. The disadvantages are that recesses around an internal fireplace can add interest to a square room and bricking is a long, tedious process.

MAKING A FIREPLACE

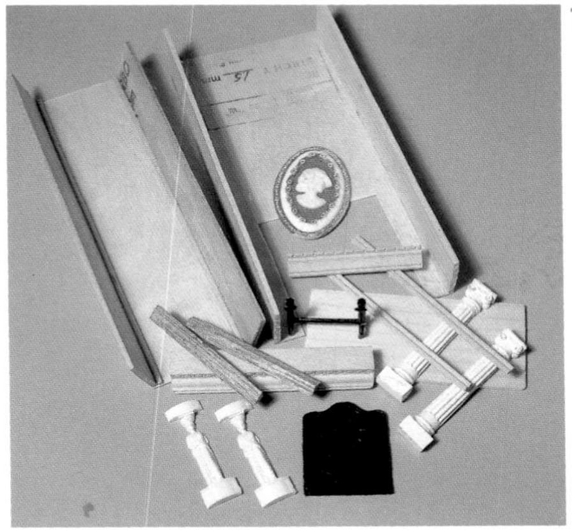
1

1 For the main room fireplace you can use a mixture of oddments and shelf and pillars from a doll's house specialist. The caryatids came from a small spirit bottle and the cameo was a broken brooch – both bought on junk stalls. The fireback is merely a shaped thin ply with a smooth, unravelled strand of string for the surround and jewellery oddments for decoration.

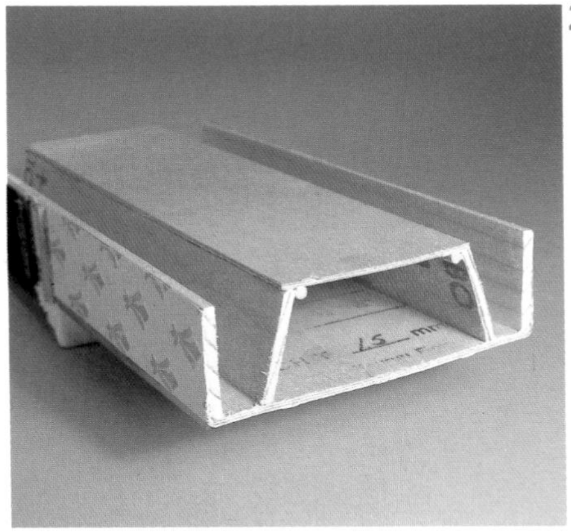
2

2 If you need to drop the light bulb down a hollow flue into the main grate, make the chimney breast in two parts.

3 The front of the fireplace before decoration.

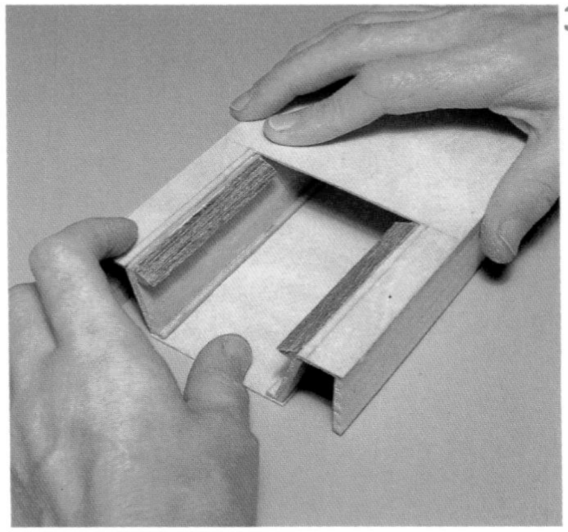
3

4

4 The fireplace in position. The cameo is supported with doll's house wax, so it can be replaced with a mirror or picture if you wish. The fire surround can be enhanced by any strip of decorative beading.

Making Curtains with a Pelmet

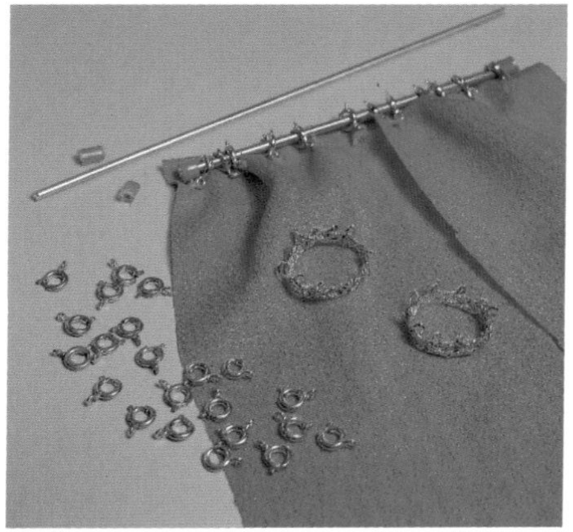

1

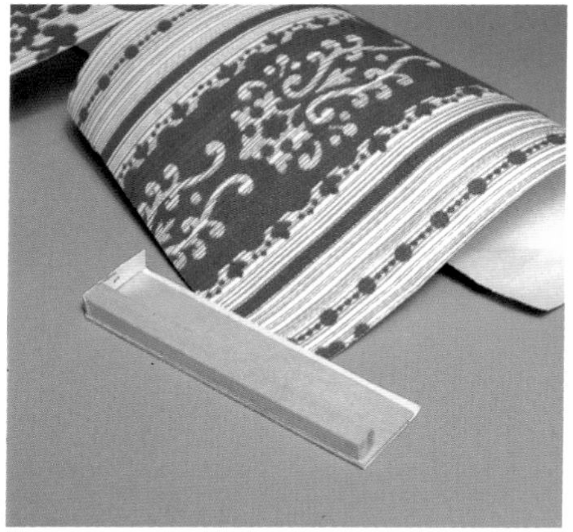

2

2 This small free sample of wallpaper was intended for the chimney breast, but the pattern was too big. The border though, was ideal for the pelmet, which was made from plywood and ¼ in (6 mm) beading.

3 Pre-drill tiny holes in the architrave for screw rings to take the curtain rods.

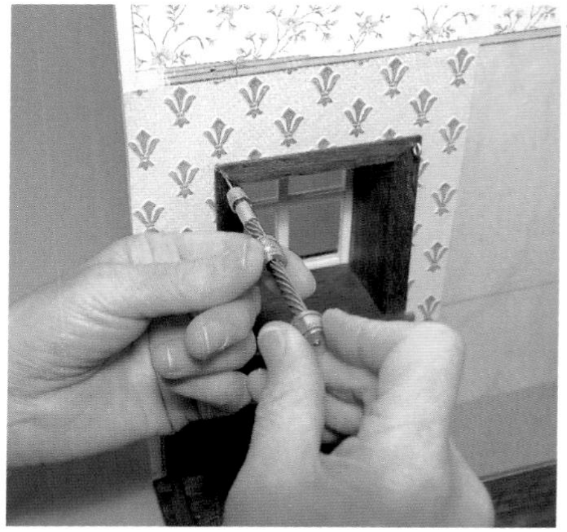

3

1 Authentic curtain rods, rings and end caps can be expensive and are not readily available. Necklace clasps are a good substitute for the rings, and they can be threaded on brass rod with plastic tubing for end caps.

4

4 The pelmet is held in place with doll's house wax so that the curtains are accessible if you ever want to change them. Always dress the window that is behind a chimney breast before you add the ceiling.

Making a Blind

1 Blinds can be made by soaking material in wallpaper paste. Allow it to dry and then press, before sticking to a brass rod.

1

2 Add a piece of cord and a bead or seed for the blind pull.

2

Curtains

Curtains should be made of thin material, and if patterned, make sure it is in scale. You may want to change your curtains when you redecorate the house in years to come, so make them removable. Spring necklace clasps make good curtain rings: sew the loops to the material and run the wider rings on brass rods. Snippets of plastic tubing will make rod caps. Hold pelmets in place with doll's house wax so they can be taken off to allow you to reach the curtains.

Blinds can be made from any material that has been stiffened by soaking in wallpaper paste and glued to rods. Only the dedicated make blinds that roll down!

The Staircase

Tape the upper stair treads to the cardboard mock room in the position it will occupy in the house. Banisters are best purchased ready made, but if you cannot obtain these, they can be made with dowling and small blocks of wood. This is a very fiddly and frustrating process and perhaps not ideal for the beginner, so you may decide to opt for solid panels which are an easier alternative.

To be realistic, the banisters should sit in the middle of the tread on the outer edge of stairs that are made with stringers, treads and risers. In practice, you need to be a master craftsman to keep them upright and firmly fixed. If this is your first doll's house, glue them not only to the stair treads but also further back so that they are supported by the risers. This method makes them less fragile and easier to fix. Because the staircase is supported on the cardboard, the banisters can be glued in a true upright position.

As you near the top of the stairs, the banisters will be taller than the ceiling. You can either cut them progressively shorter or add a solid piece of ply, cut to fit this space.

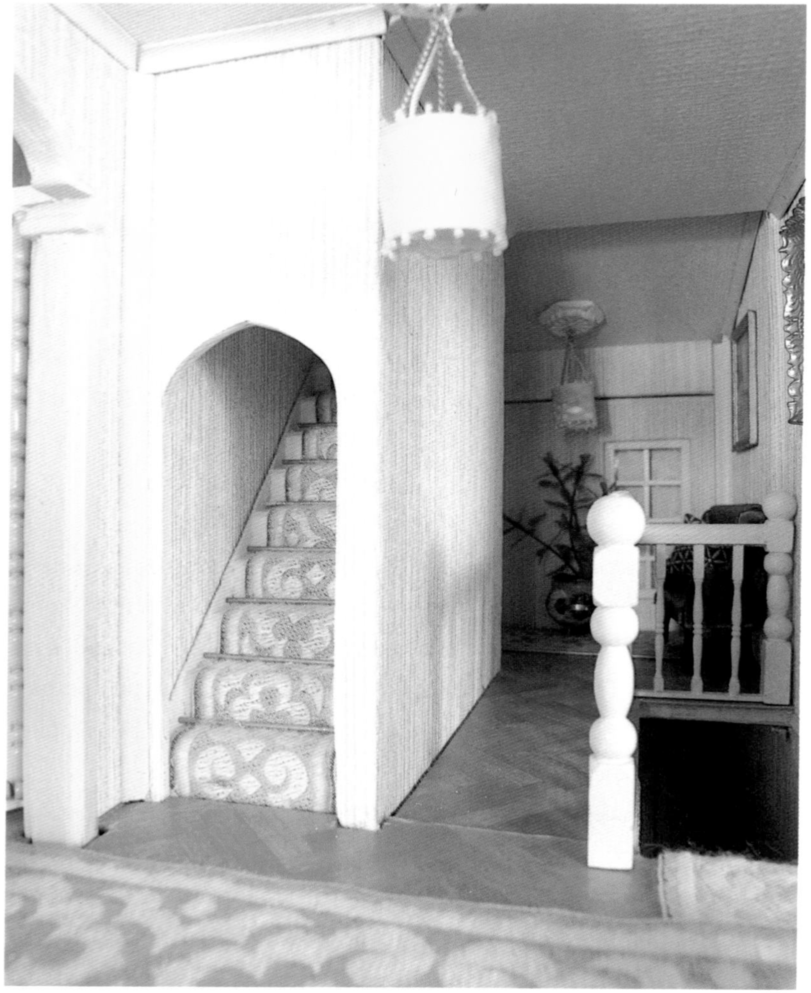

If you used triangle wood for stairs, the length of ply added to the outside edge should, in theory, be more solid and the banisters would sit on the top. In practice, you will find it more practical to glue the banisters in the angles between the treads, risers and outer support. This may not be strictly authentic, but it is easier for the inexperienced.

Newel posts for the top and bottom of the stairs can be bought ready-made or they can be carved out of wood. A simple method is to build them from square wood, dowel and beads. To make them stronger, drill holes through the component parts and force a length of brass rod through them.

The handrail is always a problem. Again, it is possible to buy ready-made ones or you can make something serviceable yourself. Cord glued to the top of each banister is often used, stiffened with paint or glue. Brass or plastic channelling is available in most hobby shops.

You will need to have a rail around the stairwell on the upper landing. You can use solid panels between the newel posts or make a surround of banisters. These are stuck to a thin strip of wood, fitted on the floor

ABOVE An enclosed staircase means that you will not need banisters. It is useful, too, for making a false staircase. In the Manor, the space under these stairs was used to extend a tiny bathroom.

RIGHT A boxed upper stairwell can be used to make a bedroom cupboard as in this room.

FINISHING A STAIRCASE

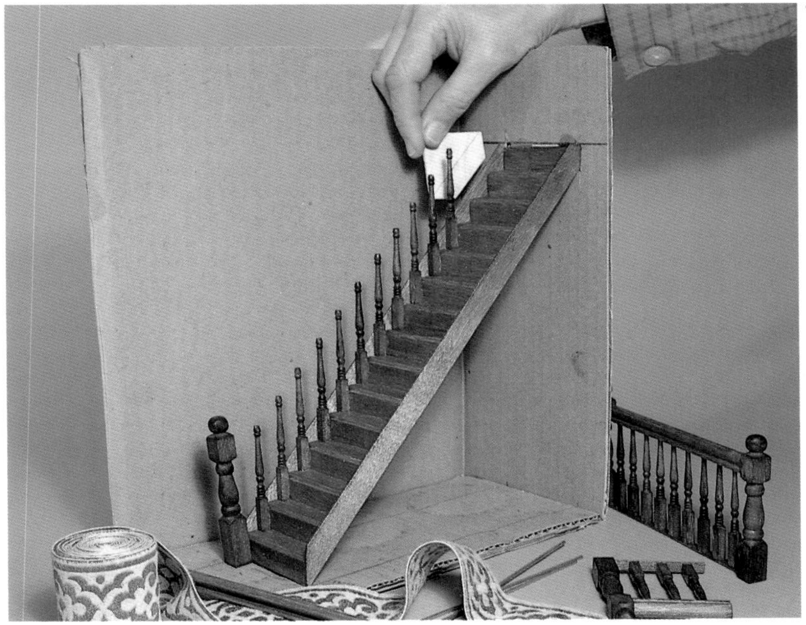

1 Use the mock cardboard hall to keep the glued banisters in an upright position.

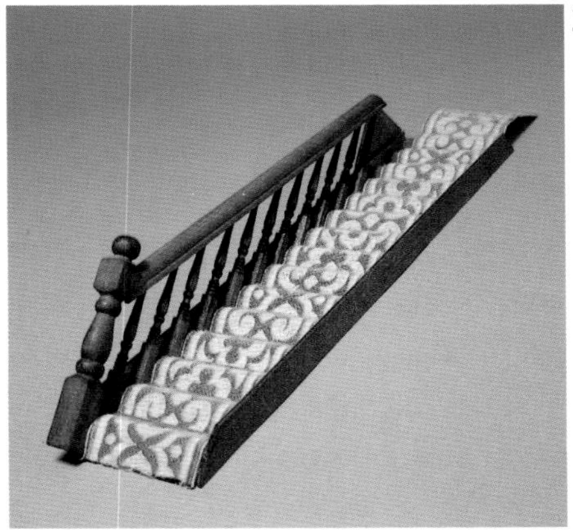

2 The staircase needs a newel post at the foot of the stairs and three for the stairwell surround above. Stick carpeting to the staircase and glue brass rods in the angles. A triangular piece of wood will fill the gap near the ceiling.

3 Do not secure a staircase until the hall or the room is complete.

between the newel posts and the handrail on top. Stair rods can be cut from brass rods and glued into the angles between treads and risers.

Do not secure any staircase permanently into your house until you have decorated and carpeted the hallways.

A simple method of fixing stairs is to have them supported not only by the room divider wall but also by another ceiling-height wall, which can be used in place of banisters. This is a useful device when staircases do not go anywhere. A solid surrounding wall allows you to partition off a stairwell, and you can make a cupboard over the stairs for added interest. You could, for example, use the space under a false staircase to extend a tiny bathroom.

In the doll's house made as a project here, part of a bedroom has been used to create a bathroom. It would have been possible to move the bathroom wall right up to the staircase and so to retain a larger bedroom. However, the landing area is more useful for a linen cupboard and for other furniture or toys.

FINISHING THE OUTSIDE

Once you have finished the interior, you should re-hinge the front opening. Many people merely paint the outer walls, but this has the effect of making them look more like toys than true miniature houses. It is possible to add a variety of features to create an authentic appearance. Outside features can also hide a multitude of sins! Remember, it's the finished product people see, not the mistakes made on the way.

The style you have devised for the interior will dictate how you decorate the outside. The walls can be covered by rendering made from an exterior strength proprietary filler or emulsion paint mixed with sand, and even painted sawdust looks effective. Weatherboarding (clapboard siding) is long strips of $\frac{1}{16}$ in (2 mm) ply stuck to the walls with impact adhesive. Start at the bottom of the wall and slightly overlap each layer.

BRICKS

Much trial and error has shown that one of the best ways to make all brickwork is with F2 grade sandpaper. First, paint the surface wood to represent mortar. Then stick on the bricks individually with a clear spirit glue which dries quickly. Bricking is a long, tedious business, but using tweezers helps considerably.

A cutting gadget from pieces of scrap wood is perfect for cutting the strips to an even width without slicing your fingers. Paint and stipple the sandpaper and cut the strips first, then cut the brick lengths, using the width of a length of wood as a guide. Leave some strips uncut for the halves and odd shapes around the windows.

ABOVE An external-strength proprietary filler is usually used for cement rendering, as on this little shop. Paint and sand, paint and sawdust (powdered or in little curls) or embossed wallpaper can also be used.

WEATHERBOARDING THE EXTERIOR

1

1 With only a base coat of paint, the house is ready for its outside decoration. The choice is unlimited: you could paint, cement render, brick, tile, weatherboard or add Tudor beams. You can use any combination for the upper and lower halves of the building. Other possibilities are to add shutters, a veranda, balconies, a porch, plain or gingerbread trim, a garden or even a street scene. In this case a weatherboard finish was chosen.

2 Start at the bottom, slightly overlapping each board. If you use strong contrasting colours, paint the contact tips of every strip, or you will end up on an endless round with a brush in each hand, one black, one white!

2

3

3 Cut around the windows. Beading around the brick and roof contacts gives a neat finish.

REALISTIC BRICKS

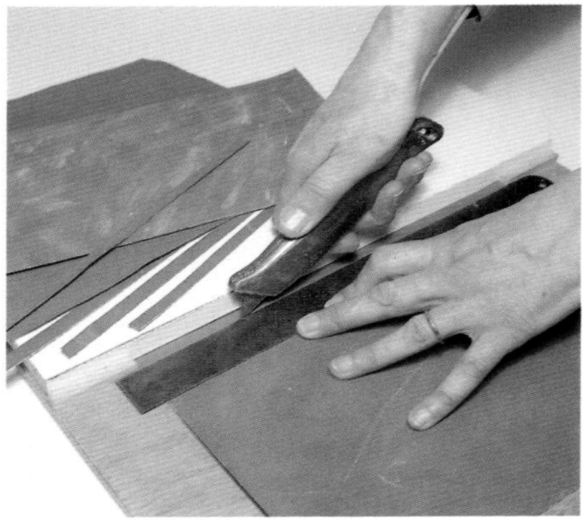

1 Paint and stipple sheet sandpaper to the shade you require. Make a cutting board from scrap wood. This will ensure the strips are an even width and keep your fingers away from the blade.

2 Cut the strips into bricks by using a strip of board ¾ in (2 cm) wide as a measure. Save some strips for the halves and odd shapes.

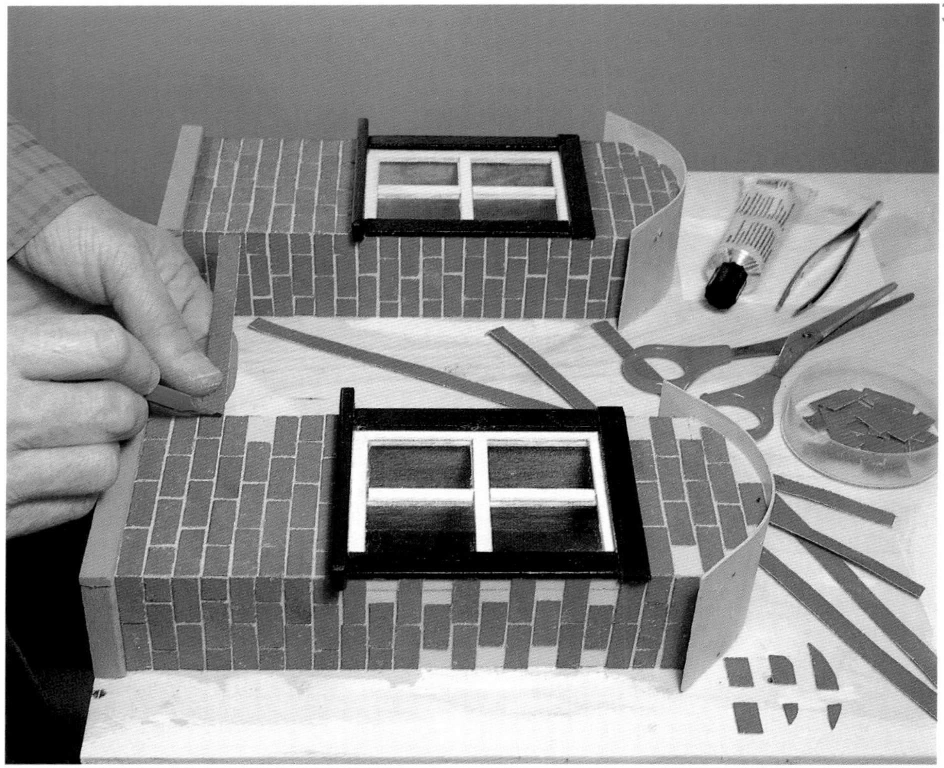

3 Paint the wall the colour of cement rendering, then glue the bricks onto the walls one at a time with spirit glue. You can brick an entire house, or just a section as I have done here.

The guide blocks on the cutting board are held in place with double-sided tape, so they can be replaced with wider pieces if, say, you want to cut large slabs for the kitchen floor. When the cutting groove grows too deep, it is not necessary to replace the board. Fill up the groove with wood glue or a glue and sawdust mix until it is flush with the surface.

If you would like to have red clay hanging wall tiles, use plain sandpaper and stick it to tiles of 1⁄16 in (2 mm) ply or scalloped shingles. Use impact adhesive to glue them to the wall and then paint all over.

THE ROOF

Do you want slate, clay tiles or stone slabs? Hobby shops sell grooved cedar shingles, but these are filmsy and are not easy to lay because they vary in thickness. They are available in straight or scalloped shapes. Shingles are also sold in a smooth wood, but these can easily be made from tongue depressors, obtained from your chemist. Use an impact adhesive because a water-based glue will cause them to warp.

To make your own roofing tiles you can either cut up lengths of

TILING A ROOF

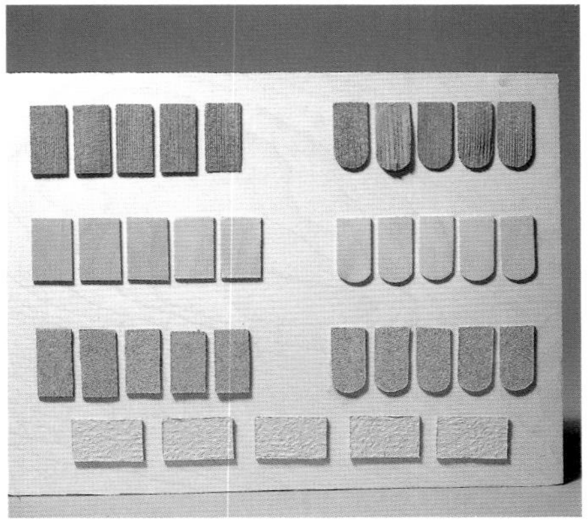

ABOVE Some samples of useful tiles (from the top): a row of commercial cedar tiles; 1⁄16 in (2 mm) ply and the scallop ends of tongue depressors; tiles covered with sandpaper to represent clay tiles; the reverse side of embossed wallpaper, glued to tiles for quarry stone slabs.

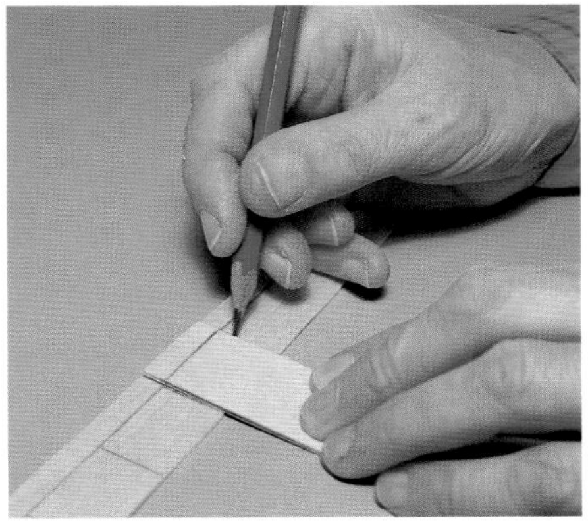

1

1 Use a scrap of wood as a measuring stick to divide a strip into equal tiles.

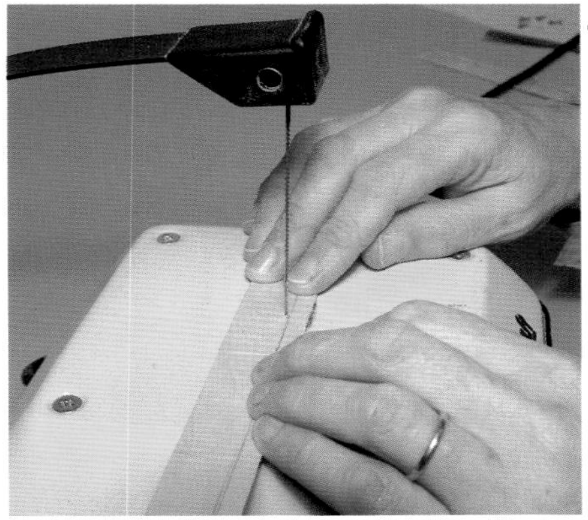

2

2 Cut along these lines, but only two-thirds of the way through.

3

3 Glue the strips to the roof so that the tiles overlap the lower row and also so that the divisions alternate by half a tile in each row.

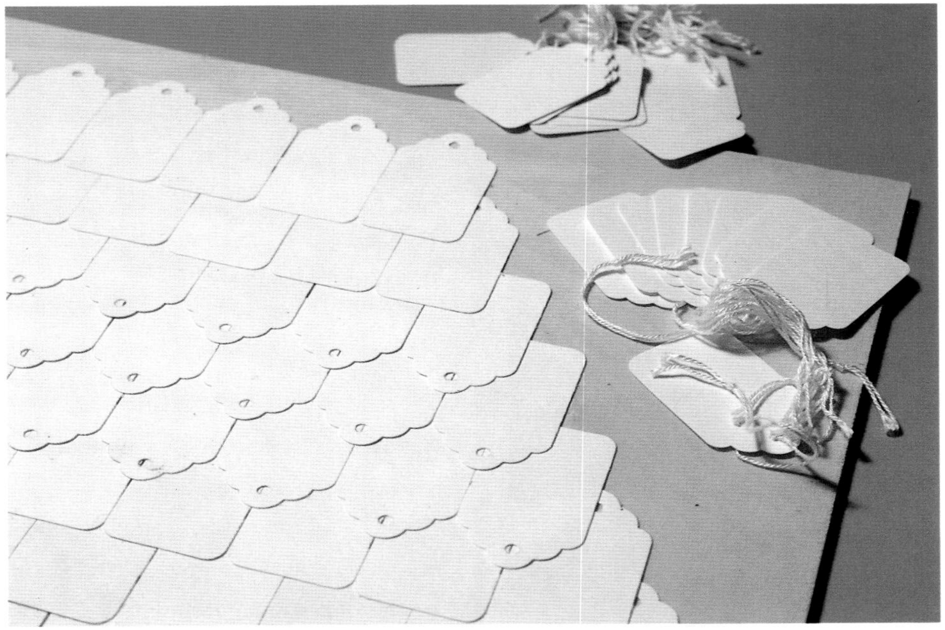

LEFT Price tags or plain card can be used as cheap roof tiles.

TILING A ROOF

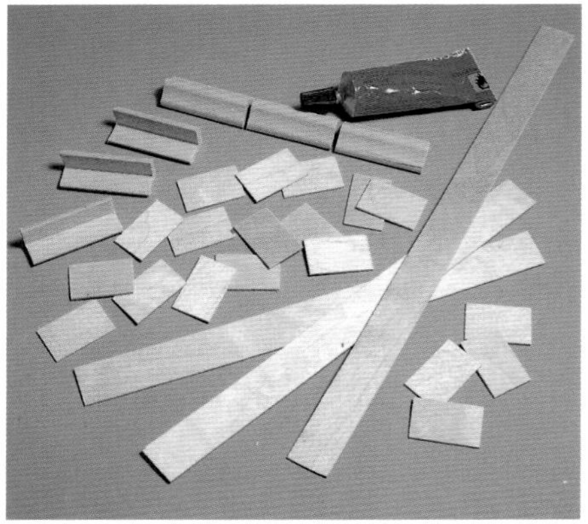

1 The tiles were made from 1⁄16 in (2 mm) ply, but curved right-angle beading was used for ridge tiles.

2 You should add a narrow strip beneath the lowest row in each of the three separate units of the front opening to keep the appearance of overlapping.

3 Cut the tiles around obstructions.

4 Paint the tiles in whatever colour you choose and neaten the hollow ends with cement filler.

1⁄16 in (2 mm) ply into individual pieces or simply cut the strips two-thirds of the way through and glue them onto the roof in their strips. The uncut portion will be hidden under the upper row.

Cross-cutting is another effective way of producing tiles, but it is more complicated and you will need a machine. Slice a length of square strip wood in the way you slice bread. These pieces have an attractive, grained effect.

Look out for different patterns of embossed white wallpaper. Choose a small, bubbly pattern and squash the lumps with a piece of wood. Stick plywood strips to the wallpaper and chop them into tile lengths. The reverse side of the wallpaper is often more realistic if you want to simulate stone slabs. This method can also be used to make paving stones.

Strips of thin card make cheap and effective tiles. Ordinary price tag labels can be used either way: a straight edge on one side, or turn them around to create a scalloped pattern, enhanced by the holes intended for the string.

Hollow triangle moulding cut into short lengths and butted together are ideal for ridge tiles across the peak.

Depending on the style of your house, plain or decorative barge-boards under the roof edges of gable-end walls give your roof a final touch of realism.

THATCH

There is something irresistibly nostalgic about thatch, but the problem is to find a material to work with that lends itself to the 1:12 scale and at the same time looks realistic.

One of the best materials is hay, although unravelled garden string is a good alternative and is considerably easier to apply – it is purely a matter of personal preference.

Whatever you use, you must thatch in the manner of real houses,

A Thatched Roof

1

2

2 While the hay is held in the clamp you have two hands for tying the bundle.

3 If your strip of wood is the correct length, you also have a measure to cut the bundles uniformly.

3

1 A simple gadget will help hold the loose hay in a narrow channel. Velcro stapled to the board and flap gives a quick clasp.

4

4 Use a non-drip contact adhesive and also sew the bundles to a painted plastic embroidery mesh.

RIGHT Thatch from unravelled string as used here is another alternative, but remember that you cannot have an opening roof if you thatch it.

stitching and/or gluing individual thumb-sized bundles to the roof. You will find it useful if you make a simple gadget that leaves both hands free for knotting. A thatched roof is practical only if your roof is a fixture with no opening.

Baseboard

Adding a baseboard means that there is less stress on your house when it is moved around, and it also prevents chipped corner walls. If you have external chimney flues or other extensions then a base is essential; it need not protrude more than 1–2 in (2.5–5 cm) around the bottom of the house.

You should use ¼ in (6 mm) or ⅓ in (9 mm) wood because the corners in particular are likely to come in for some rough treatment. Draw around the outside of your house on the board and make another line ¼ in (6 mm) inside this outline. Drill holes in the centre between the lines and marry them with drill holes on the underside of the house. Remember to countersink the screws on the underside of the baseboard to avoid scratching your furniture.

You may have a problem opening the front of your house if the bottom of the doors catch on the baseboard. Either take off the hinged doors and shave them down a fraction, or glue a length of quality beading, ¼ in (6 mm) or less, all around the base of the house before you screw on your baseboard. This will give sufficient clearance for the opening front without looking obtrusive.

Making a Baseboard

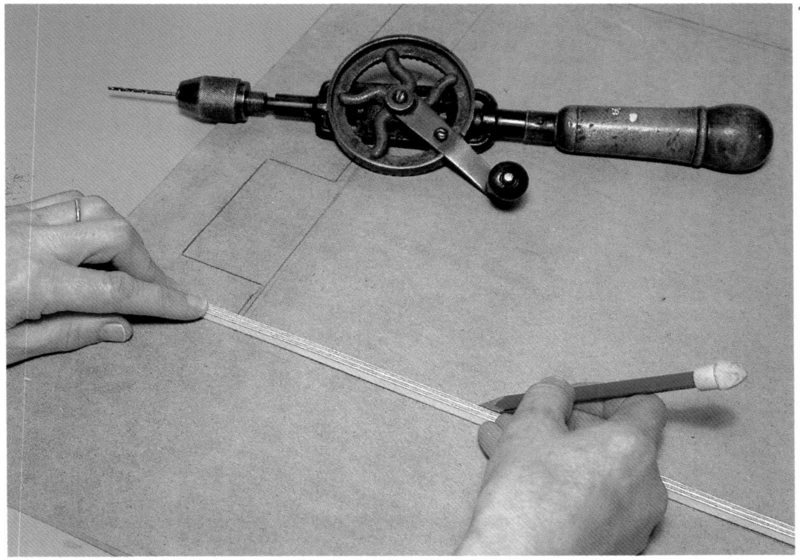

1

1 Draw round your house on the baseboard. Allow a small border all the way round, allowing more for any anticipated extras such as a veranda. Using a strip of ¼ in (6 mm) wood as a guide, draw a line ¼ in (6 mm) inside the outline. Drill holes between these lines to correspond to the lower wall ends of your house.

2

2 On the underside, countersink the screw holes. Glue and screw the board to the base of your house.

ABOVE A Bavarian chalet with plank shutters.

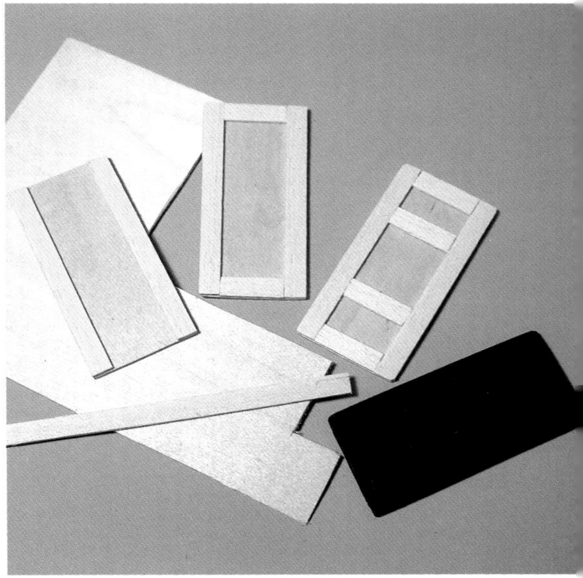

ABOVE Simple shutters can be made from thin ply with beading trim on one side only.

Shutters

Simple shutters can be made from 1⁄16 in (2 mm) ply base, with beading added to one side only. The Bavarian plank shutters were made from ice lolly sticks.

Chimneys

If you have an external chimney flue this automatically extends to a similar square shape. Chimneys that are on the roof centre have to sit astride the peak, and they should be fitted before you add the ridge tiles. You can also add a chimney halfway down the slope of the roof.

Always position the chimneys realistically in terms of the internal fireplaces, and remember that the number of chimney pots should correspond to the number of fires up each flue.

CHIMNEYS

1 Chimneys can be made any shape or size according to the style of your house. Use scrap wood to build them. This one was built to fit snugly over the roof of the house. Rough wood can be disguised by first painting with glue, then dipping it in sawdust. When dry, paint the "concrete".

2 Once the chimney has been finished to fit the style of the house, simple chimney pots can be made from dowel with trim. This pot was made from a filigree metal ribbon and dressmaking elastic. Because the pots are liable to be damaged while the house is being moved , make them removable with a peg of brass rod.

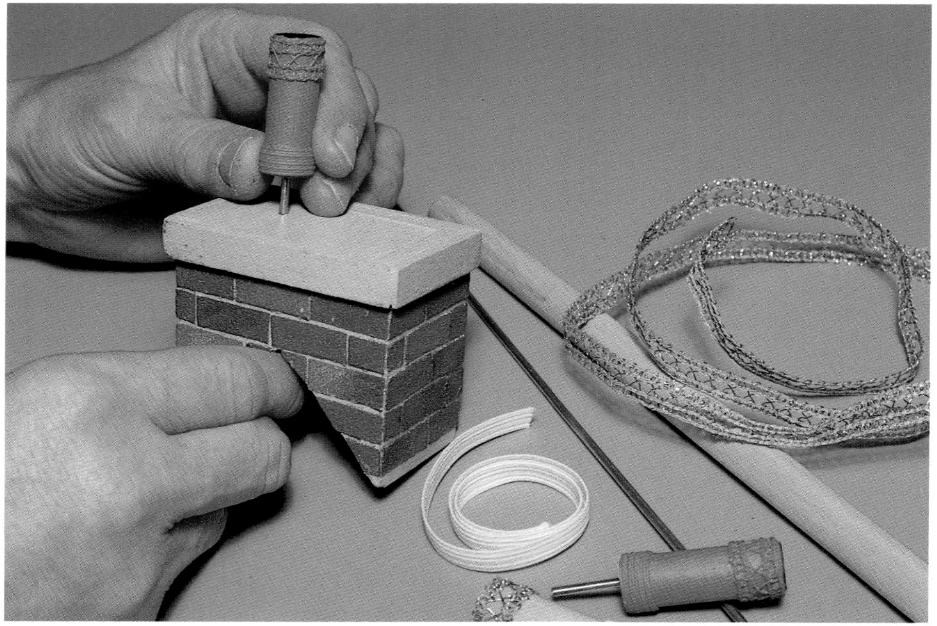

VERANDAS

You can make a veranda in any style or shape that you fancy and it can be as ornate or plain as you wish.

Although the aim is to be architecturally correct, purists will always find anomalies. If a house is pleasing to look at and appears to be authentic, you can feel happy. This is not a competition, but a satisfying and creative pastime that requires a variety of skills and techniques.

Now you have the completed house, ready for furniture and its people, although you will probably go on adding refinements for several months to come. Like your own home, no doll's house is ever really finished, but for the time being you can switch on the lights and admire your own dream home. The sense of achievement is exhilarating.

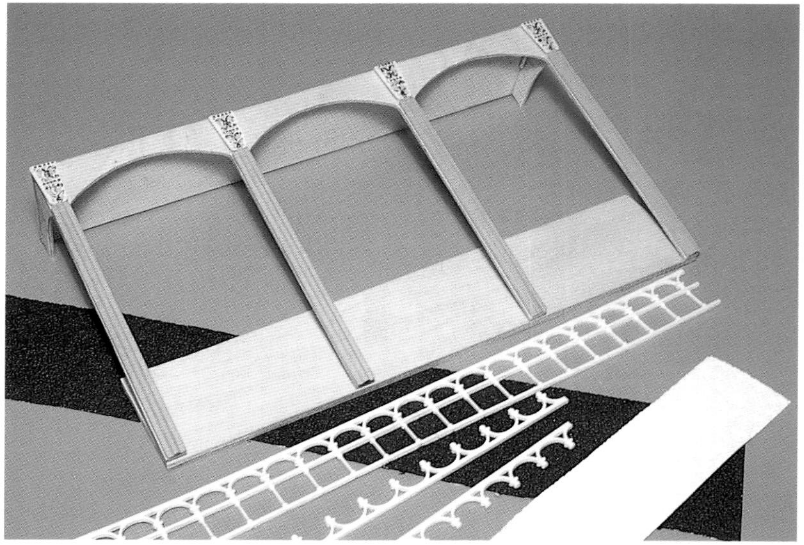

ABOVE The veranda was made up piecemeal from cut ply, wood beading and fancy trim, with ¼ in (6 mm) for the roof. The base was glued then screwed to the house front before the wall panelling was glued inside.

RIGHT The addition of shutters gives the house a different look. The contrast of black and white is effective.

LEFT The veranda and the porch over the kitchen are further delicate details which can be added if you wish.

LEFT The house is now complete and waiting to be furnished.

DOLL'S HOUSE FURNITURE

Headley Holgate & Pamela Ruddock

DOLL'S HOUSE FURNITURE

The projects in this book are set out room by room to give you ideas to fill your entire doll's house. Each room has three to four major pieces of furniture and also some smaller accessories. The larger pieces are made entirely from wood and the smaller projects use a range of materials (a full list is given at the beginning of each mini-project).

All the projects have figure diagrams showing the exact measurements of the components of the pieces. These are not drawn full size, but can be enlarged easily.

Tools and Equipment

The main pieces of wooden furniture can be made with power or hand tools, depending on what equipment you already have, and which you are most familiar with; the step-by-step photographs show the furniture being constructed with the range of power tools listed below. The other pieces of equipment and accessories you will need are also listed.

Accuracy is of prime importance when working on such a small scale. It is therefore important that you constantly check the way the pieces are fitting together: whether all the legs sit squarely to the floor, for example. If you are using power tools, remember to check them regularly: for example, check that all saws are vertical to the machine table; check that your mitre gauge is set at 90°.

You will find it useful to make a basic assembly jig, which will help to check that corners are square; you can easily make one from three pieces of 12mm (½in) plywood glued at right angles to each other (see figure drawing).

Multi-Purpose Assembly Jig

~

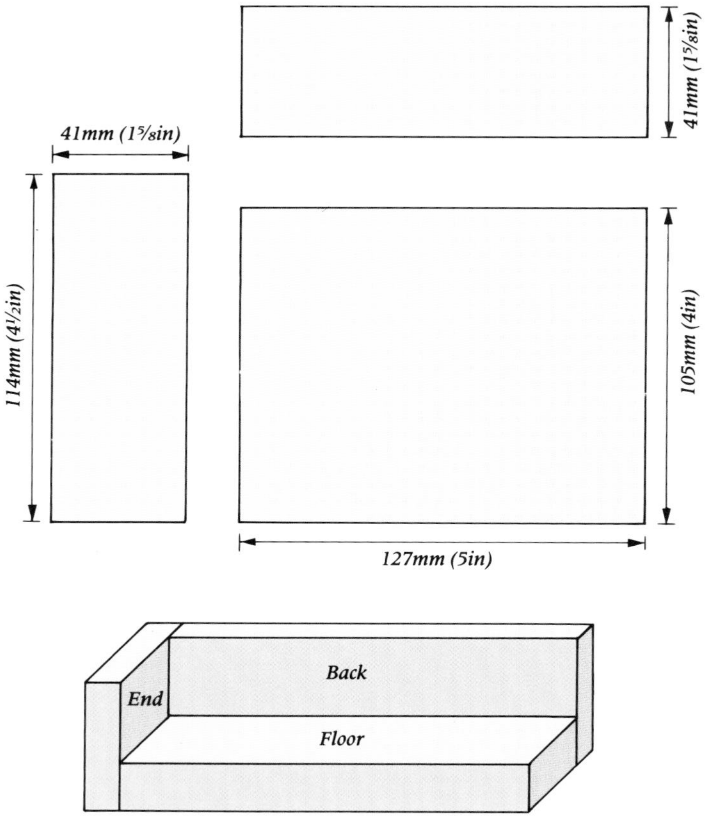

All parts are made from 12mm (½in) plywood

Hand Tools

~

Carpenter's hammer
Tack hammer
Chisels, Gouges
Screwdrivers, Craft knife
Punch, Hand fretsaw
Handsaws, Pliers
Tweezers, Vice

Power Tools

~

Bandsaw with fence and circle cutting pin, Mitre gauge
Power drill and stand with bits
Router and moulding bits
Circular saw, Belt sander
Small lathe and tools
Fretsaw
Drum sanders

Accessories

~

Set square, Steel rule
Bulldog clips, Elastic bands
G-clamps, Panel pins
Wooden cocktail sticks
Metal tape measure
Brass knobs, Brass feet
Garnet papers

Materials and Techniques

Timber

There are specialist shops which deal in equipment for making doll's house furniture, and they will sell small amounts of wood to the thicknesses required for this scale of working. Alternatively, you may find a timber merchant, joiner or carpenter who will supply you with cut sections. You will probably find it most useful to obtain pieces about 300 × 125mm (12 × 5in) long and wide and from 3mm to 16mm (1/8 to 5/8in) thick. This will give you a choice of sizes that can be sliced to the required size.

The projects use three types of wood, although you may find alternatives. They are:

MAHOGANY Danta – a mahogany-type timber from the Ivory Coast – has been used in some projects. It has a very small and pleasing grain, but has the disadvantage of moving and twisting.

PINE Always make sure you use good-quality pine, since poor-quality pine is difficult to saw and sand.

PLYWOOD Available in a range of thicknesses, from 1.5mm (1/16in) upwards. It is often used for the backs of pieces, since this side is not often seen. Plywood does not twist as wood strips are apt to. It is often used as a backing to veneer.

Glues

Always suit the glue to the job in hand.

WOOD GLUE This is the type used most often in the main projects. It is used for gluing wood to wood.

TWO-PART EPOXY RESIN This is used for gluing wood to metal. Use the slow-drying variety, which takes approximately 16 hours to dry. This glue consists of an adhesive and a hardener mixed together; follow the manufacturer's instructions carefully.

MULTI-PURPOSE ADHESIVE This clear or white household glue is used for gluing fabric, such as chair seats and other upholstery.

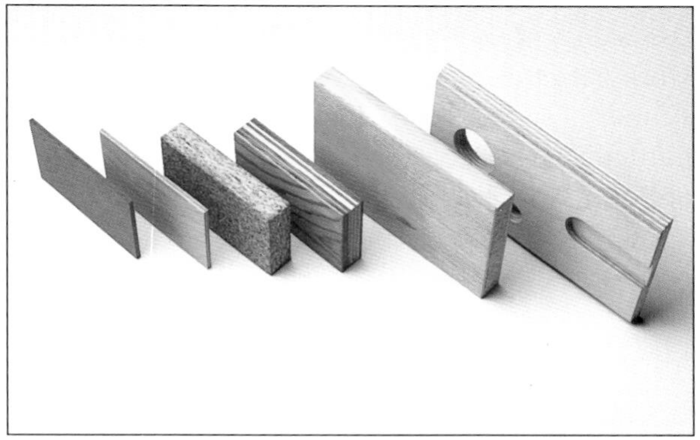

Man-made boards including MDF and plywood

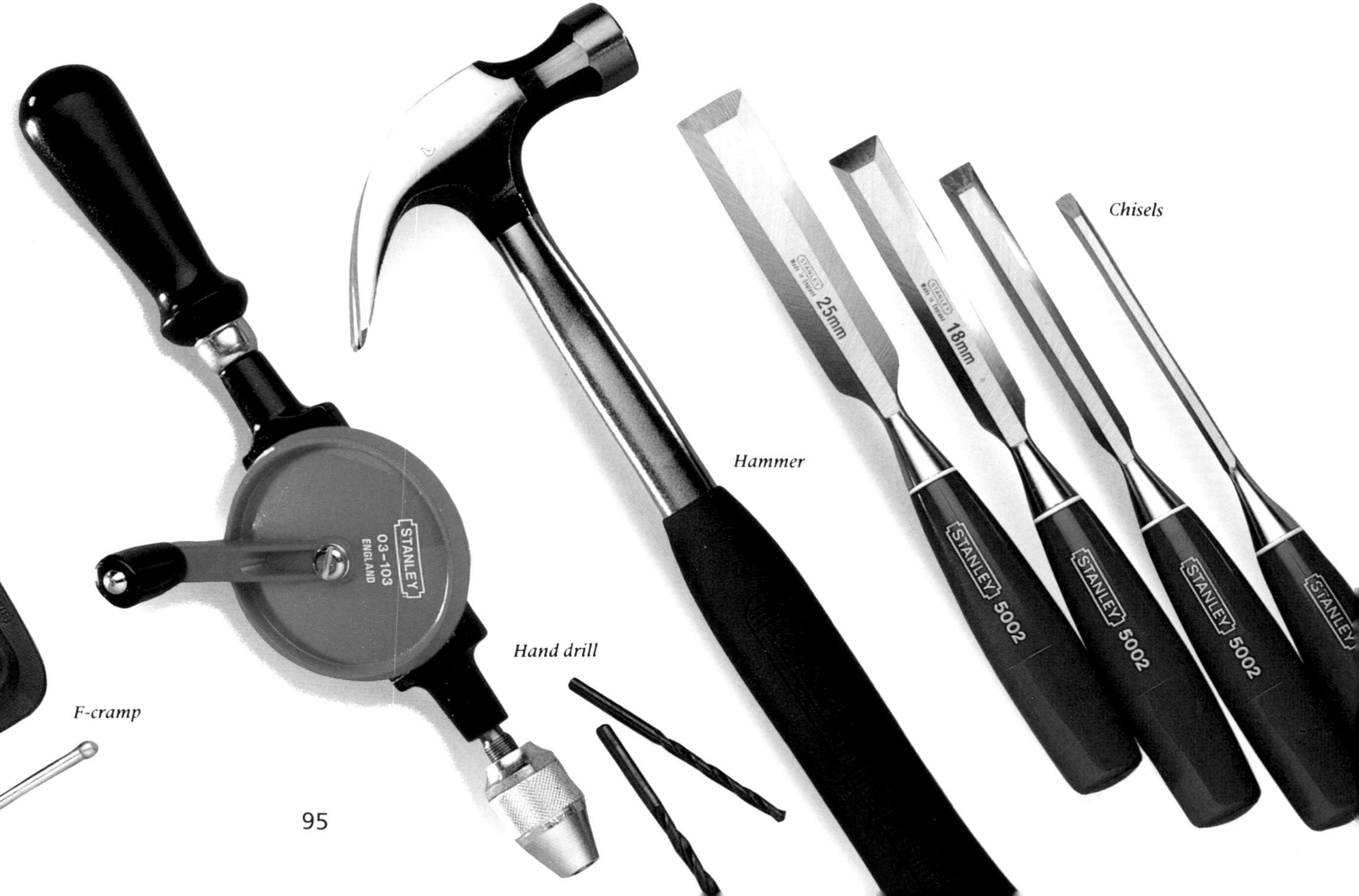

Finishing

All the instructions indicate when and how each piece should be finished – that is, when it should be sanded, stained, polished and waxed. Where a piece has a large and prominent surface, for example the top, you will have to take a lot of care to finish it properly, applying up to eight coats of polish and leaving to dry overnight.

SANDING It is better to do as much finishing as possible to individual parts before you undertake any assembly. Garnet papers are best for cutting and smoothing work. They are graded by grit numbers, the lower numbers being coarse, the higher numbers finer. Grade 40 or 60 paper should be used first for rough-sawn surfaces. Use 100 or 120 grit for a planed or smoother surface, then use 180 or 200 grit. Next use 240 grit, before giving the wood a final rubbing down with 320 or 360 grit. This programme is for perfectionists, and it can be modified if you wish. You can make or purchase a sanding block around which the paper is wrapped to produce a more even surface. All the dust that is generated must be removed with a cloth or brush before you begin to apply stain or to use any other finishing technique.

STAINING Apply the stain with a rag, although a small brush is useful for getting into difficult corners. Work with the grain. When the work is covered, wipe off any surplus stain with a clean cloth, before leaving the piece to dry overnight. When it is completely dry the surface may appear to be slightly rough. This will be the result of dust or the stain raising the grain. Use a very fine grit paper to smooth the surface.

SEALING Sealer is applied for several reasons: it affords some protection to the wood; it slightly hardens the surface; and it prevents the stain from bleeding. You should apply the sealer with a brush or a cotton cloth. The first stroke is made across the grain to lodge the talc filler that is in the sealer into the grain lines. Work quickly because sealer becomes tacky in a very short time. Leave it to dry for 24 hours. If the sealer is absorbed by the wood, apply a second or even a third coat. Rub down with a fine-grade sandpaper between coats.

WAXING A paste in which beeswax is the main ingredient is the most suitable. The first application of the wax should be made with a small piece of the finest grade, 0000, steel wool. Use plenty of wax for this first application and work with the grain. Wipe off any surplus or strands of steel wool with a clean cloth. Leave to harden overnight. The surface can then be polished with a clean, soft duster.

FINISHING EQUIPMENT

~

Garnet papers in a range of grits from 40 to 360
Dusters, Cotton cloths, Stains, Sealer
Wire wool, grade 0000
Wax (containing beeswax)
Methylated spirits, Cotton wool, Polish
Burnishing cream

Wire wool grade 0000

TOP TO BOTTOM: *fine garnet paper, coarse garnet paper, coarse aluminium oxide paper*

SAFETY

~

Almost all finishing materials and adhesives are toxic. Take great care when you are using or handling them. Work in a well-ventilated room and avoid inhaling either fumes or dust. Store all materials safely and make sure that all waste is disposed of in the proper way. Observe fire precautions at all times, and never smoke in your workshop. Wear protective clothing in case you spill anything. Never store finishers in old food containers and keep them all out of the reach of children.

French Polishing

~

You will need

- 1 piece of thin cotton rag, approximately 51 × 51mm (2 × 2in)
- Methylated spirits
- Cotton wool
- Polish

FORMING THE PAD

1. Soak the cotton rag with methylated spirits and squeeze out any surplus.

2. Place the rag on a flat surface, add a ball of cotton wool and pour on the polish.

3.Turn up the edges of the rag to form a pad.

1

2

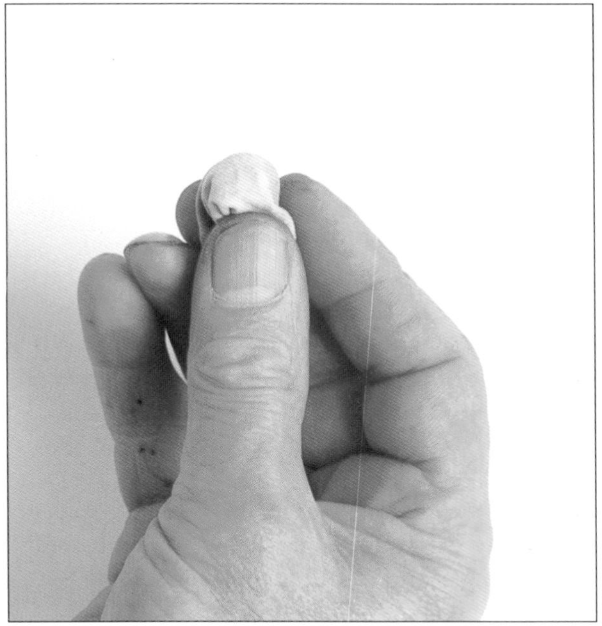

3

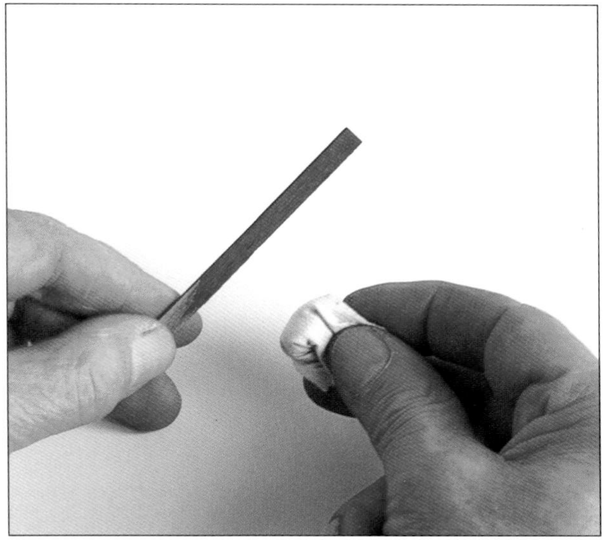

4

4.Tap the completed pad against a clean surface or the palm of your other hand until the polish appears through the rag. It is very easy to overload a pad with polish. If you do, squeeze out the pad to remove the excess. If the pad is too dry, add more polish. With practice you will learn to put in the correct amount.

POLISHING Stroke the pad along the grain. If you are polishing one piece at a time, allow each coat to dry for three to five minutes before you apply the next. For larger, more visible surfaces apply up to eight coats; five or six coats should be sufficient for smaller surfaces. Allow to dry overnight.

BURNISHING Use a burnishing cream on a piece of rag for the final finish. Apply as for French polish. When it is dry, rub with a soft duster.

Pinning blanks

Between six and eight blanks can be pinned together depending on their thickness and the length of the drill bit. This will produce several identical shapes from just one cutting process.

The position of the pins will depend on the piece being made – under the seat between the legs for chairs, for example. The length of the pin should be such that, when it is driven into the block, the heads are flush with the top of the block, but the pointed ends protrude by 1–2mm (approximately 1/16in) at the bottom.

Place the assembly jig on the drill table. Adjust the depth of drilling to 1–2mm (1/16in) from the jig floor. This will fasten the bottom blank more firmly and stop it from falling off. Place the blanks on the jig and drill both pin holes. Hold the blanks together with your fingers and drive the pins into the holes with a heavy hammer. Sand the pin tips so that they are flush.

Drill a hole through the blanks for the pin.

Drive the pin into the block until the head is flush with the top.

Glossary of Terms

CARCASS The basic framework of a piece.
CHAMFER A narrow, flat surface angled at 45°, planed or carved on the edge of a section.
COLUMN The decorative part of the leg, attached to the underside of the table, that is moulded and shaped.
COVER SLIP A small, thin strip of wood that covers the rough front edge of a slice of wood.
CROSS-CUT Cutting across the grain.
GROOVE A long, narrow channel cut into the wood. Grooves act mainly as shelf bearers.
JIG A guide to accuracy used in assembly to ensure the correct angles are held while the glue sets, and also as a guide when sawing.
LATERAL The pieces of the *carcass* that fit horizontally.
LEG HOLDER The second component of a complex leg construction. It is a small, round section of wood with three slits cut at 120° to each other, into which the legs fit.
LIPPED DRAWER A drawer which has an additional front piece which overlaps the drawer front beneath by approximately 1.5mm (1/16in).
MIDDLE UPRIGHT The pieces of the *carcass* that fit vertically.
MITRE A corner joint formed between two pieces of material, for example wood, by cutting the ends at equal angles, for example two angles of 45° joining to make a right angle of 90°.
REBATE A step cut along the edge of a piece of wood, into which another piece of wood fits – often used to hold the back of a piece.
SPLAT A piece of wood that forms the horizontal central part of a chair back. The splat may be plain or a decorative feature.
STOP A small square of wood which fits into a groove to prevent a shelf, for example, from moving in the groove.
UPSTANDS The decorative edging on the top of the desk that consists of three strips of wood fitted into grooves in the top.
VENEER A thin layer of wood with a decorative or fine finish that is bonded to the surface of a less expensive material, for example plywood.

THE KITCHEN

Kitchen Table

~

This lovely pine table is a perfect centrepiece in any kitchen. Choose a good piece of pine with a pretty grain for the top, since this element will be the most visible. The construction is relatively simple, but the detailing – such as the mitred edging and the shaped legs – makes the piece very special.

~

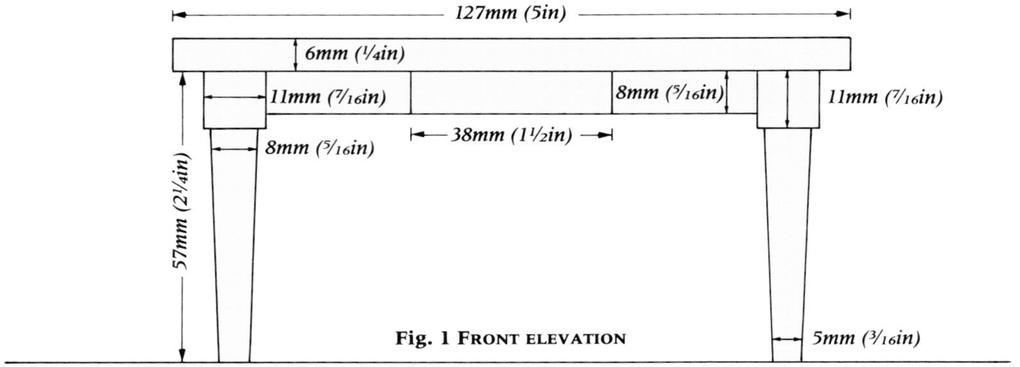

Fig. 1 Front elevation

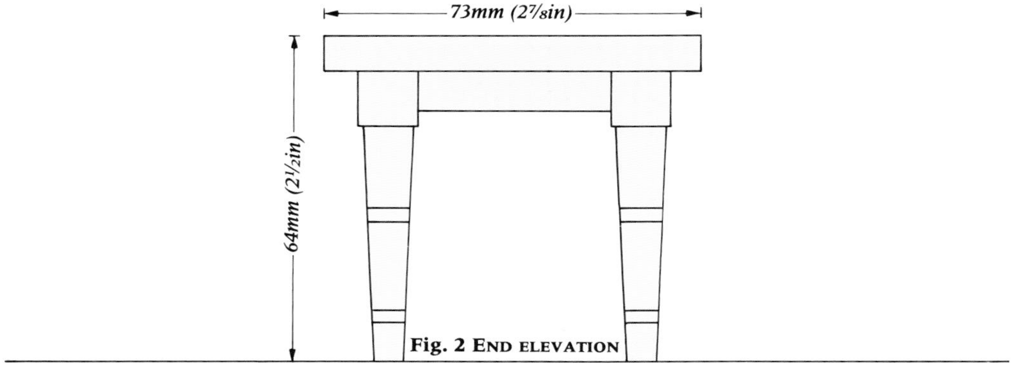

Fig. 2 End elevation

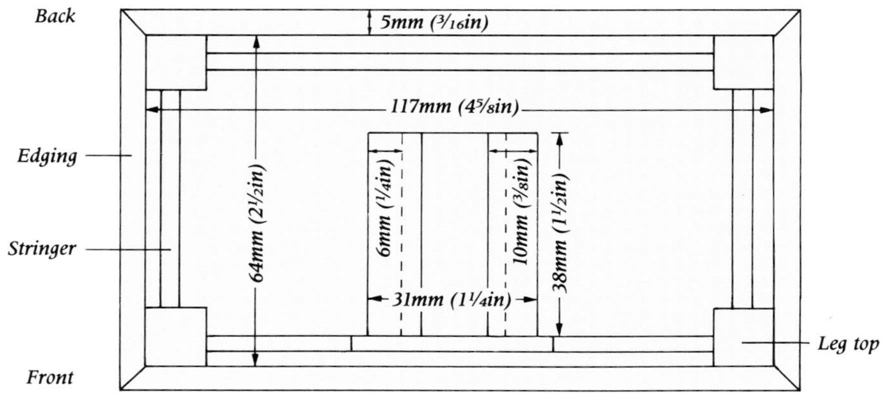

Fig. 3 Underside of top

Making the Top

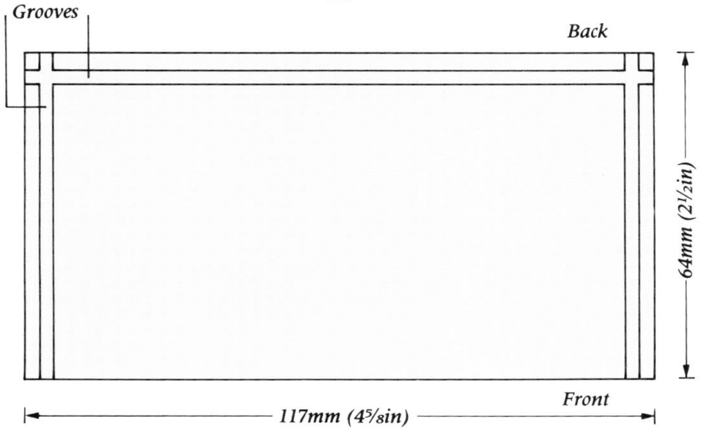

Fig. 4 Underside of top to show grooves

1

1. Cut a piece of pine for the table top 117 × 64 × 6 mm (4⅝ × 2½ × ¼ in). Run grooves for the back and end stringers 3 mm (⅛ in) wide and deep and 3 mm (⅛ in) from the edges.

2. For the edging, cut a section 51 × 5 × 137 mm (2 × 3/16 × 5⅜ in). You will need a 137 mm (5⅜in) strip for the back and two end strips 83 mm (3¼ in) long. Mitre the ends of the edging strips to 45°, testing for fit against the table top. Glue the strips to the table top. Hand sand or belt sand the table surface.

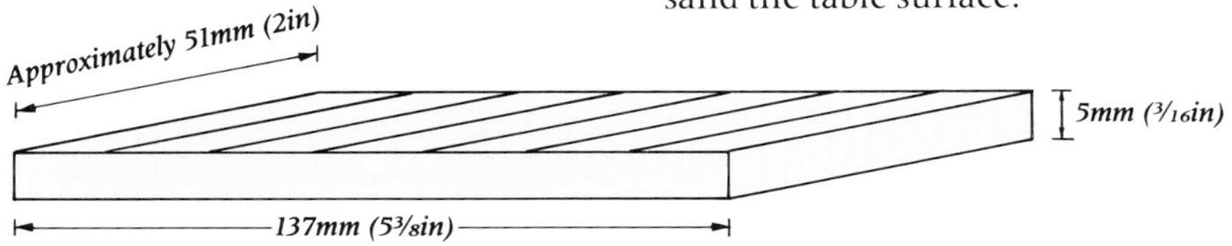

Fig. 5 Section for edging

2

Making the Legs

Fig. 6a Legs

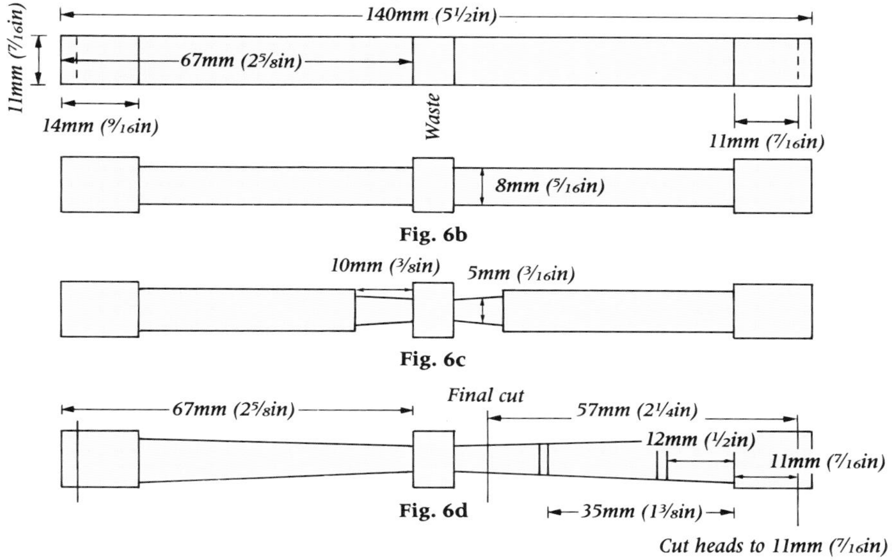

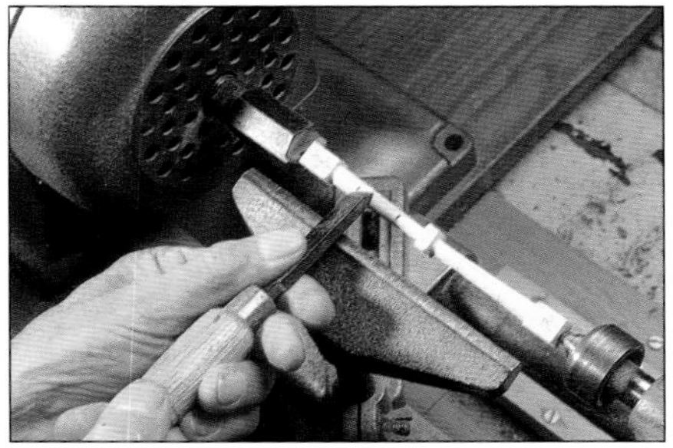

3

4

3. Cut two square blanks for the legs. Each blank will make two legs – the centre of the blank is the foot. Shape the blank in the sequence illustrated: turn the blank until it is 8 mm (5/16 in) in diameter; turn the foot until it is 5 mm (3/16 in), cut it at a slight taper to match with the total taper; taper the legs and sand; run the rings. Sand the square heads. Dust, wax and polish.

4. Cut the leg heads to 11 mm (7/16 in), making sure that all the leg heads are exactly the same height. Make the final cut to the legs to give a total length of 57 mm (2¼ in). Sand the end of the legs and heads with fine sandpaper.

5. For the back and end stringers, cut a piece of pine 11 × 108 × 3 mm (7⁄16 × 4¼ × ⅛ in) long. Check the fit across the width of the groove. Sand, dust and wax one side of all the strips. Measure each piece against the underside of the table, with the legs in place, and then cut to fit.

6. For the front stringer run a section 10 mm × 108 mm (⅜ × 4¼ in). The front stringer, which is initially glued to the drawer front, will have two cuts made in it to free the drawer front, and it needs to be cut slightly longer than the back stringer to compensate for this. Make two cuts to the drawer front strip and check that the three joined pieces exactly match the back stringer.

7. Choose the two best legs for the front of the table. Apply glue to one back leg and to the table top and glue in place. Put glue into the back groove and insert the stringer, checking for upright. Glue the second back leg. Glue the end stringers and front legs in the same way.

5

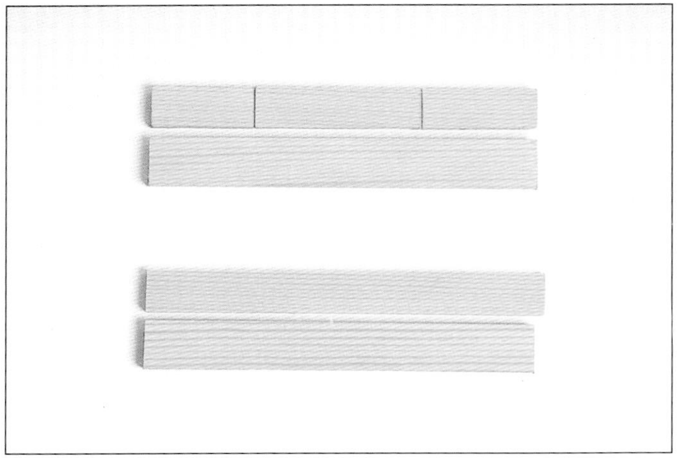

6

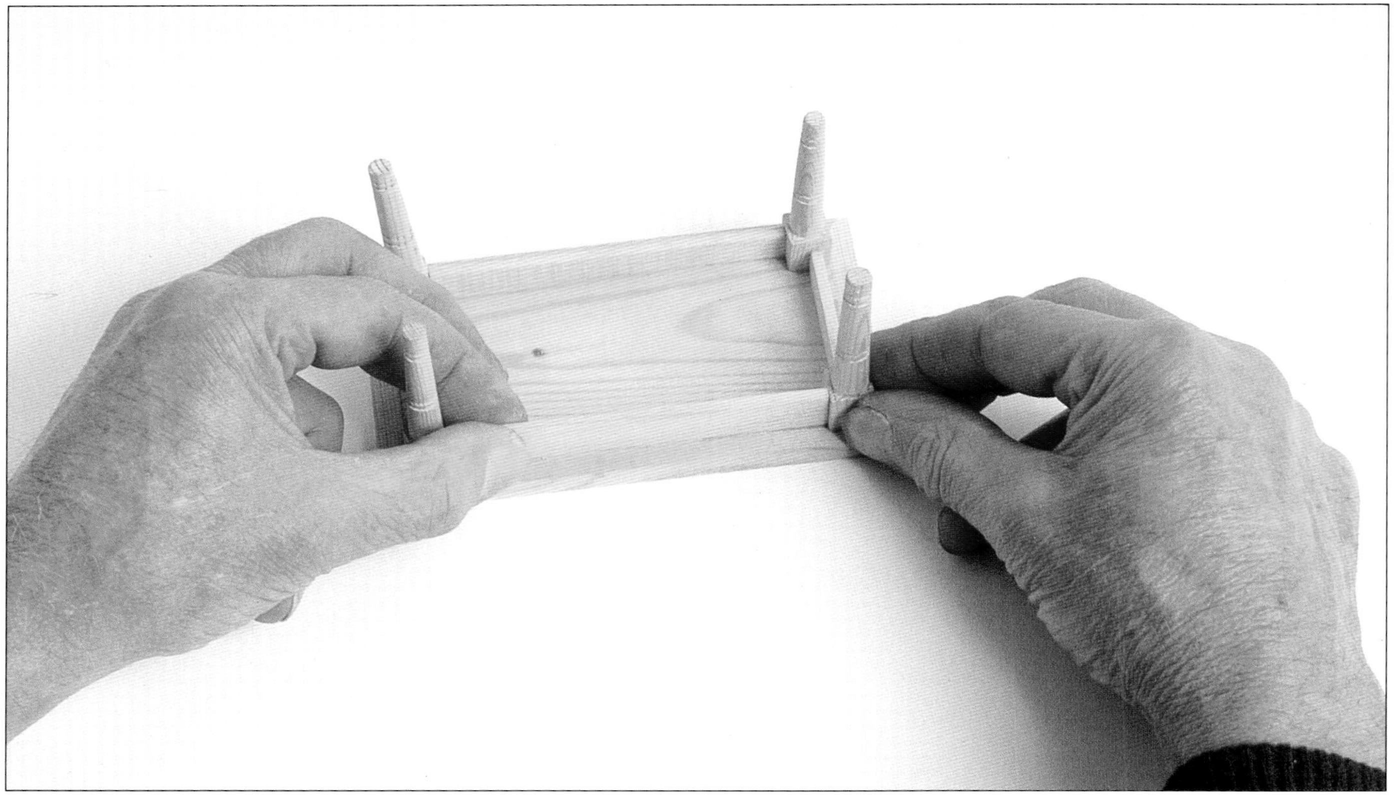

7

8. Cut the drawer bottom 1.5 mm (1/16 in) thick. Cut a section (see Fig. 5 as for edging) and slice strips 6 × 38 mm (1/4 × 1 1/2 in) for the drawer sides. Glue the sides to the bottom and leave to dry. Glue the front stringer to the drawer front matching the centre of the drawer to a centre mark on the stringer.

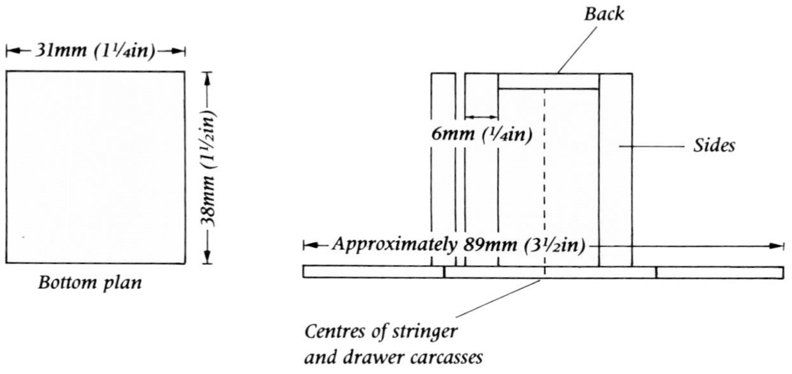

Fig. 7 The drawer

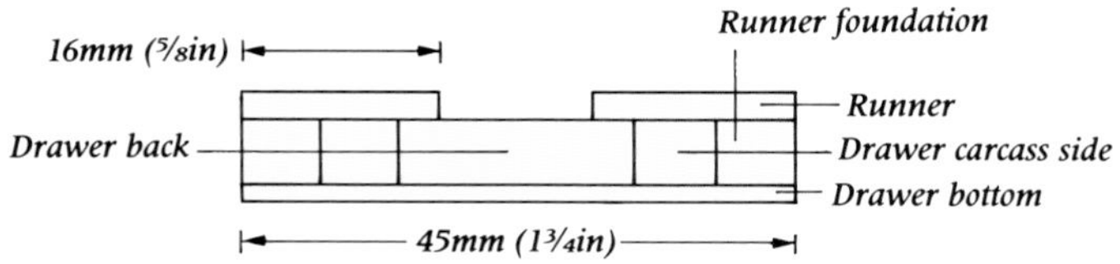

8

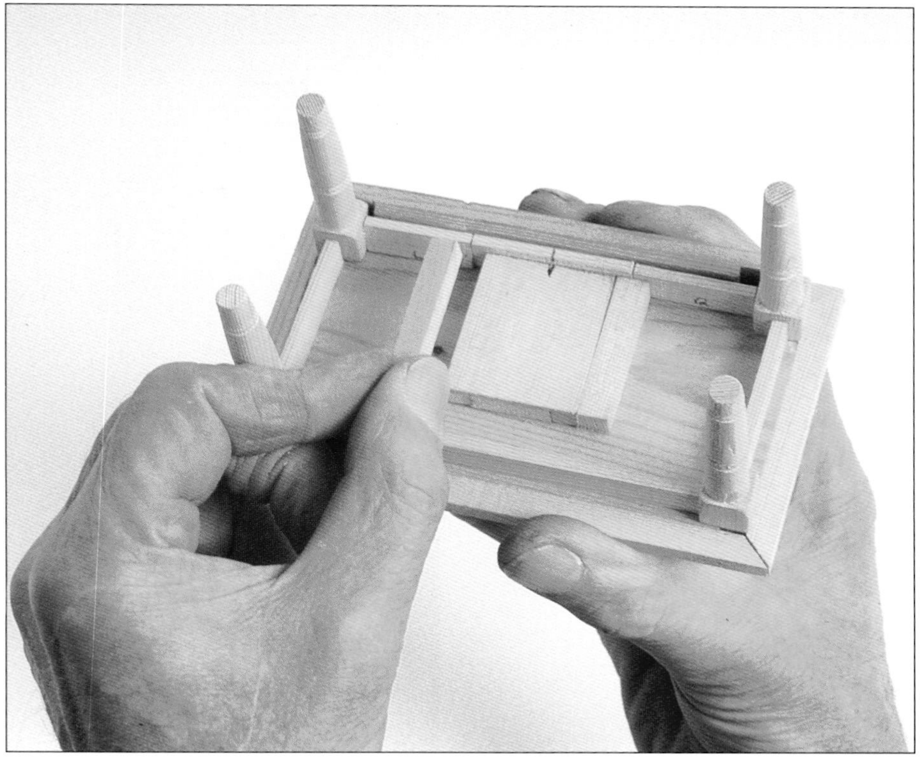

10

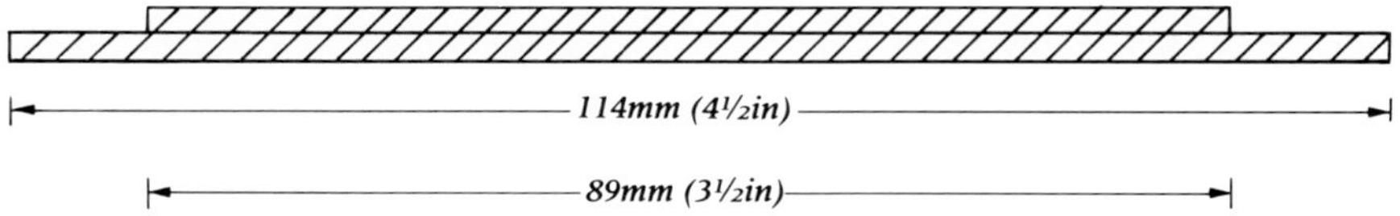

Fig. 8 Assembly jig

9. Separate the drawer front from the rest of the stringer. The ends should protrude 3 mm (1/8 in) from the drawer sides. Cut and fit the drawer back (Fig. 7).

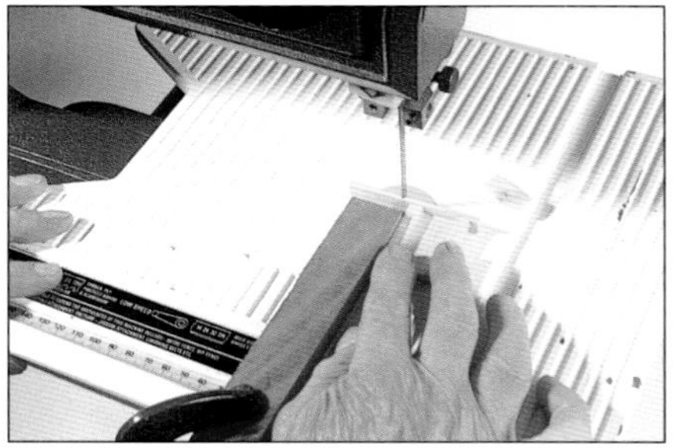

9

10. Make the assembly jig (see Fig. 8). Position the drawer and front stringer and push the assembly jig against pieces. Make sure that the gaps between the ends of the drawer front and the stringers are the same. Cut a section for the drawer runner foundations (as Fig. 5) but add the height of the drawer bottom to the thickness of the piece. Slice two foundation strips 6 mm (1/4 in) wide. Cut the strips 38 mm (1 1/2 in) long. Glue the foundations to the drawer. When the glue is dry, glue the side parts of the front stringer to the table top.

11. Make the drawer runners by cutting two strips 10 × 1.5 × 38 mm (5/8 × 1/16 × 1 1/2 in). Glue the strips to the runner foundations. Make sure the glue does not jam the drawer. Drill a hole in the drawer front for a brass knob 3 mm (1/8 in) in diameter.

11

Alternative Method

~

You can make this table without the grooves. Proceed in the same way, but make the stringers 8 mm (5/16 in) high. Instead of placing the back and end stringers in grooves, they will have to be assembled using the jig as described for the front stringers and drawer front. Make a smaller jig in the same way for the end stringers, or assemble them by eye.

Kitchen Bench

~

A lovely accompaniment to the kitchen table (page 100), this bench, also made in pine, uses some of the same design features, such as the mitred edging. The legs are made by constructing an A-frame and slicing cross-sections from the frame. This means the leg pieces are exactly the same height and shape, and it also makes it easier to create more than one bench at a time.

~

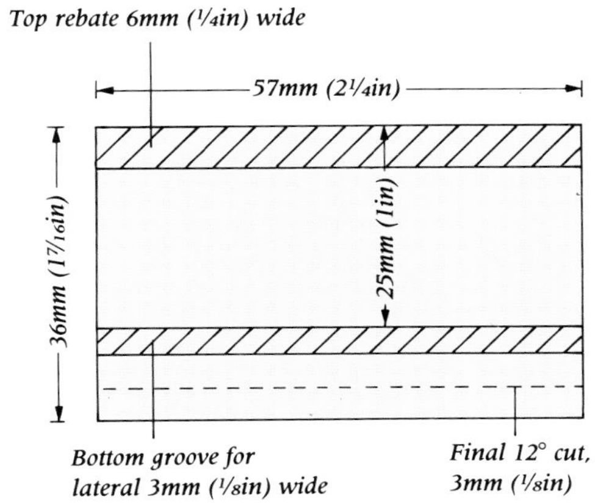

Fig. 1 Legs section

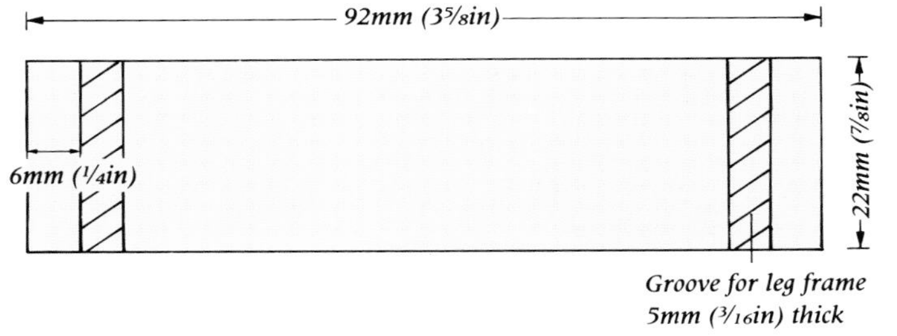

Fig. 4 Seat

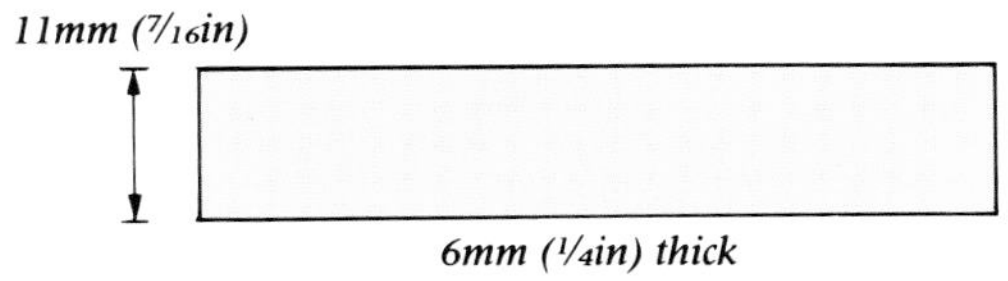

Fig. 2 Top lateral

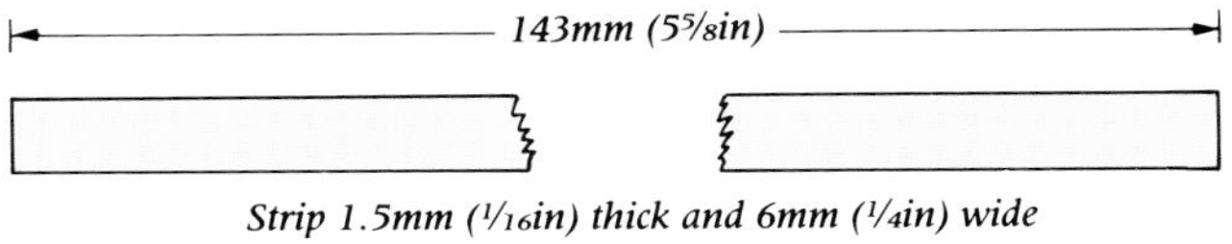

Fig. 5 Seat edging

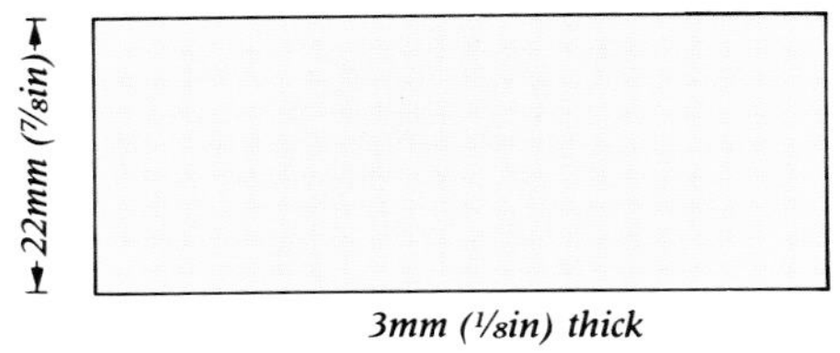

Fig. 3 Bottom lateral

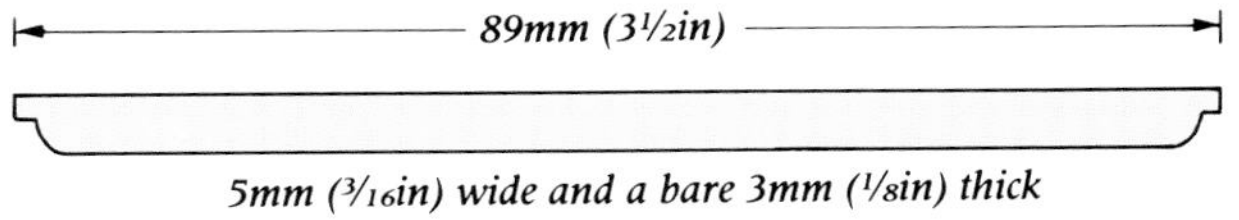

Fig. 6 Sides under seat

1

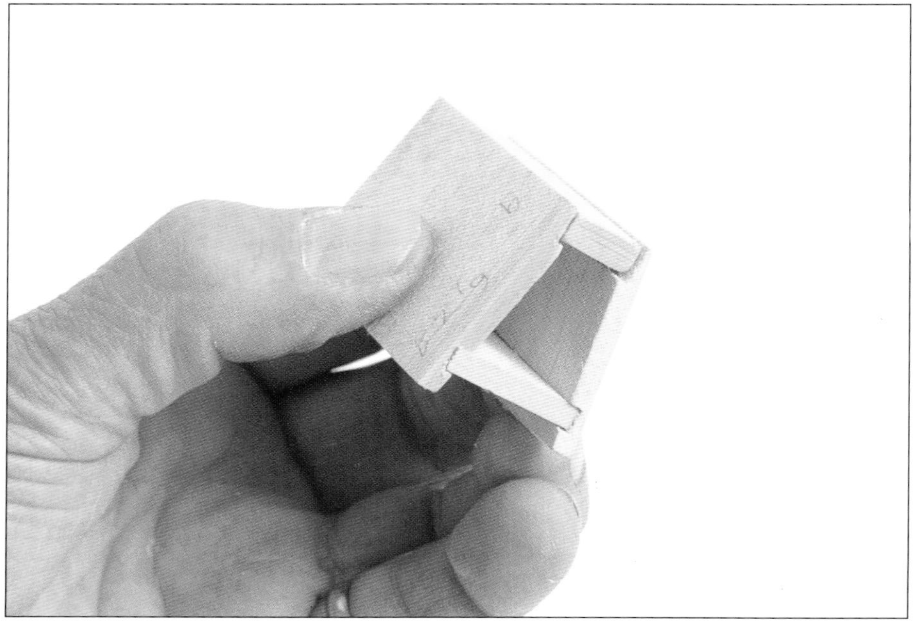

3

1. Cross-cut a section 37 × 25 × 25mm (1 7/16 × 1 × 1in). From this section cut two strips 3mm (1/8in) thick across the grain. Cut a 3mm (1/8in) groove 25mm (1in) from the edge and at a 12° angle. Cut a 6mm (1/4in) wide rebate, also at a 12° angle, along the opposite side of the strips. Make the final cut (see Fig. 1) at a 12° angle.

2. Cut the two lateral pieces (see Figs. 2 and 3).

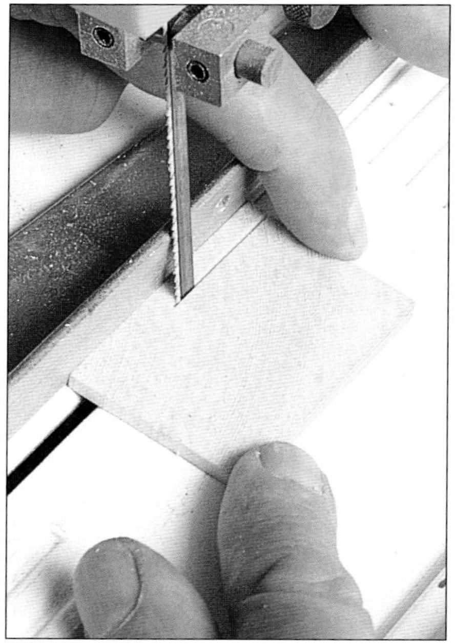

2

4

3. Put glue in the grooves and rebates on the leg slices. Insert the bottom and then the top lateral. Wait for the glue to dry.

4. Slice off the leg frames as cross-sections 5mm (3/16in) thick.

5. Cut the bench seat (see Fig. 4). Cut 5mm (3⁄16in) wide grooves in the underside to take the leg frames. Cut two seat edging strips (see Fig. 5). Mitre and glue the edgings to the seat.

6. Glue the leg frames into the grooves in the seat.

7. Cut two strips and mould them to the shape shown in Fig. 6. Glue these strips to the underside of the bench. Sand and wax the top surface and edges of the seat, the leg frame and one side of the bench sides.

5

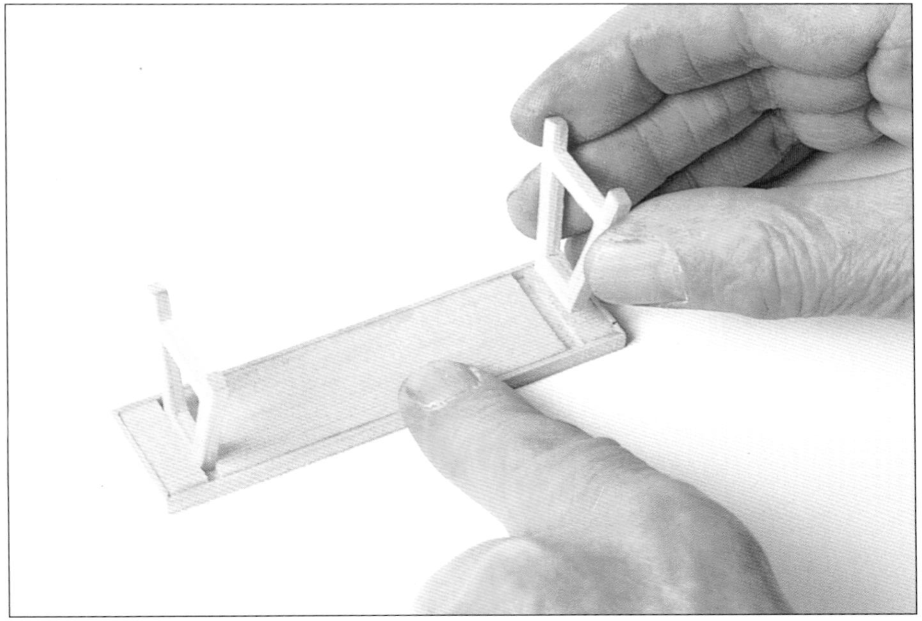

6

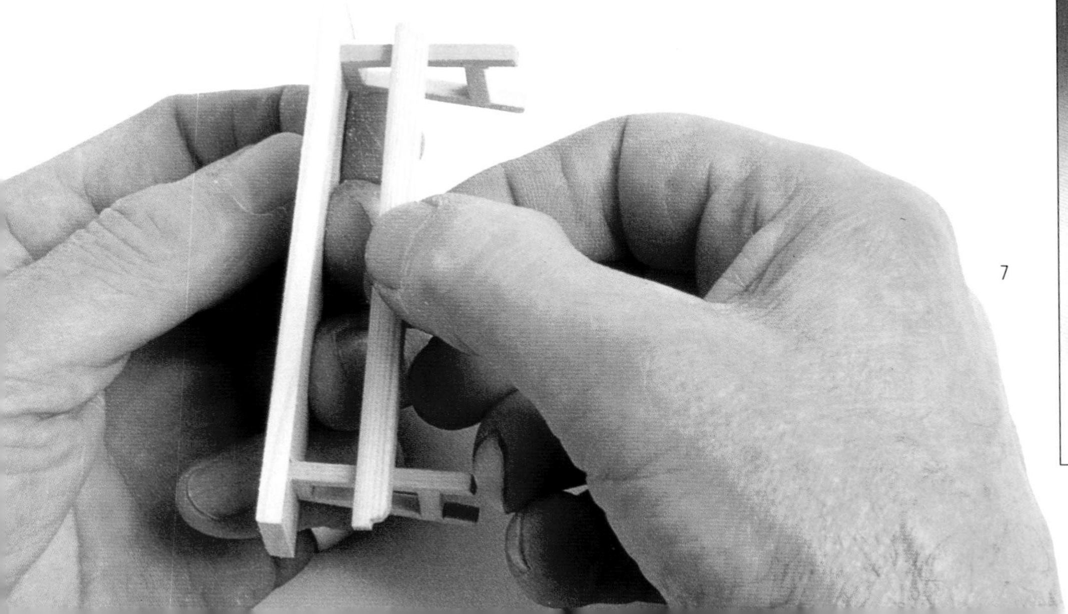

7

Pine Corner Cupboard

~

The clever construction of this cupboard – slicing the shelves from a triangular block – will ensure that all the shelves are exactly the same size, that the back pieces fit properly and that the cupboard will fit into the corner snugly. The moulded pieces at the top and bottom, and the shaped shelf fronts add a decorative touch.

~

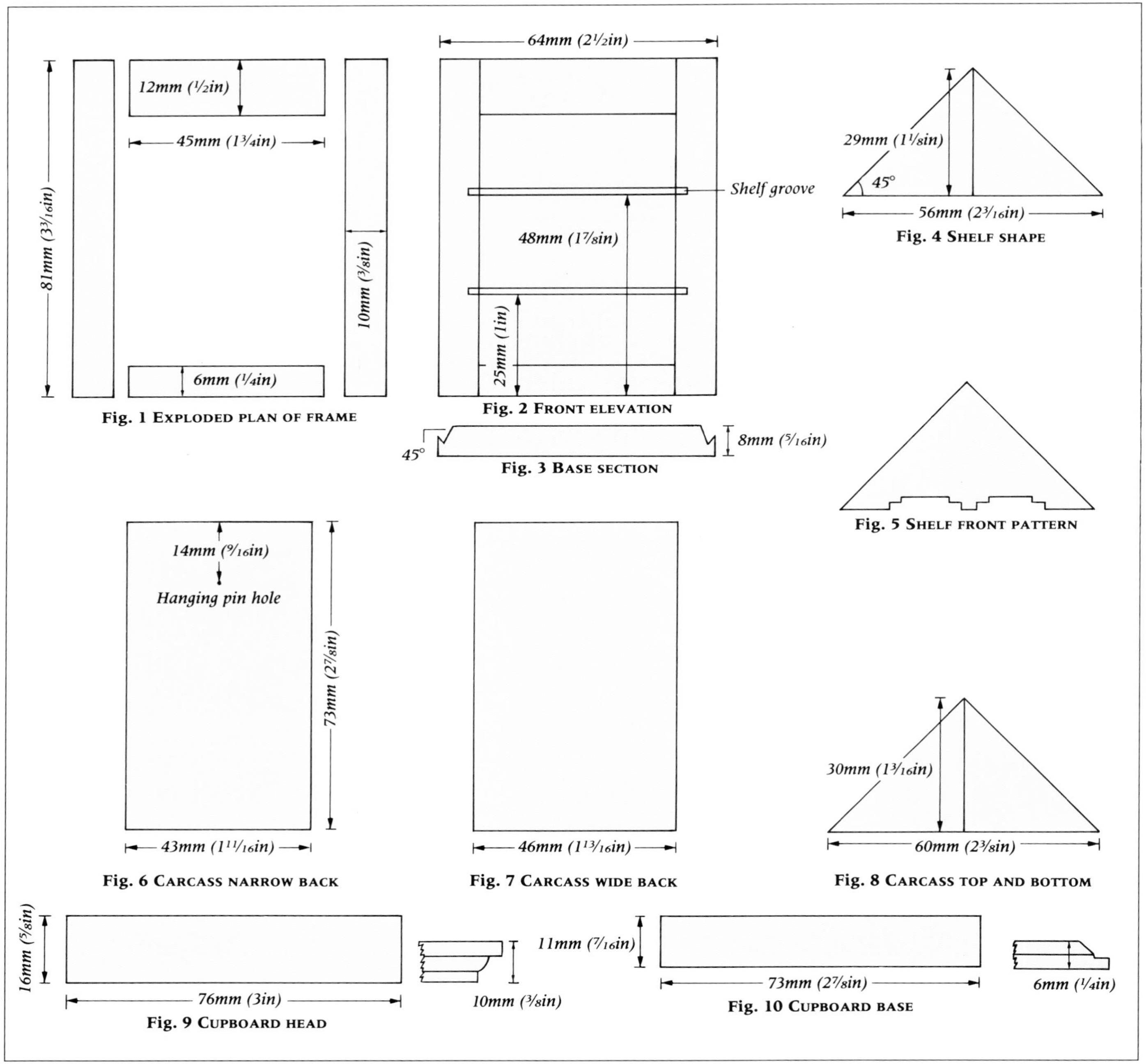

Fig. 1 Exploded plan of frame

Fig. 2 Front elevation

Fig. 3 Base section

Fig. 4 Shelf shape

Fig. 5 Shelf front pattern

Fig. 6 Carcass narrow back

Fig. 7 Carcass wide back

Fig. 8 Carcass top and bottom

Fig. 9 Cupboard head

Fig. 10 Cupboard base

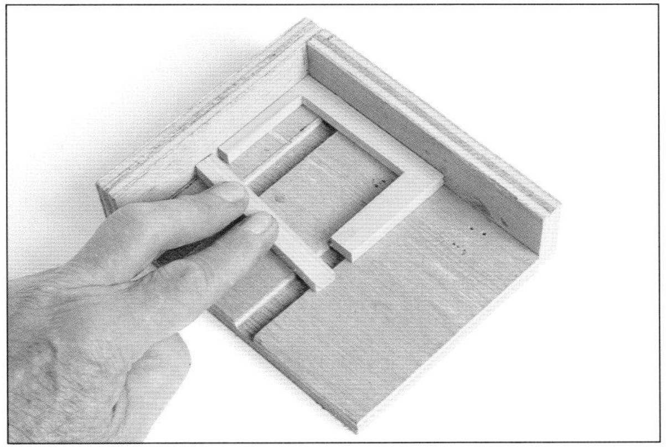

1

1. Cut the components of the basic frame 8mm (5⁄16in) thick (see Fig. 1). Assemble and glue the frame together.

2

2. Cut the base section, as shown in Fig. 3, to a 45° angle. Cut two 3mm (1⁄8in) grooves in the frame for the shelves. Sand and wax the front and side edges.

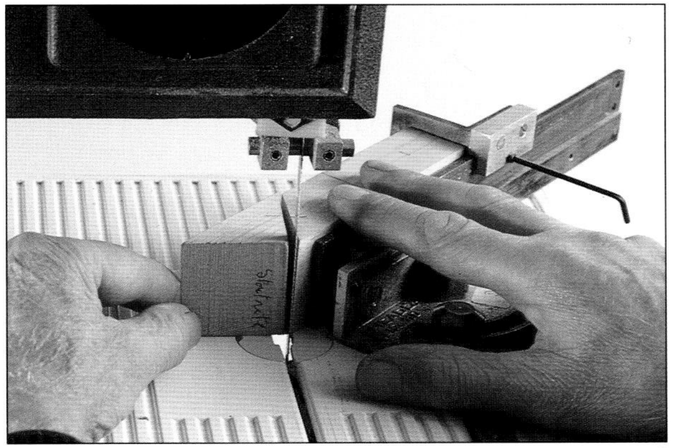

3

3. Cut a section 38 × 18 × 150mm (1½ × ¾ × 6in) along the grain.
Cut a triangular block from this section to make the shelves (see Fig. 4). Keep any remaining pieces to form the top and bottom of the carcass.

4

4. Shape the front of the triangular block as shown in Fig. 5.

5. Slice shelves from the block to the width of the shelf grooves already cut. Assemble the shelves in the carcass.

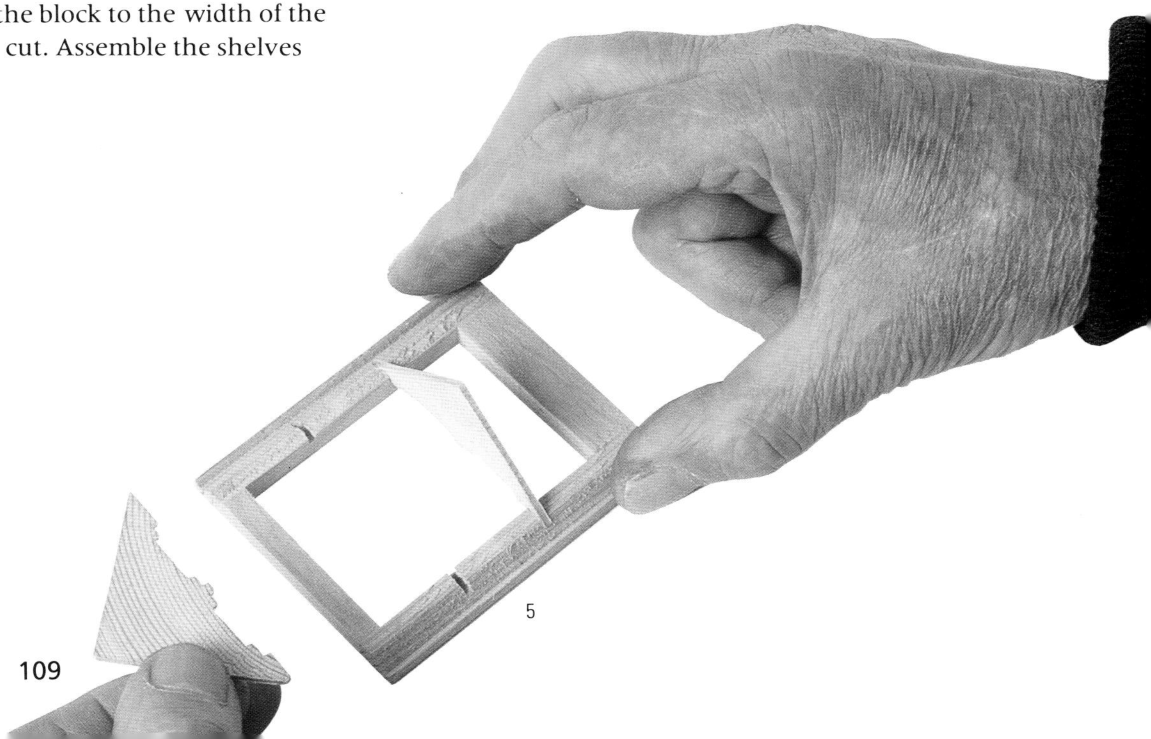

5

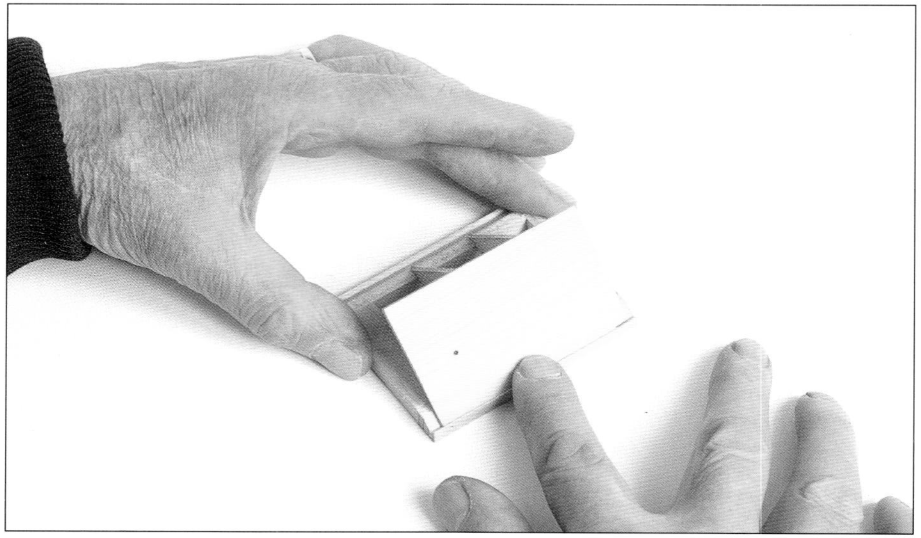

6

6. Cut pieces for the carcass back 1.5mm (1/16in) thick. Drill the hanging holes in the narrower piece. (see Figs. 6 and 7.) Fit the narrow piece first.

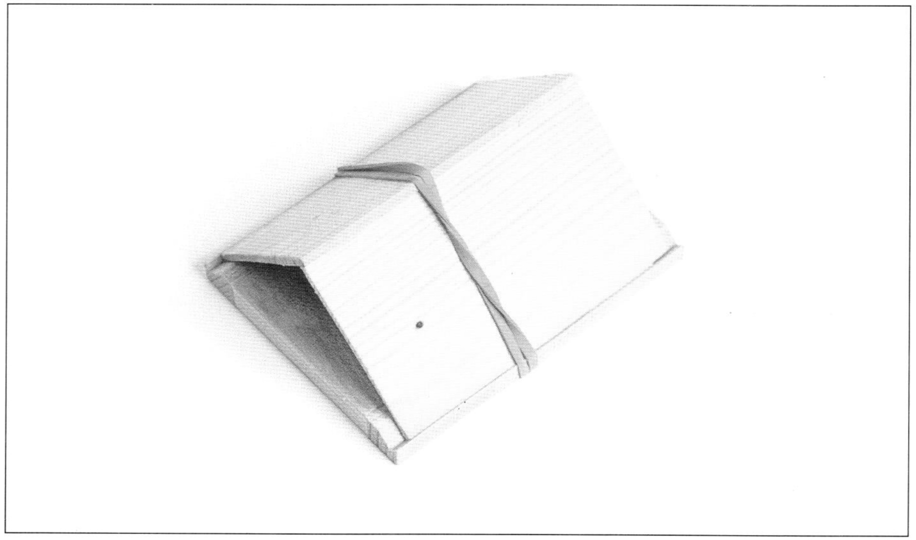

7

7. Use an elastic band to hold the back pieces in place.

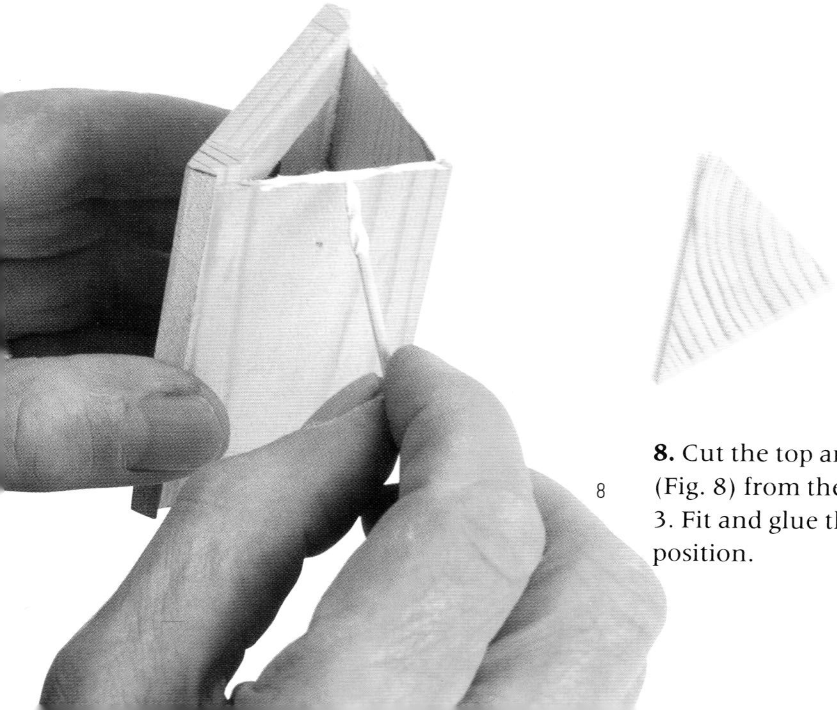

8

8. Cut the top and bottom pieces (Fig. 8) from the block made in step 3. Fit and glue the base and top in position.

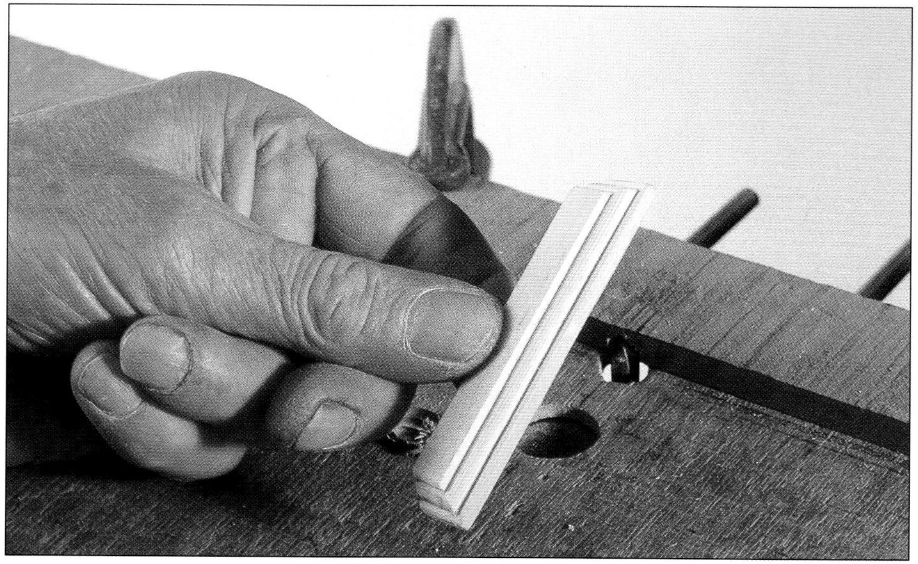

9

9. Cut blanks for the cupboard head and base. Mould the fronts and ends. (see Figs. 9 and 10.)

10. Make a 45° cut to the corners of the base and head pieces. This cut will be 5mm (3⁄16in) from the front edge of these pieces. Sand and wax the base and heads.

11. Glue the base and head in place. Cut a pad 12mm (½in) square and 6mm (¼in) deep and glue it to the underside of the carcass.

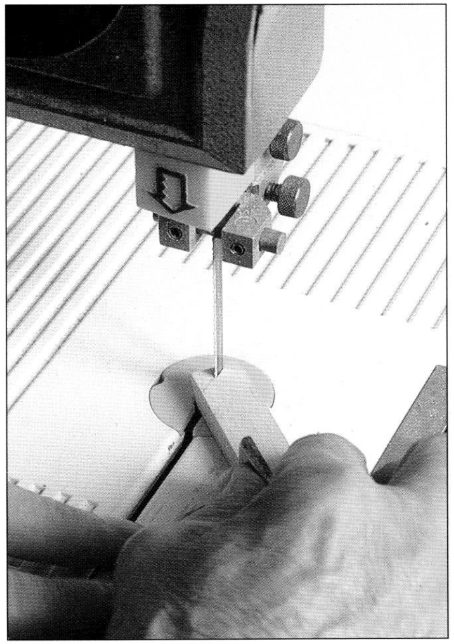

10

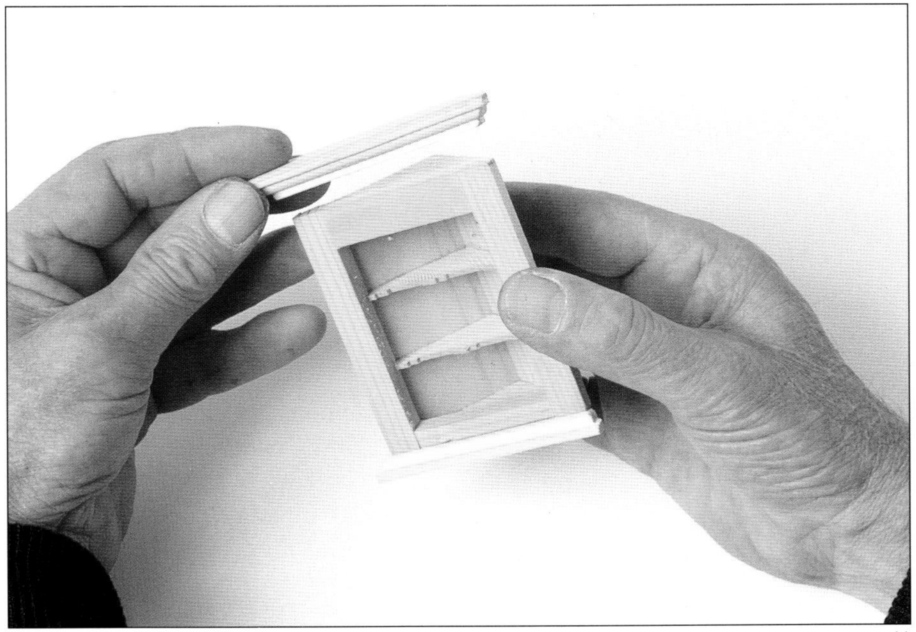

11

Note

Each time you make this cupboard, it will have slightly different measurements. The measurements in Fig. 2 form the basis for all subsequent measurements; all pieces made after the basic frame should be measured against the frame and cut to fit; the measurements given are approximate.

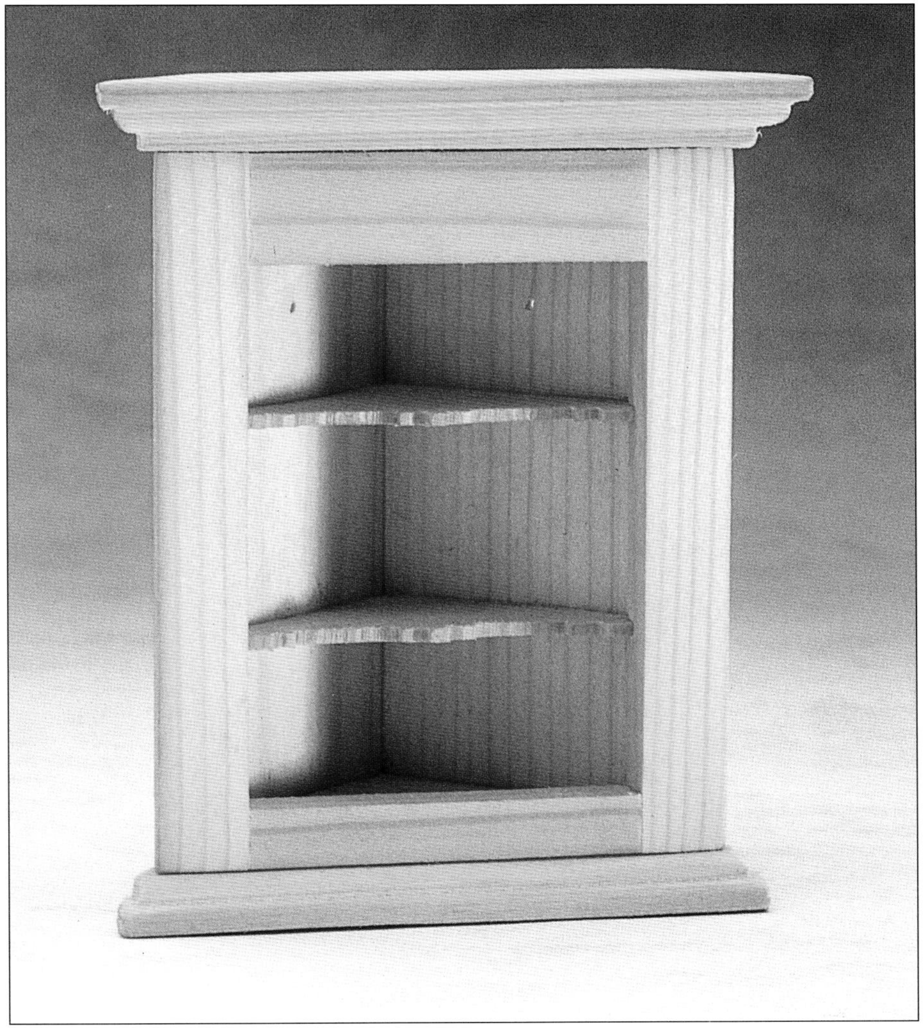

Pine Hanging Shelves

~

A decorative but useful piece for any kitchen, these shelves work best in pine since the light colour and simple designs complement the bright colours used in many kitchens. The small drawers beneath the bottom shelf are constructed in exactly the same way as the drawers in the other projects.

~

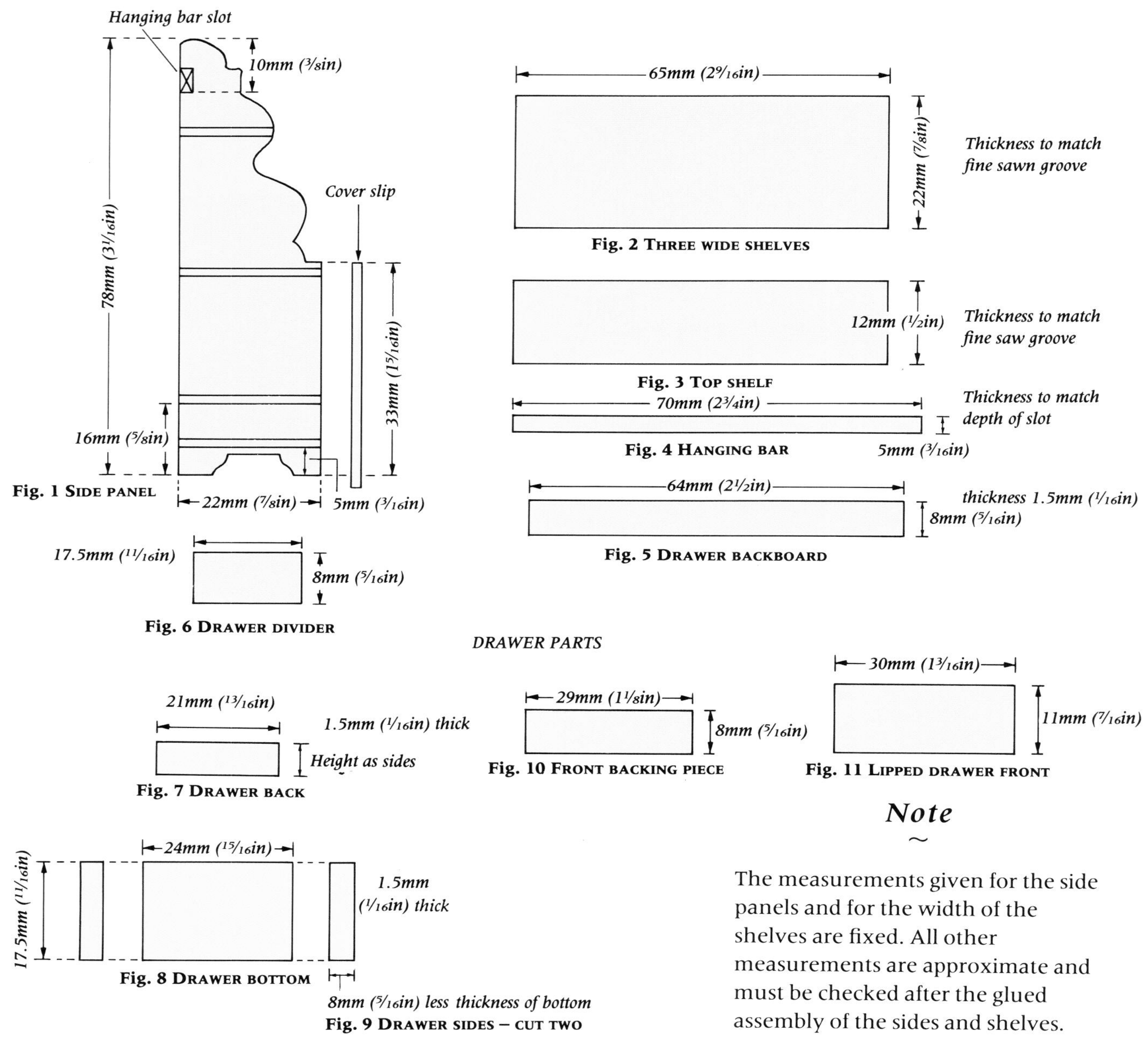

Note

~

The measurements given for the side panels and for the width of the shelves are fixed. All other measurements are approximate and must be checked after the glued assembly of the sides and shelves.

1

2

1. You will need a section 22mm (7⁄8in) wide and 81mm (3 3⁄16in) long and sufficiently deep to provide slices for the sides, the shelves and the cover slips. Cut generous 78 × 22 × 1.5mm (3 1⁄16 × 7⁄8 × 1⁄16in) slices for the side pieces. Run grooves to the measurements shown in Fig. 1.

2. Draw the pattern onto the sides. If you are cutting more than one set of sides, you can pin several slices together and cut all the sides in one go (see *pinning blanks*). Cut the hanging bar slot in the sides.

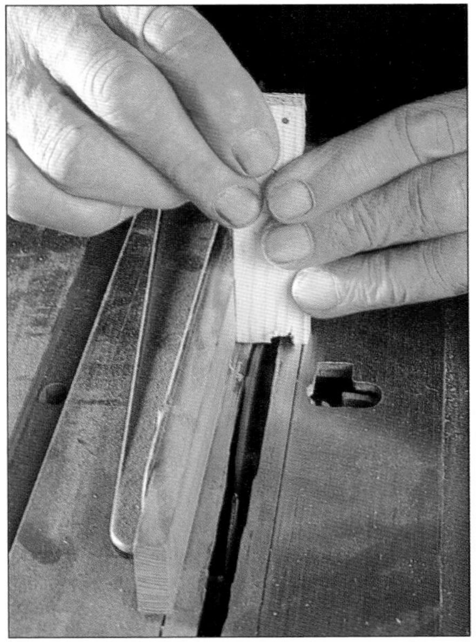

3

3. Make the moulded cuts for the feet.

4

4. Cut out the pattern.

5. Slice two cover slips from the blank already made and cut them to 33mm (1⁵⁄₁₆in) long. Glue the cover strips to the sides. They should be flush with the top edge of the front and protrude by 3mm (⅛in) at the bottom, where they are trimmed off with a craft knife.

6. The unpinned block, showing the sides with pattern and grooves cut.

7. Cut four slices from the section made in step 1 for the shelves. Reduce the width of one slice to match the depth of the top shelf groove. Cut all the shelves to a finished length of 65mm (2⁹⁄₁₆in) (see Figs. 2 and 3). Sand and wax the visible surfaces. Glue the shelves to the side panels on the jig.

8. Cut the drawer backboard (see Fig. 5) and test for fit against the carcass. Sand and wax.

9. Cut the drawer divider (see Fig. 6) and test for fit. Sand and wax.

10. Cut the hanging bar (see Fig. 4) and make the holes marked, test for fit and then sand and wax it. Make sure the ends of the hanging bar are flush with the sides.

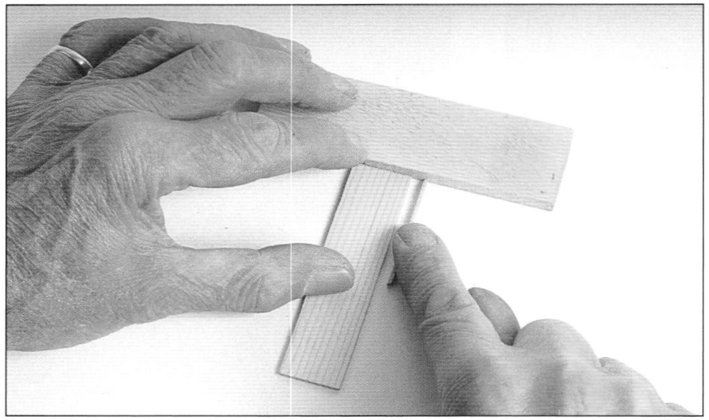

5

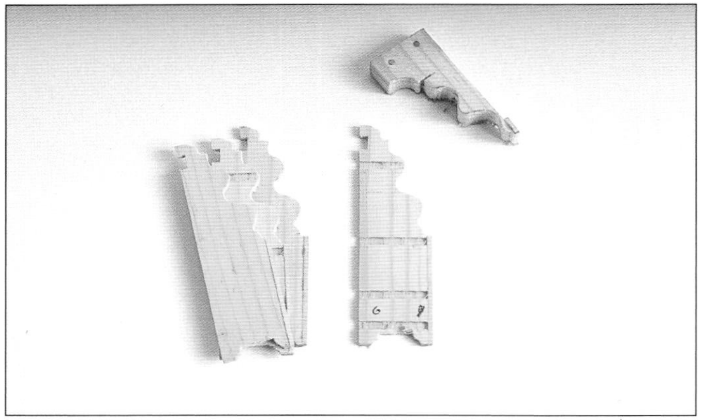

6

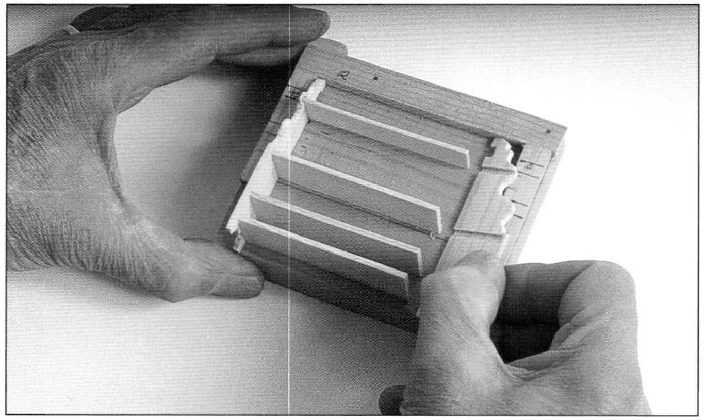

7

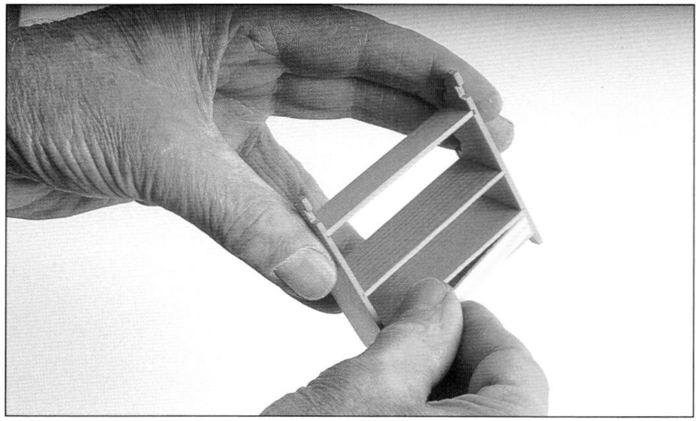

8

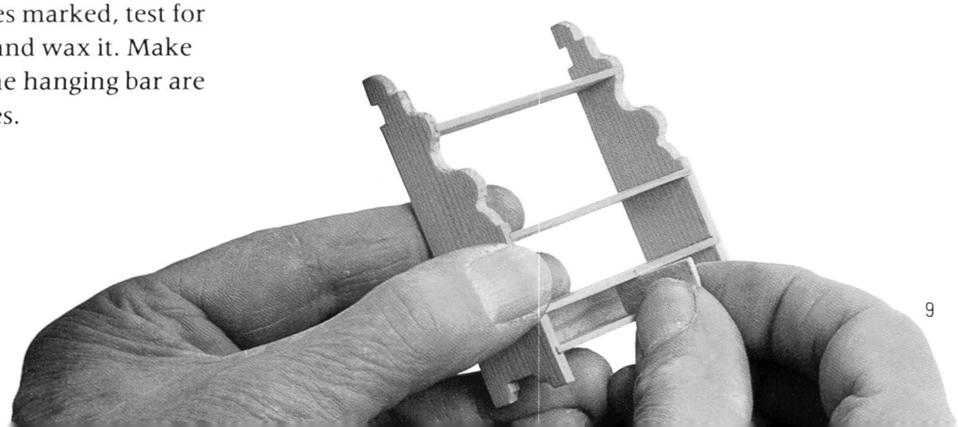

9

10

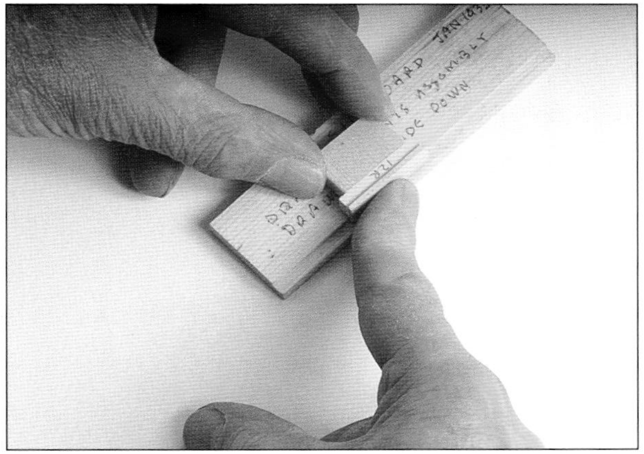

11

11. Cut, sand and wax the drawer components (see Figs. 7–11). Apply glue to the front edge of the bottom piece and glue to the front piece. Apply glue to the front and bottom of the right side. Leave glue to set and then assemble left side in the same way. Test for fit against the assembled carcass. The lipped drawer front should overlap the top, bottom and sides by about 1.5mm ($^1/_{16}$in).

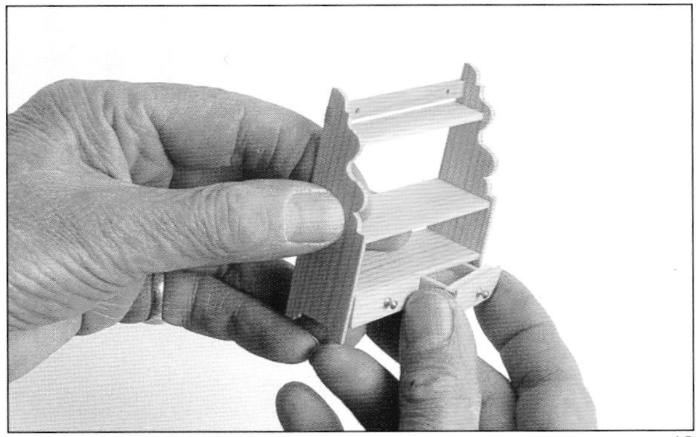

12

12. Make small holes in the drawer fronts for the knobs, apply glue and insert. Place the carcass on its back and leave to dry overnight.

THE BEDROOM

~

Bed

~

This design is one of the simplest in terms of the number of components. However, you will still need to work as carefully and accurately as possible. As with any piece with separate legs, you will have to be especially careful to ensure all the legs are level. You could shape the bed head to any design you wish – perhaps a simple rounded shape.

~

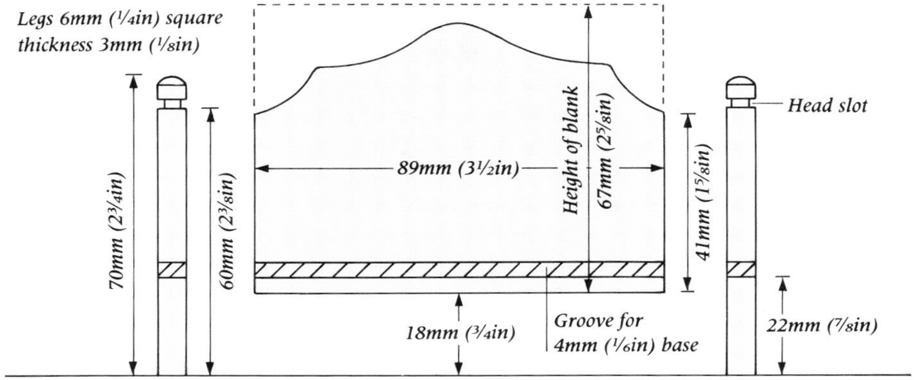

Fig. 1 Bed head panel and legs

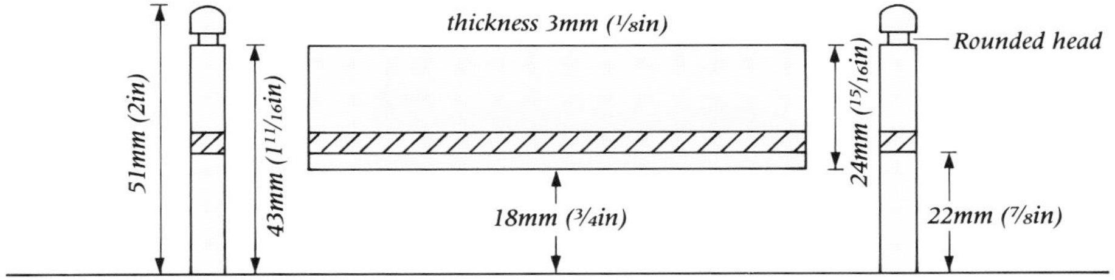

Fig. 2 Bed end panel and legs

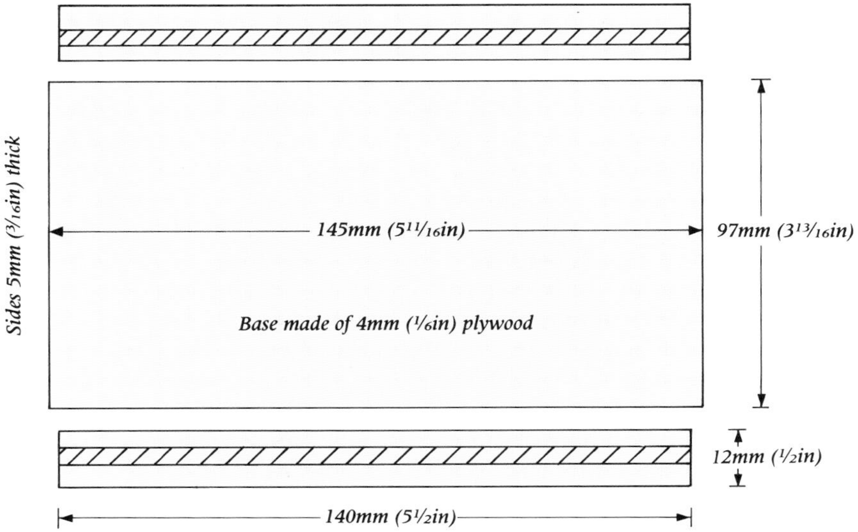

Fig. 3 Bed base and sides

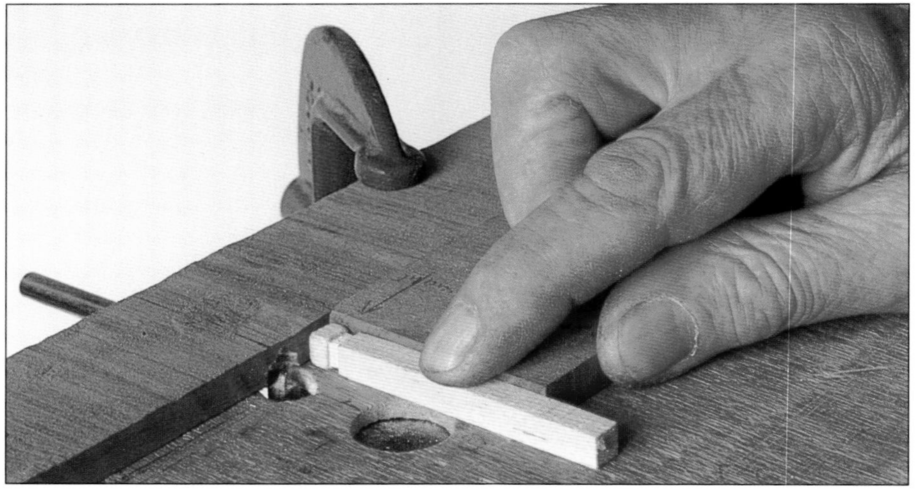

1

1. Cut out four pine legs. Make slots in the heads and round the tops (see Fig. 1).

2. Take a piece of pine to the dimensions shown in Fig. 1 for the headboard. Make a line down the middle and draw in the headboard shape, making sure the pattern is exactly symmetrical about the centre line. Cut the headboard out.

2

3

4

3. Cut the end panel out (see Fig. 2). Sand, seal and wax both panels.

4. Assemble the legs and the headboard by butting them together and fixing with glue. The top edge of each panel should be slightly below the bottom edge of the leg head slots. Allow the glue to set. Repeat for the legs and the end panel.

5. Cut 4mm (⅙in) base grooves in both the assembled panels.

5

6. Make some "stops" to fill the grooves and stop the base board moving. They need to be the depth of the groove and a bare 5mm (3⁄16in) long. Glue the stops no more than 3mm (⅛in) into the groove and running with the grain. Test the distance between the stops with a ruler – they must be at least 97mm (3 13⁄16in) apart for the base to fit easily. Sand down the stops so they are flush with the leg surface. Sand, seal and wax the legs.

6

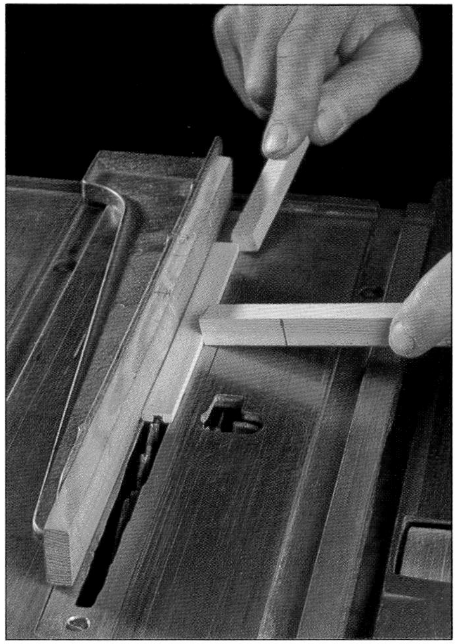

7

7. Dry-assemble the base to the head and end panels. Measure the distance between the head legs and end legs. Cut the base side pieces (see Fig. 3) so that they are very slightly longer than this measurement. Cut a 4mm (⅙in) groove in each side.

8. Sand, seal and wax the sides. Use a cocktail stick to put glue in the side grooves and offer the sides to the base so that the base protrudes equally at both sides.

8

9

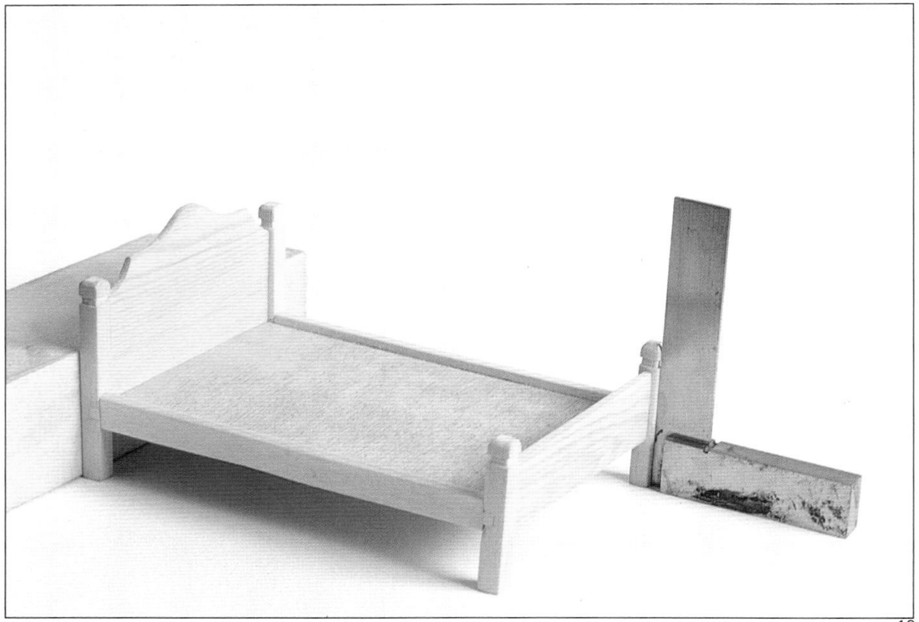

10

9. Assemble the base to the head and glue in position.

10. Assemble the end to the base and glue in position. Leave to dry, ensuring that all four legs are square to a flat surface.

Bedside Table

~

This simple but charming design is an essential piece in any bedroom, and it complements the pine bed (see page 117) perfectly. The feet are shaped by cutting out semi- and quarter circles, as are the lateral pieces beneath the table top. The legs are made of lengths of dowel.

~

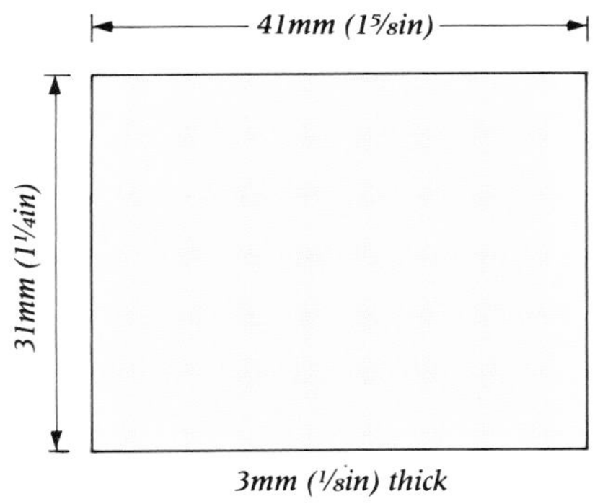

Fig. 1 Table top

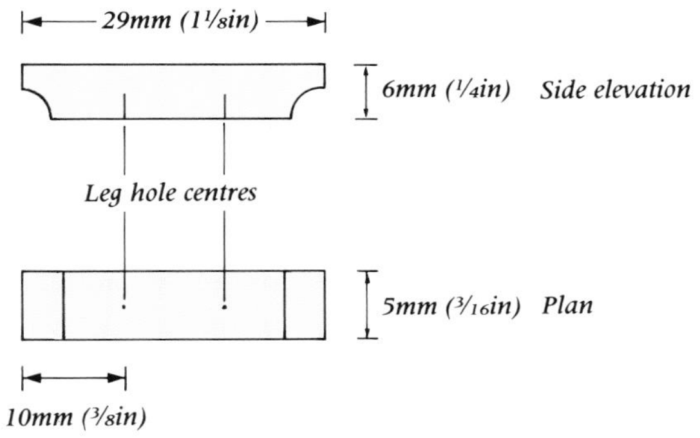

Fig. 2 Moulded top lateral

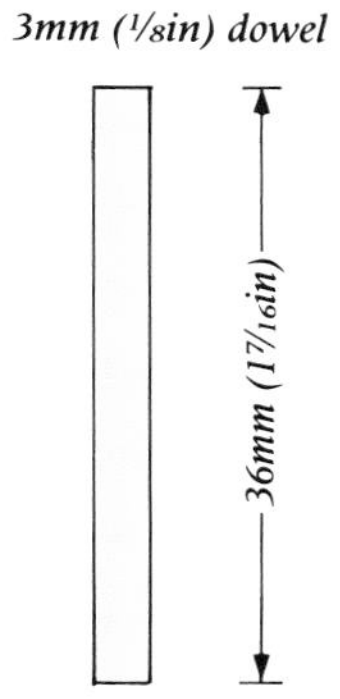

Fig. 3 Leg

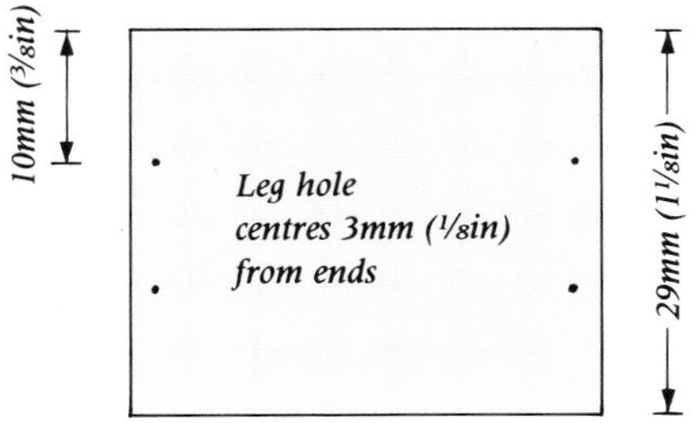

Fig. 4 Shelf blank

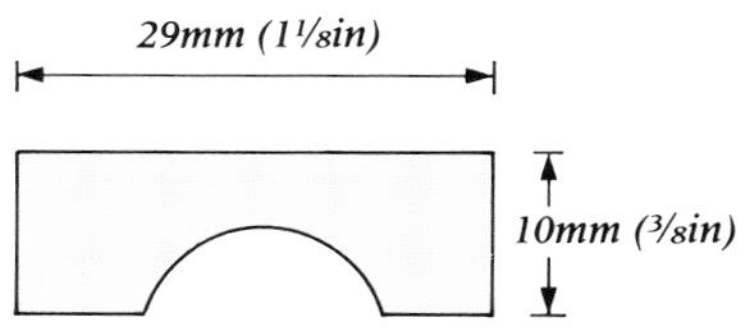

Fig. 6 Feet – first shape

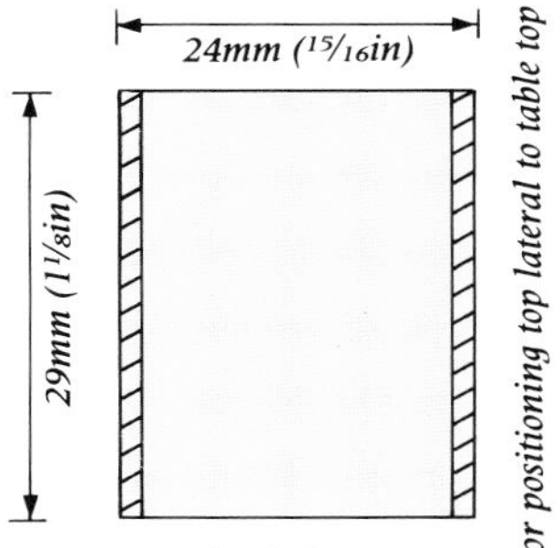

Fig. 8 Spacer

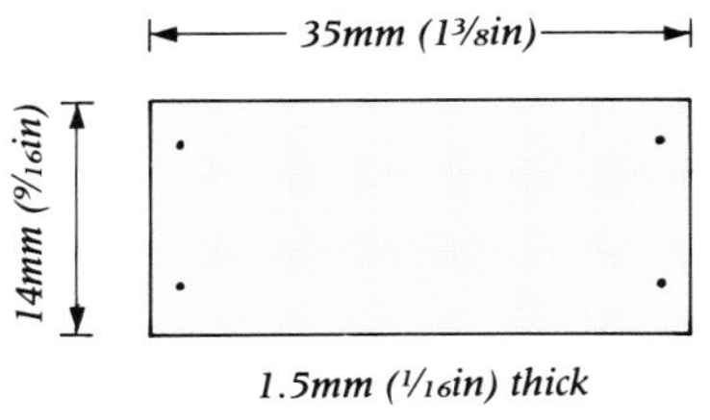

Fig. 5 Shelf – reduced to final width

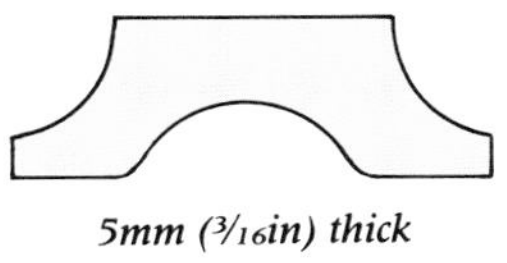

Fig. 7 Feet – final shape

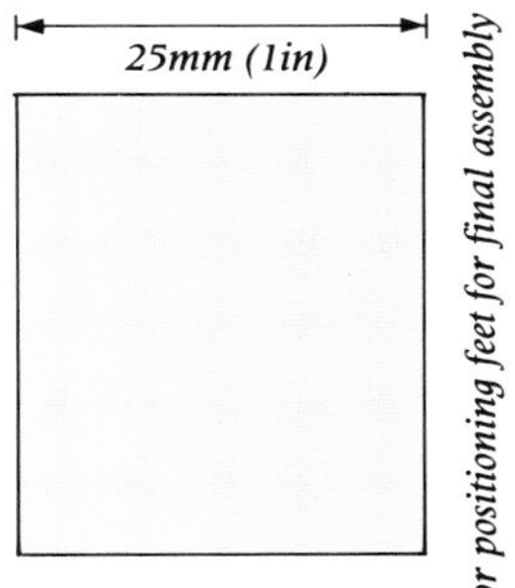

Fig. 9 Spacer

1. All the pieces shown are cut from pine except the two spacers (Figs. 8 and 9), which are cut from scrap wood. For the feet, cut two blanks 29 × 10 × 5mm (1⅛ × ⅜ × 3⁄16in). To shape the feet, first hollow out the centre semi-circle.

2. Hollow out two quarter-circles from either side to form the final shape of the feet.

1

3

3. Cut two top lateral pieces 29 × 6mm (1⅛ × ¼in) and 5mm (3⁄16in) wide, and mould to the shape shown (see Fig. 2). These pieces sit underneath the table top at the top of the legs. Drill two holes for the legs, each 10mm (⅜in) from the end of the lateral.

2

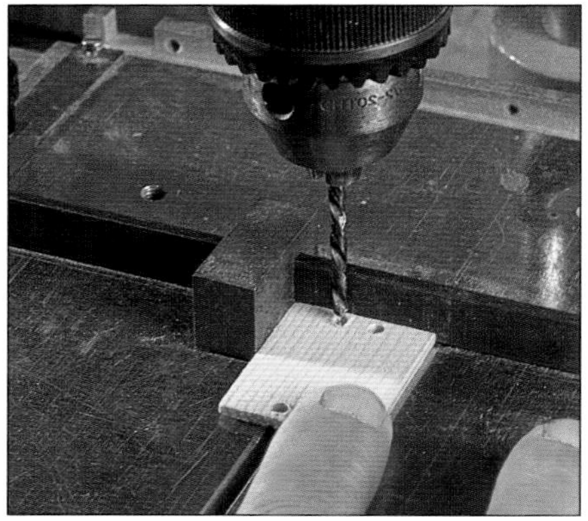

4

4. To make the shelf, cut a section 29mm (1⅛in) wide and at least 51mm (2in) long. Cut along the grain so that it is barely 3mm (⅛in) thick. Trim the section down so that it is 35mm (1⅜in) long. Make four leg holes 10mm (⅜in) from the edge as shown in Fig. 4.

5

5. Reduce the width of the shelf to 14mm (9⁄16in), which is the length of the flat surface of the feet pieces minus 1.5mm (1⁄16in). You may have to do this by a process of trial and error. The holes in the shelf must be equidistant from both sides.

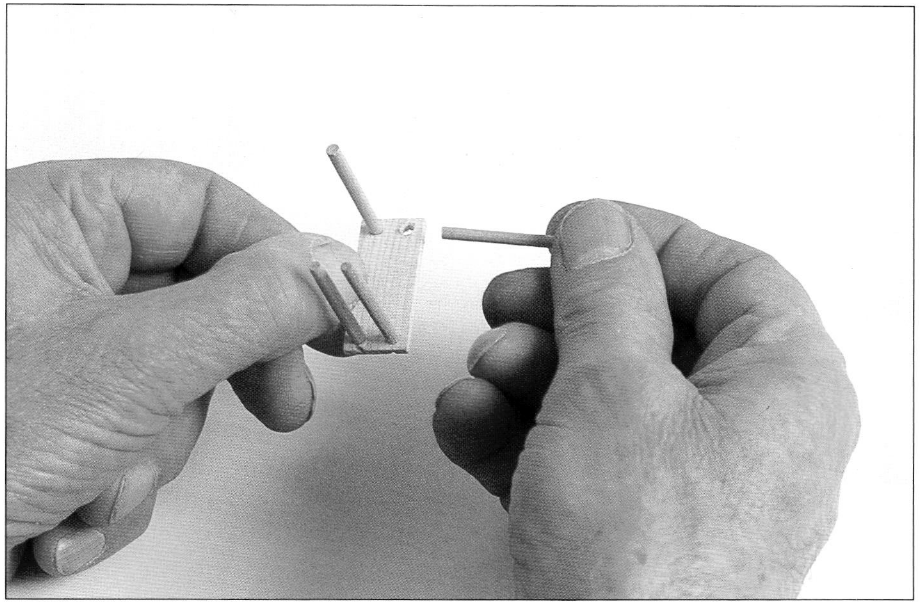

6

6. Cut the top piece (Fig. 1). Hand sand and wax the top surfaces and edges of the table top and shelf, the legs, the outside surface and moulding of the top lateral and the side surfaces and shaping of the feet pieces. Take four pieces of 3mm (⅛in) dowel (Fig. 3), insert some glue into the holes in the shelf and push in the legs. Check that the ends are flush with the underside of the shelf.

7

7. Cut the wide spacer and run "anti-glue" rebates down either side, as shown in Fig. 8. Place the table top upside-down on an assembly jig. Place the spacer on top. Put glue in the holes in the laterals and insert the legs. Check that the shelf is in line with the table top edge. Remove the table top. Check the shelf is parallel to the jig floor; check the legs are vertical from the end and the front. Allow the glued legs to dry.

8

8. Put some glue on the underside of the table top and attach it, using the spacer to ensure accuracy. Put some glue on the top, flat surface of the feet and glue them to the shelf so that the feet pieces are in line with the shelf ends and the shelf is centred over the feet pieces. Use the 25mm (1in) wide spacer to position the feet in the final assembly.

Chest of Drawers

~

This piece is made of mahogany-style wood, but could just as easily be made from pine, depending on your decoration scheme. The feet are not separate components, but are simply formed by shaping the bottom edge of the sides and the front apron. All the visible surfaces – the back is made of plywood – will need to be finished thoroughly, using several coats of polish.

~

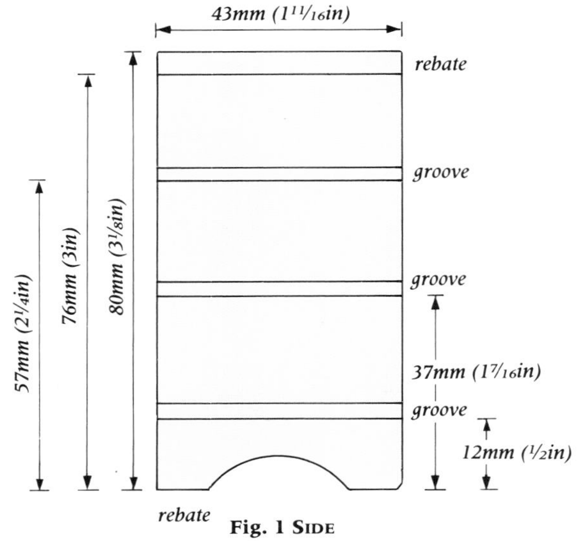

Fig. 1 Side

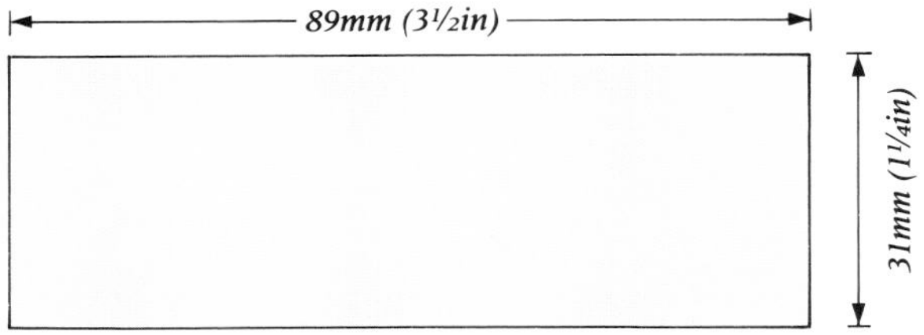

Fig. 2 Base

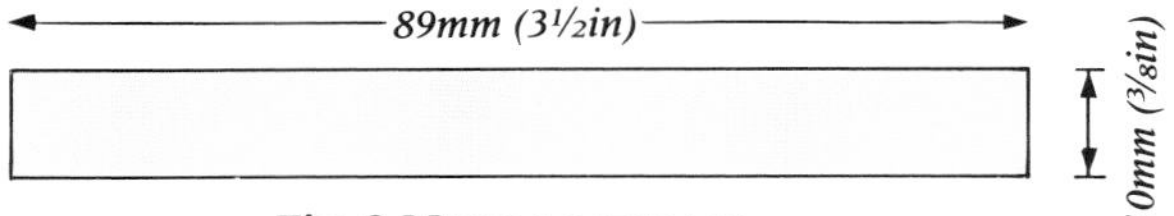

Fig. 3 Middle laterals

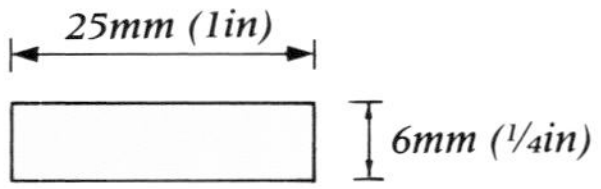

Fig. 5 Drawer runner

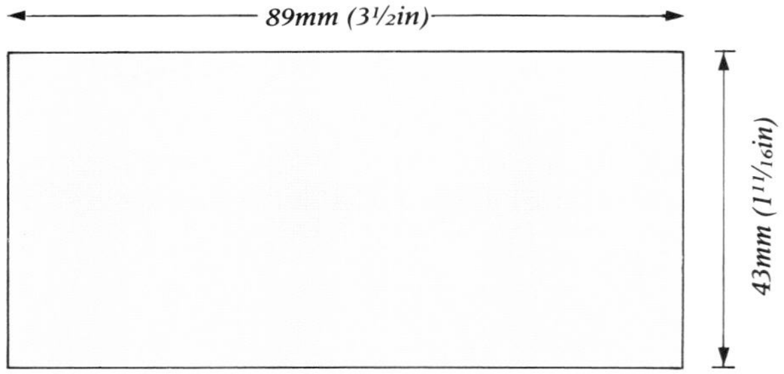

Fig. 4 Top lateral

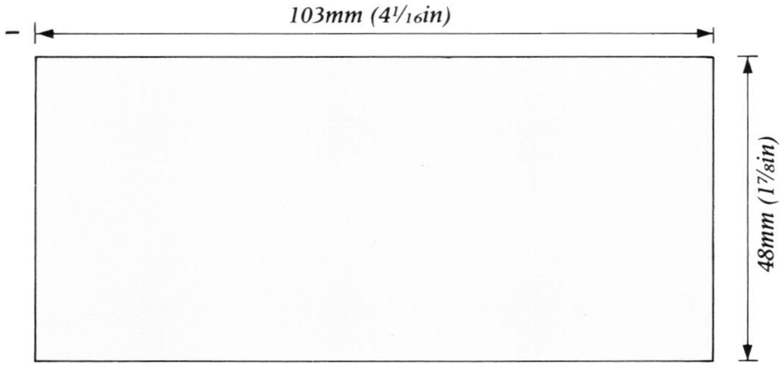

Fig. 7 Top

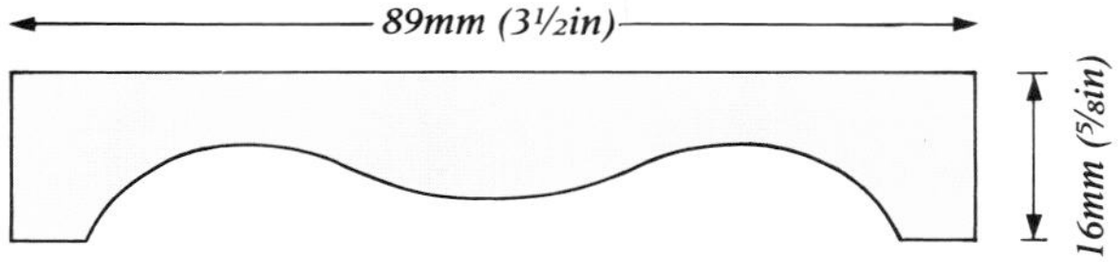

Fig. 6 Apron

1. You will need a section of wood 51 × 95 × 45mm (2 × 3¾ × 1¾in). From this you can cut two sides, one top lateral, two middle laterals, one base and four drawer runners. For the sides, cut off two slices to the dimensions shown in Fig. 1. Cut three grooves about 3mm (⅛in) wide for the middle laterals and one rebate 3mm (⅛in) wide for the top lateral. Cut a rebate down each side to hold the back.

2. To form the feet, cut out a semi-circle as shown in Fig. 1. Measure the depth of the grooves and rebate. Cut out the base, one top lateral, two middle laterals and four drawer runners (Figs. 2–5), making the width match the depth of the grooves and rebate. Cut the back (Fig. 8) from 4mm (⅙in) plywood and test for fit against the side rebate.

3. Make plugs for the front ends of the grooves cut for the base. Cut pieces to the depth of the groove and about 5mm (3/16in) long. Glue the stops to the grooves so that they protrude slightly at the front. Hand sand the inner and front sides so that the plugs are flush. Sand, stain and polish the front edges and sides, and the middle and top laterals.

1

2

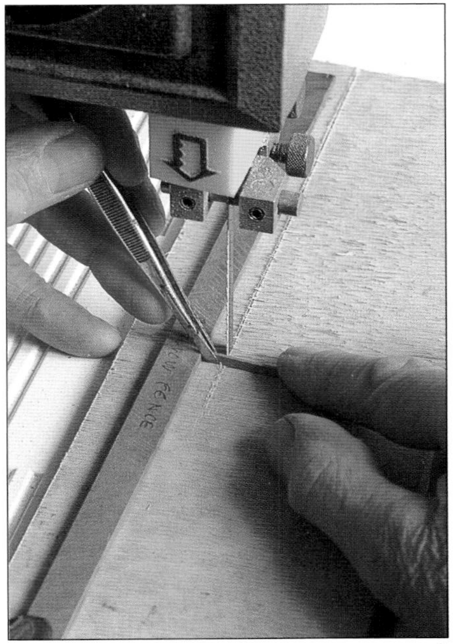
3

4. Assemble the drawer runners. Position the back end of the runners flush with the rebate for the back. Put glue in the grooves and insert the runners, using a small piece of wood to check that they are vertical.

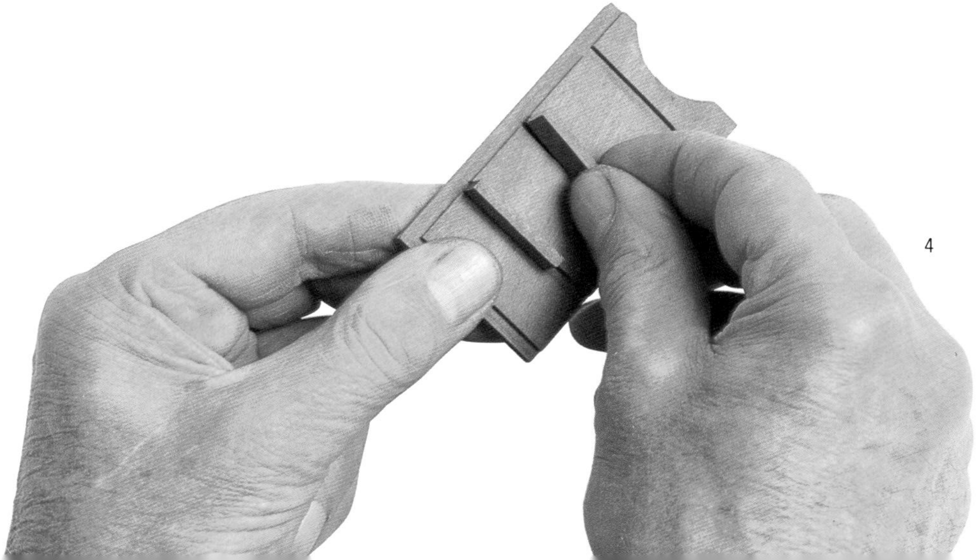
4

5

5. Assemble the carcass. Put glue in the grooves and rebates on the sides. Place the left side on an assembly jig with the feet pressed against the jig wall. Assemble the back so that its top matches the top of the side.

6

6. Assemble the base flush to the rebate wall. Assemble the right side and the top lateral.

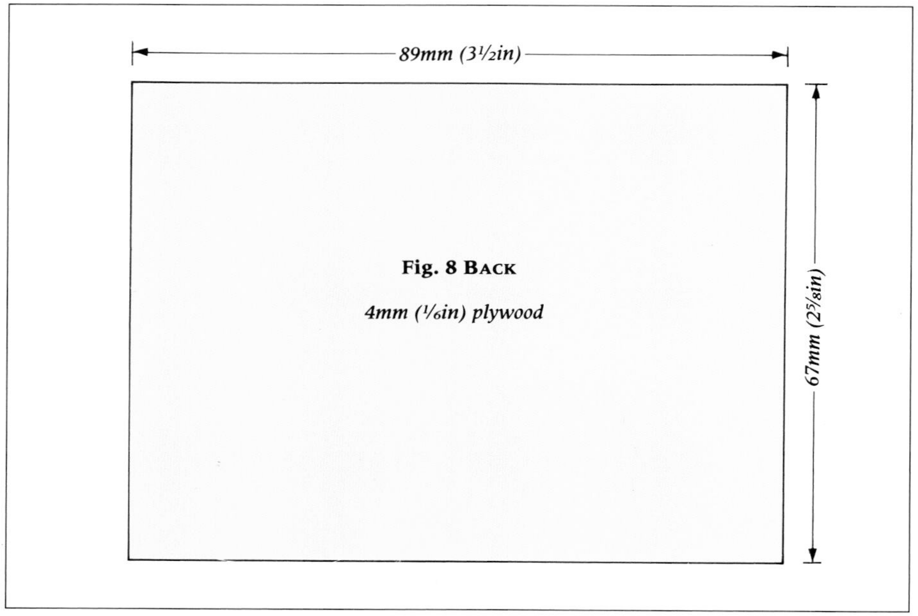

7

7. Assemble the middle laterals and the ends, which should be flush with the front edges of the sides.

8. Cut a section 16mm (5/8in) wide along the grain and 12 × 92mm (1/2 × 3 5/8in). Measure the distance between the sides of the assembled carcass to determine the width of the apron. Cut out the apron to the shape shown in Fig. 6. If you want to ensure a really snug fit, first cut out the apron in 4mm (1/6in) plywood and test it for fit.

9. Sand, stain and polish the front of the apron. Slice the section so that it is slightly less thick than the distance between the front edges of the sides and base. Fit the apron.

8

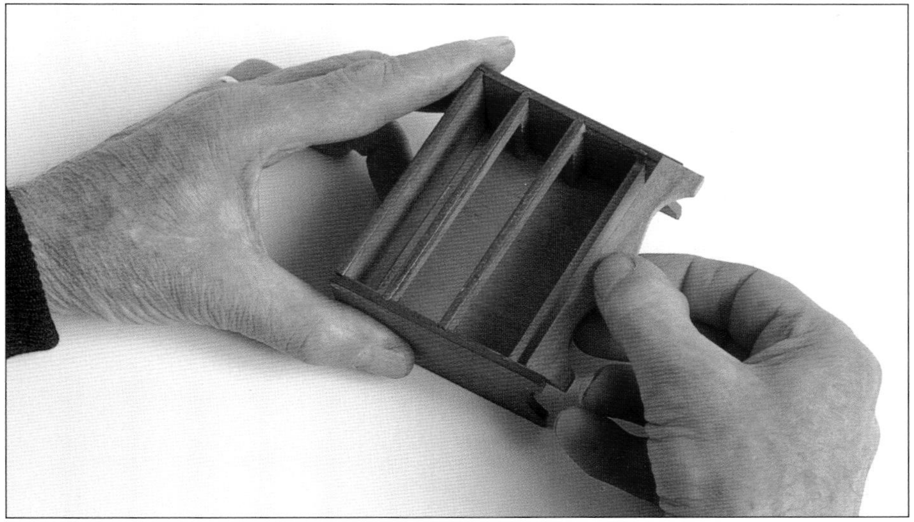

9

Making a Set of Drawers

~

Fig. 9 Drawers

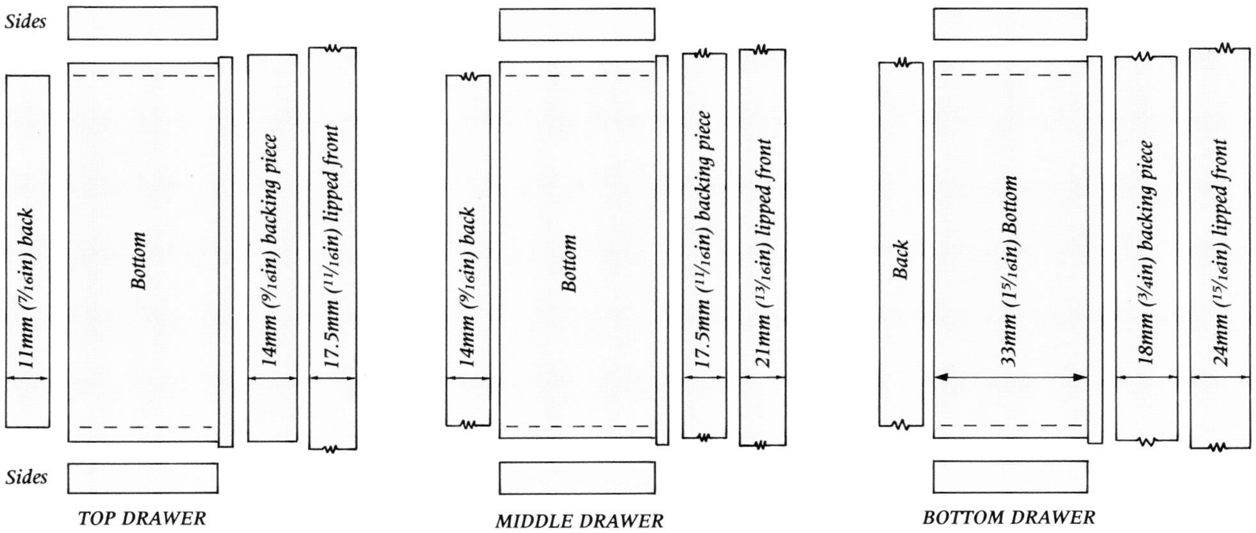

All the bottom and side pieces of the drawer are the same depth – 33mm (1 5/16in); all the backing pieces are the same width – 87mm (3 7/16in); and all the lipped fronts are the same width – 90mm (3 9/16in).

Assemble the drawers by placing the drawer front backing piece against the vertical back of a basic assembly jig. Apply glue to the front of the drawer bottom and to the backing piece. Apply glue to the front and the bottom of the right-hand side as you look at it. Holding a small square of wood in your right hand, press it against the edge of the drawer bottom and side so that they line up exactly. Push the side against the backing piece. Allow the glue to set. Assemble the left-hand side. Fit the back. Fit the lipped drawer front, which should overlap the drawer opening top, bottom and sides by about 1.5mm (1/16in). Sand, stain and polish the drawer fronts and leave to dry overnight.

10

10. Mark out where the knobs will go – about 18mm (¾in) from the edge. Make the holes, apply some glue to the knobs and insert. Remove the drawers. Sand, stain and polish the carcass sides. Cut the top (Fig. 4) and glue it to the carcass. Sand, stain and polish the top. Leave to dry overnight.

Dressing Table

~

This is one of three carcasses similar in their basic structure; the others are the desk and the sideboard. The structure of the drawers, and of course the number of grooves and rebates required to hold the drawers, differ but once you have mastered one design, you will be able to complete the other two without difficulty.

~

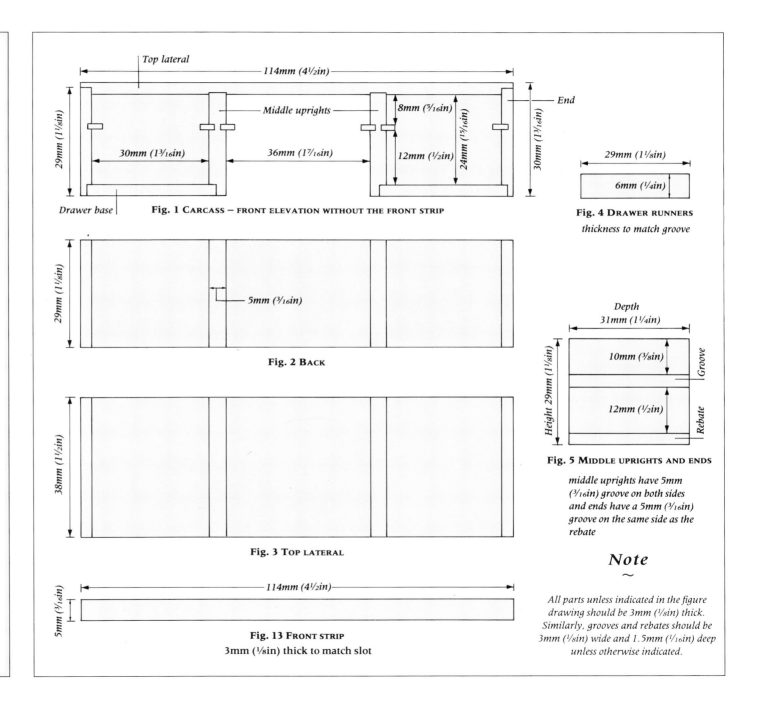

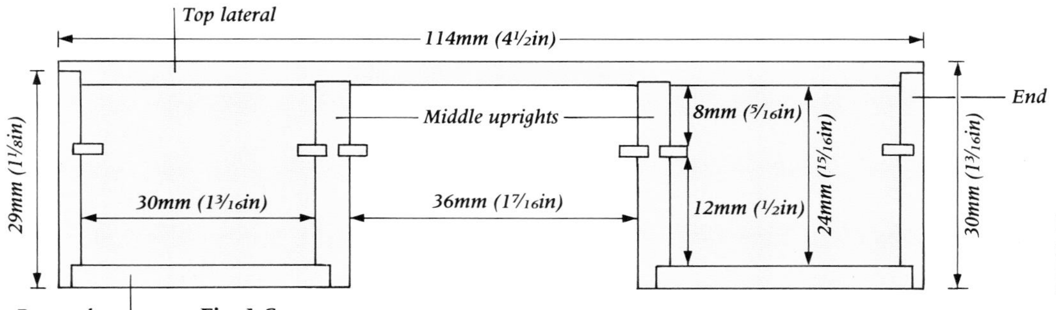

Top lateral
114mm (4½in)
End
Middle uprights
8mm (5/16in)
29mm (1⅛in)
30mm (1 3/16in)
36mm (1 7/16in)
12mm (½in)
24mm (15/16in)
30mm (1 3/16in)
Drawer base

Fig. 1 Carcass – front elevation without the front strip

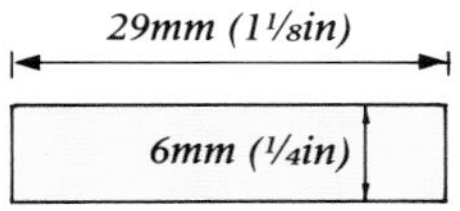

29mm (1⅛in)
6mm (¼in)

Fig. 4 Drawer runners

thickness to match groove

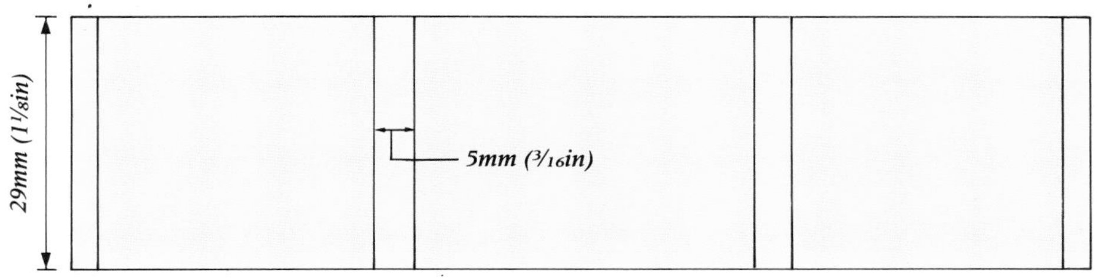

29mm (1⅛in)
5mm (3/16in)

Fig. 2 Back

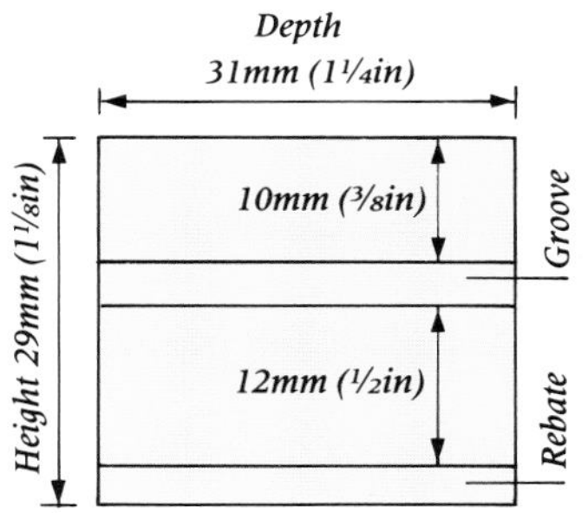

Depth
31mm (1¼in)
Height 29mm (1⅛in)
10mm (⅜in)
Groove
12mm (½in)
Rebate

Fig. 5 Middle uprights and ends

middle uprights have 5mm (3/16in) groove on both sides and ends have a 5mm (3/16in) groove on the same side as the rebate

38mm (1½in)

Fig. 3 Top lateral

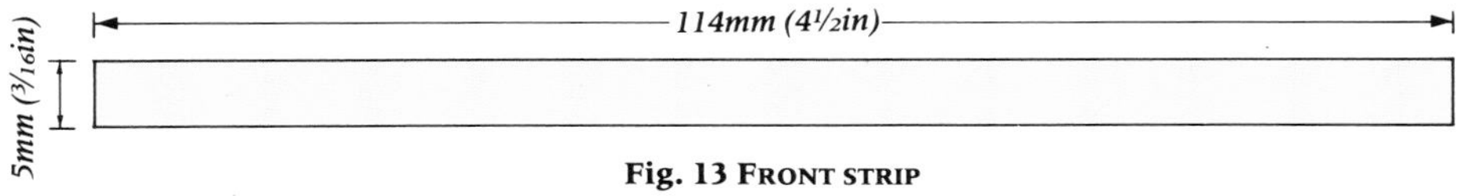

114mm (4½in)
5mm (3/16in)

Fig. 13 Front strip

3mm (⅛in) thick to match slot

Note

~

All parts unless indicated in the figure drawing should be 3mm (⅛in) thick. Similarly, grooves and rebates should be 3mm (⅛in) wide and 1.5mm (1/16in) deep unless otherwise indicated.

1

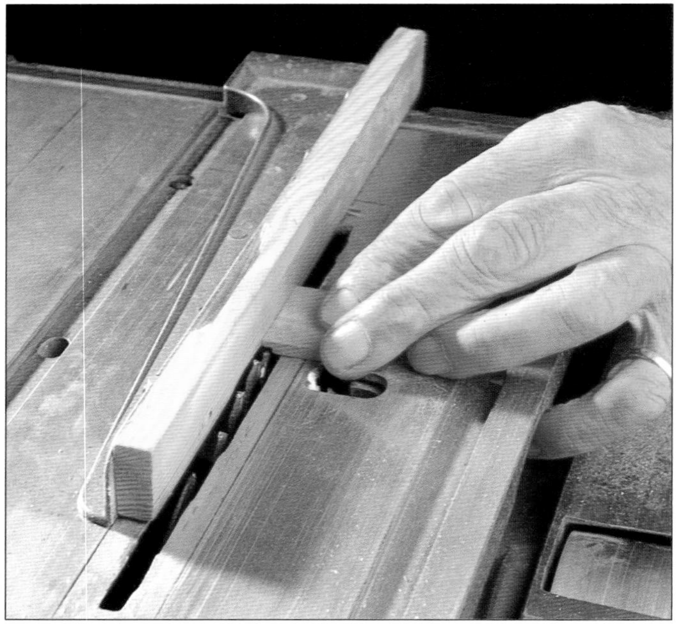

2

1. Cut out the back from 4mm ($\frac{1}{6}$in) plywood. Cut out the top lateral, two middle uprights and two ends from your chosen wood. Cut the grooves and rebates in the back and top lateral as indicated on Figs. 2 and 3.

2. Cut rebates and grooves in the middle uprights and ends (see Fig. 5). Middle upright grooves should be 5mm ($\frac{3}{16}$in) wide. Cut six drawer runners of a thickness to match the grooves (Fig. 4).

3

4

3. Holding the top lateral and back together, insert the middle uprights into the grooves and glue in place. Use a cocktail stick to put glue in the drawer runner grooves on the middle uprights and insert four drawer runners. Make sure the ends of the drawer runners butt against the back and leave a gap of 5mm ($\frac{3}{16}$in) at the front for the front strip.

4. Insert the ends into the grooves and glue in place. Glue the two remaining drawer runners into the ends, again making sure the runners butt against the back and that there is a 5mm ($\frac{3}{16}$in) gap at the front.

5

5. Cut a groove 5mm (3/16in) deep and 3mm (1/8in) wide right the way across the front of the carcass; this must exactly match the position of the grooves for the drawer runners.

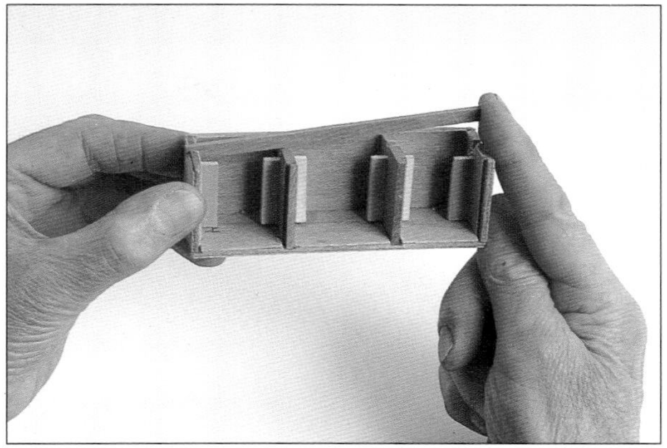

6

6. Cut the front strip (Fig. 13) and glue it into the groove in the front of the carcass. Belt or hand sand the ends and bottom of the carcass with medium sandpaper on a flat surface. The ends must be flush for gluing to the end panels and protrusions at the bottom will look untidy.

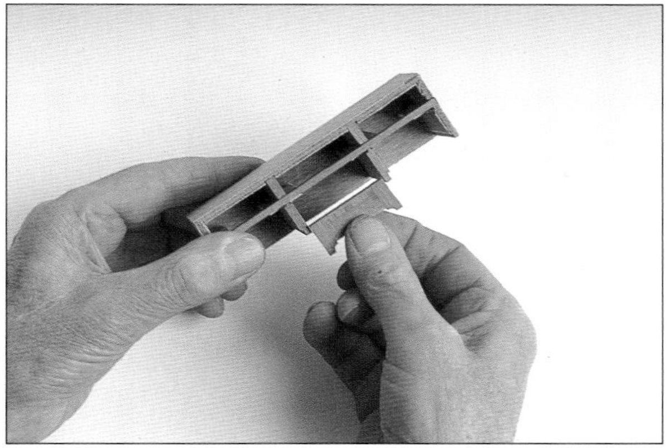

7

7. Make the apron from three pieces of wood as illustrated in Fig. 6, taking careful note of the direction of the grain on each piece. The final thickness of the apron needs to be 3mm (1/8in). Fit and glue the apron to the carcass.

8. Cut two side drawer bases (Fig. 7) and glue them in place in the carcass. Sand, stain and French polish the front of the carcass (see page 97).

8

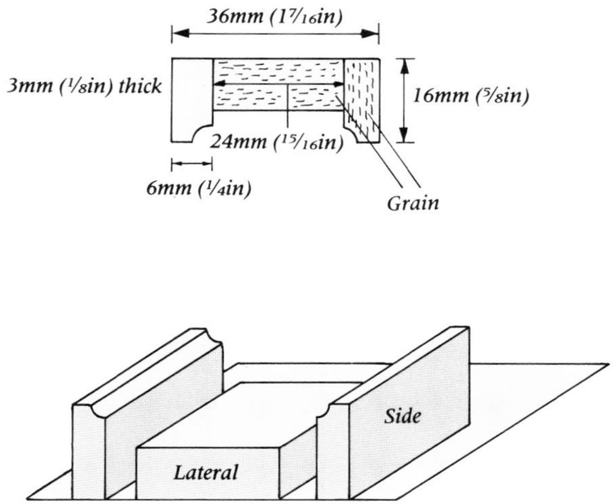

Fig. 6 Apron

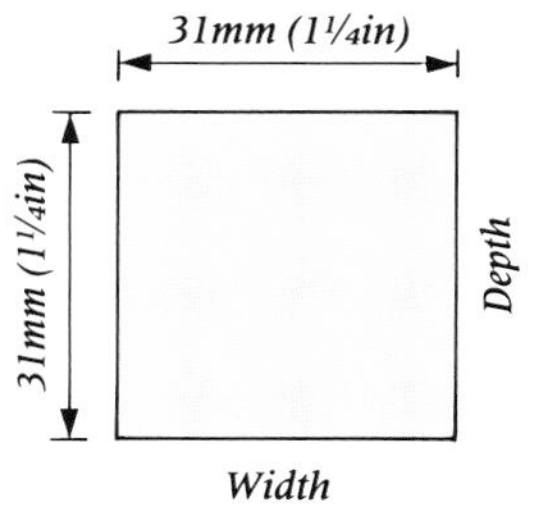

Fig. 7 Side drawer bases

Making the Legs

~

9

9. The completed carcass.

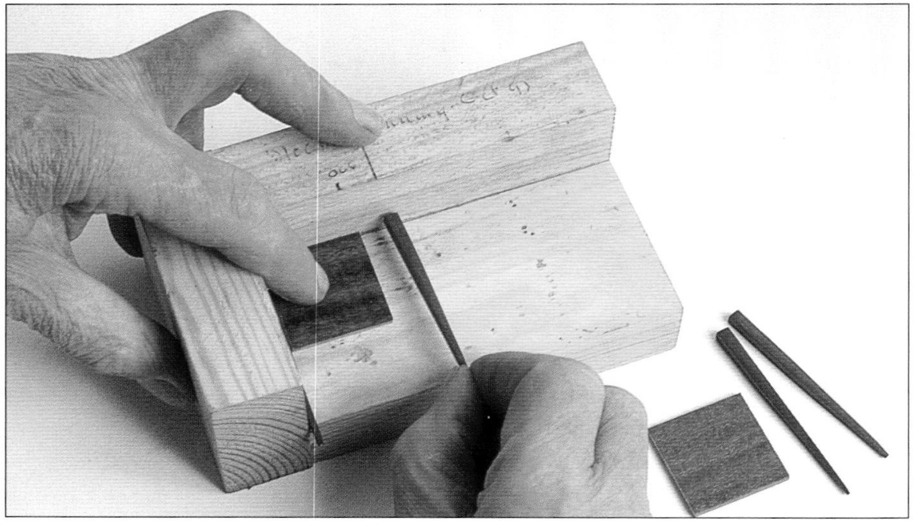

10

10. Cut four legs and taper them to the measurements shown in Fig. 11 using medium sandpaper. Fine sand, stain and polish the legs. Cut two end panels to a bare 3mm (1/8in) thick (Fig. 11). Sand, stain and polish one side. Fit the legs to the panels and assemble on a jig. The polish should be scraped off the areas to be glued. Make sure the leg tops and the top edge of the panel are exactly aligned.

11. Cut the carcass top (Fig. 12) and glue it to the carcass. Position, but do not glue, the assembled end panels and check that the overhang of the top is equal. Check that the back of the table top aligns with the back of the carcass. Remove the end panels. Sand, stain and polish the top. Glue the end panels in position. The back legs should be in line with the back and the front legs should protrude slightly.

11

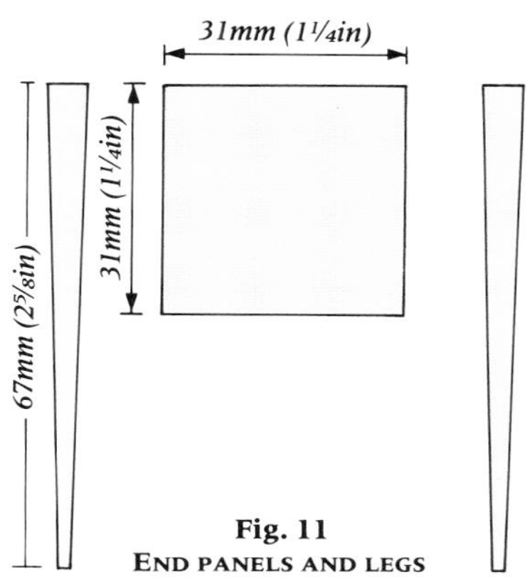

Fig. 11
End panels and legs

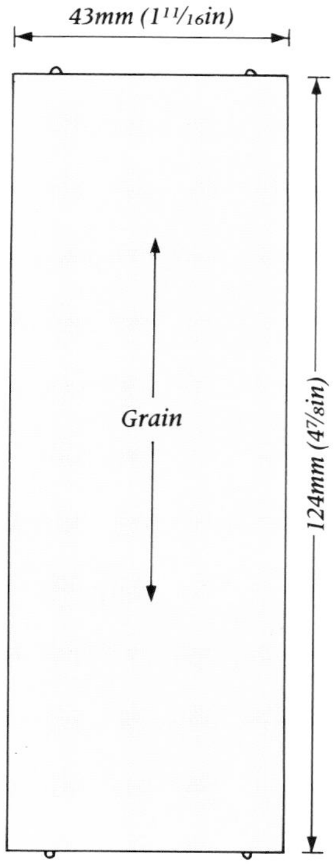

Fig. 12 top

MAKING A SET OF DRAWERS

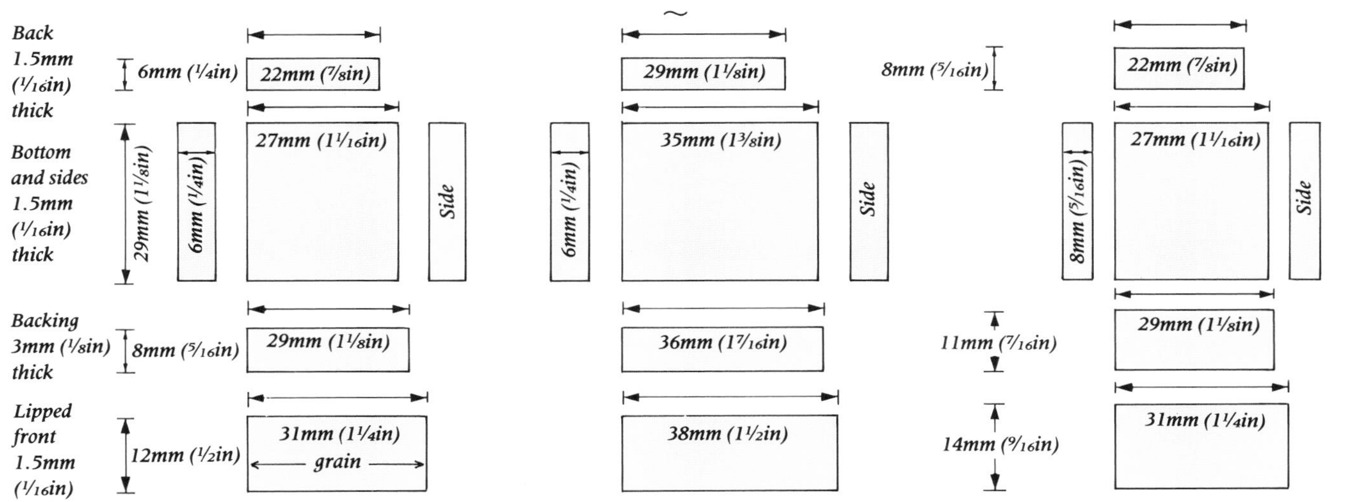

Fig. 8 Top side drawers

Fig. 9 Top middle drawer

Fig. 10 Bottom side drawers

Cut out the drawer components – two top side drawers, two bottom side drawers and one top middle drawer. Assemble the drawers by placing the drawer front backing piece against the back of an assembly jig. Apply glue to the front of the drawer bottom and to the backing piece. Allow the glue to set. Assemble the left side in the same way. Fit the drawers to the carcass. Attach the lipped front. Sand the drawer fronts with medium and fine sandpaper, dust, stain and polish. Drill holes for the knobs, insert some glue and insert the knobs. Leave to dry overnight on its back.

Doll's House

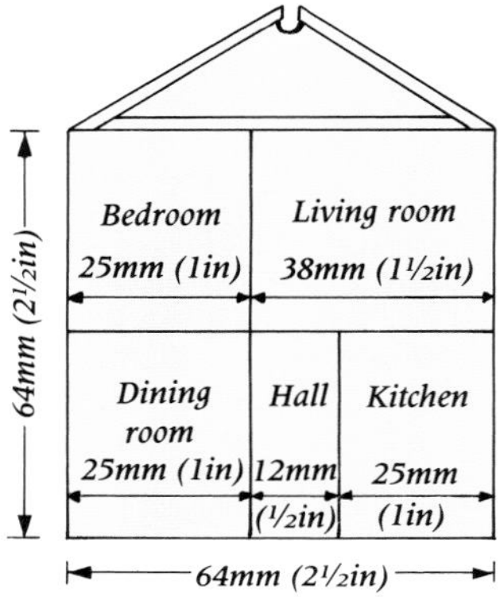

Fig. 1 House plan

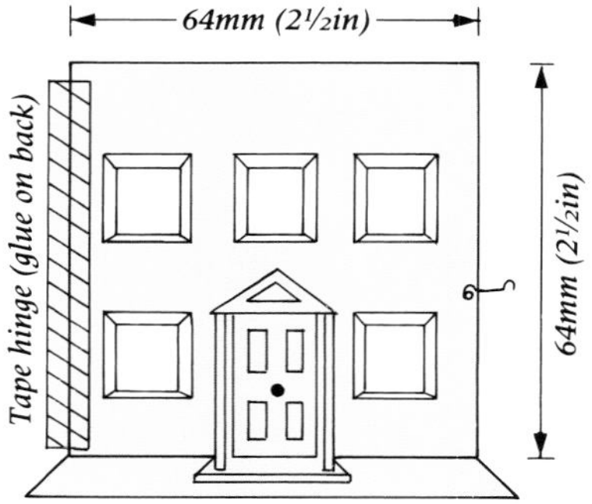

Fig. 2 House front

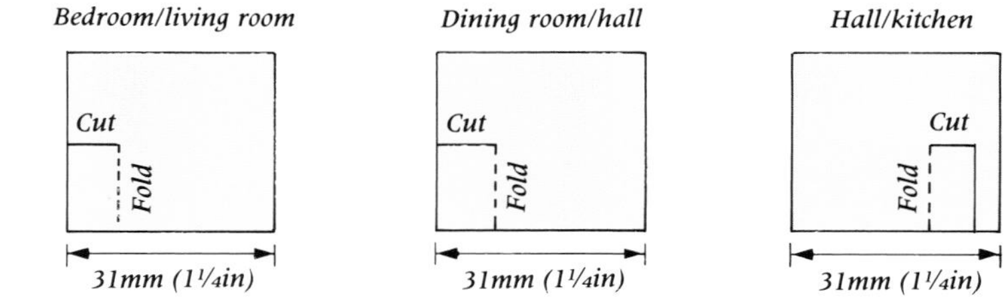

Fig. 3 The dividing walls

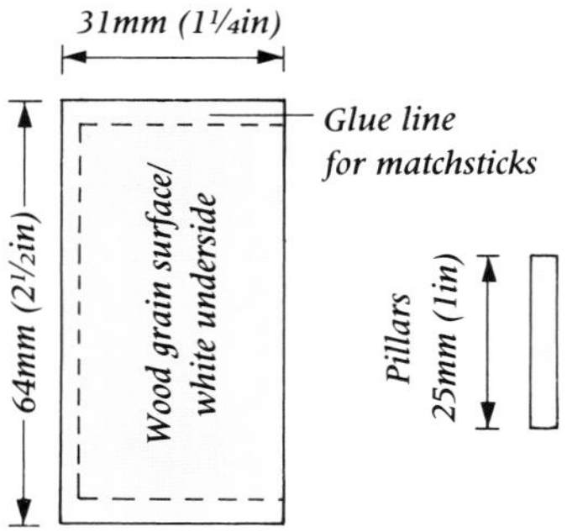

Fig. 4 The floor/ceiling

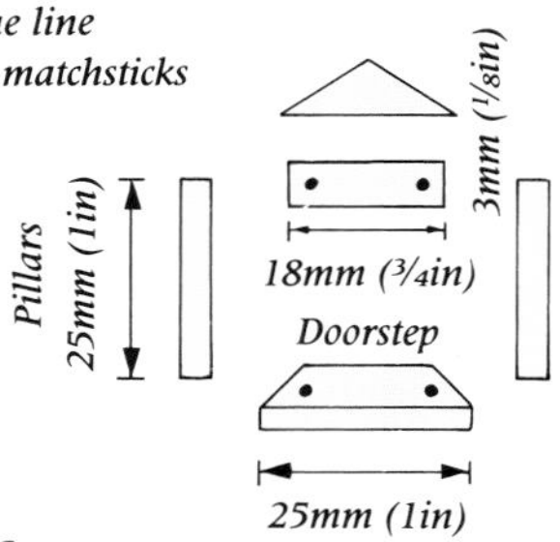

Fig. 5 The porch

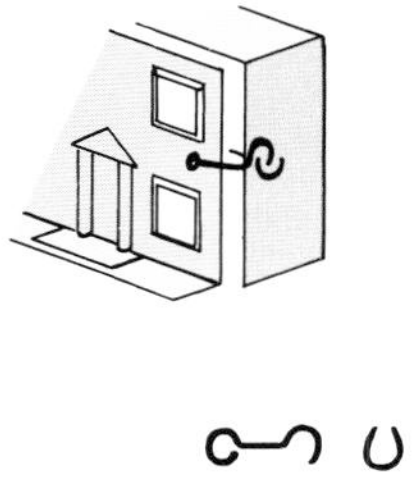

Fig. 6 The hook and loop fasting

You Will Need

~

- Box 64 × 64 × 31mm (2½ × 2½ × 1¼in)
- Card for base 64 × 45mm (2½ × 1¾in)
- Card for pediment and porch roof, 64 × 18mm (2½ × ¾in)
- Poster paint (ochre or grey) for pediment and body of house
- Matchsticks for pediment moulding and windows
- Wood glue
- Card for front, 64 × 64mm (2½ × 2½in)
- Craft knife or scalpel
- Transparent plastic for windows
- Cocktail sticks for pillars
- 6mm (¼in) tape for hinges
- 1 brass bead for door knob
- Wood 38 × 6mm (1½ × ¼in) for step
- Poster paint (black) for base and apron
- Paint (white) for door, mouldings and pillars
- 3 vertical wall dividers 31 × 31mm (1¼ × 1¼in)
- 1 horizontal floor divider 64 × 31mm (2½ × 1¼in)
- Felt-tipped pens for decoration and detail
- Tiny scraps of wallpaper for walls and floor
- Narrow lace for curtains
- Sequins for ceiling roses (optional)
- Paper glue
- Tweezers
- Wire to make door hook
- Pliers or wire cutters

1. Find or make a suitably sized box. Cut a piece of stiff card 57 × 45mm (2¼ × 1¾in) for the base; this is slightly larger than the house itself to form an apron at the front.

2. Trace the pediment from Fig. 1 and paint it ochre or grey. Punch out a circle from the apex and glue white-painted matchsticks in place. Glue the pediment to the top of the box.

3. Trace the front (see Fig. 2), marking the apertures for the door and windows – ignore the pediment, steps, porch and pillars for the time being – and transfer these to the card front. Use a sharp scalpel or craft knife to cut out the windows and the door, retaining the door piece to re-attach with tape. Paint the front ochre or grey. On the other side, glue the transparent plastic over the windows and glue strips of lace down the sides of the windows to represent curtains. Draw on a dado, skirting line and cornice moulding with felt-tipped pen and add an architrave and, if you wish, a crest over the door.

4. With the piece cut out of the door aperture, glue small pieces of card to represent door panels on the front and attach the brass bead as the door knob. Turn over the door and glue tape along the hinge side, leaving half the width of the tape free to glue to the inside surface of the house front. Paint the back of the door any colour you wish and draw on internal panels. Glue the door hinge in place. On the front draw sash glazing bars across the windows with felt-tipped pen and outline the windows. Cut matchstick mouldings for the top of each window and glue in place.

5. Cut and glue the doorstep, the porch roof, the pillars and the pediment. Use felt-tipped pen to add details to these. The house illustrated has white and gold detailing, but you may prefer to use brown or black.

6. Cut the room and floor dividers as in Figs. 3 and 4. Cut away the door edges and fold them back, so that the folds form hinges. Paper and decorate the surfaces as you wish, then glue them in place in the house. You will probably need tweezers to hold the card in place. If you glue matches close to the edges on the underside of the floor/ceiling piece, it will adhere better to the walls. When the interior is finished, glue the front to the box by means of a tape hinge. Disguise the hinge by gluing a paper cover over the box before painting the outside. Varnish the exterior of the house, adding a drop of wood stain to the varnish to give it an "antique" look.

7. Make a tiny wire hook and loop with fine gauge wire and tweezers. Pin the hook into the house front with a short dress-making pin, snipping off the excess shank on the inside with pliers or wire cutters. Make two small holes on the side of the house to accommodate the loop and glue the wire loop in the holes. You will have to bend the hook slightly so that it curves around the corner.

Cradle

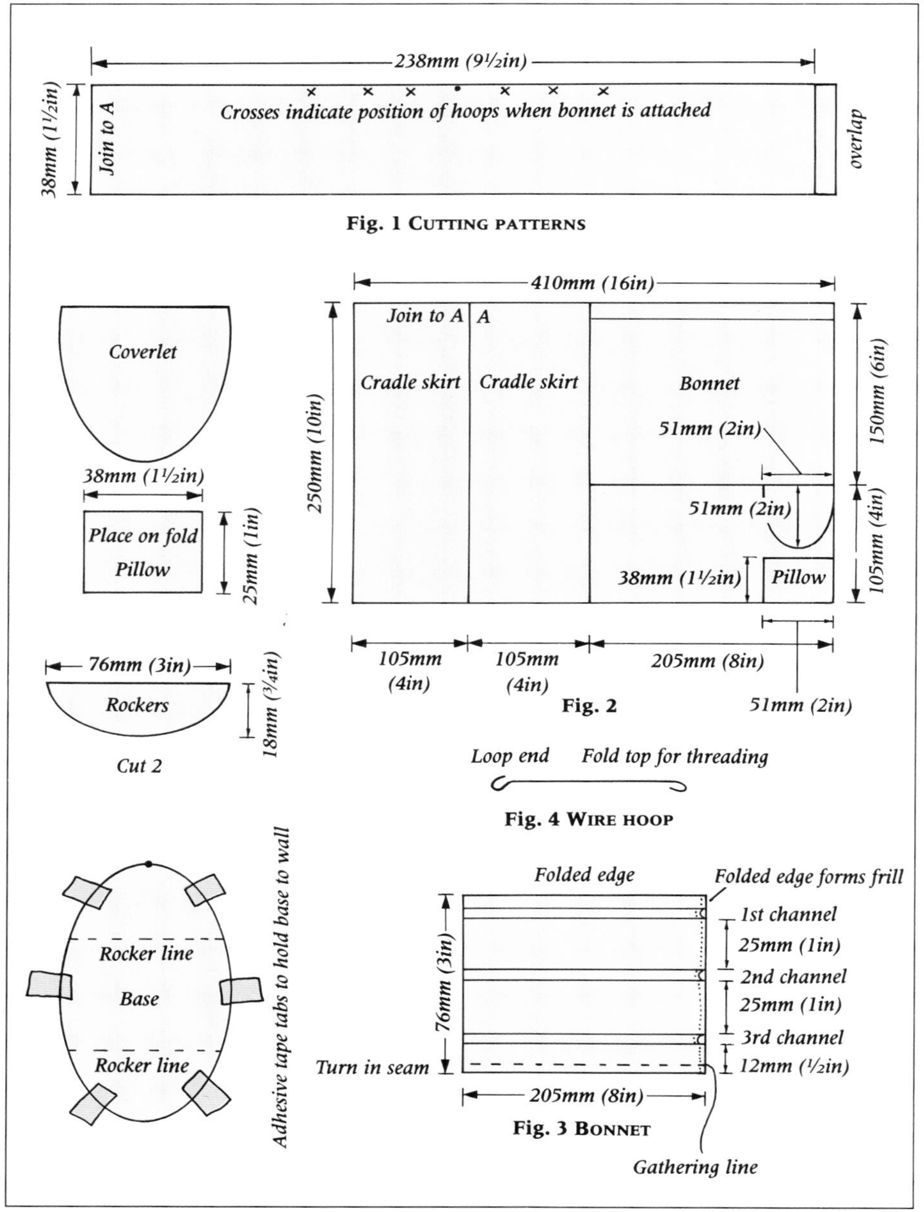

Fig. 1 Cutting patterns

Fig. 2

Fig. 4 Wire hoop

Fig. 3 Bonnet

You Will Need

- Card, approximately 250 × 130mm (10 × 5in)
- Lining silk, approximately 250 × 130mm (10 × 5in)
- 5mm (¼in) wadding, approximately 250 × 130mm (10 × 5in)
- White cotton, approximately 360 × 250mm (14 × 10in)
- Fabric adhesive
- Dress-making pins
- Ribbon to trim 460mm (18in)
- Milliner's wire or strong, fine wire 380mm (15in)
- Needle-nosed pliers
- Organdie, approximately 410 × 250mm (16 × 10in)
- Lace or braid to trim, 1m (39in)
- 6mm (¼in) balsa wood, 76mm × 18mm (3 × ¾in)
- White enamel paint (optional)
- Sealer (to seal balsa, optional)

1. Cut a template for the cradle base and wall and use it as a pattern for cutting out the silk lining, the wadding and the cotton outer covering, adding a 3mm (⅛in) turning allowance all round for the silk and cotton pieces.

2. Cut out the pieces in card and staple the foot of the cradle at the overlap. Align the dots on both pieces and glue the base to the body. You will find it easier if you place small pieces of adhesive tape under the base and use these to hold the side in place.

3. Glue a white cotton covering to the outside surface of the cradle, which will make it easier to sew the lining and bonnet to the cradle. Glue the wadding lightly in position inside the cradle.

4. Join the short ends of the silk cradle lining piece, then stitch it to the base. With the raw edges to the inside, drop it into position in the cradle. Fold the excess over the cradle rim and pin, then glue or sew in place.

5. Cut the bonnet pattern from the organdie. Fold the piece in half so that it measures approximately 205 × 76mm (8 × 3in). Sew the bottom edges – the 205mm (8in) edge – together; the dimensions given include a 3mm (⅛in) turning allowance. Turn to the right side and press flat. Turn in the raw edges at the open sides and catch down with small running stitches. Sew by hand or machine the three channels marked across the bonnet pieces (Fig. 3). Fasten off the ends. Use double thread to run a gathering line along the base of the piece, leaving the end sufficiently long to draw in later.

6. Cut three wire hoops, measuring 152, 127 and 105mm (6, 5 and 4in). Thread the longest through the first channel, bending the bottom of the wire to form a loop that will prevent the wire from slipping into the channel, and fold the top end tightly over to stop the point of the wire piercing or catching in the fabric. Use needle-nosed pliers to bend the wire. Thread the other two wires into the channels and adjust the gathers evenly. Gently arch the wires to form the bonnet shape. The finished length of the hoops should be 114, 89 and 64mm (4½, 3½ and 2½in). Snip off any excess and bend back the loops. Pull the gathering line at the back of the bonnet as tightly as possible and sew it to the entry point to close up the back of the bonnet. Pin the bonnet in place on the body of the cradle, using a pin through each loop to hold it in place, then firmly sew it to the cradle.

7. Cut out the skirt strips and join them to measure 500 × 105mm (20 × 4in). Fold the fabric in half lengthways. Run two rows of gathering stitches along the top open edges, draw up the gathers and pin in place, matching up the centre with the dot on the cradle. Arrange and pin the gathers evenly around the cradle to meet at the centre back. Tie off the thread. Sew or glue in place. Trim to taste. The cradle illustrated here has two rows of an organdie edging around the cradle edge to cover the raw edges of the skirt gathers and bands of organdie edging sewn over the bonnet. A pink bow has been sewn at either side of the bonnet.

8. Cut out the coverlet pieces in organdie, lining silk and wadding, adding a 3mm (⅛in) turning allowance all round for the organdie and lining silk. Tack the wadding to the lining silk. Place the organdie on the lining side and sew around the edge, leaving the top open. Fasten off the thread and turn the right side out. Fold in the raw edges along the top and oversew neatly. Remove all tacking stitches. Trim with lace or edging.

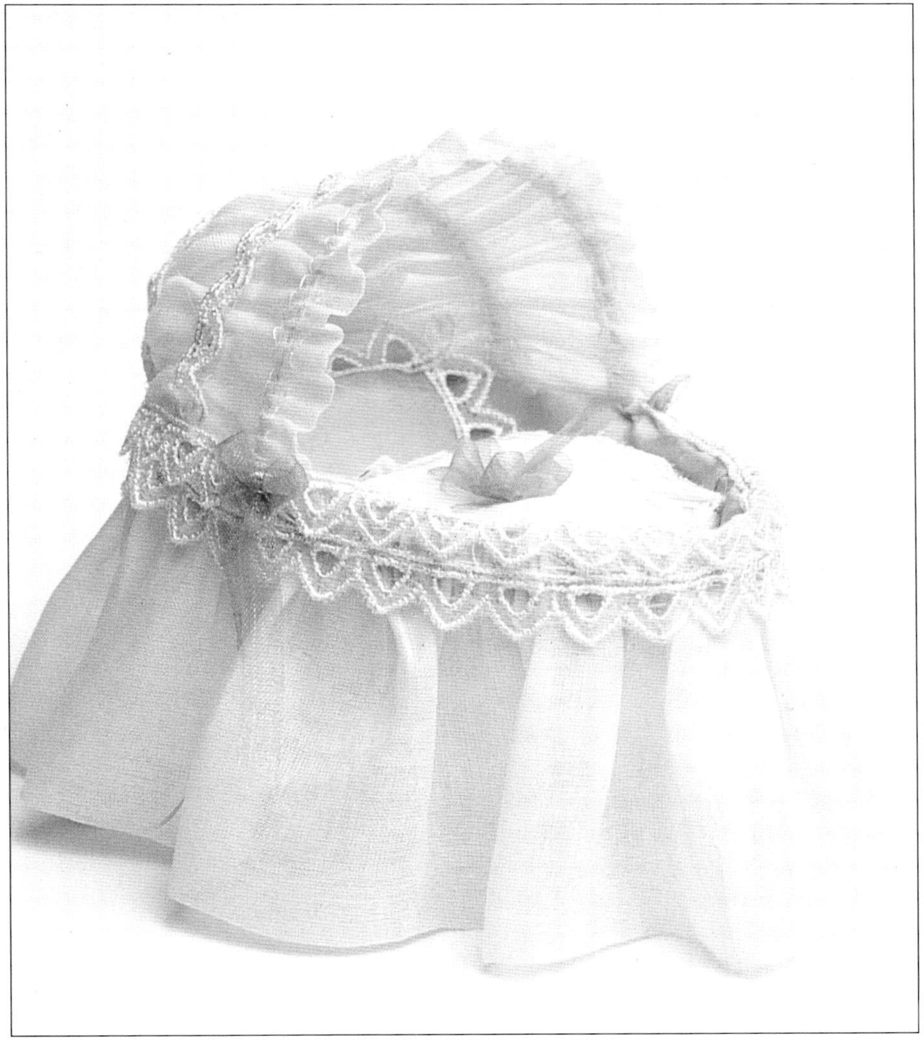

9. Fold the pillow silk in half. Sew around the edges, leaving one side open. Turn the right side out, insert the wadding, sew the end edges together. Trim with lace or edging. Decorate the coverlet and pillow with bows if wished.

10. As an added extra, cut the rockers from balsa wood, seal with a proprietary sealer and paint with white matt enamel paint. Glue them to the cradle where indicated.

Screens

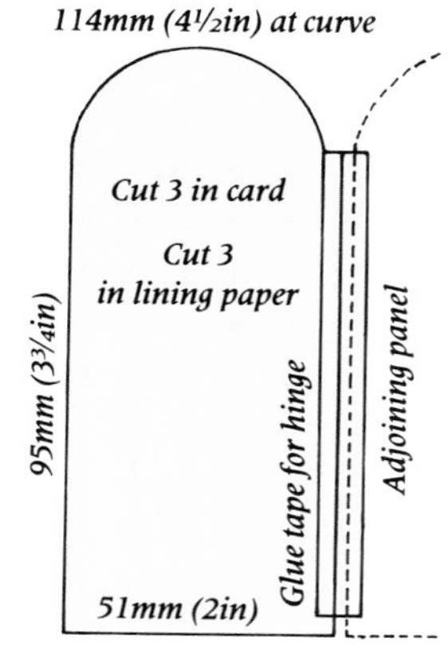

Fig. 1 Scrap screen

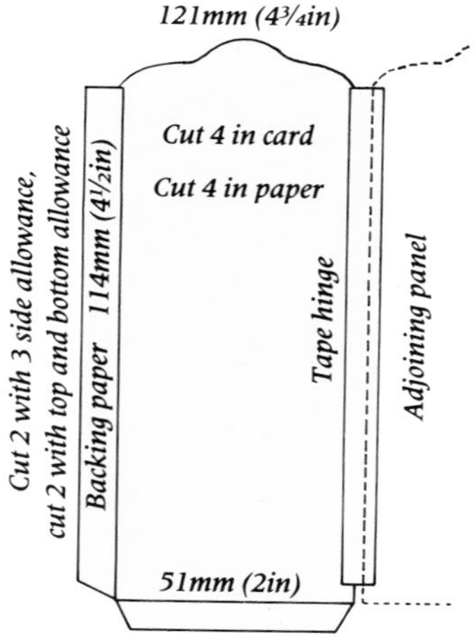

Fig. 2 Gentleman's screen

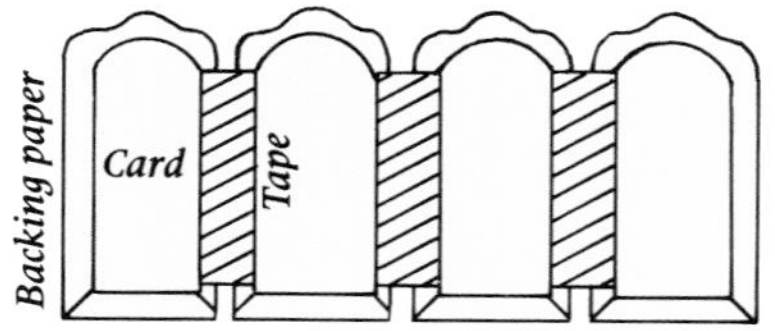

Fig. 3 The gentleman's screen with the hinges and backing in place

You Will Need

- Approximately 125 × 205mm (5 × 8in) mounting card or similar
- Craft knife or scalpel
- 460mm (18in) cotton tape, 6mm (¼in) wide, or bias binding to match screen covering
- Strong paper glue
- Fine grade glass paper
- Satin varnish to finish

For Scrap Screen

- Lining or sugar paper
- Scrap design gift wrap paper suitable cut-out pictures and so on

For Gentleman's Screen

- Textured paper, mock lizard or book binding fabric
- 6mm (¼in) tape
- Small sets of hunting prints or suitable prints from magazines or gift wrapping paper

Making the Scrap Screen

1. Cut 3 panels in card.

2. Glue tape along one edge of two of the screen sections. The tape will act as a hinge.

3. Cut 3 panels in lining paper or sugar paper. Assemble the cut-out scraps and arrange them on each panel. When you have decided on the design, glue them to the panels, overlapping them to cover the backing paper completely.

4. Glue the decorated panels to the card panels. Press them firmly and smooth them with a dry, clean cloth. When the glue is dry, check that all the glued areas are stuck down.

5. Varnish the panels. Leave to dry for a few hours. Sand lightly with fine glass paper and apply a second coat of varnish. Repeat the sanding process and apply a third coat. If you wish, mix a drop of wood stain with the final coat of varnish to give an antique finish.

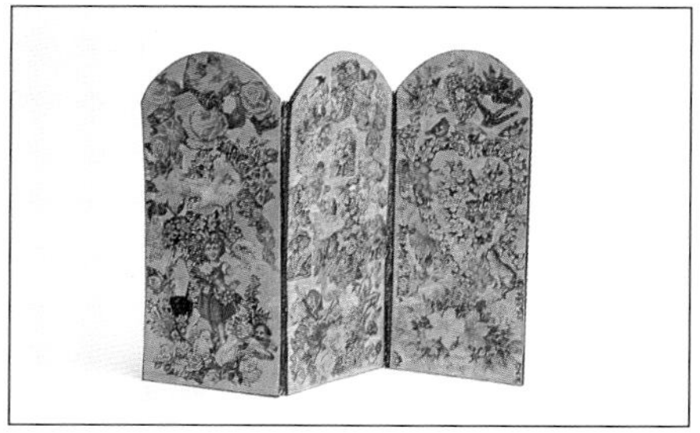

Making the Gentleman's Screen

1. Cut out the 4 panels in strong card. Cut 2 panels in textured paper, adding 3mm (⅛in) on three sides and two panels allowing 3mm (⅛in) at the top and bottom. Cut 4 panels of exact panel size for the front of the screen.

2. Glue 114mm (4½in) of tape down the outside edge of 3 of the 4 card panels to act as hinges.

3. Spread glue evenly over the paper panels and the extra allowances. Cover the card panels with paper.

4. The panels with the allowance at the top and bottom will be in the centre of the finished screen. Those with allowances on three edges will be at each end.

5. Join up the screen by gluing the tape to the adjoining panels. Glue the 4 front panels of paper to the front of the screen and decorate each panel with suitable prints, placing 3 or 4 on each panel. When they are firmly glued, varnish as for the scrap screen.

If the panels curl after decorating, sandwich between two boards and clamp, leaving overnight, to flatten.

THE DINING ROOM

Regency Dining Table

~

A beautiful reproduction table which will be the focus of any dining room. The construction of the legs – moulded column, leg holder and separate legs – is complex, but is much more elegant than the standard four-leg construction. You can of course simplify the moulding on the leg columns and leg holder.

~

MAKING THE TABLE TOP

~

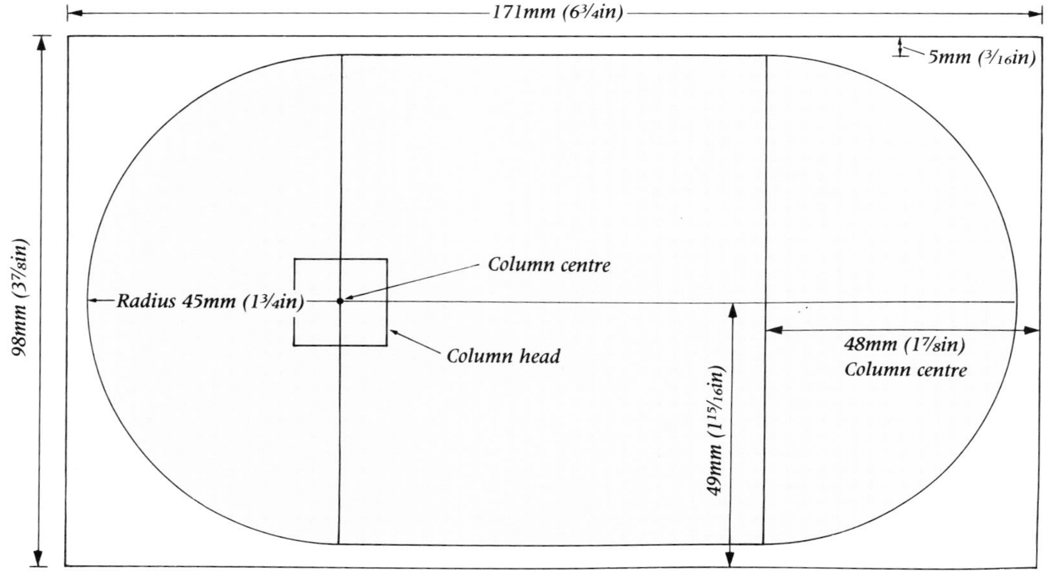

Fig. 1 Top

1

1. Cut a rectangular blank 3mm (⅛in) thick to the measurements shown in Fig. 1. Mark on the shape of the table top and the horizontal and vertical lines; use a pencil so that you can rub out the lines when you have completed the table.

2

2. Cut out one of the straight edges, then a "D-end", then the second side and finally the other D-end.

Making the Leg Columns

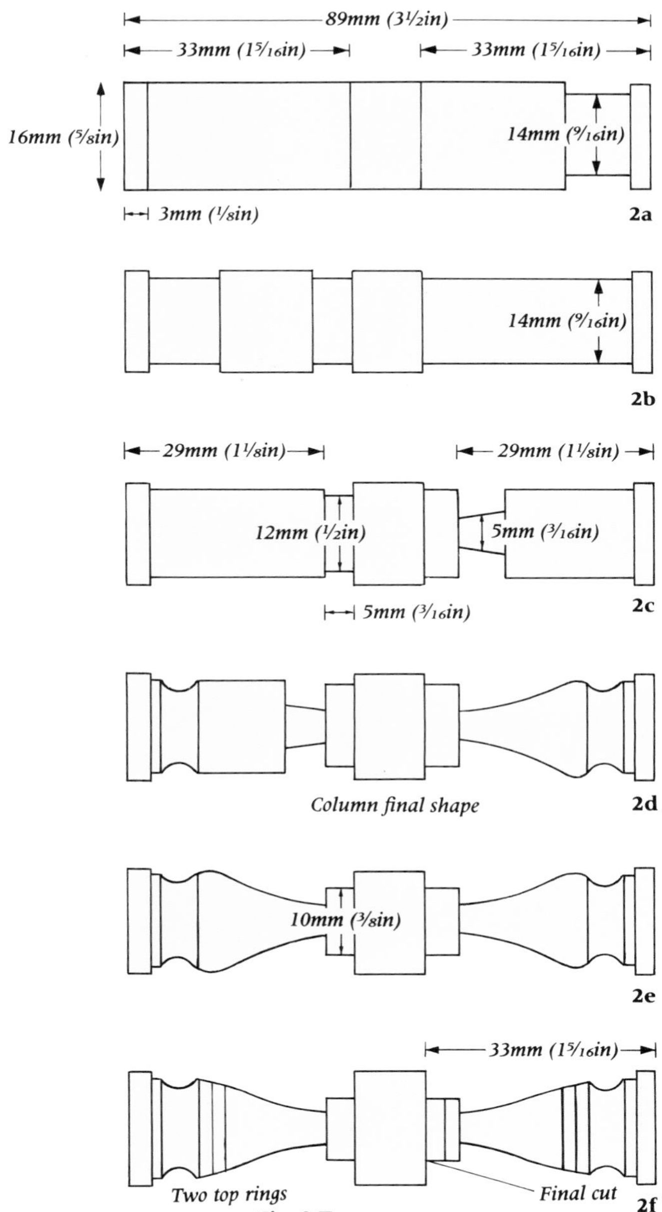

Fig. 2 Turning the column

3

3. Cut a square-ended blank – one blank makes two columns – to the dimensions shown in Fig. 2a. The leg columns will then need to be shaped according to the sequence shown (Figs. 2b–e).

4

4. Hand sand the columns. Cut the two top rings (Fig. 2f). Cut the ring on the pad. Dust, stain and French polish the columns. Cut the columns to their final length – 33mm ($1\frac{5}{16}$in).

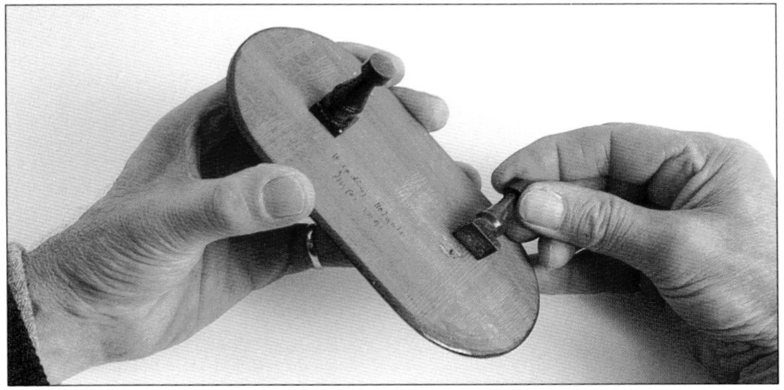
5

5. Assemble the columns to the table top.

6. Dust, sand and polish the table top.

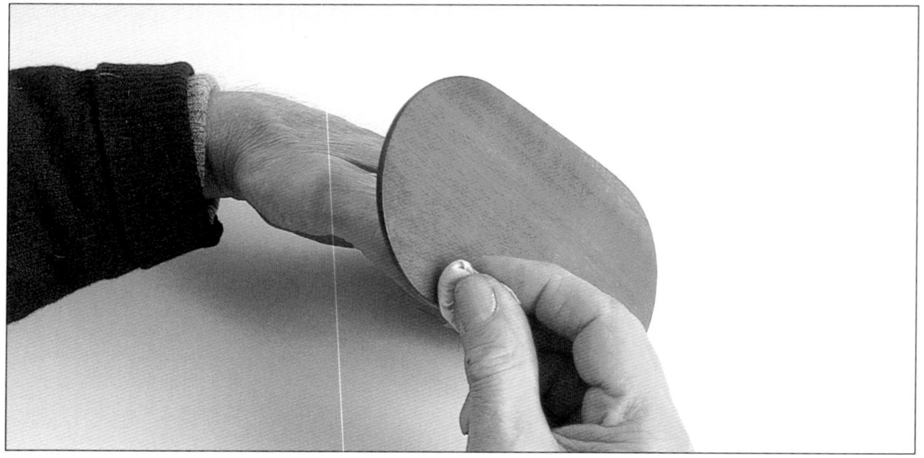

6

Making the Leg Holders

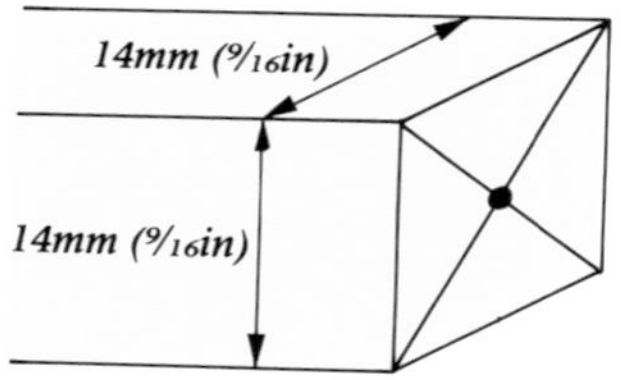

Fig. 3a

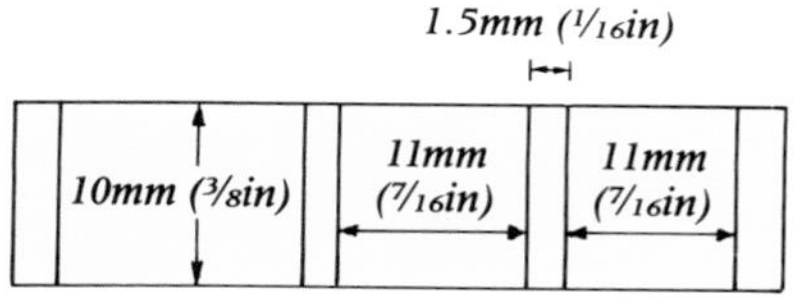

Fig. 3b Blank turned to 10mm (3/8in) diameter

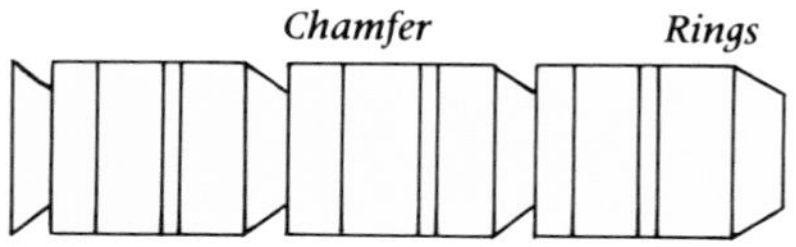

Fig. 3c Running chamfer and rings

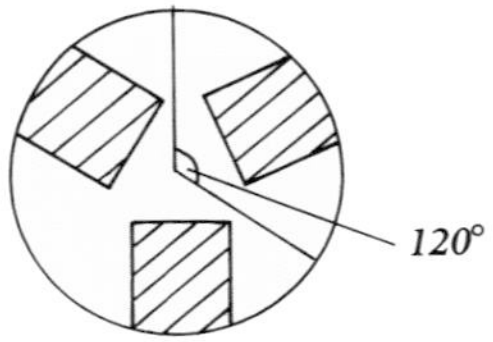

Fig. 3d Cutting slots

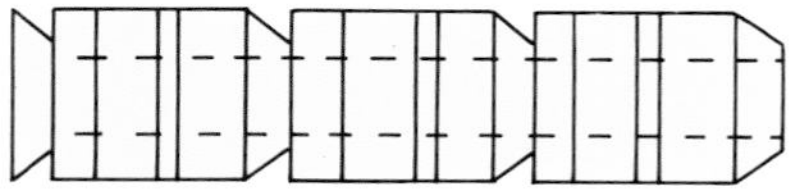

Fig. 3d Cutting slots

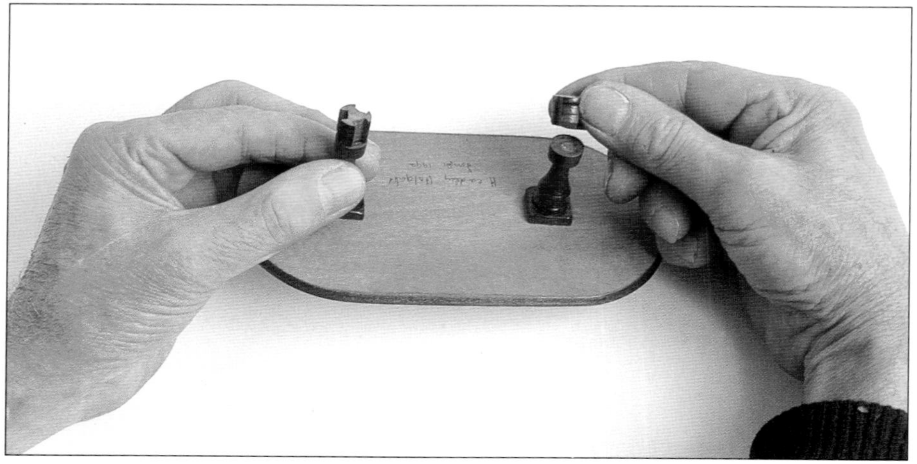

7

7. Cut a square-ended blank (Fig. 3a) and turn it so that it is 10mm (3/8in) in diameter (Fig. 3b). Cut rings and a chamfer (Fig. 3c). Stain and polish the pieces. Cut three slots down the sides of the piece at 120° to each other (Fig. 3d). Make the final cuts to give a length of 11mm (7/16in). Assemble the leg holders to the columns.

Making the Legs

~

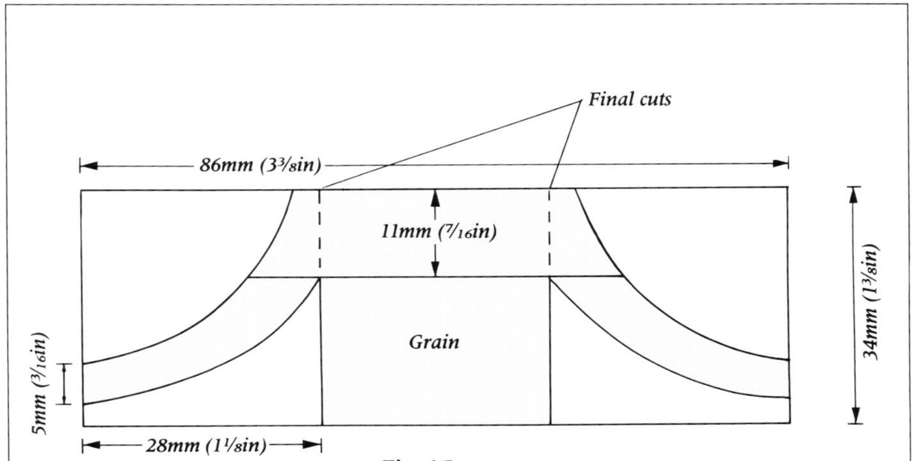

Fig. 4 Legs

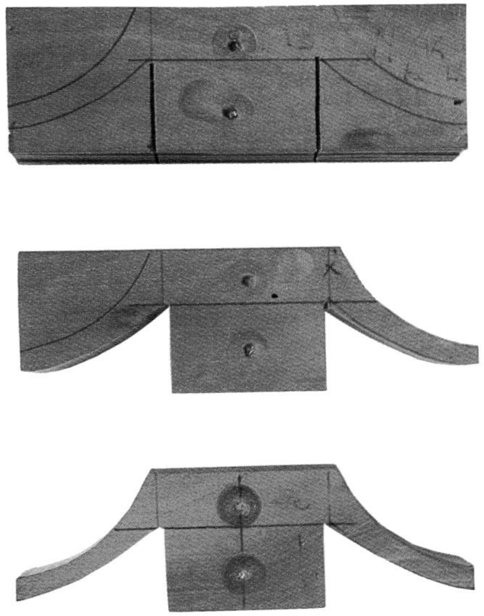

8

8. You will need six legs for one table – a pair of legs is cut from one slice. You may want to use the pinned blank method (see page 98), illustrated here, to ensure uniformity of the pieces you cut. Test the width of leg required against the slots cut in step 7, and cut the slices (Fig. 4) to this width.

9. Draw the leg shape onto a slice, or just the top slice if using a pinned blank, and cut out the number of pieces required.

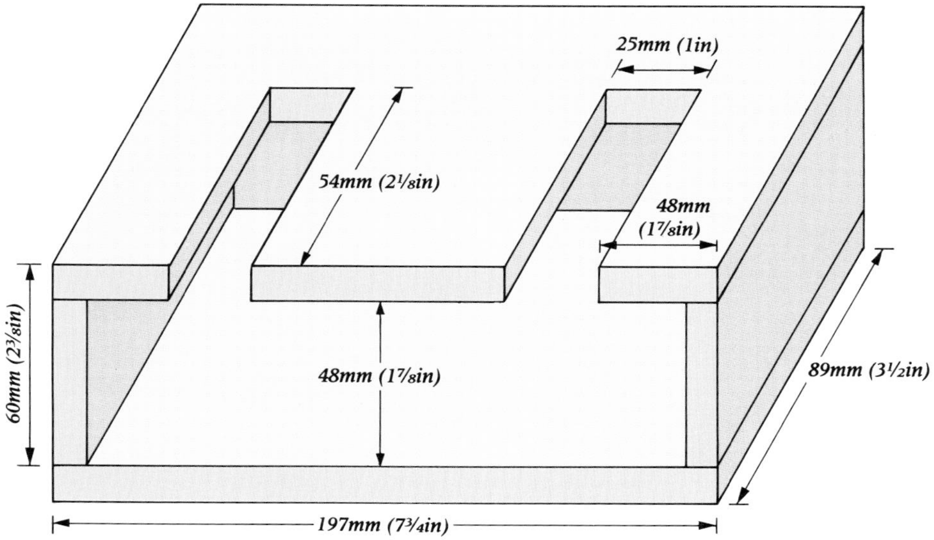

Fig. 5 Final assembly jig

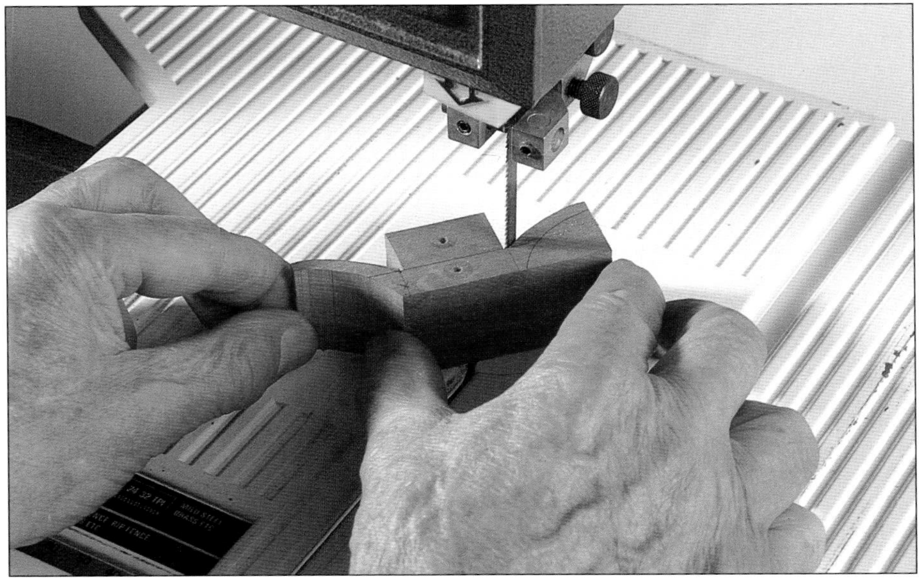

9

10. Sand the top surfaces of the pieces, or pinned blank. Keep checking the finished height of the legs against the assembly jig (Fig. 5). Do not forget to tidy the underside of the legs. Using medium and fine sandpaper and working by hand, shape the surface. Stain and polish these surfaces.

11. Dismantle the pinned blank, if used, and check the height of the legs in the jig. Taper the legs with medium and fine sandpaper, stain and polish. Make the final cuts (Fig. 4) to the legs and fit the legs to the leg holders.

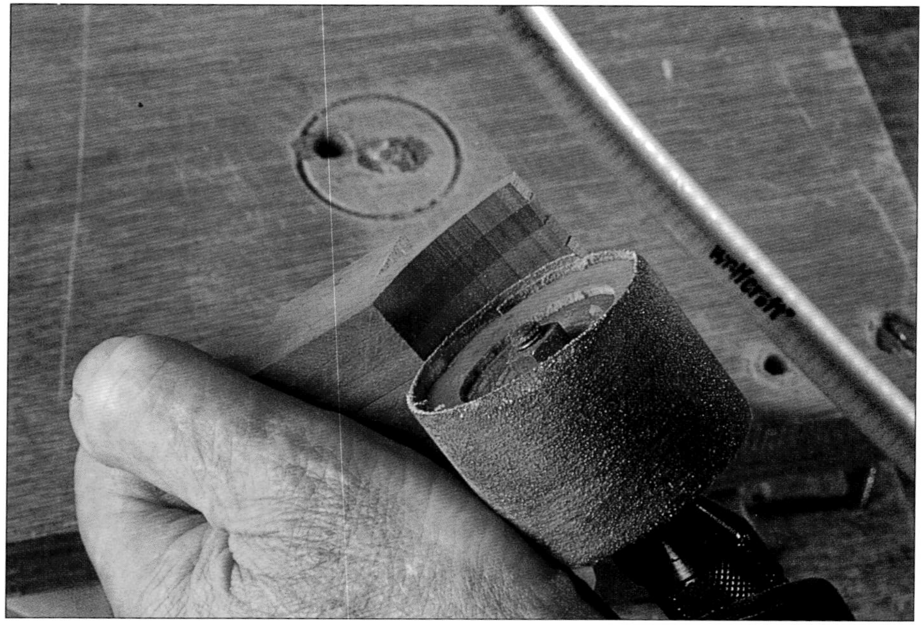

10

12. When you are satisfied with the height of the table, by checking against the jig, glue the legs in position in the leg holders and leave to dry overnight.

11

12

Chairs

~

Two delightful variations on the same design – a side chair and a carver for the head of the table – which complement the dining table design perfectly. To ensure that all four legs of your finished chairs touch the floor, choose sides that match as exactly as possible and use the special assembly jig described.

~

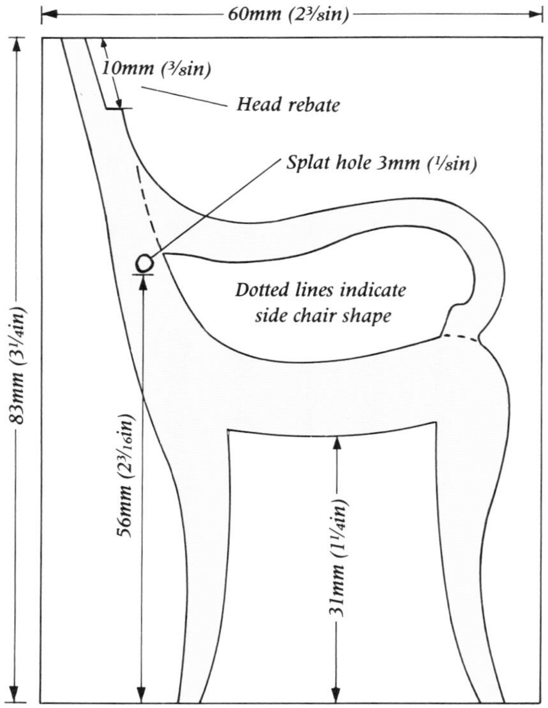

Fig. 1 Chair sides

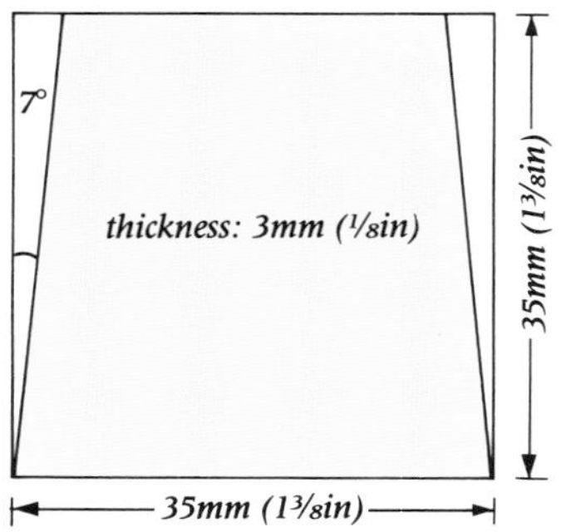

Fig. 2 Chair seat

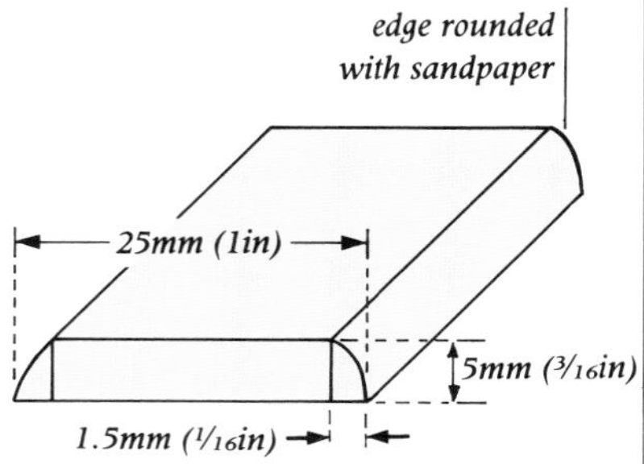

Fig. 3 Seat fronts and backs

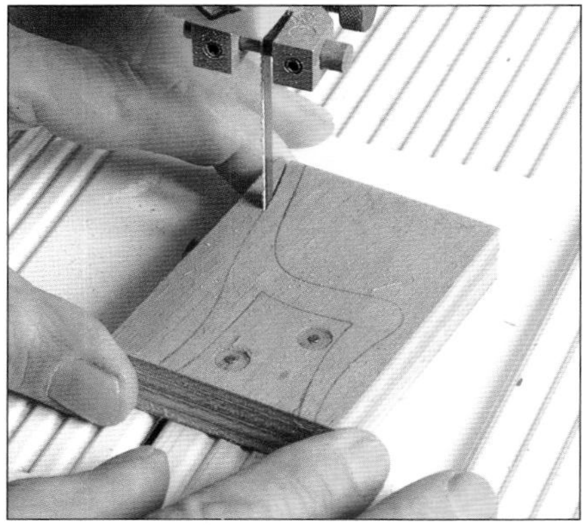

1

1. Cut slices for the chair sides to the measurements shown in Fig. 1. Make the slices 3mm (1/8in) wide. Belt or hand sand both sides of the slices. Draw the chair shapes on the slices. If you are making several chairs at once, use the pinned blank method (see page 98). Cut out the sides.

2

2. For the carver chair, you need to drill a hole in the centre of the arm as a point of entry for the saw. Finish cutting out the chair.

3

4

3. Sand all the surfaces. Keep the sides in matching pairs – mark this on the inside surface. Stain and polish all the surfaces which will show, including the underside of the carver arms. Slightly round the front edges of the sides with sandpaper.

4. Drill 3mm (⅛in) holes for the splats (decorative lateral pieces) as shown in Fig. 1.

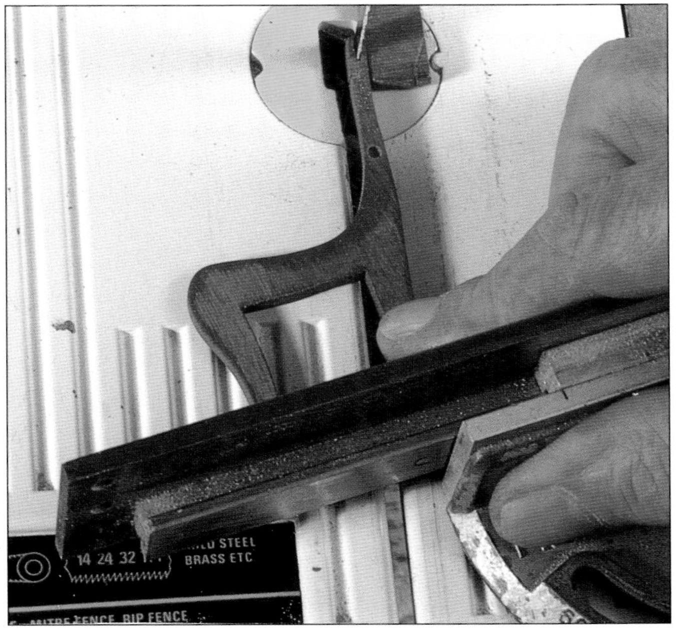

5

6

5. Cut a rebate in the top of each side to hold the head (Fig. 1).

6. Cut the seat in pine (Fig. 2). Make the seat backs and fronts – cut a section 5mm (3/16in) wide and 25mm (1in) deep and the length of the seat. Hand sand both edges to give a rounded effect (Fig. 3). Stain and polish. Cut the fronts to 45mm (1¾in) and the backs to 31mm (1¼in). Glue to the seat and trim the ends. When the glue is dry, sand the edges of the seat so that the edgings are flush.

MAKING THE ASSEMBLY JIG

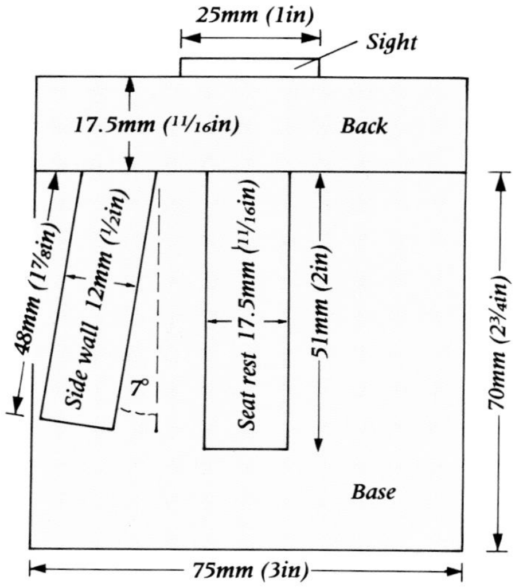

Fig. 4 ASSEMBLY JIG PLAN

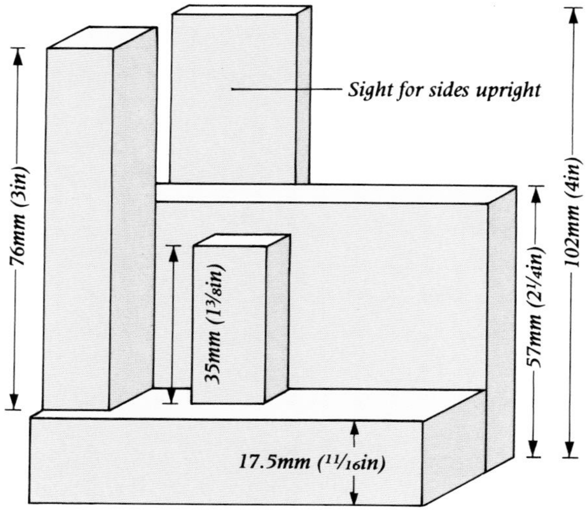

Fig. 4a ASSEMBLY JIG FRONT ELEVATION

Cut the base and mark the positions of the side wall and seat rest. Cut the back and pin and glue it to the base. Check that it is vertical with a small set square. Cut the side wall and seat rest pieces. Glue the side wall to the base and back. Check the vertical with a set square. Cut the "sight" piece and pin and glue it to the back. Check the vertical.

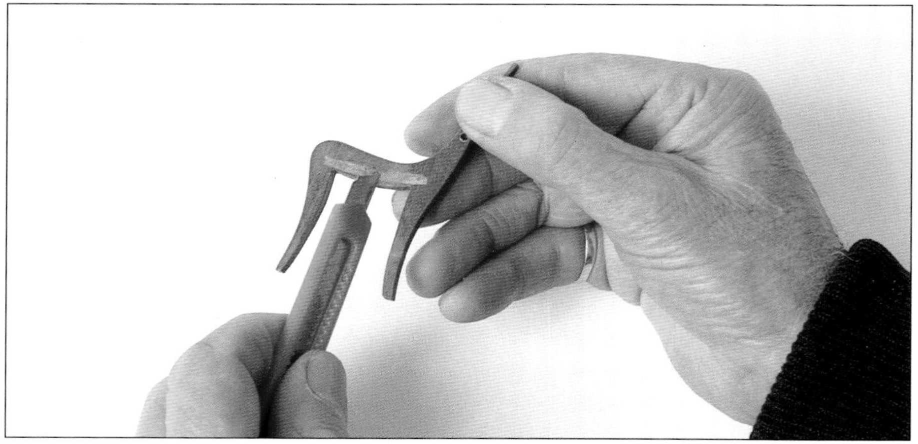

7

7. Scrape the inside area of the sides where they will be glued to the seat edges.

8. Place the left side of the chair flat against the side wall of the jig. Put glue on the left side of the seat. Place the seat on the seat rest and glue to the sides so that the front edge of the seat is 1.5mm (1/16in) in from the front of the side. When the glue has set, place the right side on the jig, lining it up with the jig sighter, but do not glue.

8

MAKING THE SPLAT

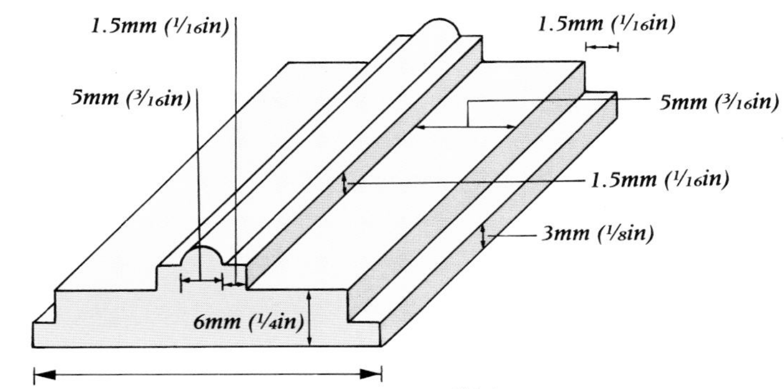

Fig. 5 Fancy splat

10

10. In this case, a whole section has been moulded to the shape of the splat, so thin sections have to be sliced off to a width of slightly more than 1.5mm (1/16in). Hand sand, stain and polish the back of the strips. Drill a 1.5mm (1/16in) hole in the centre of the splat for decoration.

9

9. Next, make the splat (Fig. 5). This can be straight or a more ornamented one as illustrated.

11

11. You may need to trim the ends of the splats to ensure a snug fit in the sides. Insert glue in the holes and assemble the splat to the left hand side on the jig. Place the right side on the jig and insert the other end of the splat in the hole. Check that all the legs are flat on the jig base.

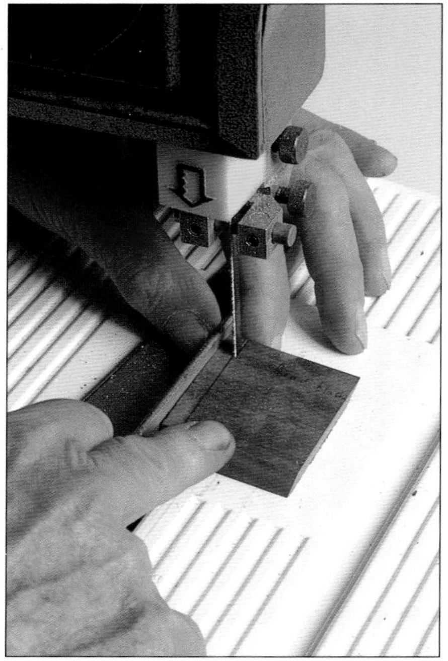

12

12. Cut the head to thickness of the rebate cut in the chair side (Fig. 6). Glue the head in position, making sure that the overhang at both ends is even.

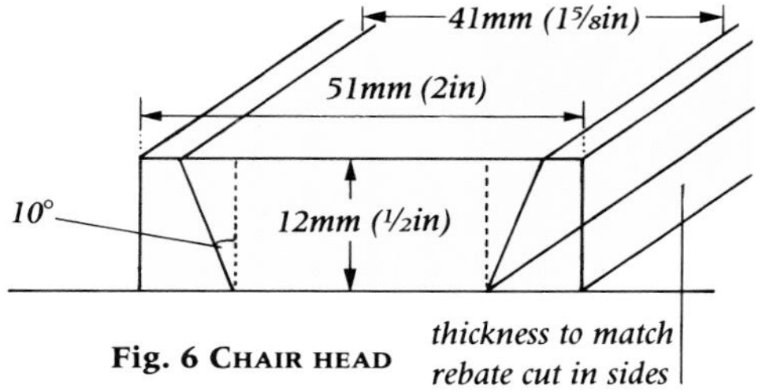

Fig. 6 Chair head

Making the Upholstered Seat

~

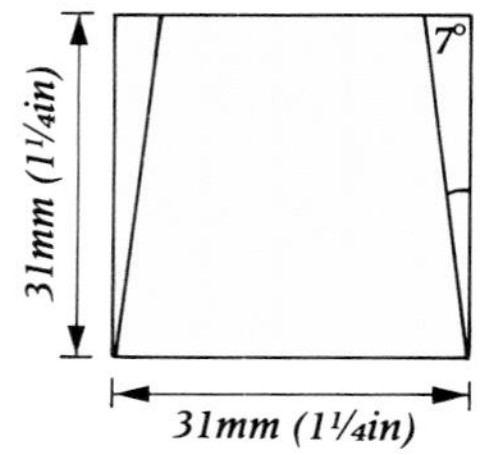

Fig. 7 Plywood base

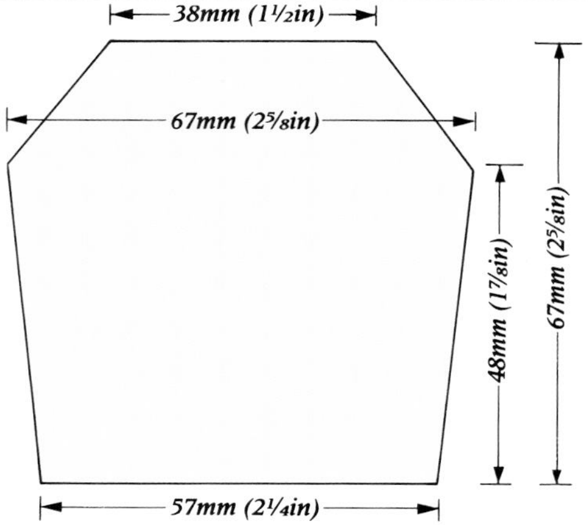

Fig. 8 Seat material

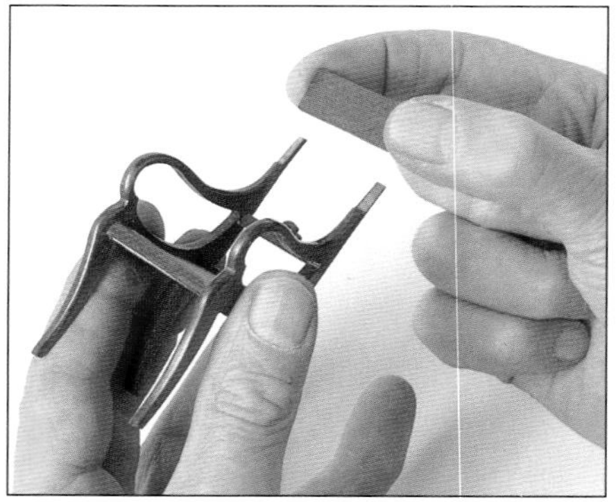

13

13. Cut a seat shape from 4mm (1/6in) plywood to the measurements in Fig. 7. Cut out a piece of foam or padding the same size. Glue the padding to the plywood. Cut out material using the pattern in Fig. 8. Cover the seat with the material and glue the edges in place. Glue onto the chair.

Sideboard

~

This design, although similar to the dressing table and desk in basic construction, has a slightly longer top and two central legs to give stability. The large surface area of the sides and top must be finished very carefully, using at least eight coats of polish for a truly professional result.

~

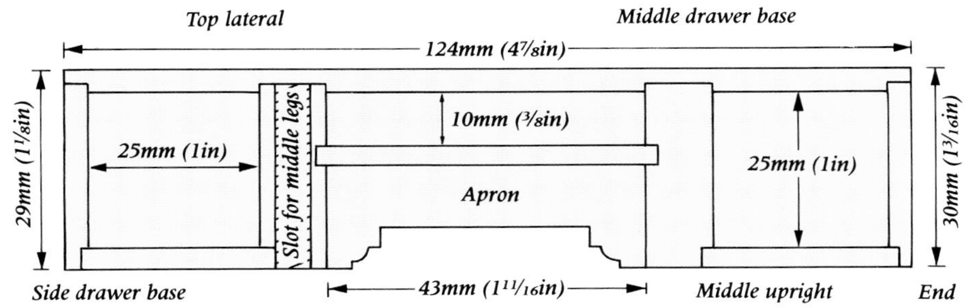

Fig. 1 Front elevation

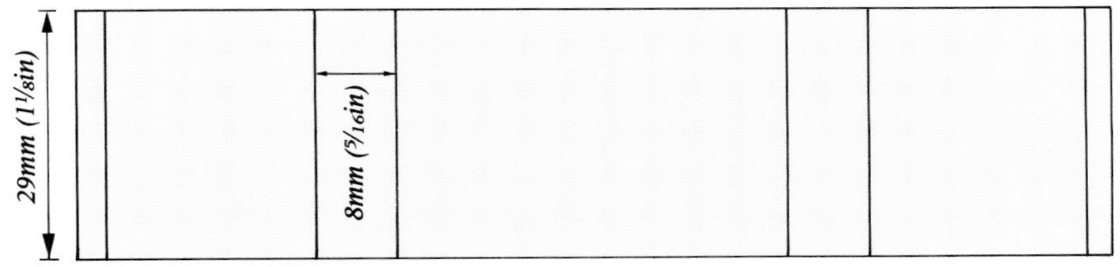

Fig. 2 Back *All grooves 1.5mm (1/16in) deep*

Fig. 3 Top lateral plan

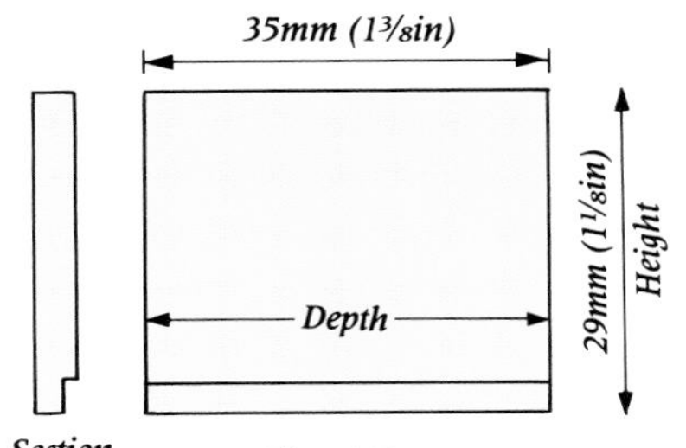

Fig. 4 End

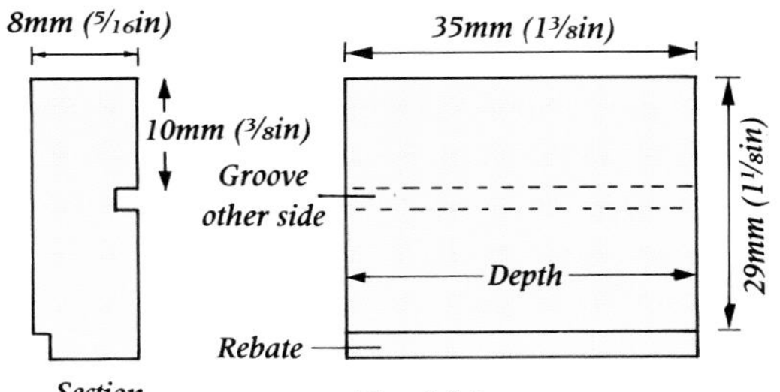

Fig. 5 Middle upright

1. Cut the back from 4mm (1/6in) plywood. Cut the top lateral, from your chosen wood, to 3mm (1/8in) thick. Run grooves and rebates as shown in Figs. 2 and 3. All grooves should be 1.5mm (1/16in) deep.

2. Cut two middle uprights to the dimensions shown in Fig. 5. Run a 1.5mm (1/16in) groove to one side and a 3mm (1/8in) rebate on the other side. Cut two ends 3mm (1/8in) thick as shown in Fig. 4. Run a rebate in the ends.

3. Run slots 5mm (3/16in) wide and 3mm (1/8in) deep in the middle uprights for the middle legs.

1

2

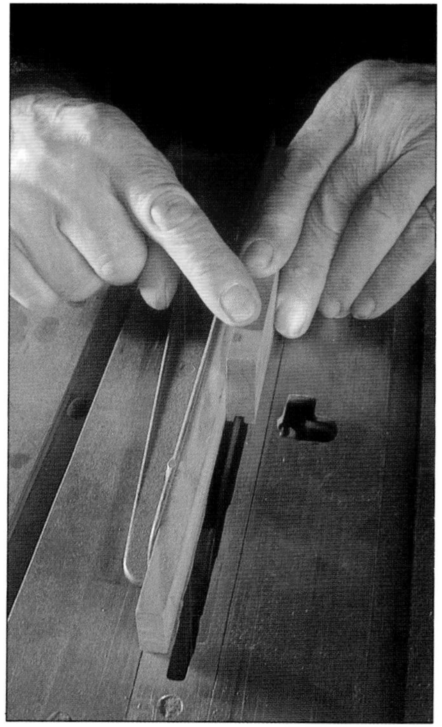

3

4. Assemble the back, top lateral and middle uprights of the carcass on a jig. Apply glue to the grooves on the back, the middle upright and the top edge. Glue the top of the lateral to the top edge of the back. Glue the middle uprights to the back and top lateral. Allow the glue to dry.

5. Apply glue to the rebates for the ends on the back and top lateral and glue the ends in place. Allow the glue to dry.

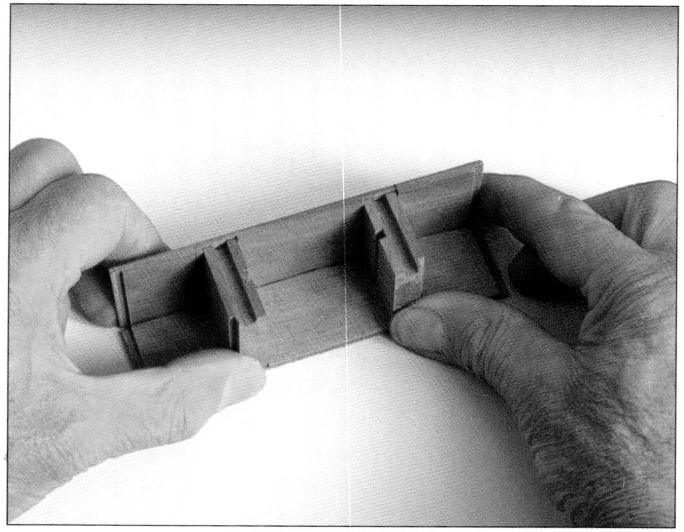

4

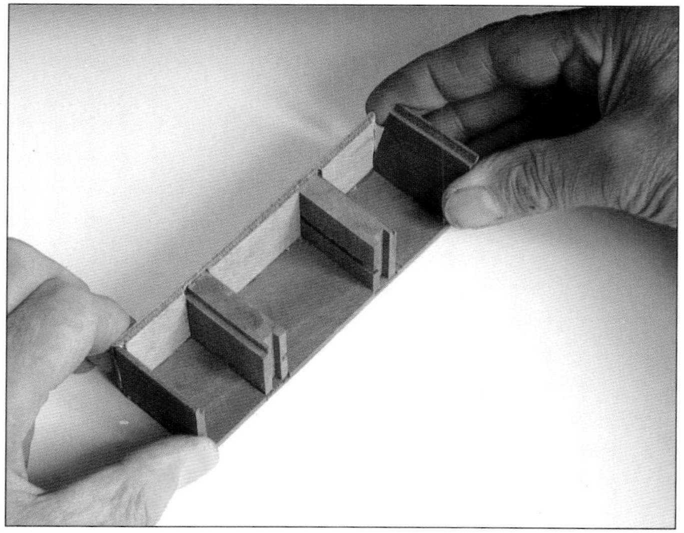

5

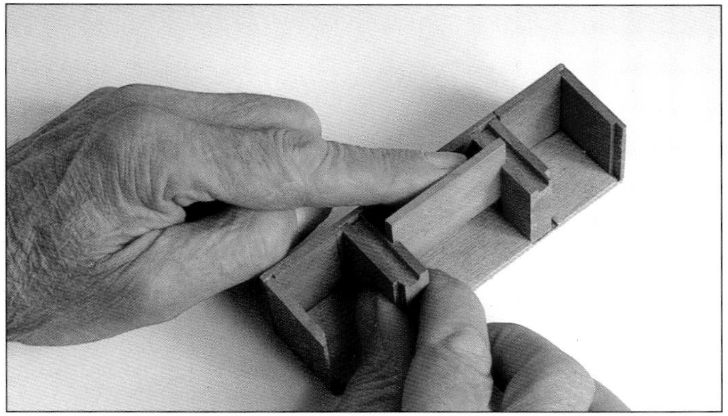

6

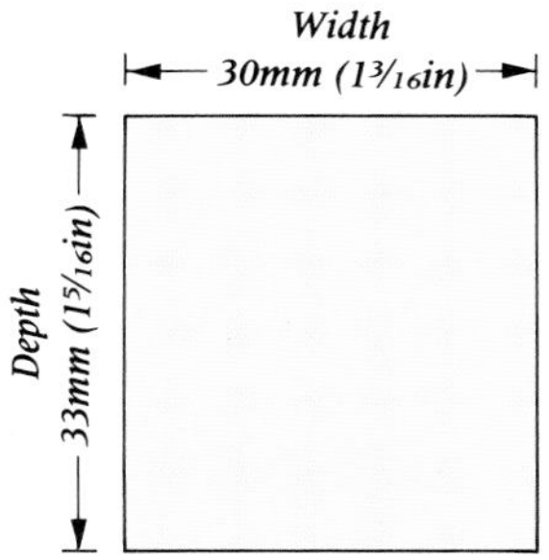

Fig. 6 Side drawer – base

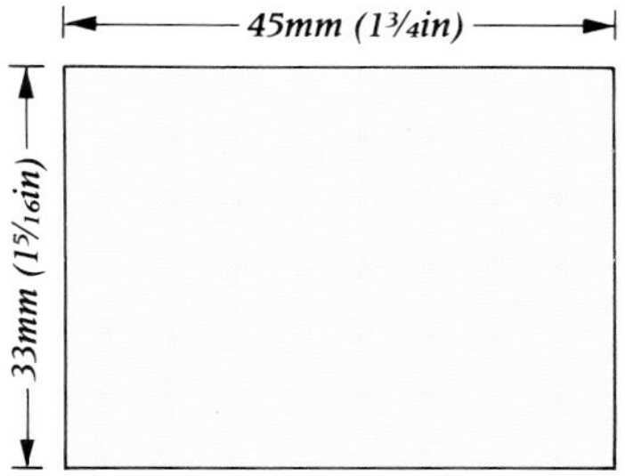

Fig. 7 Middle drawer – base

6. Cut out one base 3mm (1/8in) thick for the middle drawer and two bases 3mm (1/8in) thick for the side drawers (Figs. 6 and 7). Sand the ends and bottom of the carcass on medium paper on a flat surface. The ends must be flush for gluing the end panels.

7

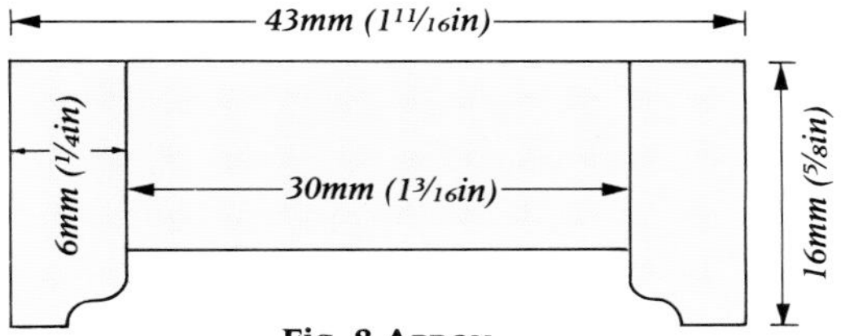

Fig. 8 Apron

7. Next cut the apron. You will need a rectangular block of wood for the central piece 30 × 10mm (1 3/16 × 3/8in) and at least 38mm (1 1/2in) long. Cut two pieces 16 × 6mm (5/8 × 1/4in) for the side pieces to the same length; these will have to be shaped as shown (Fig. 8).

8

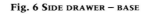

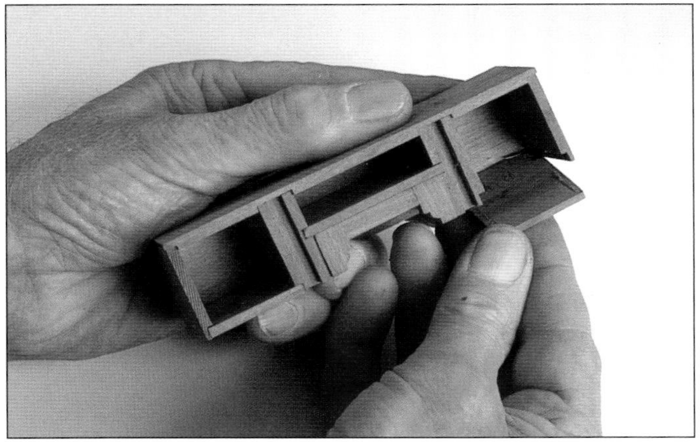

9

8. Glue the apron components together and slice off a piece 3mm (1/8in) thick .

9. Fit and glue the apron and drawer bases to the carcass. Sand the front of the carcass on a sheet of medium sandpaper on a flat surface so that all the front members are flush, dust off, stain and French polish.

Making the Legs

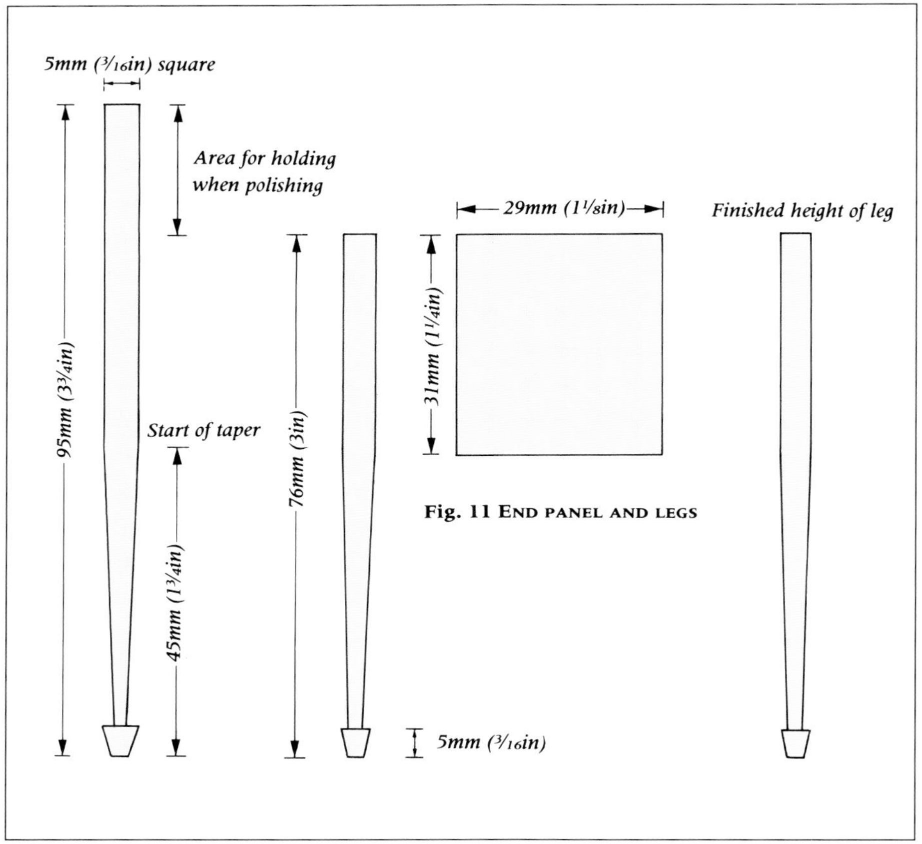

Fig. 11 End panel and legs

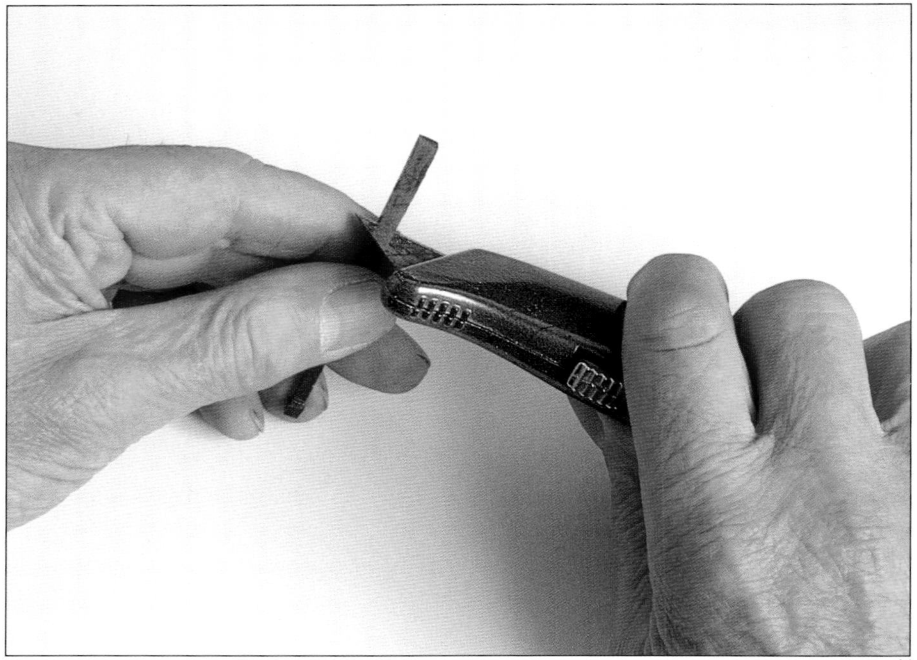

11

11. The inside of the legs and parts of the panels to be glued to the carcass should be scraped with a craft knife to remove all polish, otherwise the glue will not adhere.

12. Glue the middle legs to the carcass. Make sure all the legs touch the floor.

10. For the legs, you will need six square blanks. Taper the legs to the shape shown in Fig. 11. Fine sand, dust, stain and polish the legs. Cut the legs to the finished length. Cut two end panels 3mm (⅛in) thick. Sand, dust, stain and polish one side. Assemble the legs and end panels on a jig. Make sure the leg tops and the top of the panel align exactly.

10

12

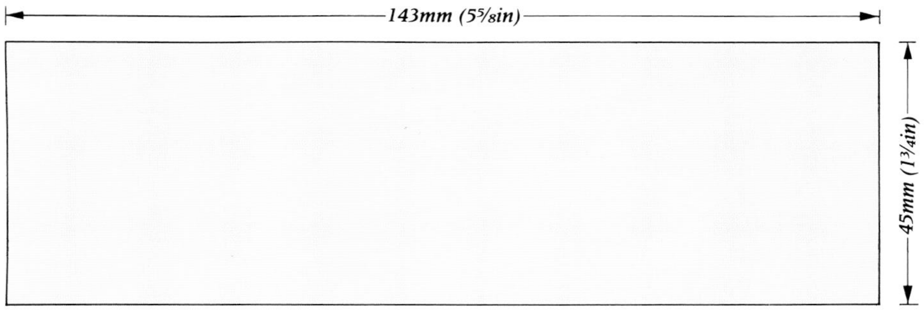

Fig. 12 Top *3mm ($\frac{1}{8}$in) thick*

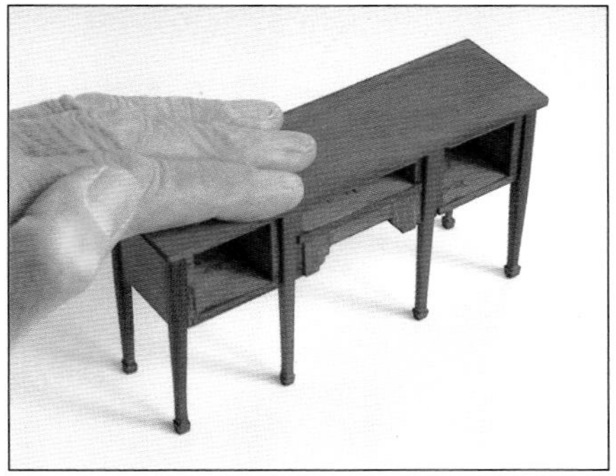

13

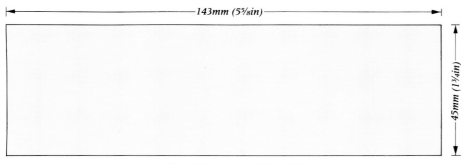

13. Cut out the table top (Fig. 12). Apply glue to the top of the carcass and position the top. Test the end panels for fit. Remove the end panels. When the glue is completely dry, dust, stain and polish the table top. Glue the end panels in position. The back legs line up with the back and the front legs protrude slightly.

Making a Set of Drawers

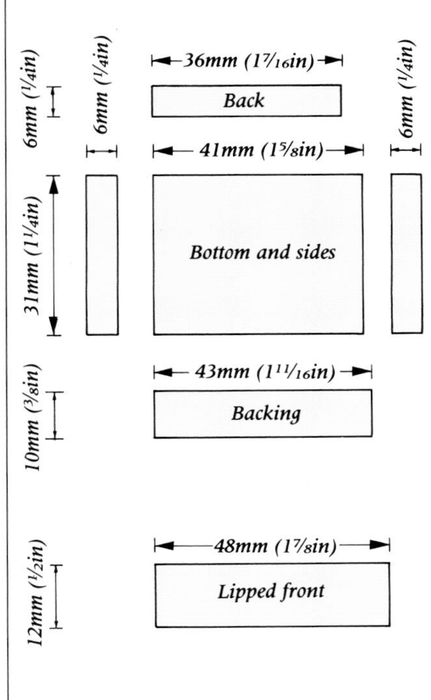

Fig. 9 Middle drawer

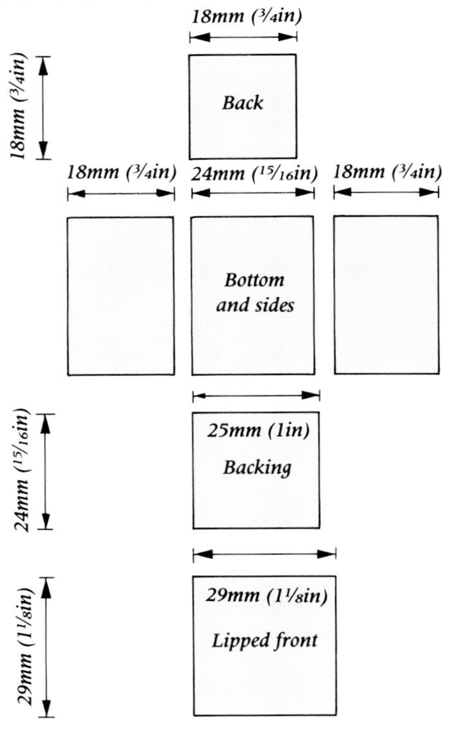

Fig. 10 Side drawers

14

14. Cut out components for two side drawers and one middle drawer. To construct a drawer, place the drawer front backing piece against the vertical back of the jig. Apply glue to the front of the drawer bottom and the backing piece. Apply glue to the front and bottom of the right-hand side. Allow the glue to dry and assemble the left side.

15

15. Fit the back by applying glue to both sides and bottom, and assemble. Fit the drawer to the carcass.

16. The lipped drawer front should overlap all the drawer edges by 1.5mm ($^{1}/_{16}$in). You can test this against a rebate 1–2mm ($^{1}/_{16}$in) deep run in a piece of scrap. Drill a hole in the centre of the drawers for the knobs and glue the knobs in place.

16

The Living Room

~

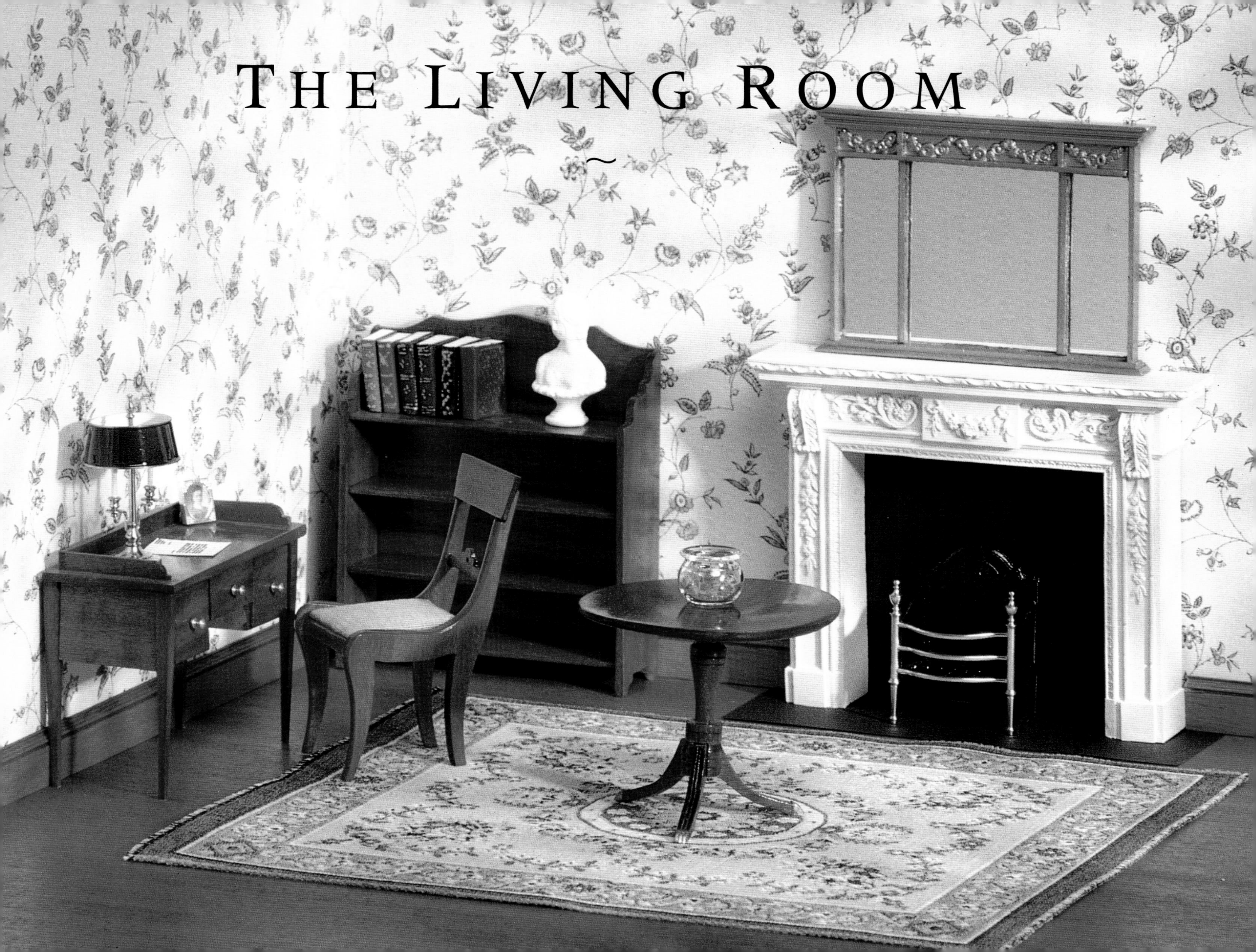

Bookshelves

~

These pretty shelves have a similar side design to the hanging shelves, but the use of a mahogany-style wood gives the piece a more substantial, old-fashioned look suitable for a drawing room. Since the back is visible and decorative, it needs to have the same level of finish as the sides and shelves; it can be made either with solid mahogany or with a mixture of plywood-backed veneer and mahogany.

~

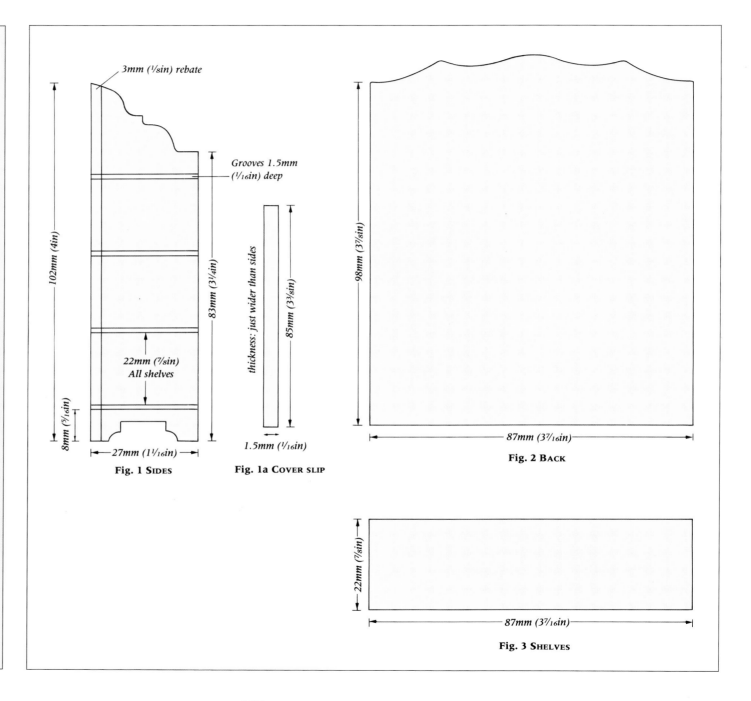

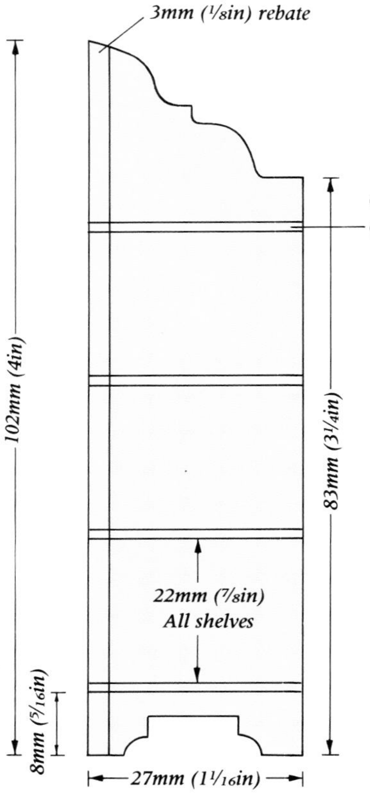
3mm (1/8in) rebate
Grooves 1.5mm (1/16in) deep
102mm (4in)
83mm (3¼in)
22mm (7/8in) All shelves
8mm (5/16in)
27mm (1 1/16in)

Fig. 1 Sides

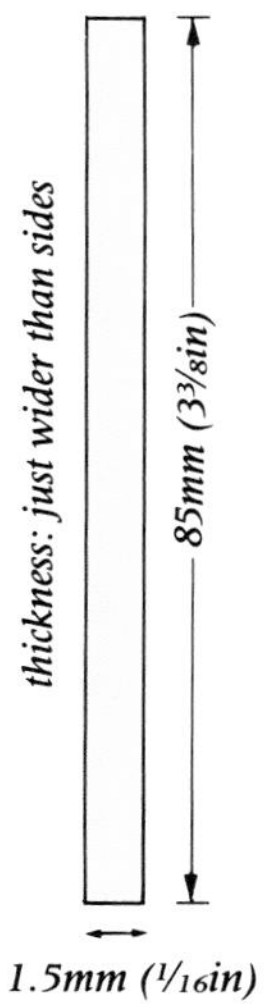
thickness: just wider than sides
85mm (3 3/8in)
1.5mm (1/16in)

Fig. 1a Cover slip

98mm (3 7/8in)
87mm (3 7/16in)

Fig. 2 Back

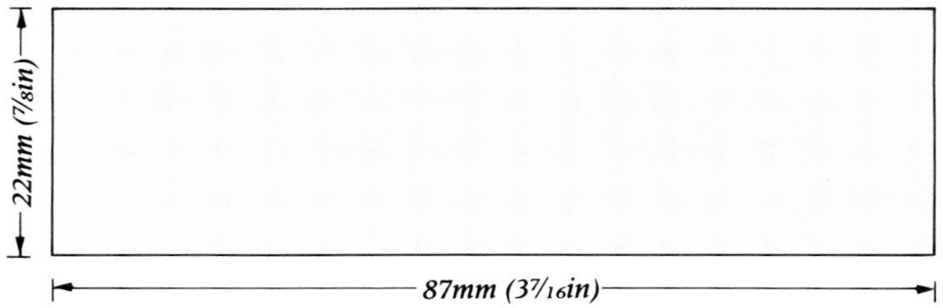
22mm (7/8in)
87mm (3 7/16in)

Fig. 3 Shelves

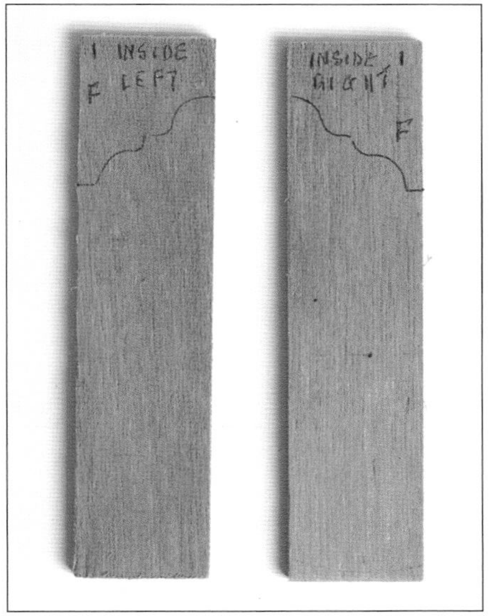
1

2

3

4

5

1. Cut slices for the sides measuring 25 × 114mm (1 × $4\frac{1}{2}$in) and 3mm ($\frac{1}{8}$in) thick. Mark whether the side is an inside left or inside right. Draw on the shape of the sides in pencil (Fig. 1).

2. Run shelf grooves and rebates. Cut two cover slips (Fig. 1a) and glue them to the front edges of the sides. Sand the edges so the slips are flush with the outside surface of the blanks. Stain and polish the inside surface of the blank. Cut out the sides. You may wish to use the pinned blank method (page 98) if you are using power tools.

3. Two polished sides with the grooves and rebates ready cut. Cut the shelves to a thickness to match the grooves in the sides (Fig. 3). Stain and polish one surface and the front edge of the shelves. Stain, but do not polish, the underside of the shelves.

4. Cut out a blank for the back to a thickness of 3mm ($\frac{1}{8}$in) (Fig. 2). Mark the head shape in pencil. Stain and polish the surface.

5. Cut the head shape. Sand, stain and polish the top of the head shape. Insert glue into the grooves and both rebates on the sides.

Alternative Methods

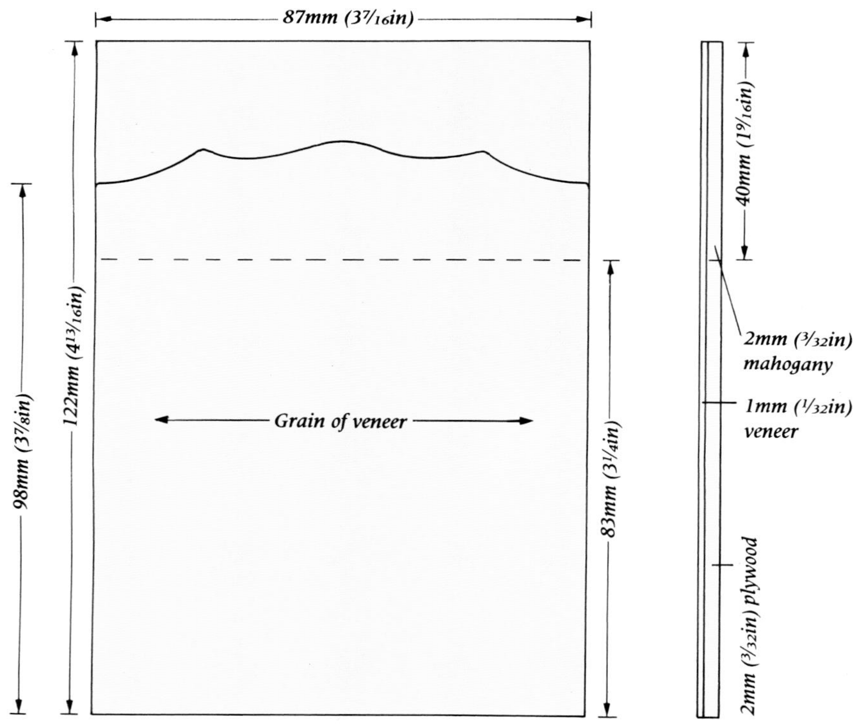

Fig. 4 ALTERNATIVE METHOD FOR BACK

Section Plan

If you are using power tools, you may find it difficult to cut the head shape due to the thinness of the wood. Instead, you can use a combination of plywood and your chosen wood covered with a veneer. The head shape is cut in the good-quality wood, so that the top edge can be finished properly. Glue the two sections of wood together to form one sheet and glue on the veneer, with the grain running across the width. Hand sand and dust. Mark the head shape and stain and polish the veneered surface to about 6mm (¼in) beyond the outline of the head shape. Leave to dry. Cut the head shape.

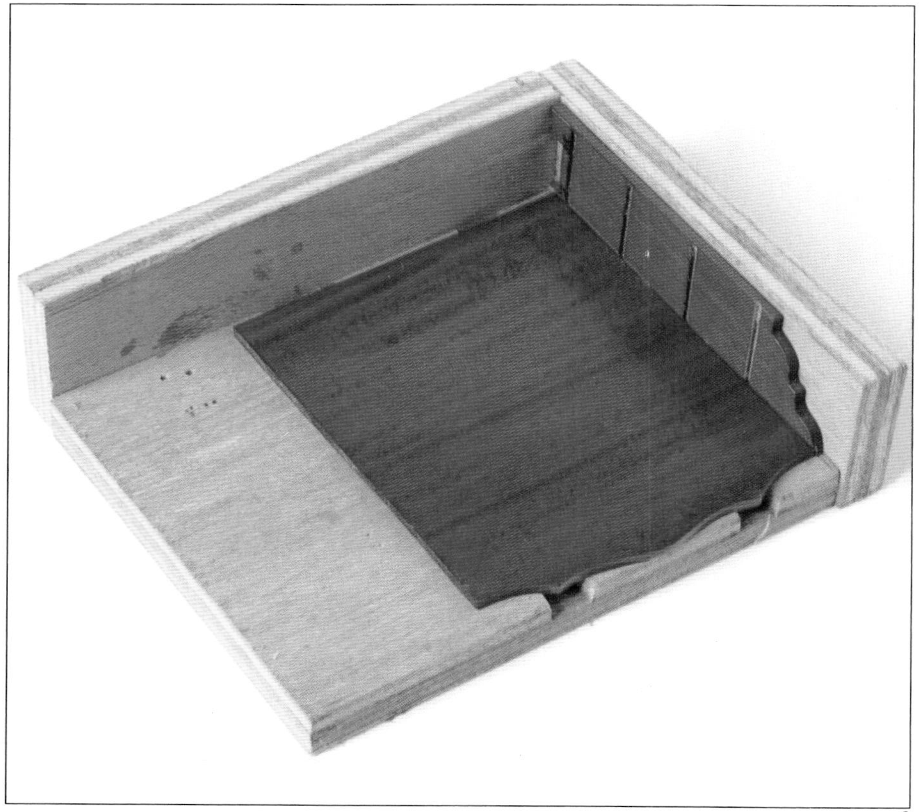

6

6. Place the right side on the jig with the feet against the adjacent jig wall. Place the back on the jig to engage the back rebate. Position the back so that the top of the side-shaped head and the top of the back head align.

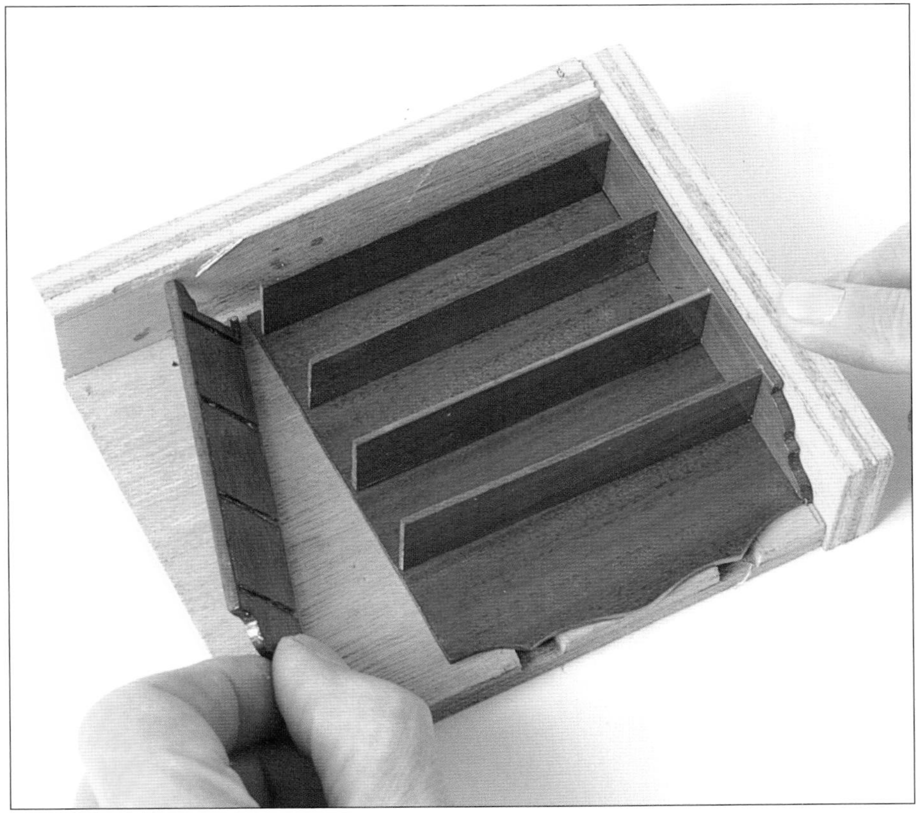

7

7. Insert the shelves so that they are at right angles to one side. Add the left side, engaging the bottom shelf first and working upwards. Leave the glue to dry. Fine sand, stain and polish the outside surfaces of the sides.

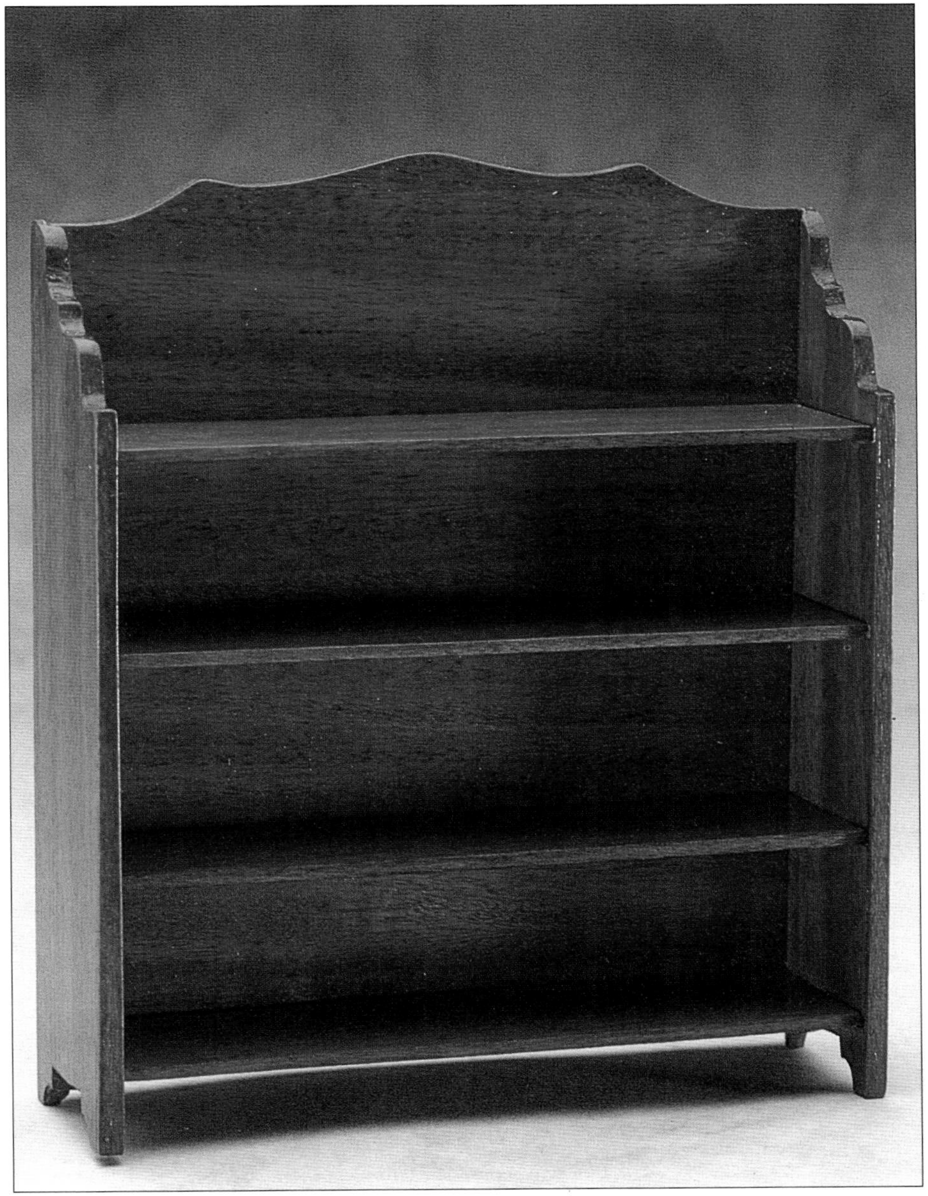

Desk

~

The desk is smaller and squarer than both the sideboard and the dressing table but it is very similar in design. The main difference is the use of moulded strips of wood – "upstands" – to decorate the top surface; these strips are inserted into grooves on three sides of the top and give the piece a distinctive appearance.

~

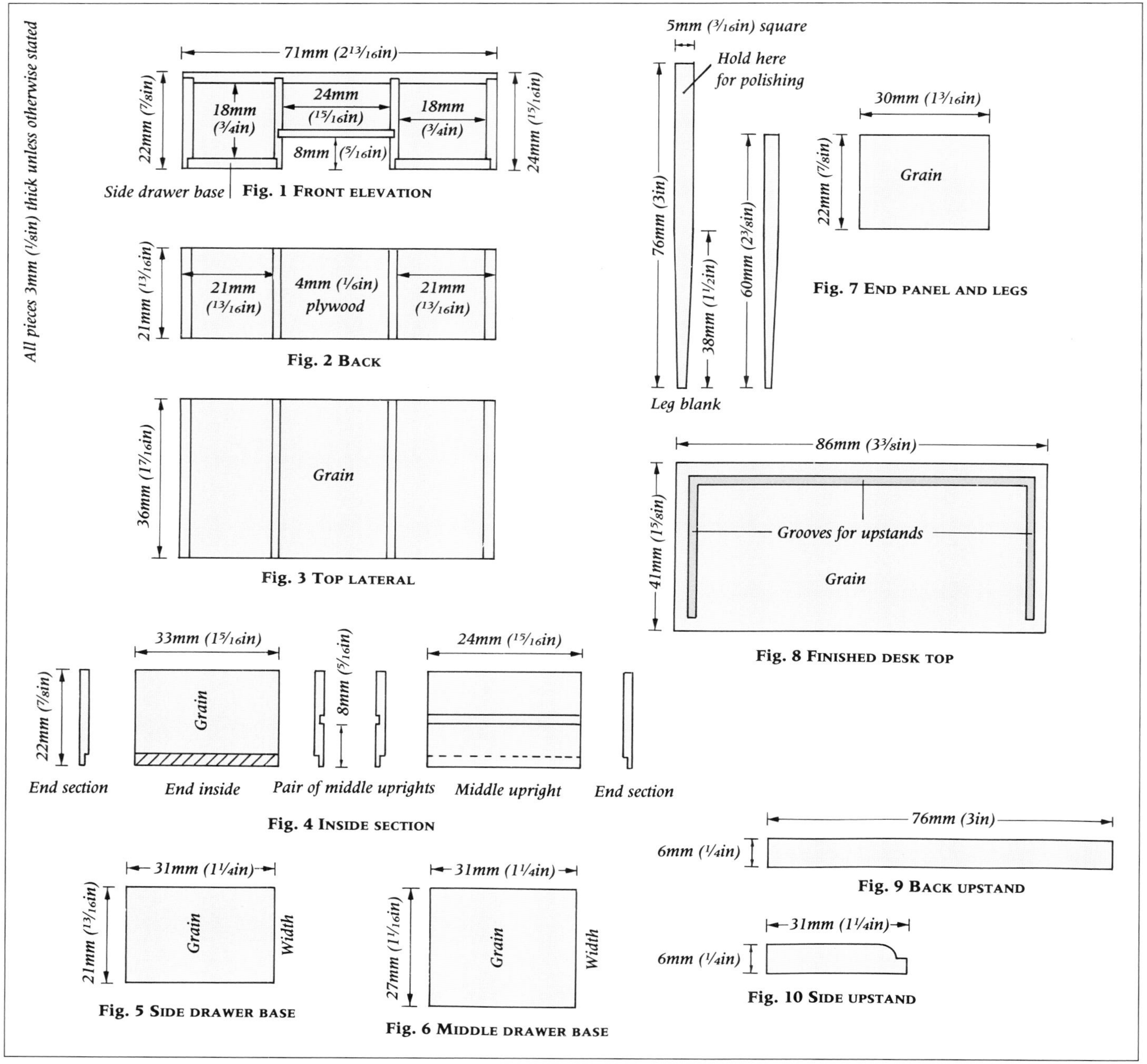

Fig. 1 Front elevation

Fig. 2 Back

Fig. 3 Top lateral

Fig. 4 Inside section

Fig. 5 Side drawer base

Fig. 6 Middle drawer base

Fig. 7 End panel and legs

Fig. 8 Finished desk top

Fig. 9 Back upstand

Fig. 10 Side upstand

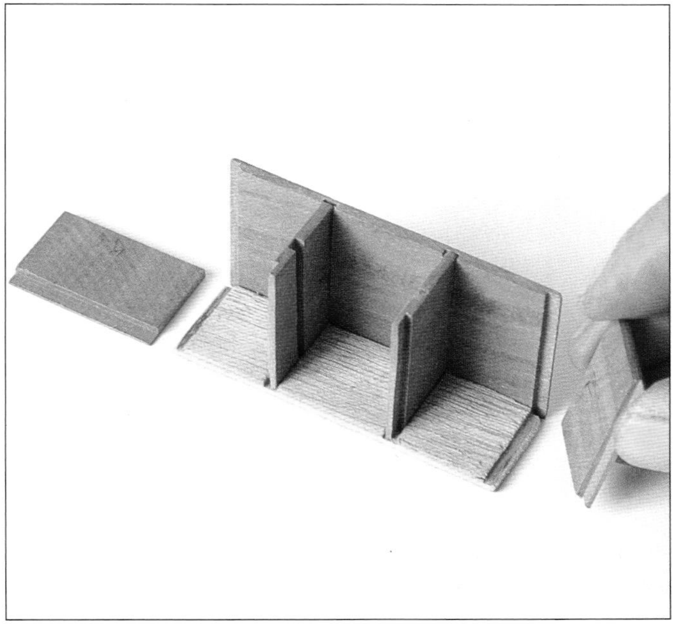
1

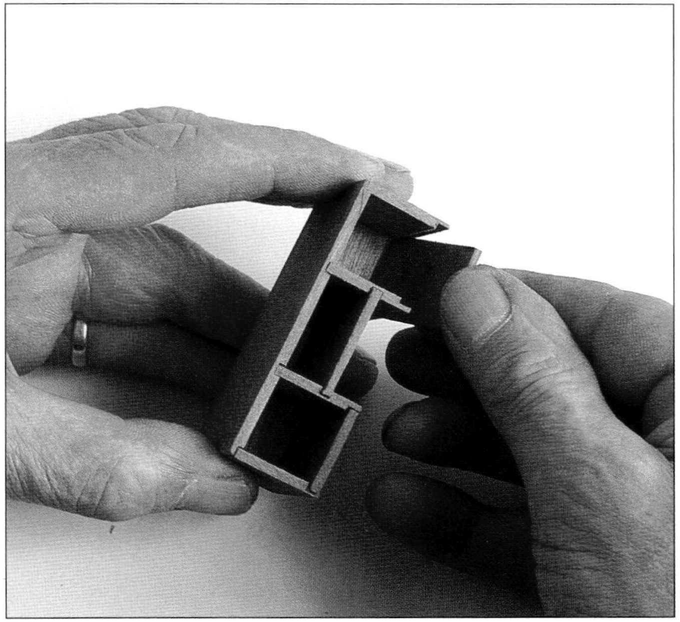
2

3

4

1. Cut out the back from 4mm (1/6in) plywood. Cut the top lateral, the side drawer bases, the carcass ends, the middle uprights and the end panels all to a thickness of 3mm (1/8in); cut the middle drawer base to a thickness of 1.5mm (1/16in). Run 1.5mm (1/16in) grooves and rebates in all these pieces as indicated. Glue the back, top lateral and middle uprights in place. Sand all the edges flush. Glue the ends in place.

2. Sand, stain and polish the front of the carcass. Assemble the bases for all the drawers. Make four square-ended blanks for the legs. Use medium sandpaper to taper the legs, starting at the point indicated on Fig. 7. Sand, stain and polish the legs. Cut the legs to their final length.

3. Assemble the legs and end panels on a jig. Scrape away the polish from any surfaces to be glued. Make sure the leg tops and the top of the panel are exactly aligned.

4. Cut the top (Fig. 8) to 3mm (1/8in). Cut 1.5mm (1/16in) grooves 5mm (3/16in) away from the back and side edges of the desk top for the "upstands". Position, but do not glue, the assembled end panels to the carcass. Glue the top in position.

5. Cut two strips 6 × 89mm (¼ × 3½in) and the thickness of the grooves in the top (Fig. 9). These will form the upstands to go around the edge of the top.

6. Polish one strip for the back upstand, holding one end. Hold the second strip in the middle and polish both ends. Leave the polish to harden overnight.

5

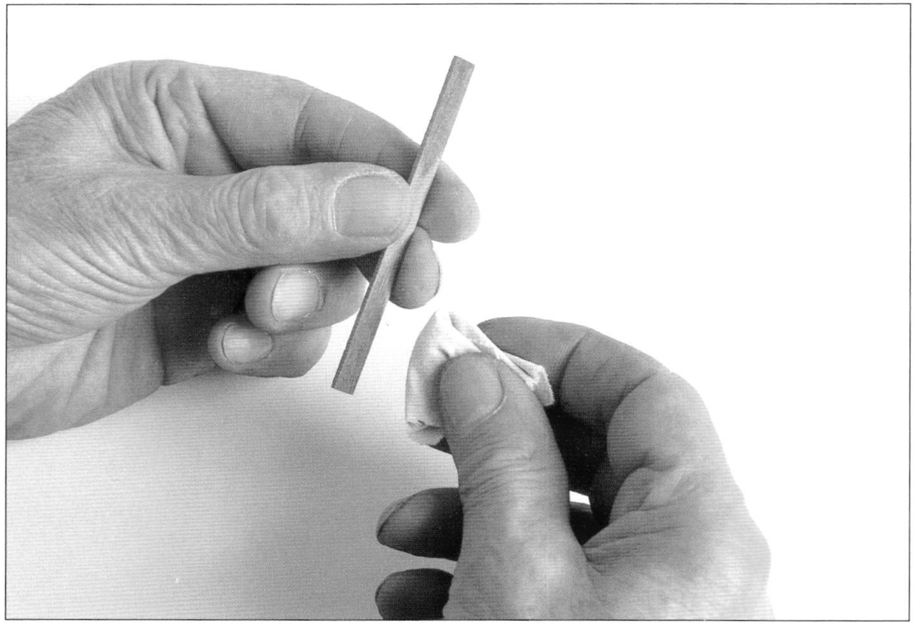

6

7. Cut the second upstand strip to form two 31mm (1¼in) lengths. Test the strips against the side grooves and cut if necessary. Mould the front ends of the side upstand pieces (Fig. 10). Sand and stain the moulding and retouch the polish.

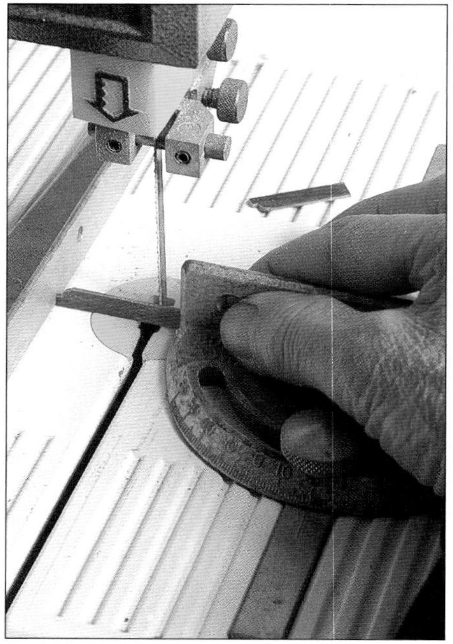

7

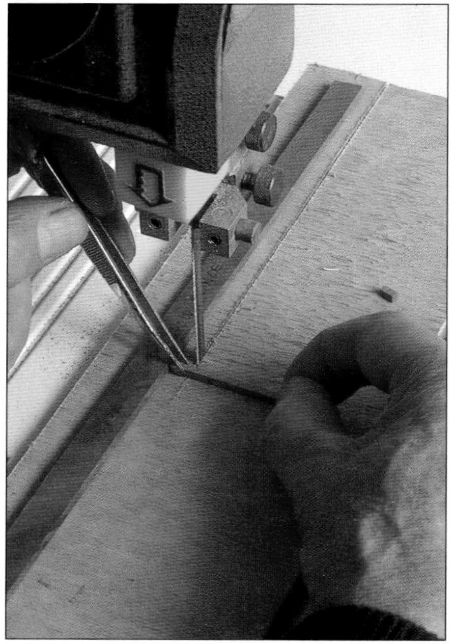

8

8. To cut two end stops for the front of the desk, cut a section 25 × 11 × 11mm (1 × 7/16 × 7/16in) and slice it to the width of the grooves in the top. Cut a strip slightly wider than the depth of the grooves, and along the grain. Now cut four stops from the leftover strip for the other ends of the grooves; these need to be the width of the grooves and 5mm (3/16in) long.

9

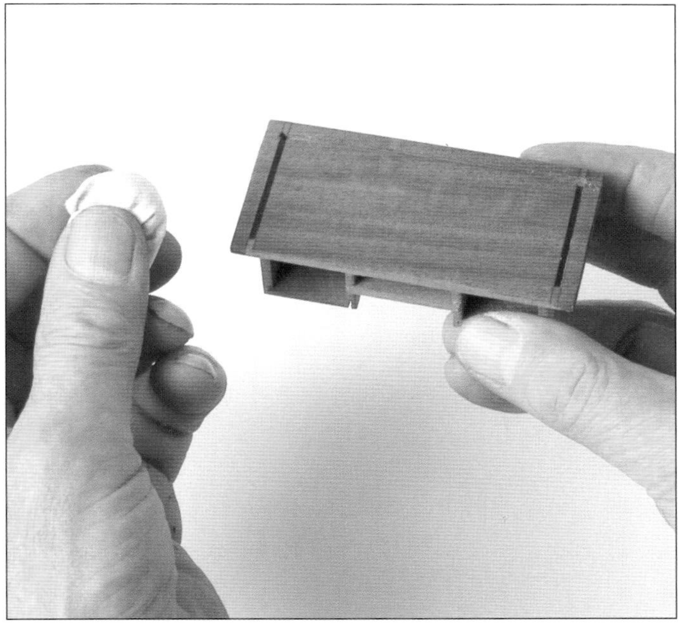

10

9. Dry-assemble the upstands to the desk top. Insert glue in the grooves for the stops and position them against the ends of the upstands. Wait for the glue to harden and remove the upstands. Trim and sand the ends of the stops.

10. Sand, stain and polish the top.

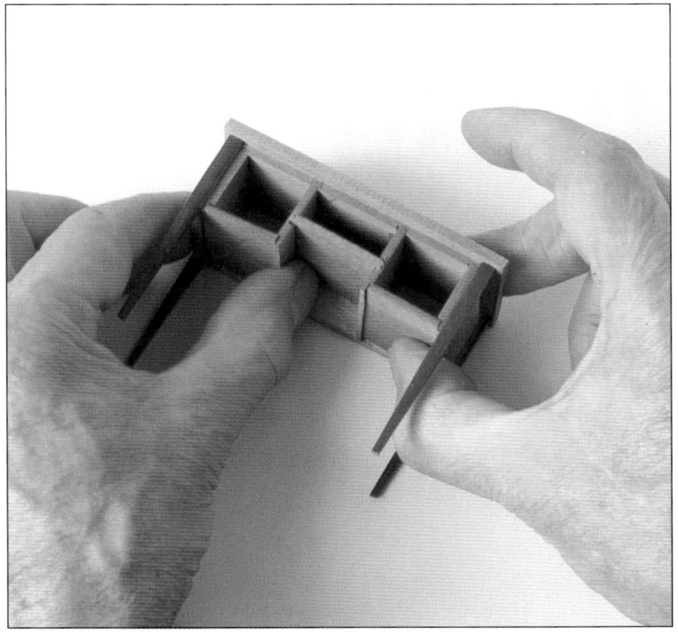

11

12

11. Check the alignment of the top and carcass against the assembled end panels and legs. Glue the end panels in position. The back legs should line up with the back of the carcass, the front legs should protrude slightly.

12. Glue the upstands in position.

MAKING A SET OF DRAWERS

~

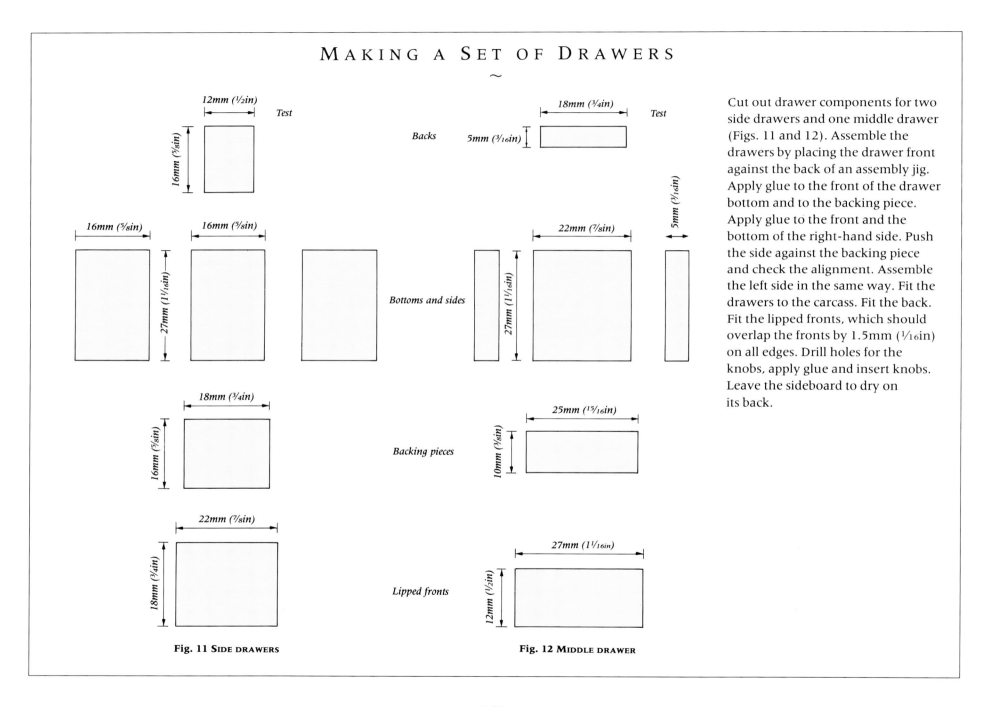

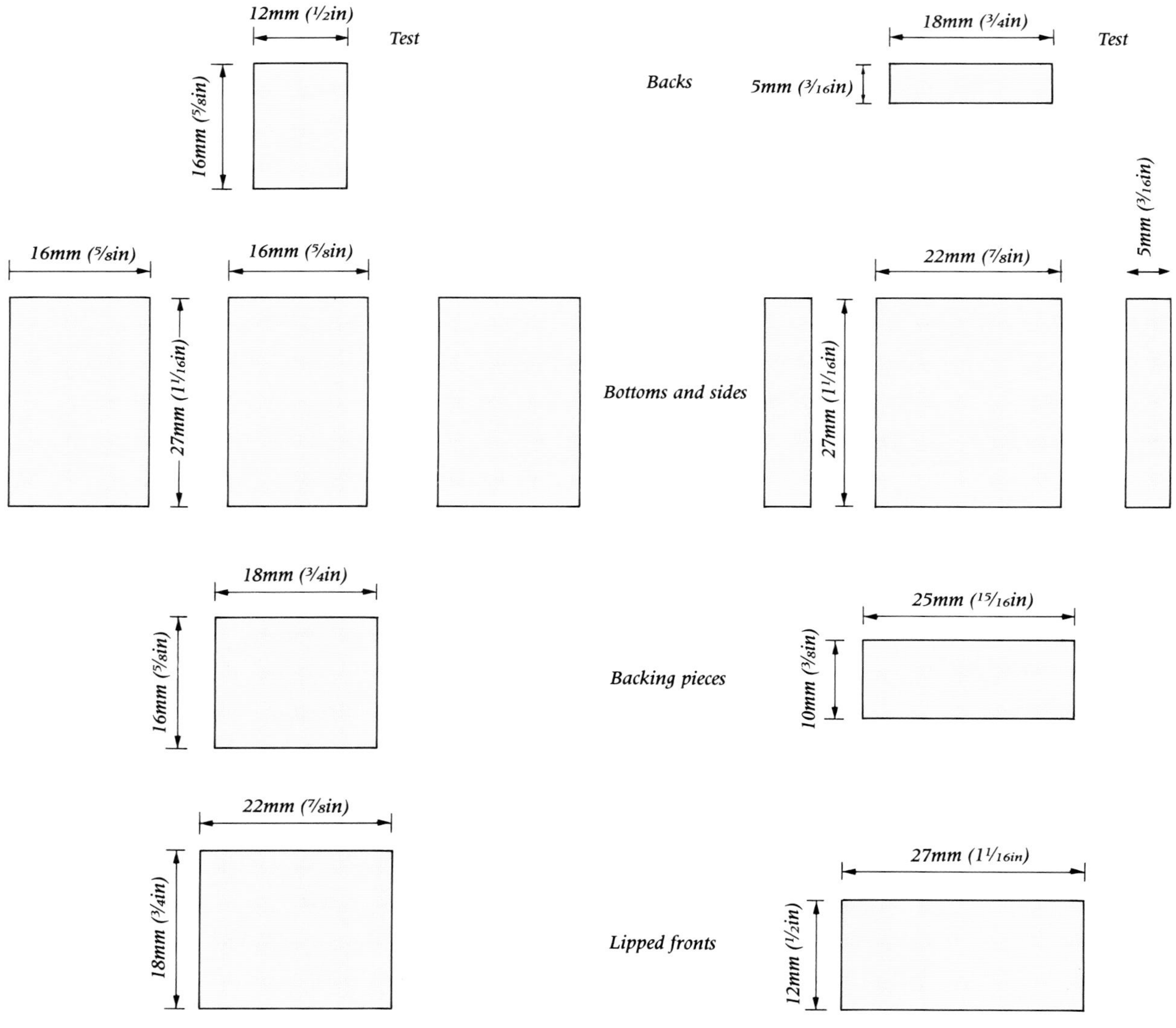

Fig. 11 Side drawers

Fig. 12 Middle drawer

Cut out drawer components for two side drawers and one middle drawer (Figs. 11 and 12). Assemble the drawers by placing the drawer front against the back of an assembly jig. Apply glue to the front of the drawer bottom and to the backing piece. Apply glue to the front and the bottom of the right-hand side. Push the side against the backing piece and check the alignment. Assemble the left side in the same way. Fit the drawers to the carcass. Fit the back. Fit the lipped fronts, which should overlap the fronts by 1.5mm (1/16in) on all edges. Drill holes for the knobs, apply glue and insert knobs. Leave the sideboard to dry on its back.

Occasional Table

~

This small table uses exactly the same construction as the Regency dining table, but it has a round top and needs only one leg, which is smaller than those on the dining table. The elegant design makes the table a splendid addition to any formal drawing room.

~

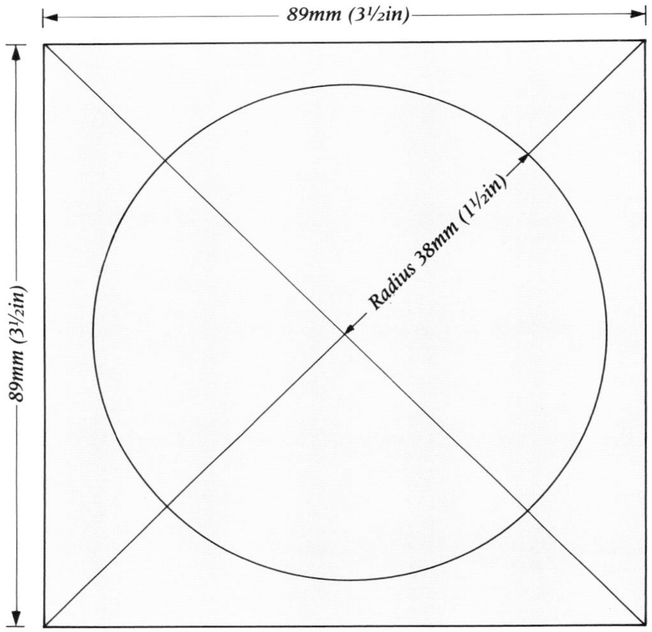

Fig. 1 Top blank

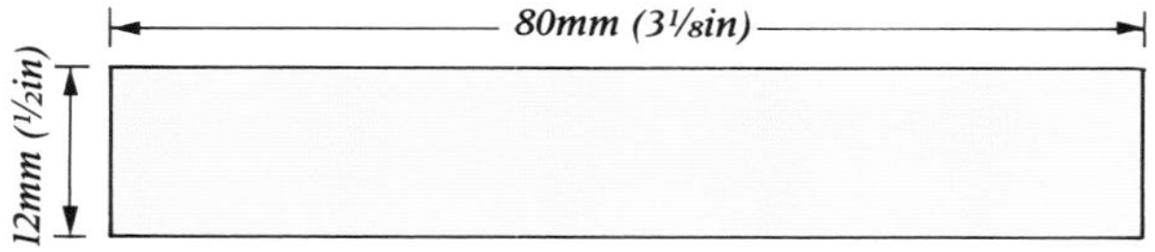

Fig. 2 Column blank

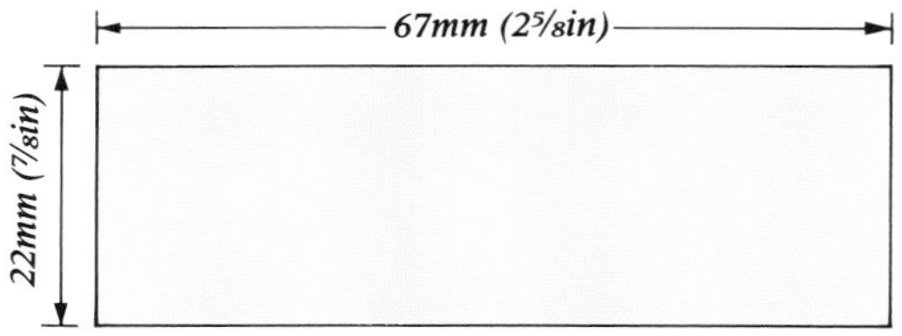

Fig. 4 Leg blank

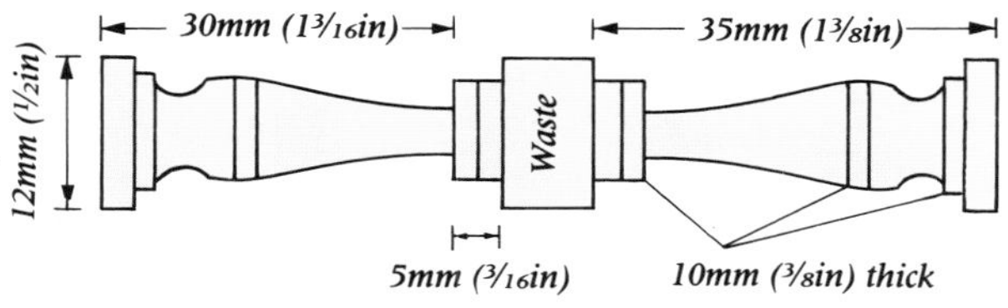

Fig. 3 Shaped column

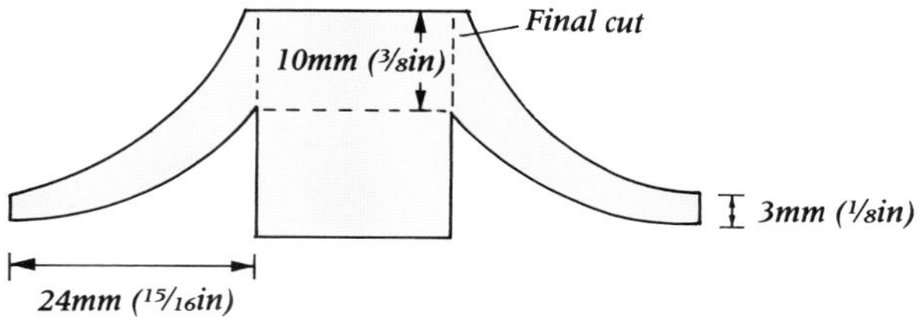

Fig. 5 Leg shaping

1. Cut the circular table top to a radius of 38mm (1½in) from a blank 3mm (⅛in) thick. These four photographs show the stages of cutting the table top on a bandsaw using a circle cutting pin.

1A

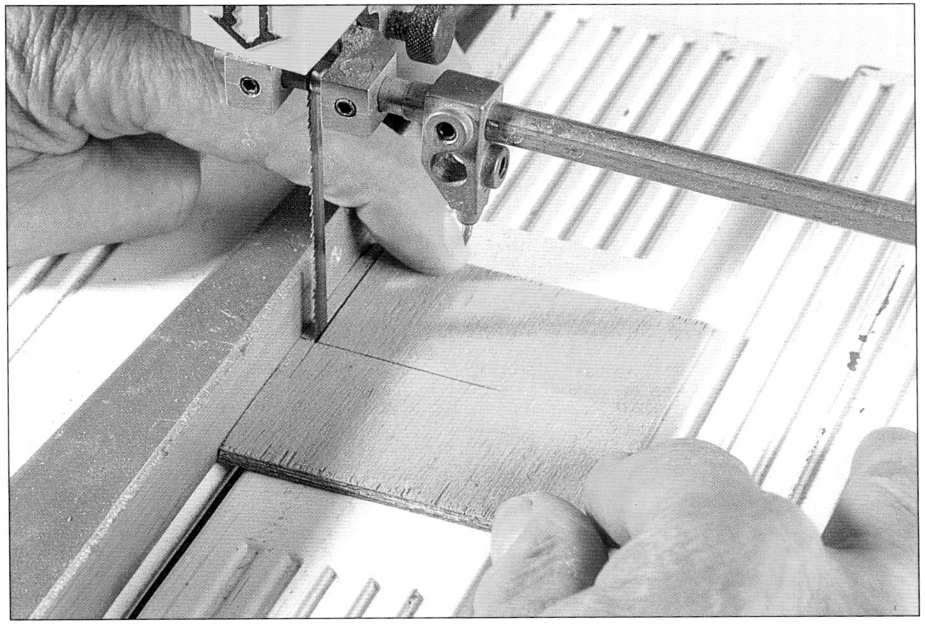

1B

1C

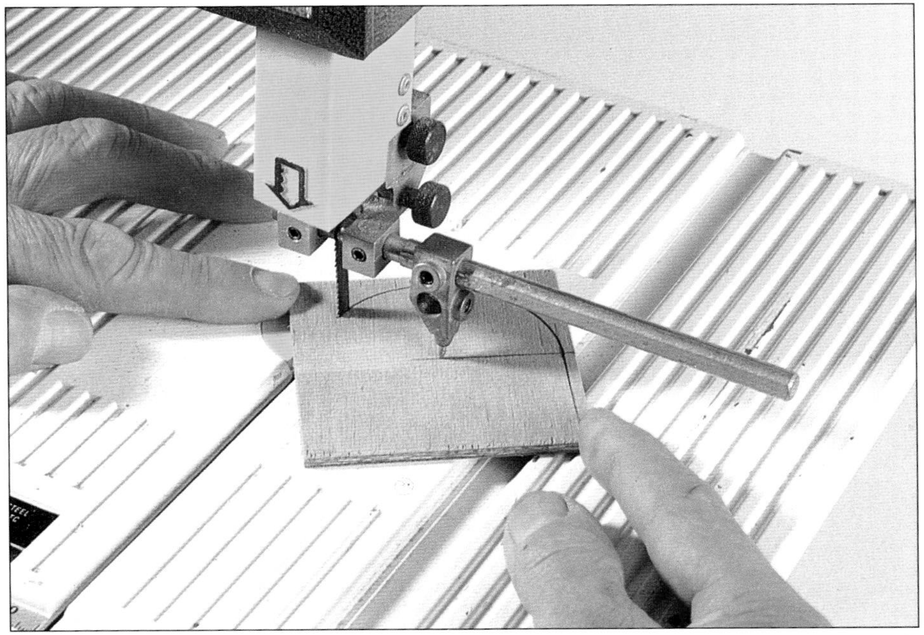

1D

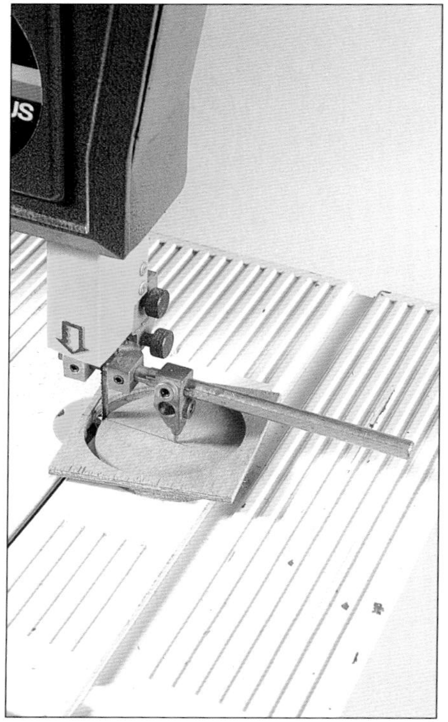

2

2. Completing the circle cut.

3. The cut table top and blocks for mounting it on the lathe.

4. Chamfer the edge of the table top. You can use a lathe if you have one, or simply sand the underside of the top. Finish by hand with medium and fine sandpaper.

5. The column, leg holder and legs are made in the same way as for the Regency Dining Table; the only difference is that this column is shorter.

4

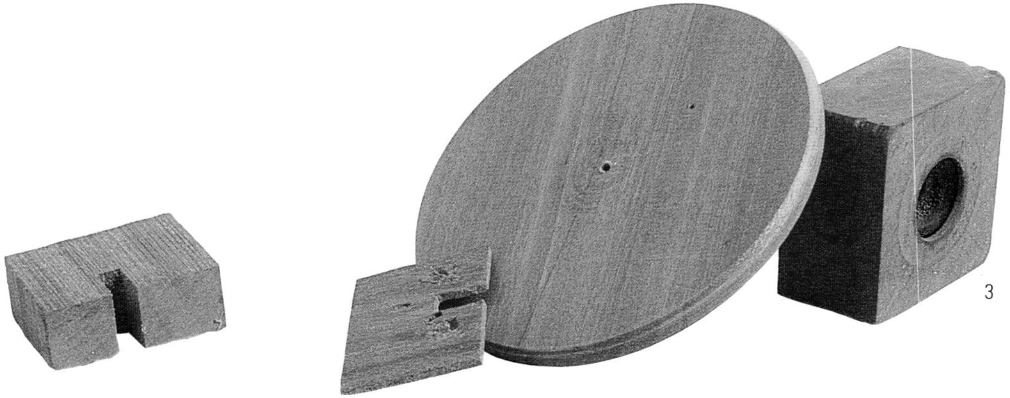

3

5

MAKING THE COLUMNS

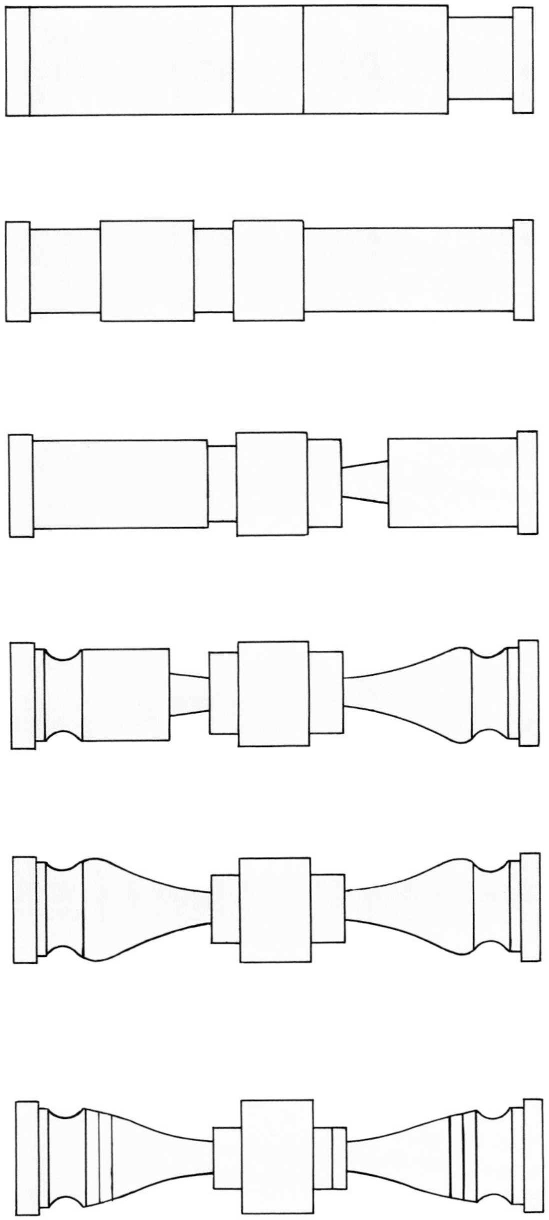

6

6. Cut a square-ended blank – one blank makes two columns – to the dimensions shown in Fig. 2. The leg column will then need to be shaped according to the sequence shown but ending up with a column to the dimensions shown in Fig. 3.

7

7. Hand-sand the column. Cut the two top rings. Cut the ring on the pad. Dust, stain and French polish the column. Cut the column to its final length – 30mm (1³⁄₁₆in).

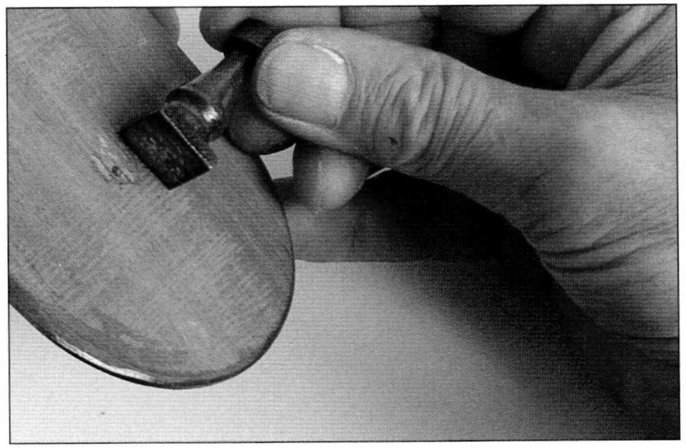

8

8. Glue the column to the centre of the table top.

9. Dust, sand and polish the table top.

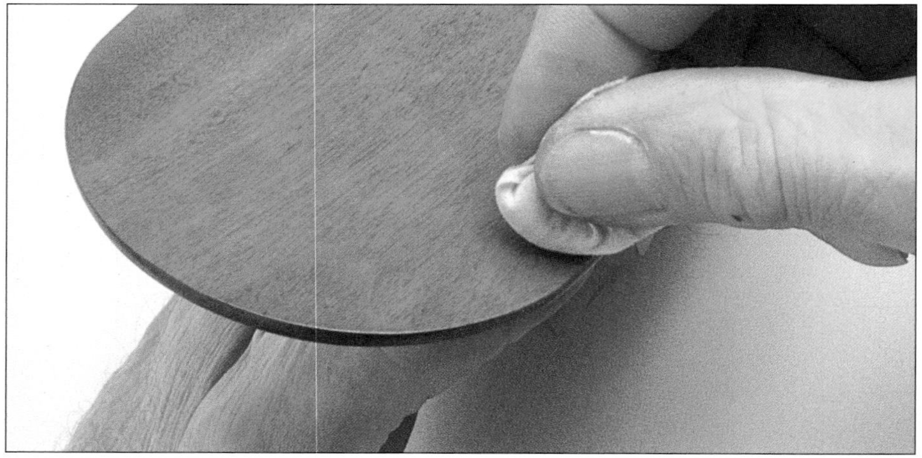

9

MAKING THE LEG HOLDERS

~

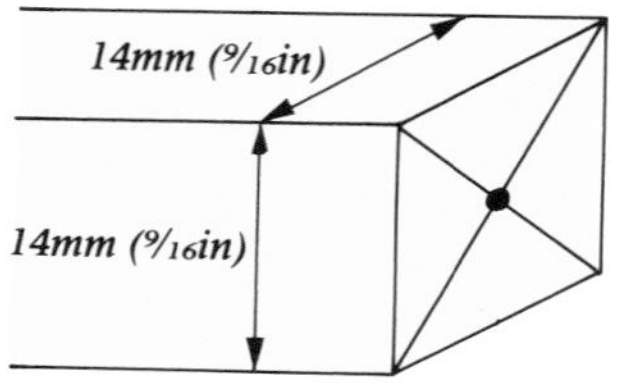

Fig. 3a

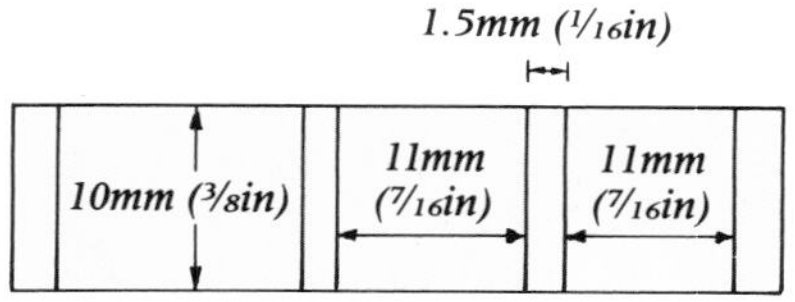

Fig. 3b Blank turned to 10mm (3/8in) diameter

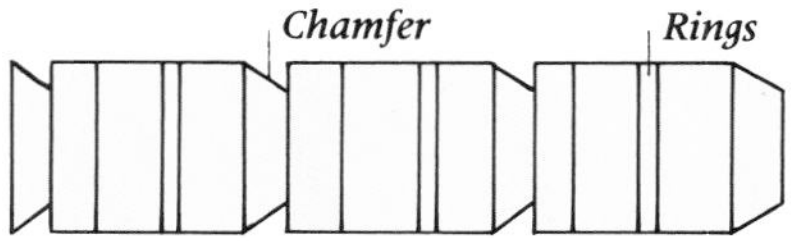

Fig. 3c Running chamfer and rings

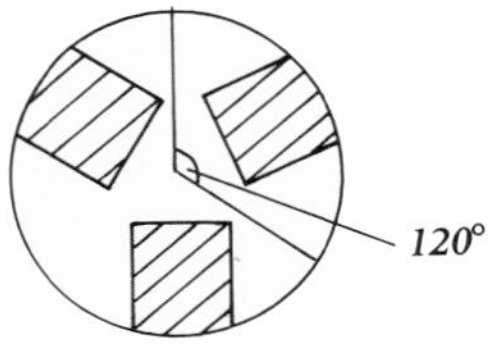

Fig. 3d Cutting slots

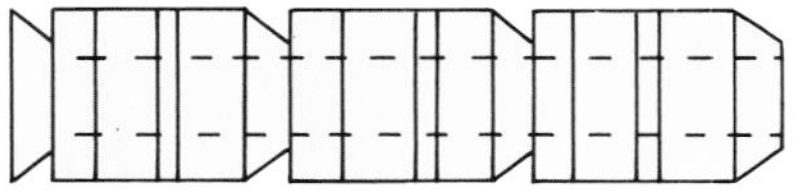

Fig. 3d Cutting slots

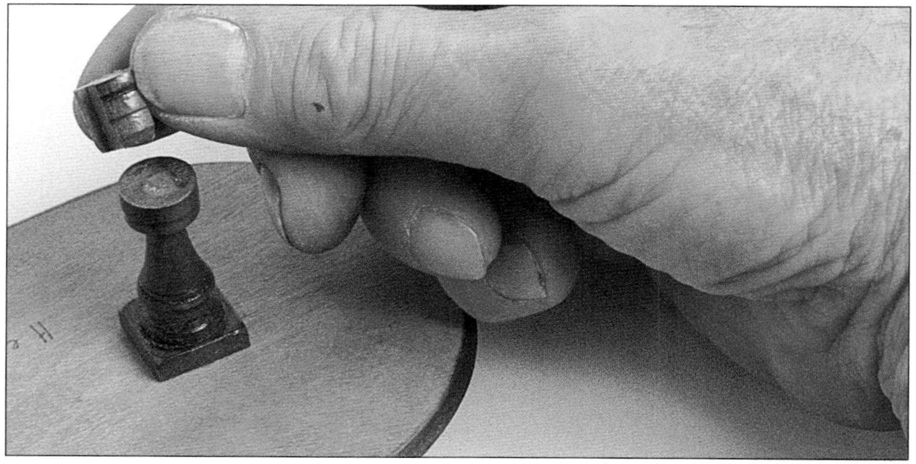

10

10. For the leg holder, cut a square-ended blank (Fig. 3a) and turn it so that it is 10mm (3/8in) in diameter (Fig. 3b). Cut rings and a chamfer (Fig. 3c). Stain and polish the pieces.

Cut three slots down the sides of the piece at 120° to each other (Fig. 3d). Make the final cuts to give a length of 11mm (7/16in). Assemble the leg holders to the columns.

11

11. You will need three legs for one table – a pair of legs is cut from one slice. You may want to use the pinned blank method (see page 98), illustrated here, to ensure uniformity of the pieces you cut. Test the width of leg required against the slots cut in step 9, and cut the slices (Fig. 4) to this width. Glue the leg holder to the column. Draw the leg shape onto a slice, or just the top slice if using pinned blank, and cut out the number of pieces required.

12. Sand the legs and attach them to the leg holders. The final assembly jig is, in principle, the same as for the Regency Dining Table, except that there is space for only one column and the height from the floor of the jig to the top surface is 35mm (1⅜in). Place the table in the assembly jig and leave the glue to dry.

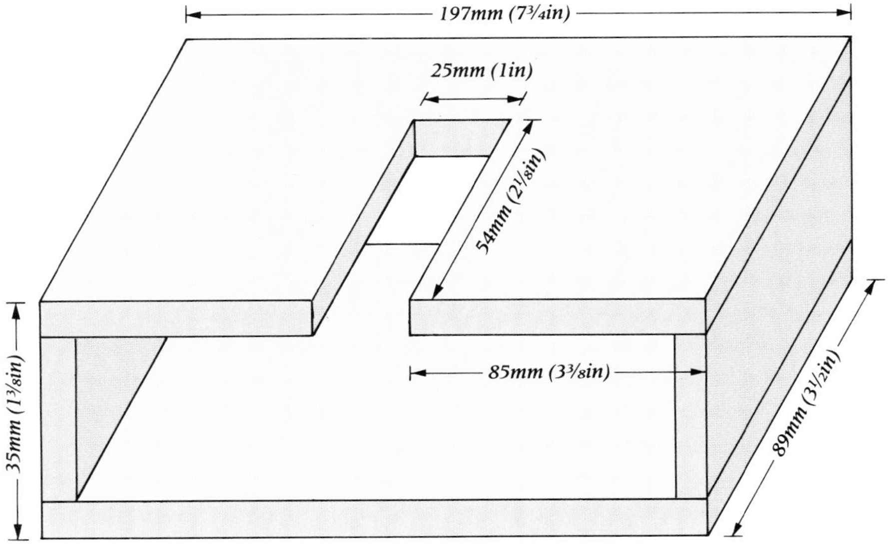

12

Fig. 12 Occasional table jig

The Occasional Table

Chesterfield Sofa

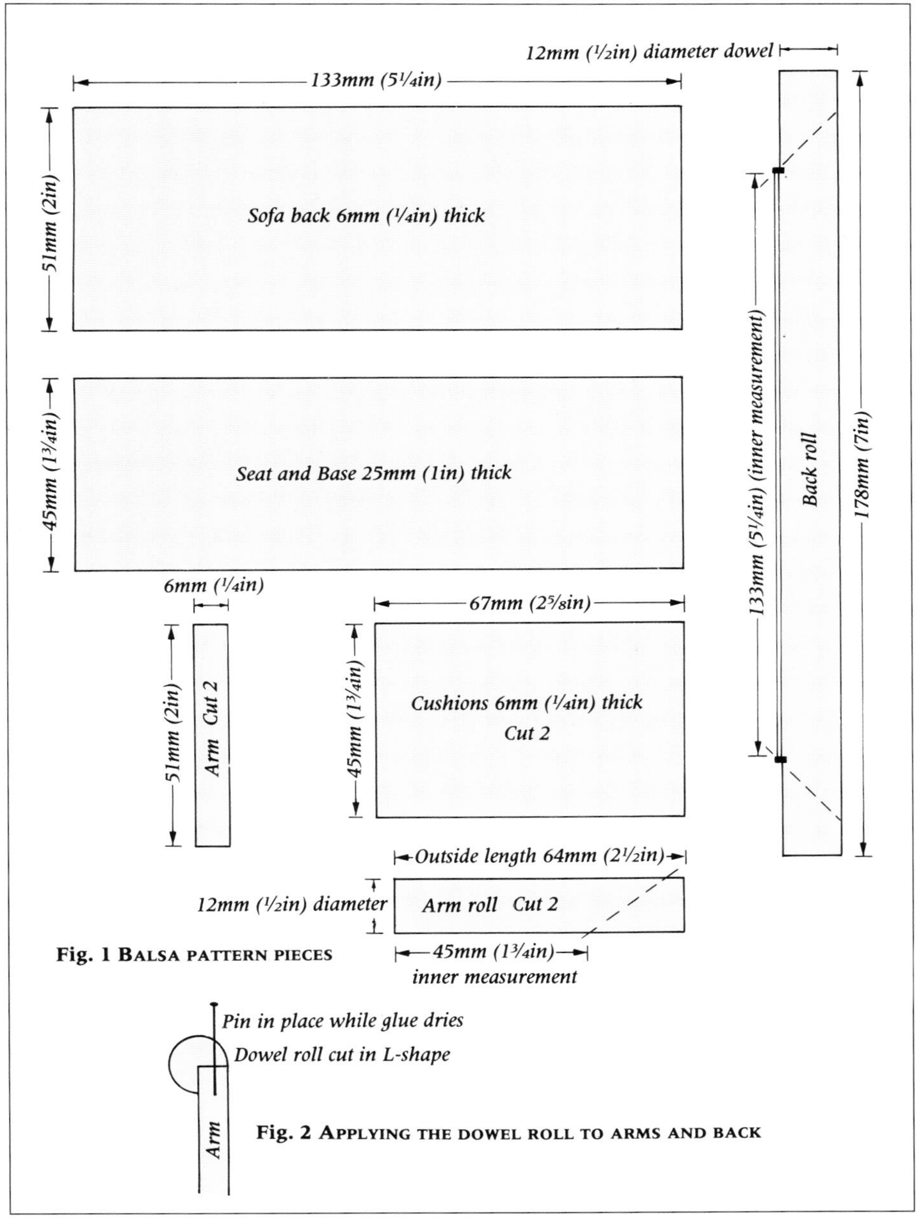

Fig. 1 Balsa pattern pieces

Fig. 2 Applying the dowel roll to arms and back

You Will Need

~

- Balsa wood for base 133 × 45 × 25mm (5¼ × 1¾ × 1in); for back 133 × 51 × 6mm (5¼ × 2 × ¼in); for arms (cut 2) 51 × 51 × 6mm (2 × 2 × ¼in); for cushions (cut 2) 67 × 45 × 6mm (2⅝ × 1¾ × ¼in)
- Sandpaper
- 380mm (15in) dowel 12mm (½in) in diameter
- Craft knife or scalpel
- Wood glue
- 25mm (1in) dress-making pins
- Wadding, approximately 205 × 205mm (8 × 8in)
- Fabric for covering (lightweight wool, cotton or silk), approximately 230mm (9in)
- Sewing thread
- Clear, all-purpose fabric adhesive
- 2 round-headed upholstery pins, 3mm (⅛in) in diameter, for ends of arms
- Hard wood, 25 × 25 × 3mm (1 × 1 × ⅛in), cut into 4 squares for feet

1. Cut out the balsa pieces. Smooth all the pieces with a sanding block. Sand the top edges of the two cushion pieces, rounding off the corners and shaving away a fraction on each edge so that they will fit onto the upholstered seat.

2. Cut the balsa dowel with the aid of a mitre block into two arm rolls, each 64mm (2½in) at the outer edge, and one back roll, 178mm (7in) at the outer edge. If you do not have a mitre block, draw a right angle with a set square on a wood-working board, divide the angle into 45° with a strong pencil line and use this as a guide for your cutting angle. Use a craft knife or scalpel to cut an L-shape out of the length of each piece of dowel (see Fig. 2).

3. Cut out the fabric pieces for the base (cut one), the back (cut one) and the arm pieces (cut two). Do not cut out the wadding at this stage. Glue the fabric for the sofa seat and front of base into position, starting at the back edge of the balsa base. When the back edge is secure, smooth the fabric forwards and down over the seat and glue it under the base. Glue both arm covers to the arms, and then glue back in the same way. Note that the fabric covers the outside surface, not the seat side, of the back. When the fabric covering is in position, glue the back of the sofa to the seat with wood glue. Clamp the pieces together until the glue is dry. Glue the arms in position. You can stick dress-making pins through the arms into the base to hold the arms.

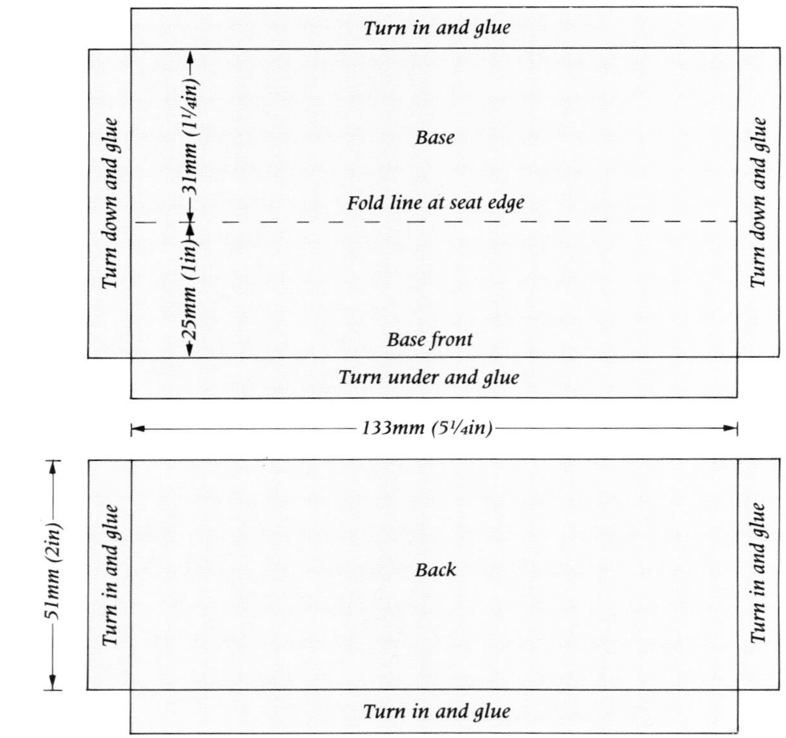

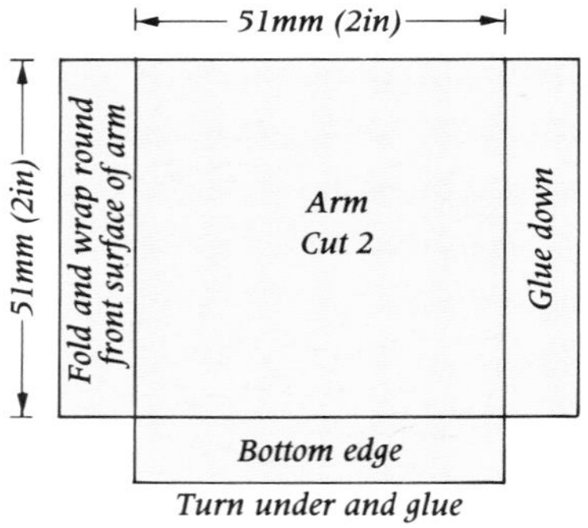

Fig. 3 Unpadded fabric pieces

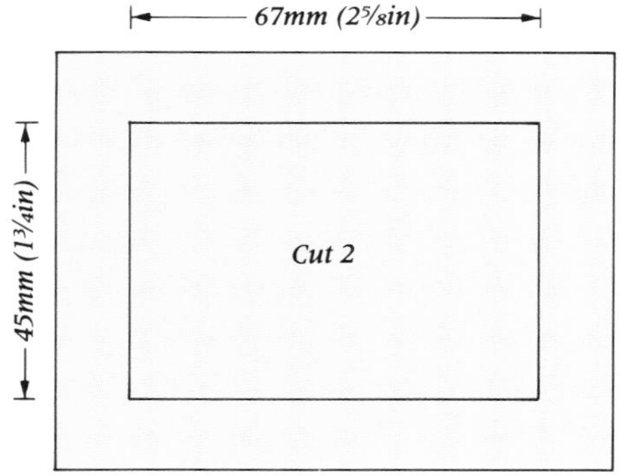

Fig. 4 Fabric and wadding pattern for cushions

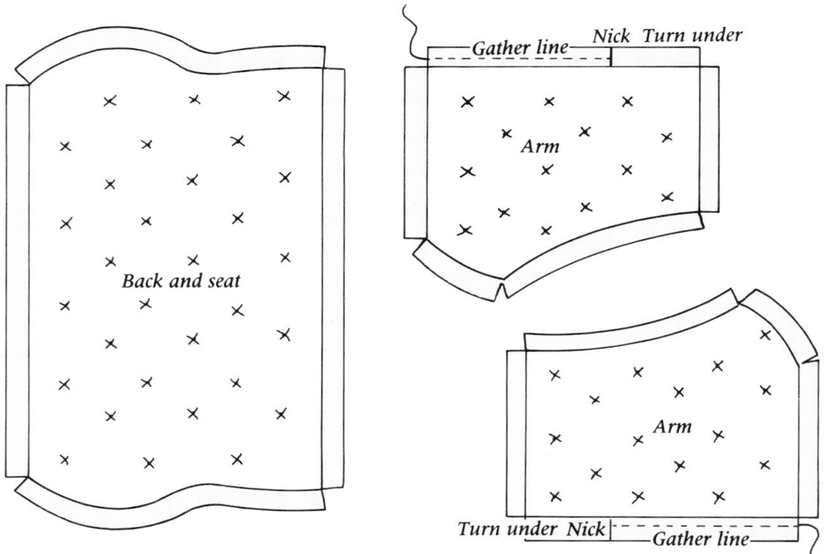

Fig. 5 Fabric and wadding patterns for back and seat and arms

4. Glue the rolls to the carcass. If the mitre ends do not fit, sand any excess or fill the gaps with a small piece of glue-soaked wadding.

5. For the buttoned-effect version, cut out the wadding and fabric pieces as shown in Figs. 4 and 5. Cut two cushion covers and two wadding pieces. Note that the wadding for the cushions should be cut exactly to size, with no allowance for edging. Draw the dots on the wadding for the arms and back. These dots must be evenly spaced or the effect will be unsatisfactory. Baste the wadding to the fabric for the arms and back, taking the tacking stitches diagonally across the fabric, from corner to corner. Shave off a thickness of wadding around all edges so that it is thinner at the gluing lines. Beginning with the centre line of dots on the back piece and using a darker-coloured sewing thread, work horizontally in a zigzag pattern. Bring the needle through from the back of the fabric and across to the first dot. Pull the thread tight enough to form a slight swelling but not so tight that the fabric puckers. Secure with a small backstitch through the dot. Continue in this way until all the dots are joined (see Fig. 6). Turn under and tack down the seam allowances. Stitch the arms in the same way but do not turn under the allowance at the top outside edge.

6. Place the back piece in position and make sure that it will fit, adjusting the turning allowance if necessary. Use fabric glue and dress-making pins to hold the back in position. When glued firmly, smooth the fabric piece forward over the roll and glue and pin it in place where the seat joins the sofa-back. Cover the arms in the same way. Do not turn under the allowances on the outer arm edges above the "nick" marked. Catch-stitch the turned under edges, below the nick, to the edge of the arm front and fasten off. Run small gathering stitches along the arm roll edge, draw them up to form a rosette. Trim off any excess fabric before pressing in the upholstery pin. Catch stitch the fabric on the mitred corners together and fasten off.

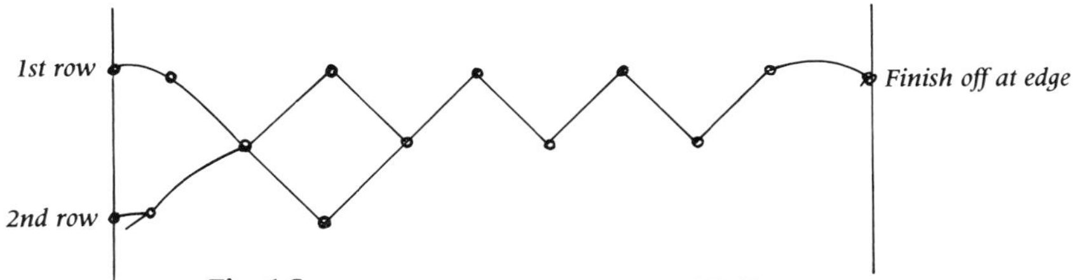

Fig. 6 STITCHING PATTERN FOR BUTTON EFFECT

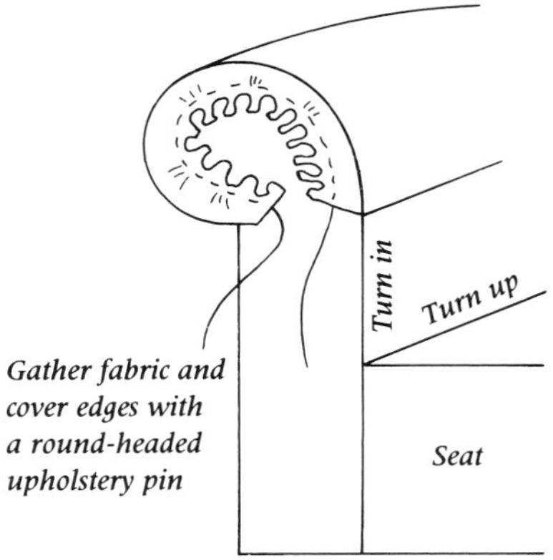

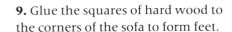

Fig. 7

7. Cut out the cushion cover pieces in fabric and wadding. Check the balsa cushion pieces for fit against the upholstered sofa, sanding off the excess if necessary. Glue the piece of wadding on the top of the cushion piece. Glue the back allowance of the fabric piece to the back of the balsa cushion, smoothing the fabric forwards over the wadding and gluing it in position under the front edge. Allow the glue to dry. Bend over the side edges, smoothing the fullness of the corners neatly and evenly around and under. Glue in place.

8. If you do not want to make a buttoned version, baste the wadding to the fabric and proceed as above. Remove all tacking stitches when the fabric pieces are glued in place.

9. Glue the squares of hard wood to the corners of the sofa to form feet.

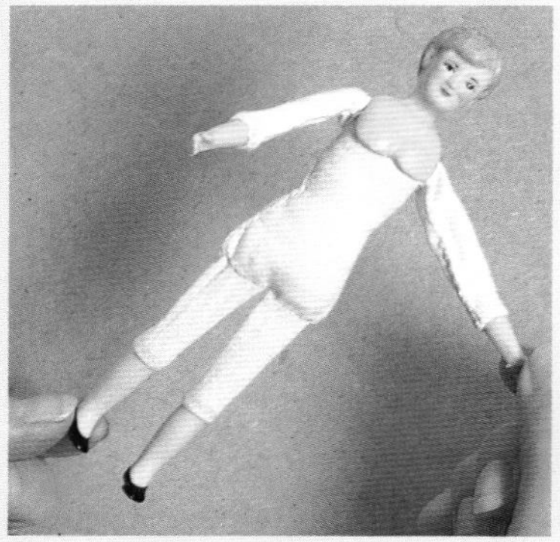

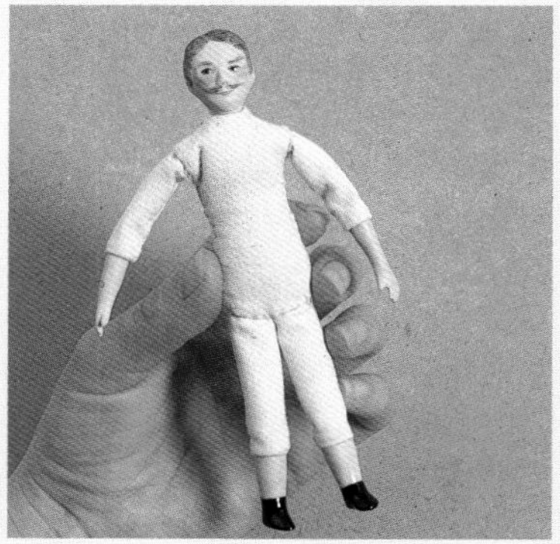

THE CORNER SHOP

DOLL'S HOUSE DOLLS

ELLEN BEDINGTON

DOLL'S HOUSE DOLLS

Miniatures depicting the human form have been found in many places and countries for centuries, and doll-making and doll-dressing have a long history. Some of the most delightful of all dolls to make and dress are the miniatures – dolls that are 15cm/6in high or less, that can be dressed to make complete families to fill doll's houses.

A doll's house doll can be dressed in any type of fabric, the decoration can be as simple or elaborate as you wish, and the dolls can be added to most collections without any fear of overcrowding. As space is often at a premium in today's smaller houses, more and more people are turning to collecting and making tiny dolls. It is an ideal way of escaping into a perfect make-believe world.

This book is designed to encourage and help you to enjoy making and dressing doll's house dolls. Each step in the assembly and making of kits and the dolls' clothes has been illustrated and clearly explained. Some short cuts are included, and there are also some do's and don'ts, garnered from many years spent teaching this enthralling subject. You will find that many of the tools and equipment you need are ordinary household items, which helps to keep this pastime within the reach of most pockets.

To enjoy the hobby of making and dressing dolls, it is important to choose your own style of doll and keep to it. The last 10 years have seen a tremendous growth in the types of dolls and costumes that are available, and even the vast range of commercially produced models available can hardly keep up with the demand for new dolls and styles of clothes.

The dolls described and dressed in this book are "artist" dolls – that is, they are dolls designed and completed by an individual. These artist's dolls differ from reproduction dolls, which are copies of antique or modern dolls and which can be purchased in kit form or made from commercial moulds. Two of the dolls described in this book have been made up from commercial kits, and two from moulds – all of them, however, have been individually dressed and wigged.

If you have a passion for detail and enjoy working with precise measurements you will find this a satisfying hobby. It also incorporates several different craft skills, which makes it additionally challenging and rewarding. It also offers the opportunity, through modelling, for you to make some unique and wholly individual dolls, but even if you do not feel sufficiently skilful (or confident) or have no wish to model with clay, you can, through the use of kits, add your own character and personality to a doll with ready-made face, arms and legs.

The dolls made and dressed in this book will suit most modern doll's houses and many antique ones. They are made to the 1:12 scale, which is the standard size.

No two makers will approach the making of doll's house dolls in exactly the same way. The instructions that follow have been designed to be as clear and straightforward as possible. However, never be afraid to change a technique or to try out something new. Put your own personality into each doll you make and remember always to make the dolls for yourself first and for other people second.

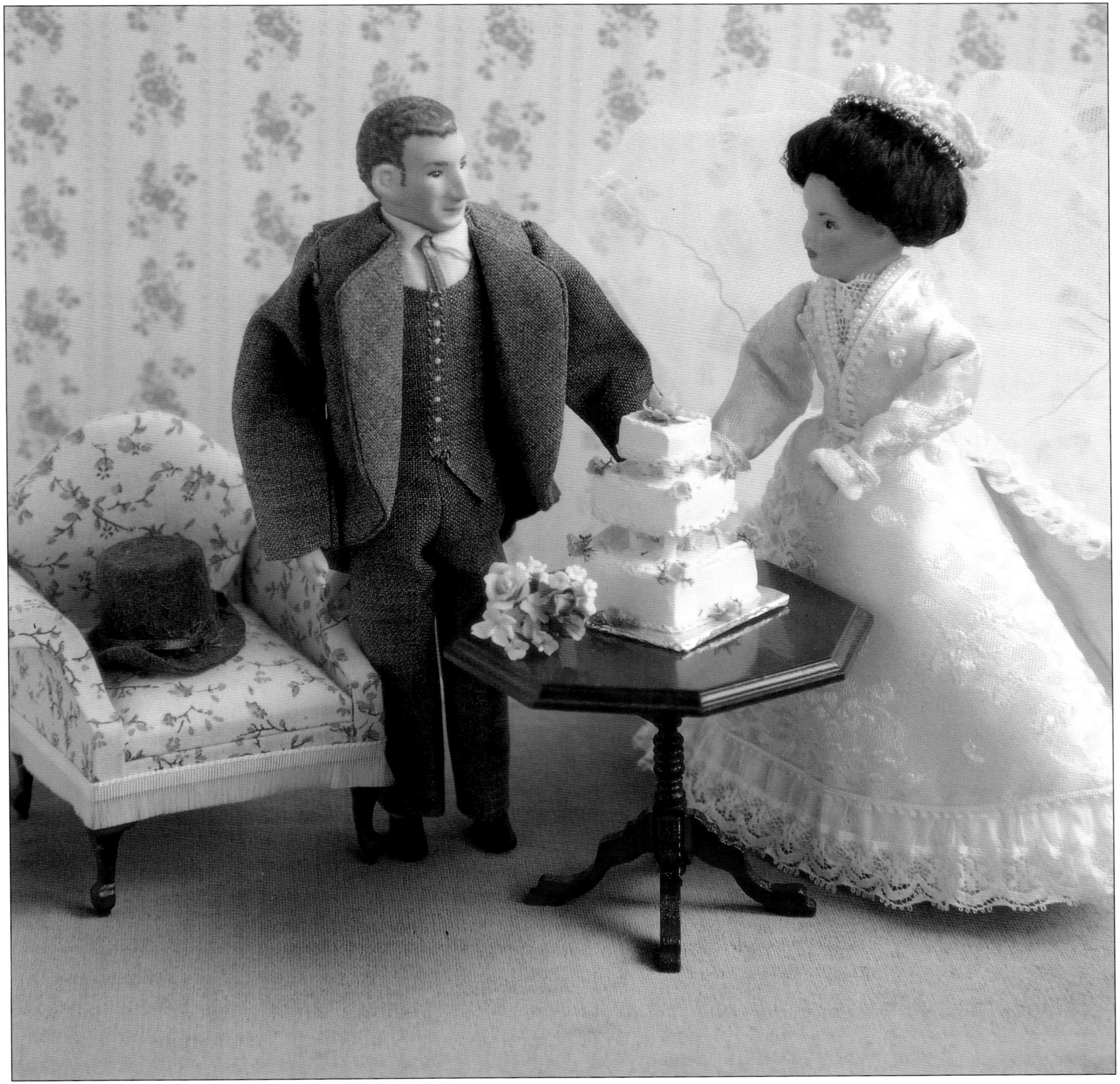

A Shoulder-plate Doll

~

The doll made from this kit has a head with an integral shoulder-plate and is complete with moulded hair. Using a doll with moulded hair eliminates the need to make a wig, and almost all antique doll's house dolls are of this type. However, you can add a wig if you wish. The body for this first kit is adapted from an original antique body. Because all that is required is to attach the arms and legs to a simple, two-piece body, it is one of the easiest dolls to understand and to put together.

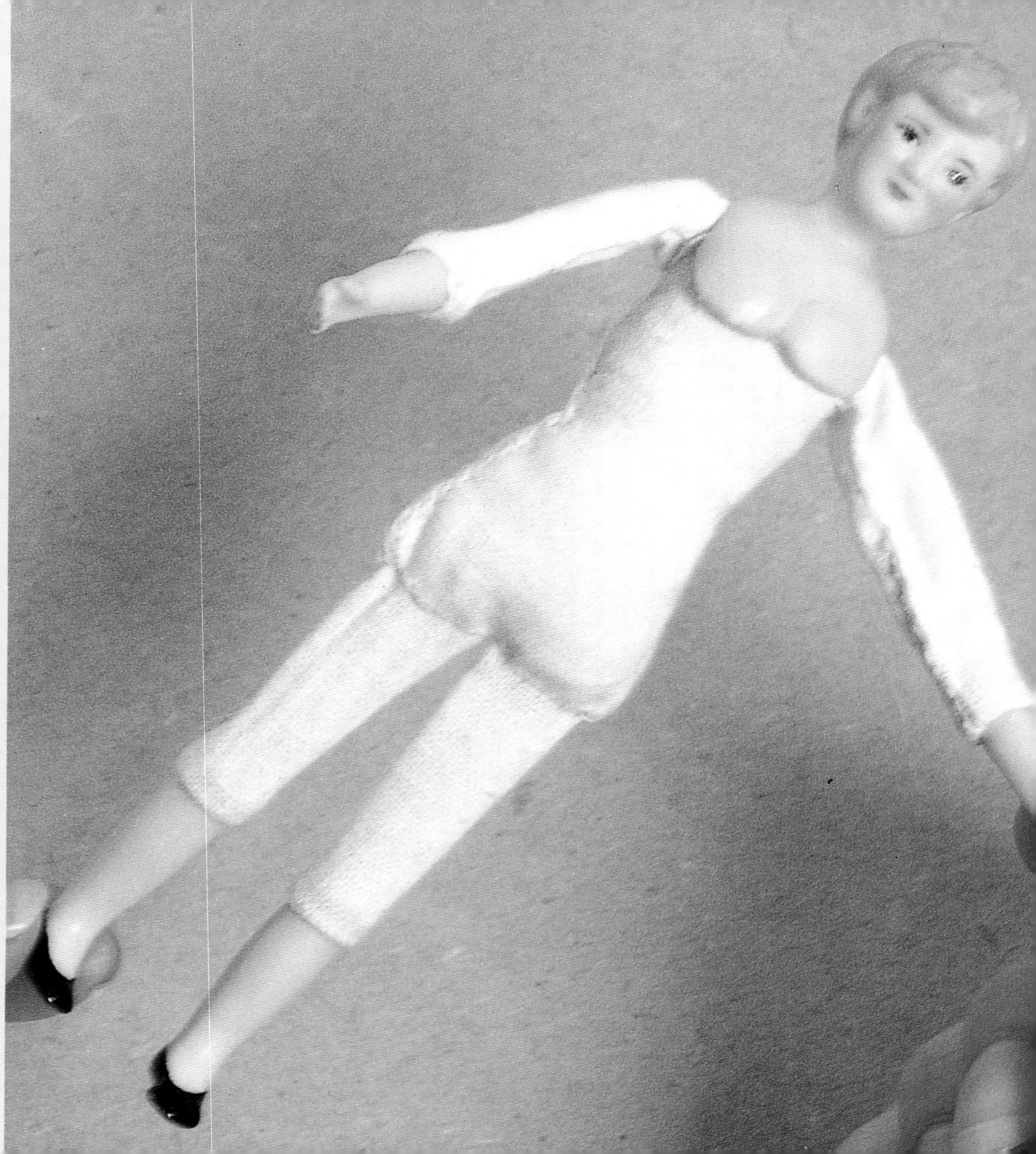

YOU WILL NEED

- Kit: painted porcelain head, lower arms and hands and lower legs and feet or shoes; the kit will usually also include the pattern for the body and pipe cleaners (6 for an adult doll, 3 for a child doll)
- Clear adhesive
- Scissors
- Tracing paper
- Pen or pencil
- 23cm/9in unbleached calico
- Needle, pins and sewing thread
- Small amount of soft white polyester stuffing
- Tweezers or small forceps

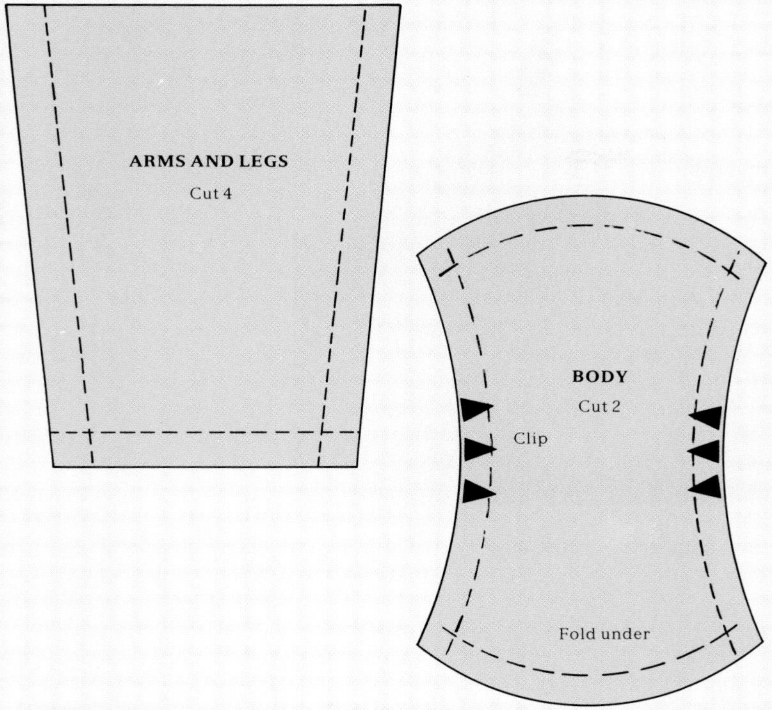

~ KITS ~

To enable you to make the shoulder-plate and flange-neck dolls to the correct size, actual size line diagrams have been included. As you make the dolls, lay the armature over the diagram to check that the finished doll will be the right height and have the correct proportions.

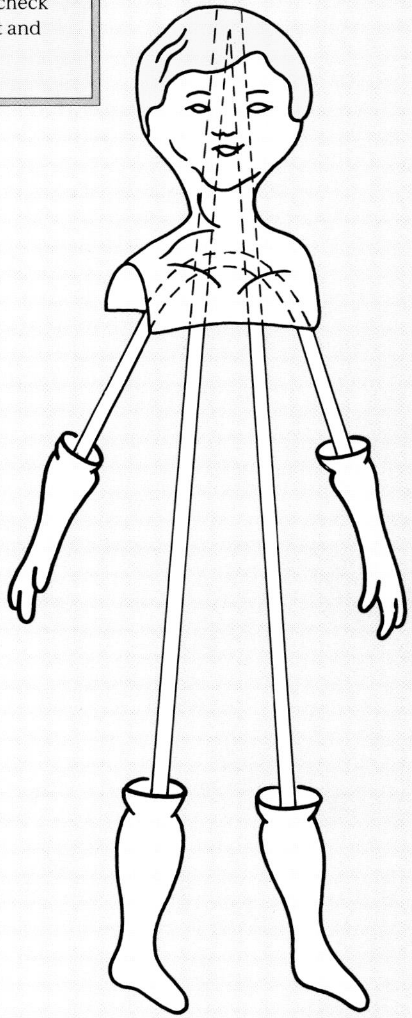

A shoulder-head doll. Note that the length of the arms from fingertip to fingertip should equal the height of the body. The wires for the leg armature pass through the shoulder-plate to the top of the head. A lady doll should be about 13cm/5¼in high.

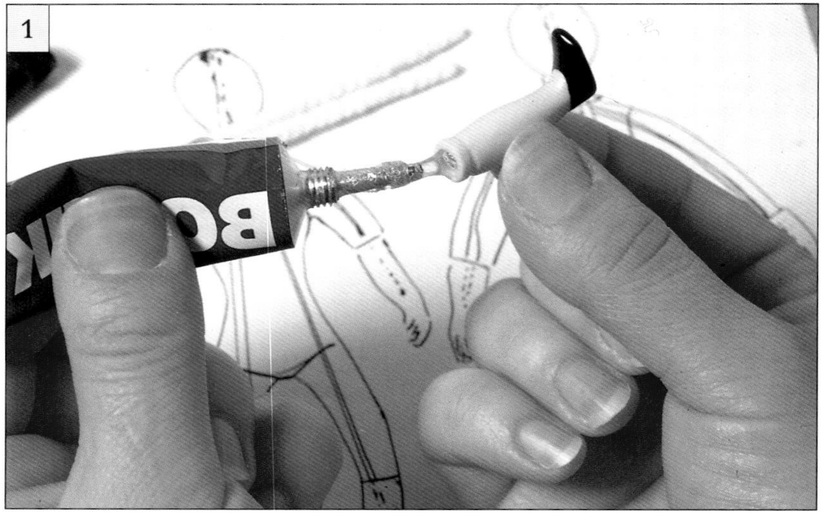

1 Glue the pipe cleaners into the legs.

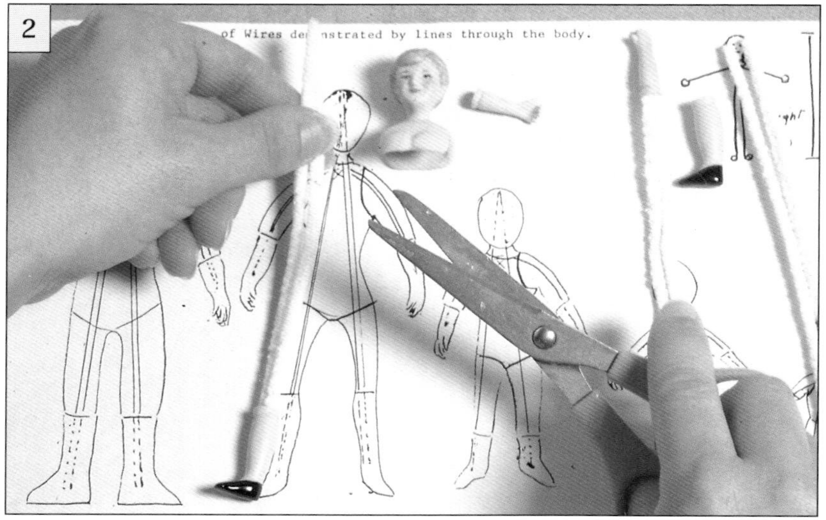

2 Lay the leg and leg armatures on top of the pattern and cut each pipe cleaner so that it reaches the top of the head. Most shoulder-plate heads have an opening through the shoulder-plate through which the armature wires can pass.

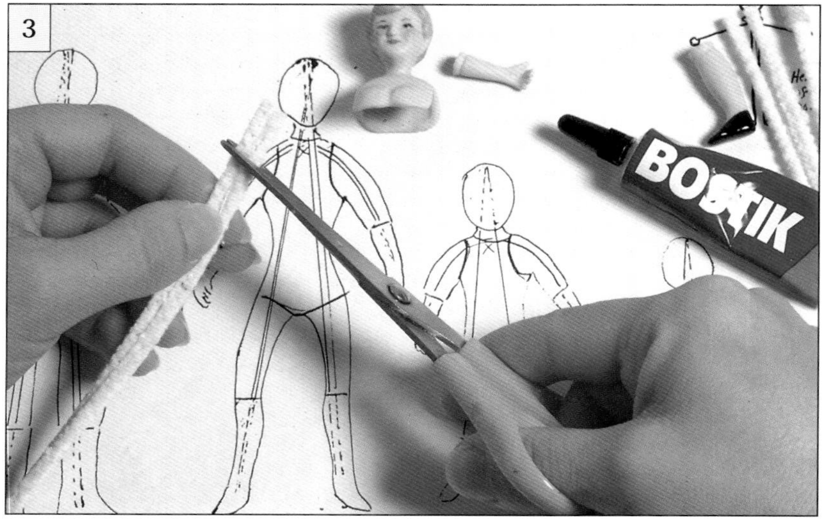

3 Glue one end of the pipe cleaners into one of the lower arm pieces and measure it against the pattern before cutting it to length. Glue the other arm piece in position. As a guide, the length of the arms from fingertip to fingertip should equal the height of the body.

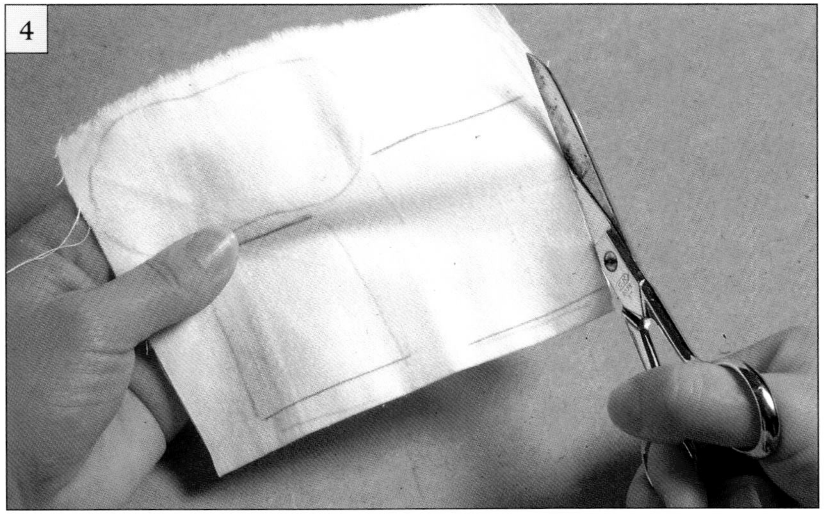

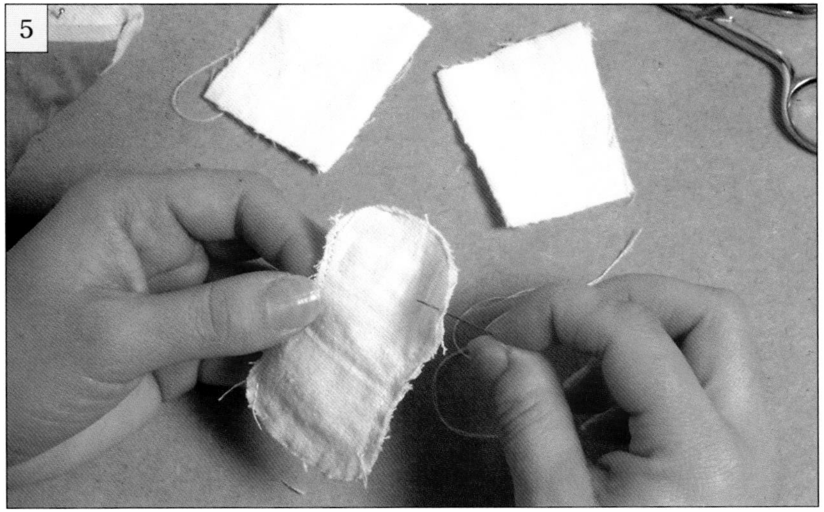

4 Trace around the templates for the body and the arms and legs and cut out two body pieces and four pieces for the arms and legs from the unbleached calico.

5 Leaving a seam allowance of 5mm/¼in, neatly stitch the two sides of the body together, leaving the top and bottom open. Clip the waist as indicated and turn to the right side.

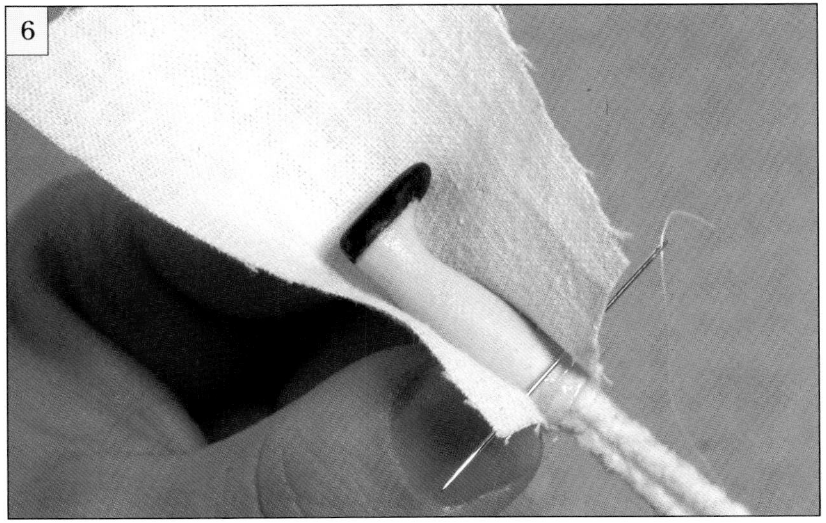

6 Make a pencil mark on the lower leg straight up from the heel to indicate where the seam will be. Put some adhesive in the groove around the top of the lower leg, place the leg on one of the cut-out leg pieces so that the fabric covers the leg, and carefully push the fabric into the groove with your thumbnail. Stitch together the part of the leg seam that is nearest to the porcelain lower leg and wind the thread around the groove three times to hold the fabric securely to the lower leg, opening out the seam allowance so that the fabric lies flat in the groove. Add a spot of adhesive to hold the thread in position. Repeat for other leg.

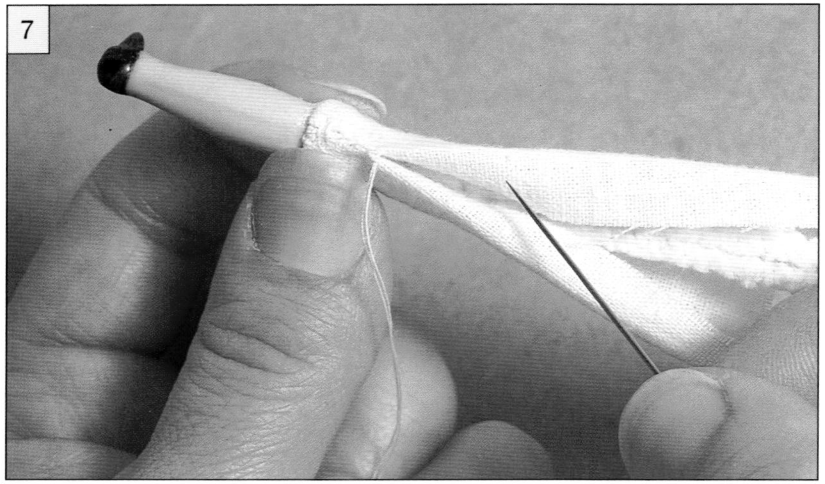

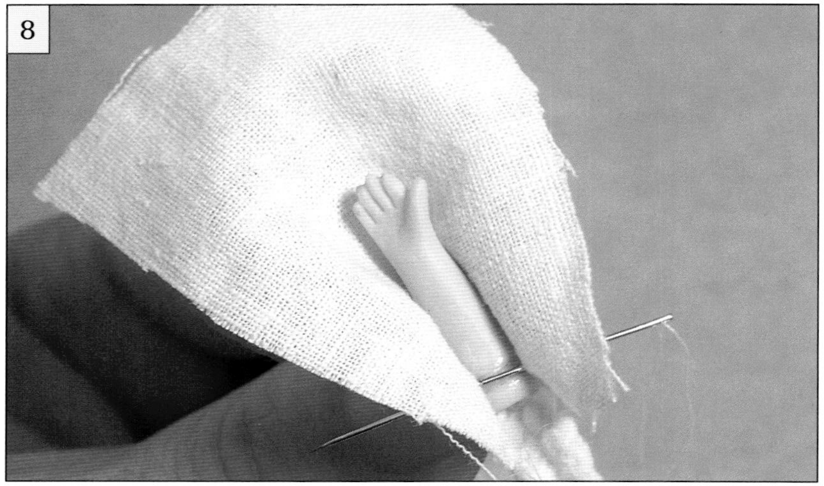

7 When the adhesive is dry, pull the fabric to cover the leg armature and neatly oversew the seam, which should run up the back of the leg in line with the heel. Stuff the leg lightly and glue the top of the fabric to the leg armature, making sure that the fabric is smooth. Repeat for the other leg.

8 Attach the fabric pieces to the lower arms in the same way, but making a pencil mark on the inside – that is, the palm side – of the arm so that you can position the seam line to run under the arms. The arms will be attached to the leg armature at the top of the shoulder-plate. Check the position of the arms on the plan. Also make sure that the arms are the same length and that when they are slightly bent the fingertips are just below the level of the hips. Place the shoulder-plate over the arms and leg armatures to double check the length and position of the arms. When you are satisfied, glue the tops of the arms to the tops of the legs.

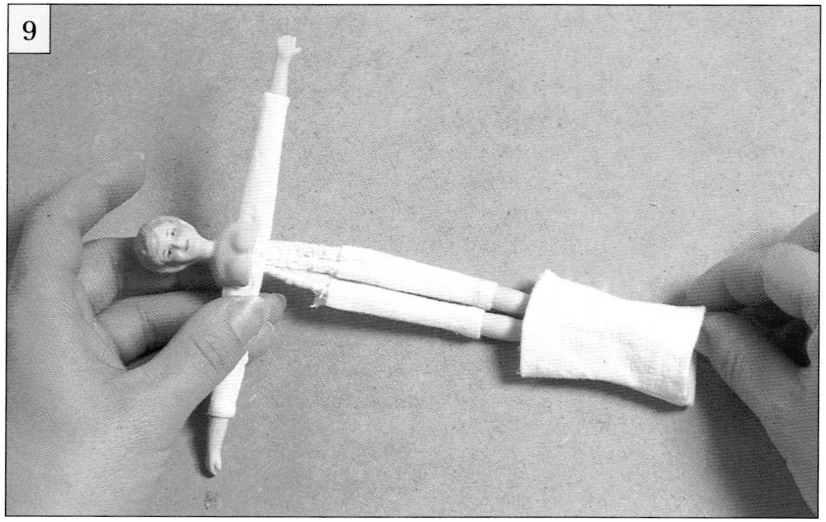

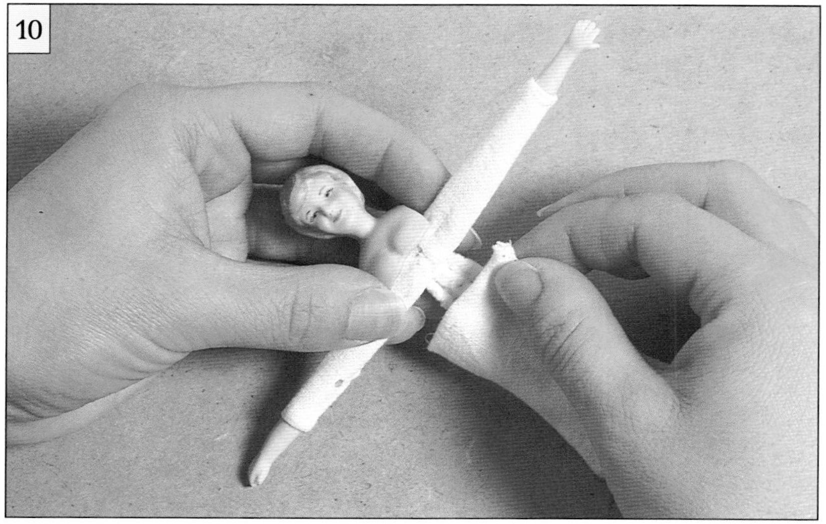

9 Push the body over the leg armatures up to the arms, checking the position against the plan.

10 With the shoulder-plate over the arms, hold the body in position at the shoulders with one or two stitches.

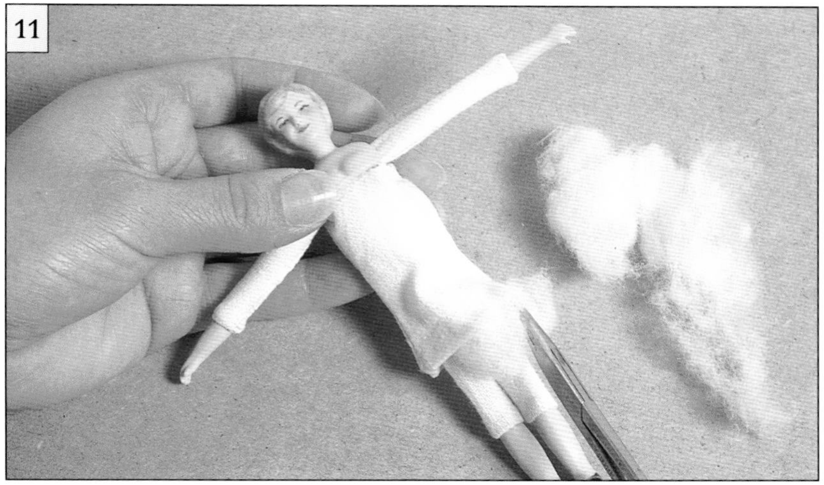

11

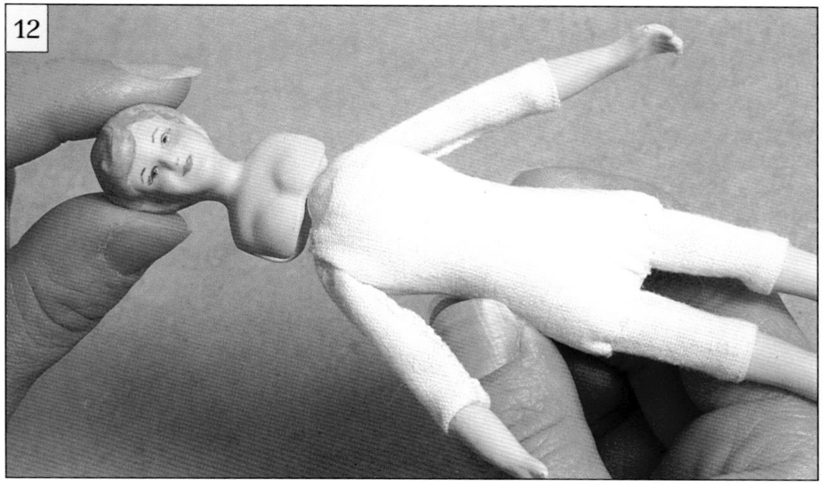

12

11 Use tweezers or small forceps to insert a small amount of polyester stuffing into the body, pushing it smoothly into the body around the front and back. Close the lower end of the body seam, turning in the seam allowance of 5mm/¼in and sewing across the legs.

12 Check again that the shoulder-plate will fit snugly over the shoulders and top of the body. If the shoulder-plate will not fit or if the body is longer than indicated on the plan, remove a small amount of stuffing and increase the size of the seam allowance at the top of the body. Oversew the top seam of the body. When you are satisfied, glue the shoulder-plate into position, pushing it well down over body.

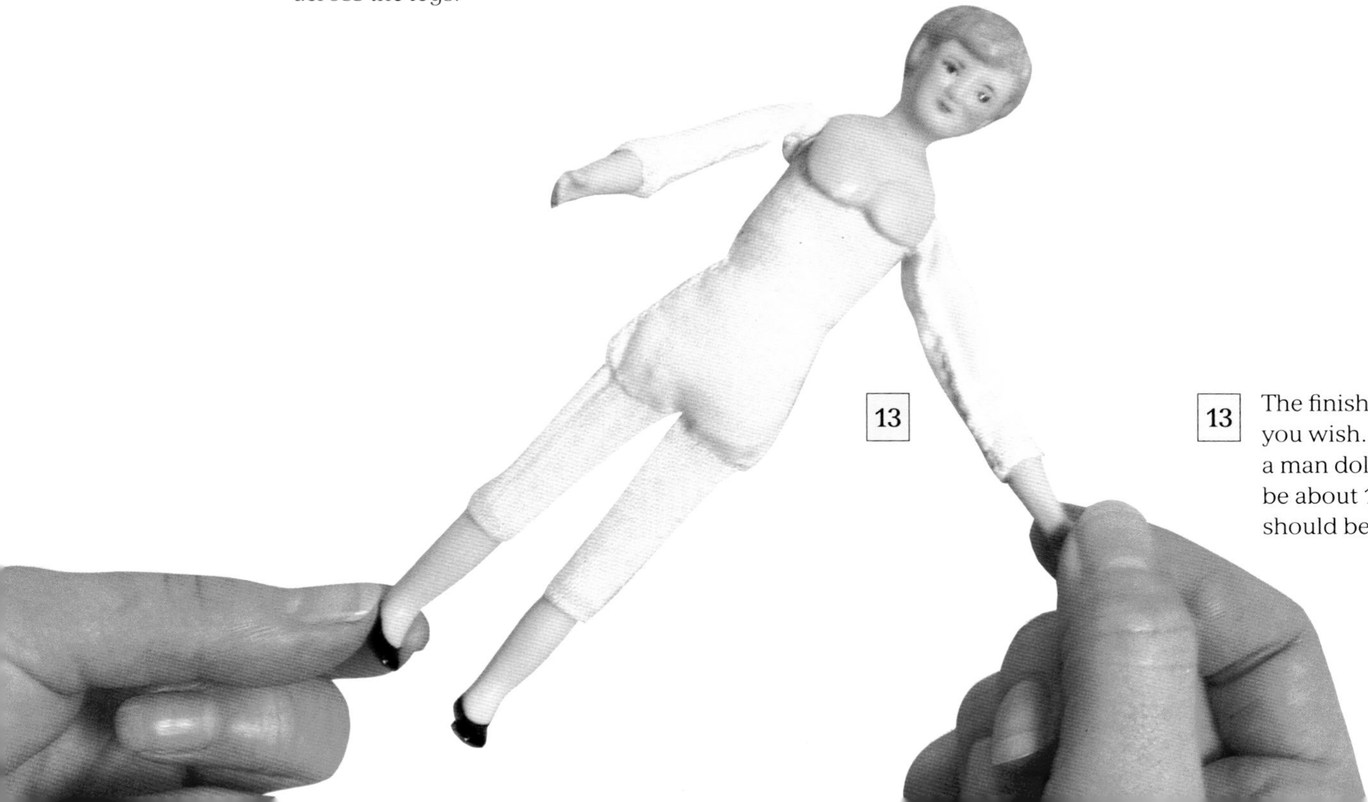

13

13 The finished doll is ready to be dressed as you wish. The kit can also be used to make a man doll. If you do this, the legs should be about 1cm/½in longer and the body should be a little fatter.

~ MAKING A MOHAIR WIG ~

The doll in the kit has moulded and painted hair. If you want to dress her as a Victorian lady or if a doll does not have moulded hair, you can either buy a ready-made wig with ringlets or make one yourself.

YOU WILL NEED

- Mohair or wool crepe for hair
- Plastic film
- Rubber band
- Clear adhesive
- Sewing thread to match mohair
- Hair setting lotion
- 2mm/00 knitting needle
- Scissors
- Tweezers or forceps

1 Gently brush the mohair, holding it down with one hand. Keep any loose hairs to one side.

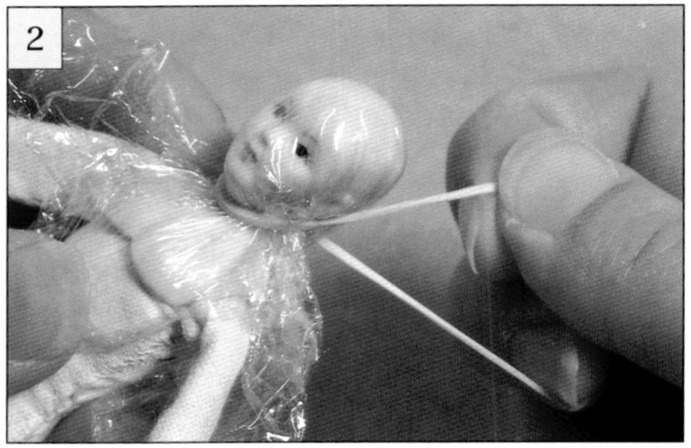

2 Cover the doll's head with a small piece of plastic film, holding it in position with a rubber band around the doll's neck.

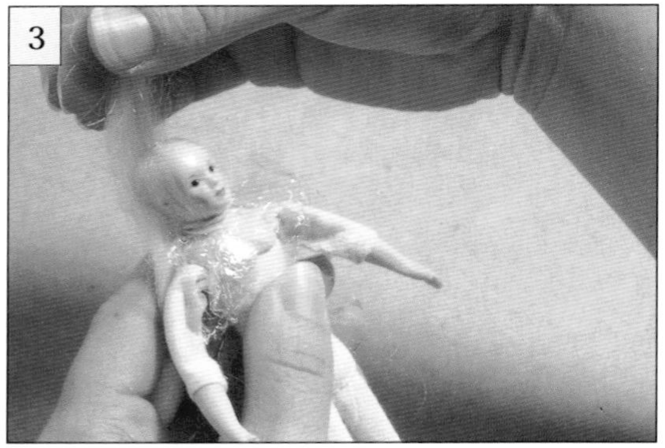

3 Put a thin layer of adhesive over the hair area of the plastic film, taking care to keep it within what will be the doll's hairline. Put some hair on the adhesive, placing it on the top of the head and taking it up and around the head to the back. Repeat the process if necessary.

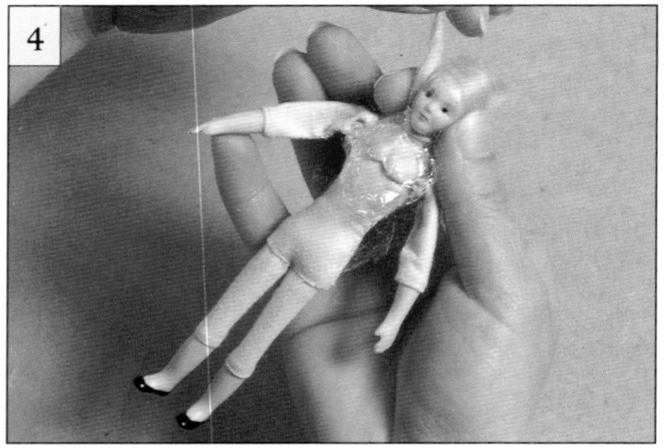

4 Twist the hair on top of the head and hold it in position with some matching sewing thread.

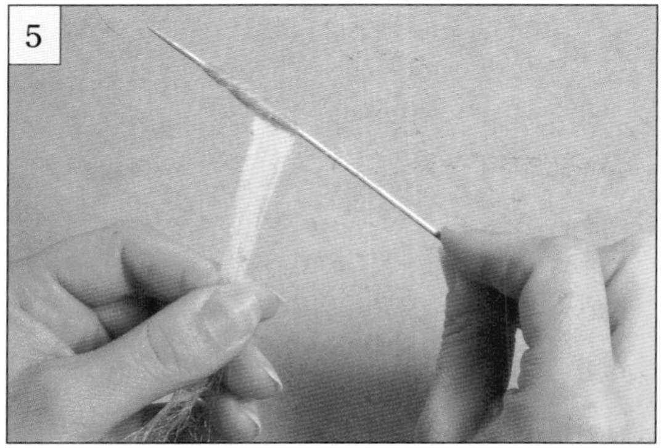

5 Take the loose pieces of mohair, dampen them with a little setting lotion and wind them tightly around a 2mm/00 knitting needle. Leave to dry, slip off the knitting needle and cut into 1cm/½in lengths to make ringlets. You will need eight ringlets in all.

6 Put spots of adhesive on the side of the wig and use tweezers or forceps to position the ringlets, so that there are four symmetrical ringlets at each side.

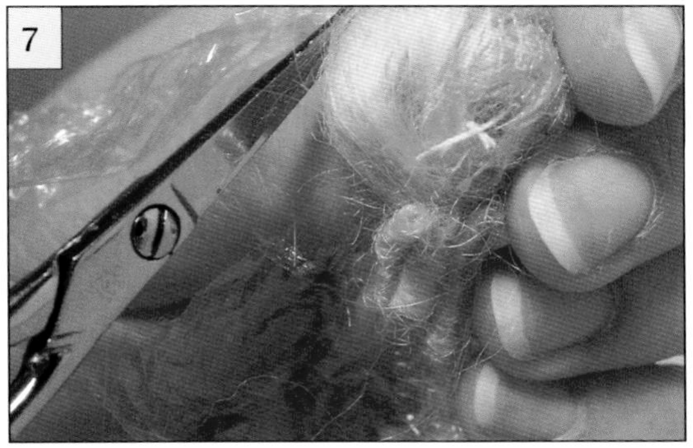

7 Remove the rubber band and peel off the plastic film with the mohair attached. Cut off the spare plastic film.

8 Trim the plastic film neatly to the hairline. Cover the head with a thin layer of adhesive and place the wig on the head, folding any visible pieces of plastic film neatly under the wig.

9 The finished wig.

A Flange-neck Doll

~

THIS FLANGE-NECK DOLL'S HOUSE DOLL CAN BE MADE FROM ONE OF THE KITS THAT ARE AVAILABLE FROM SOME CRAFT SHOPS. THE BODY WAS DESIGNED SPECIALLY TO ALLOW THE HEAD TO ROTATE, AND ALTHOUGH IT IS A LITTLE MORE COMPLICATED THAN THE SHOULDER-PLATE DOLL, IT IS WELL WORTH THE EFFORT TO MAKE.

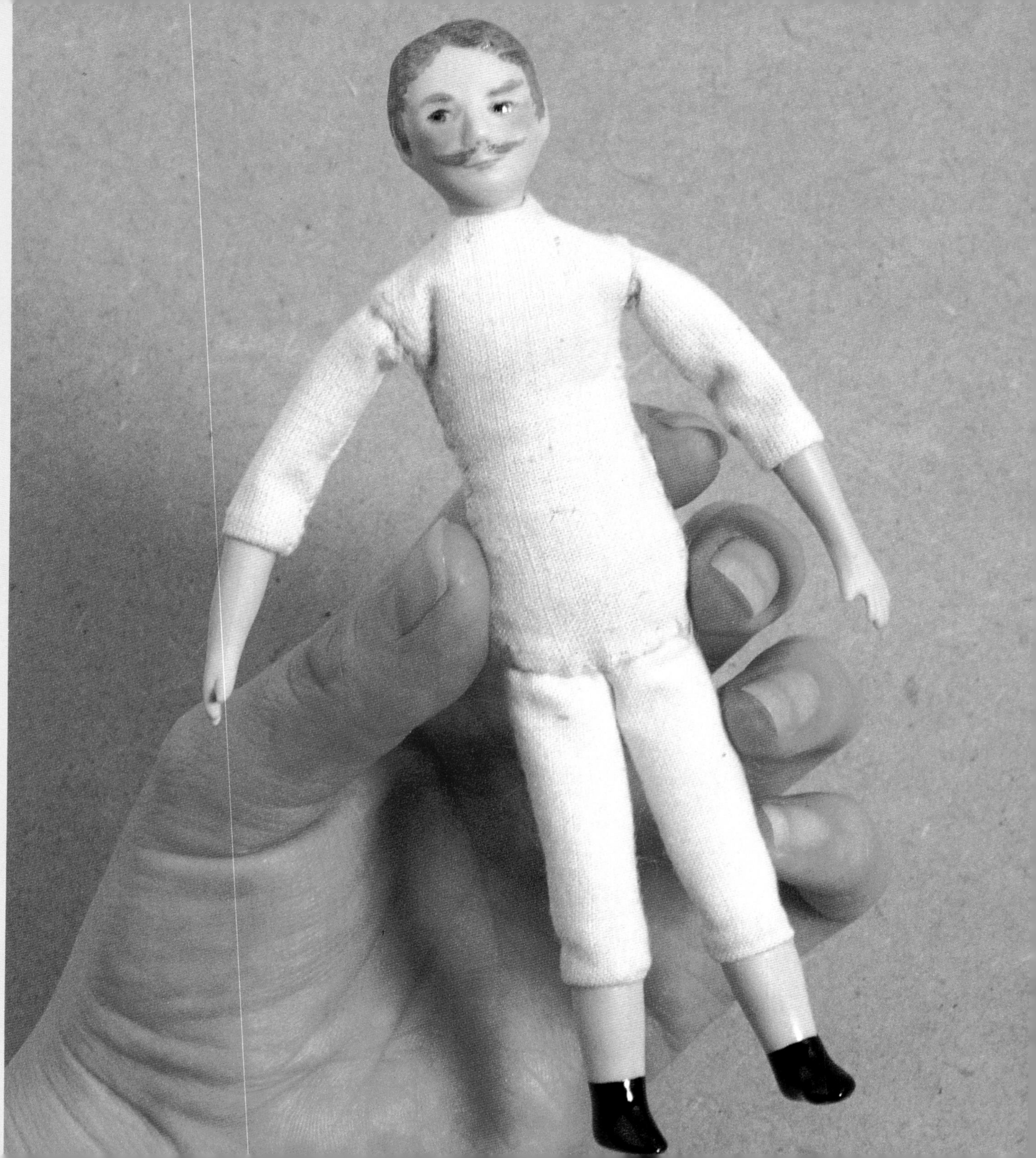

YOU WILL NEED

- Kit: painted porcelain head, lower arms and hands and lower legs and feet or shoes; the kit will usually also include the pattern for the body and pipe cleaners (6 for an adult doll, 3 for a child doll)
- Clear adhesive
- Scissors
- Tracing paper
- Pen or pencil
- 23cm/9in unbleached calico
- Needles, pins and sewing thread
- Small amount of soft white polyester stuffing
- Tweezers or small forceps

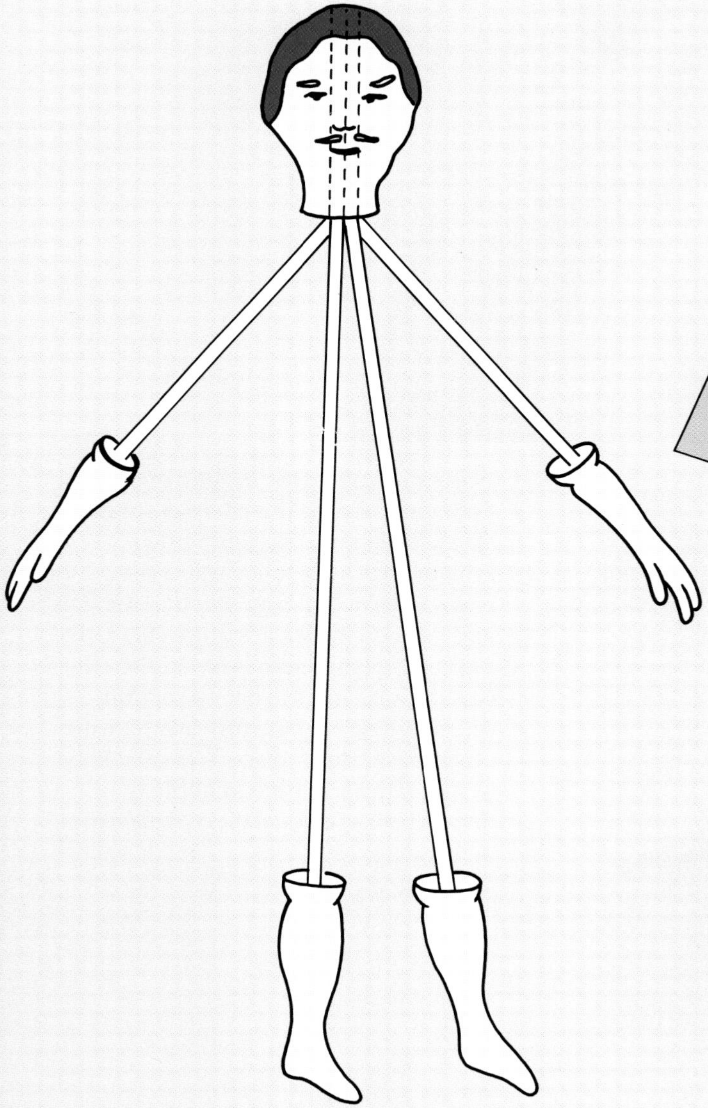

A flange-neck doll. The wires for the arm and leg armatures should be trimmed level with the top of the head. A man doll should be about 14cm/5¾in high.

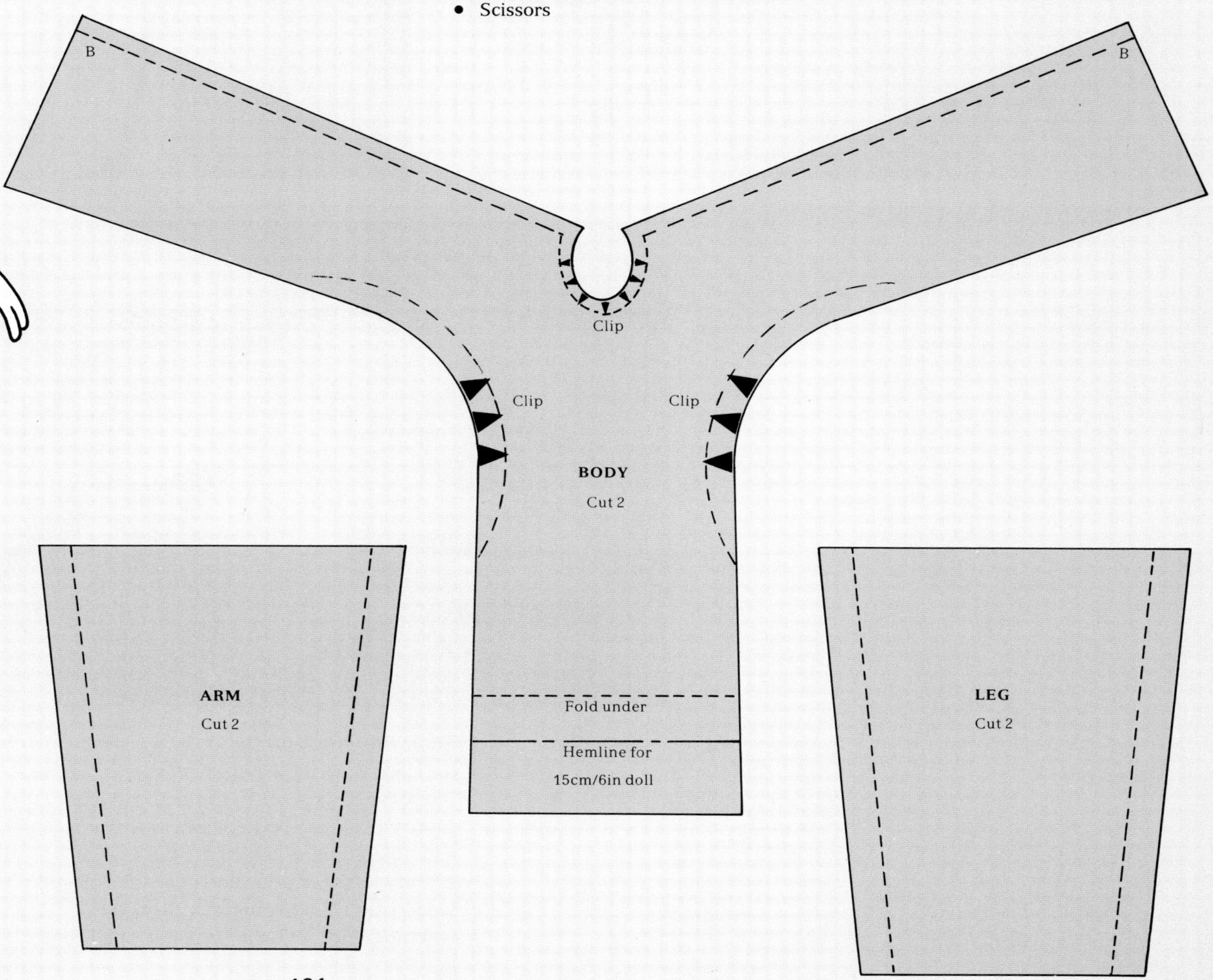

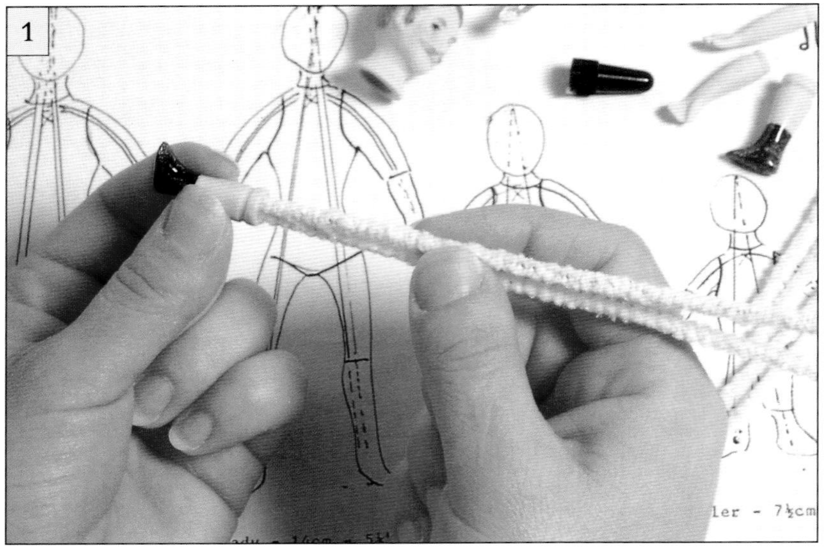

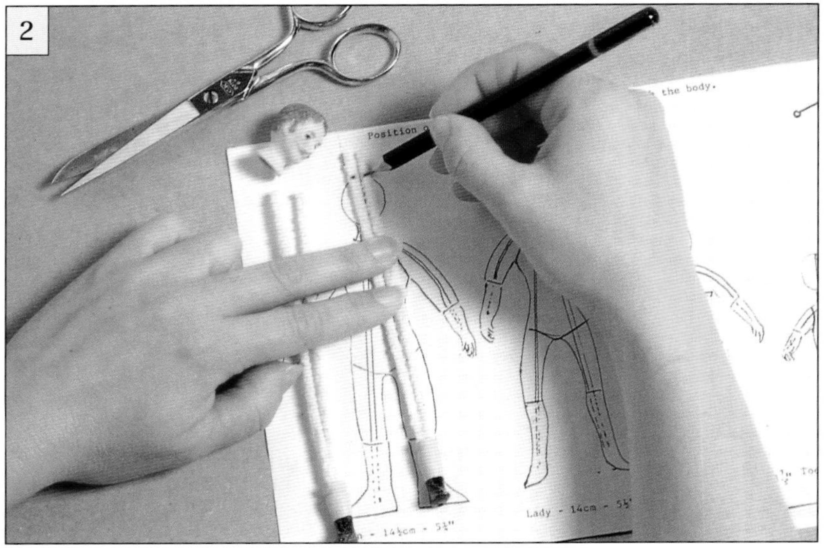

1 Glue pipe cleaners into the lower legs.

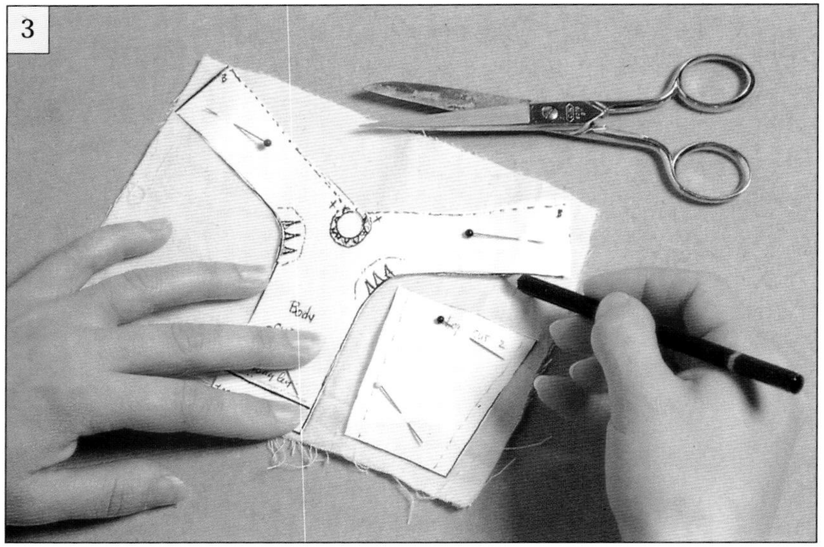

2 Place the head on the top end of the leg armatures and lay them on the pattern to check the length, marking the leg armatures at a point just below the bottom edge of the neck flange. Remove the head and mark on the leg armatures the top of the head, trimming them to this length. Glue pipe cleaners to one lower arm, measure it against the plan and glue the other lower arm in place. As a guide, the length of the arm from fingertip to fingertip should equal the overall height of the body.

3 Trace the templates for the body, arms and legs. Cut out two body pieces (one is a lining) and two each of the arm and leg pieces. Place the body pieces together, and stitch up one side of the back seam, around the neck edge and down the other back seam. Clip the neck curve to the stitching line and turn right side out. Press lightly.

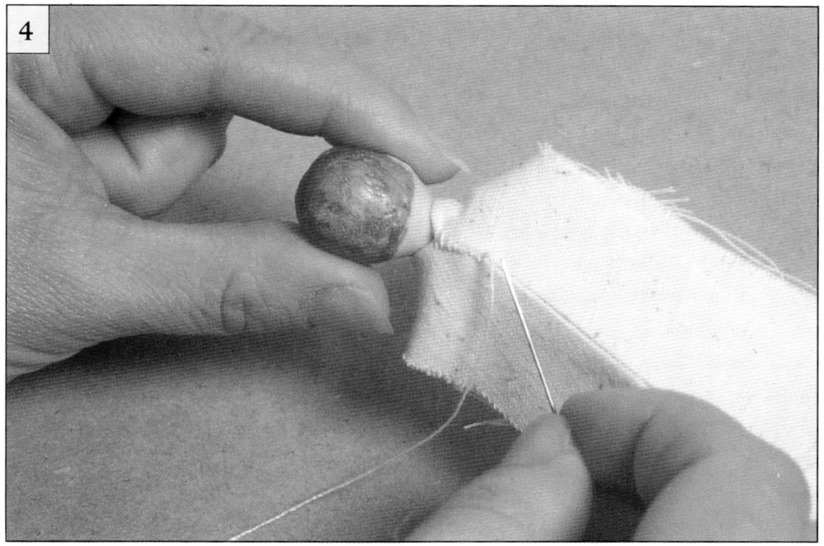

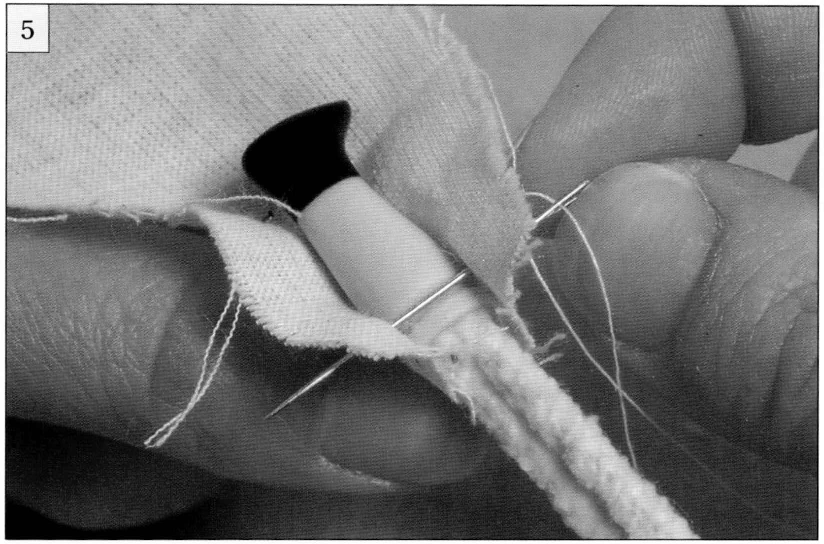

4 Stitch the neck around the flange of the neck, pulling it tight so that the neck will turn but will not fall out, then neatly oversew the back seam.

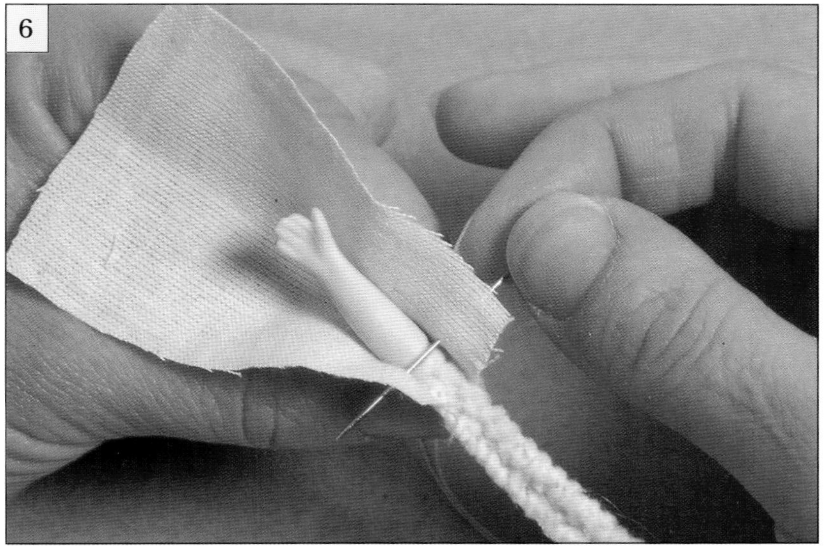

5 Mark a point on the legs with a pencil dot in line with the heel. Run some adhesive in the groove at the top of the leg and fold the fabric around the leg, using a thumbnail to push the fabric into the groove. Make sure that the seam is in line with the mark. Stitch through the seam and turn the fabric back. Wind the thread around the groove three times, fasten it off at the seam edge and finish it off with a dot of adhesive. Leave the adhesive to dry. Pull the fabric up over the leg armatures and oversew the leg seam neatly. Lightly stuff the leg, then pull the fabric up smoothly and glue it to the armature. Repeat for the other leg.

6 Mark the porcelain arm in line with the palm to indicate the position of the underarm seam. Run some adhesive into the groove in the arm and use your thumbnail to push the arm piece fabric into the groove, making sure that the seam remains in line with the dot. Stitch through the seam and turn the seam allowance back. Wind the thread around the groove three times, fasten it off at the seam edge and finish it off with a spot of adhesive. When the adhesive is dry, pull the fabric up over the arm and oversew the underarm neatly. Stuff the arm lightly and glue the fabric to the arm pipe cleaners, making sure that it is perfectly smooth. Repeat for the other arm.

7

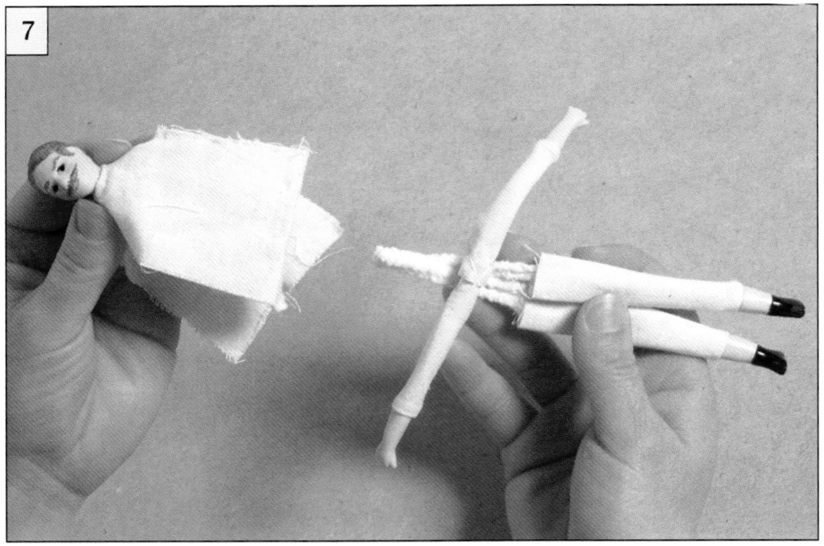

8

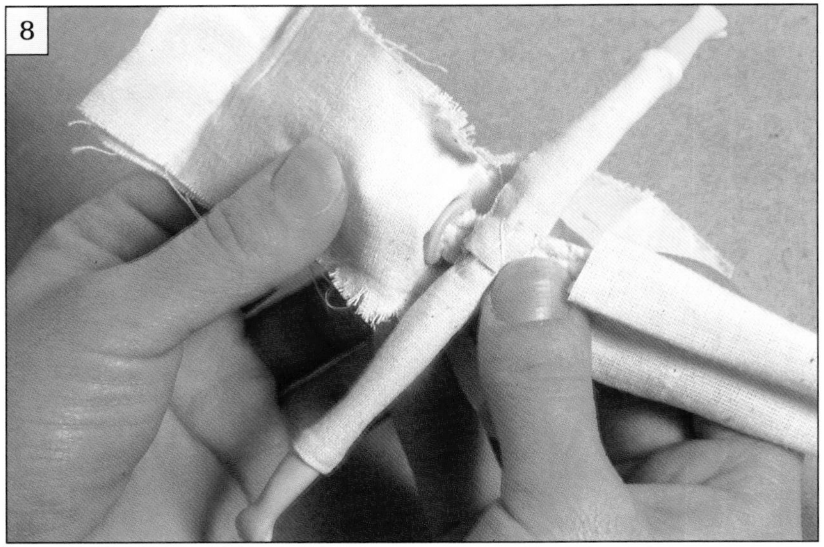

7 Glue the arms to the leg armature at the point marked for the bottom of the neck flange. Do not glue the neck flange, or the head will not move. Place the body with the head attached on the leg armature. The rim of the neck flange should rest on the wire of the arms.

8 Pull the body and head over the leg armature, pulling the body firmly down over the legs and pinning it in position. Make sure that the head is straight. Clip and turn under the shoulders, stitching them neatly to the arms. Use tweezers or small forceps to insert a little padding into the body, smoothing it evenly around front and back. Stitch the bottom seam over the legs, turning under the bottom seam allowance.

9

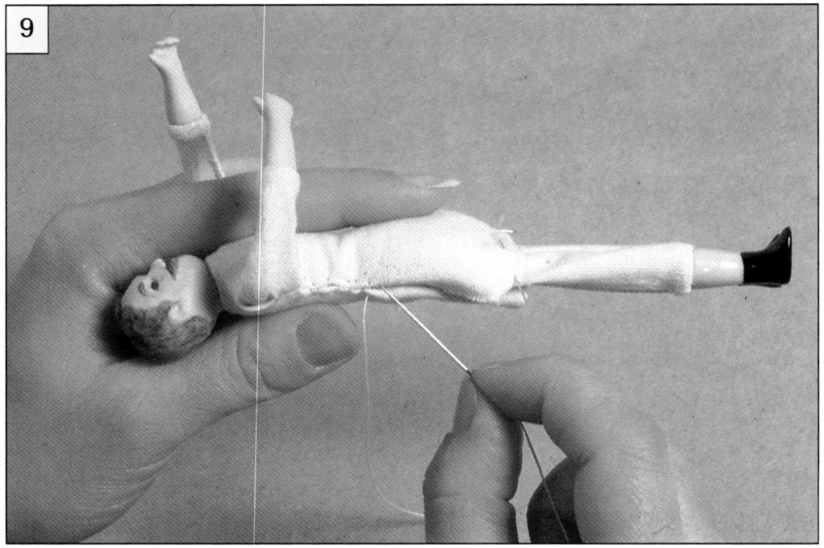

10

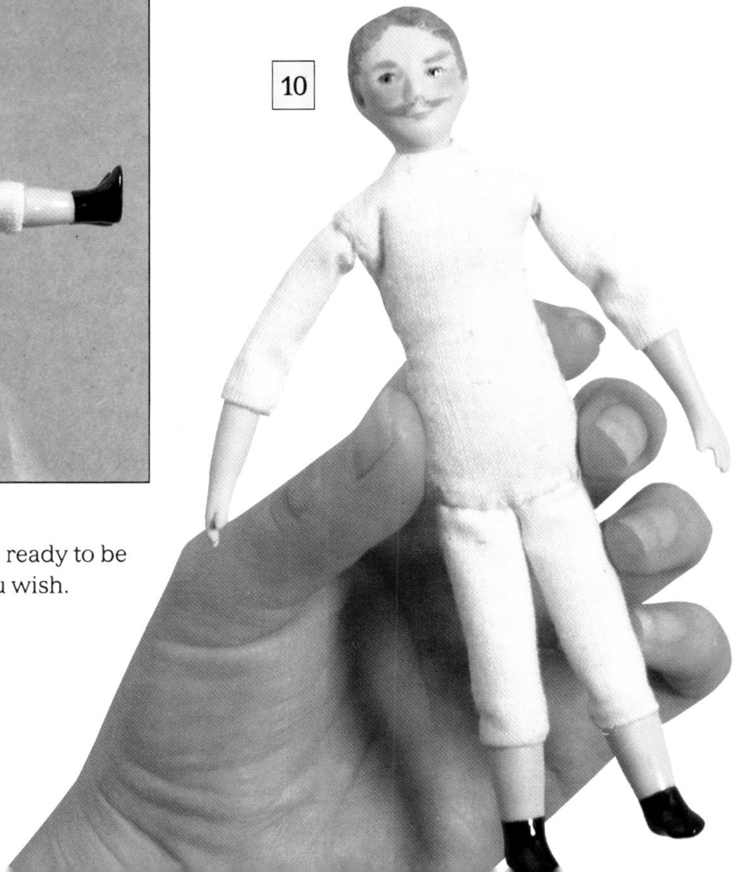

9 Pin the sides together, checking again that the head is straight. Add or take out stuffing if necessary, then carefully oversew the side seams. It will be easier to make sure that the head and body remain straight if you thread needles and sew down alternate sides for a short distance. Pull in the waist if you want a slimmer doll.

10 The finished man doll is now ready to be dressed in whatever way you wish.

Using a Mould

~

Several styles of mould are available for making dolls, but we have chosen another shoulder-plate doll. Using a mould offers opportunities to alter the facial details and the hands, and it is, therefore, one of the best ways of making a doll that is individual and, perhaps, performing a specific task.

The head of this shoulder-plate doll is bald, but you can make a wig as described on page 188.

After a kiln, the moulds are the most expensive items needed by a doll-maker. They are made from superfine plaster of Paris, which absorbs the water from the clay, and they are available from some dolls shops and from hobby ceramic suppliers. When you make doll's house dolls the slip (liquid clay) is left in the mould for only a minute at the most, then the surplus is poured out. The thickness of the cast in the mould is determined by the length of time the slip is left in the mould before decanting. If the slip is decanted after about a minute, the cast will be sufficiently thick to be handled when it is removed from the mould after about 20 minutes. Remember that every time you use a mould you are wearing it out a little, although you should get between 20 and 30 heads from a good mould.

YOU WILL NEED

- Moulds for head, arms and legs
- Large, soft brush
- Rubber bands
- Plastic tray 23 × 30cm/9 × 12in
- Commercially prepared slip (liquid porcelain) for doll's house dolls
- Boiled water
- Large, clean jug
- Wooden spoon
- Timer
- Paintbrushes (nos. 0000, 000, 00 and 1)
- Tissues
- Scalpel or craft knife
- Sharp pencil or cocktail sticks
- Underglaze paints and gloss paints
- Fine sandpaper
- Old nylon stockings or tights
- Kiln

~ PREPARING SLIP ~

Slip is liquid clay, and it is sold in 4.5 litre/1 gallon plastic containers by many doll suppliers and some potteries. There are several colours to choose from, and the quality is consistently good. It also has a long shelf-life. To prepare slip for making heads, arms and legs for doll's house dolls, you must make sure that all the containers you are going to use are scrupulously clean.

Empty the slip from its container into a bucket and mix it with a wooden spoon or with your hands. If you use your hands, wear rubber gloves, because the clay will make your skin very dry. Fasten two thicknesses of muslin or old nylon stocking or tights over the top of the original container and pour the mixed slip back. Leave to stand for an hour so that any air bubbles rise to the surface. The slip is then ready to be used.

When you have poured off the quantity you need, always clean the top of the container with a damp cloth and close it tightly. Slip dries very quickly, and if any bits are left on the rim they may fall into the clay and cause lumps or holes in the heads, arms or legs you make. Dried clay around the rim will also make it difficult to unscrew the lid next time. If this happens, try knocking the container sharply with a hammer, which should loosen the clay and allow you to unscrew the lid.

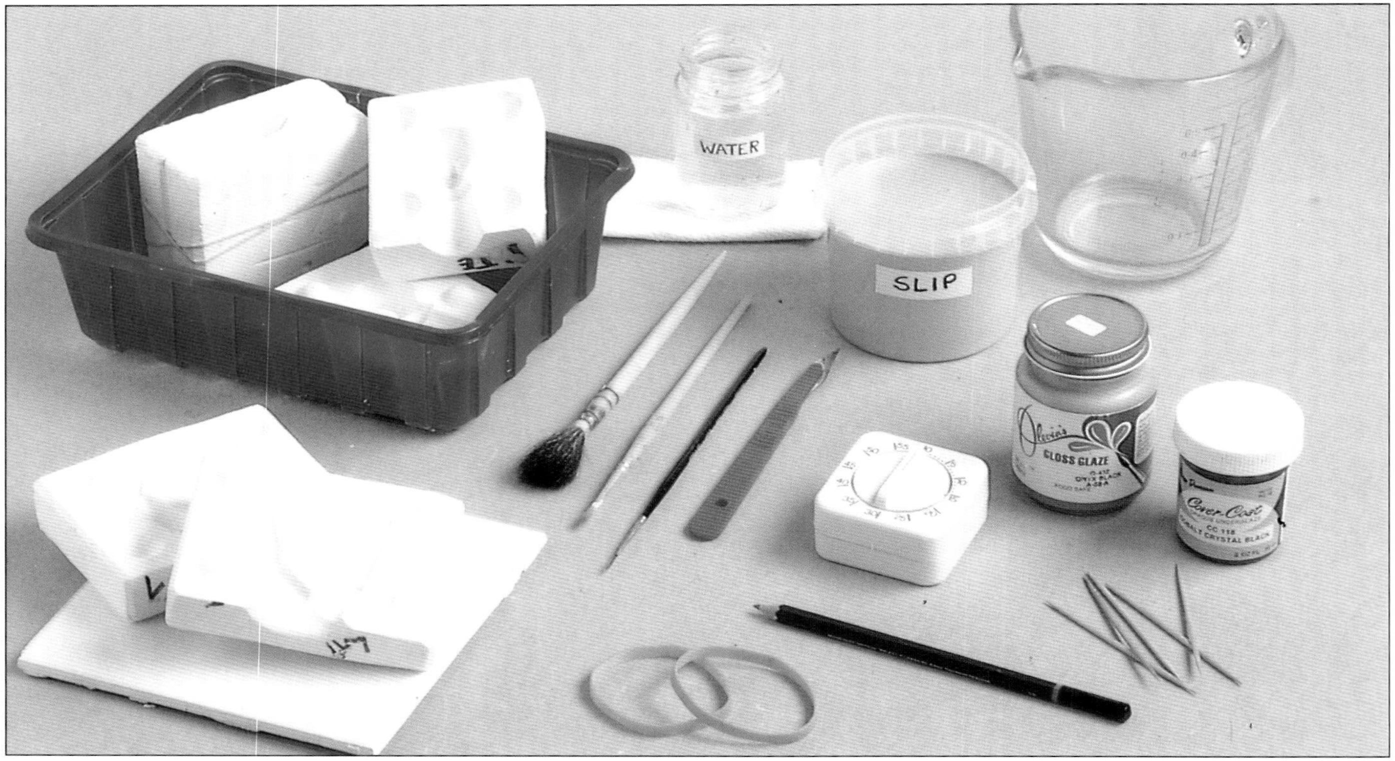

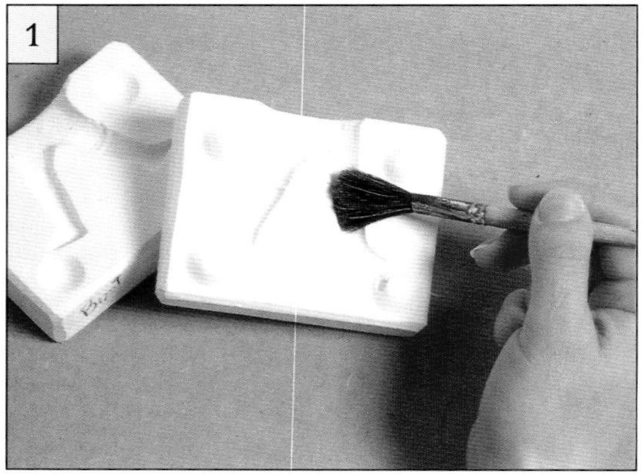

1 Clean out the moulds with a soft brush. Never use a sharp tool because plaster of Paris marks easily, and all castings will show the mark, spoiling that part of all dolls you subsequently make from that mould.

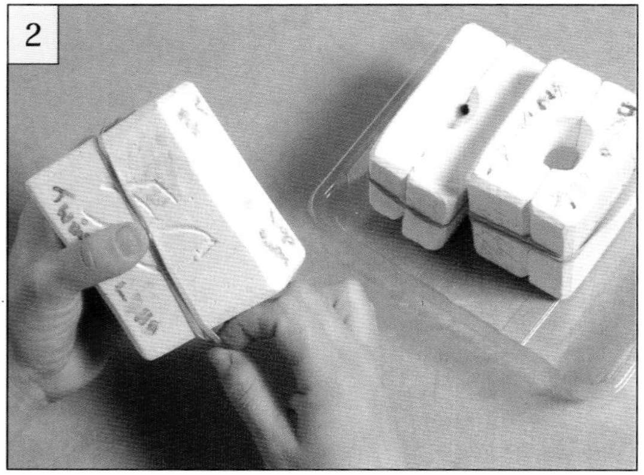

2 Hold the two halves of the mould firmly together with rubber bands and place it upright on a tray.

3

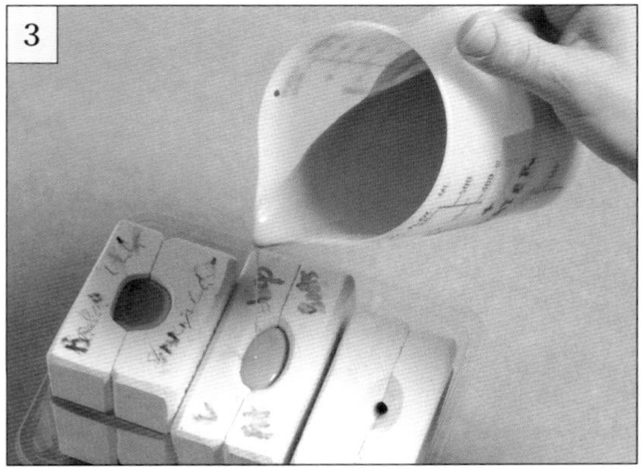

3 Pour 500ml/1 pint of prepared slip into a jug and add 60ml/2fl oz of boiled water. Mix thoroughly with a wooden spoon. Hold the jug fairly high and start to pour the slip in a very thin stream. At first you should aim for the edge of the tray, then, without stopping, move the jug across the moulds to fill each one. Do not pause and do not worry about the small amount of clay on the tray on the outside of the moulds. Try to aim the stream of slip down one side of the holes in the top of the moulds so that the air can escape.

4

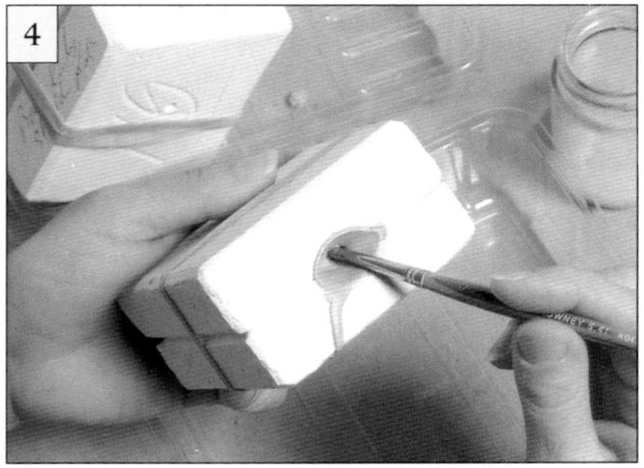

4 Leave the moulds to stand for 1 minute. Decant the moulds, beginning with the arms, then the legs, finally the head. Always decant the arms and hands first because the parts are so tiny that they dry out quickly. The decanted slip can be discarded. Leave the moulds to drain on the tray for 15–20 minutes, propping them up against the edge of the tray. Check that the pour holes in the arms and legs are clear.

5

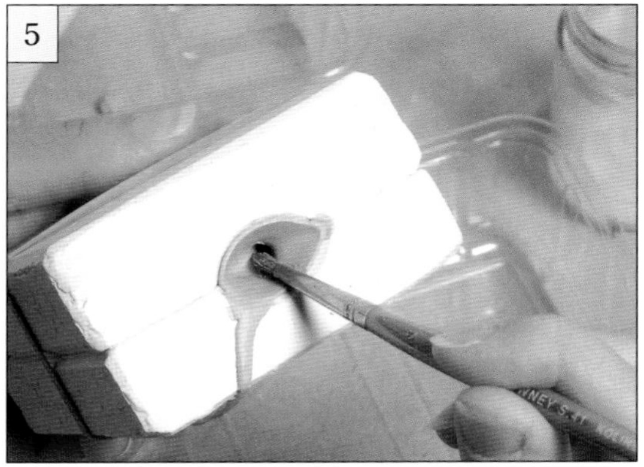

5 If the pour holes are blocked, use a no. 00 paintbrush, dipped into clean water and touch dried on a piece of tissue, to open the hole, working with a circular movement and pushing the clay away from the pour hole towards the centre. This has to be done because the pipe cleaners used for the armature are inserted through these holes.

6 Carefully remove the top part of the moulds. To separate the mould, place the bottom flat on the working surface, remove the rubber bands and hold the upper portion between the palms of your hands. Gently lift the top part away, making sure you lift it straight up so that you do not pull the casting out of shape. Never leave a cast piece in a mould for more than 45 minutes after decanting.

6

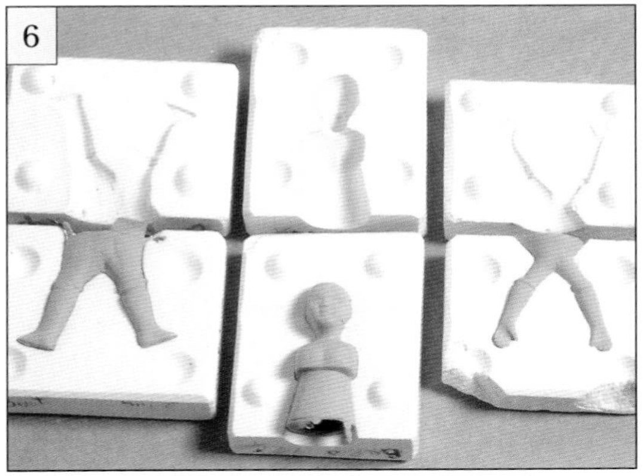

7

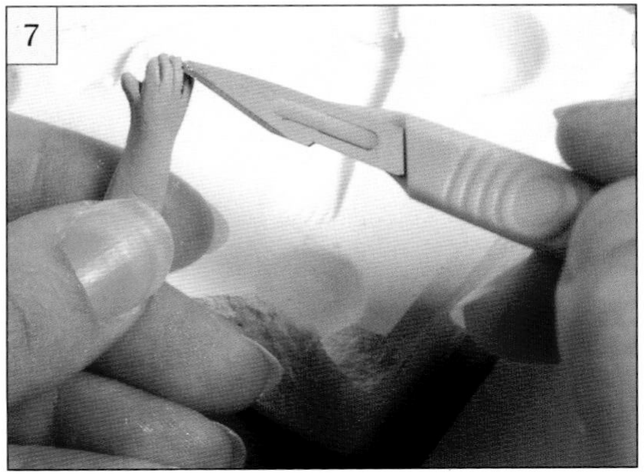

7 Carefully remove the arms from the mould. When you remove greenware from a mould, always hold the sides. If you use the pour hole you may distort the shape and it may then split when it is fired. Cut off the waste clay above the groove and clean the flash lines. Cut down between the fingers with a scalpel or craft knife. Carefully clean between the fingers with a wet paint-brush. Check that the groove around the top of the arm is sufficiently defined to hold the arm fabric in place.

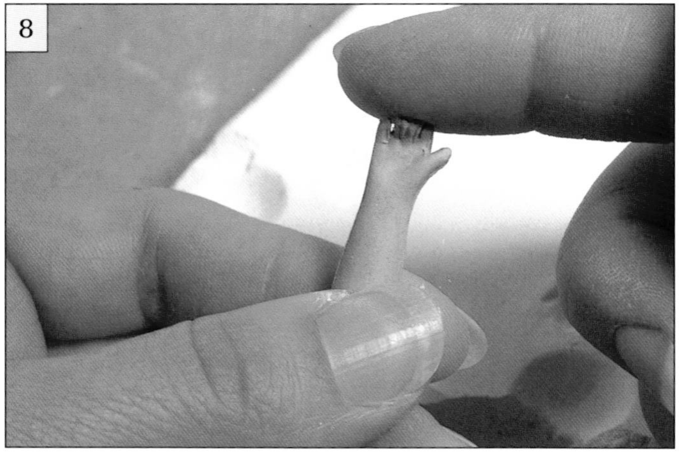

8 Delicately bend the fingers over slightly – use the handle of a paintbrush to stop them curling too far. If a finger breaks off, use a little slip to "glue" it back on. Repeat with the other hand and leave them on one side to dry.

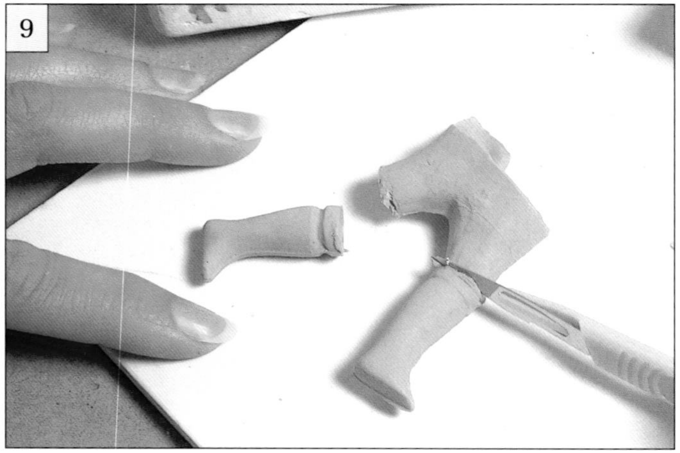

9 Remove the legs from the mould, cut away the waste clay and clean the flash lines. Hold the legs upright with the feet on a perfectly flat surface. If the legs need to be moved backwards or forwards a little, now is the time to do this.

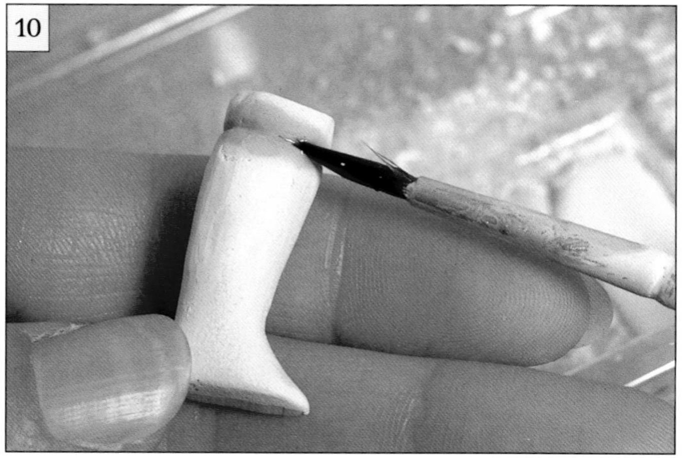

10 Make sure that the groove around the top of the leg piece is deep enough to hold the fabric securely. Use a dampened paintbrush to add definition if necessary.

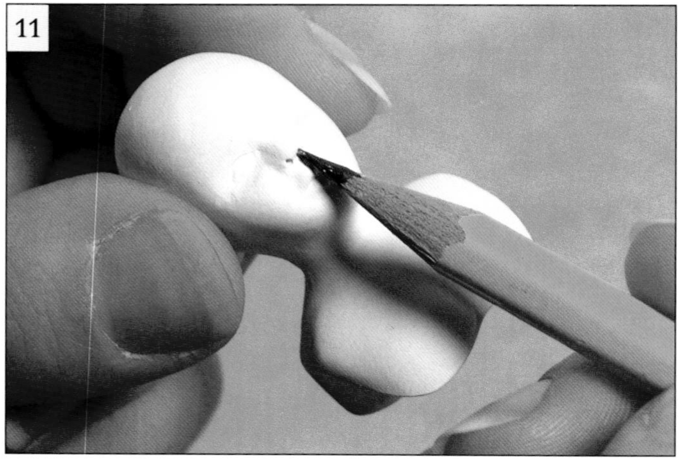

11 Check the detailing on the head: the eyes, nostrils and corners of the mouth should be sharp. If you wish, add emphasis to these features with a sharp pencil or a cocktail stick, although, if the mould was good this will not be necessary. Also check that the ears are well defined. Clean away the flash lines from the side of the head.

~ REMOVING FLASH LINES ~

YOU WILL NEED

- Paintbrush (no. 0)
- Scalpel or craft knife
- Bowl of clean water
- Tissues

When you remove the cast head, arms and legs from the moulds, you will notice the lines running down the sides that were caused by the join in the moulds. These lines can be easily removed.

Use the round, smooth handle of a paintbrush to roll away the flash lines. If the flash lines are particularly pronounced you may need to cut them away with a scalpel or craft knife. Then dampen the bristle end of the brush and dry it a little on tissue before using it to smooth over the greenware. Work on a small area, then dampen the brush again. Do not let the brush become too dry or it will pull the greenware out of shape.

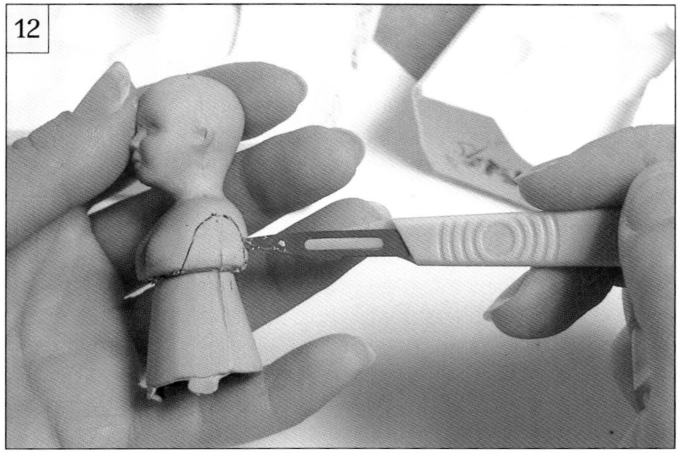

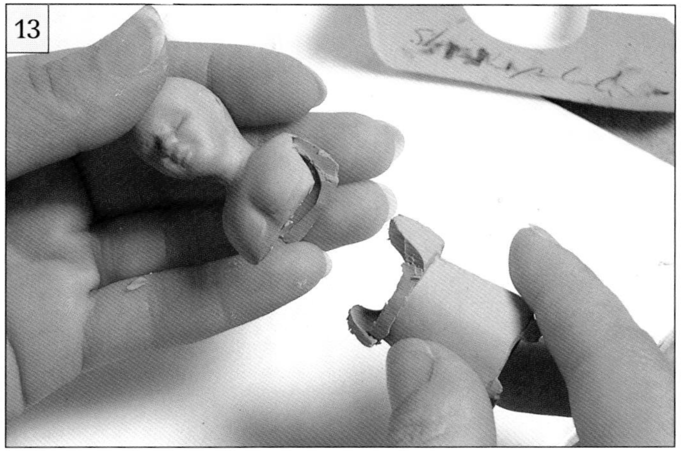

12 If you are making a shoulder-plate doll, use a scalpel or craft knife to cut away the line of the shoulder-plate.

13 Carefully separate the shoulder-head from the rest of the mould, making sure you do not distort it.

~ WARNING ~

Clay dust can be harmful to your health so it is necessary to take some precautions.

Always work in a well-ventilated room with, if possible, good dust extraction equipment. You will need ready access to water and impermeable, easily-cleaned working surfaces. It is also a good idea to wear some kind of protective clothing. All cleaning must be done with the wet method. Dust should not be blown away but rather wiped away with a damp cloth.

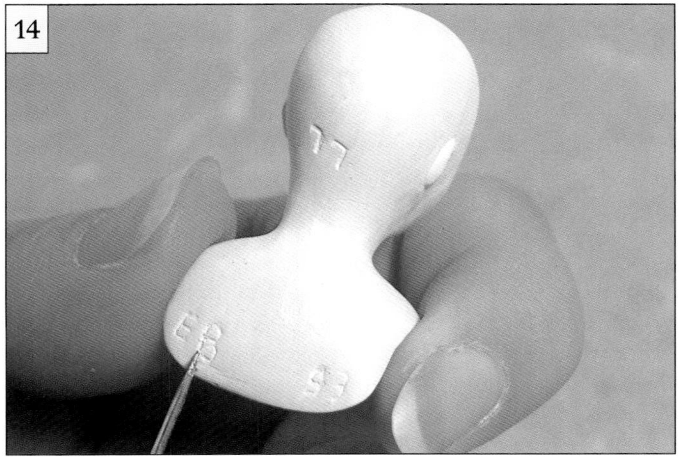

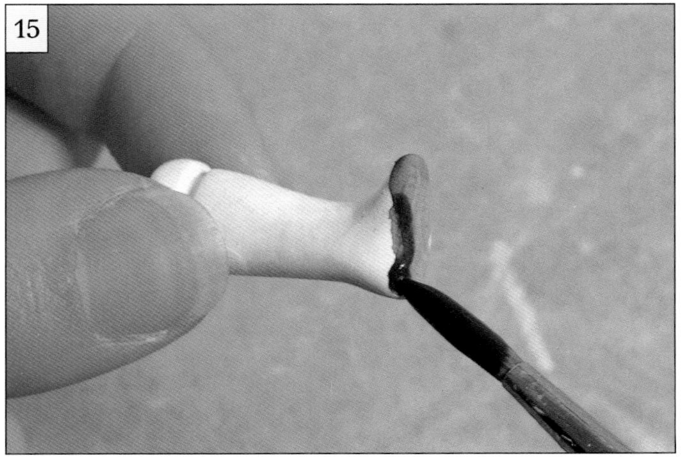

14 Remember to make an incised mark on the back of the head if it is a flange-neck doll or on the base of the shoulder-plate. You should put the date and some form of identification such as your initials. Leave the head to dry.

15 Use gloss underglaze paint for the stockings and shoes. Many doll's house dolls have black shoes or boots, but you can use any colour you wish. The paint will withstand firing at 1220°C/2230°F. When the legs are dry, gently smooth the open end with fine sandpaper so that the legs will stand upright in the kiln.

~ HOBBY KILNS ~

BELOW A typical electric kiln fitted with a series of elements that radiate heat. There is an automatic switch-off device if the kiln is opened during firing.

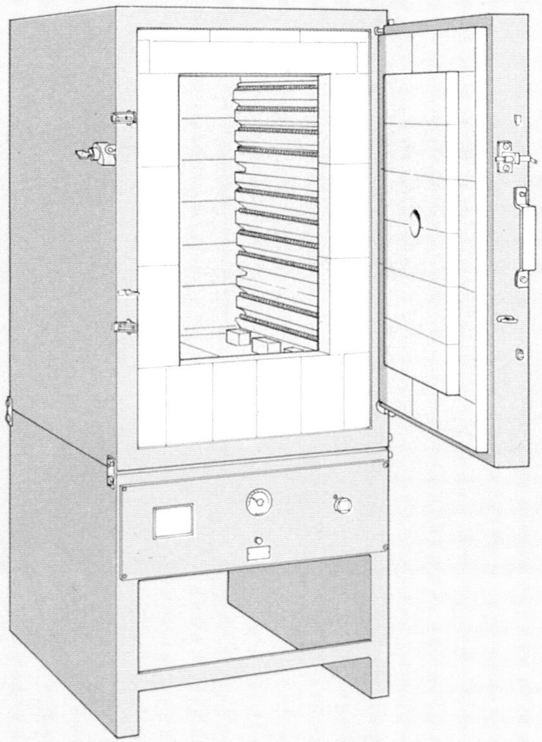

A hobby kiln is like a small oven and is just as easy to use. The firing chamber need not be larger than 23cm/9in wide and deep or, if it is circular, 30cm/12in across. Kilns can be loaded from the top or from the front. The round kilns are usually top-loading models and are generally on castors so that they can be moved. The square, front-loading kilns are too heavy to move and have to be installed in position when they are first delivered. Whichever kind of kiln you have, it must always be perfectly level because doll parts move during firing and may fall over.

Kilns can be controlled manually or automatically, and although the automatic kilns are expensive the outlay will be worthwhile if you intend to use it regularly. Many of the smaller kilns work off a 13 amp domestic electricity supply, and you should place your kiln as near as possible to a socket so that there are no trailing electric leads. The models with thermostats can be timed to switch off automatically once the correct temperature is reached. Kiln-setter type kilns are sold with full instructions and all the necessary furniture. They require special mini-bar cones. You will also need sand or kiln wash, a ceramic blanket and ceramic paper.

Modern electric kilns are fitted with safety devices that shut off the power when the kiln door is opened.

Before you stack the kiln, check the position of the thermocouple. This is the temperature unit that turns off the kiln when it is the correct temperature. It is made of a ceramic material around a wire, and it can be easily broken if, for example, it is accidentally knocked by fired bisque. Even if it is broken, the kiln is still usable because the wire in the thermostat will still control the temperature.

~ FIRING GREENWARE ~

Although each kiln will come with instructions about firing, there are really only three important points to remember:

- The greenware must be absolutely bone dry
- There should be some sand on the shelf because porcelain moves slightly during firing
- The greenware must not touch any other piece in the kiln

I always then fire on high, right from the start. You can prevent the porcelain from sticking to the floor and shelves of the kiln by using fine silica sand, a kiln wash, a ceramic blanket or ceramic paper.

Before you use the kiln, make sure that it is switched off at the plug. If you have a Kiln-setter type kiln, check that you have the correct mini-bar cone; you will need no. 6 cones for 1220°C/2230°F and no. 018 for 750°C/1350°F. Cover the shelf or shelves with sand and stack the items of greenware, making sure that they do not touch each other. Close the kiln door and, if you have an automatic kiln, select the correct temperature and switch on. The actual firing will take 1–3 hours, and you will then have to leave it for a further 5–7 hours to cool down.

~ FIRING PAINT ~

Clean all the sand from inside the kiln. This can be kept and re-used. Place all the painted heads and hands so that they are not touching and, if you have painted shoes, make sure that they are supported so that the painted area does not touch the shelf. Select the correct temperature or cone and continue as above, although this firing will take less time.

16 Dampen the eye area of the head with a paintbrush. Mix some black underglaze paint with sufficient water to make the paint just runny. Alternatively, you can wet the eyelid and add paint. Using a no. 0000 paintbrush and holding the head upside down, begin at the outside edge and paint eyelashes on the upper lid. Turn the head upside down to complete the other eye. If you make a mistake, you can use a scalpel to scrape the paint off, although you have to do this very gently and carefully. If you prefer, wait until after the bisque firing to add eyelashes.

17 The greenware must be bone dry before it is fired, which can take 1–2 days. If necessary, you can place it in a conventional oven for about 1 hour at 100°C/212°F. When it is dry you may wish to smooth the cheeks by rubbing them very gently with a piece of old nylon stocking or tights wrapped around a finger. Place the heads, arms and legs inside the kiln. If you have painted boots and shoes on the legs, you must support them so that the paint does not touch the sand. If this happens, the sand will fuse with the paint and you will never be able to remove it. Greenware should be fired at 1220°C/2230°F.

18 After the first firing you must allow at least 4 hours for the items to cool, although this will depend on the type of kiln you have. As you can see, the fired objects are approximately 20 per cent smaller than they were when you put them in the kiln.

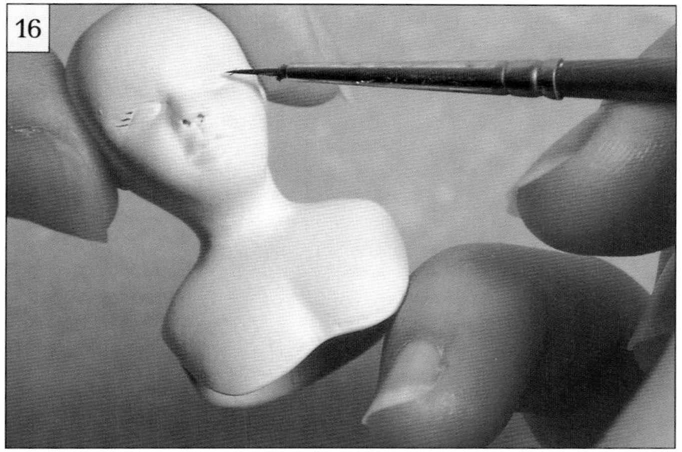

~ PAINTING THE MOULDED ~ HEAD

After the first kiln firing you will need to paint the head, arms and legs. It is important to give the dolls a good colour because they are so small that when they are dressed and wigged their little faces will disappear if they are too pale.

One of the great advantages of painting on fired clay is the ease with which the paint can be removed if you make a mistake. The complete face can be wiped off with a tissue dipped in white spirit, while an eyelash can be removed with a dot of white spirit on the point of a paintbrush. Always wipe your cleaning brush carefully on tissue before you use it again so that you do not discolour or smudge the area you are cleaning.

You must also remember that the paint will be wet until it is fired. Handling a head so that you do not smudge the paint you have just applied requires practice. However, you can overcome this problem by firing the head after every stage of the painting process, and some people prefer to do this.

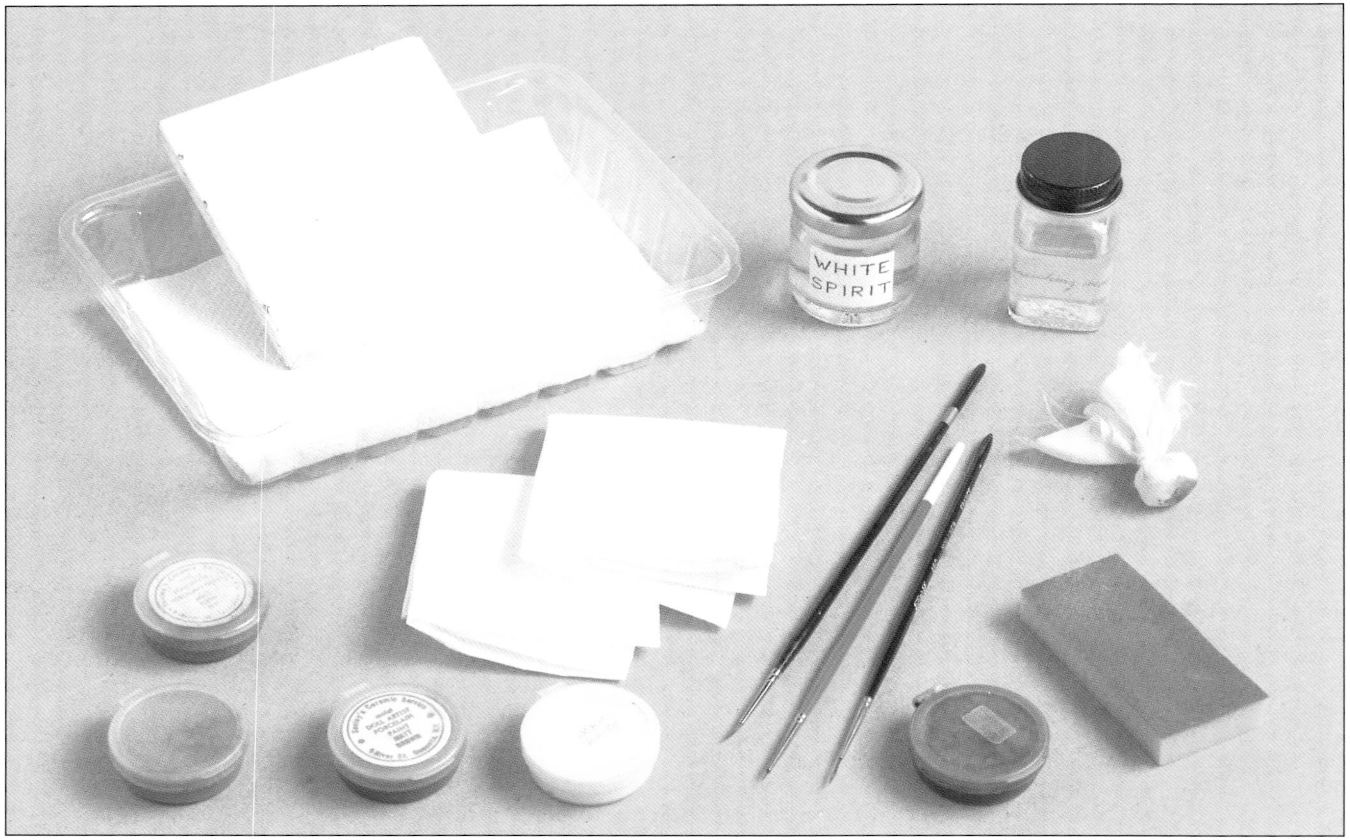

YOU WILL NEED

- Scrubber (a piece of foam with a thin layer of emery cloth glued to one side)
- Brushing medium
- Ceramic tile or saucer
- Tissues
- Wooden toothpicks or cocktail sticks
- Spatula to mix paint
- China paints
- Paintbrushes (nos. 0000, 00 and 1)
- Paintbrush (no. 000) with the bristles trimmed to about 3mm/⅛in long
- White spirit
- Pounce (a tiny piece of cotton wool or similar stuffing wrapped in a small piece of silk)
- Forceps
- Turpentine
- Copaiba medium

1 Use the scrubber to rub the head, hands and feet until they are perfectly smooth. You may need to rub very hard. Rinse and dry thoroughly. Place a drop of brushing medium on the tile or in a saucer and use the tip of a finger to rub it all over the face and hair (if the hair is moulded), the arms and legs. Wipe it all off with a tissue. The brushing medium will make the paint go on smoothly. Use a toothpick to put a minute amount of Pompadour red on the tile and use the spatula to mix it with a tiny amount of brushing medium.

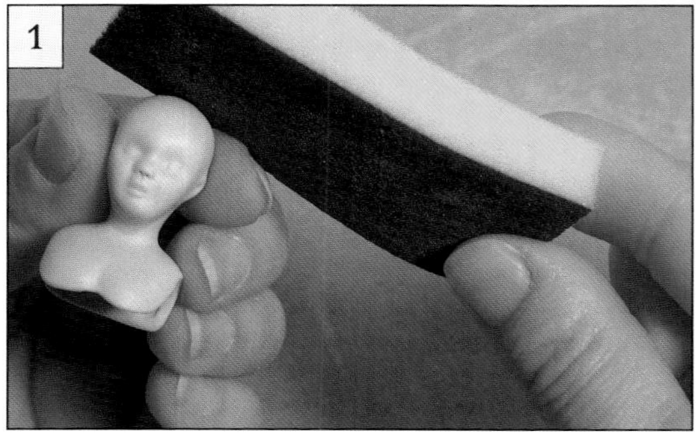
1

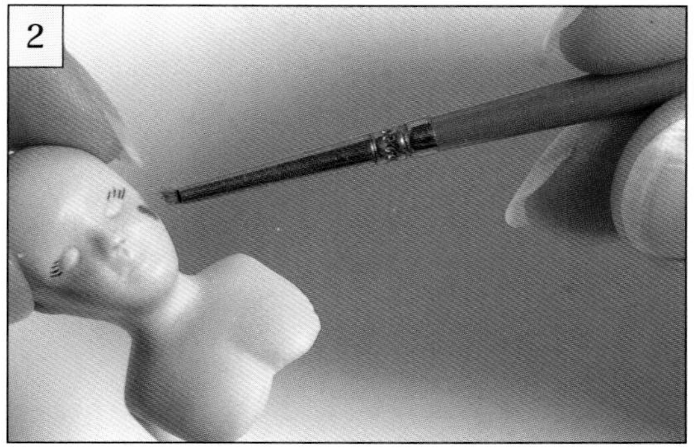

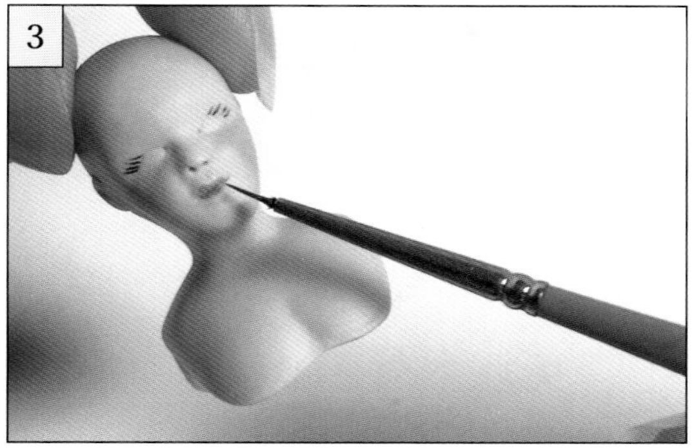

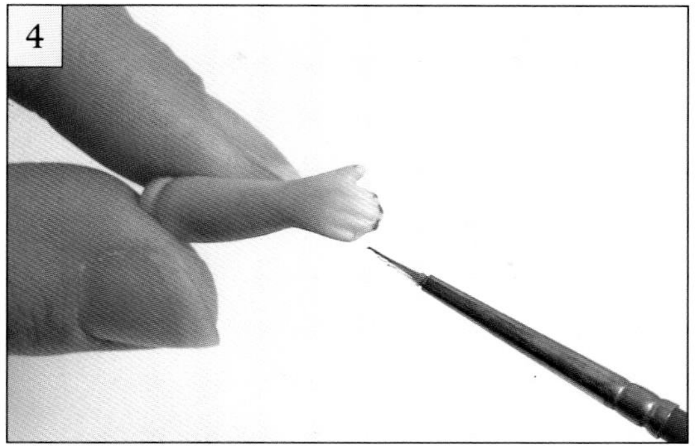

2 Use a no. 0000 paintbrush to put a dot of the paint and brushing medium mix on each cheek, then, with the cut-off paintbrush and using a circular movement, smooth the paint evenly over the cheeks. Take care that there is no harsh line between the cheeks and the neck. Keep your cut-off brush only for smoothing colour on the cheeks. Do not dip it into the paint.

3 Put dots of red in the nose (for the nostrils) and in the corners of the eyes. Use a no. 0000 paintbrush to outline the lips, then pull the brush to the centre. Pat the mouth lightly with a tissue and paint again if necessary. The top lip should be slightly darker than the lower lip.

4 If you wish, you can outline the bed of the fingernails with a thin red line. Clean your brush thoroughly in white spirit and, if you wish, place tiny spots of colour on the arms, wrists and knees. Pounce these until they are very light. When they are painted and to keep them from getting smudged, put the arms and legs back in the kiln, ready for firing with the head.

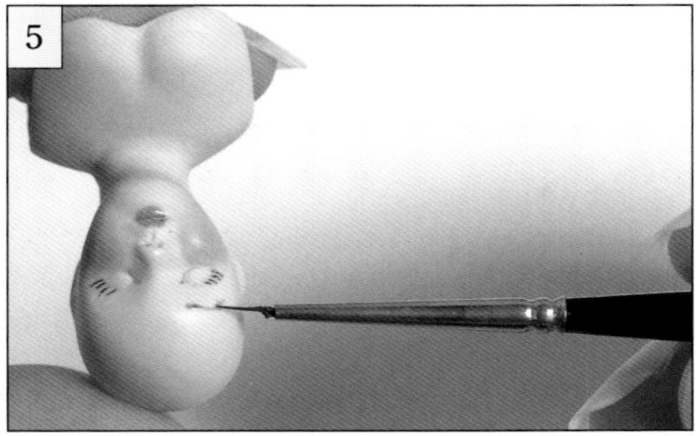

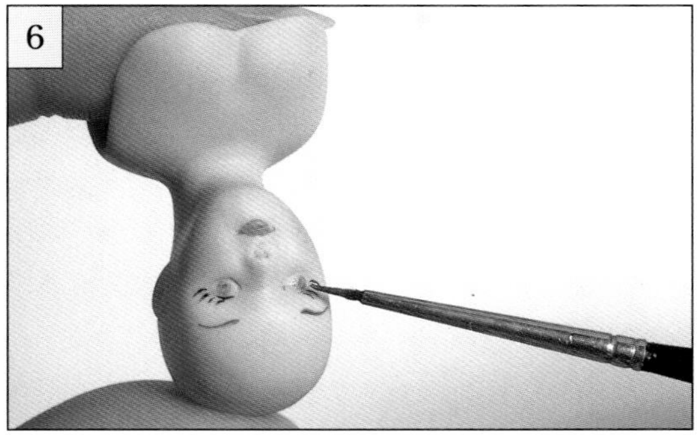

5 Paint the eyebrows with a no. 0000 paintbrush dipped in matt walnut brown. You will probably find it easier to paint the thin line if you hold the head upside down. Remember that the eyebrows should be just above the eyes and not near to the hairline. If you make a mistake, wipe the paint off with a tissue dipped in a trace of white spirit. With practice, you will be able to remove paint from under or above the eyebrow.

6 Paint the eyeball in white gloss paint. This is difficult to see, but is just visible if you hold the head to the light. If you wish, add a spot of colour to represent the iris, although this is generally not necessary because the eyes are so small. If you add colour, make sure that both eyes "look" in the same direction.

~ TIPS ~

- When you paint the white of the eye, add a drop of red food colouring to the gloss paint so that you can see what you are doing more easily. Although this makes the doll look as if it has got conjunctivitis, the red dye will be burned out during the firing.
- You may find it helpful to draw the eyebrows on in pencil as a guide before you paint them in. The pencil line will be burned out during the firing.
- If the doll's head has moulded hair, mix some walnut brown or other suitable colour with copaiba medium. The paint will dry quickly and can be handled, with care, before firing. Use only a tiny amount of copaiba and "pounce" the hair area to prevent the colour running down the doll's neck.
- Use an old scrubber to rub over the head to give it a smooth finish. The porcelain of a well-made doll has a satiny feel.

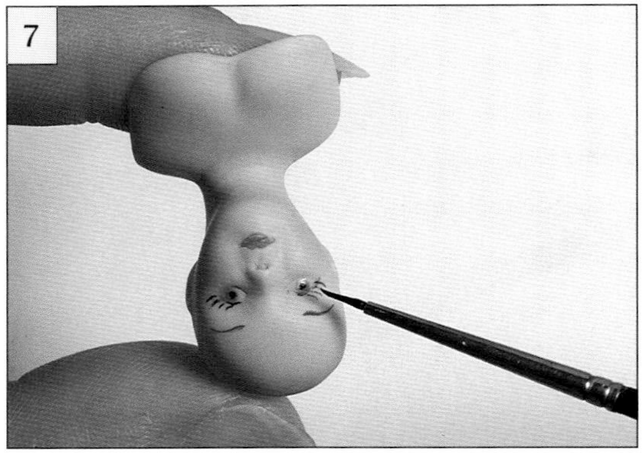

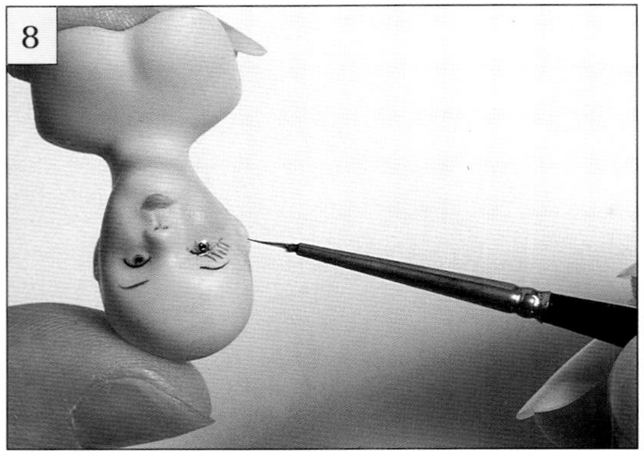

7 Use forceps to place the head in the kiln with the arms and legs ready to be refired at 750°C/1350°F. When they are cool, remove the porcelain pieces from the kiln. Use black gloss to paint a fine line at the top edge of the eyeball. Take off any excess paint with a brush dipped in turpentine. The line must be as fine as you can possibly make it.

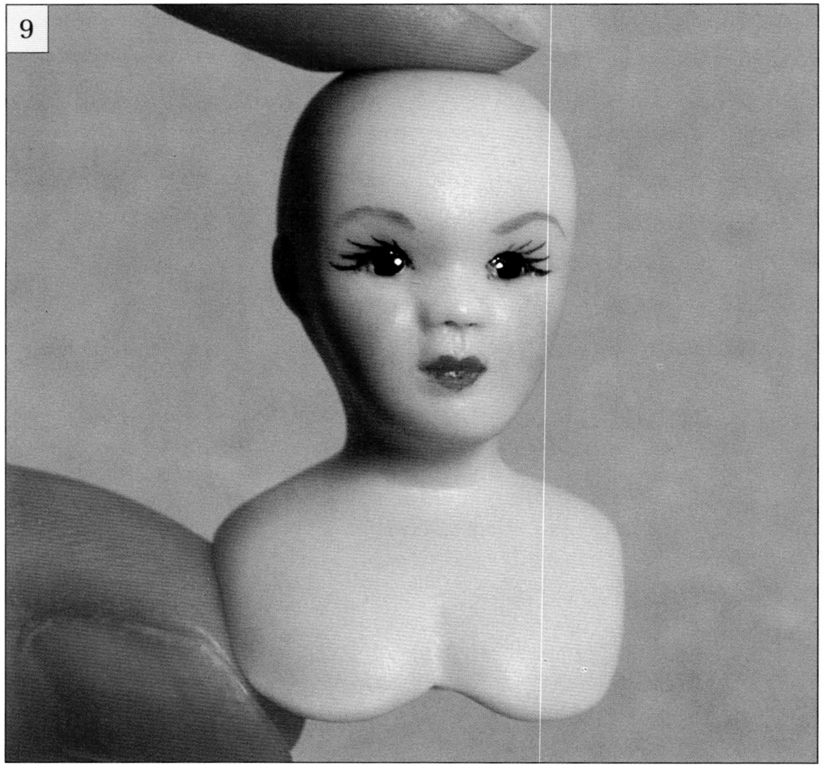

8 If you did not paint eyelashes at the greenware stage, do it now, although it has to be said that very few people bother to paint eyelashes on a doll's house doll. Use matt black paint and a no. 0000 paintbrush. Hold the head upside down and begin at the outside edge of the upper right eyelid. Paint no more than four lashes and do not paint any below the eye. Turn the head the right side up to paint the lashes on the other eye. Any errors can be wiped away with a spot of white spirit on your no. 00 cleaning brush, which should be wiped almost dry so that the paint for the next lash does not run. When you are satisfied with the lashes, clean your brush and use gloss black paint to add a pupil to each eye. Remember that the pupil should be nearer the upper lid; centrally placed pupils will give the doll a "staring" look. Clean the brush in turpentine.

9 Use forceps to place the head in the kiln and fire again at 750°C/1350°F. Heads can be fired as often as you wish provided that you do not exceed a temperature of 750°C/1350°F. The finished head is now ready to be fitted to a body and dressed in the style of your choice.

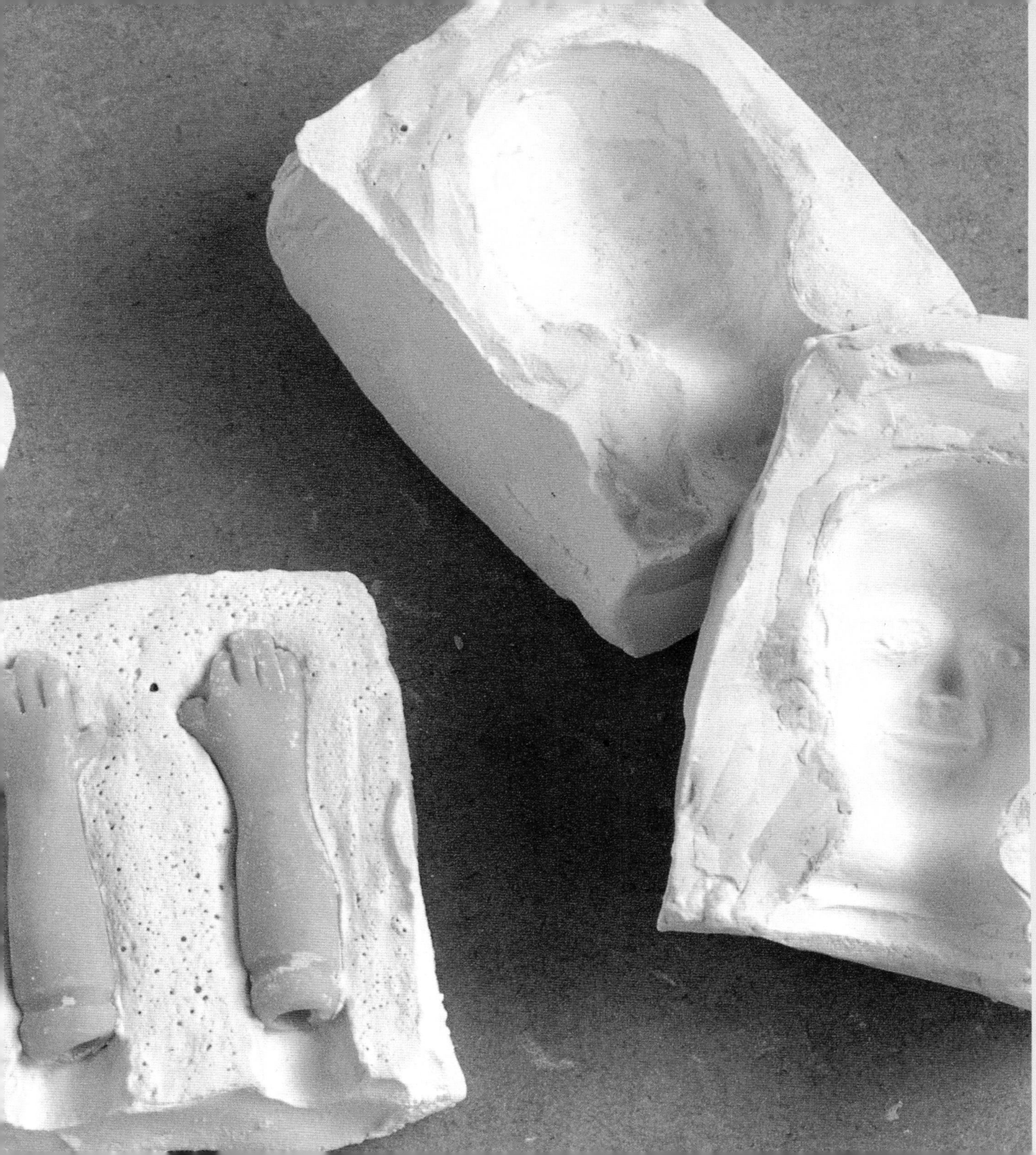

MODELLING A DOLL

~

MAKING A DOLL FROM YOUR OWN DESIGN AND IN YOUR OWN MOULD IS, MANY DOLL-MAKERS FEEL, THE BEST WAY. NOT ONLY IS IT GREAT FUN, BUT IT IS A FORM OF "ONE-UPMANSHIP" OVER OTHER DOLL-MAKERS WHO USE COMMERCIALLY MADE MOULDS AND KITS. WITH PRACTICE AND PERSEVERANCE YOU WILL FIND THAT YOU WILL BE ABLE TO CREATE A HUGE RANGE OF FIGURES – OLD, YOUNG, PRETTY OR UGLY – SO THAT YOU CAN FILL YOUR DOLL'S HOUSE WITH GENERATIONS OF A FAMILY.

I HAVE USED SUPER SCULPEY, ALTHOUGH OTHER KINDS OF CRAFT MODELLING CLAY ARE AVAILABLE. ASK IN YOUR CRAFT SHOP ABOUT THE ALTERNATIVES. YOU CAN MAKE PLASTER MOULDS FROM UNCURED SCULPEY, WHICH MEANS THAT THE SAME PIECE OF CLAY CAN BE USED AS THE BASIS OF SEVERAL MOULDS. YOU CAN ALSO COMBINE IT WITH OTHER MATERIALS SUCH AS ARMATURE WIRE, PLASTIC, PAPER, METAL, CLOTH, WOOD AND GLASS.

THE INSTRUCTIONS THAT FOLLOW DESCRIBE HOW TO MAKE A MOULD WITH MODELLING CLAY AND PLASTER OF PARIS. HOWEVER, IF YOU WOULD PREFER TO USE THE MODELLING CLAY TO MAKE A ONE-OFF DOLL, USE THE CLAY HEAD, ARMS AND LEGS FOR THE DOLL ITSELF. DUST THE CHEEKS WITH CAKE ROUGE THEN STAND THE HEAD, ARMS AND LEGS ON A TILE AND CURE THE INDIVIDUAL PARTS ACCORDING TO THE INSTRUCTIONS ON THE PACKET. PAINT THEM WITH ACRYLIC PAINTS WHEN THEY ARE COOL.

YOU WILL NEED

- Super Sculpey or similar modeling clay
- Modeling tools (you can use ordinary modeling tools or a variety of items – e.g., wooden toothpicks; manicure tools; paintbrushes)
- Plastic or marble board on which to roll clay
- "Pearl" beads
- Cake rouge
- Scissors
- Small drinking straw
- Pencil
- Plasticine
- Plastic rolling pin or straight-sided glass bottle
- Plaster of Paris
- Plastic container
- Craft knife or scalpel

~ USING MODELING CLAY ~

When you come to mold a modeling clay such as Sculpey, it should be soft enough to mold but firm enough to hold its shape. If it is too soft, wrap a piece in foil and place it in a conventional oven at 120° for about 5 minutes. This slight heating will begin the chemical reaction that will make the clay firmer. If it is left in the oven for too long it will be too firm to use. Hard clay requires a lot of kneading before it becomes workable, although it does hold its shape well if you are making large objects.

Sculpey remains pliable until it is baked in a conventional oven, when it acquires a plastic-like hardness. To cure it completely, place it on an ovenproof dish or tile and bake at 275° for 15 minutes. If you are using other types of modeling clay, follow the manufacturer's instructions.

Provided it does not get too warm, Sculpey has a shelf-life of several years.

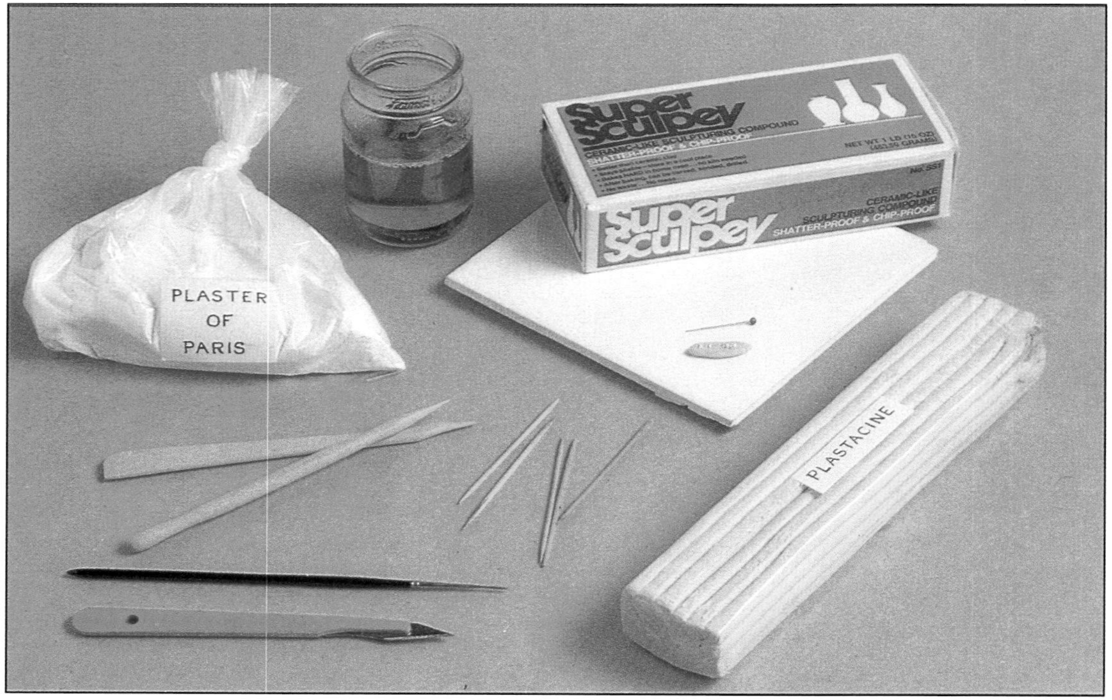

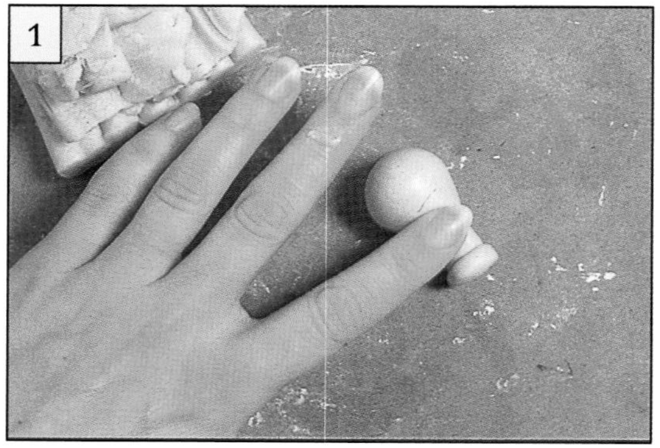

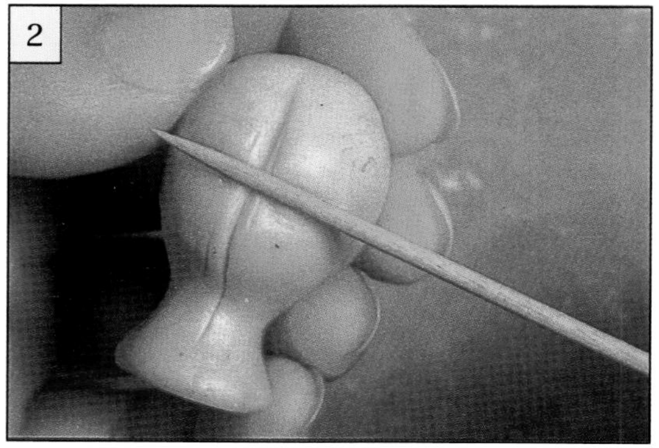

1 Make a ball for the head; this should have a circumference of about 2⅝ inches. Gently roll the base of the ball to make a flange-shaped neck, pinching it around the edge with your fingers to form the flange shape. You do not have to exert a great deal of pressure when you are working with a modeling clay such as Sculpey.

2 Divide the front of the face into quarters with a wooden toothpick or something similar.

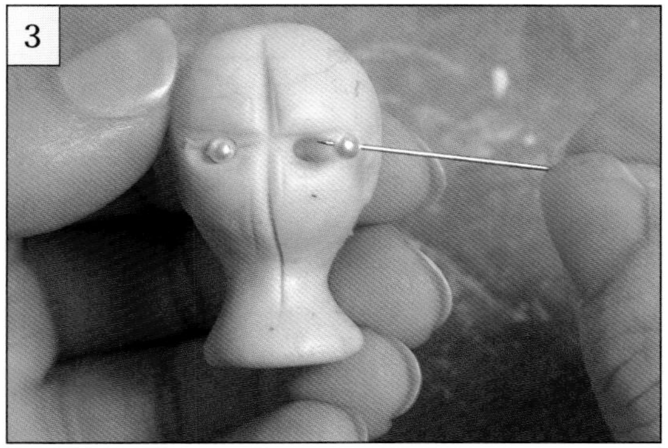

3 Use a rounded wooden tool – the end of a paintbrush, for example – to make indentations for the eye sockets. These should be just under the horizontal line and evenly spaced on either side of the vertical line. Because this head is going to be used as a mould, tiny "pearl" beads have been used. They give a smooth surface, which is easy to paint, and the plaster of Paris does not stick to them. Use a pin through the hole in the bead to position the beads. You must push them well in so that they don't protrude. If you cannot get beads use little balls of modelling clay. Beads can be used if you are making a one-off doll; they can be painted with oil paints very satisfactorily.

4 Roll out tiny pieces of clay. Add one to the chin, a tiny ball for the nose, two minute pieces for the mouth and a small piece on the forehead.

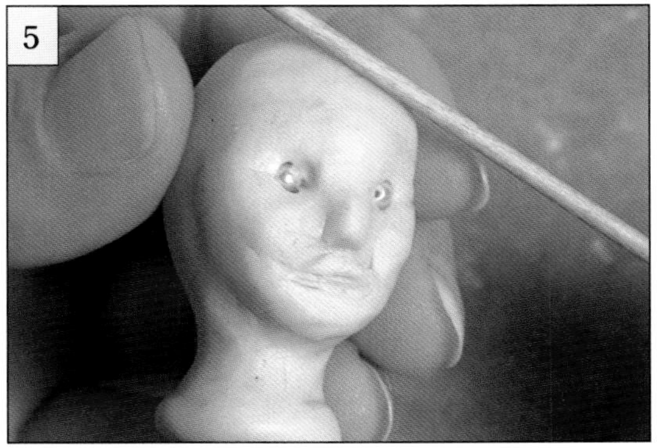

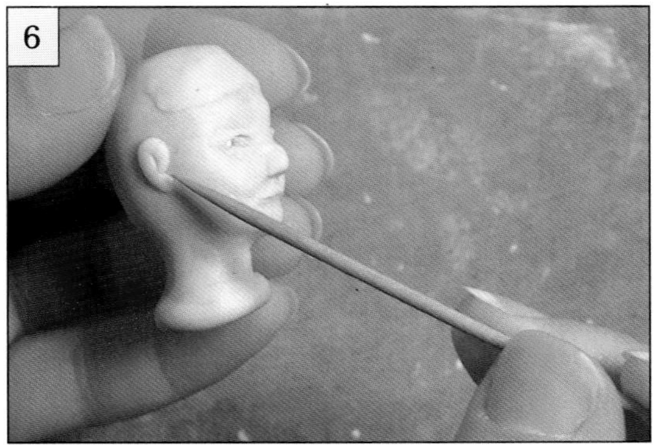

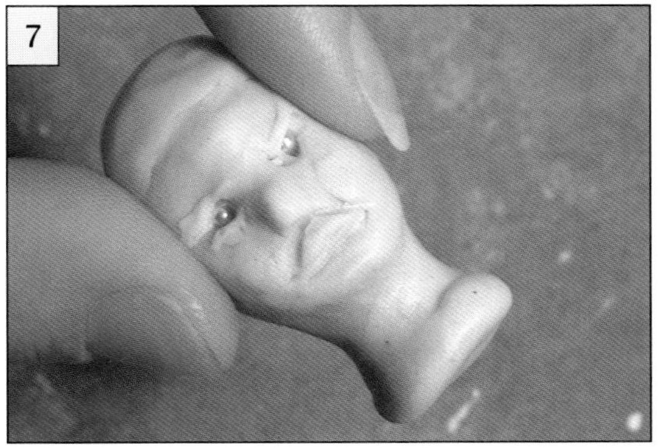

5 Smooth all the added pieces by rolling over them with a wooden cocktail stick. Add tiny balls of clay, slightly flattened, to both cheeks and smooth them gently.

6 Roll out two tiny pieces of clay for the ears and make them resemble tiny question marks. Put them in position, making sure they are level, then add two small balls inside the ears. Smooth over.

7 Gently squeeze the sides of the head and also manipulate the back of the head to make it more rounded. To make a shoulder-plate head add a ball of clay to the base of the neck and model it into shape, making sure that you smooth over the join with a cocktail stick or some similar tool.

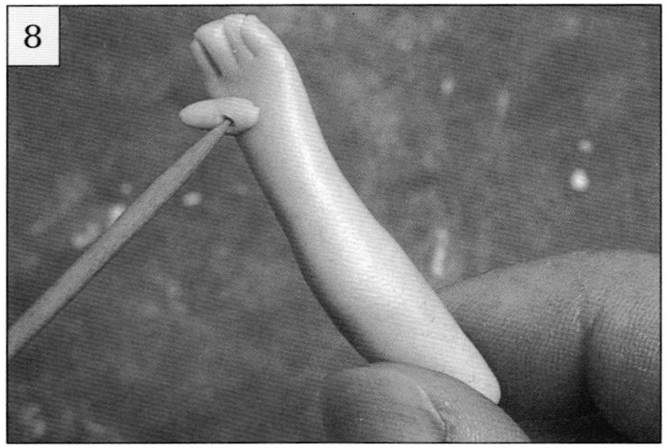

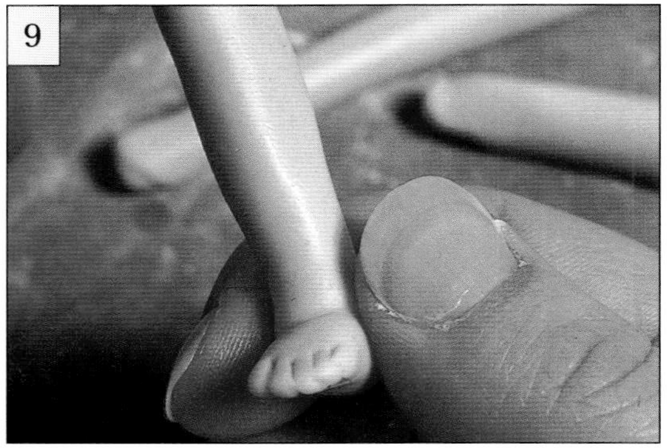

8 Prepare the hands by rolling out a piece of clay 4cm/1½in long and a tiny piece for the thumb. Flatten one end of the roll to make a hand and cut fingers with a pair of scissors. Separate the fingers with a toothpick, round the ends and push them back together again. Add the thumb and smooth it into the palm. Mark the nails with a tiny drinking straw. Make a groove at the top of the arm into which the fabric can be pressed. If the arm is to be used on a doll, curve over the fingers slightly; otherwise leave them straight. Make the second arm, remembering to make one left hand and one right.

9 Make a leg by rolling out a piece of clay 5cm/2in long. Flatten one end to form a foot and ankle and cut out toes, making sure they are not too large. Remember to make a big toe. Make a groove at the top of the leg into which the fabric can be pressed. Make the second leg in the same way, remembering to make one left leg and one right.

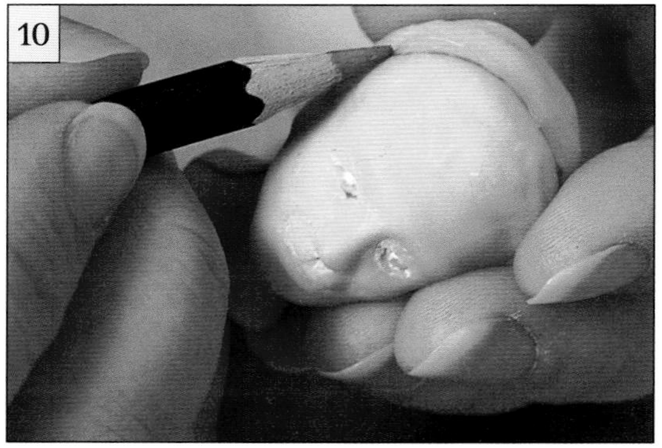

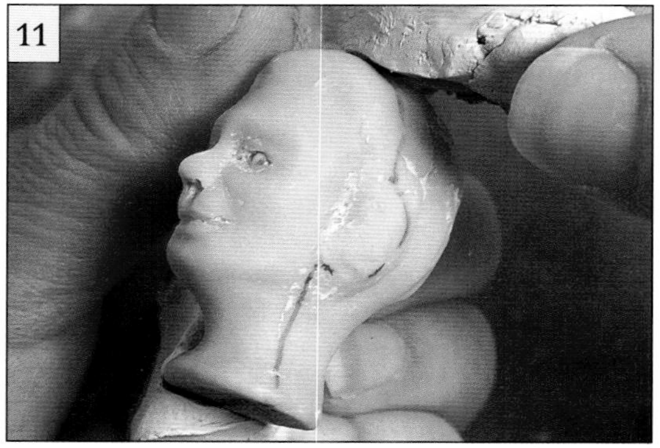

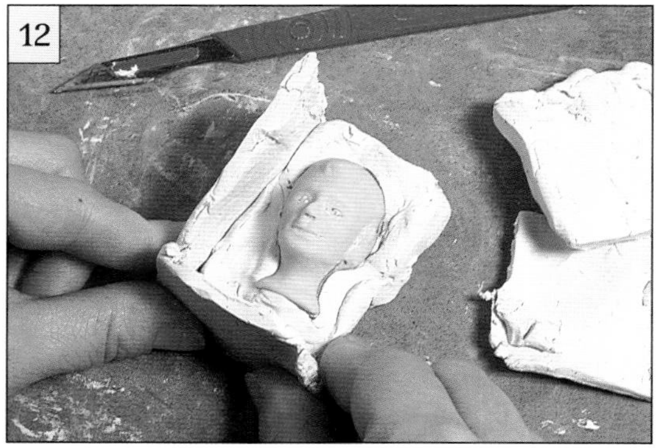

10 Take the head and draw a line right round it, making sure that you go across the highest point of the head and cheeks and exactly bisect the flange neck.

11 Use the rolling pin or bottle to roll out a strip of plasticine about 1 × 2.5 × 12.5cm/ ½ × 1 × 5in. The strip should reach right around the head, along the line, meeting under the flange neck or shoulder-plate. Build up plasticine up to this first strip until the back of the head is embedded. To make a pour hole, shape a plug from plasticine to fill the flange neck and to meet the outside edge.

12 Continue to build up the plasticine until it lies flat on your work surface and is 1–2.5cm/½–1in wider than the clay model. Flatten out strips of plasticine with a rolling pin or bottle and press them around the sides of the base, smoothing them on the work surface. Build up the sides of the walls until they are at least 2.5cm/1in higher than the tip of the nose.

13

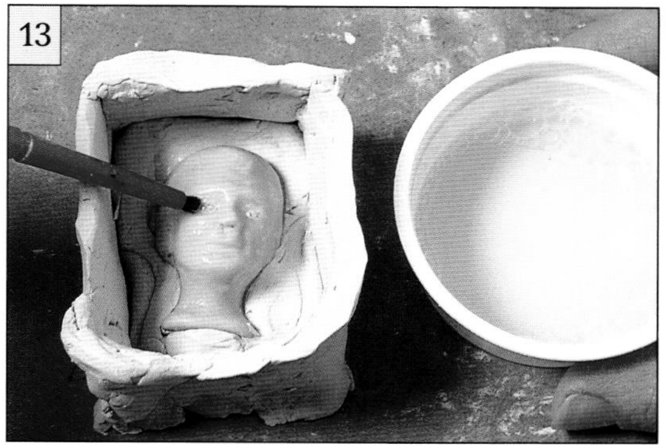

14

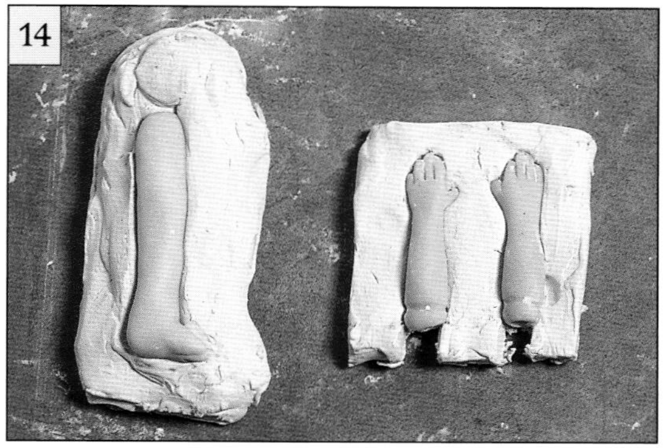

~ TIPS ~

- Mix the plaster of Paris in a large plastic container in the proportions of 1 part water to 3 parts plaster. Always add plaster to water. Stir gently so that you do not introduce bubbles of air.
- Always use plastic containers when you are working with plaster of Paris. When the plaster has dried it can be easily knocked off the surface.
- If your doll looks too large and out of scale, make another mould of the fired head, remembering to paint it with a release agent before you pour in the plaster of Paris.

13 If you have used a modelling clay such as Sculpey or used other plastic modelling clay, plaster of Paris will not adhere to the surface of the pattern. However, if you have used ceramic or wood, you must paint the surface with a release agent such as clay slip or washing-up liquid.

14 Prepare the plasticine beds for the arms and legs in the same way, building up the level of plasticine in readiness for the plaster of Paris.

16

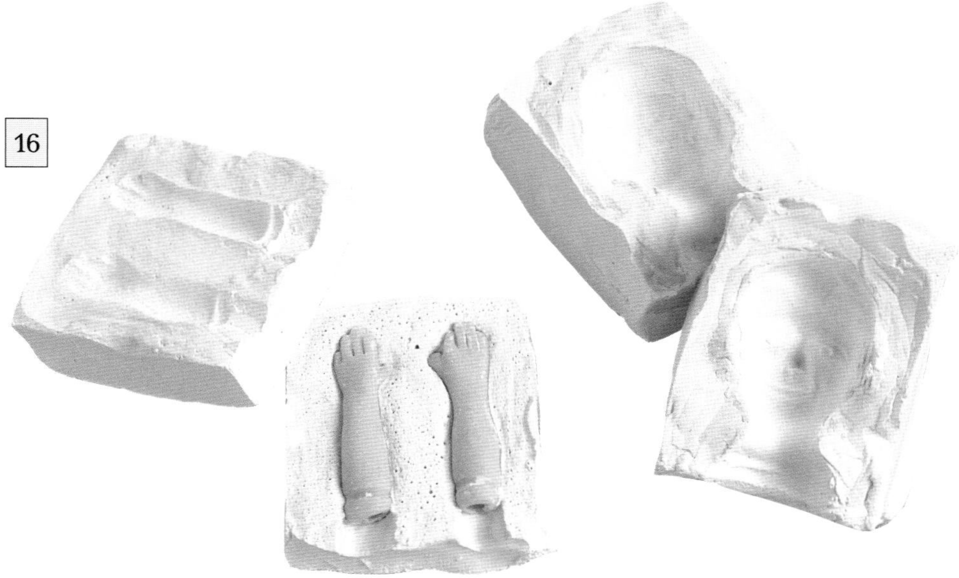

15

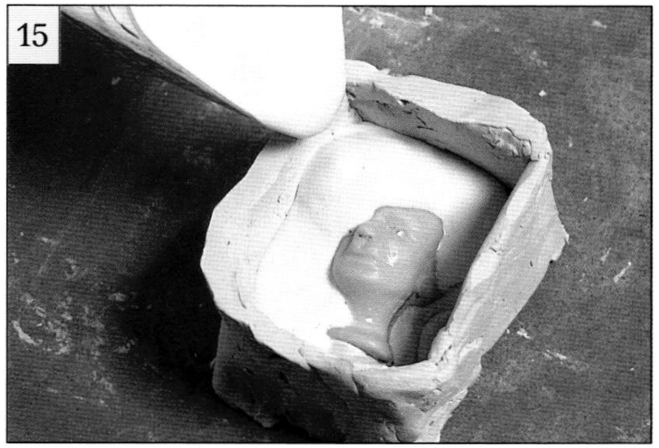

15 Mix the plaster of Paris and when it begins to resemble the consistency of thick cream, pour it down the side of the plasticine surround, filling the area to the top. Leave for 15–20 minutes. Remove the plasticine base and wall from the back of the pattern. Do not part the pattern and plaster. Use a small coin or something similar to make some indentations in the plaster while it is still soft; these will act as key marks so that both halves of the plaster mould align exactly. Rebuild the plasticine walls around your model. Coat the model and, especially, the plaster, with a release agent. Remember to make a plug for the pour hole and seal the plasticine carefully around the base and in the corners. Mix fresh plaster and, when it begins to thicken, pour it into the plasticine surround. Leave for about 20 minutes.

16 Remove the plasticine surround. Place the mould in a bowl of water for 3–5 minutes and pry apart gently. If necessary, enlarge the size of the pour hole with a craft knife. Leave to dry for 1–2 days; alternatively, place in a conventional oven at 100°C/212°F for 1 hour. When the moulds are completely dry, they are ready for you to use to make your own dolls with slip (see the previous project).

Victorian Lady

~

This is one of the easiest ways to dress a doll. When the doll is turned upside down, the lace-edged pantaloons and trimmed underskirt give the impression that the doll has a full set of underclothes. The pattern can be easily adapted for other dolls. You could, for example, make it in plain fabric with matching or contrasting lace trim and use it to dress a grandmother doll.

YOU WILL NEED

- Tracing paper
- Pencil
- Pins
- Scissors
- Narrow bonding web
- Needle
- Sewing thread
- Forceps or tweezers
- Sewing machine (optional)

FOR THE PANTALOONS

- 15cm/6in white cotton lawn
- 15cm/6in white edging lace, 5mm/¼in wide
- Shirring elastic (optional)

FOR THE DRESS

- 23cm/9in white cotton lawn
- 46cm/18in delicately patterned soft cotton or silk
- 30cm/12in white edging lace, 5mm/¼in wide
- 90cm/36in gathered white edging lace, 2.5cm/1in wide
- All-purpose adhesive

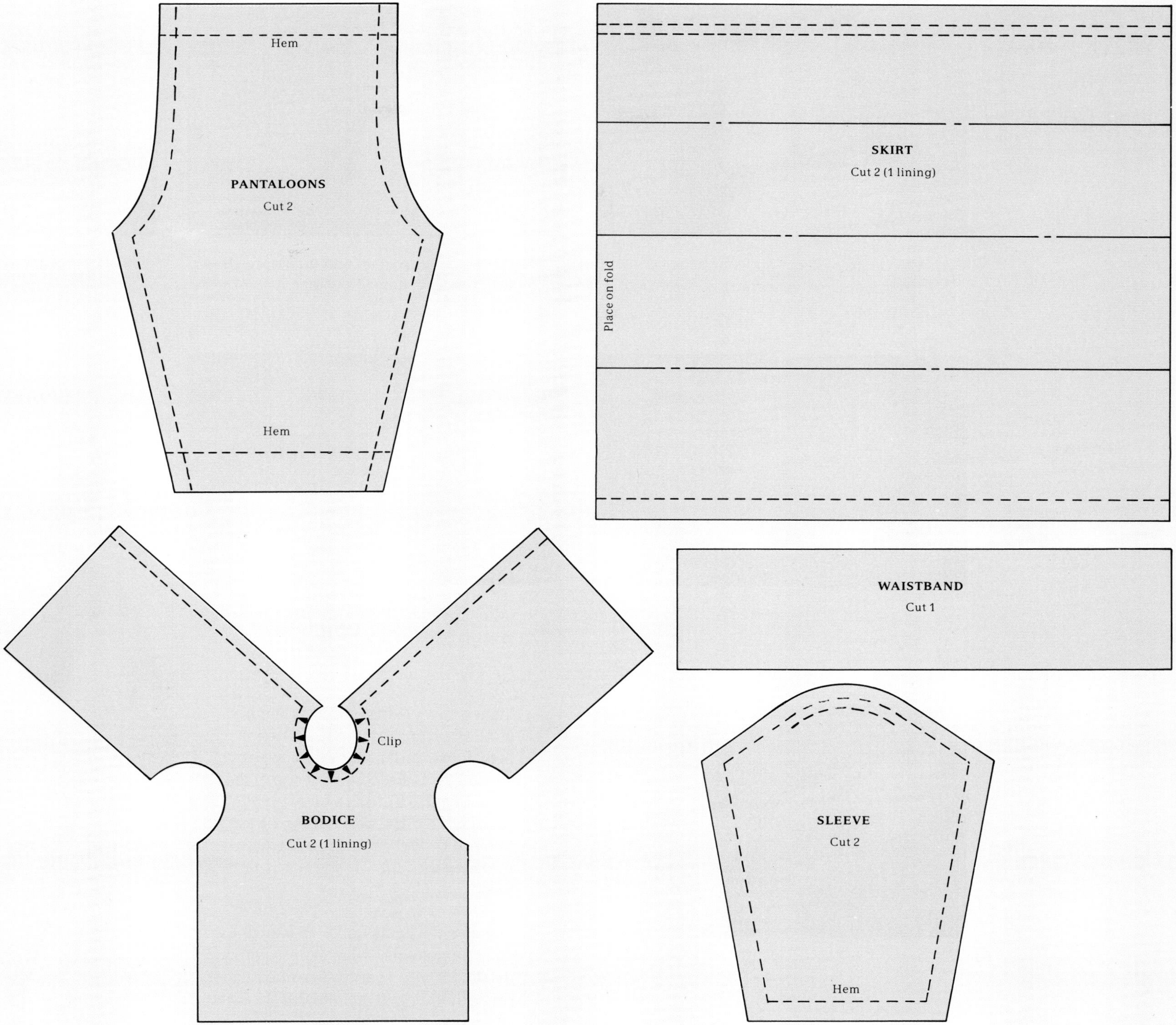

MAKING THE PANTALOONS

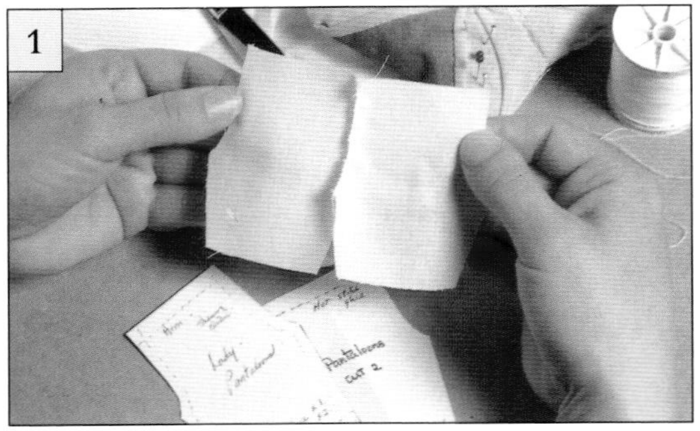

1 Cut out two pieces and stitch the centre front seam, with a turning allowance of 5mm/¼in.

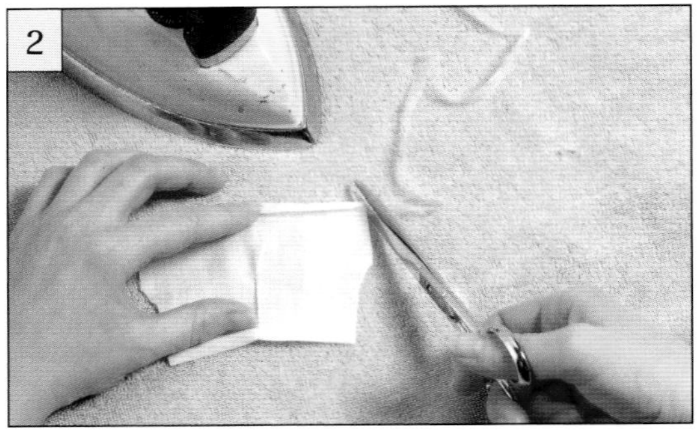

2 Press open the seam and turn down the waist and leg hem allowance with narrow bonding web.

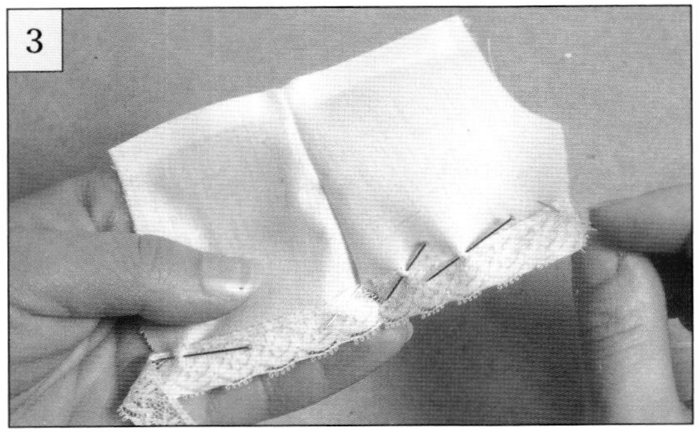

3 Pin and stitch narrow lace along the bottom edge.

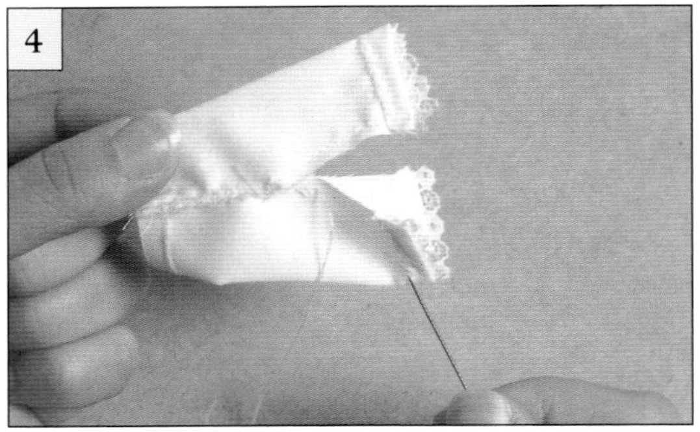

4 Turn right sides together and stitch the centre back seam.

5 Stitch the inner leg seam, catching in the raw ends of the lace.

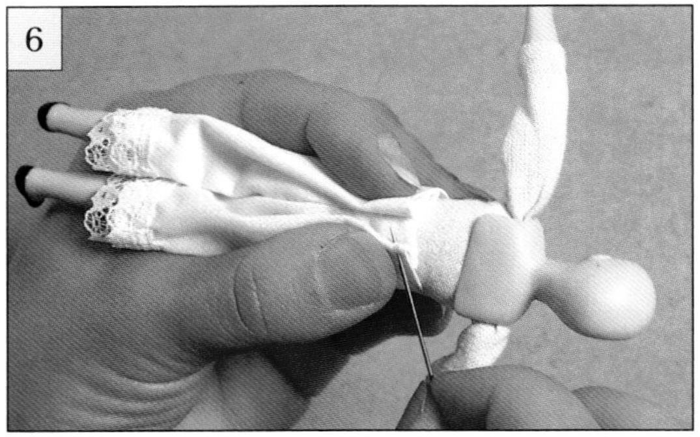

6 Make a row of small running stitches around the top. Dress the doll in the pantaloons and gather them up tightly around the waist. Stitch the top of the pantaloons to the doll's body. Alternatively, the top hem can be turned down and stitched and fine elastic threaded through. Tie the elastic tightly to finish.

7 The finished pantaloons. All lady dolls wear pantaloons of this pattern, although the length of leg varies. The maids, cook, grandmother and girl all wear the same style.

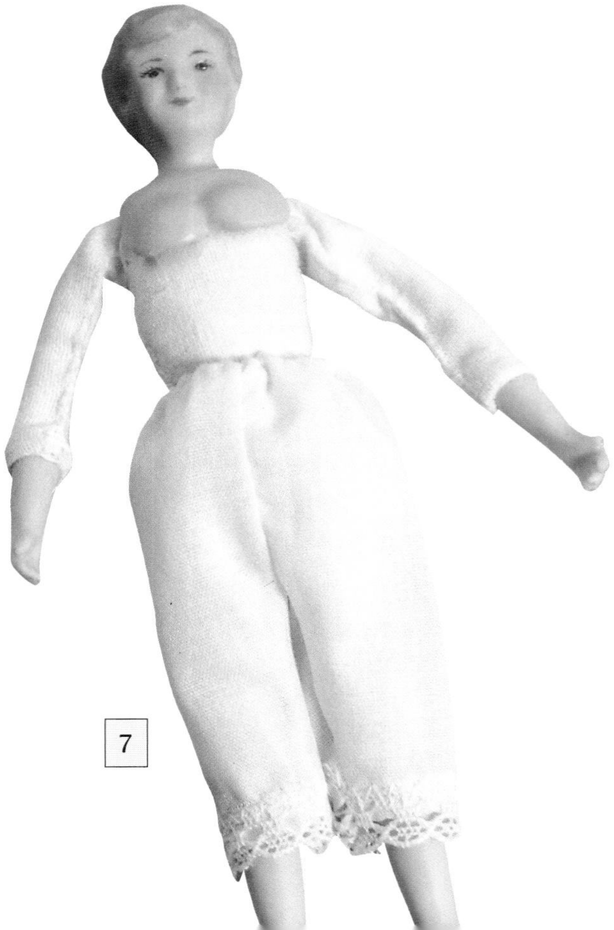

7

MAKING THE BODICE

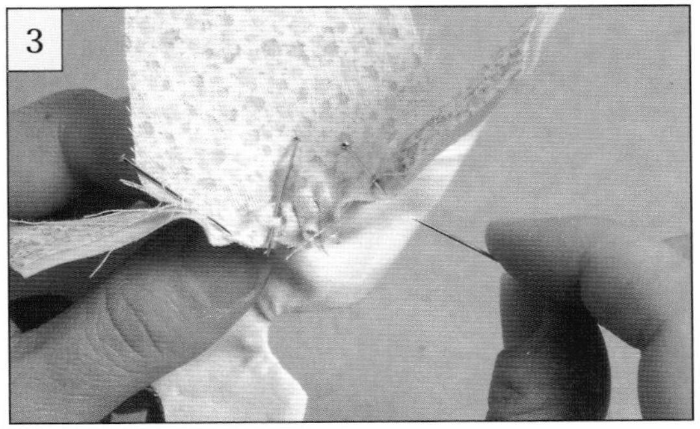

1 Cut out two sleeves in patterned cotton and two dress top pieces, one in patterned cotton and one in white lawn. Stitch according to marks on pattern.

2 Use bonding web to turn up the bottom hem of the sleeves, and then pin and stitch narrow lace around the wrist edge.

3 With right sides together, stitch the bodice pieces together. Clip around the neck seam. Turn to the right side and press the seams flat. Stitch the sleeve to the armhole.

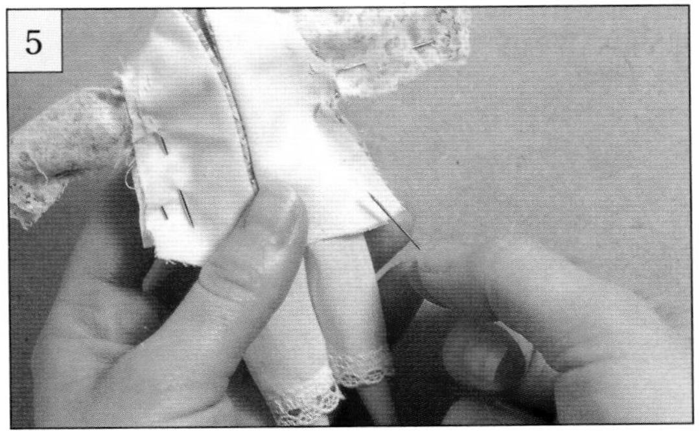

4 Stitch the sleeve top to the shoulder, easing the fullness at the top to fit.

5 Put the bodice, with the lining outwards, on the doll. Pin at the back of the neck and the waist, then pin the underarm seams and side seams to check for fit.

6 Remove the pins from the neck and waist and carefully take off the bodice. Stitch the wrist to waist seam, making an allowance of 5mm/¼in. Trim back the seam to the stitching line, oversewing it for strength if you wish. Turn the bodice to the right side, using forceps or tweezers to turn the sleeves out.

7 Stitch two pieces of 5mm/¼in lace to run from the centre front to the shoulders. Put the bodice on the doll and neatly oversew the back seam. To avoid unnecessary bulk around the waist, do not hem the lower edge of the bodice.

7

MAKING THE SKIRT

1 Cut out two skirt pieces, one in patterned cotton and one in cotton lawn, remembering to place one of the shorter sides of the template against a fold of each kind of material. With right sides together, machine or hand stitch around three sides, leaving the waist edge open.

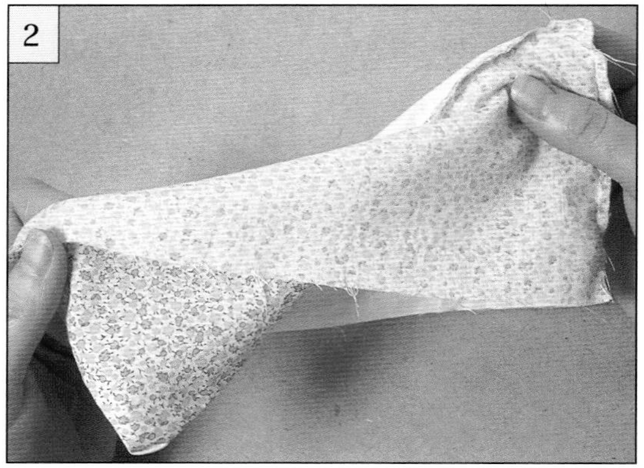

2 Turn to the right side. Press lightly to neaten the sewn edges.

3 Starting at the hem edge, stitch three or four layers of gathered lace around the skirt so that each row overlaps the previous row by 5mm/¼in.

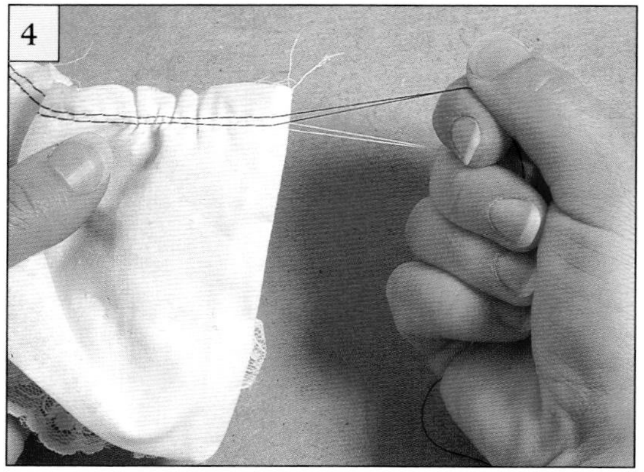

4 Stitch two parallel rows along the top edge of the skirt to gather the skirt. If you use a sewing machine, put a different colour thread on the bobbin so that you can see the gathering thread more easily.

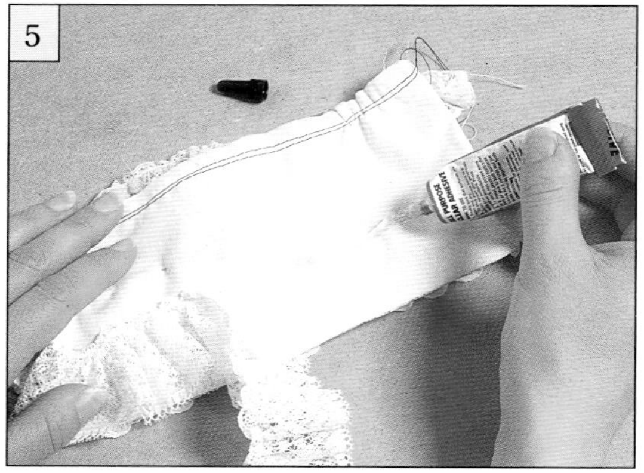

5 Glue or sew a layer of lace to the lining so that its bottom edge is perfectly level with the bottom layer of lace on the overskirt. This represents the petticoat.

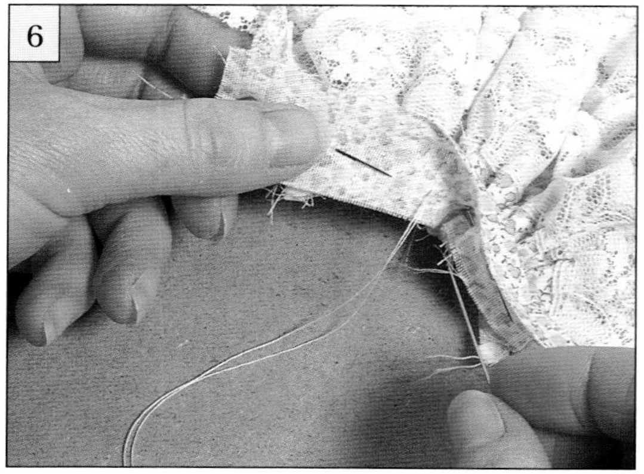

6 Cut out a waistband from the patterned material. Gather the skirt to fit the doll's waist, then, with right sides together, sew the waistband to the skirt.

7 Fold over the waistband and catch it in place on the lining to neaten the top edge.

8 Place the skirt over the bodice, pulling the waistband tightly around the doll. Sew the waistband firmly together and slip stitch the skirt together down the back.

8

~ TIPS ~

- Always clip curved seams to the stitch line so that they lie flat when the garment is turned to the right side.
- Decorate garments with paints and add lace while the clothes are still flat. You will find it much easier to work on the tiny articles before the side seams are stitched.
- Protect the doll's hair with plastic film, held in place by a rubber band around the neck, while you dress the doll.

~ MAKING A PARASOL ~

No Victorian or Edwardian lady would be seen outdoors without a parasol to protect her fair skin from the sun. Parasols varied in size, but all were prettily edged with ribbons or lace.

YOU WILL NEED

- Tracing paper
- Pencil
- Scissors
- Pins
- 12.5 × 12.5cm/5 × 5in patterned lace
- 46cm/18in edging lace, 1cm/½in wide
- All-purpose adhesive
- 10cm/4in thin white plastic tube
- Pin with coloured top

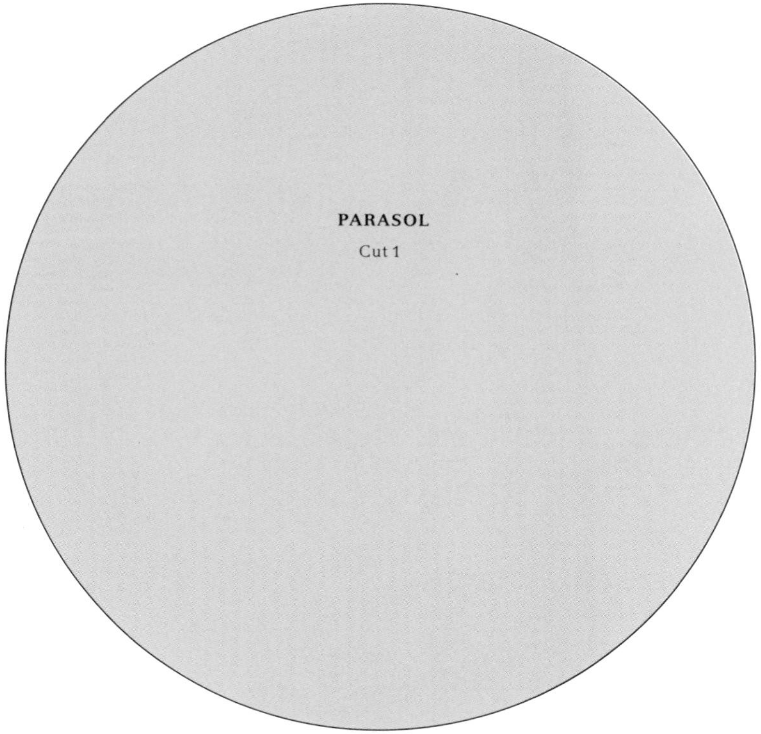

1. Place the template on the lace and cut around the edge.

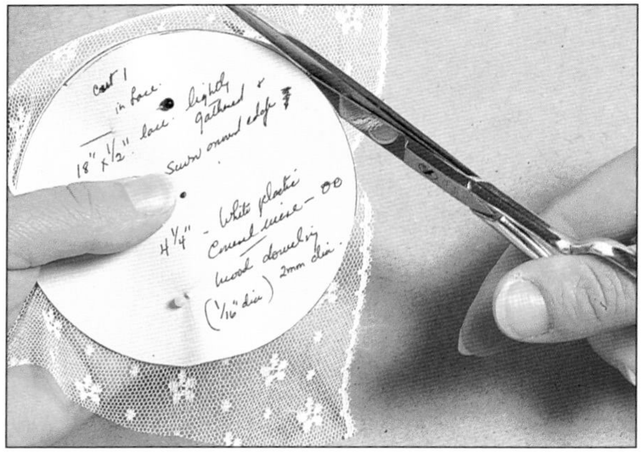

2. Either gather the lace by hand or use a pleater. Draw it up to fit the circumference of the circle and glue it in position. Fold the circle in four and place four pins to divide the circumference equally into quarters.

3. Make a small hole in the centre of the circle and push the plastic tube through it so that about 2.5cm/1in protrudes at the top. Glue the lace to the tube around the hole. Put a little adhesive on the lower part of the tube and stick the four folded edges to the handle. Stick the pin into the bottom of the tube to act as a handle.

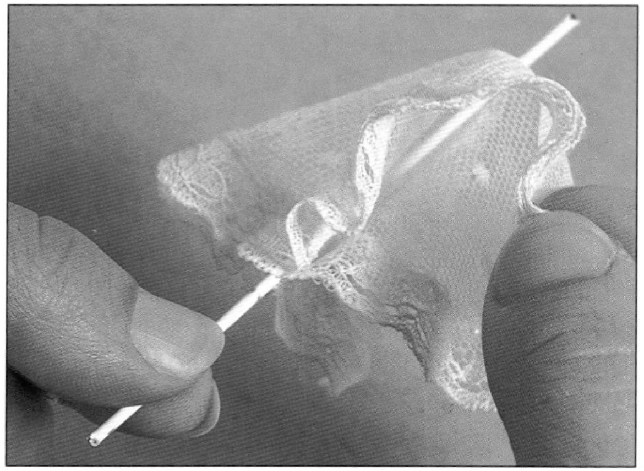

Grandmother

~

Once you have made the basic dress for the Victorian lady, you can easily adapt it for other members of the family. Make the dress in a plain, dark cotton and decorate it with only a little lace and it will be perfect for a grandmother. Add a shawl and a grey wig and you have an ideal doll for a Victorian parlour. Make a little pill-box hat with a feather in it, and she will be more suitable for an early Edwardian drawing room.

MAKING THE WIG

YOU WILL NEED

- All-purpose adhesive
- Scissors

FOR THE WIG

- 15cm/6in white mohair
- 15cm/6in string
- Small bulldog clip
- Setting lotion
- Needle
- White sewing thread

FOR THE HAT

- Piece of buckram, 1cm/½in wide, to go round doll's head
- Scraps of fabric and trimming to match doll's dress
- Feather or other decoration

FOR THE SHAWL

- Tracing paper
- Pencil
- 20cm/8in fine wool fabric
- Narrow bonding web
- Needle
- Thread
- 30cm/12in fringe to match (see box)

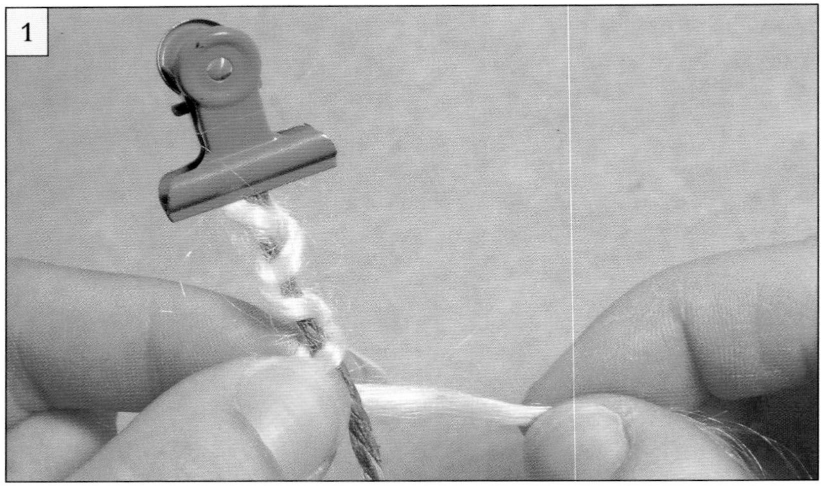

1 Because this wig is not removable, it is best to dress the doll first. Gently brush out the mohair. Divide it into two equal bunches and hold it with a piece of string in a bulldog clip. Plait the mohair firmly around the string. Wet thoroughly with setting lotion and leave to dry.

2 Remove the string and tease out the mohair, but do not brush it.

3 Cover the doll's head up to the hairline with adhesive and place the mohair across the head, taking it to the back of the head but allowing the waves to fall softly around the doll's face.

4 Twist together the long ends of hair and wind them into a bun. Use white sewing thread to hold the ends in place.

5 The finished wig. It adds instant years onto the age of the doll.

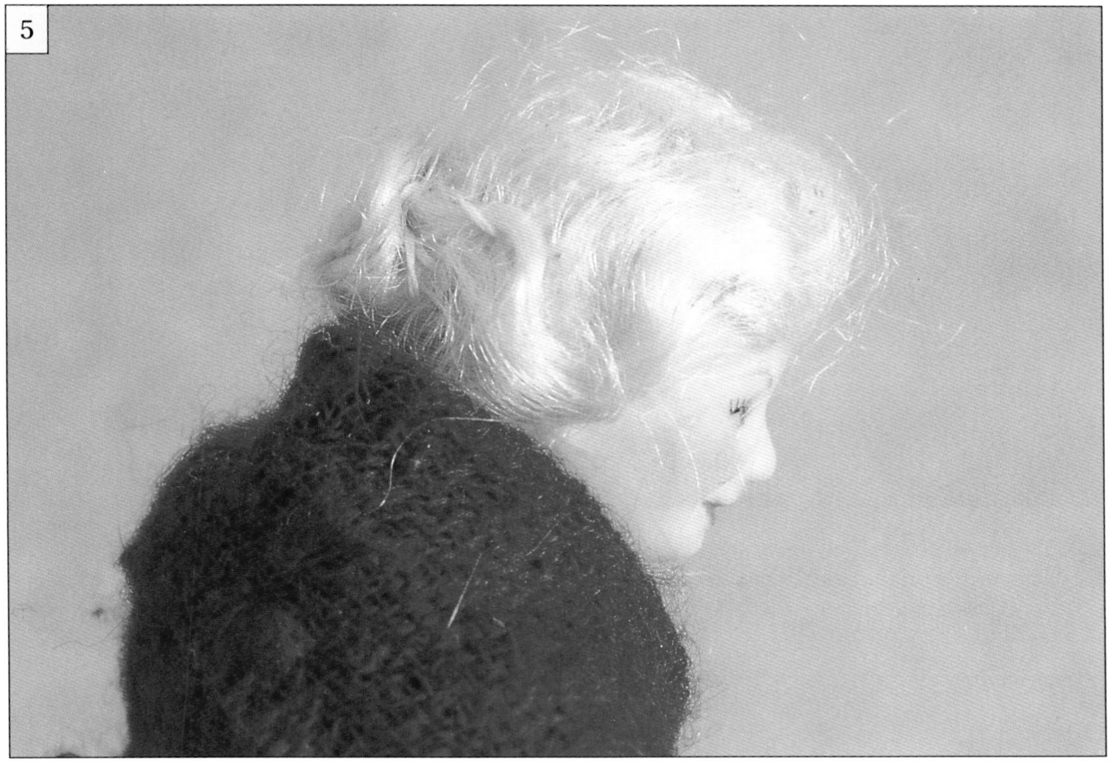

MAKING THE SHAWL

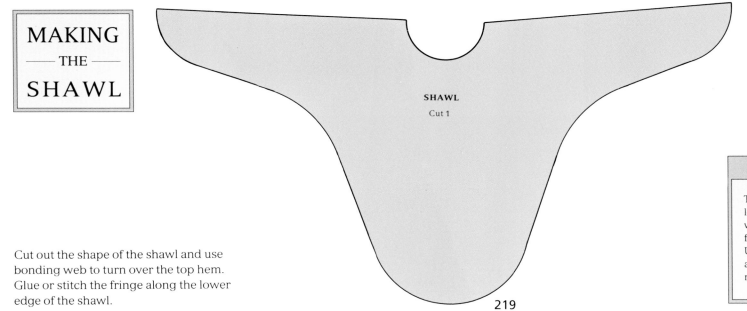

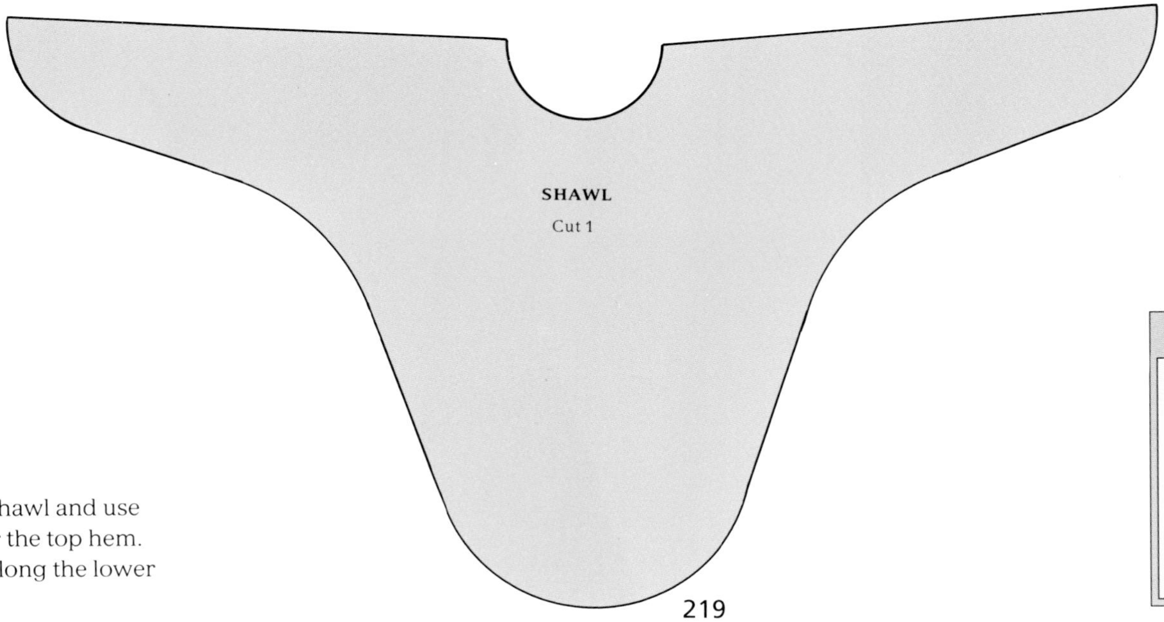

Cut out the shape of the shawl and use bonding web to turn over the top hem. Glue or stitch the fringe along the lower edge of the shawl.

~ MAKING A FRINGE ~

Trim a lady's lightweight summer shawl with a long, white fringe or add a matching fringe to a woollen shawl. Satin, which frays easily, is useful for adding fringes to clothes or even to furniture. Use scraps about 30 × 7.5cm/12 × 3in. Shawls can also be prettily finished off with a little trimming made from grosgrain ribbon.

MAKING THE HAT

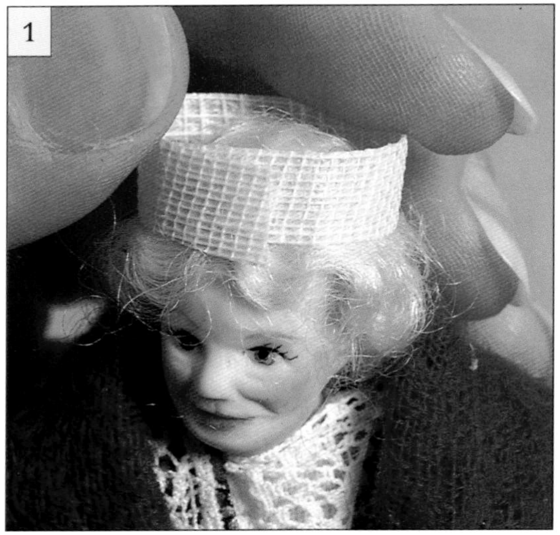

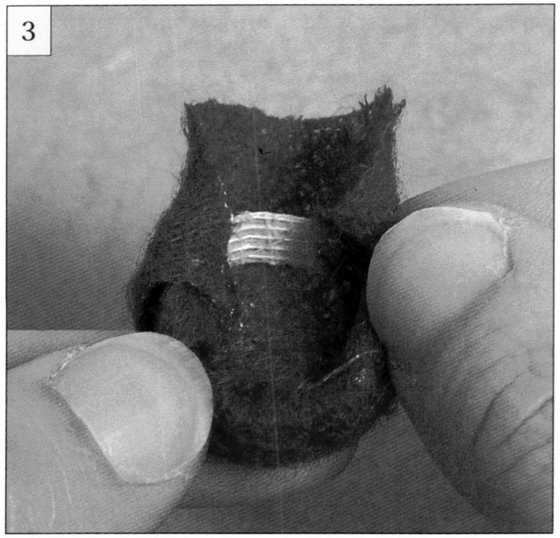

1 Measure and cut the buckram so that it sits firmly on the doll's head. Glue the ends together to form a circle.

2 Cut out a circle of fabric to match or contrast with the doll's dress and place the buckram circle in the centre.

3 Glue the fabric inside the hat, trimming it as necessary so that it is not too bulky.

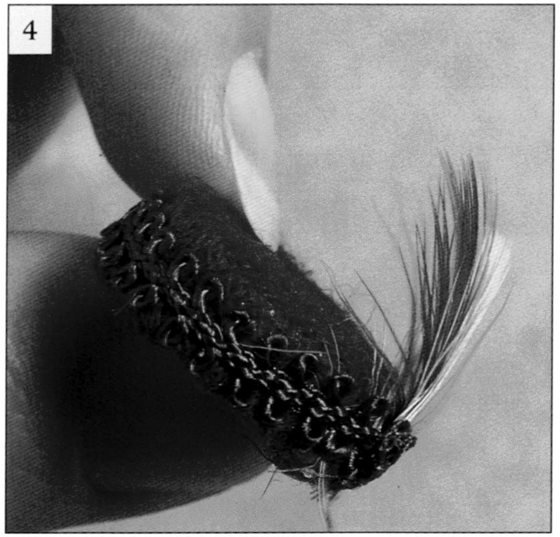

4 Decorate the rim of the hat with braid or lace to match the dress, gluing it in place. Decorate with a small feather if you wish.

Victorian Man

~

Victorian men are usually dressed in dark coats with trousers of a different material – striped or checked, for example – and often with a fancy waistcoat. Top hats, with crowns of various heights, were worn on all occasions. To eliminate unnecessary bulk, shirts do not have sleeves. For the same reason only the front of the waistcoat is made and attached to the shoulders and at the back. The coat sleeves are attached to the body at the shoulder, which is easier than fitting them into a coat. The same basic pattern for the shirt is used on all men dolls who wear coats or jackets.

YOU WILL NEED

- Tracing paper
- Pencil
- Pins
- Scissors
- Narrow bonding web
- Needle
- Sewing thread
- Forceps or tweezers
- Sewing machine (optional)

FOR THE TROUSERS

- 23cm/9in checked or striped material

FOR THE SHIRT

- 30cm/12in white cotton lawn
- 15cm/6in black or blue silk or velvet ribbon, 5mm/¼in wide

FOR THE WAISTCOAT

- 15cm/6in checked or striped material (to match trousers)
- 15cm/6in iron-on backing fabric (such as Vilene)
- Black craft paint
- Wooden toothpick or cocktail stick
- All-purpose adhesive
- Fine chain

FOR THE FROCK COAT

- 30cm/12in lightweight black suiting material
- 23cm/9in coloured satin (for lining, optional)
- 30cm/12in black bias binding

FOR THE TOP HAT

- Small pill box or similar of appropriate diameter for crown of hat
- Plastic film
- Rubber bands
- 20cm/8in black or grey felt
- 1 tbsp PVA
- Hot water
- 3 pieces card, 7.5 × 2.5cm/3 × 1in
- All-purpose adhesive
- White pencil or crayon
- 4cm/1½in ribbon, 3mm/⅛in wide to match felt

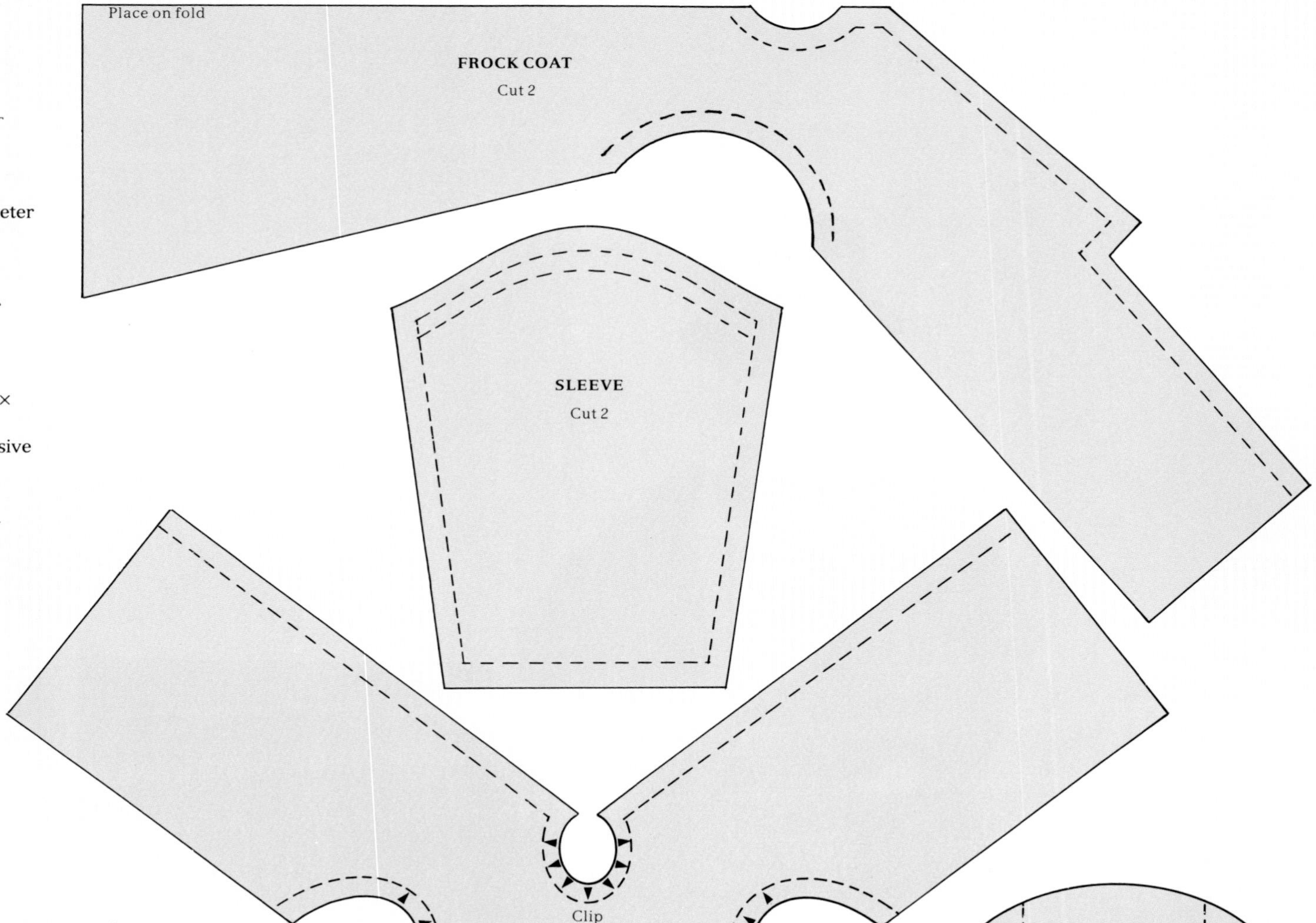

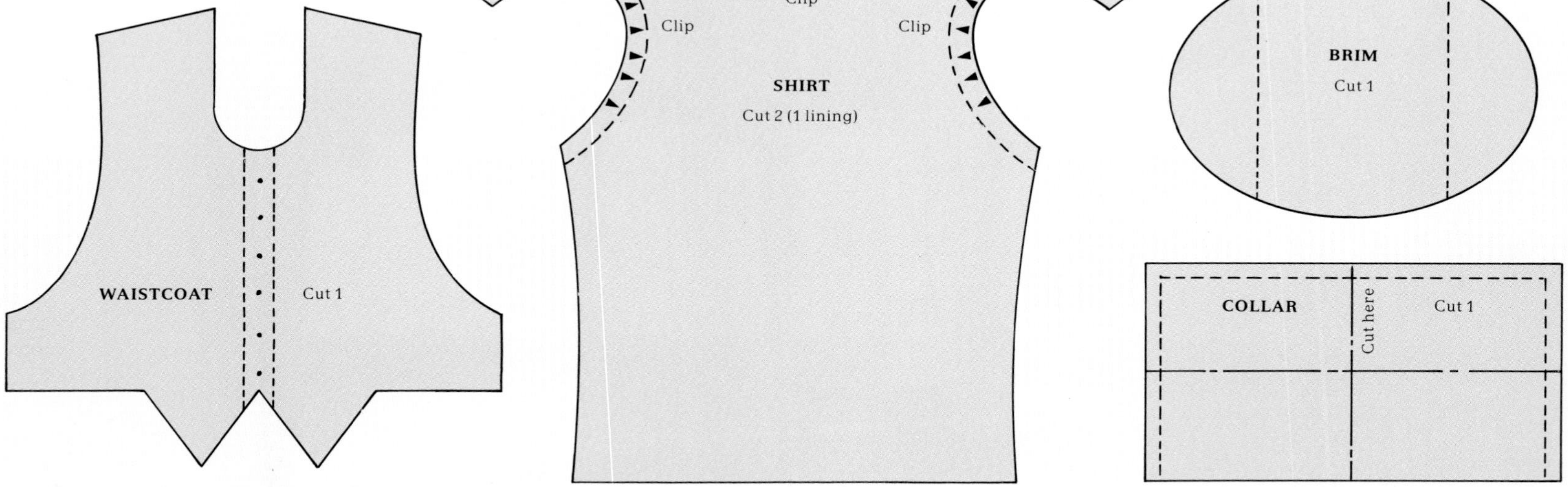

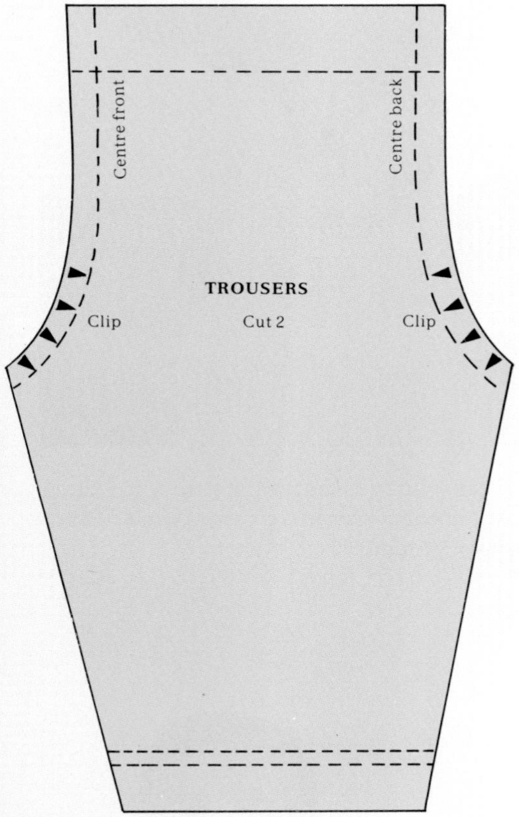

MAKING THE TROUSERS

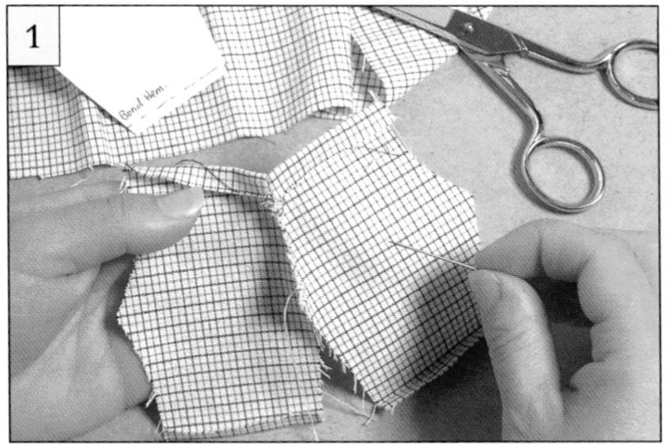

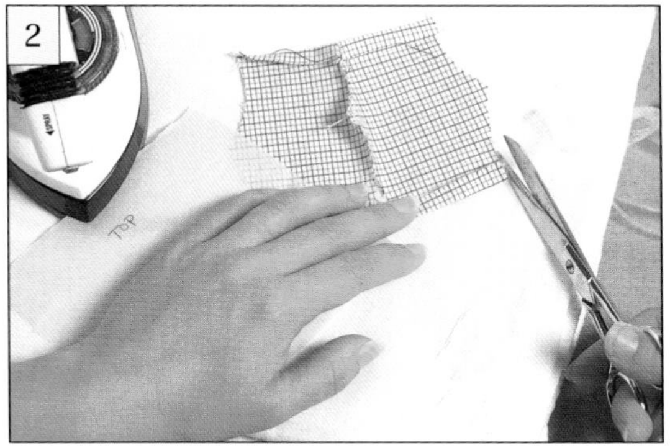

1. Cut out two trouser pieces from checked or striped material and stitch the front centre seam, leaving a 5mm/¼in seam allowance.

2. Use bonding web to turn up the hems at the bottom of the legs and around the waist.

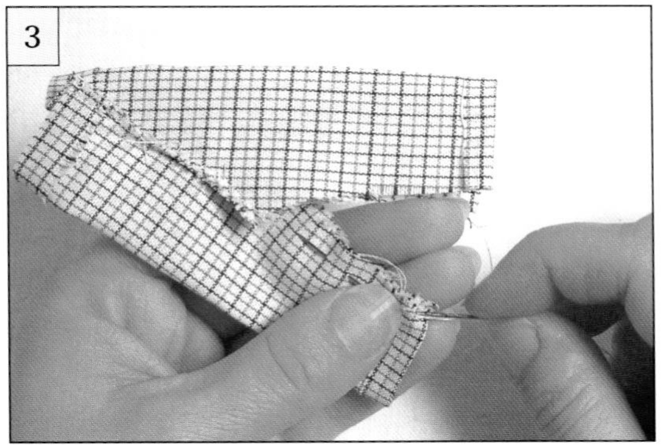

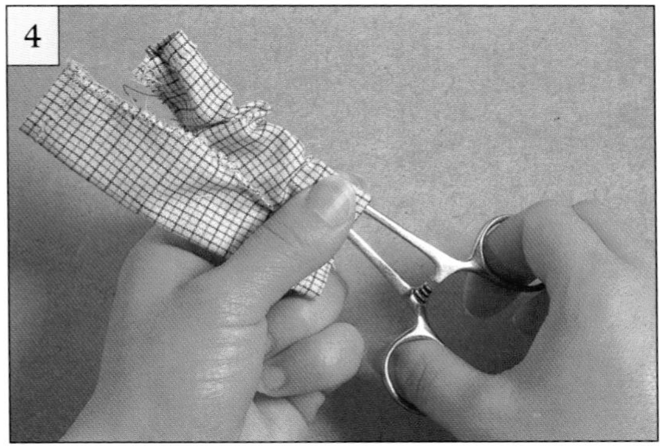

3. Turn the right sides together and stitch the centre back seam. Refold, matching front and back seams. Stitch the crotch and inner leg seams.

4. Use forceps or tweezers to turn the trousers the right way out.

5. Press the trousers and place them on the doll. Catch them with tiny stitches around the doll's waist.

5

MAKING THE SHIRT

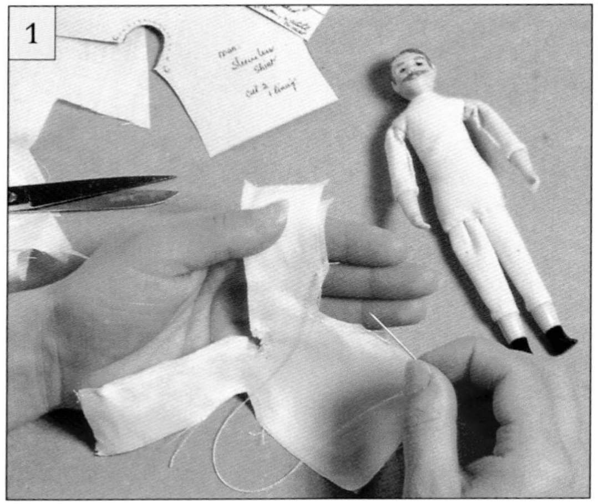

1 Cut out two shirt pieces (one as a lining) and one collar piece from white cotton lawn. Fold the collar in half lengthways and stitch the three open sides, trimming the fabric up the corner seams. Cut the collar in half, turn each piece to the right side and turn in the cut edges by hand to neaten. Press lightly and put to one side.

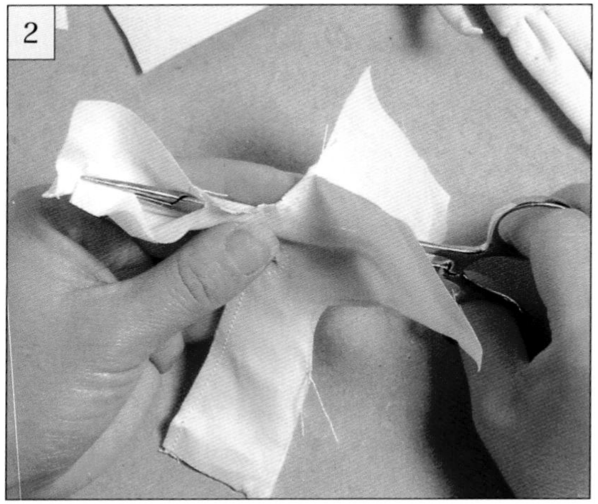

2 Stitch shirt piece and lining together around the underarm seams and up the centre back and around the neck as shown on pattern. Clip to the stitch line and turn to the right side.

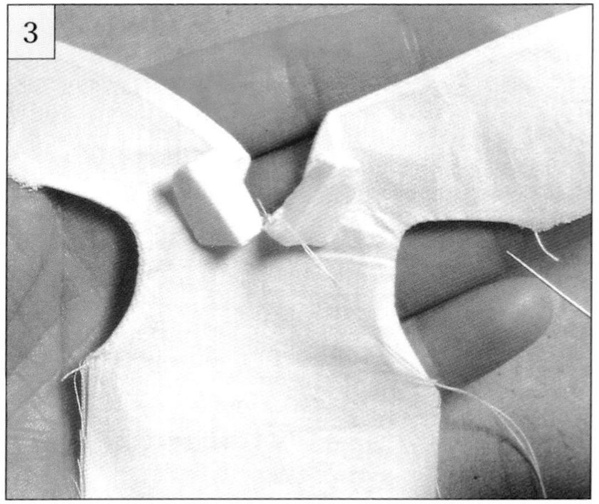

3 Press lightly to flatten the seams and stitch the collar pieces to the centre front of the neck by hand.

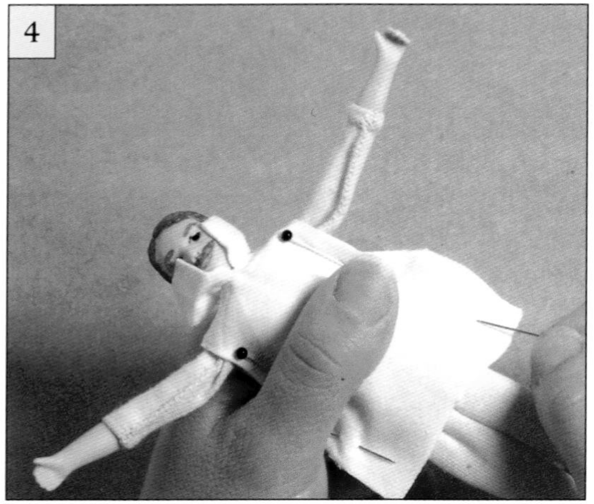

4 Put the shirt on the doll with the wrong side outwards and pin the side and back seams. Remove the pins from the back, remove the shirt and sew up the two side seams. Turn right side out and press. Put the shirt back on the doll and neatly oversew the back seam.

5 Make a tie by knotting the ribbon at the front and take the ends to the back of the neck, sewing them firmly together.

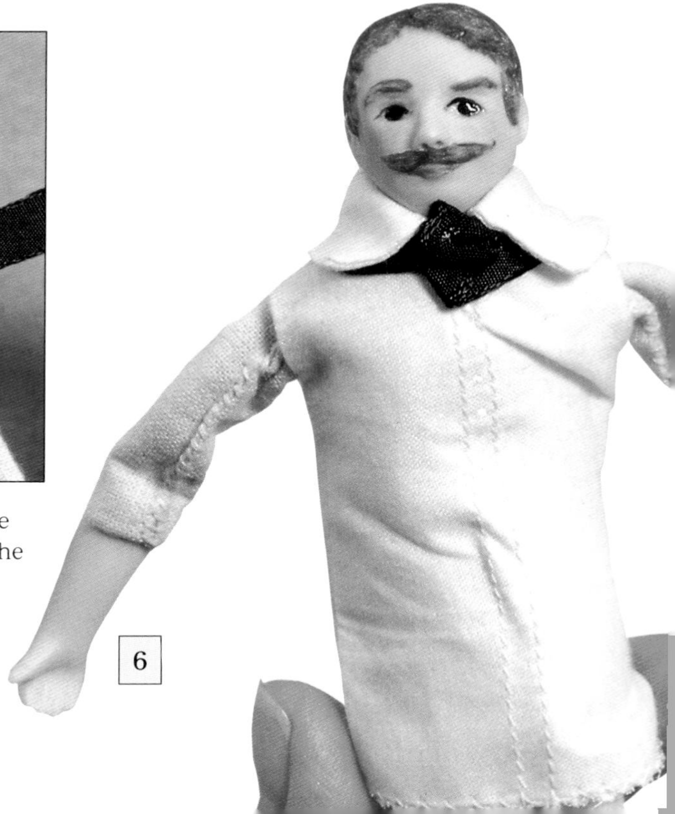

6 The finished shirt and tie.

~ ADDING SLEEVES TO THE ~ SHIRT

You may sometimes want to dress a man doll with a shirt with sleeves.
You will need
- Tracing paper
- Pins
- Pencil
- Scissors
- 15cm/6in white cotton lawn
- Narrow bonding web
- Needle
- Sewing thread

Cut out two sleeve pieces. Use bonding web to turn up the cuff hems and stitch the sides together. Turn to the right side. Slip the arms on the doll and catch them in place around the shoulders of the shirt body. Alternatively, slip the sleeves on the undressed doll and catch them directly to the arms before dressing the doll in the shirt body.

~ MAKING A SLEEVE BOARD ~

A sleeve board can be useful if you have to sew sleeves into a jacket or shirt when they have not been put in flat. You can also lightly press sleeves around a board so that they hold their shape, and it is often easier to add a cuff or lace trim to a sleeve before the sleeve is attached to the coat or dress. You can use a piece of wooden dowel, about 15cm/6in and 5mm/¼in in diameter or, as here, the empty plastic barrel of a ballpoint pen. You will also need approximately 20cm/8in of 5cm/2in wide bonding material and adhesive.

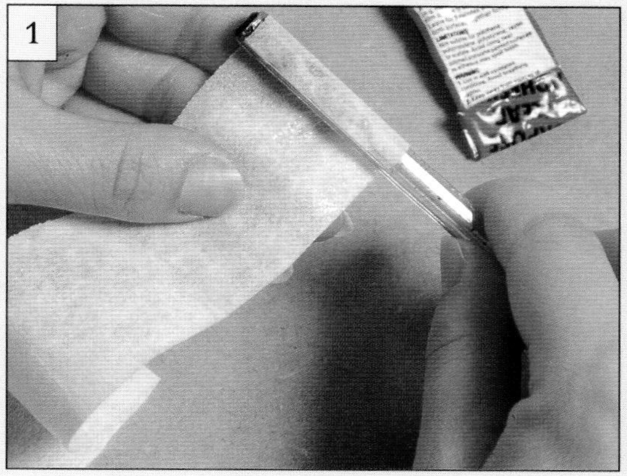

1 Wrap the bonding material around the dowel or pen, holding it down with a spot of adhesive.

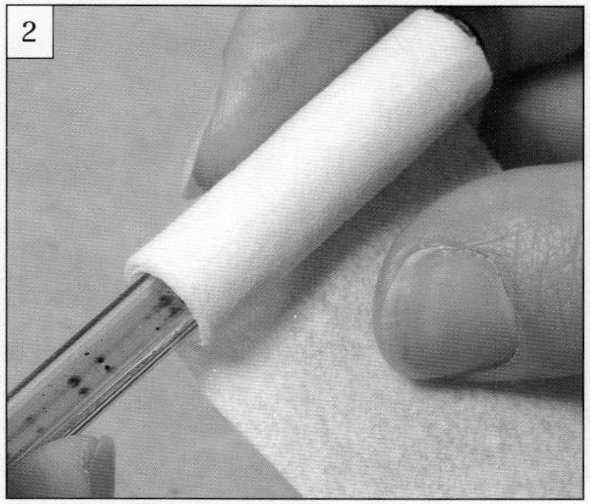

2 Continue to wrap the bonding around until the diameter is sufficient to support a sleeve but not so large that it cannot be inserted into the sleeve.

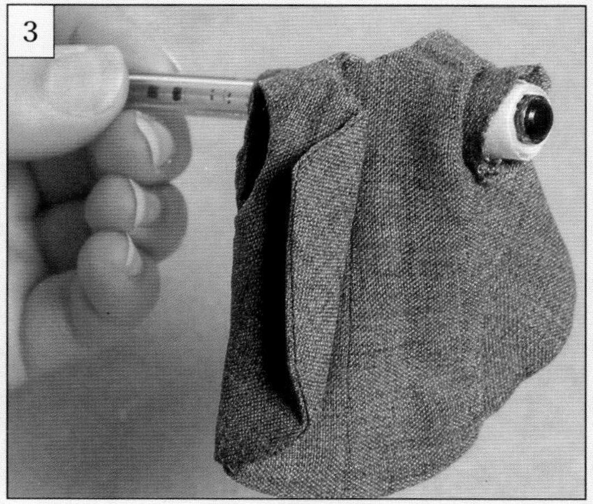

3 Finish off with a spot of adhesive and allow to dry before using.

MAKING THE WAISTCOAT

This pattern can be easily adapted to make a higher or lower neckline to suit the doll to be dressed. Once you have bonded the waistcoat material to the lining, modify the pattern as you wish before following the steps below.

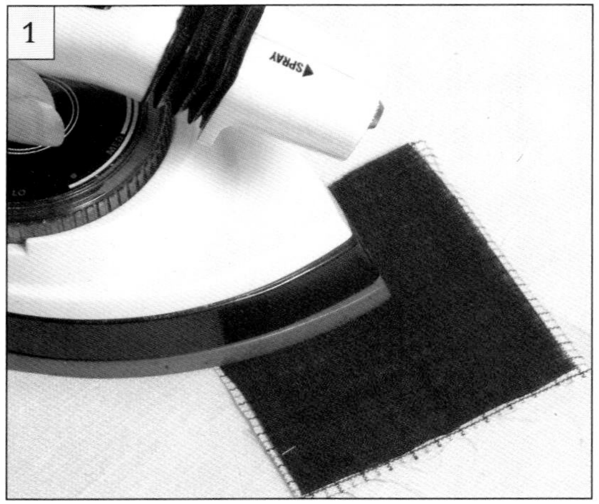

1 Fuse the backing material to the waistcoat material with an iron.

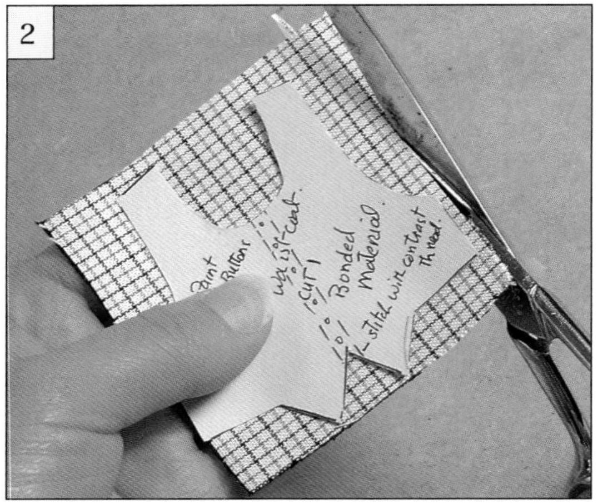

2 Cut out the waistcoat.

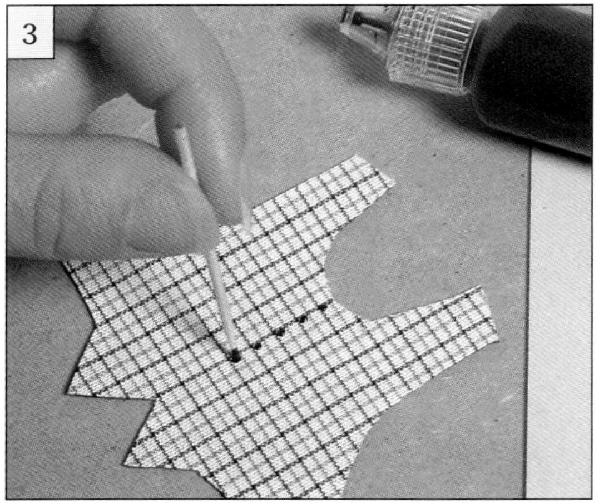

3 Use a wooden toothpick or cocktail stick to paint on buttons down the centre front of the waistcoat.

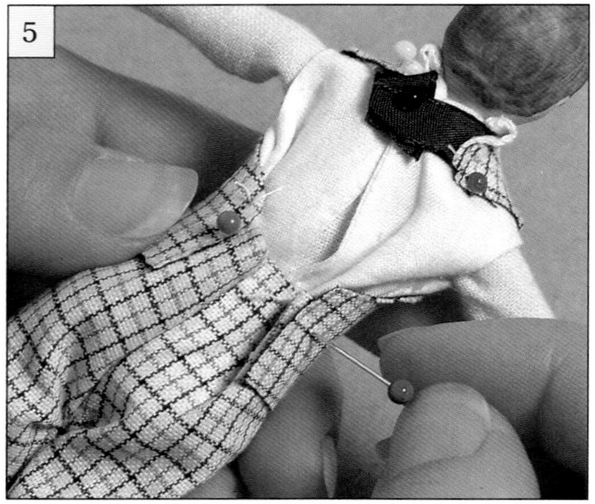

5 Place the waistcoat on the doll, pinning it in position at the shoulders and down the sides.

6 Neatly stitch the waistcoat in position.

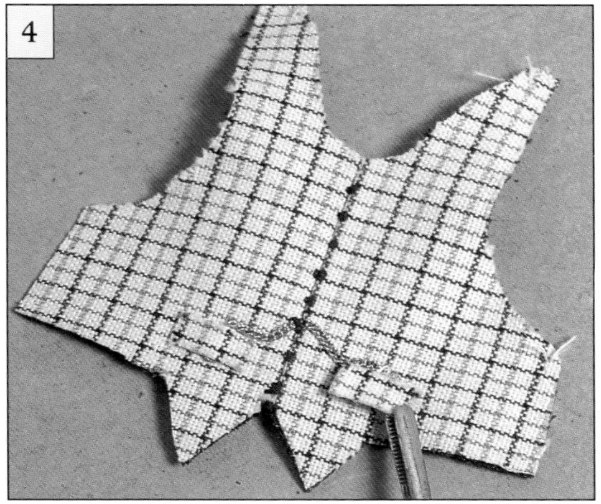

4 Cut out pocket fronts from scraps of fused fabric and glue them in position, adding a tiny length of chain running from pocket to pocket.

~ TIP ~

One way of eliminating bulk is to omit those parts of garments that are not visible. Shirt sleeves cannot be seen under a coat, for example. If you are dressing a man doll in a waistcoat, you need only make the front, which can be attached with a few tiny stitches at the shoulders and to the underarm seams of the shirt.

MAKING THE FROCK COAT

The name "frock coat" was used for several different styles. It can be a double-breasted coat with a full skirt reaching to the knees at both the front and back or it can have cut-out fronts. They are often made with lining that is the same colour as the main fabric, but if you are dressing a doll for a special occasion, you might want to use a contrasting colour of satin lining fabric.

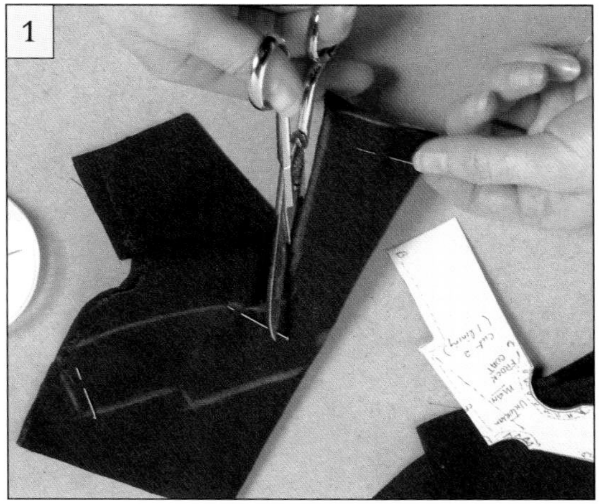

1 Cut two pieces for the coat (remembering to use a different fabric for the lining if you wish) and two sleeves, which will be attached to the doll's body, not to the coat itself.

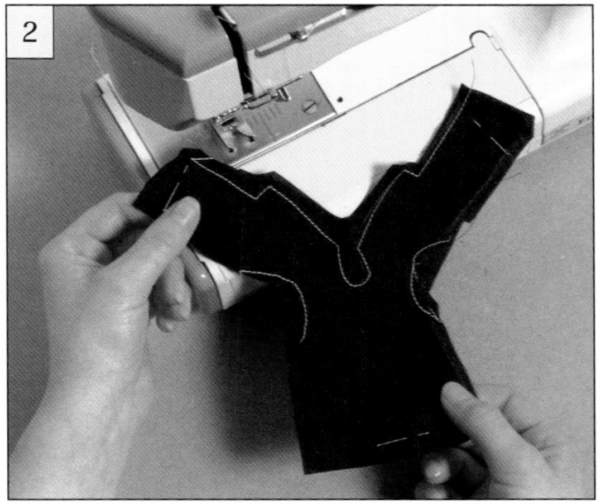

2 Machine or hand stitch the two coat pieces together around the underarm seams, and from the bottom of one front, around the neck and down the other front. Clip the arm and neck curves.

3 Turn the coat to the right side, using tweezers or forceps to pull through the material of the front, and press lightly to turn back the collar revers.

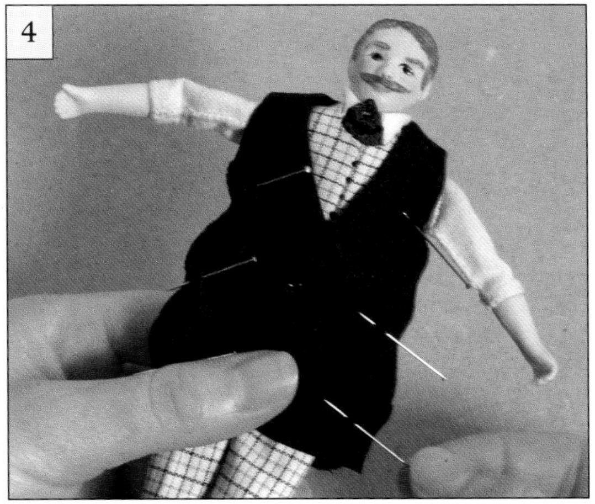

4 Dress the doll in the coat and pin the side seams together. If you have used a different coloured lining, you should put the coat on inside out. Take off the coat and neatly stitch the side seams.

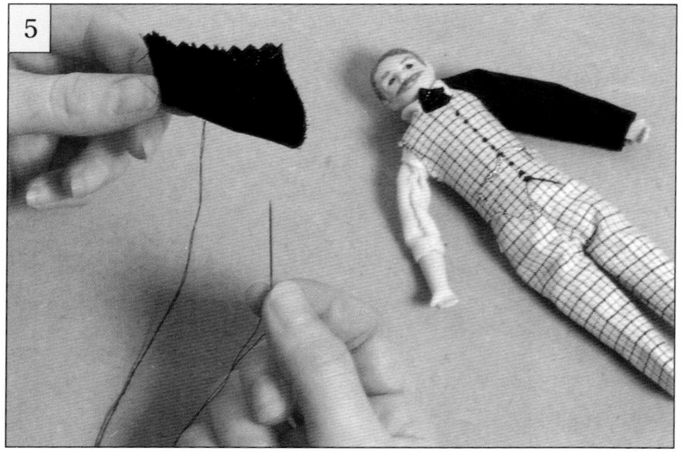

5 Use bonding web to turn up the cuff hems of the sleeves. Stitch the underarm seams and turn the sleeves the right way out.

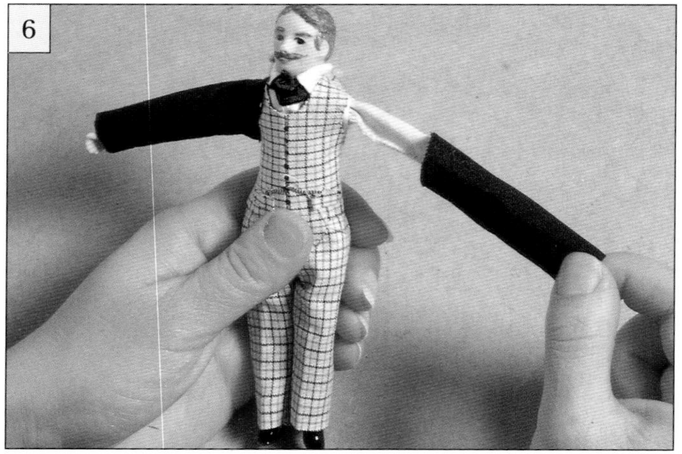

6 Slip them onto the doll and attach them at the shoulder with a few stitches.

7 Attach black bias binding to the bottom hem of the coat, turn it under and slip stitch it to the lining.

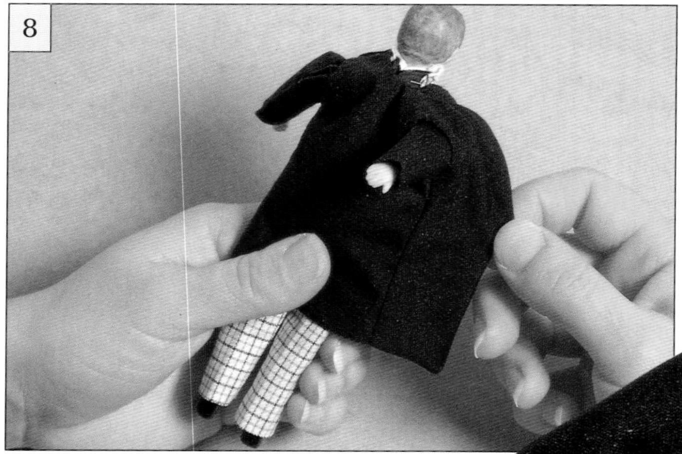

8 Dress the doll in the coat, catching it at the shoulder of the sleeves with a few tiny stitches.

9

9 The dressed doll.

MAKING THE TOP HAT

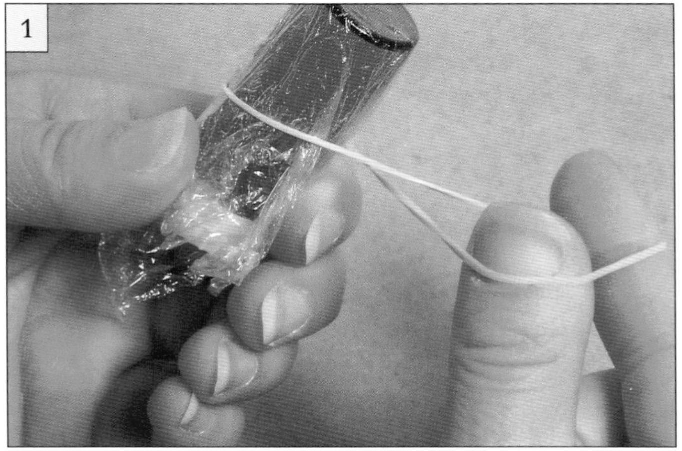

1 Cover one end of the pill box with a small piece of plastic film, holding the film in position with a rubber band.

2 Cut out one piece of felt for the crown of the hat and one piece for the brim, and soak them in the PVA mixed with hot water.

3 Pull the felt for the crown firmly down over the end of the covered pill box. Press it down as firmly as you can and hold it tightly in place with a rubber band. Leave until dry.

4 Glue the three strips of card together to make a former for the brim and cover them with plastic film. Press the soaked circle of felt firmly around the former. Leave until dry.

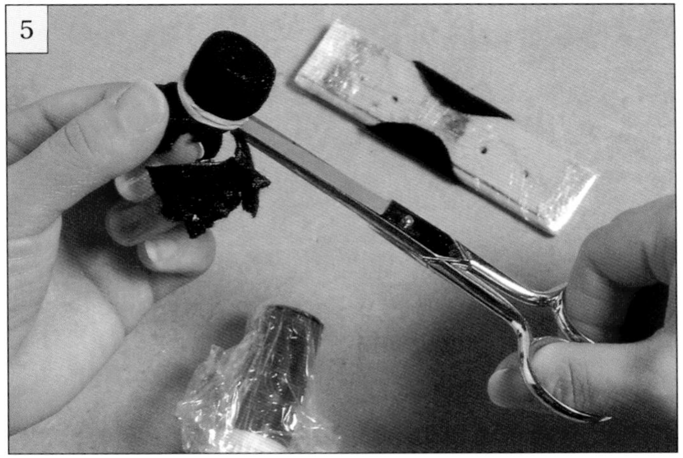

5 Take the crown from the pill box and cut the rubber band. Trim the felt so that the crown is about 2.5cm/1in high.

6 Place the pill box in the centre of the brim and draw around it with a white pencil or crayon.

7 Punch a hole in the centre of the circle you have drawn and make a series of wedge-shaped cuts out to the edge of the circle.

8 Bend up the wedges and glue them to the inside of the crown.

9 Glue a length of narrow ribbon around the bottom of the crown to cover the join with the brim.

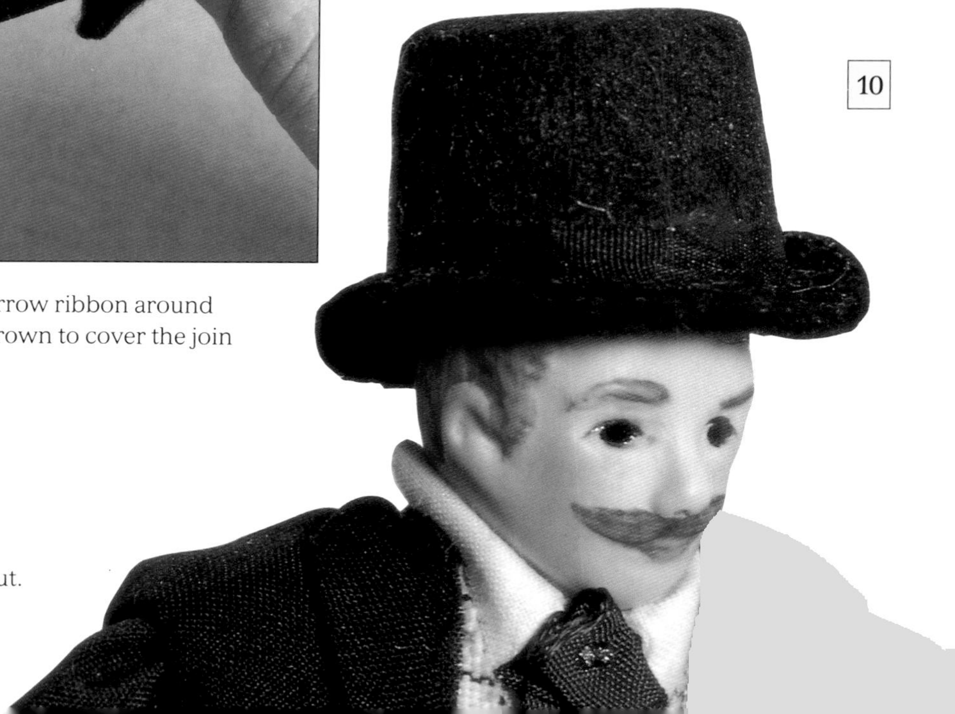

10

10 The Victorian man is now ready to go out.

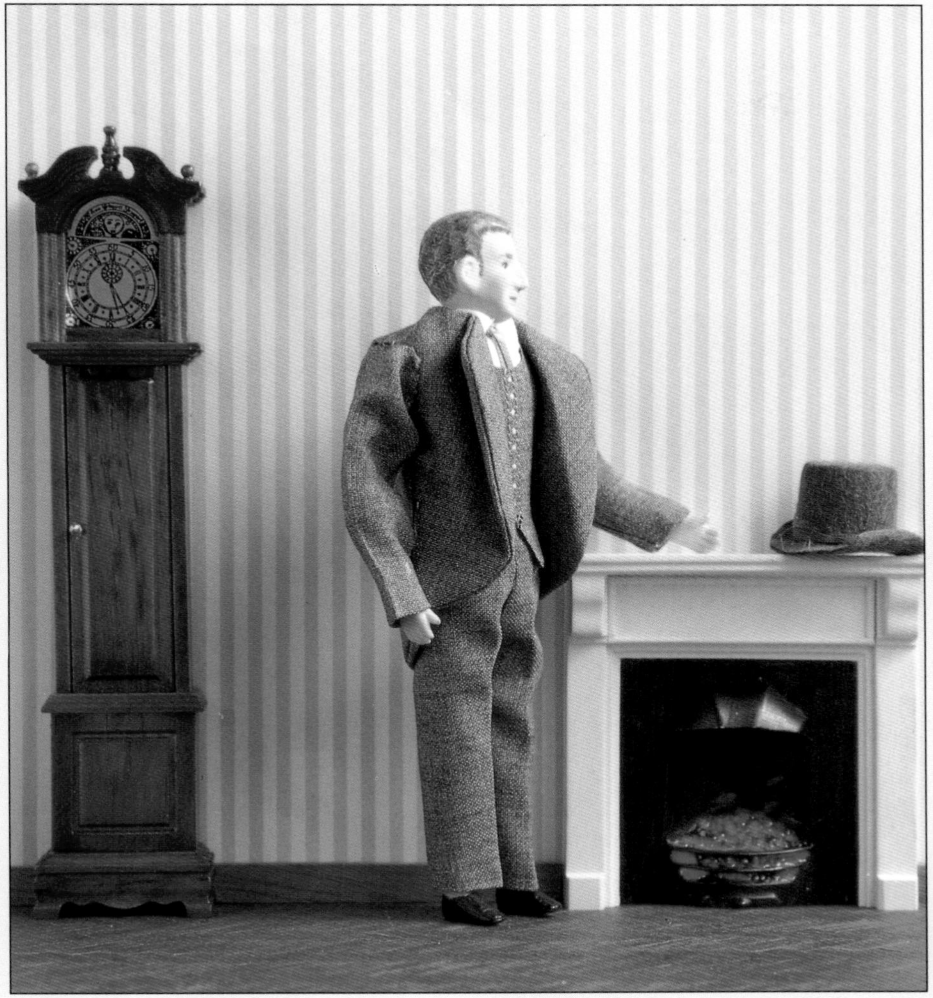

~ EDWARDIAN MAN ~

After you have made the Victorian man, it is really quite simple to alter the period of his dress. The Lounge Suit was especially popular in Edwardian times, so, by replacing the frock coat with a lounge jacket (see page 232) his dress becomes suitable for the time. This man has a grey morning suit which is versatile enough to be worn for many different occasions.

~ EDWARDIAN LADY ~

The outfit of the Victorian Lady can easily be altered to one that is suitable for Edwardian times. Follow the patterns and instructions for the bodice on page 210, but choose another fabric and use less lace. As Edwardian skirts vary, it is advisable to choose your own pattern. They are easily obtained. Add a wide-brimmed hat with an extravagant feather and the result is an elegant lady of the house.

~ MAKING A LOUNGE SUIT ~ JACKET

Being able to change part of the clothing on a doll and move it to another century is an easy way of filling your doll's house with a new family. The Victorian man is an excellent example of this. If you take off his frock coat and large tie, you can give him an ordinary lounge suit jacket, made from the same fabric as his trousers and waistcoat, and he will jump forwards in time by a century. You could make him into a business man, for example, by giving him a new tie, different hat – a bowler or a homburg, perhaps – and a walking cane.

The jacket here is made from the same checked material as the trousers and waistcoat, and it must, therefore, be made a little differently from the plain black frock coat. The jacket has shoulder seams.

YOU WILL NEED

- Tracing paper
- Pencil
- Pins
- Scissors
- 46cm/18in fabric to match trousers and waistcoat
- 15cm/6in white cotton or lining fabric
- Needle
- Sewing thread
- Narrow bonding web
- Black craft paint
- Wooden toothpick or cocktail stick
- Dark narrow ribbon for tie
- All-purpose adhesive

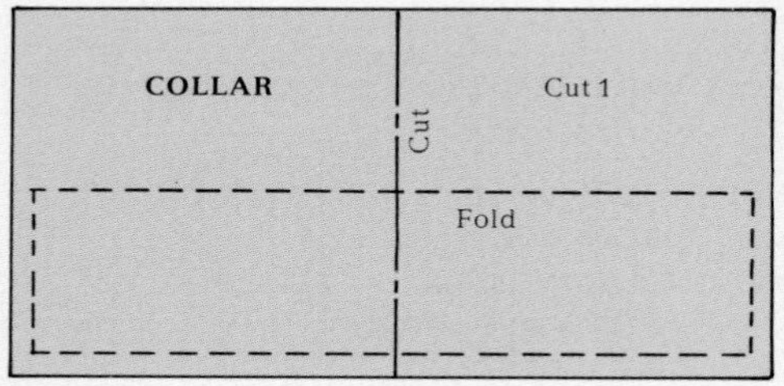

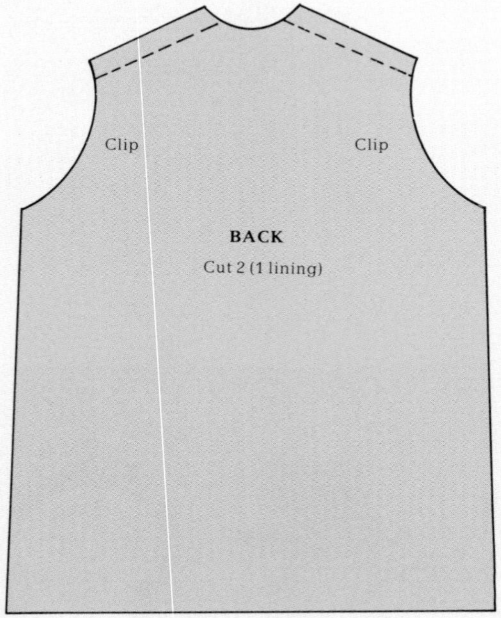

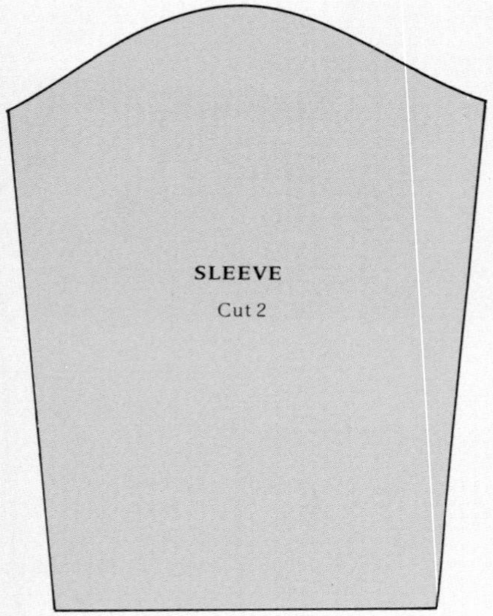

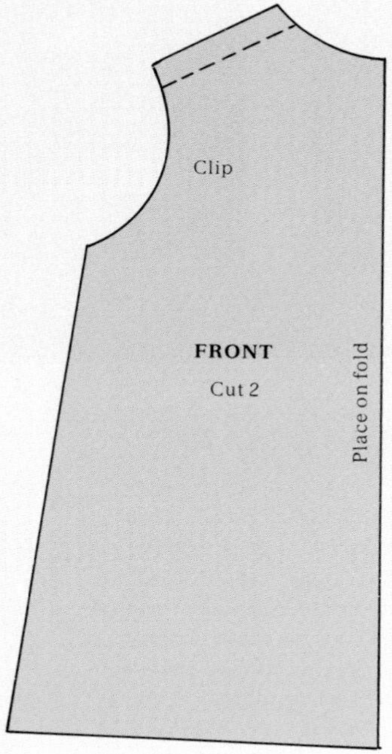

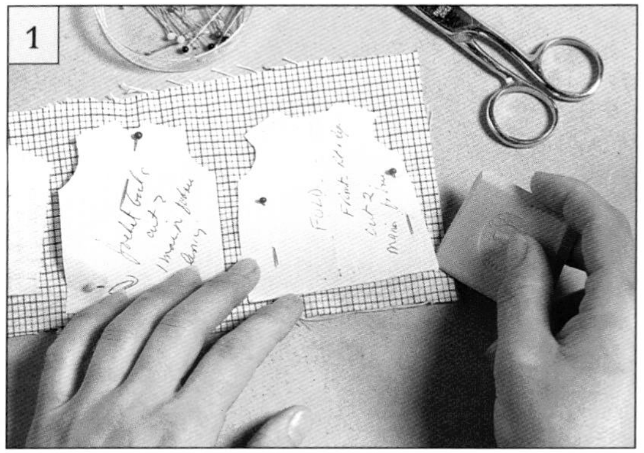

1 Cut out two front pieces from the main fabric, following the direction of the pattern carefully and remembering to place the centre line against a fold in the fabric. Because the front of the jacket is self-lined, you can fold back the top to form revers without having to include an extra seam.

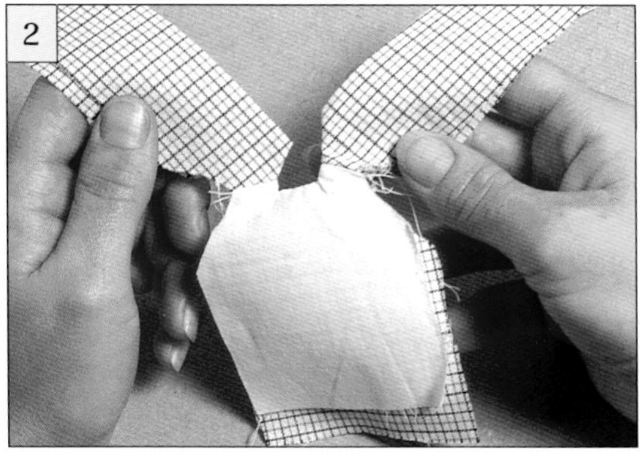

2 Cut out two back pieces, one in main fabric and one in lining. Fold the two front pieces in half and stitch all shoulder seams together, so that the back lining is attached to the front shoulders. Stitch around the neck curve, clip and turn to the right sides. Press lightly.

3 Cut out two sleeves from the main fabric and turn up the cuff hem with bonding web. Attach the sleeves to the jacket shoulders. At this stage the jacket is still flat.

4 Still with the jacket inside out, place it on the doll and pin down the front and then pin the side and underarm seams together. Remove the front pins and stitch the underarm and side seams, starting at the cuff edge and sewing to the lower edge of the jacket. Turn the jacket to the right side. Hem the lower edge by hand. Press, turning back the revers.

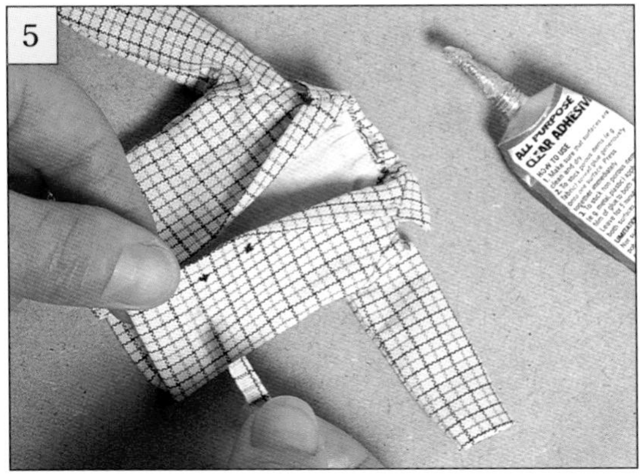

5 Cut out the back collar. Fold it in two lengthways and stitch the two short edges. Turn to the right side, turn in the long edges and stitch along the back neck of the jacket. Use a toothpick or cocktail stick to paint on some buttons and glue little pieces of fabric in place to represent pocket flaps.

6 Dress the doll in the jacket. If you wish, give him a new tie by fastening a thin piece of ribbon around his neck under the collar of his shirt.

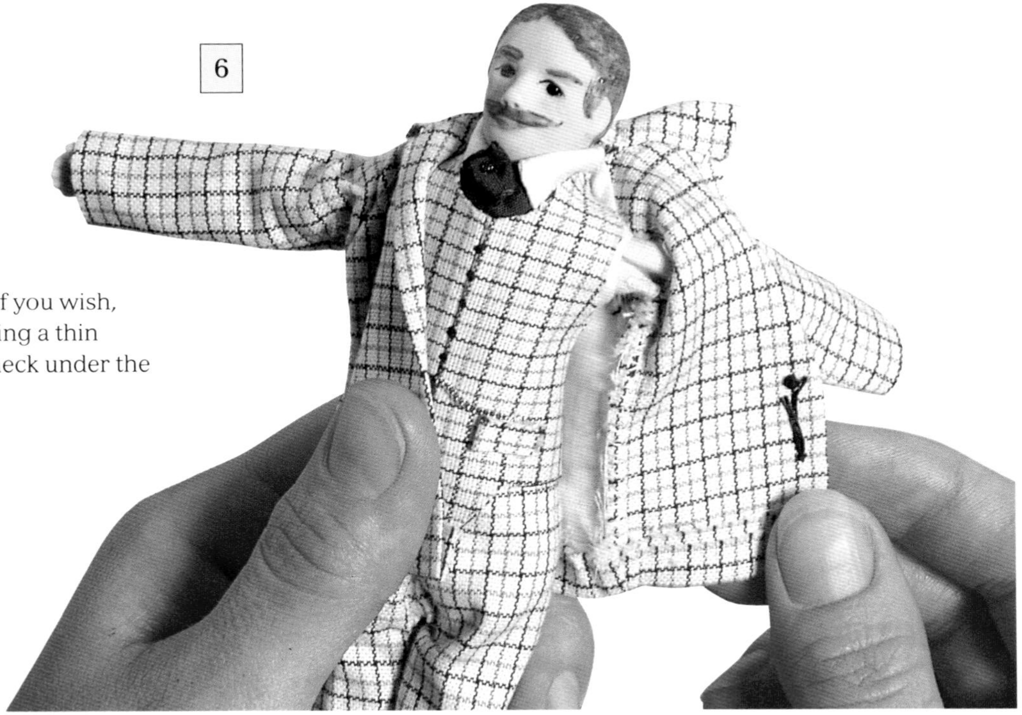

Victorian Girl

~

In Victorian and Edwardian times children of the upper classes were generally dressed as little adults. Little girls wore lace-edged pantaloons and frilly petticoats. Many paintings and prints from that period show dresses with lace, ribbons and bows and, even on the hottest days, coats. Little girls also wore highly decorated hats. The set of clothes described here is to fit a doll's house doll that is 7.5–9.5cm/3–3½in tall.

YOU WILL NEED

- Tracing paper
- Pencil
- Pins
- Scissors
- Needle
- Sewing thread
- Narrow bonding web
- Forceps or tweezers
- Sewing machine

FOR THE PANTALOONS

- 15cm/6in fine white cotton fabric
- 15cm/6in white edging lace, 5mm/¼in wide

FOR THE DRESS

- 23cm/9in very fine white cotton fabric
- 115cm/45in (total) insertion lace, 1cm/½in wide (white or coloured)
- 115cm/45in (total) edging lace, 5mm/¼in wide (white or coloured)
- 6 tiny pearl beads
- All-purpose adhesive (optional)

FOR THE COAT

- 23cm/9in fine cotton fabric with dainty pattern (or quantity of lining fabric)
- 38cm/15in edging lace, 5mm/¼in wide (white or to match pattern)
- 38cm/15in edging Picot (white or to match pattern)

FOR THE BONNET

- 25cm/10in white insertion lace, 1cm/½in wide
- 25cm/10in white edging lace, 5mm/¼in wide
- Embroidered motif
- 38cm/15in silk ribbon, 3mm/⅛in wide
- Shirring elastic

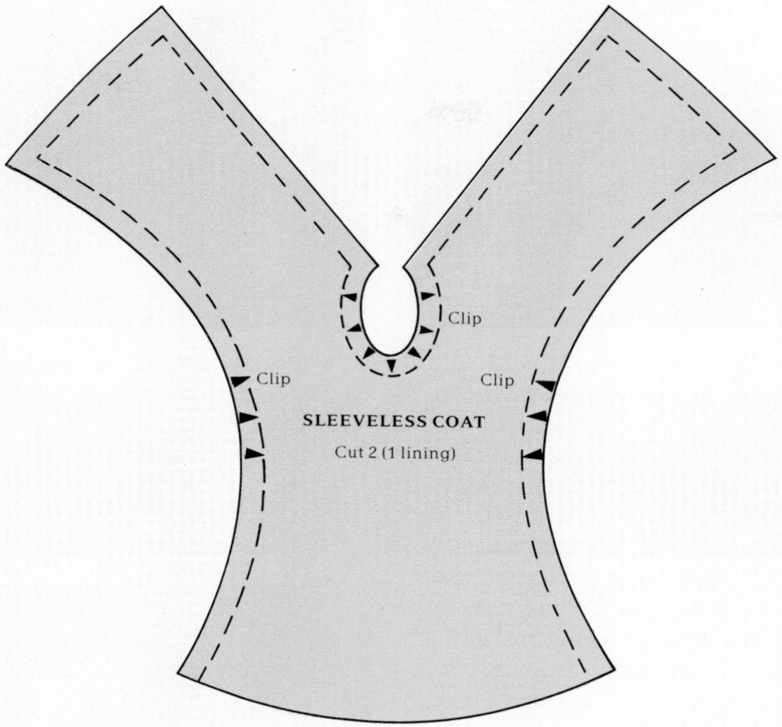

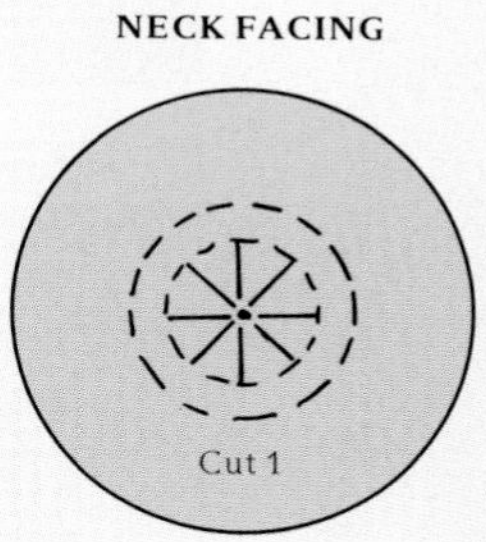

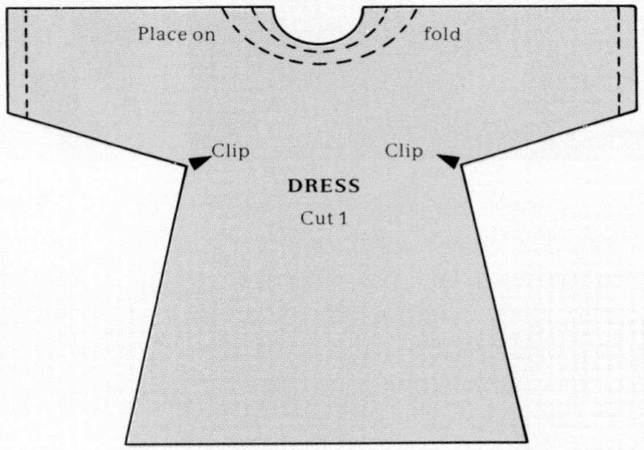

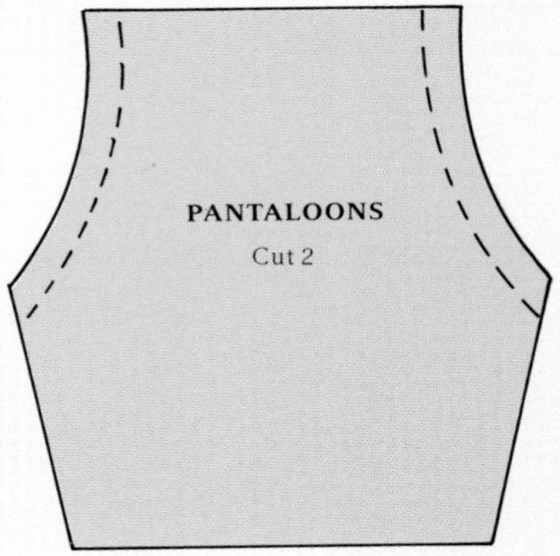

MAKING THE DRESS

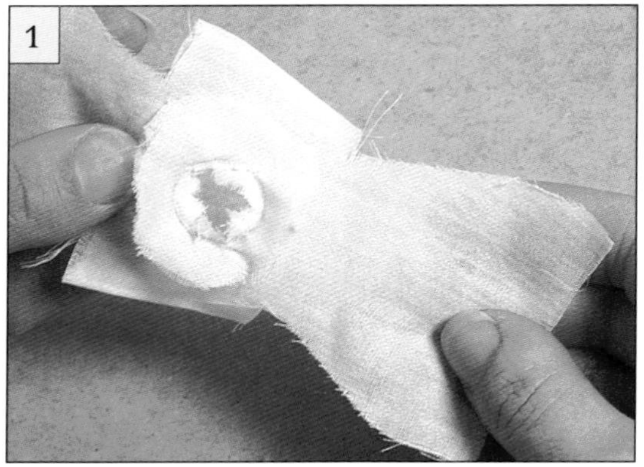

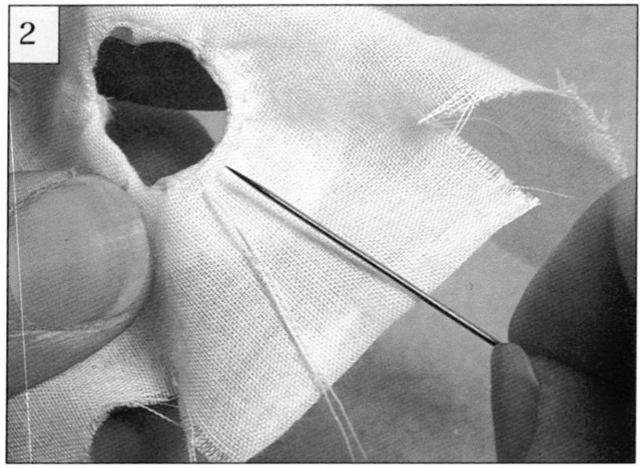

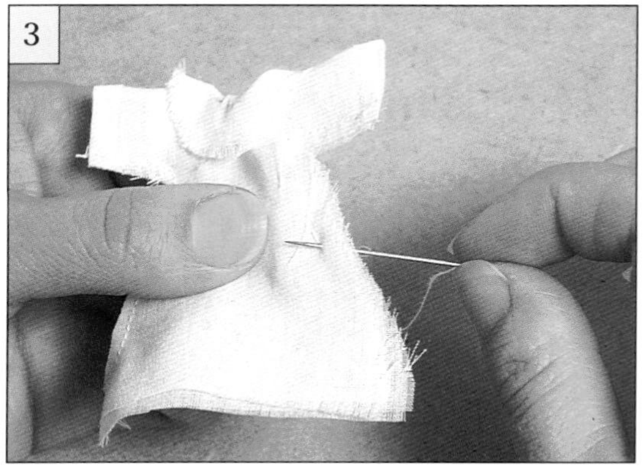

1 Before you make the dress make the pantaloons in the same way as those for the Victorian Lady (see page 212). Cut out the dress pattern and neck facing from fine white cotton fabric. Mark the centre of the neck line of the dress with a pin. Baste the neck facing to the dress, using the smallest possible stitches, cut out the centre of the facing and clip the edges of the circle. Try the dress on the doll. If it will not go over the doll's head, stitch another circle just outside the first circle and cut again. If the doll has a wig, you may find it easiest to remove the wig before dressing the doll. The wig can be glued back on once the doll is dressed.

2 Turn the dress to the right side, catch the facing to the neck edge and press lightly. Use narrow bonding web to turn up the hems of the sleeves while the dress is still flat.

3 With right sides together, pin the side and underarm seams and stitch together, clipping the underarm seam to the sewing line. Turn the dress to the right side and try it on the doll. Use narrow bonding web to turn up the hem.

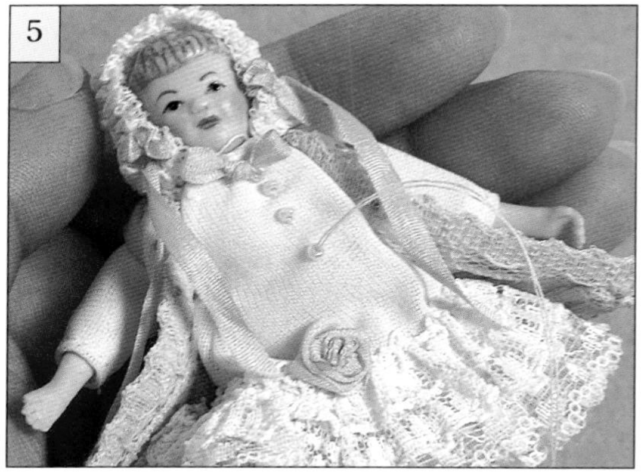

4 You will need three lengths of lace, each approximately 38cm/15in long before gathering (see page 237); you can use all white or introduce a contrasting colour to match the pattern on the coat if you wish. One strip goes on the under side of the basic dress to represent a petticoat. The second strip, which may be coloured if you wish, should be placed so that its lower edge is level with the bottom of the hem. The third strip should be placed just above the second.

5 Finish off the dress by sewing or gluing tiny pearl beads up the front. You can also decorate it with a rose and a lace trim around the neckline if you wish.

~ MAKING THE LACE FRILLS ~

Using the two widths of lace gives the frill extra body. If you prefer, however, you could use ordinary edging lace, 2cm/¾in wide, gathered by hand or on a machine. Although the lace can be sewn by hand, it is quicker and neater to use a machine.

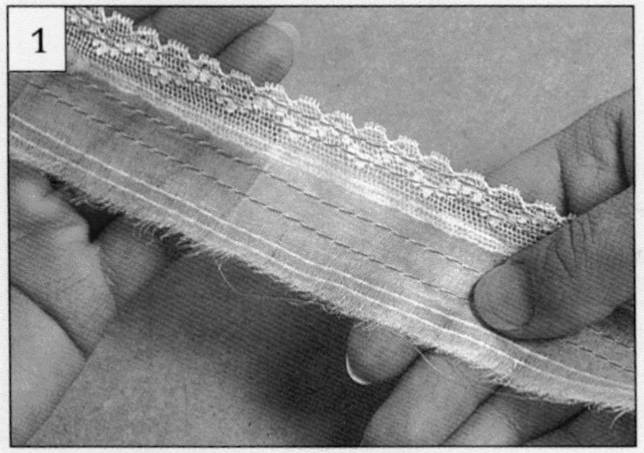

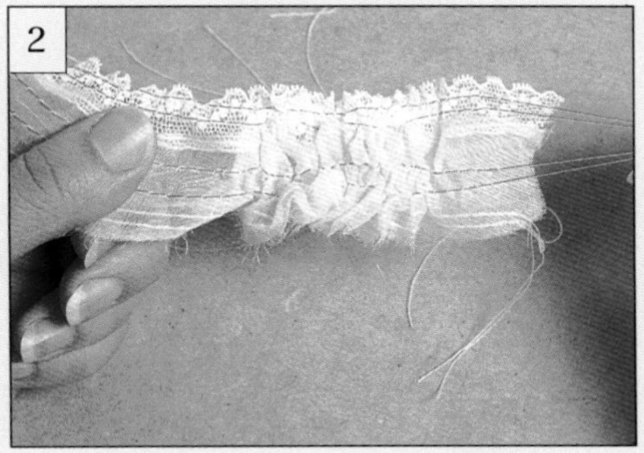

1 Lay the edging lace on the insertion lace and stitch the whole length together with a medium stitch. Cut to the required length (see instructions). Using the longest stitch on your sewing machine, sew three rows. The first row is at the top edge of the lace; the second row should be just above the line of stitching joining the three lengths of lace; and the third row shold be at the lower edge of the lace. Use a contrasting colour for the gathering thread for the second and third rows.

2 Pull the threads up as tightly as you can. Press the gathered lace under a damp cloth and allow to cool. Carefully remove the coloured gathering threads and ease out to the required length, taking great care not to break the remaining stitches. When the lace frill is the correct length, machine with a medium stitch across the first row of stitches or catch by hand.

~ MAKING A ROSE ~

YOU WILL NEED

- A fine quilling stick
- 1 metre/1 yard silk ribbon, 3mm/⅛in wide
- Clear all-purpose adhesive
- Scissors
- Needle
- Sewing thread

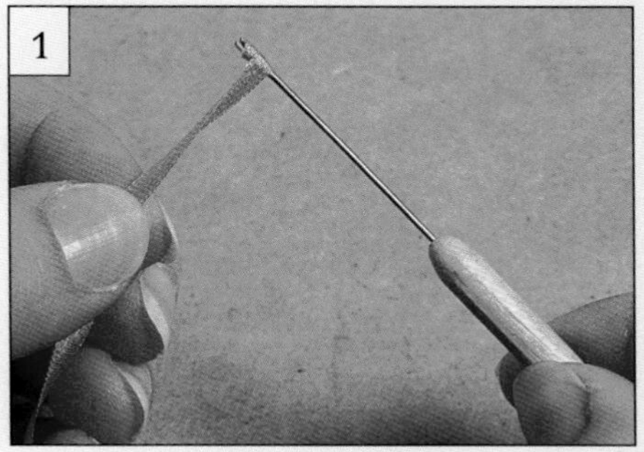

1 Slide the end of the ribbon between the teeth of the rose making tool and hold it in place with a tiny spot of adhesive. Twist the handle of the rose maker to the right and, at the same time, twist the ribbon in the other direction with your other hand, holding it in position with a spot of adhesive.

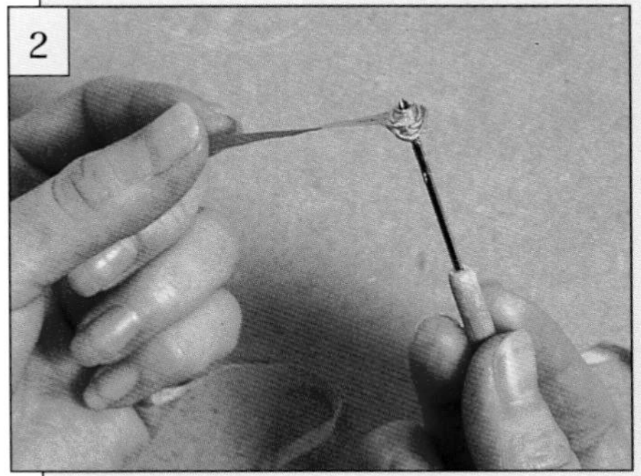

2 Continue to turn the tool and twist the ribbon, adding tiny spots of adhesive after each turn, until the rose measures the required size.

3 Glue the last turn well. Slide the rose carefully off the tool, cut the ribbon neatly, turning and gluing the end under, and stitch it through the centre to a dress or hat. These roses are usually flat enough to be glued in place if you prefer.

~ MAKING A BOW ~

YOU WILL NEED

- Wooden cotton reel or piece of wood 5cm/2in long
- Hammer
- 2 small nails
- Metal file
- 1 metre/1 yard silk ribbon, 3mm/⅛in wide
- Forceps or tweezers
- Scissors

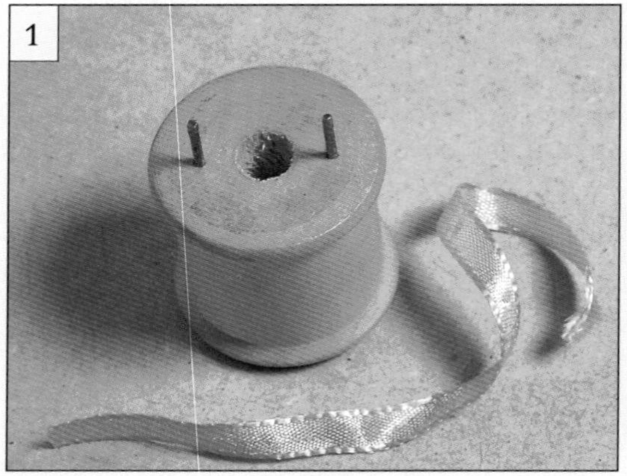

1 Hammer two small nails into the top of an old wooden cotton reel or a suitably sized piece of wood. Smooth the heads of the nails with a file.

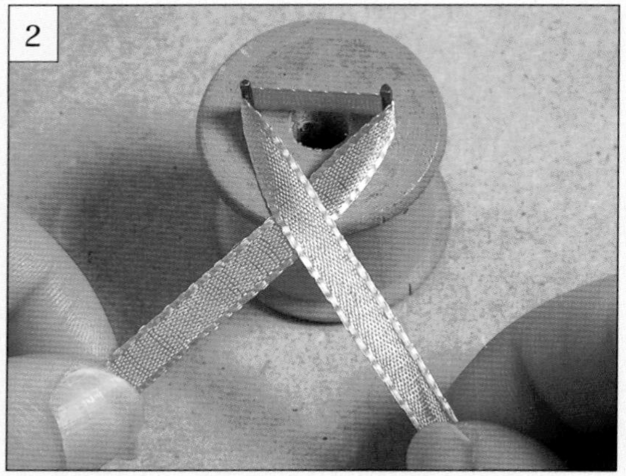

2 Place the ribbon around the nails. Bring the ends to the front and cross the left over the right.

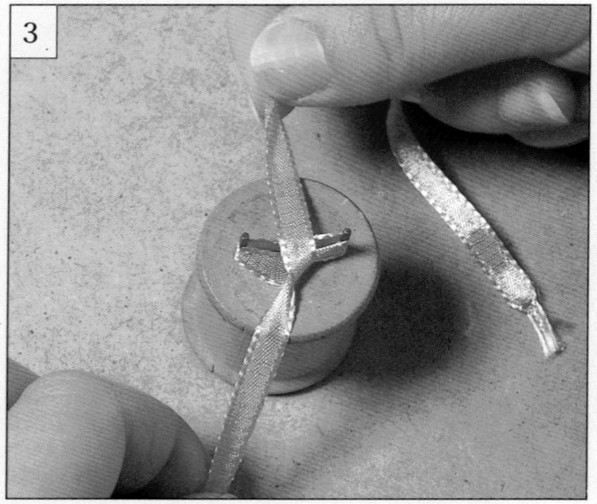

3 Take the end of the lower piece of ribbon over to the back.

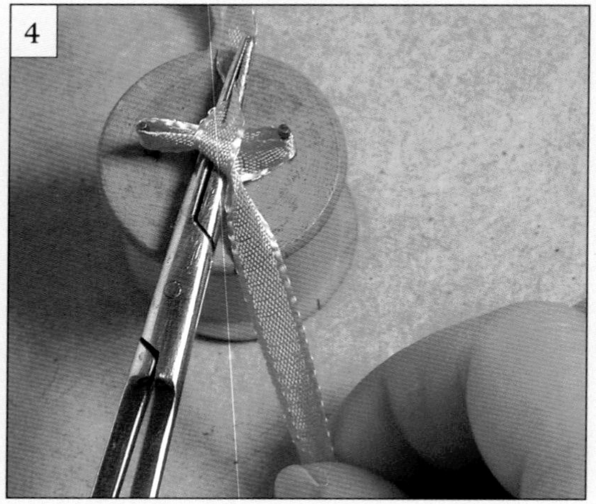

4 Use forceps or tweezers to bring it back to the front under the ribbon wrapped around the nails and under the end held at the front.

5 Tie the two ends at the front firmly together, slide the ribbon off the nails and trim the ribbons level with the bow.

MAKING THE COAT

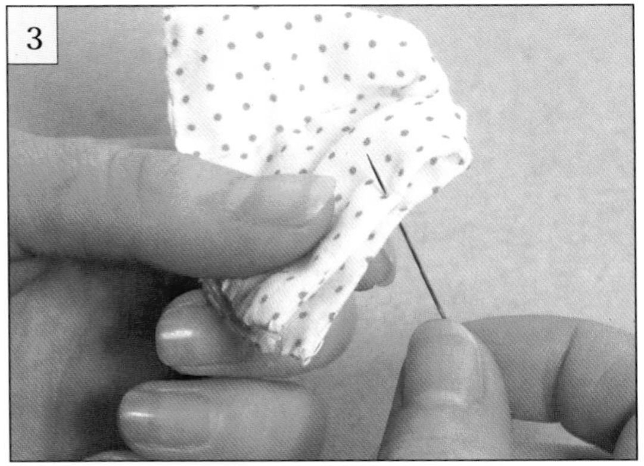

1 Cut out two coat pieces, one a lining. With right sides together, stitch around from one hem edge, right round to the other hem edge. Clip the neck and the underarm edges to the sewing line.

2 Turn the coat through to the right side. Use a needle or pin to pull the seam out. Press lightly.

3 Try the coat on the doll, placing it, with the lining outwards, over the shoulders. Hem the back so that it is level with the front. Pin, then catch by hand the side seams.

4 Turn the coat the right way out. Stitch edging lace around the inside of the front edge, then stitch matching or contrasting Picot trimmings along the top edge if you wish.

5 Make a bonnet with a lace frill (as for the dress). Pull up the gathers tightly and sew the back edge together, covering the back with a small embroidered motif or a small motif cut off a length of piqué. Add ribbons and bows to each side and fasten a small length of shirring elastic to run under the chin and hold the bonnet in place.

Sailor Boy

~

Boys were often dressed in sailor uniforms in late Victorian and Edwardian times. This uniform, which will fit a doll about 10cm/4in tall, is made from five pattern pieces.

YOU WILL NEED

- Tracing paper
- Pencil
- Pins
- Scissors
- Needle
- Sewing thread
- Narrow bonding web
- All-purpose adhesive
- Forceps or tweezers
- Sewing machine (optional)

FOR THE TROUSERS

- 15cm/6in white cotton fabric

FOR THE SHIRT

- 20cm/8in white cotton fabric
- Red felt-tipped pen
- 7.5cm/3in navy blue ribbon, 3mm/⅛in wide
- 15cm/6in navy blue cotton fabric
- 15cm/6in iron-on backing fabric (such as Vilene)

FOR THE HAT

- 7.5cm/3in white cotton fabric
- 7.5cm/3in navy blue ribbon, 3mm/⅛in wide

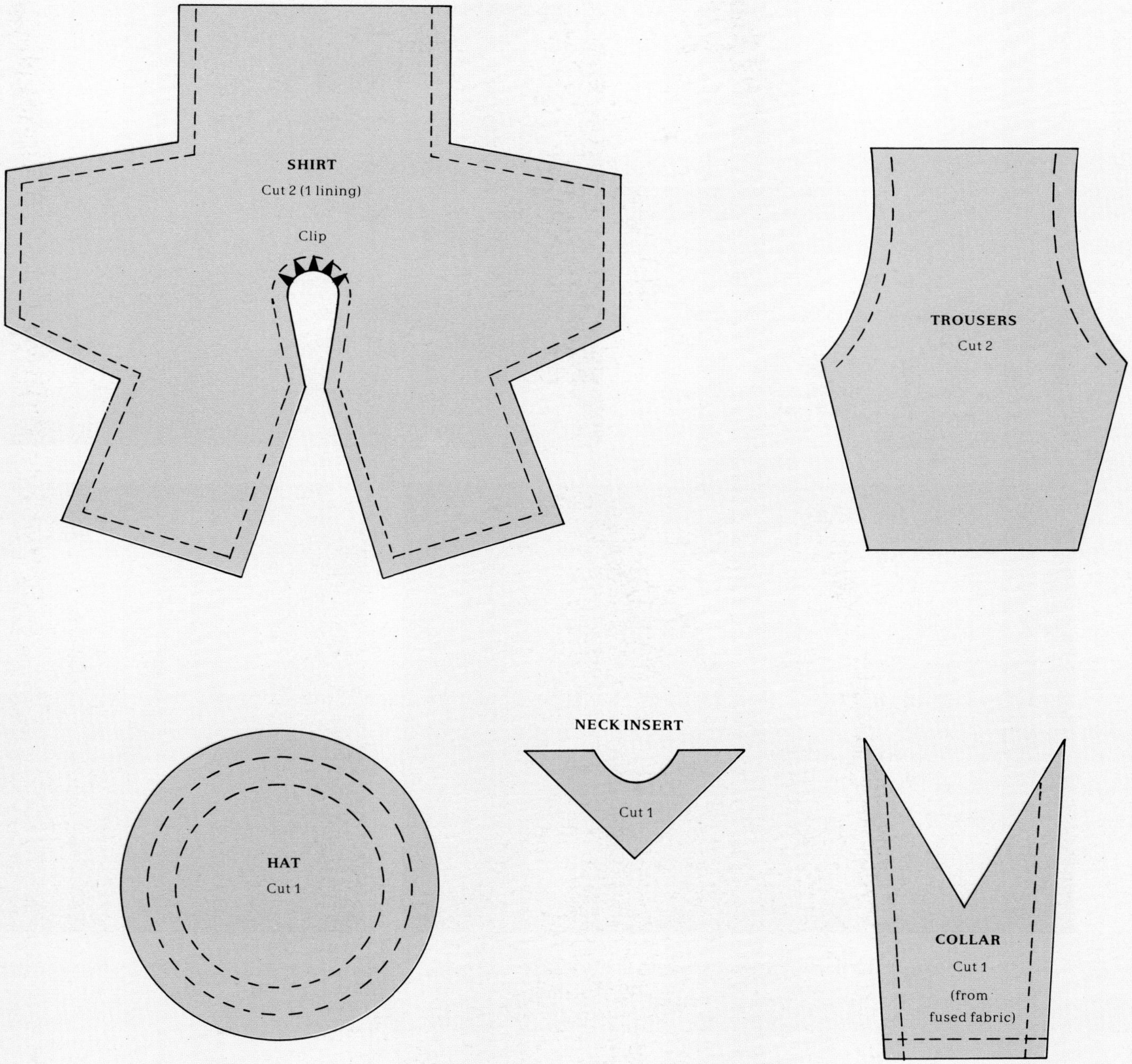

MAKING THE TROUSERS

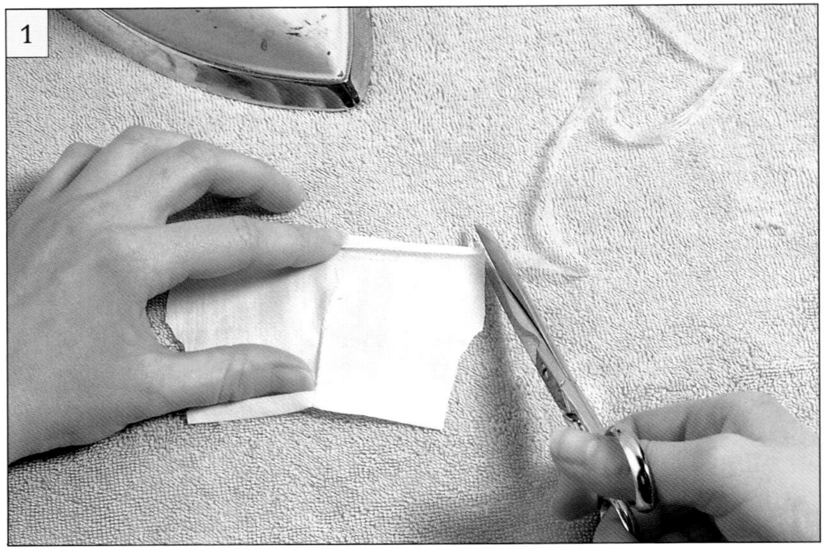

1 Cut out two trouser pieces from white cotton fabric and stitch the front centre seam, leaving a 5mm/¼in seam allowance. Use bonding web to turn up the hems at the bottom of the legs and around the waist.

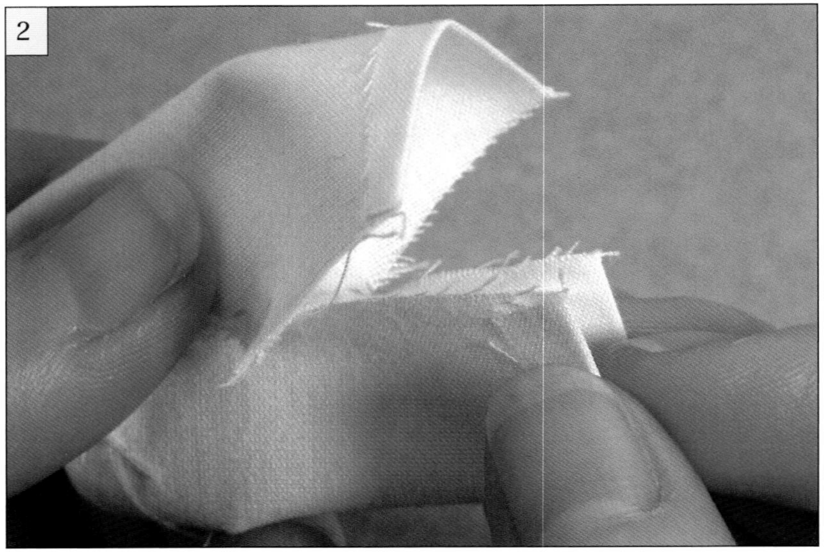

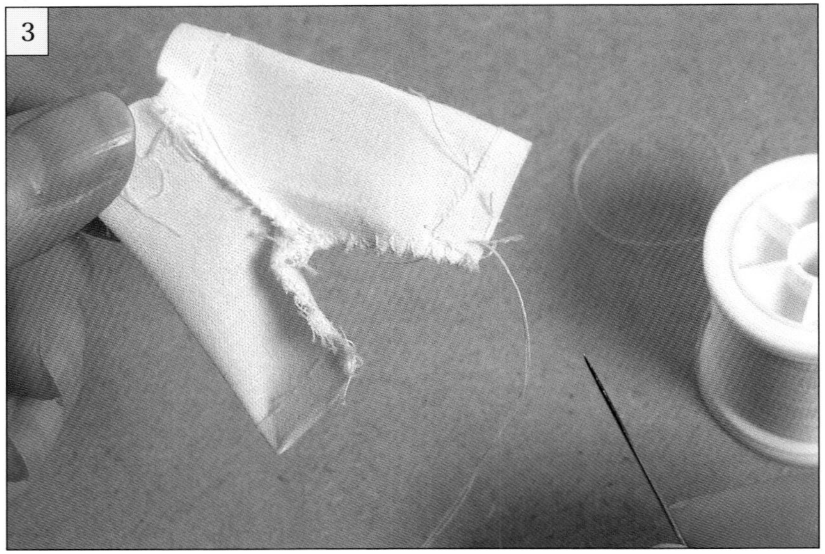

2 Turn the right sides together and stitch the centre back seam. Refold, matching front and back seams.

3 Stitch the crotch and inner leg seams. Turn the trousers the right way out. Press them and place them on the doll, catching them with tiny stitches around the doll's waist.

MAKING THE SHIRT

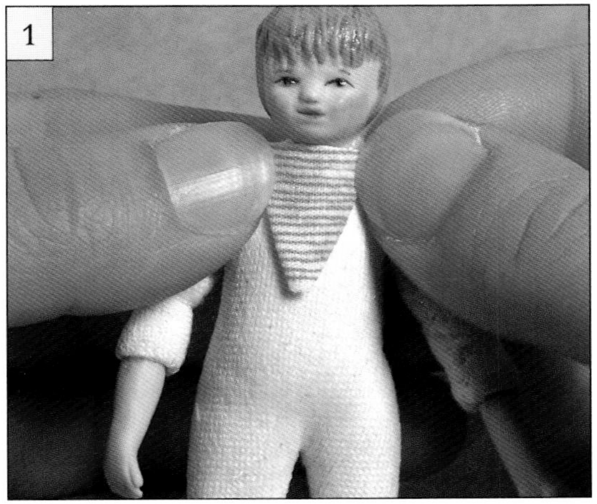

1 Cut out a V-shaped piece of white fabric for the dickey and rule fine red lines horizontally across it. Glue it to the doll's body around the neck.

2 Cut out two shirt pieces, one as a lining. Pin them together and stitch them up the back seam around the arms, up the front, around the neck and back down to the back hem. Leave the back hem open. Clip the neck to the stitching line.

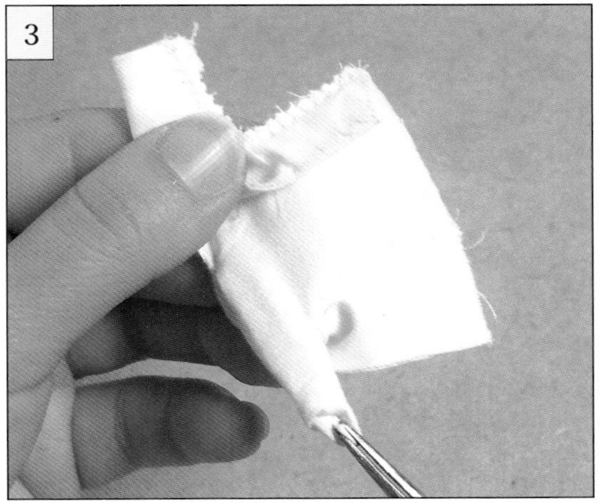

3 Turn the shirt through to the right sides, using forceps or tweezers to turn the sleeves through and to neaten the seams. Press lightly. Hem the back so that it is level with the front, turning up the outside and slip stitching it to the lining. Put the shirt on the doll, lining outwards, pinning it in place at the front and pinning the underarm and side seams to fit. Remove the pins at the front and slip stitch the underarm and side seams, beginning at the cuff.

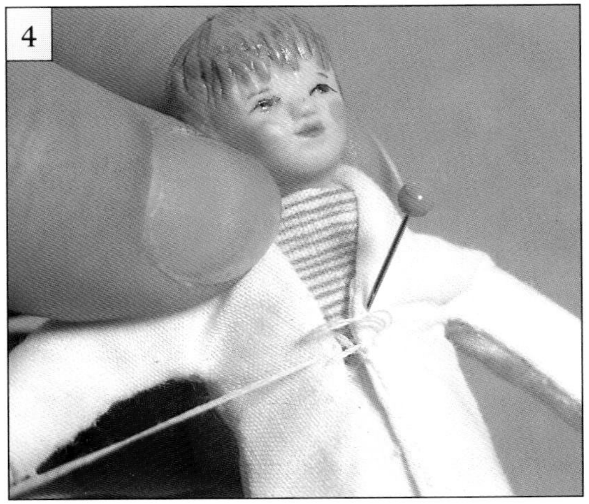

4 Turn the shirt to the right side and put it on the doll, pinning it in position so that the red-striped dickey can be seen. Catch the shirt in position down the front and use tiny stitches to attach it to the trousers.

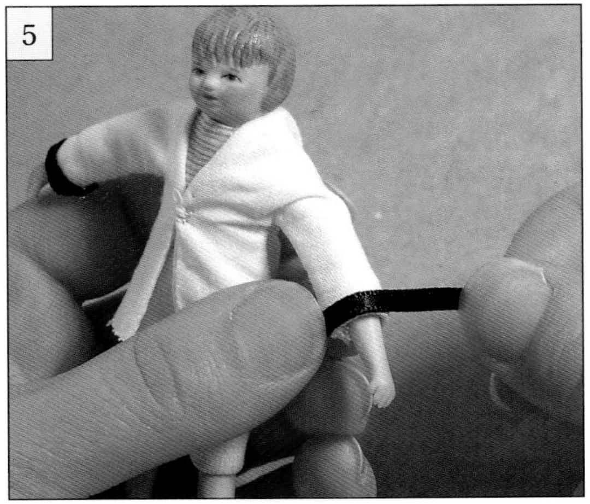

5 Glue navy blue ribbon around the cuffs of the shirt.

6

6 Fold the navy blue cotton fabric in two and place a piece of bonding material between the pieces. Press as directed to fuse the two pieces together. Cut the collar out of this piece. Use the smallest possible stitch and white cotton to sew a line 3mm/⅛in from the edge all round. Place the collar on the doll, sewing the points together and fixing them at the lower end of the V-shaped neck. If the collar will not lie flat at the back, hold it in place with one or two spots of adhesive.

7 Use narrow navy blue ribbon to make a bow (see page 238) and glue it to the bottom of the collar.

7

MAKING THE HAT

1

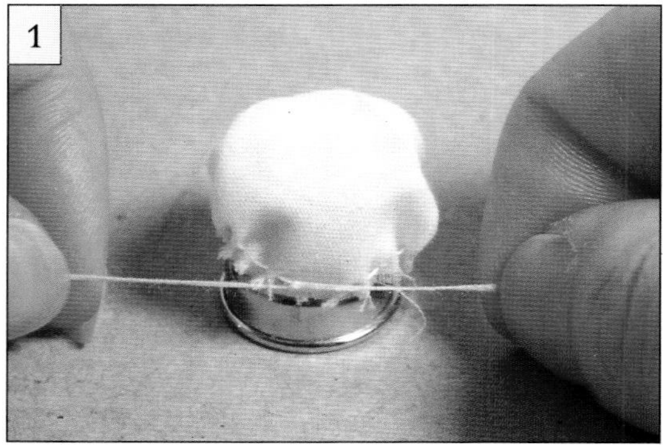

1 Cut out a circle of white cotton fabric and make two parallel rows of tiny running stitches around the circumference. Place an ordinary sewing thimble on the table in front of you as a guide and gather the circle over it, pulling it about three-quarters of the way down.

2

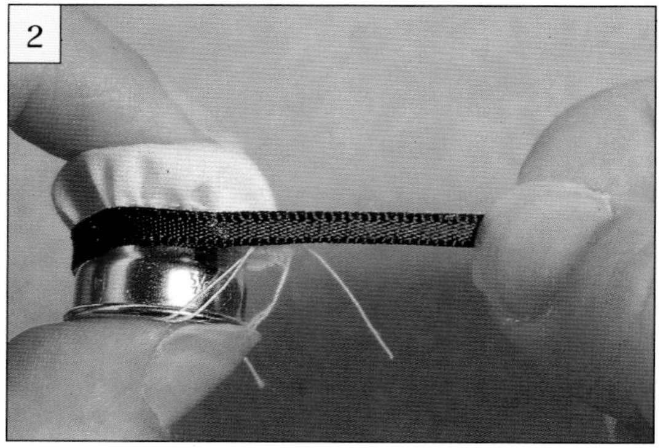

2 Run adhesive around the bottom edge of the fabric and attach a piece of navy blue ribbon. When the adhesive is dry remove the hat from the thimble and trim off any white threads that can be seen.

3

3 Put the hat on the doll's head, flattening the top so that it looks like a sailor's cap.

Cook

~

In most Victorian and Edwardian households the cook was, after the butler, the most important of the below stairs servants. Her dress was different from that worn by the maids, and her apron and cap were additional symbols of authority. This is a simple pattern to make and one that can be easily adapted for other purposes – for example, left open at the front, it could be used as a coat or it could be shortened and used as a jacket.

YOU WILL NEED

- Tracing paper
- Pencil
- Pins
- Scissors
- Needle
- Sewing thread
- Narrow bonding web
- Forceps or tweezers
- All-purpose adhesive
- Sewing machine (optional)

FOR THE PANTALOONS

- 15cm/6in white cotton lawn
- 15cm/6in white edging lace, 5mm/¼in wide
- Shirring elastic (optional)

FOR THE DRESS

- 23cm/9in blue cotton fabric
- 23cm/9in white cotton lining fabric
- 30cm/12in white bias binding
- 30cm/12in gathered white edging lace, 2.5cm/1in wide

FOR THE APRON

- 30cm/12in white cotton fabric
- 30cm/12in white bias binding

FOR THE CAP

- 6 × 4cm/2½ × 1½in piece of white cotton fabric
- Embroidered motif or motif from Picot edging
- 5cm/2in white ribbon, 3mm/⅛in wide

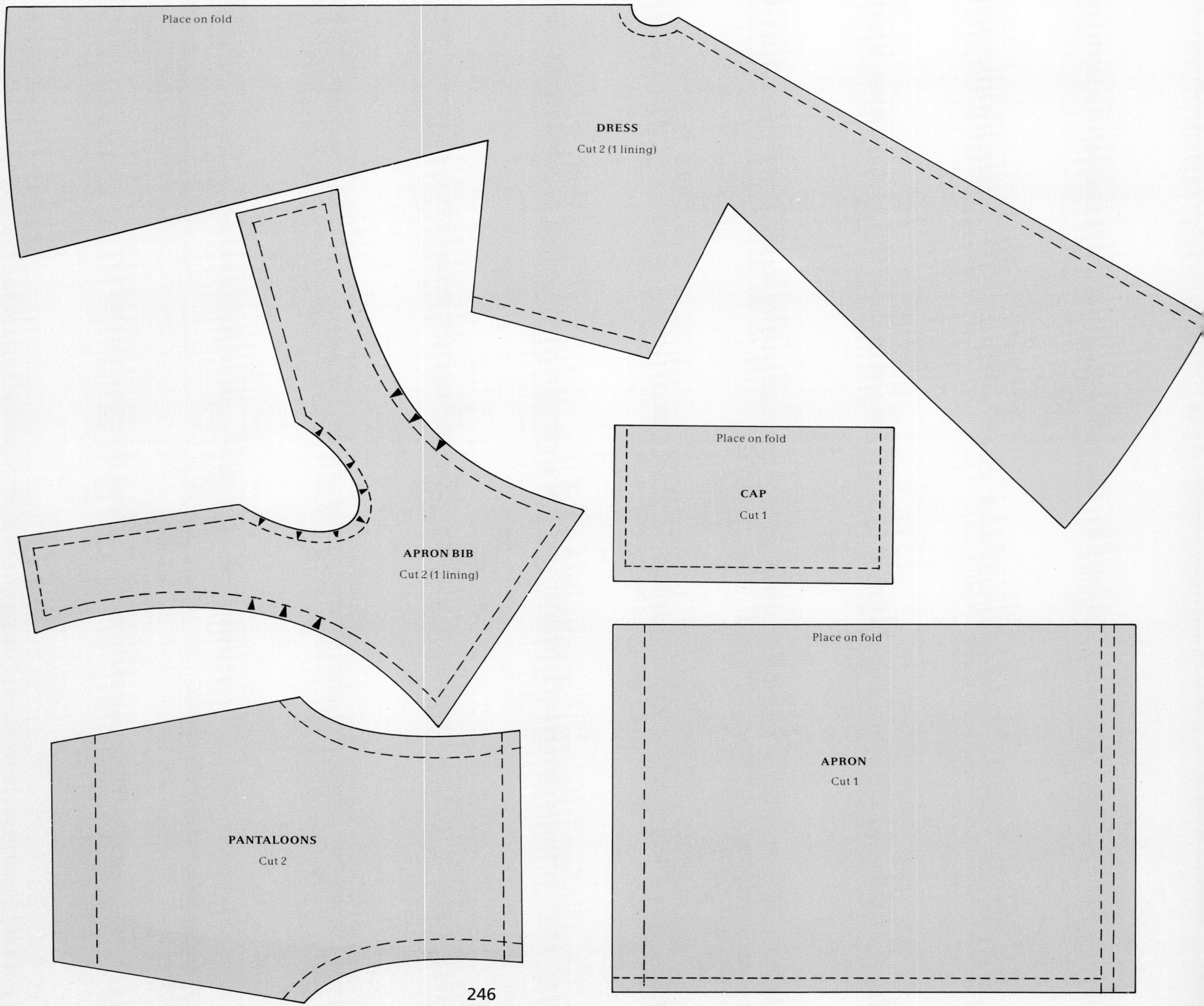

MAKING THE DRESS

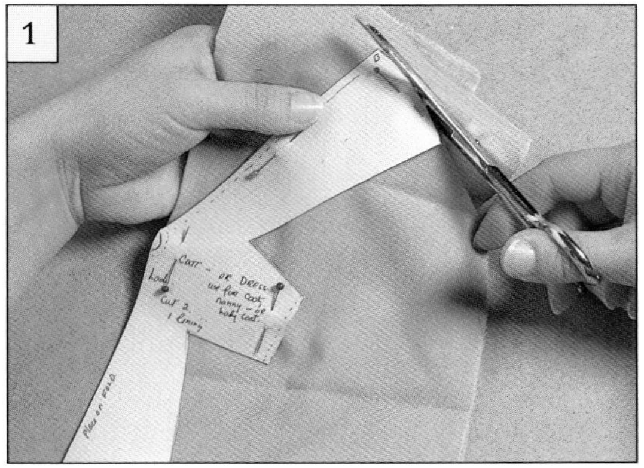

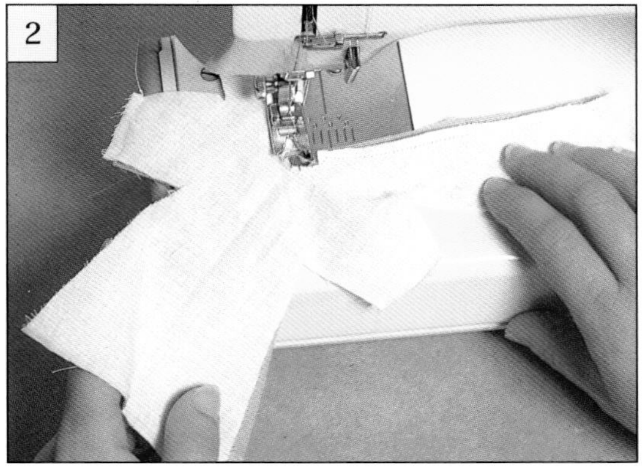

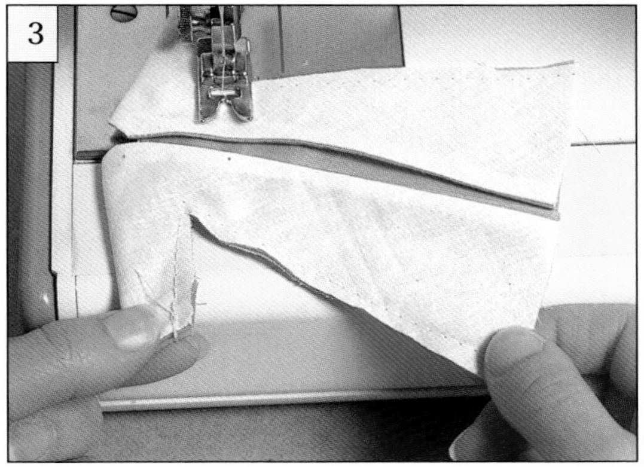

1 Before you make the dress, make the pantaloons, following the instructions for the Victorian Lady on page 212. Cut two dress pieces, one in blue and one in white lining fabric, remembering to place the centre front against a fold.

2 Pin the dress and lining pieces together with right sides facing. Stitch up one back edge, around the neck and down the other back edge. Stitch across the bottom of the sleeves. Clip the neck to the stitch line.

3 Turn the dress to the right side, using tweezers or forceps to neaten the seam edges. Press lightly. With the lining facing outwards, put the dress on the doll, pin the back opening together and pin the underarm and side seams together. Unpin the back and stitch the underarm and side seams, starting at the cuff edge. Turn the dress to the right side and turn back about 5mm/¼in of the sleeves so that the white shows as a cuff. Catch down with a few tiny stitches.

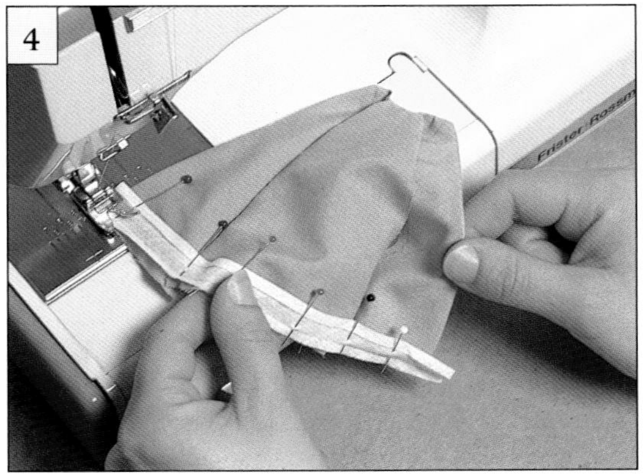

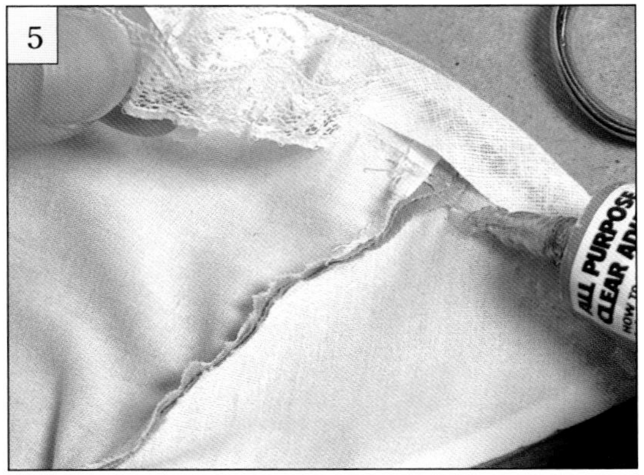

4 With right sides facing, stitch bias binding along the hem of the blue dress. Turn up the binding and glue or slip stitch it to the lining.

5 Stitch or glue a layer of gathered lace around the bottom of the lining as a "petticoat".

6 With right sides facing, stitch a short piece of white bias binding around the neck edge as a collar. Turn under and glue or slip stitch to the lining. Put the dress on the doll and slip stitch or oversew the back seam.

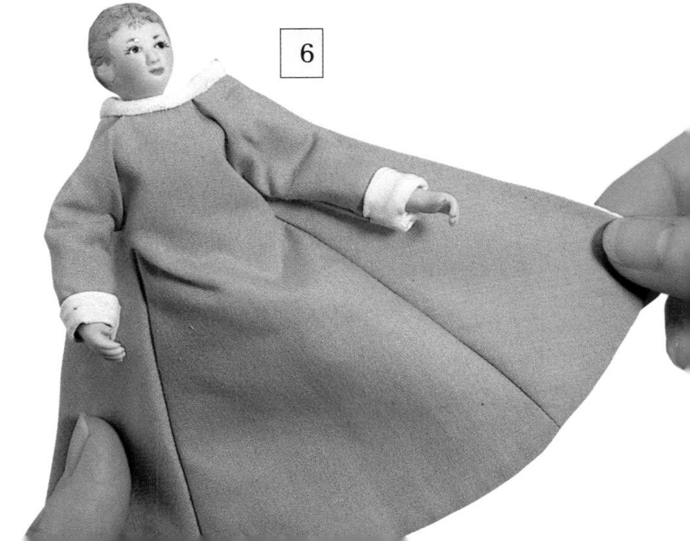

6

MAKING THE APRON

~ MAKING THE CAP ~

1 Use the template to cut a piece of white fabric. Fold it in half and stitch the sides. Turn to the right side, neaten the seam edges and press. Gather the open edge with two rows of small running stitches, pulling the fabric up as tightly as possible. Cover this with a small embroidered motif.

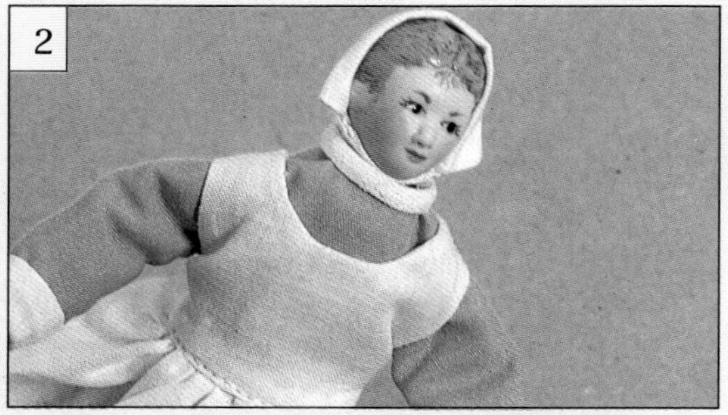

2 Turn back the front 3mm/⅛in and add two ribbon ties. Place the cap on the doll's head and tie the ribbon neatly under the chin to hold the cap on.

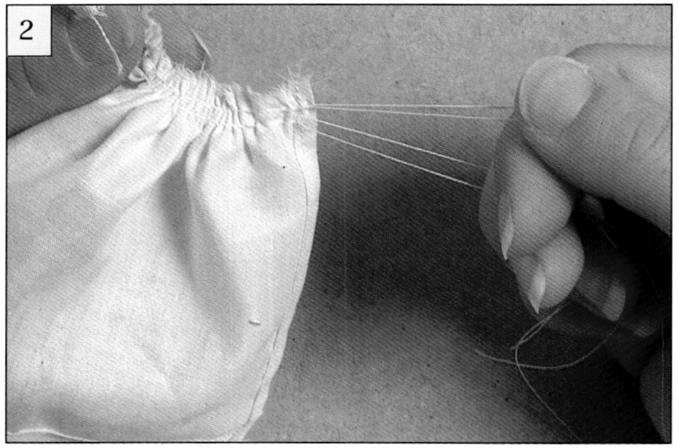

1 Cut out the skirt of the apron, remembering to place one edge of the template against a fold in the fabric. Cut out two apron bibs.

2 Turn up a hem at the bottom edge of 5mm/¼in and hems at the two short edges of 3mm/⅛in. Stitch by hand or by machine two parallel rows of stitches along the top edge and gather to fit bib. If you use a sewing machine, use the longest stitch for the gathering stitches.

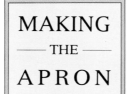

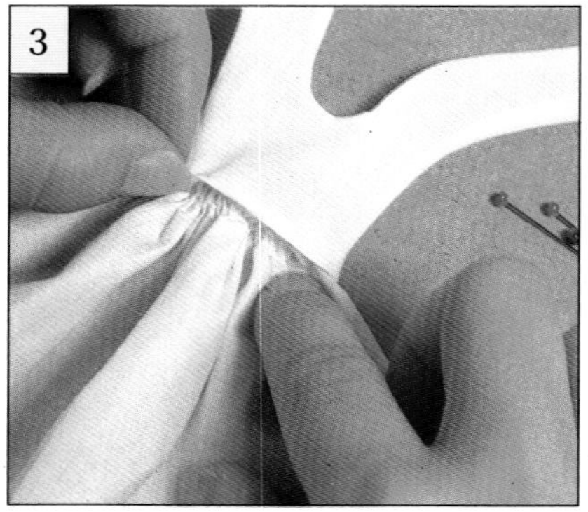

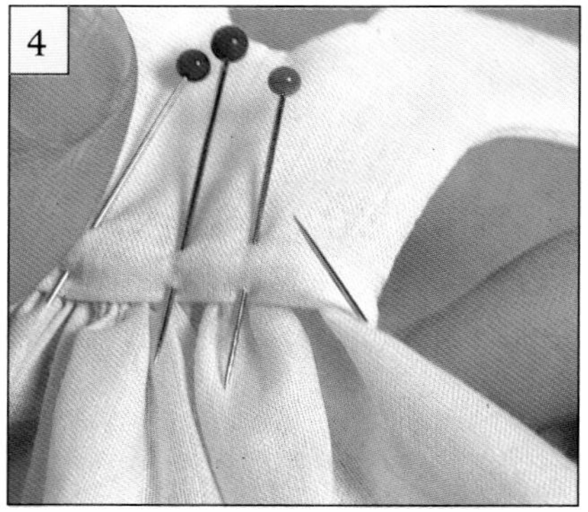

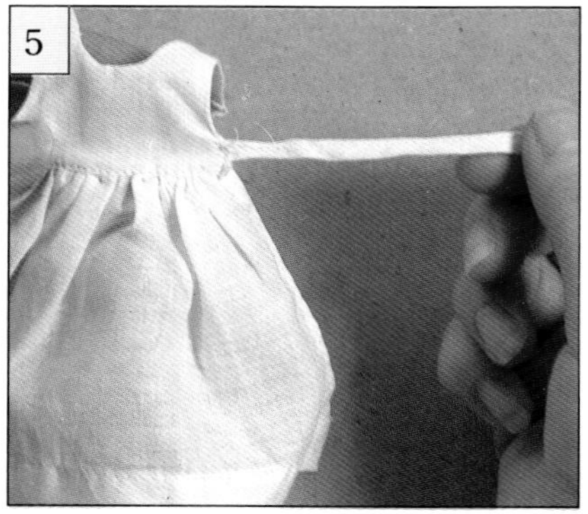

3 Stitch the two bib pieces together by sewing all around the sides and neck opening, but leaving the waist seam open. Use forceps or tweezers to turn the bib to the right side and to neaten the seams. Press lightly. Turn up the hem of the bib and insert the gathered apron skirt in the bottom of the bib, checking for fit.

4 Pin the gathered apron skirt in position between the front and lining of the bib. Stitch neatly in position from both front and back.

5 Neatly oversew the bias binding, cut it in half and attach one piece to each side of the waist of the apron. Put the apron on the doll, tying it in a bow at the back. Cross the long ends of the bib over at the back of the doll and stitch them to the apron ties.

~ BUTCHER ~

Throughout the history of fashion, some styles of clothing appear to have been worn by different trades and professions. The butcher, for example, has been described, illustrated and photographed wearing clothes that seem hardly to have changed for over a century. This butcher might be at home in a high street butcher's shop today, but he is equally appropriately dressed for the late Victorian or early Edwardian times. His trousers can be made of any dark material, and his shirt is gathered above the elbow with elastic, a style that could be used to dress, say, a butler. The striped apron is, however, typical of a butcher. Make the trousers and shirt according to the instructions for the Victorian Man (see page 221) but use the sleeve template shown here. Use shirring elastic to hold the fullness of the shirt above the elbow.

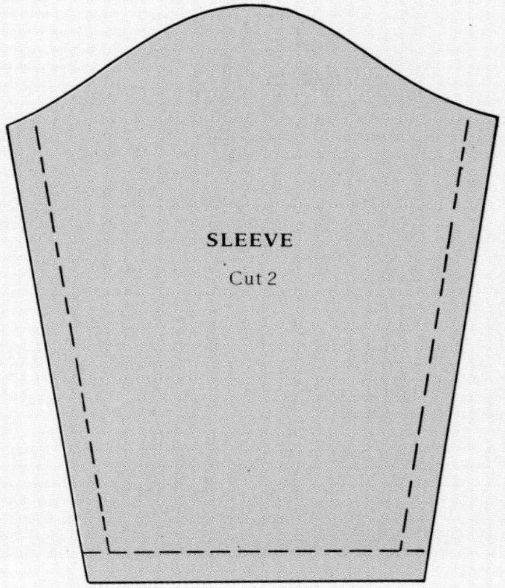

YOU WILL NEED

- Tracing paper
- Pencil
- Pins
- Scissors
- 10 × 10cm/4 × 4in blue striped cotton fabric
- All-purpose adhesive
- Narrow bonding web
- 30cm/12in dark blue ribbon, 3mm/⅛in wide

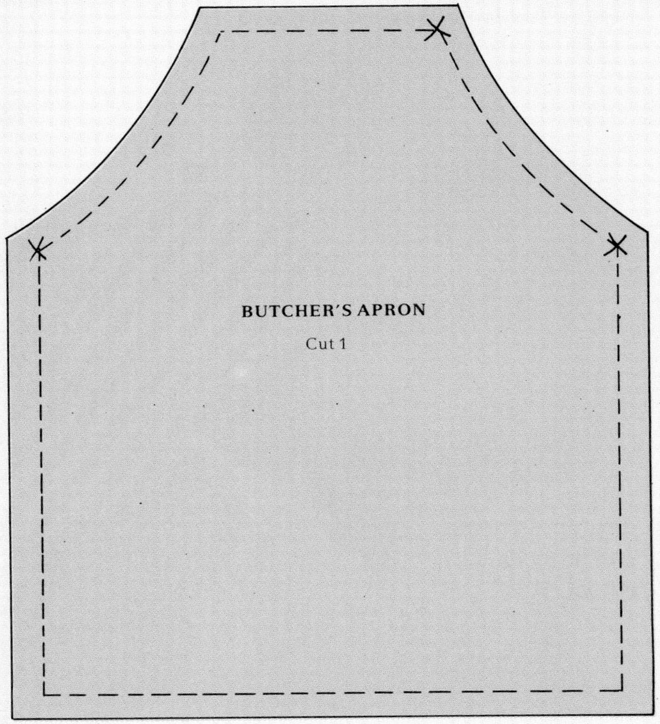

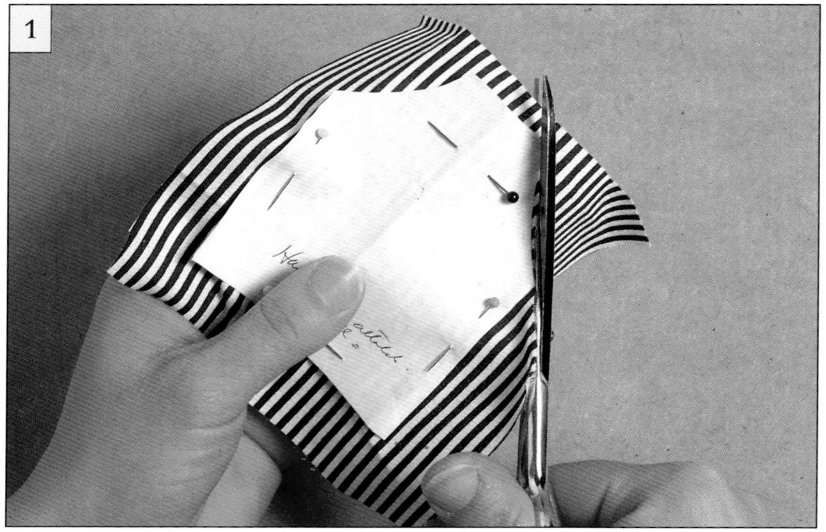

1 Use the template to cut out the shape of the apron.

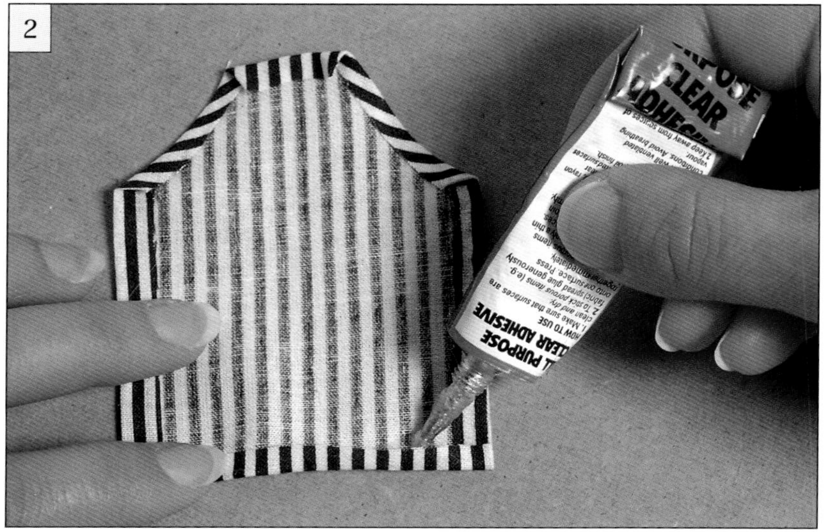

2 Glue or use bonding web to turn in the 5mm/¼in hem all round.

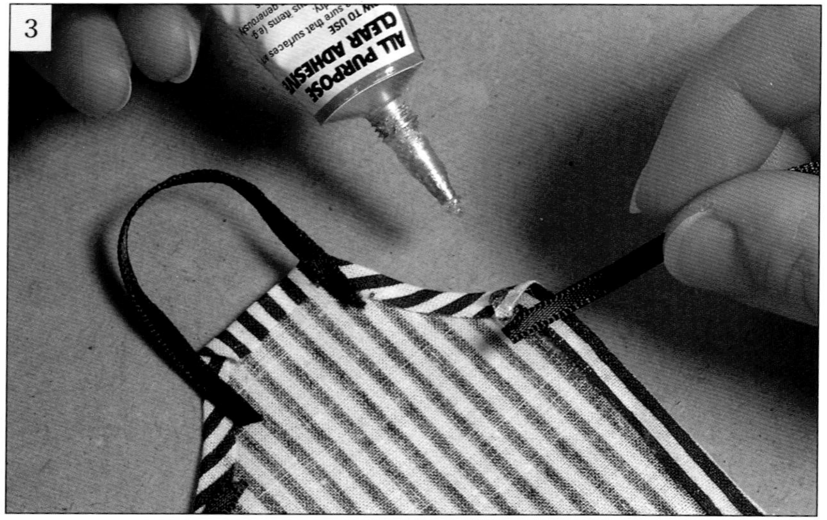

3 Glue the ties for the waist and to go around the neck. You might find it easier to glue just one end of the neck ribbon before you dress the doll, finishing the other end when the apron is in place.

4

4 Place the apron on the doll and tie it neatly at the back.

Pilot

~

One of the most delightful aspects of Edwardian life was the habit of wearing exactly the right outfit for every activity or social event. This was particularly noticeable in some of the more daring sporting events such as the new passion for driving motor cars and for flying. Our pilot, from his helmet and goggles down to his leather boots, would have been in the height of fashion. Jodhpurs and a leather, blouson-style jacket were *de rigueur*, and every pilot had a scarf and goggles. A parachute was not, however, part of his kit.

YOU WILL NEED

- Tracing paper
- Pencil
- Pins
- Scissors
- Narrow bonding web
- Needle
- Sewing thread
- Forceps or tweezers
- All-purpose adhesive
- Sewing machine (optional)
- Leather needle
- Fine black felt-tipped pen or black ballpoint pen

FOR THE SHIRT

- 30cm/12in white cotton fabric
- 15cm/6in brown ribbon, 3mm/⅛in wide
- 7.5in/3in shirring elastic

FOR THE JODHPURS

- 23cm/9in khaki-coloured fine tweed fabric

FOR THE BOOTS

- 10 × 4cm/4 × 1½in soft brown glove leather
- 4 small bulldog clips
- Black shirring elastic
- Small pieces of black leather for soles

FOR THE JACKET

- 30cm/12in soft brown glove leather

FOR THE HELMET, GOGGLES AND SCARF

- Plastic film
- Rubber bands
- 1 tbsp PVA
- 2 tbsp hot water
- 7.5 × 7.5cm/3 × 3in buckram
- 7.5 × 7.5cm/3 × 3in soft dark brown or black glove leather
- Small piece of pale brown or yellow glove leather
- Leather punch with large hole
- Clear plastic
- Ballpoint pen
- 75 × 5mm/3 × ¼in white silk

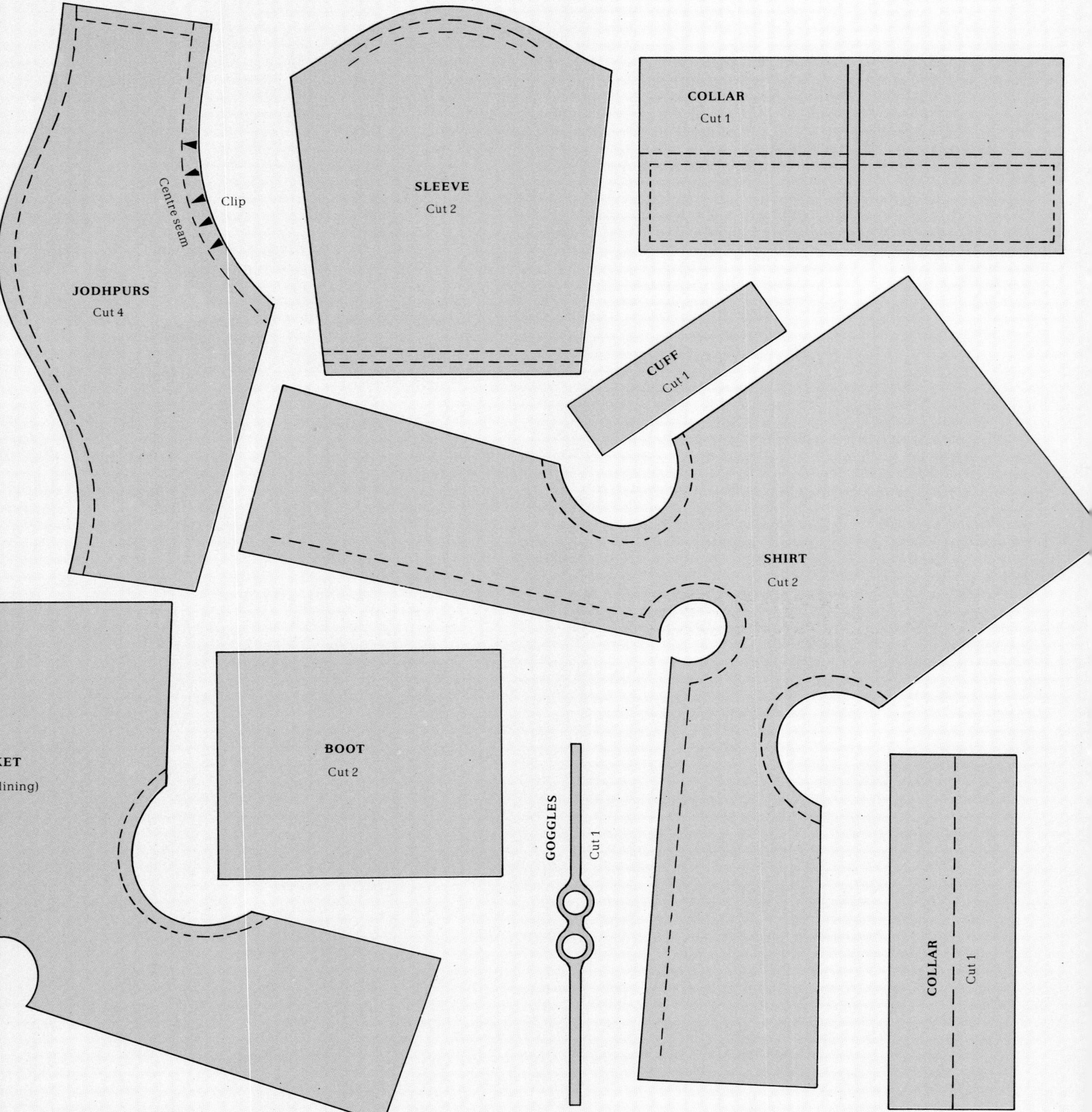

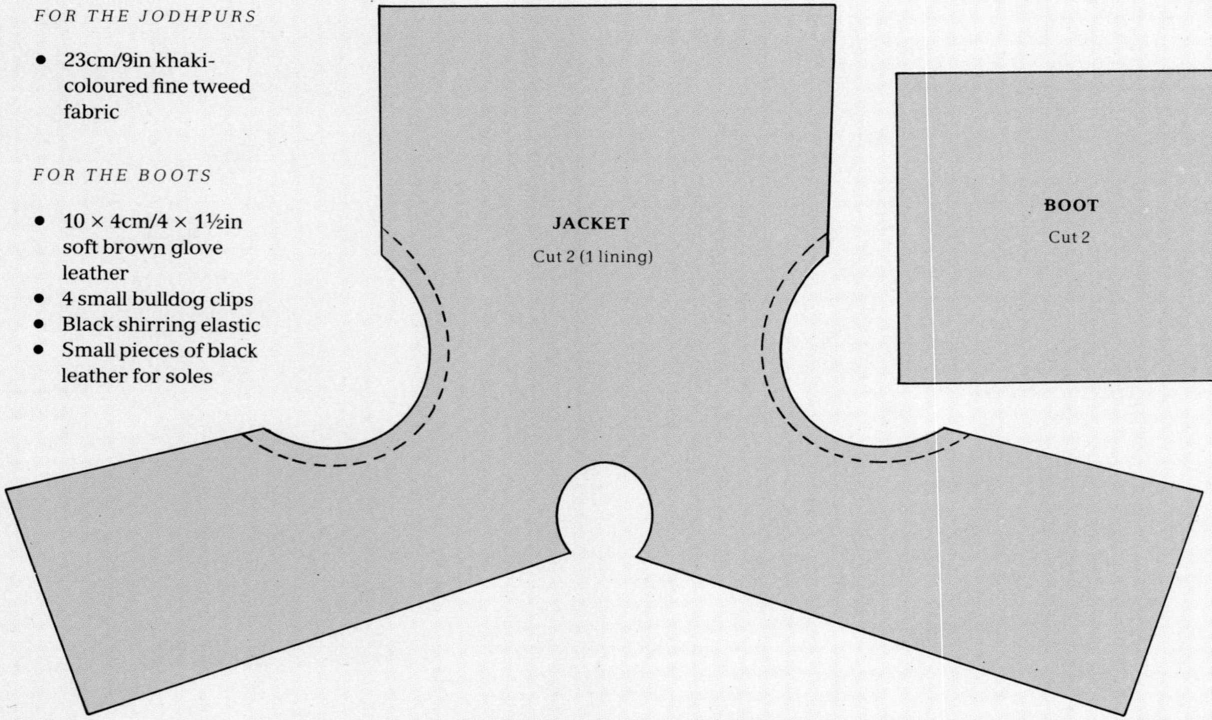

MAKING THE SHIRT

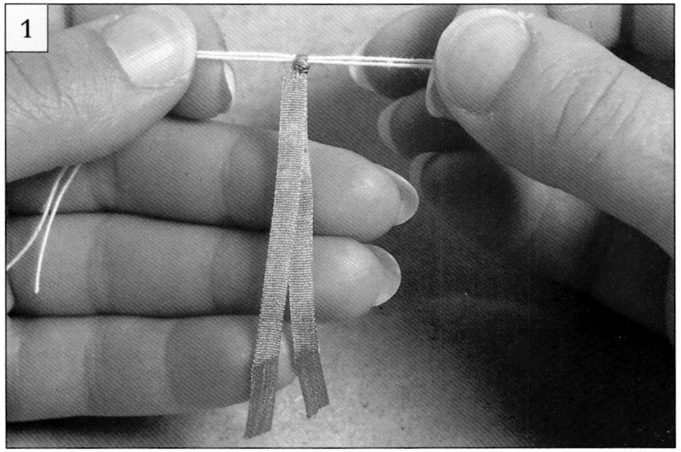

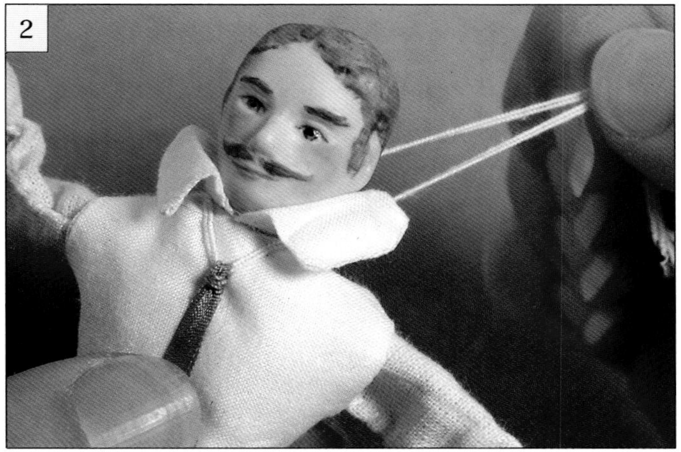

1 Make a sleeveless shirt, using the template for the front and back of the shirt and collar given here, according to the instructions for the Victorian Man (see page 221). Put the shirt on the doll. Fold the brown ribbon over the elastic and stitch it down to resemble a knot in a tie.

2 Fasten the elastic at the back of the neck under the collar.

MAKING THE JODHPURS

1 Cut out four pieces. Stitch the side seams and use bonding web to turn in the hems at the waist and ankle. With right sides together, stitch the centre back seam. Refold the right sides together and stitch the inside leg seams.

2 Clip the centre seams, turn to the right side and press lightly. Put the jodhpurs on the doll, tucking the shirt into the waistband, and stitch neatly to the shirt.

MAKING THE BOOTS

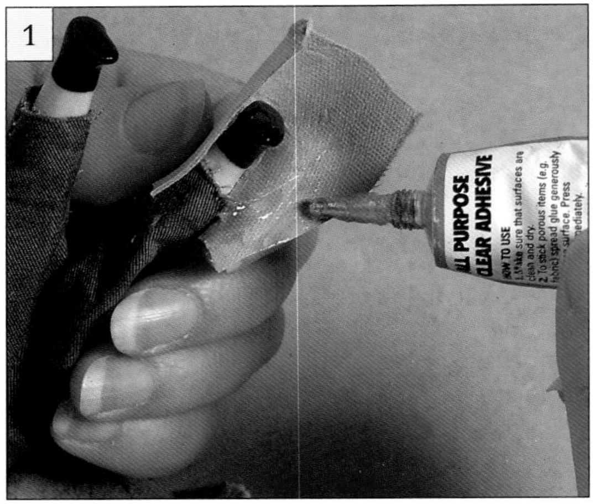

1 Use the template to cut out two pieces of glove leather. These pieces cover the bottom of the jodhpurs and are wrapped around the leg.

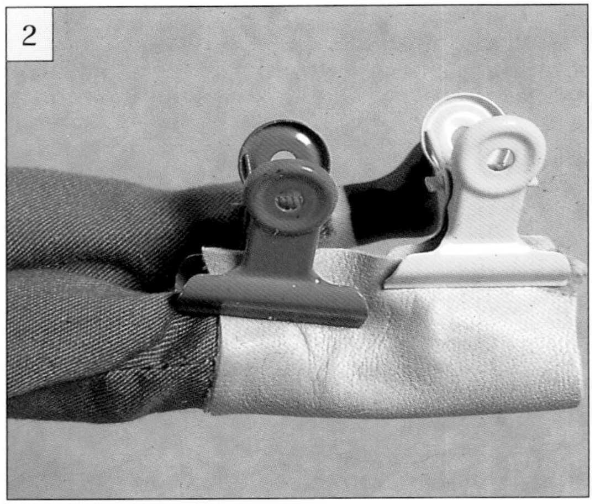

2 Glue the leather in position and hold it tightly at the front of the doll's leg with small bulldog clips. Allow the glue to dry.

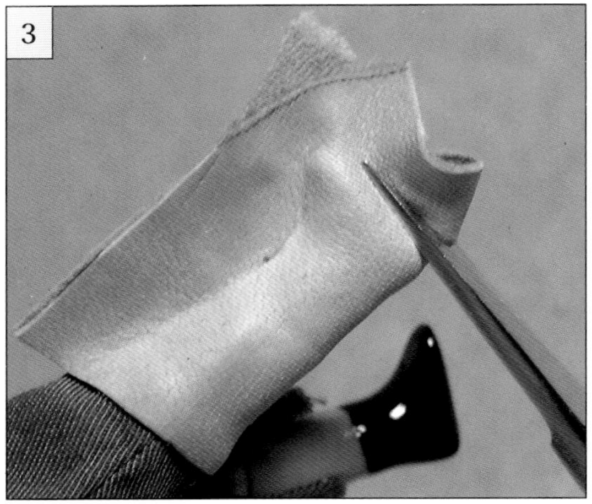

3 Use very sharp scissors to clip off the leather from around the toes and up the front of the leg. Make sure that the line up the front of the leg where the two pieces of leather meet is particularly neatly cut.

4 Use a black felt-tipped or ballpoint pen to mark buttons and laces on the front of the boots. Use a leather needle to thread a length of black shirring elastic through the top of the holes and tie the elastic in a bow. Trim off the ends.

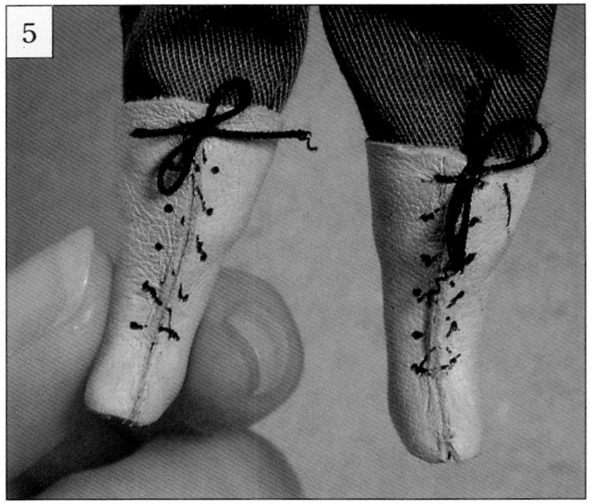

5 Trim under the soles, close to the porcelain foot, and glue small pieces of black leather under the feet to represent the soles of the boots.

MAKING THE JACKET

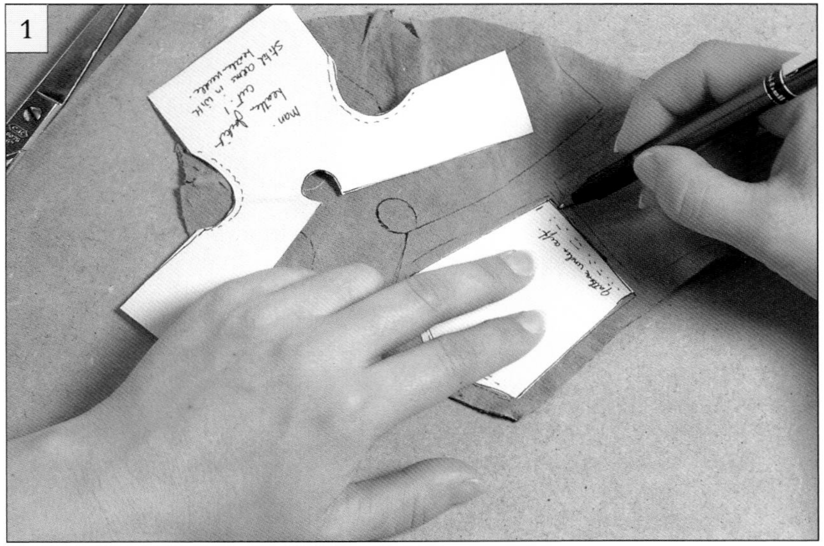

1 Cut out one jacket piece, two sleeves, one collar and two cuffs, using the smooth side of the leather as the right side.

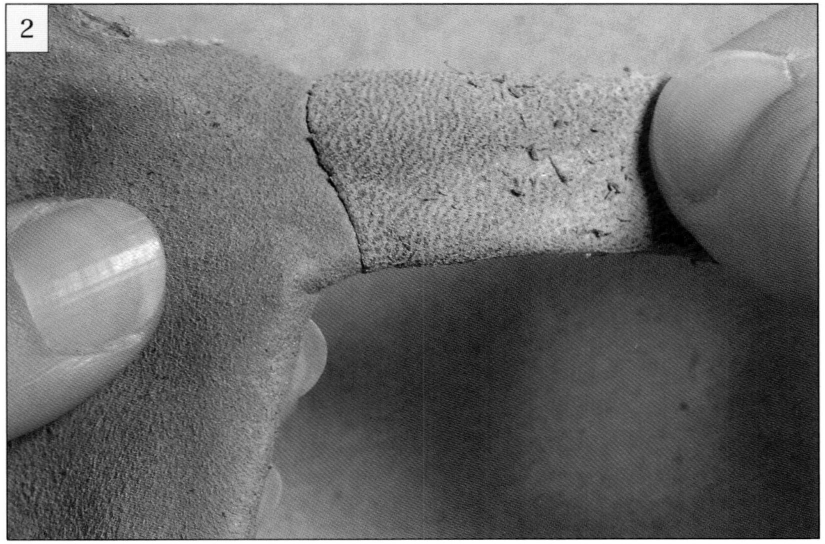

2 Use a leather needle to sew the sleeves to the jacket body. Fold the cuffs in half and glue them to the bottom of the sleeves. Oversew the underarm and side seams.

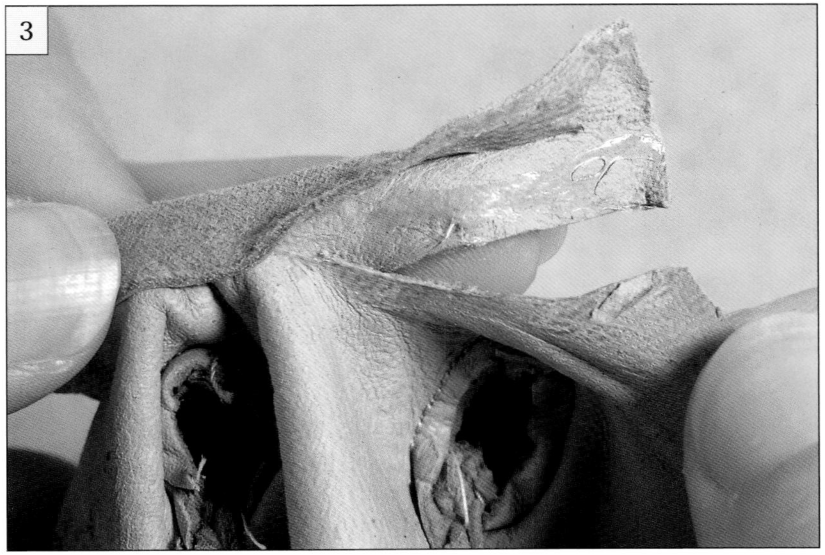

3 Fold the collar in two and glue it in position around the outside of the neck.

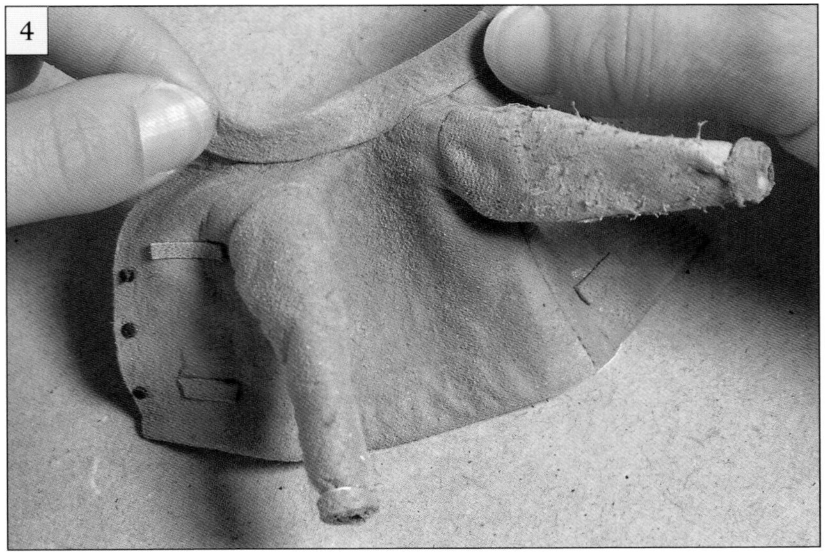

4 Turn over the collar and glue it firmly to the neckline. Glue on little offcuts of leather to represent pocket flaps.

MAKING THE HELMET, GOGGLES AND SCARF

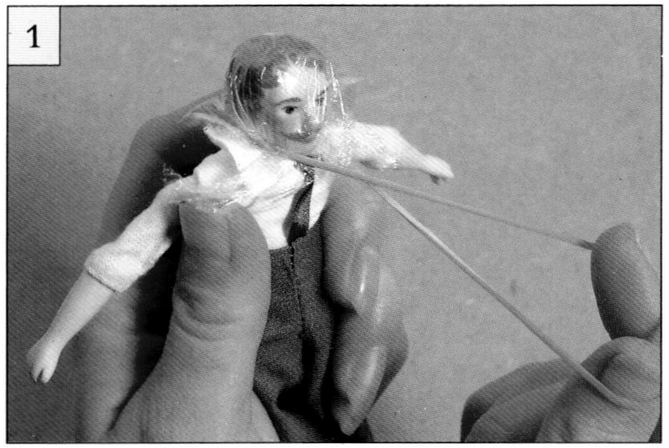

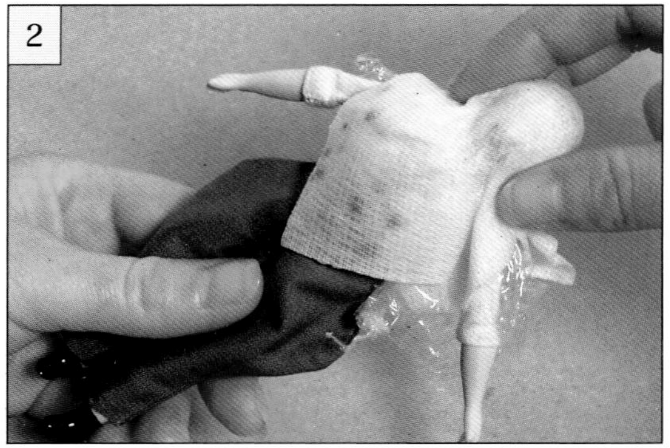

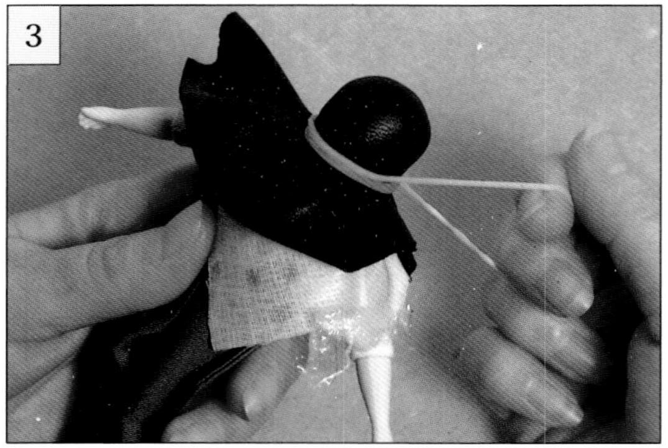

1 Cover the doll's head with plastic film, holding it firmly around the neck with rubber bands.

2 Mix the PVA and hot water in a basin and soak the buckram and leather for at least 30 seconds. Place the buckram over the doll's head and smooth it down as firmly as possible, holding it tightly in place with a rubber band.

3 Smooth the soaked leather over the buckram, using a rubber band to hold it over the doll's head. Leave to dry completely.

4 Cut out the goggles, using a leather punch to cut out the eye holes. Glue circles of clear plastic behind the eye holes if you wish.

5 Cut off the rubber bands and slide the shaped material off the head. Remove the plastic film. Use a ballpoint pen to mark the outline of the helmet, remembering that it should come well down over the forehead and that there should be earflaps. Cut around the outline a little at a time. Glue the goggles in place.

6 Finish the pilot off with strips of dark leather as a belt and strap over the right shoulder, glued in place. Tie the scarf around his neck.

Cerámica y Cultura

Detail, Fig. 3.5

Cerámica y Cultura

The Story of Spanish and Mexican Mayólica

Edited by

ROBIN FARWELL GAVIN,

DONNA PIERCE,

and

ALFONSO PLEGUEZUELO

Translations by

KENNY FITZGERALD

University of New Mexico Press ⁂ Albuquerque

This publication is funded in part by
the National Endowment for the Humanities

NATIONAL
ENDOWMENT
FOR THE
HUMANITIES

First edition

Library of Congress
Cataloging-in-Publication Data

The story of Spanish and Mexican mayólica/
edited by Robin Farwell Gavin, Donna Pierce, and
Alfonso Pleguezuelo; translations by Kenny
Fitzgerald.
p. cm.
Catalog of an exhibition held at the Museum
of International Folk Art in Santa Fe, N.M.
Includes bibliographical references and index.
ISBN 0-8263-3101-7 (cloth : alk. paper) —
ISBN 0-8263-3102-5 (pbk. : alk. paper)
1. Majolica, Mexican—Exhibitions.
2. Majolica, Spanish—Exhibitions.
I. Gavin, Robin Farwell. II. Pierce, Donna, 1950–
III. Pleguezuelo, Alfonso.
IV. Museum of International Folk Art (N.M.)
NK4320.M5 S76 2003
738.3'72—dc21
2003001150

Design: Melissa Tandysh
Printed in Singapore

Contents

List of Illustrations vii

Opening Remarks xv
JOYCE ICE

Foreword xvii
FLORENCE C. LISTER

Acknowledgments xxv

Introduction 1
ROBIN FARWELL GAVIN

1. Centers of Traditional Spanish Mayólica 24
ALFONSO PLEGUEZUELO

2. Ceramics in Domestic Life in Spain 48
MARÍA ANTONIA CASANOVAS

3. The Use of Spanish Ceramics in Architecture 76
MARÍA PAZ SOLER FERRER

4. Ceramics, Business, and Economy 102
ALFONSO PLEGUEZUELO

5. Traditional Ceramics in Contemporary Sevilla 122
ANTONIO LIBRERO

6. Baroque to Neobaroque in Barcelona 150
ANNIE CARLANO

7. Traditional Ceramic Production in Spain Today 170
JAUME COLL CONESA

8. Mexican Ceramics in Spain 186
MARÍA CONCEPCIÓN GARCÍA SÁIZ

9. The Emergence of a Mexican Tile Tradition 204
MARGARET E. CONNORS McQUADE

10. The Forgotten Potters of Mexico City 226
ANA PAULINA GÁMEZ MARTÍNEZ

11. Mayólica in the Daily Life of Colonial Mexico 244
DONNA PIERCE

12. The Revival of Puebla Mayólica in the Twentieth Century 270
BARBARA MAULDIN

13. The Mayólica of Guanajuato 296
PATRICIA FOURNIER

14. The *Loza Blanca* Tradition of Aguascalientes 314
GLORIA GIFFORDS AND JORGE OLVERA

Bibliography 339

Index 351

Illustrations

Intro.1	Jar / *Orza*, Talavera de la Reina, Spain, 17th–18th centuries	2
Intro.2	Plate / *Plato*, Chongzhen Period, China, 1630–1640	3
Intro.3	Plate / *Plato*, Talavera de la Reina, Spain, 1675–1725	3
Intro.4	Map of mayólica production and trade centers in Spain, 12th through 19th centuries	4
Intro.5	Tiles / *Azulejos*, La Alhambra, Granada, Spain, mid-14th century	6
Intro.6	Map of mayólica production centers and trade routes in Mexico, 16th through 19th centuries	8
Intro.7	Plate / *Plato*, Mexico City or Puebla, Mexico, 1650–1750	9
Intro.8	*El Parián*, Manila Market, Juan Ravenet, 1792	10
Intro.9	Plate / *Plato*, Puebla, Mexico, 17th century	11
Intro.10	Storage Jar / *Tibor*, Puebla, Mexico, late 17th–early 18th century	11
Intro.11	Storage Jar / *Tibor*, Puebla, Mexico, late 17th–early 18th century	12
Intro.12	Smoking Kiln, Workshop of Juan Almarza, Úbeda, Spain	13
Intro.13	*Plaza del Alfarero*, Úbeda, Spain	13
Intro.14	Bowls / *Tazones*, Jérez de la Frontera, Spain, 1475–1550	14
Intro.15	*An Old Woman Cooking Eggs*, Diego Rodríguez de Silva y Velázquez, 1618	14
Intro.16	Platter / *Platón*, Talavera de la Reina, Spain, 1675–1725	15
Intro.17	Storage Jar / *Tibor*, Puebla, Mexico, late 16th–early 17th century	16
Intro.18	Bowl / *Cuenco*, Puebla, Mexico, late 18th century	16
Intro.19	*Serving Nougats and Chocolate*, Valencia, Spain, 1775–1780	17

Intro.20 Chamber Pot / *Bacín*, Puebla, Mexico, late 18th century 18
Intro.21 Applying the glaze, Taller Uriarte, Puebla, Mexico, 2001 20
Intro.22 Painting, La Trinidad Workshop, Puebla, Mexico, 2001 20

1.1 Major ceramic distribution routes between the fifteenth and nineteenth centuries 26
1.2 Plate / *Plato*, Córdoba, 10th century 27
1.3 Porringer / *Escudilla*, Andalucía, 12th century 27
1.4 Baptismal Font / *Pila bautismal*, Teruel, 15th century 28
1.5 Plate / *Plato*, Sevilla, 15th–16th centuries 29
1.6 Plate / *Plato*, Talavera de la Reina, late 16th century 30
1.7 Plate / *Plato*, Talavera de la Reina, 1580–1650 31
1.8 Plate / *Plato*, Talavera de la Reina, 17th century 32
1.9 Plate / *Plato*, Barcelona, 1675–1725 33
1.10 Plate / *Plato*, Barcelona, 17th century 33
1.11 Pitcher / *Jarra de pico*, Talavera de la Reina, 17th century 34
1.12 Holy-Water Stoup / *Pila de agua bendita*, Talavera de la Reina, ca. 1700 34
1.13 Tile Panel, Sala de Cabildo, Toledo, 1698 35
1.14 Soup Tureen / *Sopera*, Alcora, Spain, ca. 1760 36
1.15a Basin / *Lebrillo*, Triana district, Sevilla, 19th century 37
1.15b Basin / *Lebrillo*, Triana district, Sevilla, 19th century 37
1.16 Commercial Stand of La Cartuja de Sevilla at the International Exhibition, Paris, 1867 38
1.17 Cruet / *Alcuza*, Granada, 19th century 39
1.18 Plate / *Plato*, Manises, 19th century 40
1.19 Deep Plate / *Plato hondo*, Ribesalbes, Spain, 19th century 40
1.20 Jar / *Jarro*, Puente del Arzobispo, 19th century 41
1.21 Inkwell / *Tintero*, Sevilla, Spain, 1898 42
1.22 Neo-Granadina Amphora / *Ánfora neo-granadina*, Valencia, ca. 1900 43
1.23 Jar / *Orza*, Juan Ruiz de Luna, Talavera de la Reina, ca. 1920 44

2.1 Mosaic Tile Panel / *Panel de aliceres o alicatado*, Tremecén Mosque, North Africa, 14th century 50
2.2 Baptismal Font / *Pila bautismal*, Sevilla, late 14th–early 15th century 52
2.3 Cistern / *Aguamanil*, Alcora, Spain, 1735–1749 53
2.4 Mortar / *Mortero*, Teruel, Spain, late 16th–early 17th century 53
2.5 Pharmacy Jars / *Botes de farmacia*, Barcelona, 15th century 54
2.6 Lusterware Porringer / *Escudilla de reflejo metálico*, Manises, 1475–1550 54
2.7a *The Last Supper*, Jaume Ferrer I, early 15th century 55
2.7b Lusterware Plate / *Plato de reflejo metálico*, Manises, 1410–1480 55
2.8 Lusterware Plate / *Plato de reflejo metálico*, Manises, early 15th century 56
2.9 *Still Life with an Ebony Chest*, Antonio de Pereda, 1652 57
2.10a *Still Life with Fruit and Cheese*, Luis Meléndez, 1771 58
2.10b Lusterware Honey Jar / *Melero de reflejo metálico*, Manises, ca. 1700–1750 58
2.11 Tiles / *Azulejos*, Sevilla, 16th century 60
2.12 Barber's Bowl / *Bacía de barbero de doble escotadura*, Villafeliche, Spain, 18th century 62
2.13 Jar / *Jarrón*, Talavera de la Reina, late 17th century 62

2.14 Spice Holder / *Especiero*, Teruel (Aragón), 18th century 63
2.15 Tapestry / *Tapiz*, Real Fábrica de Tapices Santa Bárbara, Madrid, ca. 1780 65
2.16 Trick Plate / *Plato de engaño*, Alcora (Valencia), 18th century 67
2.17 Chocolate Cup and Saucer / *Mancerina con jícara*, Alcora (Valencia), 1735–1760 68
2.18 *The Chocolate Hour*, Drawing by Manuel Tramullas, ca. 1760–1770 68
2.19 *La Chocolatada*, Workshop of Lorenzo Passoles, Barcelona, 1710 69
2.20 Writing Set / *Escribanía*, Alcora (Valencia), 1749–1798 70
2.21 Plate / *Plato*, Alcora (Valencia), 1727–1749 71
2.22 Jar / *Jarro*, Xavier Nogués, Barcelona, ca. 1930 73

3.1 St. Martin's Tower / *Torre de San Martín*, Teruel, ca. 1315 79
3.2 Tile Mosaic / *Aliceres*, La Alhambra, Granada, 13th century 80
3.3a Gothic Flooring / *Suelo gótica*, Segorbe Cathedral, Manises, ca. 1440 81
3.3b *The Prophet Isaiah*, Joan Reixach, ca. 1460 81
3.4 *The Visitation*, Francisco Niculoso (el Pisano), 1504 84
3.5 Principal Quatrefoil / *Florón principal*, Juan Fernández, The Escorial, Spain, 1570 85
3.6 Tile Walls and Benches / *Zócalos y bancos de azulejos*, Reales Alcazares, Sevilla, ca. 1543 86
3.7 Tile Altar Screen / *Retablo de azulejos*, Circle of Juan Fernández, Basilica de la Virgen del Prado, Talavera de la Reina, ca. 1570 87
3.8 Tile Flooring, Alacuás (Valencia), 16th century 88
3.9 Tile Panel, "Oliva," Salon of the Cortes de la Generalitat, Valencia, ca. 1570 89
3.10 Tiles in Diamond Pattern (*punta de diamante*), El Patriarca, Valencia 90
3.11 *St. Jerome*, Colegio de Arte Mayor de la Seda, Valencia, ca. 1700 92
3.12 *St. George*, Lorenzo de Madrid, Barcelona, ca. 1596 93
3.13 *Coming from the Oven*, Valencia, ca. 1830 95
3.14 *A Valencian Family*, Valencia, 1789 95
3.15 Tile Flooring, Doña María Disdier workshop, Valencia, 1808 96
3.16 Trade Tile / *Azulejo de oficio*, Barcelona, 18th century 98
3.17 Detail of *trencadís*, Antonio Gaudí i Cornet, Parque Güell, Barcelona, 1900–1914 100

4.1 *View of a Port*, Joseph Vernet, ca. 1754 104
4.2 Cross-section of a chapel vault where pottery was used as fill, Colegio de Santa María de Jesús, Sevilla, ca. 1500 105
4.3 *The Miracle of St. Hugo in the Refectory*, Francisco de Zurburán, ca. 1633 108
4.4 *Porcelain Traders*, Aubusson tapestry, 18th century 110
4.5 Book of *Fees to be Charged in Cádiz as well as the Ports in the Indies*, Madrid, 1720 113
4.6 *Loaded Mules on the Camino de la India*, Mexico, 19th century 114
4.7 Cart loaded with pots, Portuguese *Alentejo*, 20th century 115
4.8 Section of the hold of a galleon 116
4.9 Olive Jar / *Botija*, Spain, 18th century 116
4.10 Ceramics Market on Feria Street, Postcard, ca. 1900 117

4.11	Páramo's Collection, Oropesa (Toledo), 1919	118
4.12	Ruiz de Luna's Collection, Talavera de la Reina, 1943	119
5.1	Tile Panel, Sevilla, ca. 1600	125
5.2	The Crystal Palace, Ricardo Velázquez Bosco, Madrid, 1887	126
5.3	Detail of the Crystal Palace, Madrid, 1887	127
5.4	*Arista* Tiles, Sevilla, 19th century	128
5.5	*Plaza de España*, Anibal González, Sevilla, 1929	133
5.6	Balustrade, Plaza de España, Nuestra Señora de la O workshop, 1927	135
5.7	Jar / *Jarro*, Santa Isabel workshop, Sevilla, 2001	137
5.8	*Arista* tile for a *remate*, Mensaque Rodríguez y Cía, Sevilla, late 19th–early 20th century	138
5.9	Plates in the *cuerda seca* and lusterware techniques, CEARCO, Sevilla, 2001	139
5.10	Painting *cuerda seca* in the workshop of CEARCO, Sevilla, 2001	139
5.11	Tile Panel, Cerámica Artística Antonio González, Sevilla, 2001	140
5.12	Jar / *Orza*, Cerámica Gran Poder, Sevilla, 2001	141
5.13	Painting in the workshop of Cerámica Águilas, Sevilla, 2001	141
5.14	Ceramics from Cerámica Águilas, Sevilla, 2001	142
5.15	Jar / *Tibor*, Cerámica Águilas, Sevilla, 2001	142
5.16	Tile Panel, Cerámica Ruiz Gil, Sevilla, 2001	143
5.17	Plate / *Plato*, Cerámica Luchana, Sevilla, 2001	144
5.18	Ceramic workshop of Mercedes Ferreyro, Sevilla, 2001	144
5.19	Tiles / *Azulejos*, Mercedes Ferreyro, Sevilla, 2001	145
5.20	Plate / *Plato*, José María Campos, Sevilla, 2001	146
5.21	Tiles / *Azulejos*, Cerámica Artística Hera, Sevilla, 2001	146
5.22	Flower Pot / *Maceta*, Lucía Arriaga, Sevilla, 2001	147
5.23	Tile panel in *cuerda seca* technique, Alfar 3, Sevilla, 2001	148
6.1	Apothecary Jar / *Bote de farmacia*, Cataluña, 18th century	152
6.2	Tile Panel / *Plafón de azulejos*, Barcelona, 17th century	153
6.3	Tile / *Azulejo*, Barcelona, 19th century	153
6.4	Mallorca Tapestry, Monastery of Pedralbes, Barcelona, early 17th century	154
6.5	Trade Tile / *Azulejo de oficio*, Barcelona, 17th century	155
6.6	Detail of the main balcony, Palau de la Música, Barcelona, 1908	157
6.7	Façade of Escribà pastry shop, La Rambla, Barcelona, 1903	158
6.8	Building façade with tilework, La Rambla, Barcelona	159
6.9	*Diana*, Josep Jodi Guardiola, ca. 1925	160
6.10	Detail of vase, Cerámica Camaró, Capellades (Barcelona), 1998	162
6.11	Alejandro Jarandilla painting a plate in his studio, Capellades (Barcelona), 2000	163
6.12	Alejandro Jarandilla in his studio, Capellades (Barcelona), 2000	163
6.13	Catalan Kitchen, Cerámica Camaró, Capellades (Barcelona), 2002	164
6.14	Lizard Table Top, Lisa McConnell, Barcelona, 2000	166
7.1	Utilitarian Earthenware / *Loza utilitaria*, Manises, Spain, 2001	173
7.2	Ceramics from Talavera de la Reina and Manises in Valencia, Spain, 2001	175
7.3	Pedro de la Cal Rubio, Santa Catalina Cerámica Regional, Puente del Arzobispo	179

7.4 *Plaza Redonda*, Valencia, Spain 180
7.5 *La Escuradeta* (the pottery washing), Valencia, Spain, 1993 184

8.1a Jar / *Jarro*, Tonalá (Jalisco), Mexico, 17th century 188
8.1b Bottle / *Botella*, Tonalá (Jalisco), Mexico, 17th century 189
8.2 Bowl / *Cuenco*, Tonalá (Jalisco), Mexico, 17th century 190
8.3 Globular Vessel / *Búcaro*, Tonalá (Jalisco), Mexico, 17th century 192
8.4 Jar / *Tinaja*, Tonalá (Jalisco), Mexico, 17th century 200
8.5 Jar / *Tinaja*, Tonalá (Jalisco), Mexico, 17th century 201

9.1 Tile Flooring, Convento de San Francisco, Puebla, Mexico, 17th century 208
9.2 Altar / *Altar*, crypt of the former Convento del Carmen, San Ángel, Mexico, 17th century 209
9.3 Tile / *Azulejo*, Puebla, 17th century 213
9.4 Tiles / *Azulejos*, Puebla, 17th century 213
9.5 Façade of the Church of San Francisco, Acatepec (Puebla), 18th century 214
9.6a–c Tiles / *Azulejos*, Puebla, 17th century 216
9.7 Relief Tiles / *Azulejos de relieve*, Rosary Chapel, Church of Santo Domingo, Puebla, 1632–1690 217
9.8 Tiles / *Azulejos*, Rosary Chapel, Church of Santo Domingo, 1632–1690 217
9.9 Kitchen of the Convento de Santa Rosa, Puebla, founded 1708 219
9.10 Dome / *Cúpula*, Cathedral, Puebla, 1575–1649 220
9.11 Hospital de la Santa Caridad, Sevilla, 17th century 221
9.12 *The Virgin of the Immaculate Conception*, Puebla, ca. 1780 221
9.13 Iglesia de San Marcos, Puebla, 1797 222
9.14 Iglesia de San Francisco, Acatepec (Puebla), 18th century 222
9.15 Casa de los Muñecos, Puebla, 1792 223

10.1 Cup / *Jícara*, Mexico City or Puebla, Mexico, 17th century 234
10.2 Basin / *Lebrillo*, Mexico City or Puebla, Mexico, 1650–1700 235
10.3 Plate / *Plato*, Mexico City or Puebla, Mexico, 1650–1750 235
10.4 Plate / *Plato*, Mexico City or Puebla, Mexico, 18th century 236
10.5 Plate / *Plato*, Mexico City or Puebla, Mexico, 18th century 236
10.6 Plate / *Plato*, Mexico City or Puebla, Mexico, 18th century 237
10.7 Bowls / *Tazones*, Mexico City or Puebla, Mexico, 1700–1850 238
10.8 Plate / *Plato*, Mexico City or Puebla, Mexico, 1600–1650 239
10.9 Plate / *Plato*, Mexico City or Puebla, Mexico, 18th century 239
10.10a Cup / *Taza o jícara*, Mexico City or Puebla, Mexico, 1650–1750 240
10.10b Sugar Bowl / *Azucarero*, Mexico City or Puebla, Mexico, 1650–1750 240

11.1 Maya woman pouring chocolate to raise foam, The Princeton Pot, Guatemala, ca. 750 246
11.2 Aztec woman pouring chocolate to raise foam, *Codex Tudela*, late 16th century 247
11.3 *De Español y Negra, Mulato*, Mexico, ca. 1750 251
11.4 *Alacena*, Antonio Pérez de Aguilar, Mexico, 1769 252
11.5 Chocolate Cups / *Jícaras*, Mexico City or Puebla, 17th century 253
11.6 Chocolate Saucer / *Mancerina*, Alcora (Valencia), 1748–1798 254
11.7 Woman carrying a *mancerina*, Alcora (Valencia), 18th century 255
11.8 Chocolate Storage Jar / *Chocolatero*, Puebla, 17th century 255

11.9	Chocolate Pot / *Chocolatera*, Alcora (Valencia), 1735–1760	256
11.10	Copper Chocolate Pot / *Chocolatera de cobre*, Spain, 18th century	256
11.11	Silver Chocolate Pot / *Chocolatera de plata*, Peru, ca. 1730	256
11.12	Mayólica tile depicting a nun making jam, Valencia, early 19th century	257
11.13	Bowls / *Cuencos*, Convento de Santa Teresa, Puebla, 1750–1800	258
11.14	*Birth of the Virgin*, (detail) Arellano (signed), Mexico, ca. 1710	259
11.15	*De Chino y India, Genízaro*, Francisco Clapera, Mexico, 18th century	260
11.16	*De India y Cambujo, Tente en el Aire*, Mexico 18th century	261
11.17	*The Table Blessing*, José de Alcíbar, Mexico, late 18th century	262
11.18	*Birth of the Virgin*, Francisco de León, Mexico, 18th century	263
11.19	Mayólica Sherds, Mexico, 1600–1680	264
11.20	Plate / *Plato*, Mexico City or Puebla, Mexico, 17th century	265
11.21	Soup Plate / *Cuenco*, Cuyamungue, New Mexico, 17th century	265
12.1	Jar / *Orza*, Anonymous Puebla workshop, mid-19th century	272
12.2	Common Ware / *Loza común*, Uriarte Talavera, Puebla, early 20th century	273
12.3	Tile Panel / *Tablero de azulejos*, Enrique Ventosa and Uriarte Talavera, Puebla, 1919	274
12.4	Plate decorated in Italian Renaissance style, Enrique Ventosa and Uriarte Talavera, Puebla, 1920s	274
12.5	Plate decorated in *Art Nouveau* style, Enrique Ventosa and Uriarte Talavera, Puebla, 1920s	275
12.6	Jar decorated in Mexican Precolumbian style, Enrique Ventosa and Uriarte Talavera, Puebla, 1920s	275
12.7	Mold for creating large jars, Puebla, ca. 1917	276
12.8	Historic photo showing large jars, Puebla, 1917–1918	276
12.9	Tile panel with scene of Mexican woman holding tray, Pedro Sánchez, Puebla, 1926	277
12.10	Platter decorated with Renaissance, Mexican, Precolumbian, and Oriental willow ware motifs, Miguel Martínez, Puebla, ca. 1920	278
12.11	Tile panel with scene commemorating the founding of Mexico City, Uriarte Talavera, Puebla. ca. 1925	279
12.12	Sign commemorating the opening of the Museo de Cerámica in Puebla, 1926	280
12.13	Tile panel with floral decoration, Miguel Martínez, Puebla, 1926	280
12.14	Tile panel with scene of *Don Quixote*, Pedro Sánchez, Puebla, late 1920s	281
12.15	Tile panels with geometric motifs installed on wall and planter, Uriarte Talavera, Puebla, ca. 1940	282
12.16	Tiles with Mexican genre scenes, Uriarte Talavera, ca. 1930	282
12.17	Plate decorated with *mudéjar*-style patterns, Uriarte Talavera, ca. 1940	283
12.18	Plate decorated with Chinese-style patterns, Uriarte Talavera, ca. 1940	283
12.19	Plate decorated with Mexican genre scenes against Puebla-style blue-on-white pattern, Uriarte Talavera, ca. 1940	284
12.20	José Miguel Padierna, Puebla, 2002	285
12.21	Jorge Guevara, Puebla, 2001	285
12.22	César Torres Ramírez, Puebla, 2001	286
12.23	Angélica Moreno Rodríguez, Puebla, 2001	286
12.24	Jar / *Tibor*, Taller Talavera de la Reyna, Puebla, 2001	287

12.25	Table setting (*vajilla*) decorated with 19th-century Puebla-style pattern, Jorge Guevara, La Trinidad, Puebla, 2002	287
12.26	Jar decorated with early 20th-century Puebla-style pattern, Fermín Contreras, 2000	288
12.27	Jar decorated with serpentine handles and early 20th-century Puebla-style pattern, César Torres Ramírez, Puebla, 2000	288
12.28	Tile panel with 17th-century Puebla-style decorative scene, Magdalena Ayona Herrera, Uriarte Talavera, Puebla, 2001	289
12.29	Basin (*lebrillo*) decorated with 18th-century Puebla-style pattern, Uriarte Talavera, Puebla, 2000	290
12.30	Platter decorated with 17th-century Puebla-style pattern, Uriarte Talavera, Puebla, 2002	290
12.31	Jar decorated with early 20th-century Puebla-style pattern, Uriarte Talavera, Puebla, 2001	290
12.32	Basin (*lebrillo*) decorated with early 20th-century Puebla-style pattern, Talavera de la Reyna, Puebla, 2002	291
12.33	Jar decorated with 19th-century Puebla-style pattern, Talavera de la Reyna, Puebla, 2002	291
13.1	Pottery Sherds, Guanajuato, 19th century	298
13.2	Pottery Sherds, Guanajuato, 19th century	299
13.3	Jar / *Orza*, Guanajuato, 1825–1900	300
13.4	Plate / *Plato*, Guanajuato, 1825–1900	300
13.5	Gorky González, owner, Alfarería Tradicional, S.A., Guanajuato, 1994	301
13.6	Flower Pot / *Macetón*, Alfarería Tradicional, S.A., Guanajuato, 2002	303
13.7	Show Room, Alfarería Tradicional, S.A., Guanajuato, 2001	304
13.8	Painting a plate, Alfarería Tradicional, S.A., Guanajuato, 1994	305
13.9	Jar / *Orza*, Alfarería Tradicional, S.A., Guanajuato, 2001	306
13.10	Javier de Jesús (Capelo) Hernández, Taller de Alfarería Majolica de Guanajuato, Guanajuato, 1999	307
13.11	Jar / *Tibor*, Taller de Alfarería Majolica de Guanajuato, Guanajuato, 1996	308
13.12	Jar / *Orza*, Taller de Alfarería Majolica de Guanajuato, Guanajuato, 1999	308
13.13	Taller de Alfarería Majolica de Guanajuato, Guanajuato, n.d.	309
13.14	Plate / *Plato*, Taller de Alfarería Majolica de Guanajuato, Guanajuato, 1994	310
13.15	Bisqueware / *Juaguete*, Alfarería Aguilera Mayólica "Santa Rosa," Guanajuato, 1994	311
13.16	Jar for Preserves / *Conservera*, Alfarería Aguilera Mayólica "Santa Rosa," Guanajuato, 1999	312
14.1	Bowls ready for firing, Alfar del Caballo Blanco, Aguascalientes, 1979	316
14.2	Jorge Olvera and Maestro Juan Silva, Aguascalientes, 1979	317
14.3	Dome / *Cúpula*, Iglesia de Nuestra Señora de Guadalupe, Aguascalientes	321
14.4	Fountain / *Fuente*, Luis Fernández Ledesma, Aguascalientes, ca. 1940	322
14.5	Pitcher with *amapola* pattern, Aguascalientes, 1950	323
14.6	Platter / *Platón*, Aguascalientes, ca. 1935	323
14.7	Large jar with *amapola* pattern, Aguascalientes, 1920	324
14.8a	Preserve Jar / *Conservera*, Aguascalientes, late 19th century	324
14.8b	Preserve jar with *rosa azul* pattern, Drawing by Juan Silva	324

14.9	Bowls / *Posoleros*, Aguascalientes, early 20th century	325
14.10	Three bowls (*tazones*) with patterns *pepitalla, avellana,* and *sombra*, Aguascalientes, 1920	325
14.11	Mixing Tanks / *Pilas*, Alfar El Caballo Blanco, Aguascalientes, 1979	326
14.12	Maestro Silva at the kick wheel (*el torno*), Alfar El Caballo Blanco, Aguascalientes, 1979	327
14.13	Mill / *Molino*, Alfar El Caballo Blanco, Aguascalientes	328
14.14	Bowls / *Cuencos y posoleros*, Longino de la Rosa, Aguascalientes, ca. 1910	331
14.15	Plate with *jalón amarillo* pattern, Drawing by Juan Silva	331
14.16	Patterns / *Diseños*, including *cúchila, bocabajo, mañana, carlanga, ambar de gotas, cucaracha, mariposa*, and *perejil.* Drawings by Juan Silva	332–33
14.17	Plates / *Platos*, Aguascalientes, 1950	334
14.18	Plate with *dos hermanas* pattern, Drawing by Juan Silva	334
14.19	Soup tureen with *fresa* pattern, Drawing by Juan Silva	335
14.20	Serving platter with *tepocate* pattern, Drawing by Juan Silva	335
14.21	Maestro Juan Silva and Daughter, Alfar El Caballo Blanco, Aguascalientes, 1994	336

Opening Remarks

In a world accustomed to instantaneous communications systems, electronic transfers of funds, and high-speed travel across multiple time zones, we tend to downplay the range and importance of travel and trade in past centuries. Yet the galleons of the Spanish fleet that crossed the oceans to the shores of Spain's far-flung colonies made journeys to lands that in their time were every bit as distant as the planets are in ours. The goods they delivered to the Americas and those they brought back to Spain affected life in Europe as well as in the cultures with which they came in contact.

When the Spanish ships sailed to far-off ports, they carried not only a variety of goods, they also disseminated a worldview that spread Spain's influence far and wide. Among the goods on board were ceramics, specifically mayólica, tin-glazed earthenware that was itself a commodity as well as a container for food and other trade items. Mayólica was also a medium well suited to serve as a carrier of culture.

As material culture, mayólica illustrates the capacity of objects to mark social history and identity in place and time. Found worldwide, ceramics are at once universal and culturally specific. The historic and contemporary examples of mayólica answer basic human needs in their everyday use yet have become far more than simply functional, utilitarian objects.

Mayólica bears the marks of the various cultural influences that formed it. While Spanish missionaries taught Christianity, Spanish mayólica provided visual evidence in its design of a multicultural Spain with a multiethnic population that included Jews, Muslims, and Christians within its borders. In Mexico, another society made up of diverse inhabitants-Spanish, indigenous, and mestizo-developed its own cultural style that is both related to and distinct from its Spanish counterparts. The technical skill and artistry of pieces appeal to the eye with their beauty and the melding of form and function. They display what different cultural groups see as aesthetically pleasing. Our appreciation is further deepened and enhanced as we begin to understand the wealth of information encoded in them.

I can imagine no better guides to this emerging adventure story than the authors who have contributed essays to this publication. From Spain, Mexico, and the United States, these scholars bring perspectives framed by years of field research and careful study to the analysis of this intriguing subject matter. Their varied backgrounds in art history, Spanish Colonial art, Latin American studies, anthropology, archaeology, decorative art, material culture, and ceramics offer readers a cross-disciplinary contextual approach.

Their work provides us with a decoding of a fascinating narrative of discovery and trade encompassing the everyday and the adventurous, aristocrats, religious, guilds, and commoners. Tracing the evolution of this rich ceramic tradition, we come to an understanding of the innovations and influences that even now shape mayólica in its present-day manifestations. What fascinated early practitioners and their customers about this artistic expression continues to attract us today.

Joyce Ice, Director
Museum of International Folk Art

Foreword

FLORENCE C. LISTER

THE MAKING OF pottery was the first major technological breakthrough of humankind. In regard to receptacles, basketry preceded pottery by centuries in many parts of the world. That craft involved the manipulation of certain fibers, not their alteration. In the case of pottery, however, three natural properties-earth (specifically clay), water, and fire-were combined in such a way as to produce a unique substance not found in nature. Without question this accomplishment was a matter of chance observations followed by trial and error and not an appreciation of the innate qualities of the materials. Still, what was created would have profound significance through time for its makers and users and for those who would seek to understand them.

Once pottery techniques were learned, earthenwares became very useful to those with this knowledge. They were made in astounding volume in most such cultures, because they could be fashioned with relative speed to serve many purposes. Unfortunately, their body walls were weak, due to being fired at temperatures that often were just sufficient to solidify them. If they survived the critical baking stage, they likely soon broke because of lack of strength or from rough usage. The result was one group of intact vessels representing a small percentage of total output and another of fragments that litter the civilized world in considerable tonnage.

In one sense both categories-whole or broken- are everlasting. Unlike many other kinds of artifacts, pottery is not destroyed by insects, bacteria, rot, water, fire, wind, or other deleterious agents. Whether whole or in pieces, it comprises an invaluable resource for students of the past. The plasticity of moist clay during manufacture and the permanency of form and design resulting from the heat-induced chemical process make pottery a highly sensitive register of its cultural contexts.

At various times and places around the globe, creative minds and hands independently learned how pottery was made. Most important to the variety of pottery featured in this book was such a discovery by neolithic peoples in the Near East. As early as the seventh millennium B.C., some of them became especially dedicated to this craft. They soon recognized the value of enclosed chambers, or kilns, for firing their wares, because such constructions reduced defects from fly ash and permitted the attainment of higher temperatures. They invented horizontal wheel devices propelled by the potter's foot to speed uniform production through centrifugal force. As a by-product of glass manufacture, they formulated glazes to make their vessels impervious to liquids and to enhance their appearance. As their skills increased, in a wondrous display of aesthetic virtuosity they modeled cult figures; painted and polished objects to be used for eating, drinking, and serving; and they fashioned an array of architectural enrichments. All this fine-tuned experience eventually passed to the classical world of the eastern Mediterranean and later spread throughout Europe.

It was the Romans who brought this ceramic wisdom of antiquity to Spain. For six centuries, as they converted the Iberian Peninsula into one of the empire's breadbaskets, they maintained a pottery industry to sustain it. Served by a specialized work force utilizing compound kick wheels and two-chambered updraft kilns, dozens of small factories were responsible for millions of simple, unglazed, expendable containers to hold and transport the colony's commodities back to Rome. Prominent among them were the ubiquitous torpedo-shaped amphorae known everywhere in the Mediterranean for thousands of years. A variety of additional vessels, such as handled jugs, oil lamps, plates, and hemispherical bowls, also had long prior histories in the Near East. Many of these functional forms endured as a substratum of Spanish ceramic repertories up to modern times. There had been such successful engineering for specific uses that there was no need for change.

A secondary, shorter-lived pottery enterprise used molds to make the red gloss service vessels with delicate stamped or raised decorative embellishment that typifies Roman pottery production elsewhere. These wares vanished from the Spanish scene with the Romans.

After a lull of several centuries in pottery activity, while the pastoral Visigoths occupied Spain, a second and more decisive impact on local ceramics arrived with the Muslim invaders of the early eighth century. These conquerors quickly transplanted many aspects of their culture to the westernmost fringes of Islam. Heirs to a culture in which pottery was an integral part, artisans quickly turned out the full range of familiar functional pottery to meet agricultural and domestic needs.

A notable introduction was a bulbous, wide-mouthed jar having a shallow depression around its mid-section to facilitate its attachment to the perimeter of one of the hundreds of water wheels that soon were erected along Andalusia's rivers in order to irrigate large tracts of land immmigrant farmers planted in familiar crops. Laborers formed ponderous wellheads and casings for newly dug water sources. They molded tubing for water pipes, sewers, and downspouts for constructions. To meet the increased complexity of the lives of even the most humble colonists, they threw pitchers, cups, bottles, bowls, basins, oil lamps, casseroles, and chamber pots. Other workers in the shops applied lead glazes to some of this everyday hardware, but much was left in a bisqued state.

As the Spanish Muslim province flourished and a sophisticated caliphate made Cordoba a rival to Baghdad or Damascus, what probably was a second tier of more accomplished potters met market demands for a great assortment of finer articles. These speak of a mounting cultural refinement on a higher level than prevailed in the countryside. Potters copied modes popular in eastern emporiums stretching from Persia to Egypt. To accommodate appetites for luxury goods, they used green and amber lead glazes with abandon to cover vessel surfaces that were incised, stamped, or roughened in some way so as to catch pools of the lustrous coating. They drew fanciful decorations on open forms such as plates using green and brown pigments over a white slip background. Kufic script and quaint animal and human figures competed with formalized geometric compositions. These vessels heralded an upcoming tradition of painted wares.

With the exception of the Emirate of Granada, all of Spain was reclaimed by Christian forces in the thirteenth century. Nevertheless, the ceramic industry, from arrangement and equipment of workshops, to output, to workers, remained a Muslim enterprise. Even Castilian Spanish had incorporated Arabic terminology related to the craft. This included words for potter: *alfar* or *alfarero*. Ironically, at this historical juncture, when political, racial, and religious attitudes were to turn against the Muslims, it was they who adopted a decorative method created and long used in the Near East, which they applied indiscriminately to common and finer wares. The style known as mayólica would eventually transform Spanish ceramic production and much of that of Western Europe. It was this new direction in the craft that interested my late husband, Robert, and me, a subject ancillary to our earlier academic work in the American Southwest.

Thirty years ago, the unraveling of the history of Spanish mayólica presented a challenging research topic, because it was a kind of pottery prevalent in sites in Mexico and its borderlands dating to the Spanish colonial period and about which very little was known. From the restricted amount of excavation that had been done to that time, mayólica was presumed to be of Spanish derivation but copied in the Americas at uncertain times and places by processes only vaguely recognized. The principal explanation for this lack of knowledge and interest was the feeling then current in archaeological circles that interpretation of materials pertaining to the Spanish colonial era, with its reservoir of documentation, was the exclusive domain of social and art historians. Fortunately, this was an attitude beginning to change in the late 1960s, at which time work in historical archaeology became a valid, respectable undertaking. Hence, the mayólica project we then launched was rather like reading the last chapter of a book first; that is, we were working from colonial remains back to probable sources and inspiration in the motherland. Little did we realize the complexity of the study we were about to begin, of events in Spanish history that took that nation's products to the far ends of the world and in return, in often subtle ways, drew upon the aesthetic reserves those outposts offered.

Attempts to reconstruct the layered background of Spanish mayólicas and associated pottery types as they evolved over the centuries followed many tangential avenues. Foremost was becoming familiar with the ceramics themselves.

During the course of a dozen or so years, we made extensive surveys of museum, private, and archaeological collections in Spain. Added to those were others in Portugal, Morocco, and Italy, where Muslim-introduced mayólicas were commonplace. Other visits were to England, because medieval trade relationships brought Spanish pots to Bristol and London and sent tin from Cornwall to Sevilla.

In tracing the overseas diffusion of pots and manufacturing knowledge, the Canary Islands on one side of the Atlantic and Hispaniola on the other were important stops. A small-scale seventeenth century potting endeavor having been previously identified in Panama, we studied finds from there and followed some of these types to Colombia, Ecuador, and Peru.

A welcome opportunity to analyze a huge assortment of Spanish-tradition fragments recovered from beneath colonial sectors of Mexico City came with the construction of a subway system and the restoration of the national cathedral. The former yielded mayólicas dating to the sixteenth through nineteenth centuries. The latter produced types primarily of the years between about 1540 (the first known recorded date of a potter present) and the late 1570s, when the foundation laid for the massive cathedral essentially sealed lower deposits. The spread of some of these types to the northern reaches of the Spanish empire, from Florida to California, was confirmed by on-site examinations. Similar diffusion to the south took us to Guatemala, where there was a small colonial industry that continues today.

Finally, in hope of learning about the Chinese export porcelains that had an overwhelming influence on Mexican mayolists of the eighteenth century, we made brief visits to Taipei, Manila, Jakarta, and southern China.

To relate the generally anonymous body of potters to their social and political environments, we undertook exhaustive perusals of original and published archives. Those efforts frequently were fruitless but did provide some tantalizing tidbits about obscure individuals, their roles in community life, their ways of working, their health, and fragmentary information about the economics of the trade. Our library research reached from the halls of the Library of Congress to the stacks of a number of regional universities and to the American Embassy in Manila. Graduate-level courses in Spanish history refreshed memories left from long gone college days and led us to data pertaining to the guild and religious brotherhoods that structured Spanish artisanship. The penetration of Genoese into Spanish financial and social circles helped explain why pottery from that part of Italy was found in presumably closed Spanish America. Provocative, too, was learning of the many prejudices against Muslims in Andalusian society that were tempered by admiration for their expertise in such handiwork as ceramics.

Through studies in Spanish art history, we learned that master artists of the Siglo de Oro sometimes painted common vessels as background props. Many of these could be correlated with known extant examples.

Concurrent with these diverse inquiries, where possible we stood on the sidelines of functioning workshops to observe methods and rhythms of work in progress. We were rewarded by the observation that in conservative Spain and Morocco, some ancient patterns of operation continue. Whether this reflects a spiritual need to connect to the past or the basic cautious nature of potters remains an open question.

Drawing upon these accumulated bits and pieces of information, at last we were satisfied that we had met most of our research goals. We were convinced that most of the early Spanish pottery in the Americas was made in shops in the environs of Sevilla, to be shipped from there according to royal regulations. The earliest exports to the first colony on Hispaniola were crude containers for foodstuffs, drugs, and household items included in the colonists' baggage. Stock-in-trade tiles from Sevilla were used as ballast for the outbound galleons. So far as we were able to ascertain, no pottery was made on Hispaniola other than roof tiles and vessels used in the refining of sugar.

After Mexico was conquered, similar objects were brought to the highlands for the use of European families gathering there. Within several decades after the conquest, workshops in the capital were turning out copies of pottery types with which the potters were familiar in their homeland. These were the last vestiges of the long continuum of the Muslim ceramic tradition in Spain. Quite coincidentally, the Spanish opening of the New World occurred precisely at the time of the final expulsion of the Muslims from what had once been al-Andalus. It is entirely likely that some *moriscos* changed their identities by adopting Christian names and dress to seek new opportunities in New Spain. In some cases it would simply have been work as usual. To verify our distinctions between Spanish originals and imitations presumably made in Mexico City, chemists at the Smithsonian Institution studied the clays used. Their confirmation of our work came through the realization that Mexican clays contain volcanic inclusions whereas those of Spain do not.

As the sixteenth century wore on, the threadbare Muslim past faded, and a new body of Spanish Christians and perhaps some mestizos who had been allowed to join their ranks refined their products and copied styles then becoming popular in Spain. These were revamped according to local tastes, abilities, and resources. A significant change from previous times was that these potters made two grades of mayólicas to accommodate the rising number of wealthy colonial citizens while meeting the needs of lesser folks.

At the end of the sixteenth century a second potting industry was put in place in a prescribed potters'quarter of the new town of Puebla. The outdated, restrictive frameworks of a guild and confraternity were transferred from old to New Spain. Nevertheless, a few Italian artisans joined with Spanish colleagues to help upgrade manufacturing methods and decorative modes. Many of their painted patterns were a combination of new Spanish conceptions finally freed from the stranglehold of the Muslim tradition, along with other devices of Italian inspiration. The source for these unfolding trends was originally Talavera de la Reina, in Castile. The range of vessel forms implies increasing sophistication, as inkwells, candleholders, fountain mouths, drug jars, chocolate cups, holy water stoups, and jardinieres went on sale in Mexican markets. At the same time, Puebla was set ablaze by church domes, garden benches, and entire facades covered with brilliant mayólica tilework. Colonial artisans took a favorite Andalusian artifice and ran with it.

In the eighteenth century, polychrome types gave way to a blue on white palette and a flood of Chinese forms and formats. This shift to the Far East was stimulated by the Manila galleon trade that dumped masses of export porcelain on Mexican shores.

It was the seventeenth and eighteenth century mayólica types from central Mexico that reached the northern borderlands as the empire expanded. They were what had aroused our initial interest.

As with any pioneering effort of this sort, there were many dead ends and frustrations. Not the least of the latter was a puzzling lack of interest on the part of curators and scientists alike. Other than taking pride in the luxury pieces, they presumably were unconcerned about the run-of-the-mill materials that make up usual assortments and tell the most about their place in the scheme of things. Only now is this attitude being replaced by the realization of the value of even the lowliest pots in shedding light upon mundane aspects of daily life not easily seen otherwise. Coupled with this bias was the prevailing lack of controlled archaeological investigations in localities of possible significance for the study. Happily, this is also beginning to change, supported by legal mandates for such work prior to any renewal undertaken in historic zones.

It is to be hoped that the essays in this book, based in part upon data we collected but brought forward in time by others, will further an interest in the potential for cultural understanding afforded by a lowly craft whose practicioners turned common clay into a dazzling display of the potter's art.

Acknowledgments

THIS PUBLICATION AND the accompanying exhibition have been made possible in part by a major grant from the National Endowment for the Humanities, promoting excellence in the humanities. Generous funding has also been provided by the International Folk Art Foundation; the Museum of New Mexico Foundation; the Office of Cultural Affairs, State of New Mexico; and the US-Mexico Fund for Culture.

We would like to give special thanks to the following people for their support, goodwill, and encouragement throughout this project: Judith Espinar, Tisa Gabriel, Martha Alexandra Greenway Palacio, Willard Lewis, Darby McQuade, Feliza Medrano, Cordelia Snow, and Julie Wilson. Additional thanks go to the staff of the Museum of International Folk Art, Museum of New Mexico, particularly Jacqueline Duke, Frank X. Cordero, Deborah Garcia, Aurelia Gómez, Laura May, Ree Mobley, Tey Marianna Nunn, Paul Smutko, Chris Vitagliano, and former staff members Judy Chiba Smith and Charlene Cerny. The exhibition was completed with the expertise of the capable staff of the exhibitions department of the Museum of New Mexico, led by exhibition designer Nancy Allen, with the help of graphic designer Joseph Guglietti, of JG Designs. Preliminary designs were made by Linda Gegick. Conservators Mina Thompson, Renee Jolly, Larry Humetewa, and Teresa Myers brought out the best in the pieces.

We would also like to acknowledge our colleagues in museums in the United States, Spain, and Mexico, for the time they spent with us discussing the project, sharing ideas, and showing us through their collections. These include Tracey Albainy and Jennine Falino, Museum of Fine Arts, Boston; Susan Danley, formerly at the Meade Art Museum, Amherst, Massachusetts; Rosario Diez de Corral and M. Leticia Sánchez Hernández, Palacio Real, Madrid; Rafael Garcia Serrano, Museo de Santa Cruz, Toledo; Héctor Rivero Borrell and Julieta Giménez Cacho, Museo Franz Mayer, Mexico City; George Kuwayama, formerly at the Los Angeles County Museum of Art; Carmen Mañueco Santurtun, Museo Arqueológico Nacional, Madrid; Marion Oettinger, the San Antonio Museum of Art; Diana Pardue, The Heard Museum, Phoenix; Cristina Partearroyo, Instituto Valencia de Don Juan, Madrid; Josep Pérez Camps, Museo de Cerámica de Manises; Juan Fidel Pérez, former director of the Museo José Luis Bello y González (INAH), Puebla; Juan Carlos Rico, Museo Nacional de Antropología, Madrid; Dean Walker, Philadelphia Museum of Art; and Cathy Wright, Taylor Museum of The Colorado Springs Fine Arts Center.

Those who generously lent to the exhibition were: the Denver Art Museum and Jan and Frederick R. Mayer; Judith Espinar and Tom Dillenberg; El Rancho de las Golondrinas Museum, Santa Fe; Mr. and Mrs. Larry Frank; Gloria Giffords; Michael Haskell; the Heard Museum, Phoenix; Roberta Heckel; The Hispanic Society of America, New York; The International Folk Art Foundation; Florence Lister; the Metropolitan Museum of Art, New York; Museum of Fine Arts, Boston; Museum of Indian Arts and Culture, Santa Fe; Museum of Spanish Colonial Art, Santa Fe; Museu de Ceràmica, Barcelona; Museo Franz Mayer, Mexico City; Museo José Luis Bello y González (INAH), Puebla; Museo Nacional de Antropología, Madrid; Museo Nacional de Cerámica y de las Artes Suntuarias "Gonzalez Martí," Valencia; the Philadelphia Museum of Art; the San Antonio Museum of Art; The Taylor Museum of The Colorado Springs Fine Arts Center.

Others who contributed to this project in ways too numerous to mention are Jim, Molly, and Emma Gavin; Robert L. and Carol Y. Farwell; and Josie Caruso, Rita Robbins, Constance D. Gavin, Karen Phillips, Helen Pynn, and Ronda Brulotte.

Finally, we would like to thank the translator of essays from Spanish to English, Kenny Fitzgerald, and the very capable and accommodating staff of the University of New Mexico Press and their associates: David Holtby, Evelyn Schlatter, Melissa Tandysh, illustrator Carol Cooperrider, and editor David Margolin.

Any views, findings, conclusions or recommendations expressed in this publication do not necessarily represent those of the National Endowment for the Humanities.

> For the world's working majority, utility is a high value, the merely decorative seems trivial, and their greatest creations blend the aesthetic with the useful, just as a good meal blends flavor and nutrition.
>
> —Henry Glassie, *The Potter's Art*

Introduction

ROBIN FARWELL GAVIN

Ceramics mirror culture. Changes in style and form often reflect changes in human relationships, economy, and social status. Nowhere is this more true than with *mayólica,* one of the earliest and most enduring types of glazed and painted ceramics made in Europe and the Americas. Mayólica holds a unique position in history, for unlike unpainted earthenwares, where it is primarily the vessel form that provides us with information, mayólica has the added dimension of decoration. These two characteristics combine to reveal a story of life and art that might otherwise remain untold (fig. Intro.1).

Mayólica is the Spanish term for tin-glazed earthenware. The term is synonymous with *maiolica, majolica, faience,* and

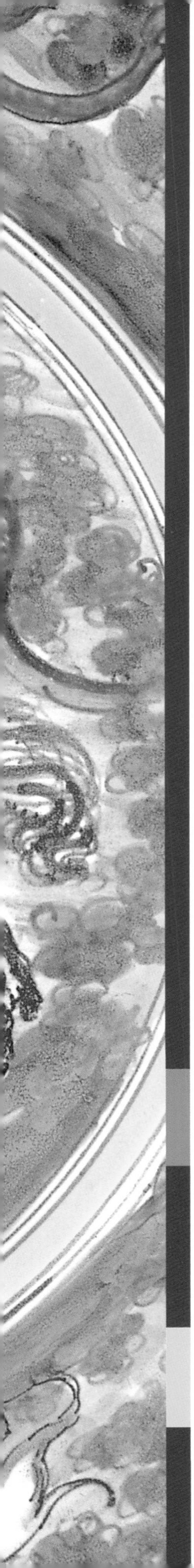

Detail, Fig. Intro.16

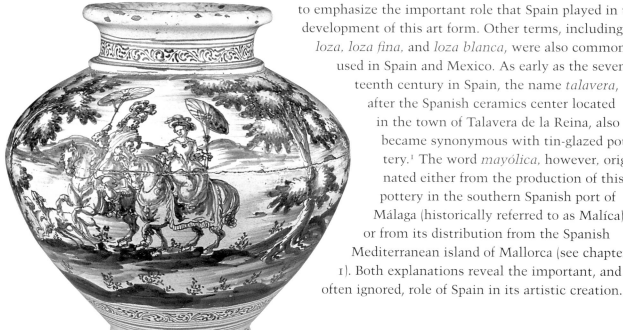

Intro.1 Jar / *Orza*
Talavera de la Reina,
Spain, 17th–18th centuries
Museu de Ceràmica,
Barcelona
Photo by Guillém
Fernández

delftware. We have chosen this term, and this spelling, to emphasize the important role that Spain played in the development of this art form. Other terms, including *loza, loza fina,* and *loza blanca,* were also commonly used in Spain and Mexico. As early as the seventeenth century in Spain, the name *talavera,* after the Spanish ceramics center located in the town of Talavera de la Reina, also became synonymous with tin-glazed pottery.[1] The word *mayólica,* however, originated either from the production of this pottery in the southern Spanish port of Málaga (historically referred to as Malíca) or from its distribution from the Spanish Mediterranean island of Mallorca (see chapter 1). Both explanations reveal the important, and often ignored, role of Spain in its artistic creation.

The Origins of Mayólica

For centuries, China held the secret to creating the world's finest pottery: porcelain (fig. Intro.2). The production of this pure white, translucent pottery that rang like a bell when struck required both kaolin, a white clay unknown in the West until the eighteenth century, and kilns that fired at high temperatures. Because of their fragility and the difficulty of overland travel across the silk roads, Chinese porcelains were rare and costly trade items in Europe in the early centuries A.D.

The most common pottery being produced elsewhere at this time was earthenware. A low-fire pottery, earthenware was typically made from colored clay. The earliest glazes, made of lead oxides, had been in use since about 200 B.C. Lead-based glazes were transparent and showed the color of the clay beneath. Certain oxides could be added to the lead glaze to create a solid background color, but painted designs would blur and run.

In the ninth century A.D., potters in the Middle East made a remarkable discovery that would revolutionize ceramic production throughout Asia, Africa, and Europe. They found that by adding tin oxide to this transparent lead glaze, they could create an opaque, white ground that not only covered the color of the clay body, but gave it the appearance of porcelain. It also provided a blank canvas for colorful designs.

Although this may seem an insignificant event from the perspective of the twenty-first century and our factory-produced tableware, this was not so in the past. The white background of the tin-glazed mayólica allowed potters to achieve the effect, if not the strength, of porcelain

Intro.2 Plate / *Plato*
Chongzhen Period, China, 1630–1640
Underglaze blue porcelain
Gift of the Heard Foundation,
Museum of International Folk Art
(Museum of New Mexico), Santa Fe
Photo by Paul Smutko

(fig. Intro.3), and the popular pristine white tableware became accessible to the most humble of homes.

Intro.3 Plate / *Plato*
Talavera de la Reina,
Spain, 1675–1725
Tin-glazed earthenware (mayólica)
Serie de los helechos
Collection of the International
Folk Art Foundation,
Museum of International Folk Art,
(Museum of New Mexico), Santa Fe
Photo by Paul Smutko

The Origins of Spanish Mayólica

In A.D. 711, Arab invaders brought Islam to the Iberian peninsula from northern Africa. For the next eight hundred years, as Muslims and Christians fought for control of what was to become modern Spain, Islamic culture became firmly established. To their new settlements, the Arabs brought an agriculture-based economy and a sophisticated network of land and sea trade derived from centuries of commerce in the Middle East. Arab merchants, who dominated Mediterranean trade in wine and spices, had long been importing tin from England. With this established source for tin, the technique of tin-glazing was introduced into the workshops of Spain as early as the tenth century (see chapter 1).[2] Arab ceramists also introduced new forms, including court wares such as jars, inkwells, trays, and chamber pots, and the idea that pottery could be beautiful as well as functional (see chapter 2).[3]

Ceramic production was eventually concentrated in Andalusia, the last stronghold of the Muslims (fig. Intro.4).[4] It was here that the art of

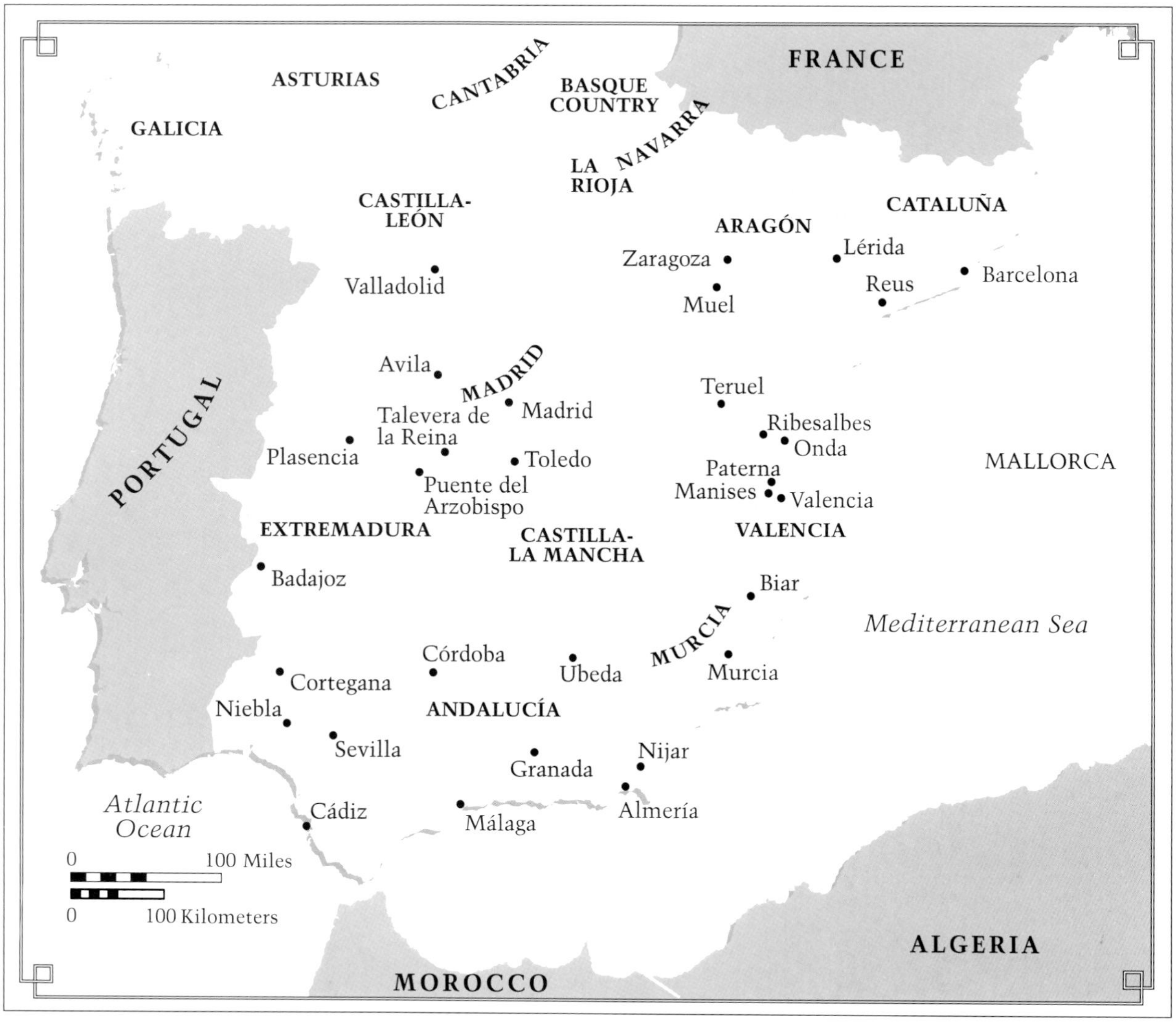

Intro.4 Mayólica production and trade centers in Spain, 12th through 19th centuries Illustration by Carol Cooperrider

covering entire walls in a tile veneer reached its zenith, under the direction of Muslim artists, who built upon the Roman use of alternating brick patterns as architectural ornament. Following the defeat of the Umayyad Caliphate in Córdoba, the Nasrid dynasty established the city of Granada in 1238, where Islam persevered in alliance with the Spanish kings for two and a half centuries more. During this time, Islamic artists constructed one of the stunning masterpieces of the Islamic world, the Alhambra. In this building, which inspired romantic writers to comment, "There is no greater sorrow than to be blind in Granada," tin-glazed tile is a basic element of its design and is at the core of its beauty. From this time forward, tin-glazed tile veneers became a hallmark of Andalusian and later Spanish architecture (fig. Intro.5; see chapter 3).[5]

In the twelfth century, Muslim potters living in Spain began to produce lusterware (*reflejo metálico*). By adding copper and silver oxides to tin-glazed mayólica surfaces, they produced an iridescent metallic decoration (see fig. 2.8). The beauty and craftsmanship of lusterware catapulted the Spanish ceramics industry to prominence. Spanish lusterwares were shipped to England and the Netherlands, as well as to Egypt, Italy, and other countries around the Mediterranean. During the Reconquest, which lasted several centuries, Islamic ceramists were often afforded great protection under their Christian rulers, so much so that in some areas only Muslims were permitted to engage in ceramic production.[6] However, as Muslim artists worked increasingly under Christian patronage in Christian-occupied territory, a new style developed in all the arts that reflected both cultures: Mudéjar (see fig. 2.7b).

The main characteristics of Mudéjar ceramics included the use of the colors copper green, manganese purple (which also sometimes appeared as brown or black, as the shade and intensity of this manganese paint could vary; see fig. 1.4), cobalt blue (brought from Persia) and lusters.[7] Patterns (almost all derived from Persia, Mesopotamia, and Egypt) included animals, plants, geometric designs, and human figures.[8] Mudéjar ceramics also featured *horror vacui*, or the tendency to fill every available surface with design; tracery, gothic and Kufic script; and both Christian and Arabic vessel forms. The outstanding legacy of this artistic collaboration is the lusterwares.

The beginning of the sixteenth century saw four events that had lasting repercussions on the production of Spanish mayólica. The first was the first expulsion of Muslims from Spanish soil, in 1502. This followed in the footsteps of the Jewish expulsion of 1492 and Spain's new fervor for *limpieza de sangre* (purity of ancestry). Although many Muslims chose to convert to Christianity, anyone of Arab North African descent held a precarious position in many parts of Spain throughout the sixteenth century. Finally, in 1609, some three hundred thousand *moriscos*, as they were then called, were forced to leave the country.[9] Secondly, following the expulsion of the Jews and the Arab loss of dominion on the peninsula, Italian merchants, artists, and potters slowly began to relocate to Spain. With them came the Renaissance artistic traditions that were enjoying such popularity in Italy. The third event was the opening of maritime trade with Asia through Portugal. In the early sixteenth century, Portugal brought to the European continent the first large shipments of Chinese export porcelains, which were subsequently traded throughout Europe. The fourth significant occurrence was Columbus's encounter with the Americas and the Spanish conquest of the Aztec city of Tenochtitlán, in 1521, transforming Spain into a world power and Sevilla into a teeming center for international commerce.

The popular appeal of the Chinese porcelains, the loss of innumerable Islamic artists, and the introduction of Renaissance art combined to transform the appearance of what had been a predominantly Islamic

Intro.5 Tiles / *Azulejos*
La Alhambra, Granada, Spain, mid-14th century
Photos by Robin Farwell Gavin, 2002

art form into an international one. And from this time forward, ceramic artistic traditions in Spain and Mexico were inextricably linked.

Beginning in 1525 and throughout the colonial period (until 1821), the convoys traveling from Spain to the Americas left from Andalucía. Before sailing, they registered at the Casa de Contratación (House of Trade), which was located first in Sevilla and, after 1717, in Cádiz (see fig. Intro.4). Owing to this monopoly on the American trade, Sevilla grew into a large, cosmopolitan city, surrounded by rich vineyards and olive groves. Although the goods shipped came from as far as Flanders, Greece, Genoa, England, Germany, Brittany, and Italy, the majority of the ceramics sent to the Americas was undoubtedly purchased at locations close to the port of departure, to reduce costs of overland transport and breakage.[10] Triana, the potter's district of Sevilla, housed some fifty mayólica workshops in the sixteenth century.[11]

Shortly after the first Spanish settlements were founded in the Americas, numerous items were shipped to the new colonies aboard the Spanish galleons; among these were ceramics. Pottery was sent both as merchandise and as containers.[12] The most common form was the "olive jar," a plain or lead-glazed jar that was used as a container for shipping liquids, such as olive oil and wine (see fig. 4.9). Mayólica, however, was sent more often as merchandise and as the personal goods of the passengers. Plates, cups, bowls, jars, candlesticks, baptismal fonts, and chamber pots were among the items shipped to Veracruz, Mexico, from Sevilla and Cádiz. Sevillian tiles were also used as ballast, taking the place of bags of sand that could not be sold at their destination. The 1592 and 1593 *flotas* to Cuba, Santo Domingo, Honduras, and Mexico carried the following ceramics: 50 cups of common mayólica from Triana; 11 large, 100-pound marked boxes of 102 dozen pieces of blue mayólica made in Sevilla; 15 dozen pieces of white mayólica made in Sevilla, all plates and porringers; 4 100-pound marked boxes that carry 36 dozen pieces of blue mayólica made in Sevilla; 3 boxes with 150 dozen pieces of blue mayólica; and 100 cups of common mayólica.[13]

Meanwhile, back in Spain, Italian merchants who were relocating to the Mediterranean coast of Spain brought with them Italian mayólica. The potters soon followed. Foremost among these was Francisco Niculoso (known as El Pisano, from Pisa), who settled in Sevilla. There he is credited with introducing the Renaissance style to Spanish ceramics. Among his earliest works is a tile panel, commissioned by Isabela la Católica for her *oratorio* in the Alcázar, in Sevilla (dated 1504; see fig. 3.4). In this single piece can be seen all the Renaissance elements that were to pervade Spanish pottery: acanthus leaves, heraldic symbols, sphinxes, griffins, putti, grotesques; a palette that extended beyond the traditional green and purple of Islamic Spain to include yellows, blues, ochres, and varying shades of each; and the innovative idea of narrative painting, using tiles as canvas, a style that slowly replaced the geometric patterning of the Islamic era.

The Renaissance style quickly caught on among patrons, if not potters, and Italian-style works were in demand. For this reason, in 1563 Felipe II summoned to Spain the Italian-trained Jan Floris, of Flanders, to instruct Spanish ceramists in the new style.[14] The center for this training was Talavera de la Reina, a small town some 60 miles from the royal residence in Madrid, that already housed some very accomplished potters. Soon the crown was commissioning all the tilework and hollowware needed for the royal palaces from potters in Talavera. By the late sixteenth century, Talavera was renowned throughout Spain and Mexico for its fine Renaissance ceramics (see fig. 1.6).

The Origins of Mexican Mayólica

In Mexico, the repercussions of these events of the sixteenth century are clearly recorded in its ceramics. Above all, there were major changes in technology. When the Spanish colonists arrived in New Spain, they found a well-established indigenous ceramic tradition. The pottery made in Precolumbian Mexico was hand-coiled and low-fired, often slipped and/or burnished, and sometimes painted (see chapter 8). To this thriving artistic industry, Spanish potters introduced the potter's wheel, glazes, and enclosed kilns. The potter's wheel both sped up and standardized production; the glazes created a glassy, impervious surface that allowed for the storage of liquids; and the kiln, or *horno árabe*, provided a controlled firing at higher temperatures that allowed the glazes to solidify and created a denser and more durable vessel.

As early as the mid-sixteenth century, tin-glazed earthenware was being produced in both Mexico City and Puebla de los Ángeles (figs. Intro.6, Intro.7; see chapters 9 and 10).[15] Much of the contemporary literature suggests that European ceramic techniques were introduced in Mexico by Dominican friars, but there is no evidence to support this assumption.[16] However, clearly some civilian potters came to the Americas to practice their art. One of them, Diego Fernández de Morón, an *ollero* (maker of utilitarian vessels, either unglazed or lead glazed), traveled to Santo Domingo on the 1509 flota, bringing with him not only his artistry but 400 mayólica cups, 140 wicker baskets of tiles, 40 green glazed jars, 100 mortars (possibly ceramic, and possibly used to grind pigments), and 2 green glazed baptismal fonts.[17] Three of the *maestros de locero* mentioned in the Puebla guild ordinances of 1653 were Juan de Sevilla, Roque de Talavera, and Juan de Valencia, suggesting that they or their families had arrived from those cities in Spain.[18]

Although Spanish designs and vessel forms were the basis for the new Mexican ceramics, even the early mayólica produced in Mexico did not faithfully follow Spanish models, but began to have an

Intro.6 Mayólica production centers and trade routes in Mexico, 16th through 19th centuries Illustration by Carol Cooperrider

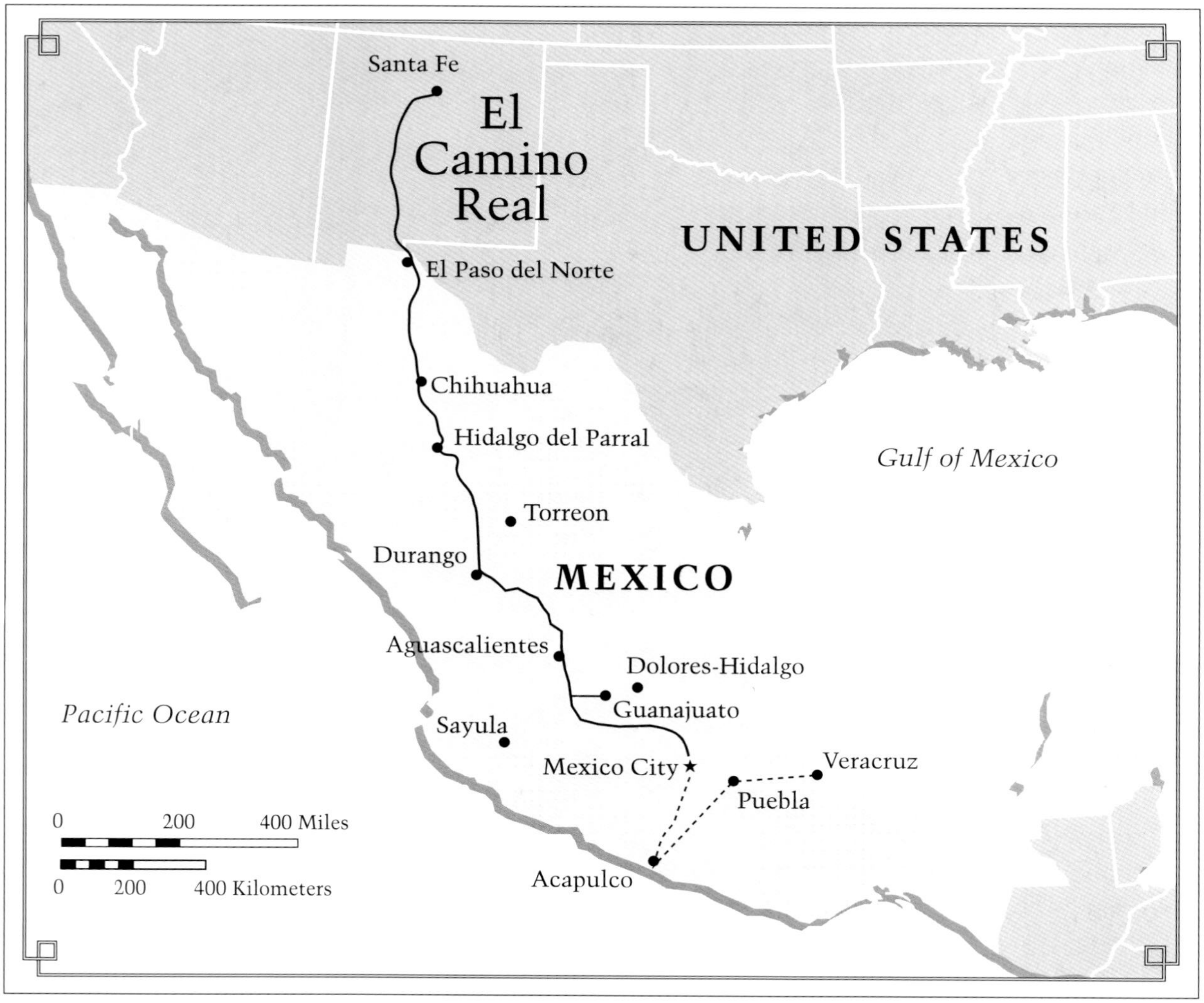

aesthetic of its own.[19] Hispano-Islamic-Christian-Renaissance forms and designs were blended with those of indigenous Mexican origin.[20] Just as much of Spain had broken with Islamic models, Mexico now took Spanish designs and interpreted them in a new way, departing from the more rigid Renaissance models (see fig. Intro.7; compare to fig. 1.6). Loose brushwork, novel combinations of motifs, and varying application of paints and glazes are elements that became part of Mexico's distinctive artistic expression.

Although archaeological excavations and guild regulations indicate that both Mexico City and Puebla produced numerous styles of mayólica throughout the sixteenth and seventeenth centuries, it is Puebla that became recognized for the quality of its ceramics (see chapter 10).[21] The seventeenth-century Franciscan chronicler Agustín de Vetancourt wrote in his *Teatro Mexicano*, "the loza [of Puebla] is finer than that of Talavera and can compete with that of China in its strength."[22] Indeed, it was China that soon became the primary source of inspiration for Puebla potters.

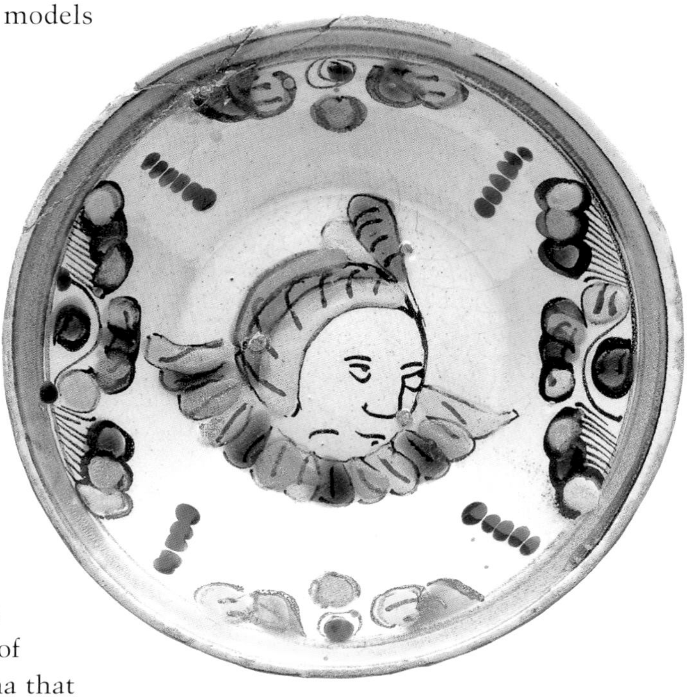

Intro.7 Plate / *Plato*
Mexico City or Puebla, Mexico, 1650–1750
Abo Polychrome
Museo Franz Mayer, Mexico City
Photo by Michel Zabé

Through its American colonies, Spain was finally able to compete with Portugal and bring spices and porcelains to its own shores. In 1565, Spain established trade with the Far East through its holdings in Mexico and the Philippines. The Manila Galleons, or *naos de la China*, left the port of Acapulco, and headed west to Manila (founded 1571). There they met other merchant ships from China and the South China Sea that brought trade items from throughout Asia (fig. Intro.8). These were then shipped back to Acapulco, where they were off-loaded and put on burros and carts for the long journey to Veracruz, on the east coast, and their departure to Sevilla.[23]

During the trip across Mexico, many of the porcelains intended for Spain were unloaded and sold to the local bourgeoisie. These vessels served as models and inspiration for the mayólica potters, particularly those in Puebla, who soon incorporated the exotic designs and motifs into their own ceramics. As in Europe, pottery in the Chinese style became the most valued, and guild regulations even specified that the finest grade of pottery was to imitate that of China (fig. Intro.9).[24] However, the combination of Spanish techniques with Chinese vessel forms, a blue-and-white color scheme, and indigenous motifs from the Americas, such as the *nopal* (prickly pear) cactus (fig. Intro.10) and the quetzal bird

Intro.8 *El Parián,*
Manila Market
Expedición Malaspina
(1789–1794)
Juan Ravenet, 1792
Photo courtesy of the
Museo Naval, Madrid

(fig. Intro.11), produced a mayólica that was uniquely Mexican and that endured for two hundred years.

The Potters

It was during the period of Muslim occupation in Spain, when mayólica production was principally in the hands of Islamic artisans, that certain occupational patterns were established and remained virtually unchanged for hundreds of years.[25] Certain areas of town were dedicated to potters, just as other areas were to other occupations. The potters' quarters were usually outside the city walls, for proximity to clays and to create distance between the city dwellers and the smoke from kilns (fig. Intro.12).[26] Triana, the potters' district of Sevilla, was established across the river from the main part of town in the twelfth century and still houses potters' workshops today (see chapter 5).[27] In the southern Spanish town of Úbeda, today's ceramists live outside the old city walls on the Calle de Alfarería (Pottery Street), adjacent to the plaza dedicated to the *alfarero* (potter; fig. Intro.13). In Puebla and Mexico City, the potters' quarters were clustered around their parish churches, then on the edge of town (see chapters 9 and 10).

Intro.9 Plate / *Plato*
Puebla, Mexico, 17th century
Houghton Sawyer Collection,
Gift of Mr. and Mrs. John F. Holstius
Museum of International Folk Art
(Museum of New Mexico), Santa Fe.
Photo by Blair Clark

Intro.10 Storage Jar / *Tibor*
Puebla, Mexico, late 17th–
early 18th century
Houghton Sawyer Collection, Gift of
Mr. and Mrs. John F. Holstius,
Museum of International Folk Art
(Museum of New Mexico), Santa Fe
Photo by Blair Clark
The crane is perched
on a nopal cactus.

Intro.11 Storage Jar / *Tibor*
Puebla, Mexico,
late 17th–early 18th century
Houghton Sawyer Collection, Gift of Mr. and Mrs. John F. Holstius
Museum of International Folk Art (Museum of New Mexico), Santa Fe
Photo by Blair Clark
The bird depicted here resembles the quetzal, a bird highly prized in Precolumbian Mesoamerica.

The *maestro*, or master potter, was the head of the *taller*, or *alfar* (workshop), which was usually run primarily by family members. Various jobs included the painters (*pintores*), the potters (*torneros*), the tenders of the kilns (*quemadores*), and the glaze makers (*esmaltadores*). Potters in Aguascalientes, Mexico, state that in the early twentieth century, it was the torneros who were the most highly paid, followed by the *maestro quemador*, who regulated the kiln solely by eye, followed then by the painters, who were "paid by each gross of pieces they decorated" (see chapter 14).

Traditionally, in Muslim, Spanish, and Mexican talleres, the maestro was a man, as were the torneros (if there were others than the master potter), the painters, and most of the rest of the workshop staff. Women appear to have had little or no official role in the production of mayólica before the nineteenth century, and then only in some localities.[28] In seventeenth-century Puebla, a widow was allowed to inherit her husband's workshop, but it was only sons that were trained in the art. [29] In eighteenth-century Alcora, Spain, "the only women permitted to enter the factory should be members of the family bringing lunch for the workers."[30] In some traditional ceramic workshops in Úbeda, Spain, superstitions still prevail, and women are not allowed in the kiln area during firing, for fear of bringing bad luck.[31] This is the exception rather than the rule, however, for in most of today's talleres, numerous women are employed, usually as painters, and in some cases women run their own workshops (see chapter 12).

Apprentices were often taken on and were promised instruction, housing, clothing, and health care in exchange for several years of indenture, before they might be qualified to take the test to become journeymen (*oficiales*) and finally masters. In the year 1677, in the city of Puebla, a young man of seventeen named Domingo de Herrera, whose father had died, was apprenticed to Hipólito de Sevilla, "maestro del oficio de losero de rueda" (master of the trade of mayólica made on the wheel), for three years. During this time, he was to be taught the trade, in the hopes of becoming a journeyman by the end of his tenure. The maestro was to pay him the wages of a journeyman, to provide housing, a bed, clean clothes, and the necessary clothing and shoes, to care for him in sickness by providing a doctor and medicine, and at the end of the apprenticeship, to give him a wool suit, a cape, shirts, pants, socks, shoes, and hat. In return, the apprentice had to promise never to absent himself from his service; if he did, he would be pursued, caught, and brought back to fill out his term.[32] In Spain, one could be apprenticed either to a "locero de pintar," or a "locero de rueda" and the apprenticeship lasted six or seven years respectively[33].

Although mayólica production had been established by the early to mid-sixteenth century in Talavera de la Reina (Spain), Mexico City, and Puebla (Mexico), guilds regulating this profession were not established until 1657, 1653, and 1681, respectively. This may have been due to the relatively high number of accomplished and recognized potters who were not full-blooded Spaniards (see chapter 10). The Puebla guild regulations specified "that no Negro, mulatto or other person of questionable color will be admitted for examination to said office, for it is important that they be Spanish to our complete satisfaction and confidence".[34] Censuses from Mexico City, Guanajuato, and Oaxaca in 1791 and 1811 clearly show that the majority of potters were in fact, not Spanish, but Indian or mestizo.[35]

The 1653 guild regulations for Puebla specified three types of pottery: yellow ware (lead-glazed) for cooking (*loza amarilla*); common ware, or tableware for everyday use (*loza común*); and fine ware (*loza fina*).[36] Most of what survives today in museum collections is loza fina, which was used less frequently and primarily for decoration. However, alongside the production of loza fina and

Intro.12 Smoking Kiln
Workshop of Juan Almarza,
Úbeda, Spain
Photo by
Robin Farwell Gavin, 2000

Intro.13 *Plaza del Alfarero*
Úbeda, Spain
Photo by
Robin Farwell Gavin, 2000

Intro.14 Bowls / *Tazones*
Hermitage of Nuestra Señora de la Defensión, La Cartuja, Jérez de la Frontera, Spain, 1475–1550
Collection of Florence C. Lister
Photo by Paul Smutko

Intro.15
An Old Woman Cooking Eggs
Diego Rodríguez de Silva y Velázquez (1599–1660)
Oil on canvas, 1618
Photo courtesy of the National Gallery of Scotland, Edinburgh
A bowl of loza común is shown in the foreground.

throughout the history of mayólica production in both Spain and Mexico, was the production of everyday wares for kitchens, loza común. These wares were characterized by thick, crude construction and surfaces of plain white or with simple designs.[37] Few examples of this work exist, as they were subject to heavy use and were discarded regularly (fig.Intro.14), but their production and use is documented in period paintings (fig. Intro.15).

Baroque and Rococo in Spanish and Mexican Mayólica

By the seventeenth century, Spanish potters were combining the popular blue-and-white palette of Chinese porcelains with European designs, particularly the Italian *istoriato*, or narrative style (see fig. Intro.1). Unlike their Italian Renaissance prototypes, however, the figures on these vessels are not framed by medallions and Renaissance motifs such as grotesques and acanthus leaves, but are rendered in a more painterly style and set in landscapes that quickly recede into the background, bringing the figures prominently to the foreground. But it was the polychrome vessels—the *serie policroma*—that most typified the Baroque, in their profusion of ornament and color (fig. Intro.16; see figs. 1.12, 2.13). These spectacularly ornate vessels, widely commissioned by both church and crown, are what most popularly distinguish the pottery of Talavera de la Reina today.

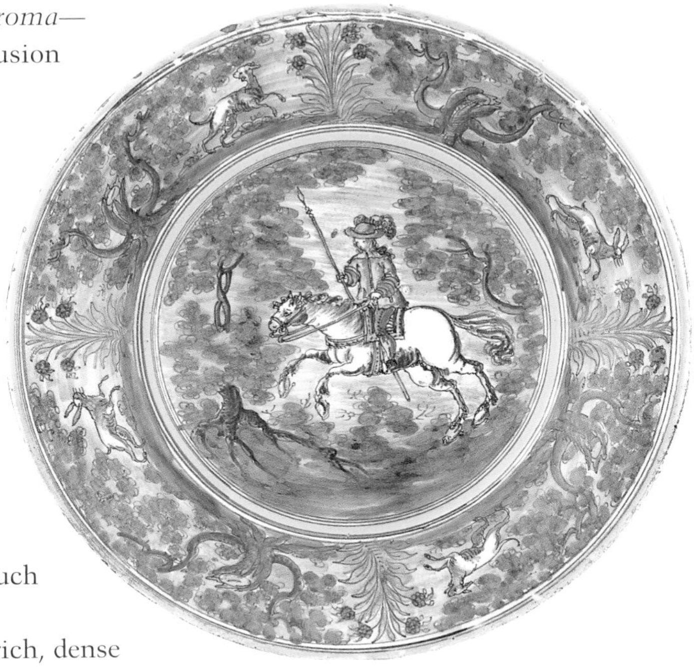

Intro.16 Platter / *Platón*
Talavera de la Reina, Spain, 1675–1725
Museu de Ceràmica, Barcelona
Photo by Guillém Fernández

In Mexico, the influence of Chinese porcelains was felt throughout the seventeenth and eighteenth centuries; however, Mexican painters brought their own unique interpretation to the designs. Cobalt blue remained the color of choice throughout this period, and it was applied both thickly and lavishly, with an aesthetic that was as much tactile as visual. The polychrome palette and Renaissance themes were abandoned for the rich, dense decorative detail that characterized much of Mexican Baroque art. Departing too from their Chinese prototypes, straight lines were made diagonal (see fig. Intro.11), seated figures began to run, and landscapes were transformed into busy patterns of floral and architectural motifs (fig. Intro.17). The serenity of the Chinese porcelain vessel became a visual cacophony of images drawn from every corner of Mexico's rich past.

By the eighteenth century, the French court of Louis XV at Versailles was at the forefront of European fashion. French paintings, furniture, architecture, and room decor were adopted throughout the continent. New ceramic forms, along with pastel colors and delicate floral patterns, began to replace the bolder designs of the Renaissance and Baroque periods. In 1708, German alchemist Johann Friedrich Böttger discovered the formula for porcelain manufacture, and production began in earnest. Felipe V, the first Spanish Bourbon king, and his court, embraced the French Rococo aesthetic, and soon the town of Alcora, in the kingdom of Valencia, became the center for production of Spanish ceramics in the French style. Artists and ceramics were brought from Moustiers and Rouen, two of the most important centers of French faience of the period, to serve as teachers and models for the new factory, established by the ninth count of Aranda, in 1727. The engravings of Jean Berain, artist and decorator at the French court, were imitated in mayólica by artists throughout Europe (see fig. 2.21), and new forms were added that reflected

Intro.17 Storage Jar / *Tibor*
Puebla, Mexico, late 16th–early 17th century
Houghton Sawyer Collection,
Gift of Mr. and Mrs. John F. Holstius,
Museum of International Folk Art
(Museum of New Mexico), Santa Fe
Photo by Blair Clark

the sophisticated and carefree life of the Spanish aristocracy and high bourgeoisie (see chapters 2 and 11 and figs. 1.14, 2.19, and 2.20).

Late Baroque (also called Estípite Baroque and Rococo) elements are clearly illustrated in the pottery of eighteenth-century Mexico.[38] Pastel glazes, delicate painted designs comprised of flowers, vines, rocaille, and latticework; and new forms of hollowware, such as oval platters with scalloped rims and fluted bowls, were characteristic of eighteenth-century Mexican mayólica. Textile patterns and the delicate designs of Meissen porcelains replaced the dense and heavy patterning of the earlier blue-and-white ceramics (fig. Intro.18). Pottery designs also incorporated more empty space, prefiguring the austere and reserved style of the Neoclassical period.

One characteristic of this late Baroque style was an emphasis on decoration, breaking away from the earlier use of somber colors and spaces and filling rooms and walls with light and air. In

Intro.18 Bowl / *Cuenco*
Puebla, Mexico, late 18th century
Houghton Sawyer Collection,
Gift of Mr. and Mrs. John F. Holstius
Museum of International Folk Art
(Museum of New Mexico), Santa Fe
Photo by Paul Smutko

Intro.19 *Serving Nougats and Chocolate*
Vicente Navarro en la calle de la Corona (?), Valencia, Spain, ca. 1775–1780
143 x 113.5 cm
Museo Nacional de Cerámica y de las Artes Suntuarias "González Martí," Valencia

many areas of Spain, tilework replaced heavy *guadamaciles* (leather hangings), and once again tile began to invade building interiors, as it had in Islamic Spain; only now the decoration was not geometric and floral, but figurative. Entire walls of palaces and grand homes were covered in pictorial tilework, illustrating scenes of domestic and courtly life, themes that were also popularized in the French and Spanish paintings of Watteau, Boucher, and Goya (see chaper 3). Interior walls depicted domestic scenes, and most popular were those related to the kitchen (fig. Intro.19). The decorative tile of the eighteenth-century Spanish kitchen revealed as much about daily life as the vessels and utensils within it.

While Mexico did follow Spain and the rest of Europe in adopting late Baroque and Rococo designs in ceramic hollowware, the use of tile murals did not follow this same pattern. In the century when Spain produced some of its most interesting and informative figurative tile wall paintings, Mexico seems to have preferred the geometric patterning and ornamentation reminiscent of both Islamic and Precolumbian design. The fascination with decorative surfaces so obvious in Islamic Spain was an aesthetic shared in preconquest indigenous Mexico. A distinctive feature of Mexican mayólica work is the tile facade. While tile had been used extensively in Spain from the Islamic era, it was characteristically placed in building interiors, covering floors and entire walls or serving as a dado. In Mexico, however, a phenomenon of the eighteenth century is the shift of this decorative feature to the exterior facade of buildings (see fig. 9.14).

Intro.20
Chamber Pot / *Bacín*
Puebla, Mexico, late 18th century
Philadelphia Museum of Art
Purchased with the Special Mexican Fund
Photo by Graydon Wood, 2002

Nineteenth-Century Mayólica

By the close of the eighteenth century, the colonial era was coming to an end. Napoleon's troops invaded the Iberian Peninsula in 1808, and Spain was preoccupied by continuous battles for the throne. The colonies saw this as the opportunity to make their final break, and in 1821, Mexico won its independence. The guilds that had been in place since the seventeenth century were abolished, and potters were now competing in a market that was flooded with creamwares and porcelains imported primarily from England. In Mexico, Padre Miguel Hidalgo, father of Mexico's independence, is credited with training potters in mayólica and bringing the art to Dolores Hidalgo and the surrounding towns of Guanajuato and Aguascalientes (see chapter 13). Without the strict requirements of the guild, glazes became thinner and less opaque, due to the use of smaller quantities of the relatively expensive tin. Green replaced blue as the dominant color in the vivid polychrome designs that varied from gay floral arrangements to political satire (fig. Intro.20; see figs. 12.1, 13.4). Patriotic themes also became popular in both Spain and Mexico, some potters portraying images of the monarch Ferdinand VII in support of the monarchy and others depicting the eagle and the snake, symbols of the independent Mexican nation (see figs. 1.20 and 14.8a).

But just as traditional Spanish mayólica was losing favor in some circles, it was gaining respect in others, mainly during the last quarter of the nineteenth century. In Spain, a new interest in historic patrimony and Spanish heritage was being fostered by the intellectuals of the country, referred to as the Generation of '98, and mayólica was a part of this heritage (see chapter 1).[39] By the beginning of the twentieth century, in both Spain and Mexico, a handful of industrious individuals had undertaken to revive the struggling traditional mayólica industry. At the forefront of this movement in Spain was Juan Ruiz de Luna; in Mexico it was a Spaniard, Enrique Luis Ventosa, collaborating with such local potters as Isauro Uriarte (see chapters 9 and 12).

Contemporary Mayólica in Spain and Mexico

Today, while walking through the contemporary workshops in Spain and Mexico, one may find large vats of glazes with huge, electric-powered mixers (fig. Intro.21), electric and gas-powered kilns and wheels, and brightly lit rooms with pristine white walls, in which some twenty painters may be working. Or one may find a small building with a courtyard, where a few family members are mixing glazes in sinks or basins, where an occasional kick wheel is still in use (see fig. 14.12), and where prints of various saints and sketches of different pottery designs are taped to the walls next to the potters' wheels (fig. Intro.22; see chapters 12, 13, 14). However varied the setting, each of the artists featured in this book has invested a considerable amount of time researching the historic methods and materials used to produce mayólica.

The ingredients for making the glazes and pigments remain a closely guarded secret. Although the standard materials and proportions have been published several times, all the artists have their own addition or pigment source that they feel makes their work distinctive. Mexican potters tend to adhere to the five "traditional" colors, or those designated in the guild regulations: green, brown, blue, yellow, and ochre. Pedro de la Cal, in Puente del Arzobispo, Spain (see fig. 7.3), would not disclose the sources for his pigments, which in the early part of the century he collected himself and ground in a *molino* (mill) powered by a donkey, as did many other potters.[40]

Intro.21
Applying the glaze
Taller Uriarte,
Puebla, Mexico
Photo by
Barbara Mauldin,
2001

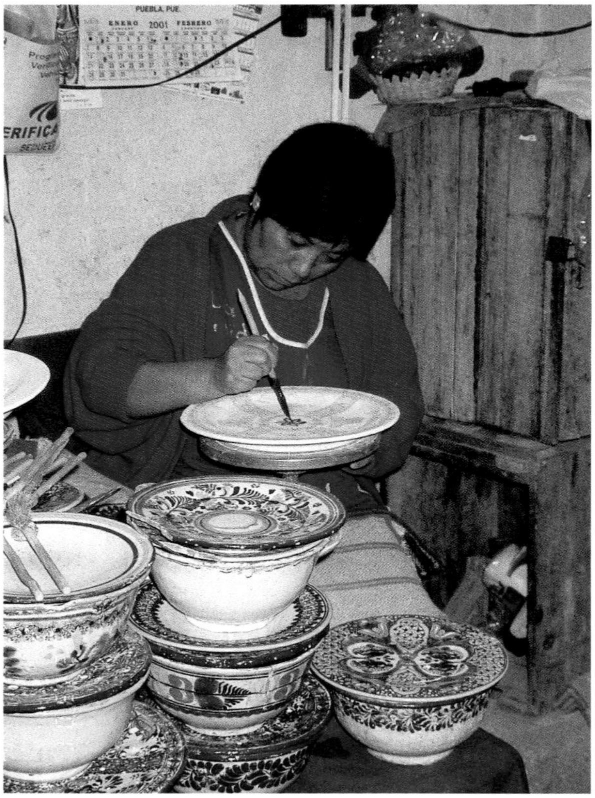

Intro.22 Painting
La Trinidad Workshop, Puebla, Mexico
Photo by Feliza Medrano, 2001

It has been and remains a struggle for these traditional talleres to maintain operation and be successful in today's market of mass-produced tableware and other utilitarian items. In both Spain and Mexico, the government has stepped in from time to time during the past century with financial support and initiatives (see chapter 7). In Mexico, the government recently issued a series of declarations that identify the qualities of "original" talavera pottery and specify the workshops in Puebla that are qualified to produce such work. The clays, the colors, and the decorations with pigments raised in relief are all indicators of the "true" *talavera poblana*.[41] Recently, however, potters in Guanajuato have reacted in anger to these decrees and have protested to President Vicente Fox, himself a guanajuatense (see chapter 12).

In a world in which individualism and idiosyncrasy are so highly acclaimed, it is remarkable that these workshops exist at all. Some critics dismiss them as copyists, making insignificant utilitarian vessels and merely imitating past designs, while others laud them as tradition bearers who pass on techniques and the accompanying folklore that are at the core of cultural patrimony. For the artists, these labels are immaterial, for this is their life and their work, and the passion they bring to it is clear to see. Each one of these artists takes with him or her the legacy of the past and carries it into the future.

Notes

1. Anthony Ray, *Spanish Pottery 1248–1898, with a Catalogue of the Collection in the Victoria and Albert Museum* (London: Victoria and Albert Publications, 2001), p. 170.
2. Alan Caiger-Smith, *Tin-Glaze Pottery in Europe and the Islamic World: The Tradition of 1,000 Years in Maiolica, Faience and Delftware* (London: Faber and Faber, 1973), p. 54.
3. Ibid., p. 53.
4. See Florence C. Lister and Robert H. Lister, *Andalusian Ceramics in Spain and New Spain: A Cultural Register from the Third Century B.C. to 1700* (Tucson: University of Arizona Press, 1987), for a thorough study of the ceramics of this area.
5. See also Alice Wilson Frothingham, *Tile Panels of Spain, 1500–1650* (New York: The Hispanic Society of America, 1969); and Alfonso Pleguezuelo Hernández, *Azulejo Sevillano: Catálogo del Museo de Artes y Costumbres Populares de Sevilla* (Sevilla: Padilla Libros, 1989).
6. This status was conferred on the potters of the kingdom of Valencia by Jaime I, who reconquered Valencia in 1238. See Trinidad Sánchez-Pacheco, "Cerámica valenciana," in *Musea Nostra: Museo de Cerámica, Palacio de Pedralbes, Barcelona* (Barcelona: Ludion, 1993), p. 17.
7. Cobalt was first used in Spain in the thirteenth century; see Lister and Lister, *Andalusian Ceramics*, pp. 74–75.
8. Regarding the human figure in Islamic art, the following quotation should be kept in mind:

   > In relation to the new figurative designs, it is worth repeating what has many times been said before, that the Moslem faith and religious law does not forbid all kinds of imagery. Though images tending to idolatry were forbidden, imagery in general is not prohibited in the Koran. There is such a prohibition in the Hadith, or Traditions of the Prophet, but these teachings were not generally accepted as obligatory. The Abbasid caliphs, and the Umayyads of Damascus before them, had not feared to represent living creatures in other arts such as wall-paintings and manuscripts. It is true that they were famed for their secular luxury rather than for piety, but they were not breaking any absolute religious precept by enjoying imagery. Considering the vast amount of figurative designs there are in Islamic art, it is surprising how persistent the idea is that all kinds of representations of living creatures were strictly avoided. The only place where this really held true was the mosque.

   Alan Caiger-Smith, *Tin-Glaze Pottery*, p. 24. See also Emmanuel Cooper, *Ten Thousand Years of Pottery*, 4th ed. (Philadelphia: University of Pennsylvania Press, 2000), p. 83.
9. Anthony Ray, *Spanish Pottery*, pp. 105, 168.

10. Kathleen Deagan, *Artifacts of the Spanish Colonies of Florida and the Caribbean, 1500–1800*, vol. 1: *Ceramics, Glassware, and Beads* (Washington, DC: Smithsonian Institution Press, 1987), p. 21.
11. George Avery, "Pots as Packaging: The Spanish Olive Jar and Andalusian Transatlantic Commercial Activity, 16th–18th Centuries" (Ph.D. diss., University of Florida, 1997), p. 214.
12. José María Sánchez, "La cerámica exportada a América en el siglo XVI a través de la documentación del Archivo Genral de Indias. I. Materiales arquitectónicos y contenedores de mercancías," *Laboratorio de Arte* (Universidad de Sevilla) 9(1996):125–42.
13. "50 vasos de loza basta de Triana / 11 cajones que llevan 102 docenas de loza azul hecha en Sevilla / 15 docenas de loza blanca hecha en Sevilla, todos platos y escudillas / 4 cajones quintaleños que llevan 36 docenas de loza azul hecha en Sevilla / tres cajas con 150 docenas de loza azul / 100 vasos de loza basta." Lister and Lister, *Andalusian Ceramics*, p. 312.
14. See Alfonso Pleguezuelo, "Jan Floris (c. 1520–1567), a Flemish Tile Maker in Spain," in *Majolica and Glass: From Italy to Antwerp and Beyond*, ed. by Johan Veekman (Antwerp, 2002), 123–44; and Alice Wilson Frothingham, *Talavera Pottery, with a Catalogue of the Collection of the Hispanic Society of America* (New York: Hispanic Society of America, 1944), p. 15.
15. Lister and Lister, *Andalusian Ceramics*, p. 221; and Efraín Castro, "Five Centuries of Talavera," *Artes de México* 3 (spring 1989):104. Enrique Cervantes, *Loza blanca y azulejos de Puebla*, 2 vols. (Puebla: Privately printed, 1939), states that production began by 1550.
16. Margaret Connors McQuade, *Talavera Poblana: Four Centuries of a Mexican Ceramic Tradition* (New York: The Americas Society, 1999), p. 14.
17. Lister and Lister, *Andalusian Ceramics*, p. 311.
18. Cervantes, *Loza Blanca*, p. 20.
19. John M. Goggin, *Spanish Majolica in the New World: Types of the Sixteenth to Eighteenth Centuries*, Yale Publications in Anthropology, no. 72 (New Haven: Yale University Press, 1968), p. 8, believed that a distinct Puebla style began around 1650.
20. Donna Pierce, "Ceramics," in *Mexico: Splendors of Thirty Centuries*, ed. by Kathleen Howard (New York: Metropolitan Museum of Art, 1992), pp. 457–81.
21. Robert L. Lister and Florence C. Lister, *Sixteenth Century Maiolica Pottery in the Valley of Mexico*, Anthropological Papers of the University of Arizona, no. 39 (Tucson: University of Arizona Press, 1982), pp. 8–9, suggest that the repeated floods in Mexico City in the sixteenth and seventeenth centuries may have contributed to the relocation of many potters to Puebla.
22. "La loza [de Puebla] es más fina que la de Talavera y puede competir con la de China en su firmeza." Agustín Vetancurt, "Tratado de la ciudad de la Puebla de los Ángeles, y grandezas que la ilustran," in *Teatro Mexicano: Descripción breve de los sucesos exemplares históricos, políticos, militares y religiosos del Nuevo Mundo Occidental de las Indias* (México: Doña María de Benavides, widow of Juan de Rivera, 1698), part 3, p. 47.
23. *El galeón de Manila* (catalog) (Madrid: Aldeasa, Ministerio de Educación, Cultura y Deporte, 2000).
24. Cervantes, *Loza Blanca*, pp. 28–29.
25. Lister and Lister, *Andalusian Ceramics*, pp. 254–57.
26. The problem of smoke from potters' kilns was to plague them for centuries. As Frothingham notes for the sixteenth-century town of Talavera de la Reina: "The rapid growth of Talavera's pottery manufacture multiplied the number of its smoking kilns, until the town officials, recognizing the fumes as a menace to public health, passed regulations to control the industry. Workmen were permitted to light their fire only at sundown and to burn them all night." Frothingham, *Talavera Pottery*, 3.

See also Diodoro Vaca and Juan Ruiz de Luna, *Historia de la cerámica de Talavera de la Reina y algunos datos sobre la de Puente del Arzobispo* (Madrid: Editora Nacional, 1943), p. 30.

27. Lister and Lister, *Andalusian Ceramics*, p. 70.
28. Trinidad Sánchez-Pacheco notes that women painted the polychrome pieces of nineteenth-century Manises, Spain particularly the idyllic plates celebrating marriage. "Cerámica valenciana," p. 29.
29. Cervantes, *Loza blanca*, p. 23.
30. Anthony Ray, *Spanish Pottery*, p. 213.
31. Interview with Juan Almarza, Úbeda, Spain, October 2001.
32. Enrique Cervantes, *Loza blanca*, pp. 55–56.
33. Trinidad Sánchez-Pacheco, "Cerámica de Talavera de la Reina y Puente del Arzobispo," in *Summa Artis: Historia General del Arte*, vol. 42: *Cerámica Española*, coord. by Trinidad Sánchez-Pacheco (Madrid: Espasa Calpa, 1997), p. 312.
34. "Item: Que no se pueda admitir a examen de dicho oficio, a ningún Negro, ni mulatto, ni otra persona de color turbado, por lo que importa que lo sean españoles de toda satisfacción y confianza." Cervantes, *Loza blanca*, 1:23; translation by James K. Gavin.
35. Node McMillen, "Alfarería: Hispanic Ceramics in New Spain. Origins, Evolution, and Social Significance" (Ph.D. diss., Texas A & M University, 1983), pp. 208–68.
36. Cervantes, *Loza blanca*; and Francisco del Barrio Lorenzot, *Ordenanzas de gremios de la Nueva España* (México: Secretaría de Governación, Dirección de Talleres Gráficos, 1920, pp. 173–75. Although no similar regulations have been documented for the guilds in Spain, José María Sánchez Cortegana surmises that similar divisions of pottery were made in Spain and were also determined by the amount of costly tin in the glaze; *Arte hispalense: El oficio de ollero en Sevilla en el siglo XVI* (Sevilla: Excma. Diputación Provincial de Sevilla, 1994), pp. 58–59.
37. "Yayal Blue on White" and "Columbia Plain," were produced in Spain, and "Huejotzingo Blue on White" (or "Yellow on White," etc.) were produced in Mexico. See Deagan, *Artifacts of the Spanish Colonies*; Goggin, *Spanish Majolica in the New World*; and Lister and Lister, *Andalusian Ceramics*.
38. Donna Pierce, in *Cambios*, ed. by Gabrielle Palmer and Donna Pierce (Santa Barbara: Santa Barbara Museum of Art, 1992), p. 81, defines Mexico's Estípite Baroque style as a manifestation of the Rococo: "Essentially Rococo, but already using some of the motifs, if not the precepts, of the nascent Neoclassical style, the Estípite Baroque combined disparate motifs in an asymmetrical, anti-architectural riot of contrasting patterns. Three-dimensional imitations of drapery and Rococo textile patterns enlivened the flattened shadows of former columns and entablatures in a dizzying amalgam."
39. Anthony Ray, *Spanish Pottery*, p. 264.
40. Interview with the artist, October 1999.
41. McQuade, *Talavera Poblana*, p. 16.

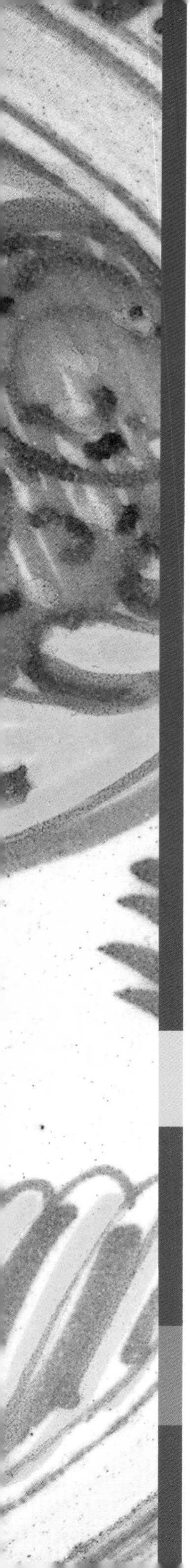

Detail, Fig. 1.6

1

Centers of Traditional Spanish Mayólica

ALFONSO PLEGUEZUELO

CERAMICS PLAYED AN extraordinary role in the Latin cultures of the Mediterranean, particularly those on the Iberian Peninsula, as it did in the pre- and post-Columbian communities of the Americas. Two great migratory tides of this ceramic development are evident in medieval history. The first wave came from China by way of Persia, Mesopotamia and Egypt, reaching the Iberian Peninsula between the tenth and fourteenth centuries. The second swept from Spain to the Americas between the sixteenth and eighteenth centuries. Minor currents that did not substantially modify the general evolutionary direction also flowed from the Iberian Peninsula toward the eastern Mediterranean and from the Americas to Spain. Of primary importance to these artistic

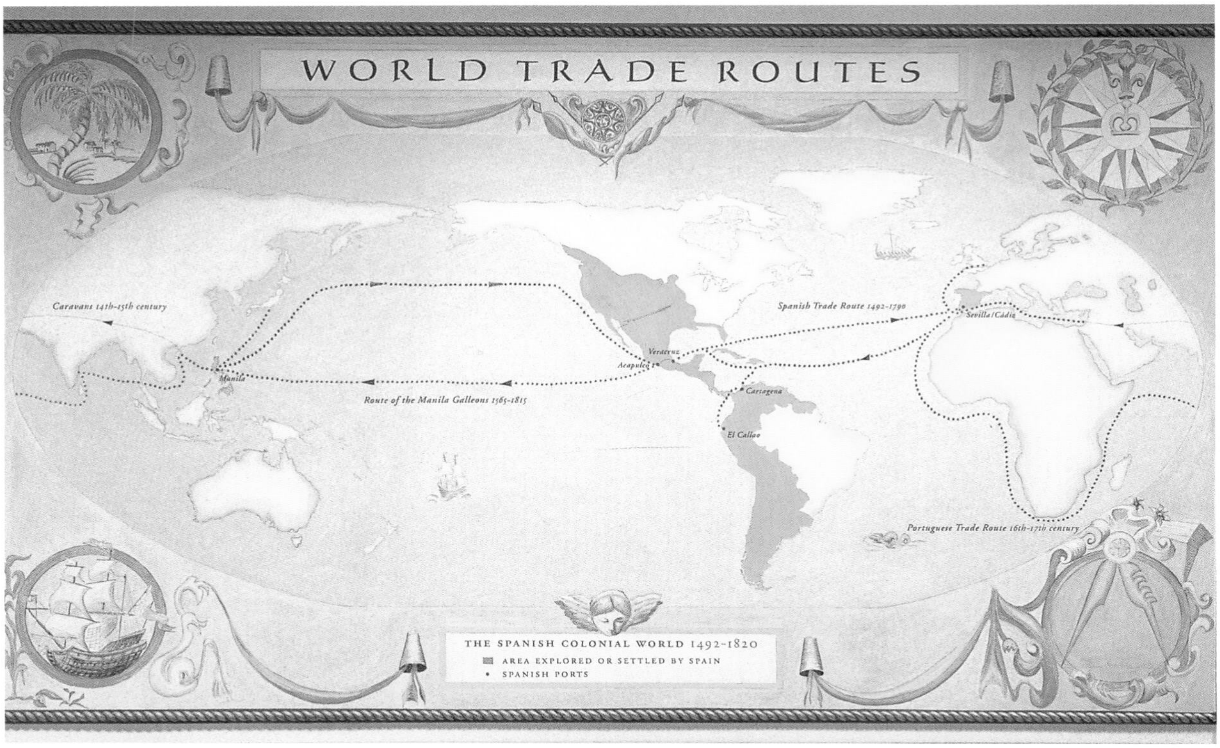

1.1 Major ceramic distribution routes between the fifteenth and nineteenth centuries Illustration by Lynn Osborne

exchanges were their vehicles of distribution: the Mediterranean Sea and the Atlantic Ocean (fig. 1.1).

Hispano-Moresque Mayólica

In the tenth century, mayólica decorated in copper green and manganese purple (fig. 1.2) or using the *cuerda seca* technique (using a resist to separate colors; fig. 1.3) was produced in Córdoba, headquarters of the Arab Caliphate in Spain. In the following century, both styles were adopted in the Taifa kingdoms of Toledo, Zaragosa, Málaga, Sevilla, Murcia, Badajoz, and Niebla, places to which Cordoban ceramists most likely emigrated (see fig. Intro.4). The palaces of Medinat–al Zahra would be the recipients of the first Asian lusterwares, which would be imitated later on.

During the twelfth century, Sevilla became the capital of King Almohade. His ceramic artists dispersed their products throughout Andalucía and northern Africa, especially their amber or white wares, their storage jars (*tinajas*), and well curbstones (*brocales*), with stamped designs and green glazes.[1]

According to the testimony of the eleventh-century Cordoban chronicler Abu Walid bin Janah, ceramic artisans from the Far East had also arrived and spread their techniques throughout the region. Archaeological findings seem to confirm this statement. Additionally, the fall of the

1.2 Plate / *Plato*
Córdoba, 10th century
Serie verde y morada
Museo Nacional de Cerámica
y de las Artes Suntuarias
"González Martí," Valencia

Fatimid Dynasty in Egypt (A.D. 1171) appears to coincide with an influx of designs from that region detectable in the lusterware of Murcia, Almería, and Málaga in the same period. The earliest production of lusterware appears to have occurred in Murcia at the end of the eleventh century.[2] Murcia's boom period corresponds to a time during which it had special commercial relations with Pisa and Genoa, as evidenced by ceramic objects (*bacini*) from Murcia that were hung as ornaments in Italian medieval towers.[3] When the Mardanisí kingdom in Murcia collapsed, some ceramists emigrated to Granada, North Africa, and Valencia, launching the production of lusterware in those centers.

The kingdom of Granada and its port of Málaga was the most important lusterware manufacturing center during the thirteenth century.[4] This center not only supplied the peninsular market but also exported its sophisticated lusterware to countries as far as Egypt in the east and England and the Netherlands in the north. This external trade was documented by the historians Ibn Batuta and Ibn al Jatib. The fourteenth and fifteenth centuries saw the expansion of lusterware technology from Granada to Valencia and Sevilla. Mallorca must have played an important role as a port of transshipment, since the name *mayólica* is interpreted by some as a derivation of *Malíca* (Málaga) and by others as *Maiorca* (Mallorca), although today it is clear that mayólica of this type was not produced on the island of Mallorca in the Middle Ages.

1.3 Porringer / *Escudilla*
Andalucía, 12th century
Serie de cuerda seca
Mértola, Portugal

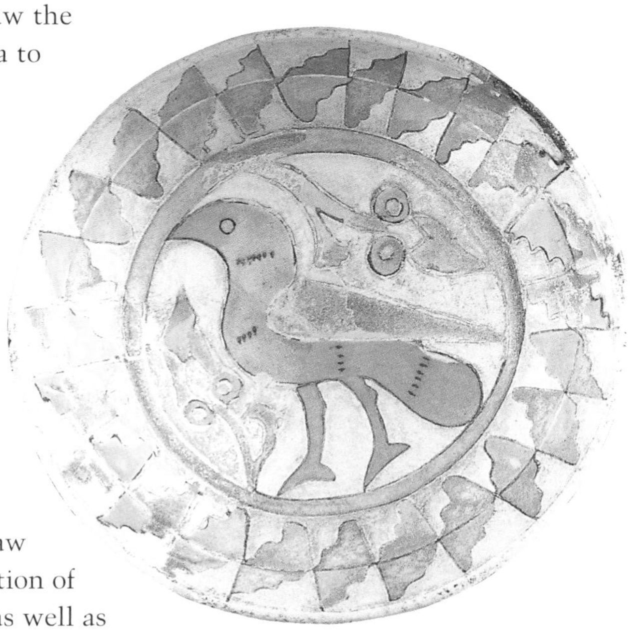

Mudéjar Mayólica

At the opening of the thirteenth century, Teruel saw the birth of intense ceramic activity in the fabrication of pieces for use in Mudéjar architecture of the area as well as the familiar green and purple tableware. The extraordinary quality of these ceramics (fig. 1.4)[5] has made some experts suggest that the wares produced in Aragón were the models for those later manufactured in green and purple at Paterna (Valencia). Ceramics from both Teruel and Paterna were widely distributed in the fourteenth century, owing to their uncontestable quality and the commercial activities of the rulers of Aragón. The obvious Sassanid (Persian) and Byzantine influences reflected in the mayólica of Teruel and the Levante (principally the regions of Valencia and Murcia) suggest a close connection between these cultures; however, although we know that textiles did come from these places and could have been one of sources for the shared designs, the documentation for such a contact is lacking.[6] The green and purple mayólica made in Cataluña, on the other hand, reveals connections with French and Italian centers. Products were shipped to these destinations, as is evident from the documented case of Collioure (France).[7] But the most important area of green and purple Christian mayólica production was that of Valencia (Paterna, Manises, Cuart, Mislata, etc.). During the fourteenth century, Valencia supplied its products to not only the local market but also to a great part of the Iberian Peninsula, southern France, and Italy. In the second half of the fourteenth century, decorations of green and purple faded in favor of those in blue, *reflejo metálico* (lusterware), or in both color schemes combined. The blue-gold decoration (using cobalt that may have been from Persia) was produced in the same centers that made green-and-purple wares, and by the end of the century had succeeded in replacing them (see fig. 2.8). Islamic Málaga was the first center to manufacture the blue-gold wares (*las azules doradas*) in the thirteenth century. From here the style most likely spread to Manises, where it was produced during the fourteenth and fifteenth centuries by itinerant ceramists who would travel from center to center. The dispersion of blue-gold mayólica follows the same path as the green-purple, but expands as well via the Atlantic Ocean to Flanders and the United Kingdom.[8]

1.4 Baptismal Font / *Pila bautismal*
Teruel, 15th century
Serie verde y morada
Museu de Ceràmica, Barcelona
Photo by Guillém Fernández

Soon Málaga and Valencia became producers of lusterware for the countries of the Mediterranean and the Atlantic coasts. How this spread of production between Málaga and Valencia in the final stages of the fourteenth century occurred is not well known. It is probable that specialists from Málaga or Murcia moved to Valencia to take advantage of its more favorable market or that the Boil family, lords of Manises and Paterna, may have brought Muslim lusterware experts to the area. What is certain is that the Boil family saw the potential of this business and around 1372 solicited from the king special exploitation privileges. The wide-spread distribution of these Valencian ceramics (which began in the port of El Grao) from the primitive Málaga or Pula types (circa 1350–75), up until the more classical types in the fifteenth century, reveals mass production, manufactured for the most modest markets as well as for the most demanding and refined aristocratic clientele. The lusterware sent to those countries of the north did not have, in general, any impact on local manufacture, but those remitted to Italy played an essential role in the adoption of lusterware in the fifteenth century, especially in Gubbio and Deruta during the sixteenth century. Some of the most popular decorative motifs of the *loza dorada* were imitated in the blue mayólica of Florence.

1.5 Plate / *Plato*
Sevilla, 15th–16th centuries
Serie azul y morada
Museu de Ceràmica, Barcelona

The role of Valencia in the establishment of lusterware technology in other peninsular centers was crucial. It is known that a family of talented ceramists of lusterware, the Eiximenis, arrived in Barcelona. It is also well established that Francesc Reyner used to bring mayólica from Valencia to Barcelona to decorate it. We know that relocation of manufacturers of this mayólica occurred from Reus to Muel (Aragón) in 1610. There is no direct evidence of the transfer of artisans from Valencia to Sevilla, but there are numerous specimens of mayólica in the area that could explain the faithful reproduction of Valencian lusterware that took place in Triana (the potters' district of Sevilla).[9]

At the end of the middle ages, Sevilla and surrounding areas became a crossroads for ceramic novelties and a center for the diffusion of these new styles to the rest of Europe and, after 1492, to the Americas. Ceramic production there in the fifteenth century was already important and served as a base for the innovations brought from Italy by "Pisano," Francisco Niculoso, an artist who decisively influenced decoration in Spain (see fig. 3.4).

However, his impact on the styling of tableware is still not known, since during the first half of the sixteenth century there is no indication that it had been affected by Renaissance trends. Although the quantity of tableware produced indicates a large market, the pieces lacked complex ornamentation. These are the so-called "Moorish" tablewares, inspired by the Gothic-Mudéjar tradition—simple designs with basic decoration in blue or glazed in green or amber (fig. 1.5). The production of luxury tableware would continue, in the medieval tradition of decorating pieces with metallic lusters in imitation of Manises ware, in blue and purple or cuerda seca polychrome. In the other Spanish manufacturing hubs during this period, one can see a generalized attempt at imitation of the prestigious and attractive mayólica of Manises.

Mayólica from the Golden Age

Coinciding with the epoch of major growth in commercial traffic with the Americas and Europe, the port of Sevilla toward the middle of the sixteenth century saw an important change in the fabrication of mayólica. This was almost certainly due to the large group of artisans from Genoa that lived in the city and who produced vast quantities of mayólica tableware. Some notable ceramists among this community were Tomás Pésaro, Virgilio Cortivas, Bernardo Cerrudo, and the Sambarino brothers.[10] Another specialist, Frans Andríes, from Antwerp, also arrived in Sevilla and began a partnership with a local ceramist. He had received his training from his father, an important Italian ceramist known as Güido di Savino in that country and as Güido Andríes in Flanders. Unfortunately, there still has not been a clear identification of the production of these talented craftsmen, but in archaeological excavations local imitations of the Genoese blue style and the white Faenza have been discovered.

1.6 Plate / *Plato*
Talavera de la Reina, late 16th century
Serie punteada
Museu de Ceràmica, Barcelona
Photo by Guillém Fernández

There were numerous shipments of ceramics to the Americas, and along with these products went craftsmen who set up shops in Mexico and Peru.[11] The commercial stream flowed not only from Sevilla to the Americas but also in the opposite direction.[12] The establishment of the Route of the Manila Galleon in 1565 connected the Philippines and the surrounding areas in the Pacific Rim with the Pacific coast of Mexico and the ports of Peru. Some of the cargo of the Manila galleons was transferred to the ships en route to Spain (*carrera de Indias*), whose final destinations were Sevilla and Cádiz. Spaniards now navigated not only the Atlantic but also the Pacific, an ocean that came to be called "the Spanish lake."[13]

An avalanche of foreign products arrived in Sevilla during this era. Among the imported pieces were salt-glazed stoneware jars that originated in Germany; mayólica from Genoa, Montelupo, and Venice; and porcelain from China. It is possible that these imported ceramics, as well as tableware fabricated of other materials, were acquired with such facility that local copies were unnecessary. In any case, we still cannot identify with certainty the Sevilla Renaissance tableware dating from the second part of the sixteenth century. On the other hand, the extreme delicacy and fragility of the known pieces from this period makes their preservation less likely. Certainly we are aware that the most magnificent tableware was not a ceramic product but rather was made of gold and silver, which arrived in abundance from the Americas.

Meanwhile, in the center of Castilla, important innovations are linked to a ceramist from Antwerp named Jan Floris (Juan Flores in Spain). His work would have major repercussions on the production of tiles. It is quite likely that his circle of Talaveran disciples manufactured the first Spanish Renaissance tableware that we know as the *punteada* series, due to the frequent dot decorations found on the rim of plates (fig. 1.6).[14] These eye-catching polychrome mayólicas, influenced by Deruta, were executed in Puente del Arzobispo and Talvera,[15] and now we know that similar versions were also realized in Úbeda (Jaén).[16] It is also possible that students of Floris in Toledo were producing these same products. The parallels between some examples of this group of Toledan ware and Talaveran tiles at the close of the sixteenth century are indisputable. Along with colored tableware produced in these same Spanish centers, series of blue plates and wine jars have recently been identified as originating in Toledo.[17]

1.7 Plate / *Plato*
Talavera de la Reina, 1580–1650
Serie Tricolor
Collection of the International Folk Art Foundation
Museum of International Folk Art (Museum of New Mexico), Santa Fe
Photo by Paul Smutko

A crisis of short duration in Talavera around 1575 was resolved quickly, so that at the end of the sixteenth century and during the first half of the seventeenth, this Spanish city was a model for many production centers on the Iberian Peninsula, especially Muel, Zaragoza, Villafeliche, Toledo, and Sevilla. But the model of Talavera, in turn, reflects the two established European modes of that period. On the one hand, the prestigious white pottery of Faenza was very much in accordance with the purist reaction experienced in Italian and Spanish art of that era. This was cause for the cessation in Talavera of the fabrication of Renaissance-style polychrome tableware and the fostering of objects completely white in color, or very simply decorated with blue, black, and ochre, a Hispano version of the Faentino *compendiario* style that now we call the *tricolor* series (fig. 1.7). These were decorated with human or animal figures, *palmetas* (palm designs), and the so-called *cenefa castellana* (Castilian rim).[18]

On the other hand, a boom in Chinese porcelain and of its Lisbon

1.8 Plate / *Plato*
Talavera de la Reina, 17th century
Serie de los helechos
Museo Nacional de Artes
Decorativos, Madrid

copies was also taking place. The latter flowed in massive quantities to Spanish cities, thanks to the solid relationship with Portugal during the period of peninsular unification (1580–1640), causing a flood of white hollowware decorated only with blue. This style is known by the generic name *mariposas* (butterflies), due to the insect-like motif applied to the rim of many of these objects. Another pattern was called *helechos* (ferns). It was predominant on works that emulated Chinese porcelain (figs. 1.8, Intro.3).[19] These designs were painted with cobalt, creating an affordable alternative to the imported porcelains during the phase of economic decline occurring at that time. The Atlantic side of the peninsula received, therefore, numerous pieces manufactured in Portugal influenced by Chinese models, while the Mediterranean coast was supplied by the substantial influx of ceramics from Liguria and Toscana. In the combined influence of these two centers are found almost all the keys to the development of Hispanic ceramics between 1550 and 1650.

The polychrome mayólica of Cataluña, dated to the beginning of the seventeenth century, received an energetic influx from Montelupo, Italy, in spite of the documented presence of Talaveran ceramists; it is not by sheer coincidence that the mayólica of that area came to be called *pisa* (fig. 1.9). The blue Catalan mayólica, on the other hand, was made according to Ligurian patterns painted only in blue or blue mixed with yellow, although its progressive separation from the original Italian models resulted in an unusual and easily identifiable style (fig. 1.10).[20] The Ligurian polychrome series, such as the so-called "calligraphic" was reproduced in Talavera as well in other centers on the Mediterranean coast.

In seventeenth century Sevilla, Talaveran patterns were followed to produce the tricolor series. Ligurian models were used for the blue series, and *faentinos* (from Faenza; known as *pisanos*) for those of the compendiario style. In contrast to Talavera, some Italian patterns were followed very literally and are indistinguishable from the originals.

In Aragón the strong influence of ceramists from Liguria can also be seen. These artisans came from well-known Italian families who had established themselves in the area and who originated the production in Zaragoza of a blue series that imitated Genoese works.[21]

The second half of the seventeenth century saw a severe economic downturn for Castilla and Andalucía. The international commercial connections of prior times were interrupted. Chinese porcelains, Delft tableware that emulated Chinese styles, and the delicate blue series *a tapetto* of Savona appeared in Seville ports. These three styles were replicated in the pottery workshops of Triana. Production in Talavera came to a standstill, since it continued to follow the models of the first half of the century, such as the older blue styles of helechos and tricolor. However, some other styles were born that represented popular tastes, for example, those that imitated lace patterns and *randas* (bobbin lace; fig. 1.11). This was a textile motif that would also be used in contemporary Portuguese mayólica as well as in the ceramics produced in Puebla de los Angeles in Mexico (figs. 10.2, 11.20). Talavera, on the other hand, produced objects almost exclusively for the market of the interior of the peninsula.

This is the period in which the American centers of manufacturing consolidated, taking advantage of the deterioration of ties with the home country and the increasing development of colonial society. Puebla de los Angeles (Mexico) is a prime example of this progress.[22] The first American ceramics began to arrive on the peninsula through the ports of Sevilla and Cádiz. For the most part these consisted of *búcaros* and *tinajas* (large, multi-purpose jars) made in the state of Jalisco, Mexico; in other words, burnished, unglazed pottery that was painted and gilded.

During the last decades of the seventeenth century, under the influence of the Baroque style, new forms of Talavera ceramics enthusiastically represented spectacular explosions of color. Without abandoning the production of blue and white mayólica, which continued to be popular and followed the fashion of new tableware styles from Holland and Genoa, these new polychrome wares with elaborate decorations were reminiscent

1.9 Plate / *Plato*
Barcelona, 1675–1725
Serie policroma
Museu de Ceràmica, Barcelona
Photo by Guillém Fernández

1.10 Plate / *Plato*
Barcelona, 17th century
Serie azul de transición
Museu de Ceràmica, Barcelona
Photo by Guillém Fernández

1.11. Pitcher / *Jarra de pico*
Talavera de la Reina, 17th century
Serie de randas
Museu de Ceràmica, Barcelona
Photo by Guillém Fernández

of the Italian series of Castelli (fig. 1.12). Early pieces of timid style, derived from the tricolor series and from tiles of this new polychrome series, gave way to pieces of great maturity that were manufactured by a group of expert painters working between 1690 and 1720. Designated for the aristocratic clientele of the court, its stately palaces, and its monasteries, these were splendidly colored ceramic works. It is likely that the best examples of this group came from the workshop of the most important of the ceramic masters, Ignacio Mansilla del Pino. The monarchs, King Felipe V and Queen María Luisa, appointed him royal supplier and permitted him, together with other prominent Talaveran craftsmen, to hang the royal coat of arms above the entrance to their shops. He also displayed his own *hidalgo* emblem, since he was granted a title of nobility. Talaveran ceramics again came into style in the elite circles of the court. The keys to the success of these objects produced in the final stages of the golden age of Talavera ceramics were their detailed and well-executed illustrations, a rich palette of eye-catching colors in attractive combinations, and a popular repertoire that followed current fashion trends, although it still contained traces of earlier works inspired by Flemish engravings (fig. 1.13).

1.12 Holy-Water Stoup / *Pila de agua bendita*
Talavera de la Reina, ca. 1700
Serie policroma
Museo de Ávila, Ávila

1.13
Tile Panel
Sala de Cabildo, Toledo
1698
Ayuntamiento Toledo
Photo by
José María Moreno

Mayólica from the Age of Enlightenment

In the eighteenth century, traditional Spanish mayólica began to encounter growing foreign competition. Only those centers that were willing to accept the drastic changes in taste demanded by their clientele continued to prosper. In 1727 the Count of Aranda founded the Alcora factory, with an aesthetic criterion very different from that of historical Spanish mayólica.[23] Fashion was now dictated by France, especially from the manufacturing centers in Moustiers and Marseilles. These ceramics are very delicate in form with complex late Baroque designs (fig. 1.14). Such techniques called for the abandonment of the potter's wheel in favor of a generalized use of molds, a palette of pale colors, and a repertoire of motifs of tiny proportions, based on the Japanese Imari porcelains that also had been introduced into the country. Alcora, whose success hinged on the group effort of some fine artists, took command of the

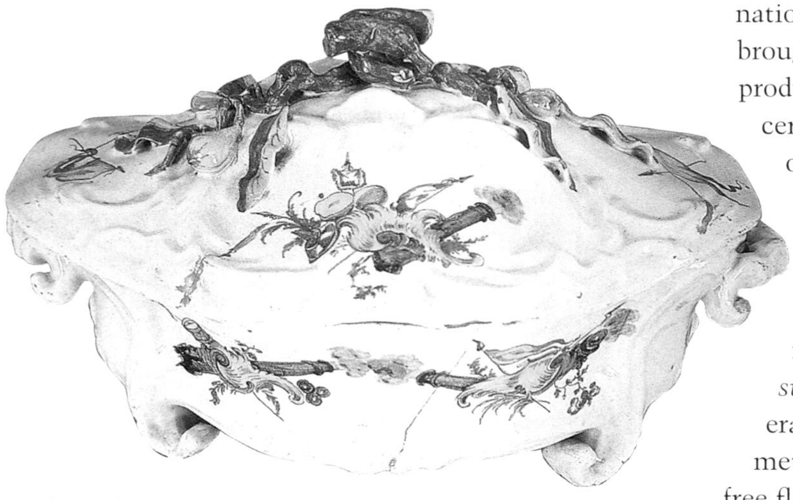

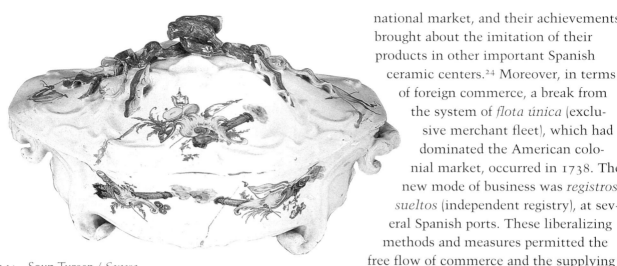

1.14 Soup Tureen / *Sopera*
Alcora, Spain, ca. 1760
Serie de trofeos militares
Museu de Ceràmica, Barcelona
Photo by Guillém Fernández

national market, and their achievements brought about the imitation of their products in other important Spanish ceramic centers.[24] Moreover, in terms of foreign commerce, a break from the system of *flota única* (exclusive merchant fleet), which had dominated the American colonial market, occurred in 1738. The new mode of business was *registros sueltos* (independent registry), at several Spanish ports. These liberalizing methods and measures permitted the free flow of commerce and the supplying of secondary coastal marketplaces that soon swelled with commercial activity.

This trade progressiveness brought to Spain the latest innovations of the English ceramics industry. The first sets of *loza de pedernal* (stoneware) arrived, manufactured in the Staffordshire region and initially imitated only by Alcora. English mayólica also found markets in Spain's American colonies, thanks to the Commercial Treaty of Madrid, signed in 1750, which allowed free commercial ventures by the South Sea Company. The foundation of the Royal Company of Barcelona in 1756 resulted in the official and permanent participation of Cataluña in the American trade, which brought about the arrival in the Americas of ceramics from the region.[25]

The Tratado de Libre Comercio (Free Trade Treaty) signed in 1778 was the decisive solution that allowed the American colonies to become consumers of ceramic products of various European origins. Although at this time the Americas were still under the political control of Spain, they would soon gain their independence.

In the face of competition from porcelain being manufactured in Germany, Carlos III created the Buen Retiro factory (1760–1808), based on the model previously founded in Naples. The high-quality luxury tableware and ornamental pieces produced by this Spanish factory were destined for consumption by the court and the aristrocracy.[26] The production was of *pasta tierna* (soft-paste porcelain) until the beginning of the nineteenth century, after which time the fabrication of genuine hard-paste porcelain began. Effects on the manufacture of mayólica were limited. Another factory founded by the crown that would play an essential role in mayólica for the middle classes of that period was La Moncloa (1817–50).[27] There Bartolomé Sureda put into practice the innovations that he brought from England after his stay there between 1793 and 1796 and those gained later at the manufacturing center of Sèvres, near Paris, in 1802–3. The importance of La Moncloa is not due to the expansion of its scarce products but rather to its having established the basis for modern industrial methods of earthenware production including, from 1830, transfer decorations (*estampadas*) in the English style. The Alcora factory, in its last stages, found itself involved in this same search for new types of industrial earthenware following English models and the tastes of the new Spanish bourgeoisie.

1.15a Basin / *Lebrillo*
Triana district, Sevilla, 19th century
Collection of the International Folk Art Foundation
Museum of International Folk Art,
(Museum of New Mexico), Santa Fe
Design in center is hand-painted

Industrial Mayólica

Although theoretically we should not confuse industrial earthenware with the traditionally manufactured products we are dealing with here, the former had obvious influences on the latter. The most important was that this new automated manufacturing process took over the fabrication of plates and bowls that until the nineteenth century had been carried out with traditional techniques. In addition, traditional earthenware imitated the industrial models in some new forms, certain types of decoration, and, especially, in aspects related to English technical approaches and management strategies (fig. 1.15a, b).

Spain would become an important center of production of industrial mayólica with the well-established factories of Sargadelos (Lugo),[28] Cartagena (Murcia),[29] La Cartuja (Sevilla),[30] San Juan de Aznalfarache (Sevilla),[31] Valdemorillo (Madrid),[32] Busturia (Vizcaya),[33] San Claudio (Oviedo),[34] etc. (fig. 1.16). The rocky history of all these factories producing everyday tableware for the middle classes, their closures and continuous reopenings, produced an erratic coming and going for the laborers, technicians, transfer equipment, and mold collections. This, combined with the continuous plagiarism of the most popular decorations, resulted in a homogeneity that makes it difficult at times to distinguish their respective places of origin, if their factory marks are missing.

1.15b Basin / *Lebrillo*
Triana district, Sevilla, 19th century
Collection of the International Folk Art Foundation
Museum of International Folk Art,
(Museum of New Mexico), Santa Fe
Design in center is stencilled
Photos by Paul Smutko

1.16 Commercial Stand of La Cartuja de Sevilla at the International Exhibition, Paris, 1867 Photo from *La Exposición Universal en París en 1867* (1867)

The founders of almost all of these plants were not cultured aristocrats, as had been the case in the previous century, but were rather middle-class entrepreneurs of the new social class that now controlled an unstable political situation. The market would fluctuate greatly, according to tariffs and taxes imposed on the importation of foreign products. When customs duties rose, they made national production profitable; but when they were lowered, more products were imported from abroad.

The most popular new form of ornamentation was monochrome or color-highlighted transfers, 1830–1900, in the English fashion, for everyday tableware. Panoramas of cities and idyllic countrysides with gardens and romantic historical representations were most frequently applied with this technique. Differing from the English mayólica, the French models were painted by brush, imitating the porcelain produced in Sèvres and Moncloa. These techniques were also followed for special orders. At the end of the nineteenth century, these laboriously painted decorations also began to be imitated with the use of decals (*calcomanías*). The resulting boom, involving mainly floral designs, would end up overtaking the monochrome versions.

The American market would continue to be very important, especially Cuba, Santo Domingo, Argentina, and Uruguay, not only because great quantities of mayólica were sold in these countries, but also because this commerce resulted at times in further investment in the Spanish factories.

Later Traditional Mayólica

In spite of the influence of industrialized mayólica production on the traditional models, many aspects of the old manufacturing ways remained unaltered—so much so that some modest local shops continued to supply tableware to the more rural areas during the nineteenth century, particularly domestic objects. Far from succumbing to the aggressive competition of the large factories producing the English-style ceramics, some traditional production centers enjoyed a boom and a new vitality in their business, more stable than those of the industrial giants. It cannot be said that these more popular products supplied only the local markets. Many of them were the object, as were the industrial ceramics, of extensive interior trade, and some even ended up being exported.

The example of white Bristol ware, as it was called in the coastal areas, encouraged some traditional earthenware craftsmen to refine the appearance of their pieces by using a much whiter clay or coating them, when they were dark, with enamels rich in tin. Numerous production centers of traditional water vessels that had used very light colored calcareous clay now were persuaded to bathe their pottery in white enamels and to embellish them with brushwork. In addition, many centers for the production of unglazed earthenwares that had been using dark, coarse pastes decided to imitate the glossy white finish found in high-quality ceramics. This was the case of Fajalauza in Granada (fig. 1.17) and Vega de Poja in Oviedo. A particularly interesting example is found in the white crockery of the Basque country. Pieces of rough pottery were transported hundreds of kilometers from their original manufacturing sites in Castilla-León, and then a lustrous white finish was applied. In the nineteenth and twentieth centuries, white slips made from a light clay produced a smooth surface that was then covered by a transparent lead glaze. Although not true mayólica, this technique advanced traditional medieval pottery methods to a point of full industrialization.

In the domain of authentic traditional mayólica, Manises, Onda, and Ribesalbes in the region of the Levante (eastern Spain) stand out for their imitation of Alcora mayólica beginning in the eighteenth century (figs. 1.18, 1.19).[35] The objects they produced included attractively decorated plates of different styles, which enjoyed wide popularity in the nineteenth century. These centers flooded the peninsula with their products, and their models served as a major influence on the pottery produced in many other localities.

During the nineteenth century, earthenware factories in Aragón, with a long and rich tradition of their own, modified their production to emulate other zones on the peninsula.[36] In Muel and in Villafeliche objects were produced that tended to imitate in form, repertoire, and decorative application the pottery manufactured in the Levante. Among these

1.17 Cruet / *Alcuza*
Granada, 19th century
Collection of Mr. and
Mrs. Larry Frank
Photo by Paul Smutko

1.18 Plate / *Plato*
Manises, 19th century
Museum of International Folk Art
(Museum of New Mexico), Santa Fe
Photo by Paul Smutko

was blue mayólica painted and ornamented with stencils (*plantillas*) or pounce bags (*muñequillas de tejido*). The evolution of Teruel is similar to that of Muel and Villafeliche. Its production also waned in the face of the vigorous competition from the factories of the Levante region.

In the south of Castilla and in Extremadura, the major centers of mayólica manufacture were Talavera and especially Puente del Arzobispo (Toledo). Workshops in these cities kept alive traditional production techniques as they supplied the major part of the market. The Talavera polychrome series was simplified in Puente, creating new motifs such as *cola de gallo* (rooster tail), *el pino* (the pine), *la pajarita* (the little female bird), *la Guerra de la Independencia* (the War of Independence), and portraits of Fernando VII (fig. 1.20). Mugs and plates that were adorned with garlands and banners were also produced, following popular versions of neoclassic and romantic styles.[37] In the finest series, a pure white enamel was employed, but in lower-priced models the finish had a creamy appearance due to smaller quantities of tin in the glaze.

In western Andalucía, Sevilla and Andújar stood out for their production of mayólica.[38] Given the enthusiastic consumption of tableware industrially manufactured by both of the important factories in Sevilla, the traditional ceramic masters of Triana focused on the production of tiles and an infinite variety of other domestic objects. Traditionally dedicated to ceramic production, this district produced utilitarian objects such as globular jars

1.19 Deep Plate / *Plato hondo*
Ribesalbes, Spain, 19th century
Collection of the International Folk Art Foundation
Museum of International Folk Art
(Museum of New Mexico), Santa Fe
Photo by Paul Smutko

(*orzas*), umbrella stands, urinals, mortars, flower pots, chamber pots, storage jars, and basins. More decorative items included writing sets and small sculptures, or *talleros*. All of these were either decorated with blue stenciled designs (plantillas, fig. 1.15b) or with expressive polychrome decorations applied by brush. Small figures, flowers, and bouquets derived from the *montería* style (depicting the practice of hunting) dominated the decoration of these ceramics (fig. 1.21).

Some regions of Andalucía had potters who attained a high degree of excellence in their imitations of mayólica, using slips and metal oxides to produce colorings. This was the case in Cortegana (Huelva), Úbeda (Jaén) and Nijar (Almería). The eastern zone of Andalucía received products produced in Valencia and Sevilla through the port of Cartagena. The interior zones were supplied with traditional domestic mayólica manufactured in the vicinity of Granada's Fajalauza Gate. Huge quantities of mayólica produced in Biar (Alicante) made its appearance throughout Andalucía. Made using molds, light pastes, and transparent lead glazes, these pieces were modest attempts at imitating jars and plates of the French mayólica (faience) style. In the first few decades of the twentieth century, objects in the art deco style reached a high point.

The majority of these popular mayólica production centers provided complementary objects for domestic life, since tableware was now dominated by industrial plants whose diverse grades of quality and enormous volume of production allowed for lower prices. They also sold items that had defects from the firing process, so that these products were accessible even to people of lower economic status.

1.20 Jar / *Jarro*
Puente del Arzobispo, 19th century
Serie de la Guerra de Independencia
Collection of Mr. and Mrs. Larry Frank
Photo by Paul Smutko

The Mayólica Revival

At the conclusion of the nineteenth century and the beginning of the twentieth, there was a resurgence in the production of traditional pottery, in response to the romantic and nostalgic movements born in Europe in reaction to industrialization and its negative aspects.[39] One strong revival arose in the last years of the 1800s, intensified as a result of the loss of the colonies. In the sphere of literature, the so-called "generation of '98" arose, affecting the educational world with the establishment of the "Institución Libre de Enseñanza" (Free Institution of Education)

1.21 Inkwell / *Tintero*
Sevilla, Spain, 1898
Serie de Montería
Casa Amatller, Barcelona

that defended the necessity of cultural recovery in order to recapture the brilliance of former periods. This era of new enlightenment had a great effect on all Spanish artisans and coincided with similar important foreign movements, such as the Arts and Crafts movement in England. Spanish artists and businesses participated in international expositions in Spain and other countries, and this contributed to the reinforcement of cultural connections. Throughout these years, the first great modern collections of Spanish ceramics were initiated, not only within the country but abroad as well.[40] Scientific studies of these collections generated, for the first time, published articles that led to the birth of new factories bent on reestablishing traditional artistic expression through imitation of age-old styles and techniques. This phenomenon reached special importance in Sevilla, Talavera, Toledo, Barcelona, and Valencia, where new factories of modern design and organization began to produce ceramics with the best qualities of the past. The technical processes were mechanized, but the artwork remained a manual operation.

One of the ambitious aims of this period was to improve the procedures for making lusterware, the singular and exceptional type of mayólica that originated in Hispano-Moresque Spain. In Cataluña, Madrid, and Sevilla, work was performed with this objective. But the centers most successful in their efforts to produce attractive vessels were in Manises and Valencia, especially the workshop La Ceramo (1885–1992; fig. 1.22).[41]

Perhaps the forerunner of all Spanish centers in this renewal was Sevilla. José Gestoso, historian and archaeologist, played a very important role as artistic consultant. The foundation of La Cartuja (1841), San Juan de Aznalfarache (1854), and Soto and Company (1855–67) was also important in this history of rejuvenation. Progressive artistic ideas emanating from England were spread from these focal points. During

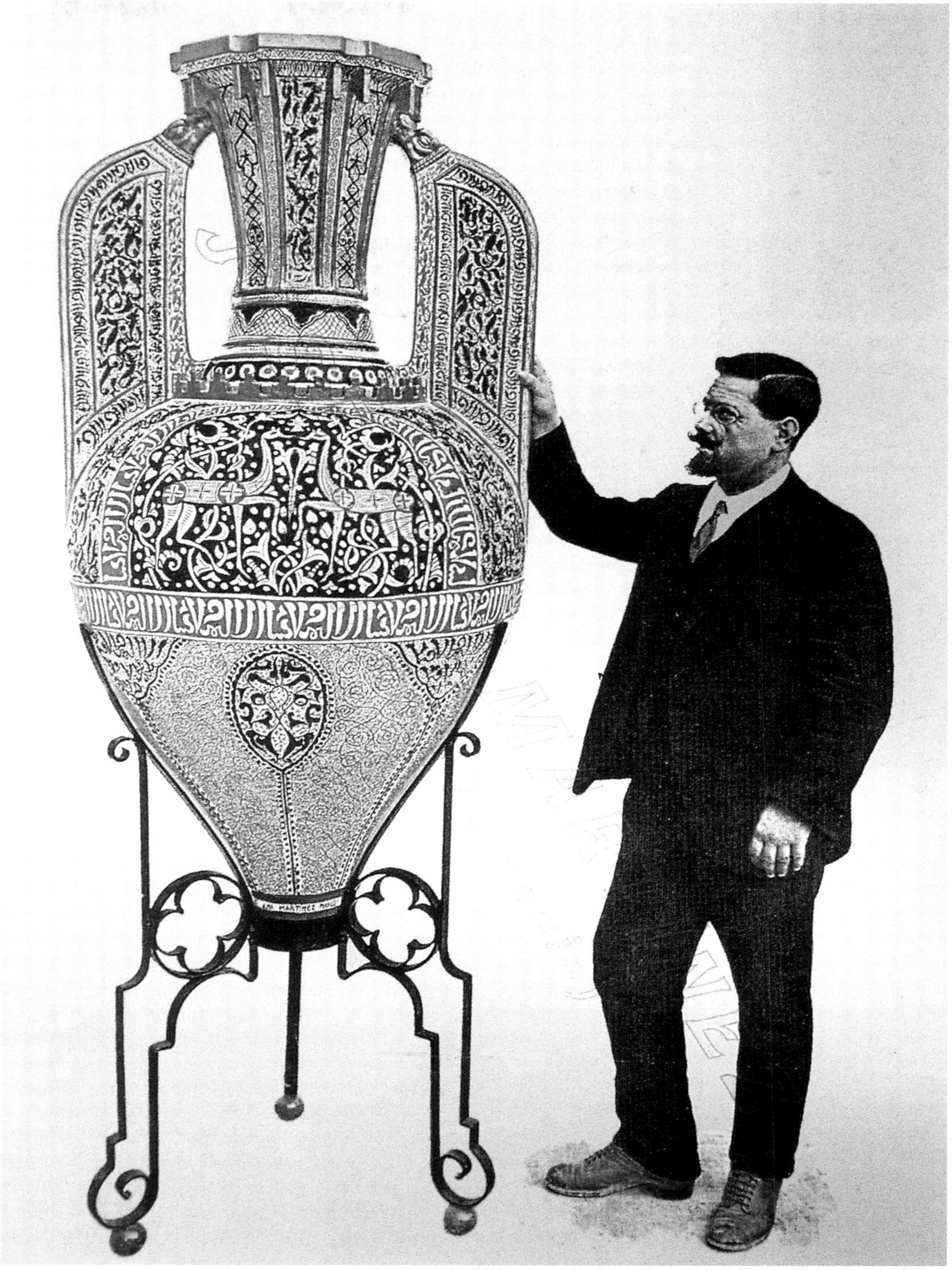

1.22 Neo-Granadina Amphora / *Ánfora neo-granadina*
Valencia, ca. 1900
Catálogo de la firma Martínez
Courtesy of the Museo de Cerámica de Manises, Valencia

the final three decades of the century, the Soto family recaptured the medieval techniques of cuerda seca and *arista* in tilework and the special enamel mixtures for the production of lusterware. Another company, operated by two brothers, José and Miguel Jiménez, made substantial contributions to the recovery of these historical manufacturing methods as well. Two other great pioneering factories were those of the Mensaque family (1880–1946) and one founded by Manuel Ramos Rejano (in 1895), managed by his widow and children after 1922. A very active and brilliant period of production preceded the celebration of the Iberoamerican Exhibition in 1929. These factories, along with those of Nuestra Señora de la O, Cerámica Santa Ana (see chapter 7), and Fábrica de José Tova Villalba presented marvelous exhibitions in the national pavilions of vibrantly colored tiles and mayólica. The industrial innovations, the well thought out techniques, the quality in designs, and the high level of artistic education achieved through the connection of these ceramists with the Escuela Superior de Bellas Artes (School of Advanced Studies in the Fine Arts) made Sevilla one of the primary centers of ceramic production. Some of these same factors also contributed to a similar process of development and recognition that took place later in Talavera.

1.23 Jar / *Orza*
Juan Ruiz de Luna, Talavera de la Reina, ca. 1920
Collection of the International Folk Art Foundation
Museum of International Folk Art (Museum of New Mexico), Santa Fe
Photo by Paul Smutko

Multicolored mayólica painted in the best Renaissance and Baroque traditions, along with tiles, were replicated in Talavera in the early years of the twentieth century. This followed a period of steep decline in manufacturing in the last half of the 1800s. The collapse in production was only roused from its deterioration by the efforts of two factories: La Menora (1860–1905) and El Carmen (1849–), whose output was heavily influenced by Valencian ceramists. The partnership of art connoisseur and collector Platón Páramo and an enterprising decorator, Juan Ruiz de Luna, in conjunction with the technical consultation provided by Enrique Guijo, an artist from Sevilla,[42] resulted in the creation of the Nuestra Señora del Prado factory (1908–61). The extraordinary quality of the decorated ceramics fabricated in this plant made it sometimes difficult to distinguish their products from genuine antiques (fig. 1.23). Besides splendid imitations of classic Talavera and Alcora models, they also manufactured pieces inspired by famous Spanish and European works and by literary sources such as *El Quijote*, by Miguel de Cervantes.

During the opening decades of the twentieth century, Talavera and Sevilla exported numerous products to Latin America and the United States, but this flourishing commerce was interrupted by the outbreak of the Spanish Civil War, in 1936.

An ambiance of modernism presided over architecture and art in Cataluña, where a similar process of recuperation arose in ceramic creations. Here it was in the architectural use of ceramics that the most original contributions were made. Individualists such as Marià Burgués, Lambert Escaler, Dionís Renart, all from Barcelona, and Peiró, in Valencia, also made domestic artifacts and sculpture that contributed to the movement and achieved wide popular dissemination.[43]

During this time, objects of great technological quality and enormous aesthetic beauty continued to be produced. However, in the 1940s and '50s these artistic accomplishments crumbled, in a Spain disheartened by a civil war and the cultural isolation that resulted under the dictatorial Franco regime.

The artistic and economic depression reached its lowest point in the middle of the twentieth century, when traditional mayólica lost even the small remaining portion of its domestic sales to objects produced with newly invented plastic materials and tableware fabricated from durable glass. After the 1950s, the precarious existence of traditional mayólica factories was maintained thanks to collectors of popular art and the tourist market for souvenirs. Only in the past few decades have official attempts been made to revitalize and give life to new forms of this specialized craft for coming generations. This has entailed efforts to find a niche in the industrial economic scheme, to foster alternative markets, and to provide work for large segments of the population who are unemployed (See chapter 8). All of this has been responsible for new growth in this productive sector. It is what we today call "new artisanship" (*nuevas artesanías*), in an attempt to identify this complex sociological phenomenon. It is an art form very distinct from the traditional crafts of the past, whose products we currently can only admire in collections and museums.

Notes

1. Pilar Lafuente Ibáñez, "La cerámica almohade en Sevilla," in *El último siglo de la Sevilla almohade (1147–1248)*, coord. by Magdalena Valor Piechotta (Sevilla: Universidad de Sevilla–Gerencia Municipal de Urbanismo, 1995), pp. 285–301.
2. Julio Navarro, "Murcia como centro productor de mayólica dorada," in *Congreso Internacional de Cerámica Medieval en el Mediterráneo Occidental*-3, 1986.
3. Graziella Berti y Ezio Tongiorgi, *Ceramiche importate dalla Spagna nell'area pisana* (Firenze, 1985).
4. Isabel Flores Escobosa, *Estudio preliminar sobre la loza azul y dorada nazarí de la Alhambra* (Madrid: Instituto Hispano-Árabe de Cultura, 1988).

5. Isabel Alvaro Zamora, "La cerámica en el mudéjar turolense," in A.A.V.V. *Teruel Mudéjar: Patrimonio de la Humanidad..* (Zaragoza: Ibercaja, 1991), pp. 203–37.
6. Josep Vicent Lerma, *La mayólica gótico-mudéjar en la ciudad de Valencia* (Valencia: Ministerio de Cultura, 1992).
7. Albert Telese Compte, "Cataluña" en *Medi-terra-neum: Cerámica medieval en España e Italia* (Barcelona: FAUL Edizioni Artistiche, 1992), pp. 92–102.
8. Christopher Gerrard, Alejandra Gutiérrez, J. Hurst, and Alan Vince, "Guía sobre la cerámica medieval española en las islas británicas," in *Cerámica medieval española en España y en las Islas británicas*, by Christopher Gerrard, Alejandra Gutiérrez, and Alan Vince, *British Archaeological Reports International Series*, no. 610 (Oxford: Archaeopress, 1995), pp. 281–97. See also Alejandra Gutiérrez, *Mediterranean Pottery in Wessex Households (13th to 17th Centuries)*, *British Archaeological Reports International Series*, no. 306 (Oxford: Archaeopress, 2000), p. 143.
9. Alfonso Pleguezuelo, *Cerámicas de Triana en la Colección Carranza* (Sevilla: Fundación El Monte, 1996), pp. 63–87; and Anthony Ray, *Spanish Pottery 1248–1898* (London: V&A Publications, 2000), pp. 140–41.
10. José Gestoso y Pérez, *Historia de los barros vidriados sevillanos desde sus orígenes hasta nuestros dias* (Sevilla: Tipografía la Andalucía Moderna, 1903–4).
11. José María Sánchez, "La cerámica exportada a América en el siglo XVI a través de la documentación del Archivo General de Indias, Parte I: Materiales arquitectónicos y contenedores comerciales," and "Parte II: Ajuares domésticos y cerámica cultural y laboral," *Laboratorio de Arte* 9 (1996):125–42, and 11 (1998):121–33.
12. Concepción García Sáiz and María Angeles Albert de León, "La cerámica de Tonalá en las colecciones europeas," in A.A.V.V., *Tonalá: Sol de barro* (México: Banca Cremi, S.A., and De la Fuente Ediciones, S.C., 1991), p. 47.
13. Oskar H. K. Spate, *The Spanish Lake* (Minneapolis: University of Minnesota, 1979).
14. Albert Telese Compte, "Platos de cenefa punteada," *Galería Antiquaria* 108 (1993).
15. Domingo Portela, "Apreciaciones sobre la evolución de 'las talaveras,' siglos XVI al XX," *Boletín de la Sociedad Española de Cerámica y Vídrio* 4 (1999):38.
16. Cayetano Anibal and Carlos Cano, "La cerámica pintada de Úbeda: Avance de un estudio sistemático," *Revista de Arqueología* 20(224) (2000):38–45.
17. Mariano Maroto, "Jarras y jarros toledanos de mediados del siglo XVI," *Quadrivium* (Toledo) (1999):27–36.
18. Natacha Seseña, "Doble mirada a las lozas de Talavera y Puente," in *Las lozas de Talavera y Puente* (exhibit catalog) (Madrid: Mercado Puerto de Toledo, Junta de Comunidades de Castilla–La Mancha, Ayuntamiento de Talavera de la Reina, 1989), pp. 19–35.
19. Diodoro Vaca González and Juan Ruiz de Luna, *Historia de la cerámica de Talavera de la Reina y algunos datos subre la de Puente del Arzobispo* (Madrid: Editora Nacional, 1943).
20. Albert Telese Compte, *La vaixella blava catalana de 1570 a 1670* (Barcelona: Carrera Edició, 1991).
21. Isabel Alvaro Zamora, "Sobre los modos de irradiación de la cerámica ligúr y la presencia de ceramistas de esta procedencia en la Zaragoza del siglo XVII," *Revista Artigrama* (Departamento de Historia del Arte, Universidad de Zaragoza) 4 (1987):137–56.
22. Enrique Cervantes, *Loza blanca y azulejos de Puebla*, 2 vols. (Mexico City: Privately printed, 1939); and more recently Margaret Connors McQuade, *Talavera Poblana: Four Centuries of a Mexican Ceramic Tradition* (New York: The Hispanic Society, 1999).
23. Manuel Escribá de Romaní, Conde de Casal, *Historia de la cerámica de Alcora* (Madrid, 1945).

24. María Antonia Casanovas, "Influencia de Alcora en otras manufacturas españolas," in *El Esplendor de Alcora* (Barcelona: Museo de Cerámica, Ayuntamiento de Barcelona, 1994), pp. 29–31.
25. Alejandro Artucio Urioste, *Azulejo en la arquitectura de Río de la Plata, siglos XVIII–XX* (Montevideo: Intendencia Municipal de Montevideo y Junta de Andalucía, 1996).
26. Carmen Mañueco Santurtún, "La Real Fábrica de Porcelana del Buen Retiro a través de sus documentos (1760–1808)," in *Manufactura del Buen Retiro (1760–1808)* (Madrid: Ministerio de Educación y Cultura, Comunidad de Madrid y Museo Arqueológico Nacional, 1999), pp. 17–128.
27. José Sierra Álvarez and Isabel Tuda Rodríguez, "Sureda y la renovación de la cerámica española durante el primer tercio del siglo XIX," in *Bartolomé Sureda (1679–1851): Arte e Industria en la Ilustración tardía* (Madrid: Museo Municipal de Madrid, 2000), pp. 89–158.
28. Felipe Bello Piñeiro, *Cerámica de Sargadelos,* (La Coruña: Ediciones El Castro, 1972); and Xosé Filgueira Valverde, *Sargadelos* (Santiago: Ediciones El Castro, 1951).
29. Manuel Jorge Aragoneses, *Artes industriales cartageneras: Lozas del siglo XIX* (Murcia: Academia Alfonso X el Sabio, 1982).
30. Beatriz Maestre de León, *La Cartuja de Sevilla: Fábrica de cerámica* (Sevilla: Fábrica de Cerámica La Cartuja, 1993).
31. Alfonso Pleguezuelo, "Una breve historia de 100 años," in *Estampaciones para lozas de los siglos XIX y XX: La fábrica de San Juan de Aznalfarache, Sevilla (1854–1954),* ed. by Marcos Buelga (Oviedo: Museo de Bellas Artes de Asturias, 2000), pp. 11–24.
32. José Sierra Álvarez and Isabel Tuda Rodriguez, *Las lozas de Valdemorillo (1845–1915)* (Madrid: Comunidad de Madrid, 1996).
33. Ángel de Apraiz, *La cerámica de Busturia* (Valladolid, 1952).
34. Marcos Buelga, *La fábrica de loza de San Claudio 1901–1966* (Oviedo: Museo de Bellos Artes de Asturias, 1994).
35. María Antonia Casanovas, "Alcora, Onda y Ribesalbes," in *Cerámica española,* ed. by Trinidad Sánchez-Pacheco, *Summa Artis* (Madrid) 42 (1997):389–436. See also for this region and period the complete listing of factories published by Josep Pérez Camps, "Artesanía e industria cerámica en el país valenciano durante la primera mitad del siglo XX," *Forum Cerámico* (Alicante) 1 (August 1993).
36. Isabel Alvaro Zamora, "La cerámica aragonesa," in *Cerámica española,* ed. by Trinidad Sánchez-Pacheco, *Summa Artis* (Madrid) 42 (1997):223–88.
37. Natacha Seseña, "Producción popular en Talavera y Puente del Arzobispo," *Archivo Español de Arte* 41(161) (1968):120–35.
38. Ray, *Spanish Pottery*, pp. 266–80.
39. Natacha Seseña, *La cerámica popular en Castilla la Nueva* (Madrid: Editora Nacional, 1975).
40. Ray, *Spanish pottery,* and various authors in *El reflejo de Manises: Cerámica hispano-morisca del Museo de Cluny de Paris* (Valencia: Museo de Bellas Artes de Valencia, 1996).
41. Josep Pérez Camps, *La ceràmica de reflex metàlic de Manises 1850–1960* (Manises: Museu d'Etnologia de la Diputació de Valencia, 1997).
42. María Isabel Hurley Molina, *Talavera y los Ruiz de Luna* (Toledo: Excelentísimo Ayuntamiento, 1989).
43. María Pía Subiás, "La cerámica decorada en la época del Noucentisme," en *Cerámica española,* ed. by Trinidad Sánchez-Pacheco, *Summa Artis* (Madrid) 42 (1997):529–50.

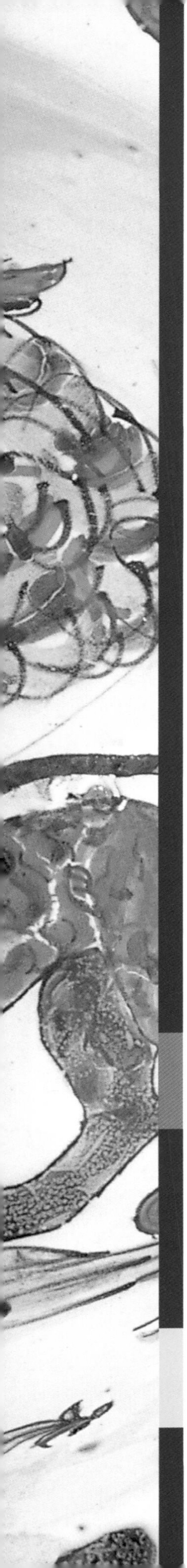

Detail, Fig. 2.12

2

Ceramics in Domestic Life in Spain

MARÍA ANTONIA CASANOVAS

SINCE THE TIME Neolithic people discovered the plasticity of clay and began to mold the first mud vessels, they developed both the practical and the artistic facets of their nature. They transformed the surface of common vessels into pictorial and sculptural compositions. For this reason, even the simplest items fashioned for daily use have come to be objects worthy of collection. Few commonplace household items have survived in Spain, a country somewhat cavalier with its personal effects.[1] However, certain pieces, in spite of their private and individual use, have been preserved with the same consideration as works of painting and sculpture and have been handed down from generation to generation. Legal documents, such as inventories, and graphic representations, such as paintings and engravings (the latter beginning in the sixteenth century), have underscored the importance and the function of each one of these artifacts in everyday life. Through them we can appreciate that ceramics served not only a practical purpose but had ornamental significance as well.

The Middle Ages and the Renaissance (Thirteenth through Sixteenth Centuries)

Three dissimilar cultures —Christianity, Judaism, and Islam —were living together in Spain in the Middle Ages. Survivors of the Umayyad Arabic dynasty brought with them, in the tenth century, the opulence and sophistication of the courts of the Abbasids of Baghdad. This included their table manners, recipes, silk and cotton fabrics, perfumes, music and poetry, and ornamented ceramics (fig. 2.1). Up until that time in Spain, all earthenware objects had been porous, contributing to the spread of illnesses and causing the retention of undesired odors. This also made them unsatisfactory containers for prolonged preservation of liquids or the application of pictorial designs. Spanish families had also been using vessels of wood or metal, as had the rest of Europe in the thirteenth century. Once the techniques of tin-enameling became known, making it possible to hide the clay color by glazing and decorating the pottery, they began to order the improved crockery from pottery shops. From that point on, the richness and variety of designs permitted potters to follow the shifting tastes and fashions of the times.

2.1 Mosaic Tile Panel / *Panel de aliceres o allicatado*
Tremecén Mosque, North Africa, 14th century
Museu de Ceràmica, Barcelona
Photo by Guillém Fernández

The Middle Ages also saw a revitalization of the middle class—the class that led to the decline of the feudal system. This growing group of entrepreneurs not only managed the rapid commercial development of businesses but also participated in the political life of their cities. Many of the potters of Spain during and following the reconquest were *Mudéjares* (Muslims living under Christian rule who kept their religion and customs). In the provinces of Valencia and Aragón, they worked under the patronage of rulers who both exacted an annual tax from them and demanded free earthenwares. In Cataluña, however, all the potters were Christians and, like all other artisans, belonged to a guild, an association that supervised the work and quality of the manufactured objects.

Workshops throughout the country were run by families, and each member was responsible for a particular task: mixing the clay, throwing the pots, glazing, painting, gathering firewood, or tending to the kilns. In the ornamentation of their pottery, the ceramic centers of the Middle Ages used standard Islamic patterns and motifs that were popular well into the sixteenth century. The main decorative features were diametric bands, symmetric axes, the radial disposition of ornamental motifs, and *horror vacui*, a tendency to decorate the article's surfaces so thoroughly that almost no area was free of embellishment. The first Christian potters who manufactured *loza* or mayólica (tin-glazed pottery) were from Paterna, Barcelona, and Teruel and employed three symbolic colors: green, the color of Islam; black, the color of the Prophet Mohammed; and white, the color of the Umayyad dynasty. The symbiosis of the Christian and Islamic elements that comprise Mudéjar art is best reflected in the ornamental repertoire of this bicolor (green and black/purple) series and is characteristic of medieval Spanish art.

Religious Ceramics

After the reconquest, the unification of the country meant the ban of any religious rites other than those observed by Christians. For this reason, beginning in the late fourteenth century, the need for baptismal fonts and urns for blessed water burgeoned. The churches and chapels of palaces and castles in rural areas of southern Spain had large baptismal fonts manufactured in the pottery shops of Sevilla. These sacramental basins were also exported to the Canary Islands and the Americas. Documents of the era have revealed that many Andalusian aristocrats procured fonts for the churches of their states. These were constructed in a hemispherical shape and set on a cylindrical base, coated with a lead glaze, and profusely bedecked with relief and stamped patterns (fig. 2.2). Few specimens have survived the unavoidable destruction that followed the ordinances of Fray Alonso de Santo Tomás of the Málaga archdiocese, who in 1671 insisted that, "the fonts will be made out of stone and not of clay" and "where any one was left, it was to be disposed of within two months and replaced with one of stone."[2] One can suppose that the power of the church obliged the use of more impressive fixtures in place of the simple earthenwares that had always been thought of as humble. On the other hand, the survival of some fonts from private chapels and public churches proves that the ordinances were not always obeyed. Between the thirteenth and nineteenth centuries, several of Aragón's pottery workshops produced baptismal fonts of lesser dimensions. The medieval specimens from Teruel have a globe-like or hemispherical body with a conical cover and a large pommel (see fig. 1.4). Decorated in green and purple, or in blue, they followed the Mudéjar style of ornamentation, which included no decorative allusion to the Christian religion. During the sixteenth and seventeenth centuries, Muel produced specimens decorated in metallic

2.2 Baptismal Font / *Pila bautismal*
Sevilla,
late 14th–early 15th century
Earthenware with a green glaze with stamped fleurs-de-lis, eagles with wings spread and rampant lions decorating the rim. Pineapples appear in relief.
From the church of Castilleja de Talhara, destroyed in 1756 during the earthquake of Lisboa
Private Collection

oxides and green. Surviving fonts from the eighteenth and nineteenth centuries are much rarer; they utilize zoomorphic depictions on the lugs of the hemispherical cover and have small, semicircular lateral handles. In Talavera, portable fonts for private chapels and churches were manufactured in the shape of covered *lebrillos* (large basins).

Medieval Ceramic Kitchen Utensils

The kitchen was a space reserved exclusively for the female members of the family, a place where they could be together in private, not only to cook the daily meals, but also to preserve seasonal foodstuffs for later use. It was also a place for weaving and chatting. This small space was divided into two areas, one set aside for food storage in ceramic containers and the other where the cooking fire was located. The hearth, in the homes of the upper classes, was built against the wall or in the center of the room, with chimneys that allowed smoke and odors to be channeled to the outside. In the homes of the less prosperous, it was against the wall of the single common room of the dwelling.

The concept of privacy was completely different from that of the present. Members of a family shared spaces, furniture, and their meager personal belongings.[3] Since there were no cupboards or pantries, tableware was kept on shelves or hung from walls. Pots and pans were placed adjacent to the fireplace. Vessels of different sizes and shapes were used to prepare and cook food: cooking jars (*ollas*); casseroles (*cazuelas*); large, steep-sided, flat-bottomed bowls (*lebrillos*); and large bowls (*cuencos*). Other types were employed for the preservation of liquids: pitchers (*cántaros*), measuring vessels (*medidas*), one- or two-handled jars (*jarras*), and olive oil containers (*aceiteras*).[4] All the recipes stipulate that containers for olive oil should be glazed, to avoid the risk of oxygen seeping through porous clay and causing a chemical reaction that would alter the oil's properties. Likewise, cruets (*alcuzas*) were to be glazed to prevent grease from oozing out and to facilitate their cleaning. Doctors tried to instill the habit of cleaning these vessels to prevent the growth of mildew or verdigris.[5]

Ceramic cisterns (*aguamaniles*) contained water for washing hands before and after meals. Influenced by Arabic practices, the water was frequently perfumed with an extract of roses. The oldest examples date back to the fifteenth century, but these vessels were most abundant during the eighteenth century, when there was a notable rise in the importance of personal hygiene (fig. 2.3). Those glazed in green, black, or amber, intended for the rural home, had pillar-shaped bodies and long, conical necks. Decorations on handles and lids often depicted reptilian forms.

Large earthenware jars known as *alfabias,* or *tinajas,* were used for the maritime transport of goods and in homes for storing wheat, flour, and wine. Their dimensions were substantial—140, 245, and 280 liters—and they were sheathed in raffia fiber for easier handling and to avoid breakage. Since they were quite costly, a market existed for used, broken, or restored jars. To enhance their stability, the jars were sunk into pits in pantry floors.[6]

As mentioned earlier, ceramic objects as well as furniture and other domestic goods were scarce, and for that reason the same object often had multiple uses. Ceramic mortars, which took the same shape as those made of bronze, served in the kitchen to crush condiments, prepare sauces, and mince and mix food, while they were used in pharmacies to prepare medicines (fig. 2.4).

In similar fashion, apothecary jars were used not only for storing medicinal herbs in drug stores but for the preservation of aromatic herbs and candied fruit in the kitchen as well (fig. 2.5). The science of pharmacology saw a notable development during the fifteenth century. The Muslims, and later the Benedictine monks who translated Greek and Roman texts dealing with illnesses and their treatment, were responsible for the popularization of remedies based on plants cultivated in the gardens of palaces, castles, and monasteries, where a pharmacy would also be maintained. In Italy apothecary jars were called *arbarelli,* from the Persian *al barani,* which means "spice bottle." In Spain they became known as "Damascus bottles" (*botes de Damasco*), since the first specimens arrived during the thirteenth century on board ships that traded along the route that linked Europe with the Near East. The smaller arbarelli, approximately 10 or 12 cm high, were specially designed to hold pills.[7] Jars for syrup (*xaruperes*), were used not only for balms and oils

2.3 Cistern / *Aguamanil*
Alcora, Spain, 1735–1749
Serie de chinescos
Acquired from Luis Plandiura in 1932
Museu de Ceràmica, Barcelona
Photo by Giullém Fernández

2.4 Mortar / *Mortero*
Teruel, Spain, late 16th–early 17th century
Collection of the International Folk Art Foundation
Museum of International Folk Art (Museum of New Mexico), Santa Fe
Photo by Paul Smutko

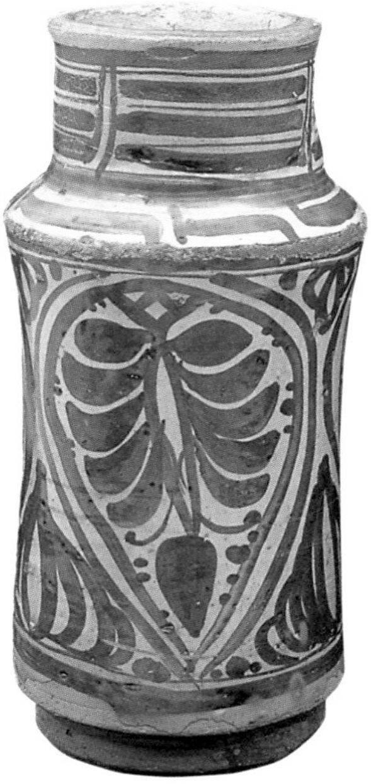

2.5 Pharmacy Jars / *Botes de farmacia*
Barcelona, 15th century
Museu de Ceràmica, Barcelona

in pharmacies and herbariums but also to keep olive oil in the kitchen.

Tableware

Before the fifteenth century there were no dining rooms or dining room tables, as we know them today. A wide board was simply placed on top of two trestles for the duration of the meal, and this makeshift table was dismantled when dinner was over. Ceramics decorated in green and purple, or in blue, were luxury items in rural areas but were everyday objects in urban areas, where the wealthy used tableware made of fine metals. In the Middle Ages, guests shared plates, goblets, knives, and spoons. Tableware consisted of few items, and all of them were multifunctional. Porringers (*escudillas*), for example, were ceramic saltcellars, but they were also used as soup or bouillon bowls (fig. 2.6). In addition, these small bowls were utilized for dispensing holy water in churches for the baptism of children and in the medical practice of bloodletting. Documents of the times mention the *scudella amb orelles*, a bowl with flat, triangular handles, and the *scudella duplorum,* which consisted of two bowls with conical necks that fit one inside the other and were used to keep soups and stews warm. Footed bowls and plates of various sizes, platters for stews and other foods, and saltcellars (*saleros*) for the most important condiment on the medieval table, made up the dinner service. The daily ritual at the medieval table was based on Christian liturgy and represented the celebration of the Eucharist; the saltcellar was a symbol of the union between the dinner guests and God, and by extension, the symbol of the presence of God at the table.[8] Therefore the saltcellar was the first vessel to be set on the table and the last to be put away.

Jars for water and wine had long conical

2.6 Lusterware Porringer / *Escudilla de reflejo metálico*
Manises, 1475–1550
Collection of the International Folk Art Foundation
Museum of International Folk Art
(Museum of New Mexico), Santa Fe
Photo by Paul Smutko

2.7a *The Last Supper*
Jaume Ferrer I,
early 15th century
Museu Diocesia i
Comarcal de Solsona,
Solsona
This painting for the
predella of an altar
faithfully reproduces
tableware from the
Ave María series of
Manises

necks, a globular body, and a pedestal. Bread and wine, symbols of the body and blood of Christ, were also never absent from the table. We have to remember that the predominant way of thinking in medieval society was symbolic. These symbols were as real to people as the objects used to represent them. Paintings from this era depicting scenes such as the Last Supper authentically portray the kind of crockery actually used on the medieval table. Pictorial documentation has been instrumental in expanding knowledge of the customs of this era (figs. 2.7 a, b).

Lusterware Table Services with Cobalt Blue Ornamentation

Increasing commerce throughout the Mediterranean brought imports from Italy to Spain and exported Spanish-made ceramics. This pottery maintained Muslim themes until the sixteenth century, since practically all production sites were then operated by Morisco potters—Arabs who had converted to Christianity. The Boil family, shipowners and ambassadors of King Jaime II in the Nasrid kingdom of Granada,

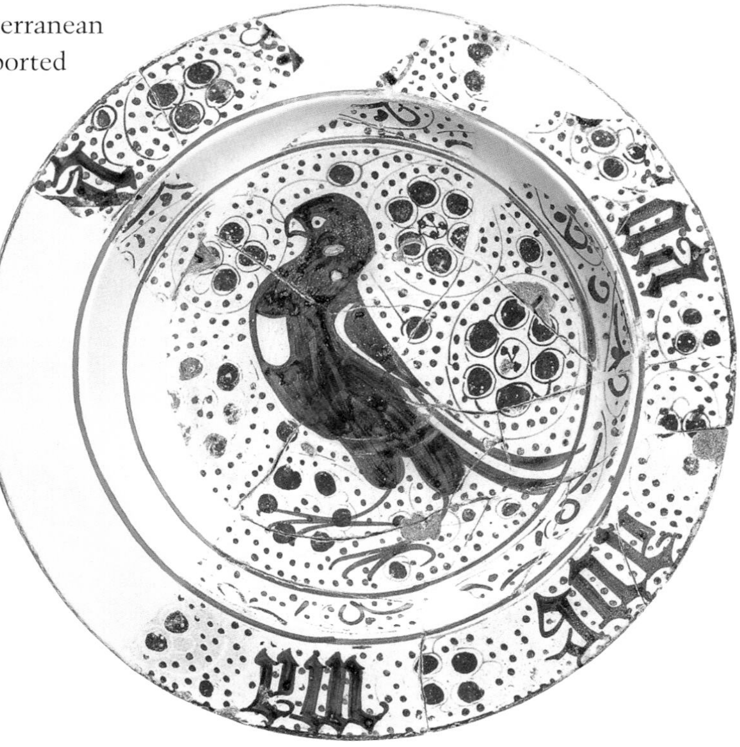

2.7b Lusterware Plate / *Plato de reflejo metálico*
Manises, 1410–1480
Serie Ave María
Collection of the International
Folk Art Foundation
Museum of International Folk Art
(Museum of New Mexico), Santa Fe
Photo by Paul Smutko

observed the commercial success of the lusterware of Málaga. At the close of the fourteenth century, they contracted with potters from Andalucía to work at their estates in Manises (Valencia). According to the terms of their contracts, these potters could charge a certain percentage on the sale of their goods. The period from this time until the first quarter of the sixteenth century is considered the golden age of Valencian lusterware, a unique product that was destined for consumption exclusively by the upper classes (fig. 2.8). Coinciding with the decline of the Nasrid dynasty, Paterna and Manises, in Valencia, became the only production centers of these luxury items and thereby the sole producers for the courts of Europe. Popes, kings, and nobles throughout Europe ordered lusterware table services and tile decorated with their individual coats of arms from Valencian potters. For this reason, it is common to find remainders of these beautiful services not only among the possessions of palaces and museums but also amid the merchandise salvaged from shipwrecks off the English, Dutch, Danish, French and Italian coasts. Lusterware producers became authentic entrepreneurs, and it was necessary to hire apprentices or acquire slaves, because the family-run workshops of the era were inadequate to meet the increasing demand. In Spain, artisans belonged to a guild in order to maintain control over the quality of their products and to gain, as a group, a voice in local politics.

2.8 Lusterware Plate / *Plato de reflejo metálico*
Manises, early 15th century
Museu de Ceràmica, Barcelona
Photo by Guillém Fernández
Decorated in blue with parsley leaves and bryonies

The popularity of Spanish lusterware throughout Europe was such that it was frequently used as a motif in Spanish, Flemish, German and Italian paintings of the Gothic period. Painters of miniatures, altarpieces, triptychs and dowry chests, reproducing traditional religious themes such as The Last Supper, The Annunciation, The Adoration, and the Virgin and Child, also applied their talents to the most beautiful and sumptuous objects of the times: background drapery, fabrics brocaded with gold, glass objects, and lusterware. The exceptional state of preservation of some of the surviving lusterware pieces is due to the fact that they were also used as ornamental pieces.

During the fifteenth century, the table ritual, as a result of the new Humanist attitudes, fell away from a spiritual emphasis and developed a more secular mode. The image of God was replaced by the master of the house, who assumed the role of host during the banquet ceremony. (The word *banquet* comes from the Italian *banchetto*, which means "bench," and it recalls the custom of eating while seated on a bench prior to the year 1000). The room where the formal meal took place was decorated with tapestries, carpets, and a credenza. The latter, placed against the wall, could contain as many as twelve shelves and was used to exhibit the collections of the host, such as gold or silver pieces, crystal objects, sea shells mounted on ornate metal stands, ivory boxes, and lusterware. It was the duty of the nobleman to exhibit his wealth and thus his social status, in front of his guests.

These luxurious ceramics, intended for affluent families, consisted of highly refined vessels that imitated designs in silver and gold. Originally lusterware had been created as a substitute for gold and silver table services, whose use had been prohibited by the prophet Mohammed. Jars, cups, and goblets for wine were highly decorated, with gadrooned rims and molded stands. Platters attained considerable sizes and displayed gadroons or vegetal designs in relief. In many cases this decoration was evocative of repoussé designs on gold and silver tableware. Skillfully combined gold and blue tones formed a rich ornamental variety that alternated between a detailed symbiosis of vegetal, calligraphic and geometric elements and figurative or allegorical themes. The immense variety of embellishments, some derived from the Islamic world and others from Gothic-Christian traditions, was adapted to the equally abundant repertoire of extant forms: wine coolers for the table, oil lamps (*candiles*), pharmacy containers of different sizes, basil pots, porringers of several

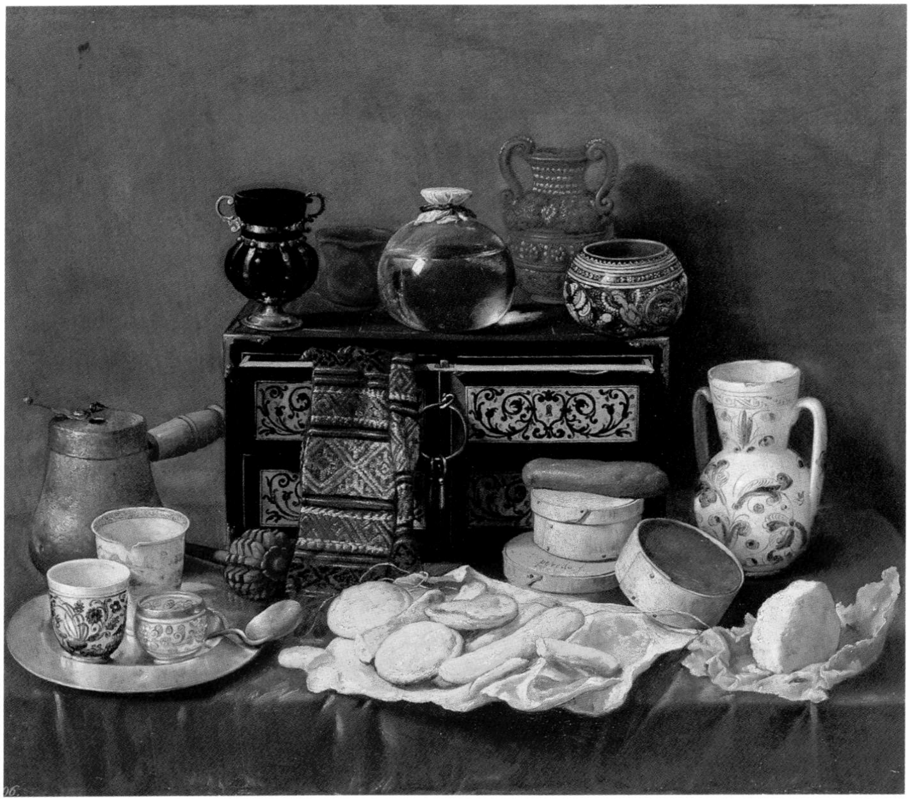

2.9 *Still Life with an Ebony Chest*
Antonio de Pereda, 1652
The State Hermitage Museum, St. Petersburg

2.10a *Still Life with Fruit and Cheese*
Luis Meléndez, 1771
Museo Nacional del Prado, Madrid

2.10b Lusterware Honey Jar / *Melero de reflejo metálico*
Manises, ca. 1700–1750
E. Boyd Memorial Fund purchase
Collection of the International Folk Art Foundation
Museum of International Folk Art, (Museum of New Mexico), Santa Fe
Photo by Paul Smutko

sizes, bowls, and large flat-bottomed serving platters (*braseros*), among many others.

From the second half of the sixteenth century, lusterware declined in popularity in Europe but continued to be manufactured for the Spanish market, not only in Manises but also in Muel (Aragón), Barcelona and Reus (Cataluña), and Sevilla (Andalucía). Even as the pieces lost their original magnificence and refinement, they retained the Hispano-Moresque character that makes them unique even today. By the seventeenth century, there was no longer a real demand for lusterware, although it was often included in still lifes of painters such as Juan Sánchez Cotán, Juan Van der Hamen, Antonio de Pereda (fig. 2.9), and Thomas Hiepes. Luis Meléndez repeatedly painted pots designed especially for preserving honey well into the eighteenth century (figs. 2.10 a, b). During the nineteenth century, lusterware reached another period of splendor, thanks to the collectors of that epoch. Spain was rediscovered during the French invasion and mythicized by French writers and travelers, who described it as an exotic country filled with mystery. The Romantic Orientalist movement defended the Hispano-Arab legacy and fueled the collection of historic lusterware. Throughout the second half of the nineteenth century, the best collections emerged. The most prominent were the collections of Conde Valencia de Don Juan in Madrid, the Godman collection of the British Museum of London, and the collections of the Hispanic Society of New York, the Louvre, and the Thermes de Cluny Museum in Paris. In addition to aristocrats and the upper class, merchants and businessmen also became interested in acquiring these works. Painters converted their studios into large and sumptuous exhibit spaces, where they kept furniture, tapestry, rugs, suits of armor, lusterware, glass objects and costumes of previous eras used to attire their models.

Azulejería—*Decorated Tilework*

Following the Mesopotamian tradition of ornamenting palaces with glazed bricks, Muslims covered interior floors and walls and the exterior facades of their buildings with *alicatados* (mosaic panels composed of glazed tile) and tiles (see figs. 2.1, Intro.5). At the end of the thirteenth century, the production of painted tiles was initiated, and by the end of the fifteenth century, they had become a substitute for the alicatados, which were inspired by Roman mosaics and of extraordinary beauty, but which were very expensive and difficult to manufacture. As in Syria, square, rectangular, star-shaped, and hexagonal tiles were fabricated. Triangular shapes were produced specifically to fit into corner areas. As was the case with tableware, the first tiles were decorated in green and purple, with themes rooted in Islamic traditions. After the beginning of the fourteenth century, blue was used to emulate Chinese porcelain of the Ming dynasty, which had begun to arrive in Europe. Heraldic and vegetal motifs were favored throughout the country. Potters decorated by sketching *a mano alzada* (free hand). But in Cataluña, during the sixteenth century, a preindustrial technique was created that allowed the ornamentation of a large number of tiles in a short period of time. A metallic or wooden stencil (*plantilla*) was applied to the white enamel coating just before firing. The decorative details were then inscribed into the tile with a punch.

The origin of polychrome

During the fifteenth century, European families had ordered their crockery and flooring tiles from local pottery makers. At the beginning of the sixteenth century, thanks to the changes brought on by the artistic innovations of the Renaissance that took place in various Italian principalities, new styles rich in polychrome finishes spread with force throughout Europe. They became immediately popular and gradually replaced traditionally designed pottery of Muslim origin.[9] With the new polychrome techniques, initially scarce and expensive, ornamental subject matter of Classical origin reappeared. Frequently used motifs were acanthus leaves, cherubim, griffins, grotesques, and fruit garlands (see fig. 3.4).

Diamond points and volutes were common. The *istoriato* style was utilized with a decorative technique for tiles that employed a stencil with perforated lines (*estarcido*). In the sixteenth century, the printing press made an important contribution to the distribution of designs through the production of prints of popular subjects. Potters acquired prints that allowed them to copy religious, allegorical, historical, and mythological scenes, along with all sorts of intricate patterns. Although medieval life remained basically unchanged until the middle of the sixteenth century, a slow, subtle shift in home decoration was initiated. Rooms (*estancias*) began to have specific functions and acquired a certain warmth. Rugs were placed on floors. Retablos were replaced by canvases. Walls were decorated with tapestries, curtains, and Cordovan or embossed leatherwork (*guadamaciles*). In fact, tile murals depicting figurative scenes and botanical or geometric motifs were a cheaper alternative form of decoration and better suited to the high temperatures of the warmer areas of Europe.

The introduction of Renaissance trends in Spain took place through different channels. One was the settlement, beginning in the sixteenth century, of Italian potters in Aragón and Cataluña, as well as in the cities of Talavera and Sevilla. The ceramic industry in the latter erupted in the sixteenth century, after the discovery of the Americas, when it acquired a commercial monopoly and became the most important port in Europe. Churches and palaces were built with dados (*zócalos*) and floors surfaced with tiles using the Islamic mold technique called *arista* or *cuenca* (fig. 2.11). These tiles were also exported to the New World. Another conduit for the arrival of Renaissance trends was the importation of Italian table- and kitchenwares, which arrived in massive quantities through the Mediterranean ports of Barcelona and Valencia (see figs. 1.9 and 1.10 for sixteenth-century Spanish ceramics based on Italian models). The third and last path was through Flemish potters,

2.11 Tiles / *Azulejos*
Sevilla, 16th century
Arista, or *cuenca*, technique. Museu de Ceràmica, Barcelona
Photo by Guillém Fernández
In this technique, colors were divided by small ridges of clay, which kept the glazes from running.

who founded their workshops in Talavera de la Reina and worked in the Italian style.

One way to learn about Spanish domestic ceramic goods of the Renaissance era has been through the study of merchandise exported to the American colonies, systematically recorded in item inventories starting in the year 1520. Daily life in Latin America could be considered a mirror of that in Spanish metropolitan societies. Ceramic objects competed with those made out of metals such as tin, pewter, or silver and were cheaper, more decorative, and hygienic. Common ceramics were exported for use in the storage of grain, honey, and jam, but ceramic kitchen utensils were not, because merchants did not find them as profitable as metal implements. Inventories also list small quantities of storage jars (tinajas), pharmacy jars (botes) and basins (lebrillos) of different sizes, urns (*tarros*), squat jars (*orzas*), pitchers (cántaros), mortars, cruets, cooking pots, and casserole dishes. Prices for these wares were listed, as were the ingredients they held. Chamber pots, perfume bottles, and small handleless cups (*búcaros*) to cool water were also made out of varnished clay, as were baptismal fonts and holy-water stoups. Tin-glazed tableware was sold in greater quantities. Sets included different size plates, porringers, jars (*jarros*), sauceboats, and saltcellars from Valencia, Talavera, Sevilla, and Italy. The items were packed and transported in baskets, hampers, or boxes. Inventories also mention white and yellow loza, which is undoubtedly a reference to a form of lusterware from Sevilla of a lesser quality.[10]

Baroque, Rococo, and Neoclassicism (Seventeenth to Nineteenth Centuries)

Baroque

During the seventeenth century, the concept of luxury and interior decorating was further developed. Villas and palaces became elegant places for social events. The proprietors converted their sitting rooms, patios, studies, and assembly rooms into comfortable spaces where balls, official receptions, and banquets were held. These residences were in fact theaters for the social activities of the times. The Baroque epoch was the age of three great monarchies—-France, England, and Spain. For Spain it was to become known as El Siglo de Oro—The Golden Age. The population, which was becoming more and more fashion conscious, was not satisfied with locally manufactured objects and ordered furniture, chests, painted glass, tableware, and tortoiseshell items from abroad. It is worthwhile pointing out that Spanish pottery production benefited greatly from the *sumptuary* laws, which prohibited the nobility from manufacturing and using their gold and silver tablewares. When this law was promulgated in 1600 by the duke of Lerma, prime minister to Philip III,[11] Spanish potters began to produce customized tin-glazed wares with emblems for aristocratic families,

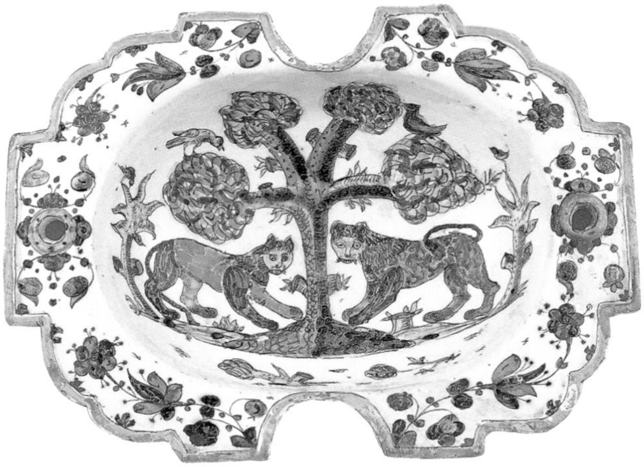

2.12 Barber's Bowl / *Bacía de barbero de doble escotadura*
Villafeliche, Spain, 18th century
Museu de Ceràmica, Barcelona
Photo by Guillém Fernández

religious orders, and the royal palace; this in spite of the fact that their clientele considered the pottery inferior and suitable only for the lower classes. Tirso de Molina (1564–1648) incorporated this sentiment in his historical comedy *Prudence in Women* (1634). In scene 9, act II, Queen María de Molina speaks to her mayordomo:

> A single goblet of silver
> I will keep for myself today.
> The pottery of Talavera
> costs little and 'tis of clean clay.
> But while a parching thirst
> drives some serf crazy. . .
> caution can never be coerced.
> So see to this then, head attendant,
> that while continues the confrontation
> if from plates of dirt I must now eat
> my land does not meet desecration.[12]

While styles based on curves, the avoidance of straight lines, and ornamental exuberance predominated in other decorative arts, Spanish potters held on to their outmoded technology. They maintained simple styles while focusing their attention on the application of polychrome adornment to their works.

Ceramics and Metalworking

During this period potters fashioned their works using objects of silver and tin as models. One example is the jars with spouts shaped like a mask, pedestal base, and a single spiral handle (Sevilla, latter part of the sixteenth century). This jar was used at table for wine or

2.13 Jar / *Jarrón*
Talavera de la Reina, late 17th century
Serie policroma
Acquired from Luis Plandiura in 1932
Museu de Ceràmica, Barcelona
Photo by Guillém Fernández

water, as well as for personal hygiene. It was reproduced in Manises in the *pardalot* series, in Cataluña in the Escornalbou and transitional series, and in Muel in lusterware. The salver (*salvilla*), of English origin (1660), was a tray mounted on a pedestal used to serve glasses, goblets, or ice cream saucers. It also served as a platter for sweets, pies and cakes, or pyramids of candied fruit. Its use was widespread during the eighteenth century, when it became a standard part of table decoration, supporting towers of fresh fruit or floral arrangements.[13] Cataluña and the cities of Manises, Teruel, and Talavera also reproduced this versatile platter, which became a standard component on tables of the Baroque period. Another item fabricated in emulation of metal vessels was the "barber's bowl." With an opening on the side (in Talavera they were manufactured with two openings), it was derived from metallic versions used in the medical procedure of bloodletting (fig. 2.12).

The gadrooned bowls and jars with twisted handles and masks that were born in the pottery shops of Talavera are noteworthy not only for their substantial size but also for their eye-catching allegorical (*historiada*) embellishments, inspired by ceramics produced in Urbino and Faenza. The vigor of the colors of the Italian ceramics, the high quality of their paste, and the subtle decoration made by well-known painters and experts in the art of perspective, had an aesthetic impact in Spain. Although Spanish pottery did not achieve the same degree of refinement and perfection as its Italian Renaissance counterparts, it is conspicuous for its spontaneity, exuberance of color schemes, and intrinsic popular appeal, which have remained its most alluring characteristics ever since (fig. 2.13).

The square saltcellar with a single concavity or the triangular form with three depressions for salt, pepper, and paprika or nutmeg, are novelties of this century. Ornamented with masks in relief set in the center of each side, they display the most arresting designs of each series. The first of these vessels were made in Talavera and later, during the eighteenth century, were replicated in Aragón (fig. 2.14).

2.14 Spice Holder / *Especiero*
Teruel (Aragón), 18th century
Serie tricolor
Collection of the International Folk Art Foundation
Museum of International Folk Art, (Museum of New Mexico), Santa Fe
Photo by Paul Smutko

The Rhenish custom of furnishing dining rooms with storage cabinets for plates, jars, and platters, has contributed to the preservation of many of these items. A renewed interest in Classical antiquities reinforced the appreciation of symmetry. Therefore, every item was placed on the table according to the balanced *servicio a la francesa,* a disciplined order of arrangement determined by squared pleats in the tablecloth. Each guest had a separate plate, butter knife, spoon, and napkin. The saltcellars, alternating with the sauce boats, platters, and soup tureens, were placed on the table in precise harmony with the candleholders.[14]

Rococo

Throughout the eighteenth century, known as the Age of Enlightenment, the French upper classes enjoyed a sophistication unequaled in any other era and which was emulated by all the courts of Europe. Rococo style predominated in interior decoration and supplanted the aspiration to impress with the desire to please. For that reason, decorative motifs that referred to pleasurable and novel forms of diversion were prevalent. Scenes of gallantry, hunting, music, and rural landscapes, as well as more bizarre subject matter such as mob scenes or *singeries* (where the characters in human situations were simians), were popular decorative themes. Sinuous curves and countercurves, colors accentuated by the addition of gold and white, naturalistic ornamentation inspired by engravings of botanical subjects, and a tendency toward asymmetry are its key characteristics. It was also a period that focused on elegance in dining. Dining areas were built as separate, small, and intimate rooms and were furnished with drop-leaf tables following the English design. Auxiliary furniture, such as the dumbwaiter (*servidor mudo*), was introduced to eliminate the need for servants.

The culinary arts gained greatly in importance. Food and its preparation became an area of investigation (fig. 2.15). Special sauces and sweeteners were added to the cuisine to augment its flavor and yet conserve its original taste. The link between visual pleasure and the savoring of foods was the impetus for the invention of complementary tableware that was sold in large quantities and developed into dinner services. Some of these dinner services would become *surtouts de table.* These groupings of bisque porcelain depicted garden scenes containing white sculptures reminiscent of the ancient sugar figures of the Middle Ages. Along with this crockery came new specialized objects, such as mustard holders, butter dishes, fruit juice pitchers, coolers for bottles and goblets, stands for chocolate cups, soup tureens, and platters for fruit and flower arrangements. At this time the ostentation of the credenza from earlier times was relocated to the surface of the table.[15]

The most radical change in Spanish pottery took place at the beginning of the eighteenth century, with the importation of French fashions and social customs by Philip V, first Spanish Bourbon king. In addition to the decorative objects, textiles, carriages, paintings, and tableware introduced from France, there came dances, *fiestas*, and theatrical representations. Vintage wines, liqueurs, crystallized fruit, and other specialized food and drink contributed to the spread of the vogues that flourished in Versailles, the city that set trends in fashion for all of Europe. At the same time, a transformation was experienced in architecture and interior decoration that gave priority to smaller, cozier rooms that could be accessed directly instead of having to pass through another room. The result was a luxurious, comfortable, and more intimate atmosphere within the home. Each room was reserved for a particular activity and hence was decorated with distinctive furniture appropriate for a specific function. Walls previously covered with painted skins or embossed painted leather murals (*guadameciles*), were replaced by Damask fabrics, ornamented paper, and murals on canvas that portrayed landscapes, religious scenes, imitation marble, and floral patterns.

This interior decor was noted for *trampantojo,* or trompe l'oeil, an effect to which eighteenth-century European society was greatly attached. Ceramics also were influenced by period changes in artistic preferences. Valencia tiles were now used not only to decorate dados (zócalos) but also entire walls of palaces, in the form of depictions of courtesan life, hunting, and *chinoiseries.* Ornamentation in kitchens faithfully detailed domestic scenes that today are of great anthropological value (see figs. 3.13, Intro.19).

2.15 Tapestry / *Tapiz*
Real Fábrica de Tapices Santa Bárbara, Madrid, ca. 1780
Patrimonio Nacional, Madrid
Based on design by Francisco Bayeu

Alcora and Luxury Ceramics

European nobles were not only collectors of luxury objects but also patrons and founders of centers dedicated to the manufacture of such objects. Significant among these was the factory of Alcora, founded by the ninth count of Aranda in 1727. It was the first ceramics factory in Spain in which—as at Meissen—the work was conducted in specialized departments, coordinated by directors who chose their Spanish staff from the factory's apprentice school. Since the first artists were French, emigrants from Moustiers and Marseille, initial pottery production was indistinguishable from that of Provençal. As time went on, however, these same artists began to imitate and incorporate Spanish styles and ended up with products rooted in the creativity of the country they now inhabited. The Alcora factory, which had sophisticated manufacturing equipment, diligently investigated various processes of fabrication, in the hopes of discovering the secret of porcelain. Although the porcelain process eluded them, their efforts nevertheless were rewarded when they obtained superior quality clay, well purified white glaze, and a large decorative repertoire inspired by foreign models. In this era, concepts of functionality and ornamentation were closely linked: objects had to be beautiful as well as practical.

The workrooms were lit by candelabras consisting of multiple branches, suspended from the ceiling. However, for a more intimate and informal environment, other forms of illumination were sought. Candles in candleholders were the solution, with the latter constructed in pairs or in series. They were placed on consoles, cupboards, desks, or tables. In Alcora, aside from metalworkers' designs, sculptural models were also used for the creation of these objects. Ornamental plaques used to adorn drawing rooms and studios were sometimes signed in a diminutive script by the factory's most famous artists. They drew upon topics in vogue at the time for ornamental inspiration. Many of these were based on mythological, allegorical, religious, and historical themes copied from engravings.

Given that the eighteenth century is known as the century of gastronomy, the dining area became one of the key rooms in the household. Entry into the room was intended to be spectacular for the guest. Incense burners or vessels with aromatic fragrances were situated in the corners of the room (to mask pungent odors stemming from inadequately preserved food). Wash basins and cisterns for the cleansing of hands before and after meals were positioned near the door. The table was elegantly set with a long tablecloth that reached the floor, highlighting the carefully placed pleats. The servicio a la francesa, observed until the middle of the nineteenth century, dictated that platters, soup tureens, and plates be meticulously arranged when the guests entered the dining room. Ceramic sauceboats, copies of objects forged by silversmiths, and spice or condiment trays were never amiss. Salt, pepper, paprika, vanilla, and cinnamon were some of the condiments used at table, along with aromatic herbs, cultivated in patios and the surroundings of the palaces and castles. For use on honeyed fruit and fruit salads, sugar casters in the form of balustrades were used. These were also imitations of silver and silver gilt vessels.

2.16 Trick Plate / *Plato de engaño*
Alcora (Valencia), 18th century
Museu de Ceràmica, Barcelona
Photo by Guillém Fernández

The beverage attendant was in charge of serving and keeping water and wine cold; bottles and goblets were kept in containers especially designed for cooling. One kind of item used for the ornamentation of the dining room was the *plato de engaño* (fig. 2.16). This vessel was decorated with ceramic sculptures of fruits, vegetables, or reptiles, whose images in relief were surprisingly realistic. These ornamental pieces demonstrate the interest of eighteenth-century society in nature, as well as its affection for surprise, fantasy, and optical illusion. Toward the end of the century, sets of dishes including soup tureens, sauceboats, and spice containers were produced with zoomorphic forms. These vessels, in the shape of sheep, lions, partridges, ducks, and roosters were called "Alcora fauna" and were imitated by craftsmen in Cataluña. The fondness of the affluent for recreating the popular ambiance of the poorer classes and dressing themselves as *majos*, (i.e. in provincial dress) is also reflected in the popularization of the tableware of the last decades of the eighteenth century, which shared its existence with refined productions of soft-paste porcelain. This material, emblem of the Rococo style in France and Germany, was indispensable for the imported drinks in fashion at that time: coffee (from the Near East), tea (from West Asia) and chocolate (from Central America). These heated drinks, first appreciated for their therapeutic qualities, by the beginning of the seventeenth century had became sophisticated and expensive beverages. As they became more fashionable, porcelain became more important, because it was the best material available for withstanding high temperatures. The first silver teapot was fabricated in England (1670), and the production of porcelain teapots, introduced at Meissen, was rapidly copied by manufacturing centers throughout Europe. Alcora and Buen Retiro were the only Spanish pottery factories that were able to produce them, since they were knowledgeable in the techniques of producing French-style soft-paste porcelain. It is interesting to note that some of the saucers in these Spanish tea sets had a raised rim similar to those produced at Sèvres. This design conformed to French etiquette, which allowed the practice of pouring hot tea into a saucer and then sipping from it.

2.17 Chocolate Cup and Saucer / *Mancerina con jícara*
Alcora (Valencia), 1735–1760
Serie de chinescos
Museu de Ceràmica, Barcelona
Photo by Guillém Fernández

Chocolate consumption was one of the customs of the eighteenth century encouraged, in particular, by King Carlos III. He was so fond of this beverage that in the kitchen of his palace a pot with the capacity for 23 kilograms of cacao was used to brew it daily.[16] The Alcora factory was the only fabricator of the single truly genuine Spanish piece of hollowware. It was the *mancerina,* a server specially designed to hold the *jícaras,* small handleless cups for the hot chocolate (fig. 2.17). Don Pedro Álvarez de Toledo, marquis of Mancera and viceroy of Peru between 1639 and 1648, designed with the help of his metalsmith a plate that had a small ring, whose function was to prevent the chocolate from spilling from the jícara.[17] Although the silver mancerinas had circular forms decorated with garlands, the Alcora ceramic models took on the shape of shells, grapevine leaves, or doves (in Talavera and Teruel they were made only in the shape of shells). The consumption of chocolate, like that of tobacco, became a habit that Spaniards of all social classes soon became

2.18 *The Chocolate Hour*
Drawing by
Manuel Tramullas,
ca. 1760–1770
Museo de Arte de
Cataluña, Barcelona

2.19 *La Chocolatada*
Workshop of Lorenzo Passoles, Barcelona, 1710 (detail)
From the estate of Marqués de Castellvell in Alella
Museu de Ceràmica, Barcelona
Photo by Guillém Fernández

addicted to (figs. 2.18, 2.19). Francisco de Quevedo wrote in *The Guest, the Lady and the Tattletale*, "There arrived the Chocolate and the Tobacco Devils, whom although I had suspicions, never thought were really devils. They said that they had taken their revenge on Spain on behalf of the Indies [America] since they did more evil when they introduced into Spain powders, smoke, chocolate cups [jícaras] and the chocolate whippers than all the evil done by The Catholic King, Columbus and Cortés combined." Numerous recipes providing the proportions for sugar and other spices to be mixed with cacao are found in travel books about Spain in that era (see also chapter 11).[18]

Initially, chewing tobacco, which was imported by Columbus from the Americas, was considered in bad taste. However, halfway through the seventeenth century it became an enjoyable pastime among European courtesans. This change was the impetus for pottery and porcelain makers to produce not only tobacco flasks for the ground tobacco but also containers for tobacco leaves and pipes, with their accompanying holders.[19] The young Queen María Amalia de Sajonia is supposed to have savored tobacco for the first time on the day of her wedding and developed such a taste for it that she became addicted to cigars.

Among the 303 different forms of ceramics produced in Alcora, those associated with botanic purposes particularly stand out, especially pots and flower stands intended for the beautification of interiors with flowers. Country estates had become popular among the aristocrats who had their own orchards and gardens, which they allowed to grow freely. They built nurseries where they raised and studied exotic plants brought from abroad. The first botanical treatises illustrated with engravings were published at this time, and they became sources for the models used in floral decoration. For offices and libraries, portable writing sets were manufactured, with ceramic blotters containing sand, ink, and compartments for the pens. The oldest samples date back to the fifteenth century, although only two specimens with the characteristic green and purple decoration of Teruel have survived; they were abundant during the eighteenth century (fig. 2.20). The first productions from Alcora, Talavera, Teruel, and Sevilla kept the basic rectilinear form. However, during the last two decades, complex models with two and three levels were fabricated in Alcora. These portable writing sets were sold with matching pieces such as candleholders, clock boxes, or racks for the pens.

Social decorum, travel, dietary customs, hygiene habits, modes of dress, and production of consumer goods in Spanish society all were modified under French influence. Objects produced for use in the dressing room included sets consisting of compacts, perfume bottles, wig stands, soap holders, wash basins, spittoons, jars in the shape of an inverted Greek helmet (modeled after works of the Renaissance silversmiths), bowls for shaving, and boxes for combs, sponges, and artificial beauty spots, worn to stress the whiteness of the skin and to hide smallpox scars.[20] There are numerous specimens of "Dompedro,"

2.20
Writing Set / *Escribanía*
Alcora (Valencia), 1749–1798
Serie de las flores naturalistas
Museu de Ceràmica, Barcelona
Photo by Guillém Fernández

cylindrical chamber pots with a wide, flat rim and two handles on the upper section. During the Middle Ages, these objects were fabricated with red clay and glazed on the interior. Later they were ornamented to correspond with other objects designed for personal hygiene.

Products from Alcora became popular throughout the country and in France, Portugal, and Italy as well. Other pottery factories in Spain soon produced popular versions of the commercially successful series. In Manises, Cataluña, Talavera, and Teruel, objects with borders decorated in the delicate point lace style known as Berain were reproduced (fig. 2.21). Alcora's *chaparro* series was copied in Talavera and Teruel, while *las flores de ramito* was imitated in Villafeliche and Cataluña. In Sevilla, they copied platters (*fuentes*) decorated with garlands and refined the clays and glazes. The penchant of the times for Asian motifs had an effect on the decoration of tiles in Valencia and on the pottery of Sevilla. The high quality of the pottery from Alcora and its tremendous acceptance by the upper classes was a catalyst for renewed interest in the loza created in family-run workshops throughout Spain. Although these smaller facilities were not able to reach the same degree of technical perfection, they nevertheless did reinvigorate their production.

2.21 Plate / *Plato*
Alcora (Valencia), 1727–1749
Serie Berain
Museu de Ceràmica, Barcelona
Photo by Guillém Fernández
This plate illustrates the style that became popular in France through the engravings of Jean Berain, artist and decorator at the French Court. The blue-and-white Berain pattern is characterized by its lace-like edging and the vertical orientation of the painted design.

Ceramics and Religion

All Spanish pottery centers, without exception, manufactured holy-water stoups in great quantities. These were placed in bedrooms, next to the bed, so that people could dip their fingers into the blessed water and make the sign of the cross before going to sleep. The types made in Aragón, intended for a less demanding clientele, were the simplest. They were decorated with themes of Christ, the Deesis, or the Virgin, and after the seventeenth century, they were executed in relief.[21] In Manises and Cataluña, lusterware fonts with triangular pediments, molded columns, and gadrooned semispherical reservoirs were made (from the sixteenth to eighteenth centuries). The fonts of Talavera, Puente del Arzobispo, Sevilla, and Alcora stand out for the vivid polychrome applied to religious themes, either painted or in bas-relief (see fig. 1.12).

Neoclassicism

The arts of the nineteenth century encompassed a wide range of styles, from those of Imperial France (disseminated during the reign of

Napoleon), to those evoked by the treasures of the Classical world. It was an eclectic century in its political as well as its artistic history, which began with the reintroduction of the canons of Classical art rediscovered in the middle of the eighteenth century. Spain, like the rest of Europe, was enthralled by the archaeological discoveries in Pompeii and Herculaneum (1750), sponsored by Carlos III, King of Naples and Sicily. In these two ancient towns, houses were excavated with interior decor still intact, with immediate consequences for the decoration of European homes. The soft-paste porcelain products manufactured in Alcora, Buen Retiro (1760–1808), Moncloa (1817–50) and Pasajes (1857–78) were the only ones that embodied all the characteristics of the newly recognized styles, which indicated a return to the appreciation of "quality": notably, the predominance of straight lines over curves, severity and austerity of forms and decorations, and pale colors.

Spanish potters continued their production of traditional wares decorated with contemporary themes, but in a less elaborate manner more acceptable to a public with limited resources. The quality of clays, enamels, and decorations declined with the lack of artistic incentives in the absence of a critical clientele. The pottery workshops of Manises were the ones that most expanded their artistic capabilities during this period. From these factories emerged huge covered jars, octagonal dishes called *platillos* for serving sweets, and table- and kitchenware rich in color and painted for the most part by women. These vessels were adorned with vegetal themes, suns, and coarsely molded feminine figures. Women who were going to get married decorated their own objects, known as "idyllic wares," in which they represented themselves next to their fiancés. Religious objects were copious and diverse, such as holy-water stoups in the form of tabernacles with monstrances, Calvary scenes, and Virgins flanked by columns and Atlas figures, profusely ornamented with tiny flowers and birds in relief. Due to the special reverence that people in Manises held for the Holy Sacrament, monstrances sometimes as high as 65cm (25.5 in.) were produced for domestic altars. These were glazed in yellow, the color that most resembled gold. They consisted of several pieces joined together and ornamented with many details in relief alluding to the Passion of Christ.[22] In Talavera, Alcora, and Aragón, tombstones of mayólica with the names and dates of the deceased were manufactured on request, as were large numbers of holy-water fonts for bedrooms. Patriotic themes alluding to the victory of Fernando VII over the French were frequently made in Talavera and Puente del Arzobispo (see fig. 1.20).

In Sevilla, motifs dealing with bullfighting and hunting were abundant and were often applied on large ornamental vessels and tiles used to decorate stair risers. In Aragón as well as Cataluña, pottery characteristic of each center continued to be produced but was of a lesser quality than that manufactured in previous centuries.

Traditionally manufactured ceramics did not disappear completely, but their number decreased considerably, due to the establishment of factories dedicated to the production of tablewares that imitated patterns utilizing British transferwares. Their cost was reasonable and their production was much more economical than that of hand-painted wares. Factories such as Sargadelos (1806–75), Pikman y Compañía (later la Cartuja de Sevilla, 1839), Busturia (1842–55), Cartagena (1843–93), and Valdemorillo (1845–1915) sprang up along with others of lesser importance. They produced products with white earthenware (*tierra de pipa*) and copied the British Neorococo porcelain wares, typical of the second half of the nineteenth century.

Historicism and Neopopulism (Late Nineteenth and Early Twentieth Centuries)

The last quarter of the nineteenth century was a period of adaptation for all artistic styles and marked the production of ceramics that replicated the most important types of the Middle Ages. The brothers Daniel, Guillermo, and Germán Zuloaga, upon reopening the Real Fábrica de Moncloa (1874–92), dedicated their efforts to the manufacture of large jars, plates, and tile friezes for the decoration of interiors. Their creations were based on styles popular during medieval, Hispano-Moresque, and Renaissance periods. Reproductions of Manises-style lusterware stand out for their striking technical perfection. The Persian pieces in the Minai series, ornamented by the Islamic *cuerda seca* method and with reliefs following the Lucca della Robbia style, are other examples of their mastery. Coinciding with the birth of the Art Nouveau movement (1890–1920) and the outburst of industrialization was the special significance given to the production of historical ceramics that were integrated into the facades and interiors of buildings, along with colored glasswork and wrought iron. Ornamental jars in the style of those of the Alhambra of Granada and dados of arista-style tiles formed part of the interior design of a home, along with marble and porcelain sculptures, mosaics, and transferwares (see fig. 1.22).

Traditional mayólica had practically lost its domestic function and was essentially relegated to

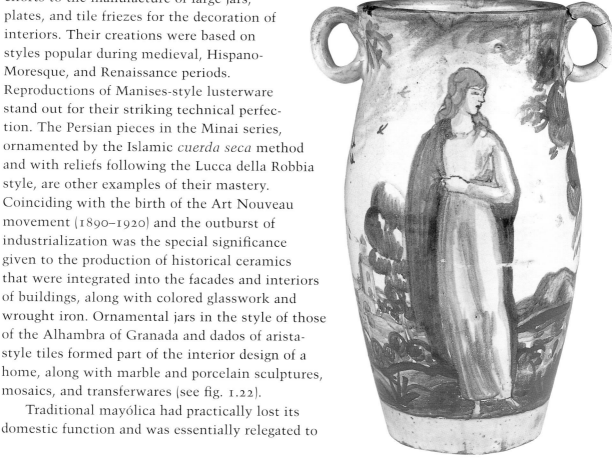

2.22 Jar / *Jarro*
Xavier Nogués (1873–1941), Barcelona, ca. 1930
Museu de Ceràmica, Barcelona
Acquired from Isabel Escalada, widow of Xavier Nogués, in 1967
Photo by Guillém Fernández

kitchen use. It was not until the idealists of the Novocentista movement of Cataluña (1911–30) began searching for their roots, and a corresponding renewal of interest in popular artistic expertise in Sevilla was born, that this form of pottery was temporarily liberated from oblivion. Famous artists of the times were hired by factories to decorate tableware, tiles, and jugs of popular styles, using traditional techniques and pigments (fig. 2.22). These specimens shed superfluous and elaborate decorative elements and were, as in earlier times, basic, practical and austere.

Since the outset of the decade of the 1940s, loza manufacturing has survived through its production of ornamental rather than functional objects. Lacking genuine domestic uses for their products, contemporary potters, without providing innovations to their craft, have been reduced to repeating models of the eighteenth and nineteenth centuries, recreating the forms, splendor, and polychromatic traditions of their predecessors in Spanish ceramics.

Notes

1. N. Seseña, *Los disparates de la comisaria: Vida cotidiana en tiempos de Goya* (Madrid: Sociedad Estatal Goya, 1996), pp.12–14.
2. José Gestoso y Pérez, *Historia de los barros vidriados sevillanos*(Sevilla, 1903), pp.140–43.
3. Mónica Piera and A. Mestres, *El moble català* (Barcelona: Angle, 1999), pp.27–33.
4. Since the Classical period of the Greeks, medicinal benefits have been ascribed to the consumption of olive oil. It has also been touted for its flavorsome and tonic qualities. During Roman times in rural areas, olives were an essential part of the diet. In the most cultured circles of Italy, olives from Spain were imported, because they were considered to be much more flavorful. Texts on agriculture, recipes, and medical advice from al-Andalus are plentiful. These manuscripts offer various ways of preserving and seasoning olives with salt, thyme, oregano, and ginger; ingredients that from early times have been included in the Mediterranean diet.
5. E. García Sánchez, "El consumo de aceite de oliva y otras grasas vegetales en Al Andalus," in *La Mediterrània, àrea de convergència de sistemes alimentaris* (Palma de Mallorca: Institut d'Estudis Balears, 1995), pp.19–24
6. Julia Beltrán de Heredia, *Terminologia i ús dels atuells ceràmics de cuina a la baixa Edat Mitjana: Del rebost a la taula, cuina i menjar a la Barcelona gótica* (Barcelona: Electa, 1995), pp.50–57.
7. María Antonia Casanovas, *Colección de botes y morteros farmacéuticos* (Barcelona: Laboratorios Novartis, 2000), pp. 5–7.
8. A.A.V.V., *Le dressoir du prince: Service d'apparat à la Rennaissance* (Paris: Réunion des Musées Nationaux, 1996).
9. María Antonia Casanovas, "Cerámica arquitectónica catalana de época medieval y renacentista," in *La ruta de la cerámica* (Castellón: Diputación de Castellón, 2000), pp.72–75.
10. José M. Sánchez, *La cerámica exportada a América en el siglo XVI a través de la documentación del Archivo General de Indias 2: Ajuares domésticos y cerámica cultural y laboral* (Sevilla: Publicaciones de la Universidad de Sevilla, Laboratoria de Arte, Departamento de Historia del Arte, no. 11, 1998), pp.121–33.

11. Don Juan Sempere y Guariños, *Historia del luxo y de las leyes suntuarias de España*, vols. 1 and 2. Facsimile ed. (Madrid: Atlas, 1973).
12. Con un solo vaso de plata / He de quedarme este dia / Vajillas de Talavera / Son limpias y cuestan poco / Mientras la codicia fuera / Vuelve a algún vasallo loco / Nunca la prudencia yerra / Haced esto mayordomo / Que mientras dura la guerra / Si en platos de tierra como / No se destruirá mi tierra.
13. A.A.V.V., *Objets civiles domestiques* (Paris: Imprimerie Nationale, 1984).
14. Zeev Gourarier, *Arts et manières de Table en Occident, des origines à nos jours* ed. by Gérard Klopp (Thionville, 1994), p.137.
15. Ibid., p.151.
16. María Emilia González Sevilla, *A la mesa con los reyes de España: Curiosidades y anécdotas de la cocina de palacio* (Madrid: Ediciones Temas de Hoy, 1998).
17. Manuel González Martí, *Mancerinas* (Faenza, 1956).
18. Pérez Samper, "La integración de los productos americanos en los sistemas alimentarios mediterráneos," in *La Mediterrània, àrea de convergència de sistemes alimentaris* (Palma de Mallorca: Institut d'Estudis Balears, 1995).
19. Roger Mc Ilroy, *Tabaco y rapé: Técnicas de los grandes maestros de alfarería y cerámica*. 2d ed. (Madrid: Herman Blume, 1985), p.183.
20. María Antonia Casanovas, *La manufactura de Alcora: Innovaciones técnicas y primicias artísticas*. Offprint from *El conde de Aranda y su tiempo* (Zaragoza: Institución Fernando el Católico [CSIC], 2000), pp. 463–77.
21. María Isabel Álvaro Zamora, *Cerámica aragonesa*. 2 vols. (Zaragoza: Pórtico, 1976 and 1978), p.68.
22. M. Paz Soler, *Historia de la cerámica valenciana*, vol. 4 (Valencia: Vicente García, 1987 and 1988), pp.21–29.

Detail, Fig. 3.3a

3

The Use of Spanish Ceramics in Architecture

MARÍA PAZ SOLER FERRER

GLAZED TILE IS undoubtedly the ceramic form most frequently employed in architecture. It has an eminently decorative character and is used to veneer baked brick, the basic element in building construction. Other ceramic objects are incorporated as embellishing components, but it is tile that is most often used to beautify both the exterior and interior of buildings.

Before the Muslim invasion of Spain in the year 711, ceramics had been utilized in Spain in structural design in the form of unglazed bricks, mosaic pieces, roofing tiles, water channels, eaves, etc. However, the introduction of glazed tiles or tiles enameled with metallic oxides was a contribution of Islamic culture. The first European use of such tiles was in Spain, and their use eventually spread throughout the Western world. In the Far East, the implementation of glazed ceramics in architecture dates back to 2700 B.C. The first known example is in the pyramid of Saqqara in Egypt. Other examples from 2494 B.C. are located in Ur, Mesopotamia.

The immediate precursors of decorative tiles in Spain, however, must be sought in North Africa. Among the best known of these is the Kairouan Mosque in Tunisia, where lusterware techniques were prominent. The route by which these tiles eventually reached Spain, through Egypt, Tunisia, and Morocco, undoubtedly began in Iraq.

Middle Ages

The Almohad invaders from North Africa are responsible for the dissemination of methods of manufacturing glazed tile. Due to the almost complete absence of written records, we must rely on manuscripts produced, for the most part, centuries after the creation of the tiles, as well as on archaeological discoveries and extremely rare surviving examples.

The earliest certain date for mayólica tile is the twelfth century and refers to incomplete specimens rather than complete facings. The first type that we find is the *alicer*, or *alicatado*, initially utilized as isolated panels and later assembled to form entire dados or wainscots, water tanks, fountains, water channels, ornate portals, etc. The alicer is a single colored piece of tile, cut to its desired shape from a large square or rectangle. Usual shapes are rhombuses, rectangles, arrows (*cola de Milano*), stars, and other geometric figures that fit together perfectly in innumerable combinations (see fig. 2.1).

These decorative combinations became more intricate as time went on. Producing such a tiled surface was a complex task requiring great manual dexterity. First, an outline was traced of the complete panel, generally with the aid of a compass, a setsquare, and a ruler; then it was colored, forming stylized designs within polygons of varying complexity (*lazos de a cuatro, de a seis,* etc.) This drawing was then transferred to larger enameled tiles according to the corresponding colors of the sketched original. Once this was accomplished, the geometric forms were cut, using a hammer and a pin punch to follow the traced outline. A file was used to smooth rough edges. The cut pieces were then reassembled on top of the original pattern, glazed side down. If the panel was destined to be mounted on a wall, a layer of plaster was poured on the inverted side. Lime mortar was used to form a solid backing for the tiles if they were intended for use as flooring. Once the cast was hardened, the panel was turned over and affixed to its desired place. The installation process also required highly skilled artisans, usually from the same factories that had fabricated the tiles.[1]

In this early era of aliceres, curved tile disks were inserted between bricks to accentuate details in the decoration. Dating from the thirteenth century this type of ornamental tile is found in the Torre del Oro in Sevilla, the Tower of San Sebastián in Ronda (Málaga), and the Puerta de Armas in the Alhambra, Granada. In all these buildings and later in the Mudéjar towers of Aragón, tin-glazed components served to enhance the lattice pattern accomplished by means of an intricate arrangement of bricks embellished with lace-like plastering (*yesería*). Most of the buildings that have survived from the period were decorated in this manner.

The range of colors was limited, due to the fact that some of the oxides later utilized for formulating pigments were not available, and the technology to apply them to ceramics had not yet evolved. The colors applied to these designs were manganese black, purple, or brown; yellow from antimony; amber created from a base of lead and iron; and copper green (the hues of which varied depending on the base with which it was mixed). Cobalt gave blue, and tin was used for white. The tonalities of these colors varied according to the region, and we find, for example, that the spectrum of colors produced in Aragón tended to be more somber than that of Andalucía.

3.1 St. Martin's Tower / *Torre de San Martín*
Teruel, ca. 1315
Photo by J. Escudero

Towers from thirteenth-century Aragón still reveal signs of this early form of construction using aliceres, disks, column shafts, and curiously, whole plates inserted into wall facings. Some of the earliest examples of this architecture are the Tower of Santo Domingo, in Daroca, and the towers of Santa María and San Miguel, in Belmonte de Gracián, but the best known edifices are those in Teruel, San Martín (fig. 3.1), and Santa María de Mediavilla. In succeeding centuries we find richer examples of this tradition in ornate structural designs that continued up until the expulsion of the *Moriscos* in the mid-seventeenth century. Perhaps the most interesting feature to be found in buildings in this part of Spain during the thirteenth and fourteenth centuries is the incorporation of plates of fine domestic tableware as decorative adjuncts, just as was done during the same period in Italy, where the famous *bacini* were set into the facades of bell towers, churches, convents, and some public buildings.[2]

Surviving friezes of aliceres that have been restored are numerous. For example, all through the palace and gardens of the Alhambra there are

3.2 Tile Mosaic / *Aliceres*
La Alhambra, Granada,
13th century
Photo courtesy
of La Alhambra

collections of tiled panels (fig. 3.2). A Christian work dating from the fourteenth century survives in the Alcázar of Sevilla, and a thirteenth-century example is in the Cuarto Real de Santo Domingo, in Granada.

Over time, the complex production of aliceres was simplified, first by the use of molds of different shapes and later by employing tiles decorated with the *cuenca*, or *arista*, techniques, by which geometric drawings were traced on the unbaked tiles by means of a mold that left a slight relief (see fig. 2.11). Each portion of the drawing was then filled in with an oxide. The small ridge left by the mold prevented the different colors from mixing. This is the same technique used for champlevé enamel. Once the tiles were fired, the panel appeared to be composed of several differently shaped pieces. In reality, it was composed of square or rectangular tiles whose colors were separated by dividers of clay.

The Christian World

As the fourteenth century drew to a close, in Valencia, and specifically in Manises, a new type of tile was produced, in an almost industrially organized manner. The Hispano-Moresque world had already used this type of tile, although in limited quantities. The new wave of large-scale production coincided with the increased demand for tableware and domestic ceramics, which were beginning to be exported to other sites within the kingdom of Aragón. In the early decades of the fourteenth century, some individual examples of green and purple tiles appear. These were similar to the tableware then in daily use, but their novelty lay in the application of cobalt beneath, and sometimes on top of, the creamy white tin oxide finish. In these rectangular (14 by 19 cm) tiles with an iconographic repertoire strongly connected to the Islamic world, we see the use of Persian-style pineapples; symmetrically facing peacocks; the *hom*, or tree of life; the keys of Paradise; four axes emerging from the center of the tile and vanishing in the corners, representing the four rivers whose source is the center of that same Paradise and which flow through all of Eden. All these motifs were permeated by a rich array of symbolic associations not always explicitly expressed.

Such tiles were almost exclusively used in flooring, although rarely was the entire floor made up of tin-glazed tiles. The usual custom was to combine them with unglazed bricks or with stucco (fig. 3.3a). Sometimes an unglazed bisqued tile had a groove in the center for the insertion of glazed tile. Straight lines were avoided, and a preference was shown for patterns of lozenges and combinations of square and hexagonal forms. In this way, with a great economy of means, a very pleasing visual effect was created. Islamic influence continued to be present, since most of the artisans who produced these pieces were Muslims, although their clients were Christians.

No entire tile flooring arrangement has survived from the fifteenth century, but some survive from the sixteenth. Moreover, we have indirect testimony through many Gothic paintings of the times, in which they are reproduced in minute detail (fig. 3.3b). In the fifteenth century, hexagonal tiles, now commonly known as *alfardones*, are found along with square tiles of varying sizes.

The fifteenth-century iconographical repertoire was copious. On one hand we have tile

3.3a Gothic Flooring / *Suelo gótica*
Hall in the Segorbe Cathedral, Manises, ca. 1440
Photo by Paco Alcántara

3.3b *The Prophet Isaiah*
Joan Reixach, ca. 1460
Oil on wood showing Gothic flooring
Museo de Bellas Artes de Valencia, Valencia
Photo by Paco Alcántara

series that present vegetal themes, geometric themes, or common slogans, produced indiscriminately for any customer. On the other hand, there are those that were custom made, following particular patterns provided by the client. These normally involved names, coats of arms, emblems for monasteries or guilds, or depictions of medieval legends related to a family.

Custom floors, such as that made for King Alfonzo V for his Castel Nuovo de Napoles and for his royal castle in Valencia, had complete iconographic programs, often with a political agenda, praising the king and his accomplishments.[3] Carlos III of Navarra also ordered similar works for his castle in Olite. People of lesser means emulated this fashion. Convents, for example, wanted emblems of their order or their abbesses. Guilds of artisans, who during the Middle Ages enjoyed great prestige, constructed chapels or headquarters with floorings that displayed their insignias, such as a card and a pair of scissors for wool workers' guilds, a horseshoe for blacksmiths, woolen caps for hat makers, and a tassel or a silkworm chrysalis for the fringe makers.

These floor tiles were immensely successful. They were much easier to export and above all, much less complicated to apply than the Islamic aliceres. Sometimes orders were placed at Manises. There were also requests for the potters to work at the installation sites, as was the case with Cardinal Audoin for his palace in Avignon or with the Duke of Berry for his royal edifice at Bourges. At times this movement of master tile makers gave birth to new industries in the places where they went to work.[4]

In the late Gothic period, Valencia was unrivaled as the most important tile-producing center. There were other places within the kingdom of Aragón at the close of the fourteenth century and into the fifteenth that manufactured tiles, but their products were of poorer quality and generally only supplied local demands.[5] Catalan ceramics factories imitated Valencian models but had a much darker tone of blue and would frequently apply designs with the use of a stencil. Ceramists in Aragón produced flat tiles in green and purple, but also used blue and a combination of blue and purple. The flooring in the throne room in the palace of La Aljafería de Zaragoza is an outstanding example from the time of the Catholic monarchs Ferdinand and Isabela. In these pieces we find the beginnings of the arista technique that subsequently spread throughout the territory of Aragón.

The Renaissance

One of the first changes that we can authenticate in the Renaissance period is that many works of major importance were signed. Pieces whose designs were more conventional are also identifiable, since there are bills of sale specifying the name of the artist and the destination of the ordered objects. In contrast to the anonymity of the Middle Ages, Renaissance artisans tended to assert themselves and took pride in their creations, which they now frequently signed. The desire for recognition is also evidenced in the proliferation of coats of arms and family trees, a vanity that did not exclude the clergy. As a general rule, geometric drawings gave way to emblems, shields of ancestry, and other symbols of personal or guild-related identity.

Another novel phenomenon was the social recognition granted to some painters who mingled with the aristocracy, and not only as a result of their work. The profile of ceramists had changed. They were no longer the simple artisans who worked in an empirical manner, transmitting their knowledge orally; rather, they were well-informed professionals, versed in the arts of Classical antiquity, the models for Renaissance style. They were people who had traveled and had a cosmopolitan outlook. They were open to new ideas and were familiar with the great artists of the times, whose works were available in printed form. These artisans utilized famous works as models, while at the same time drawing upon their personal knowledge to create their own designs. Moreover, the projects they were contracted to produce for specific places were meticulously studied and analyzed prior to their realization. These works were no longer like the friezes or floorings of the Middle Ages, which embraced a simple, repetitive design. They now were panels whose figures were adapted to the scale of the places where they would be exhibited. For example, if the creation was a retable for an altar, considerable calculations were necessary, taking into account the size of the room, doors, windows, and the angles from which it would be observed. Ceramists now not only had to know the secrets of varnishes and firings, or other technical aspects of the trade, but were also required to be well informed regarding the social and cultural environments in which they now had to interact.

Sevilla was the city that most quickly adopted the Renaissance style, owing to its cosmopolitan character. After the discovery of the Americas, it had exclusive commercial contracts through the Casa de Contratación for trade with the Indies. It grew enormously and became a nucleus of wealth and a magnet for Spaniards as well as for foreign entrepreneurs.

Shortly before the end of the fifteenth century, Francisco Niculoso Pisano established residency in Sevilla. Pisano was an Italian ceramics painter, probably educated in the workshop of Della Robbia. He brought with him Italian methods of manufacture and an iconographic repertoire characteristic of the Italy of that day. Among them were formulas for a very fine, purified white paste with an even coating of paint applied over the tin-based glaze in which the objects were bathed. He expanded the chromatic palette and rendered the familiar blue in

3.4 *The Visitation*
Francisco Niculoso
(el Pisano), 1504
Cuarto de la Reina,
Reales Alcazares,
Sevilla
Photo courtesy of
the Reales Alcazares

chiaroscuro, something never attempted in Hispanic mayólica before this time. But his most important contribution was the development of tiles as a medium for storytelling. His subject matter was almost exclusively religious, and background elements were taken from antiquity—classical architecture, *candelieri* and grotesques popularized following the discovery of the *Domus Aurea*. Other motifs included caryatids, fantasy figures, snakes, and *putti*, along with laurels and garlands of flowers or fruit. All of these were applied in the Classical manner. It is interesting to note that even though Niculoso's style was Italian, his work reflects a certain Flemish influence. For instance, the garments and jewelry with which the characters are attired seem more characteristic of Flemish than Italian paintings.

One of Pisano's earliest and best-known works is the altar scene depicting the Visitation of the Virgin, commissioned by the Catholic monarchs for their private chapel in the Reales Alcázares (fig. 3.4). Another renowned work of exceptional quality is the facade of the Santa Paula monastery in Sevilla, which unites the Gothic arch with Renaissance decorative elements. Both of these works were completed in 1504. His pictorial mastery can be appreciated in the balance of the compositions and the recurring use of architecture as a frame for figures, grotesques, and candelieri. Although his masterpieces are large-scale representations with known figures, he also produced exquisite dados, such as the altar frontal in the church of Tentudia, or the friezes that are preserved at the Museum of Fine Arts in Sevilla. These latter panels exhibit well-known Renaissance themes and stylized floral and vegetal motifs fashioned from four tiles in the formation known as *de a cuatro*.

To this purely Italian style, originally introduced by Niculoso (and known as *pisano*), another style was added that had Renaissance influence, but whose roots were Flemish. It is commonly known, particularly in painting, as the Italo-Flamenco style, and is a mixture of elements from both countries.

The first painter of ceramics of Flemish origin about whom we have information is Jan Floris. Born in Antwerp, and brother of the engraver Cornelis Floris, he emigrated to Spain and established a workshop to produce tiles in Plasencia, in the middle of the sixteenth century. One of his works, signed and dated 1559, is the collection of panels in the church of the nearby town of Garrovillas. His masterly touch is especially notable in the figures of San Pablo and San Andrés. His fame was such that King Phillip II commanded him to move to Talavera and commissioned him to create the tiles for the Alcázar and the palaces of El Pardo and Valsain (Segovia). Floris also worked in Toledo, which continued to be the imperial city of Spain, even though Phillip II moved the royal court to Madrid. It was in Toledo that he completed his work on the chambers of the sovereign in 1565, in the Alcázar Real. The dados were made of tiles from Talavera and the flooring of bricks and tiles manufactured in Toledo.

3.5 Principal Quatrefoil / *Florón principal*
Juan Fernández,
The Escorial, Spain, 1570
Photo by
Robin Farwell Gavin,
2002

When Jan Floris passed away, Juan Fernández, a member of the Loaysa family, known for their fine ceramics, inherited Floris's royal ceramic production responsibilities. Fernández also had a workshop in Talavera and in 1570 received an order for nine thousand tiles for the construction of the Escorial, to be ornamented with a motif called *florón principal* (fig. 3.5). An additional request was then made for two thousand tiles of a type known as *florin arabesco*. They can still be seen in this monastery-palace. The florón principal, or acanthine rosette, design consists of four tiles of equal size; each one exhibits an acanthus leaf that, once they are assembled, forms a complete drawing within a set of borders composed of chains and circles. They are painted in an accented chiaroscuro style, which gives them a three-dimensional appearance, almost as if they were in relief. This design, undoubtedly of Flemish origin, enjoyed great success and was imitated with slight variations in many other regions of Spain. However, the most important extant work of this ceramic master is the altar of a parish church in Candeleda (Ávila). The altar is divided into three sections. The upper part displays the Calvary scene, the middle portion illustrates the Last Supper, and the lower segment exhibits the figures of two evangelists and Saint Zachariah with his son, Saint John. We also know that he owned another workshop, where craftsmen worked on tiles and sculptural pieces for the same monastery.

In the second half of the sixteenth century, there were three major

3.6 Tile walls and benches / *Zócalos y bancos de azulejos*
Cristóbal de Augusta, Cenador de Carlos V, Reales Alcázares, Sevilla, ca. 1543
Photo by M. L. Menéndez

centers producing works of importance: Sevilla, Toledo, and nearby Talavera. Each area had outstanding ceramists, whose styles blended and became more homogeneous, resulting in a differentiation of products not by decorative motifs but by technical factors. For example, Toledo clay is more reddish than that from Sevilla, and the colors from one area are slightly more subdued or more vivid than those of another. In regard to decorative motifs, we have already seen that they continued to intermingle and were utilized indiscriminately by artists from different regions and even different countries. Once a particular design was successful, it was repeated over and over again, either exactly or with slight modifications. Around 1590, influenced by the Herreran style exemplified by the Escorial, tilework tended toward a marked simplicity in decoration, a style that became known as *desornamentado*.

In Sevilla, in the late sixteenth century, the most important workshop was that of Roque Hernández, who produced tiles in the arista technique. In 1561, he became a partner of Francisco Andries, who had already made an altar for the cathedral of Córdoba in pure Flemish style. However, a son-in-law of Hernández, Cristóbal de Augusta, was the most successful of the three. Between 1573 and 1578, he received numerous orders for the Alcázar, in Sevilla. Augusta's creative talents are best exemplified in the wainscots displayed in the chambers of Carlos V (fig. 3.6). These were composed of six alternating, different models, divided by caryatids or allegorical figures, whose principal motifs were large floral patterns (*florones*) interspersed with strapwork patterns (*ferroneries*) and motifs resembling folded parchment, both designs of Flemish origin.

The magnificent ceramic retables achieved wide recognition (fig. 3.7). They replaced the wooden *retablos*, as they were less costly and easier to maintain, but equally beautiful. They are to be found in small parishes in little-known towns or in convents, which normally would not have been able to afford expensive works of art. This accounts for the wide geographic dispersion of these sophisticated pieces, especially in Talavera, Sevilla, and Toledo, three important centers, but also in distant locations such as Valladolid, Priedralabes, Ávila, or Calera de León, in Badajoz.

Sevilla, Toledo, and Talavera reached such a high level of success on the Iberian Peninsula that they exported their products to other areas that had lost touch with the new styles. Early on, Valencia as well as Cataluña turned to Andalucía or Castilla for inspiration when it came to important compositions. It was only later that they began to follow the forms and methods emanating from the major centers, producing objects according to currently popular models and creating their own styles.

The case is somewhat different for Valencia. During the fifteenth century, Valencia had experienced great cultural and economic splendor. After the discovery of the Americas, however, the center of activities moved from the Mediterranean to the Atlantic, and Sevilla became the hub of economic power. Added to this shift in influence and wealth were other factors that benefited Castilla. One of these was the loss of political importance of the kingdoms that composed the crown of Aragón, after the merging of the two monarchies, first under Doña

3.7 Tile Altar Screen / *Retablo de azulejos*
Circle of Juan Fernández, Basilica de la Virgen del Prado, Talavera de la Reina, ca. 1570
Photo by Alberto Moraleda

3.8 Tile Flooring
Alacuás (Valencia),
16th century
Photo by
María Paz Soler
Redona tiles with a
border that gives
the appearance
of a carpet

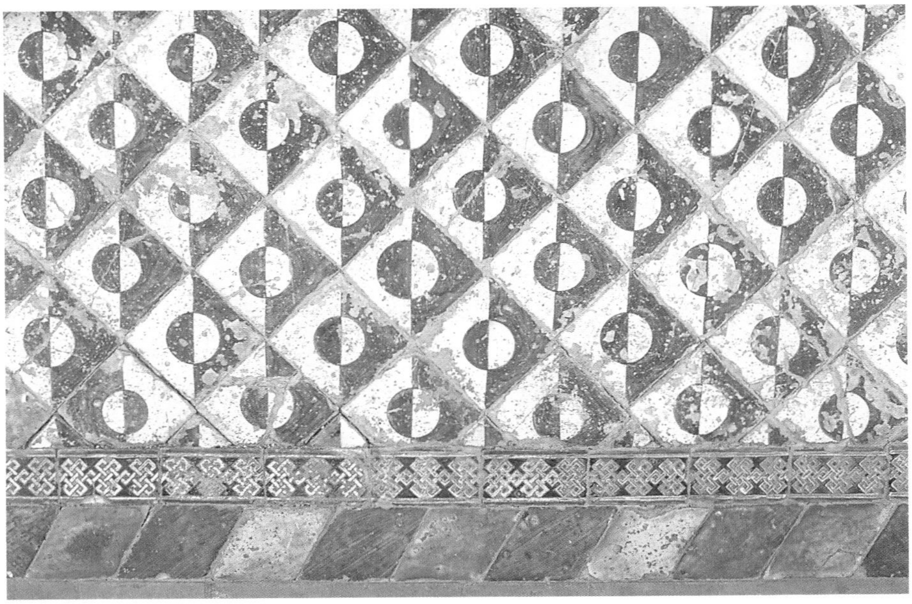

Juana la Loca and immediately afterwards under the emperor Carlos V. Another factor that for many years has been considered the true cause of the decline in the ceramics industry in Valencia was the expulsion of the Meriscos that occurred in 1609. However, when this event took place, ceramic production was no longer exclusively in their hands; many Christians were already engaged in this trade when the decline began. Ultimately, the demise was due more to the lack of vigorous desire on the part of Valencian artisans to evolve and adopt the new trends. They stubbornly clung to a Gothic world, while the major arts were embracing the Renaissance. Because of this, they lost favor in the eyes of the dominant classes, who chose to commission the new styles from other production centers. It was not until the eighteenth and the first half of the nineteenth centuries that production was finally rejuvenated in the city of Valencia and its outskirts.[6]

Until well into the sixteenth century, there was very little change in the styles of Valencia. Only a few designs changed, with a tendency toward the geometricization of patterns that produced the effect of optical illusion (*trampantojo*), as with the Italian work of intaglio in woodcuts. The Borgia pope, Alejandro VI, requisitioned tiles for his son from Valencia; Manises was incapable of filling the order quickly enough. The duke of Gandia complied rapidly with the papal request and also saw to the installation of the tiles in the ducal palace. They bore the well-known coat of arms and papal themes: the bull of the Borgias, the double crown, and the papal umbrella. Also included in this order were models whose style was known as *redona*. These were square tiles divided on the diagonal, one half white and the other blue, and each of these halves had a perimeter also in contrasting blue and white. We find this design not only in the palace of Gandia, but in the castle of Alacuás and other places as well, all constructed in the early part of the sixteenth century (fig. 3.8).[7] This pattern of diagonally separated halves of white and blue, or white and green, was enthusiastically accepted, so much so that from the sixteenth century until modern times, its production has never ceased. A good part of its success is due to the innumerable design combinations that can be created with it.

Regarding the pure Renaissance style, the most significant work that has survived to modern times is the tile veneer in the salon of the Cortes de la Generalitat. While the floor tiles were ordered from Manises, the eye-catching dados were produced outside of Valencia. The three medallions that represent the branches of the Cortes (parliament)—ecclesiastical, military, and political—were manufactured and signed by Oliva, an artisan who operated a workshop in Toledo. His style reveals Flemish influence, especially in the manner in which the figures are encircled by the medallions (fig. 3.9). The rest of the dado, however, was produced by other artists. One of them was Herrando de Santiago, from Sevilla, who had worked in Talavera and on the site of the project in Valencia, in association with the silversmith Juan Elias. (This was not an unusual association, since ceramic pieces were frequently designed by silversmiths.) The same designs found in the panels of the salon of the Cortes appear in the gardens of the Alcázar, in Sevilla. We know that after Santiago left Valencia, he went to work in Toledo, leaving his shop in the hands of a craftsman named Villalba, who after working for a time in Valencia, moved to Sevilla. This relocation of ceramists was a constant occurrence.

Another exemplary Valencian work, constructed somewhat later and fashioned in the desornamentado style, is the Capilla del Colegio de Corpus Christi, popularly known as El Patriarca. The patriarch referred to was San Juan de Ribera, son of the marquis of Tarifa, owner of the famous Casa de Pilatos, in Sevilla, filled with numerous Sevillian tile works. Ribera was well versed in the modes of Renaissance art. Consequently, when he was named archbishop of Valencia, it is not surprising that he embarked on the great venture of constructing the Colegio. Built between 1586 and 1609, practically all of the wainscots

3.9 Tile Panel
Salon of the Cortes de la Generalitat, Valencia
Signed "Oliva," ca. 1570
Photo by
Estefanía Martí

3.10 Tiles in Diamond Pattern *(punta de diamante)* Capilla del Colegio de Corpus Christi, El Patriarca, Valencia Photo by Estefanía Martí

are finished with tiles. In the cloister, a wall covering was produced in the cuenca, or arista, technique, uncommon in Valencia, although not unknown to artisans there. In this work, more emphasis is given to the color green than the normally predominant blue. It is not farfetched to assume that the archbishop may have had it shipped by sea from Sevilla itself. Two renowned Talaveran ceramists, Lorenzo de Madrid (who later went to Barcelona to create his masterpiece, La Diputación) and Antonio Simón, worked on this project. Both artists established themselves in the nearby town of Burjasot, a feudal territory of the patriarch that had deposits of fine clays.

The rest of the building exhibits other well-known designs of that era: the diamond pattern (fig. 3.10); the nailhead; egg and dart surrounded by strapwork; and several friezes with allegories of the Eucharist, fantasy figures, and jars. In short, the quantity of tiles in this building is enormous. The themes, although somewhat varied, are mostly of a repetitive and solemn nature. This expression of austerity is what the patriarch wished to convey throughout the edifice, and its splendor lies in its conservatism. Its ambiance is a reflection of the spirit of its founder, with all the elements that in his day were considered appropriate for a church, and in this case, the chapel of La Purísima as well. This is one of the few places where one can study a structure from that period as it was originally envisioned.

One novelty that we find in El Patriarca is the covering of the cupola with glazed roofing tiles, a decorative system from Andalucía that became extremely popular in Valencia. The cupola was covered almost entirely with blue tiles, but lines formed by white or gold tiles divided the dome into sections.

The patriarch founded and rebuilt numerous convents and monasteries, many of which contain tiled wainscots. Some of these were located in the newly introduced *transgrarios* (small chapels built behind the sanctuary). An example of this can be found in the church of San Nicolás, in Valencia. The main altar of the church of Santa Ursula is another work supported by the patriarch, and like many others he inspired, it alludes to the Eucharist. The decorative styles found in these edifices rapidly commanded much admiration, and we find them in many structures erected without his patronage. Some decorative motifs have continued to be used up to the present, especially the nailhead and the diamond pattern.

To summarize the brief period of the Renaissance movement in Valencia, we can say that in the early part of the sixteenth century, ceramics were imported from Andalucía or Toledo. Shortly afterward, potters relocated to Valencia. Local ceramists quickly developed models of their own, based upon those brought by these artisans. All of the tiles fabricated in imitation of imported tiles used the same chromatic palette as the original models, and their size averaged around 13 cm on a side. Some styles immediately became popular, and certain combinations of tiles became classic. For example, one design that appeared in many flooring schemes used alternating large bisqued tiles of a reddish hue with smaller tiles, called *azuelos de cartabón*, or *mocadoret*, tiles with designs of alternating solid colors painted on the diagonal in green and white, and eventually florones, with geometric vegetal themes. We can find this kind of floor covering in the Ayuntamiento de Potries or in the impressive palace-monastery of San Miguel de los Reyes, in Valencia. Another version, applied to wainscots, is the combination of *azulejos de cartabón*, forming rhombuses and leaving space in the middle for a large floral pattern composed of four tiles (*florón de a cuatro*). These were produced in blue and yellow. Well-preserved samples are located in the church of Rubielos de Mora, Teruel, and the tomb of Felipa Sans, in the chapel of Santo Domingo, today known as the church of the Capitanía General de Valencia.

The Renaissance style can be traced up to the beginning of the eighteenth century. One example is the panel of San Jerónimo, dated to 1700 and conserved in the Colegio de Arte Mayor de la Seda, Valencia (fig. 3.11). It is painted in blue, yellow, and green, with a medallion formed by a laurel branch encircling the figure of a saint. Surrounding him are interwoven floral motifs, applied in a looser manner than in pure Renaissance style, and a rocaille shell that bears the date. From this point on, up to the termination of the eighteenth century and the birth of the nineteenth, it can be said that the Valencian creations belonged more to the Baroque than to the Renaissance style.

The situation of Cataluña was similar to that of Valencia. Until the first third of the sixteenth century, Catalan tilework was based on models from Valencia, although certain techniques in the application of decoration differed. The *trepa* (stencil with cut-out designs) was used in place of the *estarcido* (stencil with dotted outlines) or free hand methods, and the predominant color scheme was blue on white. The ornamental repertoire also included new elements, such as dolphins and Classical portrayals of dragons. But here the impact of the Renaissance was more substantial and quickly developed into a local expression, probably due to the port of Barcelona, which provided a closer association with Italy and France. Nevertheless, the first pieces that truly emulated Renaissance style were produced by master ceramists from Talavera and Sevilla. One of the first was Lorenzo de Madrid, who had lived in Talavera and came to Manresa after spending some time in Valencia. In 1596, he was hired to work on the palace of the Generalitat.

3.11 *St. Jerome*
Colegio de Arte
Mayor de la Seda,
Valencia, ca. 1700

This first contract took the form of a wainscot whose central theme is the figure of Saint George fighting the dragon, with the princess shown in the background (fig. 3.12). This panel incorporates the typical tones of blue, yellow, and green, and is framed by other tiles that display patterns of volutes, fruit, grotesques, and acanthus leaves. Madrid was also later commissioned to produce for the same palace a floor composed of marbleized tiles edged with Classical ornamentation.

In later works, such as the wainscots and stairways of the Casa de la Convalencia de Barcelona, today the Biblioteca General de Cataluña, one can appreciate a style more typical of the Baroque period than of the Renaissance. Almost all of the tilework in this structure, wall panels as well as floors, are the creation of Lorenzo Passoles, who began to work on the project in 1662. His mastery is demonstrated in several representations of episodes of the life of Saint Paul, undoubtedly in honor of the founder of the hospital, Pablo Ferrán. The last great works that we can classify as Renaissance are the soffits that allude to the battle at Lepanto. These are also attributed to Passoles and are located in the chapel of the Virgen del Rosario, in Valls, Tarragona.

An interesting detail associated with the advent of the Renaissance in Aragón is that, although ceramists adopted the new decorative styles, they did not apply them to flat tiles, as was the practice on the rest of the peninsula, but rather continued to employ the arista technique that was deeply rooted in the region, due to contacts with the kingdom of Andalucía. Even though these two sovereignties were far apart, the migration of ceramists kept Mudéjar traditions active throughout the territory, especially with respect to architecture.

The sixteenth century was a period of great activity in the construction and adornment of edifices within the ancient realm, especially in its capital, Zaragoza, where the number of workers from other regions grew tremendously. For its cathedral, completed in the second half of the century, artisans from several nearby towns composed wall coverings as well as floors using the arista method. They also carried out the installation of tiles in the cathedral of Huesca, those in the chapel of La Comunión being the same type that had been sent to Leo X for the castle of Sant' Angelo. Nevertheless, they continued with the tradition of alternating glazed tiles (azulejos) with either bisqued or stucco tiles. Another surviving tradition was that of placing loose pieces or friezes on the exteriors of towers and walls that previously had a brick facade. This new form, covering some cupolas or roofs of important buildings with flat tiles in two or more colors arranged in a shingle pattern, gave them a certain eye-catching elegance. An excellent example of this technique is the Diputación (parliament building) in Zaragoza, where Lorenzo Madrid also worked, from 1586 to 1589.

3.12 *St. George* Lorenzo de Madrid, Palace of the Generalitat, Sala del Consistorio, Barcelona, ca. 1596

White, blue, green, purple, and amber continued to be the most popular colors and, along with the styles most typical of the times, show little innovation. Designs followed the characteristic four-tile arrangement with crowns or floral patterns and friezes or garlands formed with the repeating egg-and-dart pattern, urns, acanthus leaves, and columns. Sometimes these patterns originated from designs introduced by itinerant ceramists, but for the most part they were taken from books of prints of Classical architecture. One element that was popular toward the end of this era was the typical *cartabón*, divided in two halves and always linked with others to achieve an impressive decorative pattern.

Baroque

The eighteenth century marked a resurgence for Valencia in ceramics. If its golden age was the fifteenth century, the eighteenth was its silver period. This rejuvenation and regeneration began with the tile industry. Not only had the quality of the tiles improved, but decorative motifs were more varied, resulting in increased demand. New uses were found for tiles in other parts of buildings. They were applied to floors, walls, windowsills, balcony ledges, stair risers, garden benches, altarpieces, sundials, etc. This decorative innovation, tied to the era's construction boom, caused the number of tiles produced to skyrocket.

Until the final decades of the seventeenth century, artists continued to work with a chromatic palette that was very constrained. In Valencia, this consisted of white, which was mainly used as a background hue, and different shades of blue, green, and yellow. But around the middle of the eighteenth century, the range of colors broadened; two tones of green were added (an emerald shade and one slightly darker), along with ochres, purples, and new yellows and blues. These were all silhouetted with a dark line produced by manganese. The background was a creamy white, in contrast to the commercially produced pure white that would be used after the beginning of the nineteenth century. This is a defining feature between it and the eighteenth century, when ceramists still mixed their own paints. These pigments never were pure oxides, and it is precisely this lack of purity that gave them their unique nuances and particular beauty.

Regardless of the theme, tiles were used as much for floors as for dados, although scenes with human characters seemed to be more appropriate for the latter. These could depict outdoor events, such as picnics, country fairs, hunting scenes, pastoral scenes, landscapes, or lakes with boating activities. In them we encounter a certain chivalrous air, and popular reminiscences of eighteenth century French paintings, such as those of Watteau and Boucher. Floors usually displayed symbolic themes relating to the four elements, the four seasons, or the four sections of the world. Most popular, however, were kitchen scenes including the gadgets and utensils used in them (fig. 3.13). There are illustrations of servants bringing baskets from market, others engaged in butchering animals, cooks frying fish, and cats that would like to snatch those same fish. The tiles present a splendid array of everything from the pottery used for cooking and storing to the different foods that were hung from hooks—ducks, small wild game, goats with their bellies split open, codfish, sausages, etc. These scenes have an air of innocence and great charm and are an important source of cultural details of the times (fig. 3.14).

Other frequently recurring themes employ religious subject matter: symbols of the Passion of Christ, the Eucharist, or the Holy Scriptures are displayed on panels covering the walls of chapels of churches and convents. Images of saints were placed on the facades of homes. The names of these patron saints were often given to streets or entire neighborhoods. The Stations of the Cross were also found on facades within a town or on some small commemorative structure on a nearby hilltop. There were images of many kinds of flowers, generally not realistically depicted but of great beauty, and fruit was also a popular motif, especially pomegranates and apples. The repertoire was inexhaustible, and the rocaille that frames the central theme was almost always present.

The same themes were apparent in the nineteenth century, although changes in tonality can be noted, in part due to the availability of commercially produced pigments, which imparted a more uniform quality and consistent hue to the colors. There was a tendency to dispense with dados representing one large scene and to replace them with small, individual representations. Tiles were also used as street signs, such as those depicting a house on fire, indicating that that home was insured. One with the picture of a coach drawn by a horse might be used to designate the direction of traffic flow for carriages.

This century marks the advent of the first true tile factories in Valencia. Although the division of labor was initially rudimentary, the work was

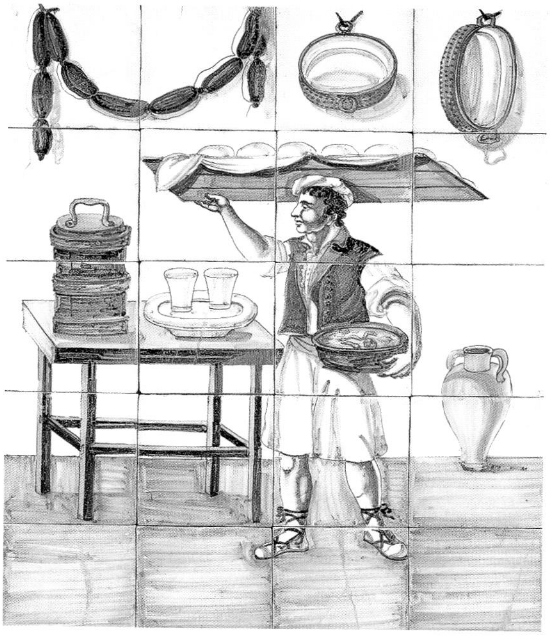

3.13 *Coming from the Oven*
Valencia, ca. 1830
Museo Nacional de Cerámica y de las Artes Suntuarias "González Martí," Valencia

3.14 *A Valencian Family*
Valencia, 1789
Museo Nacional de Cerámica y de las Artes Suntuarias "González Martí," Valencia

3.15 Tile Flooring
Doña María Disdier
workshop (detail)
Valencia, 1808
Museo Nacional de
Cerámica y de las
Artes Suntuarias
"González Martí,"
Valencia
Photo by
J. M. Liébana

divided into specialties, and each operator was assigned a certain responsibility. These factories also utilized designs that were urbane and sophisticated, resulting in splendid works. One example is preserved in the Museo Nacional de Cerámica González Martí. Created in the Reales fábricas de Doña María Disdier, named after the daughter of the entrepreneur who founded the factory, this magnificent tile floor has the appearance of an opulent oriental carpet. Its central *chinesco* theme is surrounded by scenes of Pompeiian subject matter (fig. 3.15).

There is a tendency among individuals and antique dealers or collectors to attribute pieces made at the Reales Fábricas de Disdier to Alcora. The fact is that the output from Alcora was almost exclusively devoted to tableware, and the small number of tiles manufactured there were produced solely by commission. Their quality and elegance are instantly recognizable in the few examples that have survived. Not only are the tiles flawlessly made, but the superiority of the glazes and the grace of their skillfully applied designs is outstanding. Their yellow tone gives them a distinctive light golden hue. One panel fabricated at Alcora is housed in El Museo de Cerámica de Barcelona, along with a series of large plaques that present the Stations of the Cross in exquisitely executed illustrations.

Not surprisingly for a period of great creativity and splendor, the Baroque tiles of Valencia were in high demand and were exported to many areas. They were highly prized within the ancient kingdom of Valencia and in other parts of Andalucía and Castilla as well. Even today, southern Aragón is rich with Valencian works. Following the loosening of restrictions on trade with the Americas, shipments left the port of Valencia for Cuba, Argentina, Uruguay, Mexico, Chile, Guatemala and Peru, although the bulk of exports were directed to countries in North Africa, especially Algeria and Tunisia.[8]

The story of tilework in Barcelona is similar to that of Valencia, although the Baroque style emerged earlier. Great compositions were produced, such as the famed panel *La Chocolatada*, which portrays an afternoon "tea" (*merienda*) in a garden; the focal point is the chocolate being prepared and served by servants (see fig. 2.19). Companions to this piece are a representation of a bullfight and many other panels depicting saints. However, more characteristic of this period of Catalan ceramics is the individual tile with a distinct meaning. These included tiles *de oficio*—or logos for professionals, with the representation of a person occupied in a particular trade or business (see fig. 3.16). Narrative tiles were also very popular and focused on the literature of the *cordel*, or popular stories, ballads, and romances recited in the streets by the blind or peddlers. There were also burlesque topics, with caricatures of musicians or dancers with large heads.

Around this time, Andalucía fell into a slump in production and resorted to the fabrication of individual tiles similar to those produced in the city of Delft, in Holland. However, we still find admirable panels from this era, including a number of panels of saints destined for the facades of homes, as we have seen in Valencia or Cataluña. The manufacture of dados also continued, with Baroque themes such as rocaille combined with Renaissance characteristics. One such example is found in the archbishop's palace of Málaga, where the characters depicted are attired in fashions of the eighteenth century but are framed by Renaissance motifs. In any case, although the production of these panels was sparse, their designs and overall quality remained excellent.

Aragón was not able to compete with the tile production of Valencia and Cataluña either. Production there was geared mostly to local consumption, abandoning the deeply rooted Mudéjar style and the cuenca method of manufacture in favor of flat, or pisano, tilework. This form of

3.16 Trade Tile / *Azulejo de oficio* Barcelona, 18th century Museu de Cerámica, Barcelona Photo by Guillém Frenández

tile was manufactured in Zaragoza, Muel, Villafeliche, and Teruel. Colors were subdued in comparison to those used in other regions. Blue was dominant, followed by yellow and green, but a full polychrome range was missing. Illustrations lean toward popular religious themes. The primary source of orders for this art was naturally churches, convents, and hermitages.

Modernism and Historicism

At the conclusion of the nineteenth century, Spain saw a spectacular increase in its population, with a corresponding expansion of its cities that tore down the walls constraining them. New neighborhoods were built and old ones renovated. This construction boom, coupled with new trends in health consciousness that were spreading all over Europe, was a catalyst for tile production. Tin-glazed tiles were thought to be an ideal solution to community health problems, especially in places like hospitals, maternity houses, hospices, markets, spas, and railroad stations.

The Universal Exposition in Barcelona, celebrated in 1888, served as the impetus for Spain to break away from old, established styles and to align itself with recent Modernist trends in Europe. However, it did not want to renounce the past completely. Spain, like many countries in the region was, at that moment enveloped in an aura of enthusiastic nationalism and therefore chose to hold on to great moments of its glorious history. For this reason, so-called "neo" characteristics became accepted and admired. This attitude applied to all designs, especially those of the Islamic or Mudéjar styles, which had parallels with Romanticism.

The National Exposition of Industrial Arts that also took place in Barcelona, in 1912, established the use of ceramics in architecture just as these new styles were being encouraged. Architects, especially Antoni Gaudí i Cornet (1852–1926), who was known for his unique style, enthusiastically made use of ceramic pieces in facades, friezes, balustrades, cupolas, capitals, garden fountains, and other areas considered appropriate for their installation. This massive employment of tiles resulted in a reduction of production costs, because more efficient methods of manufacture were developed. The consequence of this flurry of activity in the ceramics industry was the creation of modern factories with presses, *hornos de pasaje*, highly purified commercially produced colorings, and the specialization of workers. Another point that should be emphasized is the availability of talented and skilled artisans, who rescued techniques of the past, such as those for producing lusterware, while they perfected new methods.

Modernism gave rise to a true moment of ebullience with respect to the application of ceramics in architecture. Barcelona was the city through which these styles first entered and where they are best exemplified. But this enthusiasm spread to other locations, often thanks to the same architects, who left to work outside of Cataluña. Gaudí used ceramics in a very personal manner, as seen in his *trencadí*, which give the impression of being *teserae* gathered from broken pieces. Actually, they are intentionally formed in this manner and precisely planned to take advantage of the way light is reflected and plays across the projections of the composition. The celebrated Parque Güell in Barcelona is a superlative example of this strategy of design (fig. 3.17). Gaudí was one of the first to integrate ceramics into buildings in a diverse mixture of formats and was also the innovator of a movement whose goal was the amalgamation of all parts of an edifice: its iron, glass, and even its furniture and the objects used to enhance the atmosphere of a room.

Domenech i Montaner, Puig i Cadafach, and Galissa were other outstanding architects whose designs were symbols of Modernist philosophy in Barcelona at that time. One cannot fail to mention the work performed at the ceramic factory of Pujols i Bausis in the town of Espulgues de Llobregat. Its artisans produced enormous quantities of tiles in a wide array of decorative styles for these avant-garde buildings.

In Valencia, tile production continued, especially in nearby communities such as those of Cabañal, and their use in construction was prominent. But the style of this ornamentation, which was also applied to facades, fits more closely that of the Vienna Sezession than that of Modernism. There was, however, a certain cultural tide that generated a popular use for tiles in doorjambs, wall facings, shelving, and panels; within this current of fashion, a number of fine buildings were constructed—the Estación del Norte, the Mercado Central, and the Mercado de Colón among them. One of the notable effects of this trend was the establishment of a new ceramics factory, La Ceramo. It undertook the important task of reproducing lusterware and reviving ancient techniques and practices. The best examples of works turned out by this plant are its unrivaled imitations of the *jarrones* of the Alhambra (see fig. 1.22). The factory also produced plaques for roofing, tiles for cupolas, finials for garden walls, gargoyles, and many other items. Nolla was another important factory; it followed English processes to fabricate mosaics of excellent quality that embraced traditional geometric patterns and used subdued tones in their coloring.

3.17 Detail of *trencadís*
Antonio Guadí i Cornet,
Parque Güell, Barcelona,
1900–1914

In Sevilla, by contrast, the influence of Modernism was almost imperceptible, but there was, nonetheless, a true flourishing of ceramics following historical styles, especially those of the Mudéjar and the Renaissance. Here, the work of the Pickman factory stands out. Its primary production was devoted to decorative ceramics and tableware, but it also manufactured tiles of superb quality, while trying at the same time to recapture ancient ceramic techniques.

At the beginning of the twentieth century, the major volume of production was concentrated in the area of Valencia. Gradually it filtered into the surrounding areas of Castellón. This period was a bonanza for ceramic production, but was interrupted by the bloody fratricidal conflict of the Spanish Civil War. The industry regrouped when hostilities ceased on the peninsula, due in large part to the tremendous external demand resulting from the destruction of ceramic factories throughout Europe during the Second World War. Orders poured in, not only from Europe, but also from Africa and the Americas. However, the massive increase in volume led to the deterioration of quality and aesthetics. The workforce was no longer as skilled, and the decorative processes were reduced to a minimum, in order to save production time and to keep pace with demand. There were ups and downs in fabrication, and a slump occurred in the late 1950s; a true resurgence came only with the advent of natural gas. The factories refitted their kilns for this energy source, which was much cleaner and cheaper.

Today the thinking of ceramic producers has changed a little. They are conscious that this vigorous industry must rely on investors and must continually update its technology if it wants to be competitive. At the same time, it must forge ahead with the indispensable tasks of researching new production techniques and finding more cost-effective and efficient methods of manufacture. It must develop new products that will find a demand in the marketplace. At present, that part of the ceramic industry concerned with providing materials for construction is centered primarily in the area of Castellón, concentrated in huge industrial centers and in various towns that have experienced spectacular growth. The tendency is toward total automation of the fabrication processes. This would result in a soaring volume of production and would make Spain the world's leading exporter of these products.

Notes

1. For a complete explanation of the alicer technique and its place in a particular work, see Josep María Gomis Martí, *Evolució històrica del taulellet* (Castellón: Diputación de Castellón, 1990).
2. Thorough studies of the Italian bacini have been published by Graziella Berti. The most complete of these publications is Graziella Berti and Liana Tongiorgi, *I bacini medievali delle chièse di Pisa* (Rome: Lérma di Bretschneider, 1981).
3. See Victor M. Algarra Pardo, "Espacios de poder: Pavimentos cerámicos y escritura en el Real de Valencia en época de Alfonso el Magnánimo," in *Actas del 15 Congreso de Historia de la Corona de Aragón* 1 (1996):271-89, for a study of custom-made Valencia tile and its use as an object of political propaganda.
4. The Duke of Berry contracted ceramists from Valencia to work on several floors, thus initiating a tradition in France. See Philippe Bon, *Les premiers "bleus" de France* (Mehun-sur-Yèvre: Conseil Général du Cher, 1992).
5. The earliest examples we know of are green and purple and come from the cathedral of Tarragona and the Gerona baths.
6. See Inocencio V. Pérez Guillén, "La azulejería valenciana en los siglos XVII, XVIII y XIX," in A.A.V.V., *La ruta de la cerámica* (Castellón: Ascer, 2000), pp. 112–22 on tile factories founded in Valencia.
7. In the castle of Alacuás, there are other floors recorded as having individual green and yellow tiles that were never combined and were always formatted in geometric compositions. All floors of the castle of Alacuás, some no longer in existence, are reproduced in the study by María Bordón Ferrer and María Paz Soler Ferrer, "Pavimentos valencianos de los siglos XIV–XVI," in *Actes du 6 Congrès de la Céramique Médiéval en Méditerranée* (Aix-en-Provence: Narration Editions, 1997), pp. 667–75, pl. 15.
8. A pioneer study on recent exports to Latin American countries is Inocencio V. Pérez Guillén, "Las exportaciones de azulejos valencianos a ultramar: Siglos XVII–XIX," in A.A.V.V., *La ruta de la cerámica* (Castellón: Ascer, 2000) pp. 123–25.

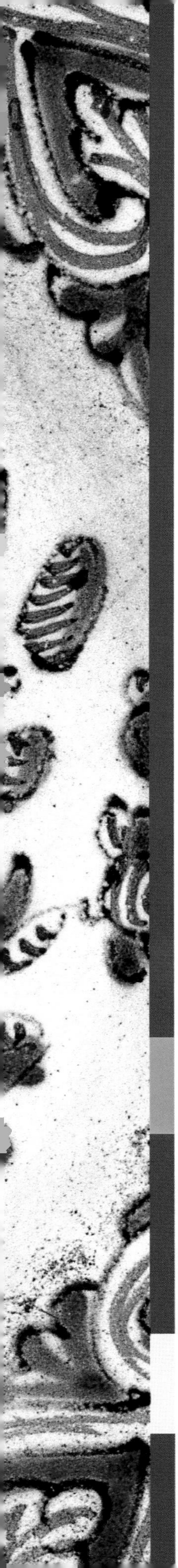

Detail, Fig. 1.7

4

Ceramics, Business, and Economy

ALFONSO PLEGUEZUELO

EVERY CERAMIC OBJECT is subject to scrutiny from a completely economic standpoint. The expediency of such analysis is indisputable, since it reveals an important dimension of the object, closely related to the multiple facets that it can represent: aesthetic, functional, technical, social, and symbolic. We might begin by asking ourselves if this investigation is usually the goal of those who occupy themselves on a daily basis with the history of ceramics; the answer would be uncertain. Some aspects connected with economy usually appear in isolation in art historical ceramic studies, although these considerations are more frequently the preoccupation of archaeologists, who attempt to decipher such information from the detailed statistical analysis of excavated

4.1 *View of a Port*
Joseph Vernet, ca. 1754
Musée de la Marine, Paris

materials. Generally, such ceramic studies are carried out from the point of view of business and the economy as a whole. It stands to reason, however, that we historians should emphasize this analytical perspective that is so tied to the interchange of ceramic products between Spain and the Americas. It is a theme that affects us in Spain to an extraordinary degree and offers us the opportunity to embark upon a wide-ranging investigative voyage (fig. 4.1).

But we need to clearly stipulate the specifics of this area and ask ourselves to what extent this economic factor affects our work. The answer, in principle, is quite simple. A ceramic object is no different from a painting, clothing, furniture, or any other artifact in our material culture. From the moment of its conception, an object is influenced by economic factors. These considerations include the stocking of raw materials, investment in the methods of production, manufacture or industrial fabrication, the payment of fees and taxes, labor costs, the organization of companies, apprenticeship contracts, and the buying, selling, and transportation of the finished products. In fact, even before an item is produced and long after it has been discarded, it is intrinsically linked to economic issues.[1]

One question that should concern those who are investigating this field is the connection (whether cooperative or competitive) between ceramics and other decorative materials (whether architectural or involving domestic furnishings). For example, in the case of coverings, tin-glazed tiles may be only one option in addition to possibilities such as marble or other polished stone facing, ornamented mortar and stucco, wooden wainscots, embossed hides, or textile hangings. Awareness of these alternatives can shed light on the reasons for fluctuations in the supply and demand for ceramics products. It can also occasionally reveal the origins of the ornamentation found in models produced in other materials that frequently were imitated in ceramic objects. In the case of tableware, the matter is of great significance. The importance accorded to ceramic possessions depended on the relative abundance of similar objects made from other materials; for example, tableware made from wood in medieval Europe, that made from tin in the Nordic nations, tableware of glass or porcelain in Venice during the sixteenth century, or tableware fashioned from the gold and silver that arrived in great quantities in Spain during its golden age.[2] From this standpoint, an awareness of the prices and costs of production of other products is of importance. Official lists of rates, pay scales for artisans, estimates recorded in the registries of custom offices and port authorities, established prices for contracted work, etc., all are important, especially when they can be related to one another in time and space.

Another phenomenon that plays an important role in the economics of ceramics is its frequent reuse for cost effectiveness. This applies as much to ceramic vessels originally designed for liquids and solids as to tile coverings used in architecture. Defective crockery items were recycled as lightweight fill in vault construction or to form partitioning layers to counter moisture beneath floors in humid areas (fig. 4.2).[3] Broken pitchers and jars have always been used as flowerpots or water containers for pets and other domesticated animals. Only items that were completely shattered were discarded. At times, even these fragmented items were used as rubble to level terrain, to make forms for wall construction, or were ground into temper for use in clay to make other earthenware containers. This also applies to damaged tiles, which were almost never disposed of; when possible, just as is still done with bricks, they were reused in some part of a building. Consequently, within the same floor or wall covering, a mixture of pieces can be found from different time periods, offering historians of today the possibility to track different stages in the construction of a building and the history of the consumption of these products.

One key point, as yet unstudied, is the relationship between the ceramics industry and that of the glass and textile industries. Such an examination would reveal not only the similarity in raw materials and technical processes employed for the production of both glass and ceramics, but also the shared aesthetic relationship, particularly between ceramics and textiles. But most significant would be the coincidence that almost all the important ceramic production centers were also equally important sites for the fabrication of these other art forms. This is not only true for the great manufacturing areas of Asia, such as China, Persia, Mesopotamia, and Egypt, but also in such cities of the Iberian Peninsula as Granada, Toledo, Sevilla, Talavera, Valencia, and Barcelona, not to mention the city of Puebla, in Mexico.

Two valuable sources of information available for the

4.2 Cross-section of a chapel vault where pottery was used as fill Colegio de Santa María de Jesús, Sevilla, ca. 1500 Drawing by Pedro Mora, 1992

reconstruction of this history are historical documents and the extensive collections found in museums and private collections. Manufacturing centers that concentrated on luxury wares have always enjoyed the interest of collectors and specialists, but the more common ceramics, sometimes even more important in terms of general commercial value than the luxury items, have traditionally received much less attention. The few advances in the history of ceramic commerce have occurred in recent years, thanks to historical archaeology, both on land and under water. This discipline, whose journey to uncover the past has only been launched in quite recent times, and is dedicated to a period that is sometimes indiscriminately called "postmedieval" is, therefore, still in its embryonic stages in Spain and Latin America.[4] As a result, only a few general research activities have begun in this area.[5]

However, archaeology enjoys a stronger tradition in Northern Europe and North America.[6] This prior research has acted as a powerful catalyst for the examination of this area in Spain and Latin America. But the particular and justified interest of English archaeology in the medieval period and that of the North Americans for the age just before colonization, known as 'the contact period," always leaves an enormous gap from the middle of the seventeenth century to the present.[7]

This brief panorama does not permit the synthesis of an extensive approach to Hispanic ceramic production. That has already been presented in universal terms in a previous work on earthenware and tilework in Spain, which the interested reader may consult.[8] For this reason, these pages will discuss general issues relative to both the domestic and foreign commerce of mayólica. Our goal is to encourage the undertaking of new studies that will provide answers to the questions formulated here and to introduce this complex phenomenon, which awaits a more profound and extensive study.

Earthenware, Mayólica, and Porcelain

In the wide and complex world of ceramics, the mobility of specific objects stands in an inversely proportional relationship to the number of centers in which they were produced and their degree of specialization. Some forms of ceramics, easily fabricated in any location, would therefore not be transported great distances, except on rare occasions. For this reason, it is important to distinguish between the very different levels of technical complexity involved in the manufacture of these products, which in turn correspond to varying price levels.

Earthenware

At the lowest levels of complexity and cost would be what is customarily known as earthenware *(alfarería),* or common ceramics. Taking into account the simple procedures and ubiquity of raw materials necessary for its fabrication, this group can be considered the most widespread, with production details decided within the nucleus of each city, town, and even the smallest village. Only a few types of ceramics from this group, and almost always for historical or very specific commercial reasons, have been objects of exchange reaching beyond their areas of origin. In short, cooking pots, roofing tiles, bricks for the construction of houses, and containers to haul water from a fountain or spring are usually manufactured by potters from the area in which they are used. Buyers of these objects are not generally disposed to pay high prices for transportation from some far-off factory, especially when the same items most probably can be produced nearby if clay, water, and fuel are available. There are, of course, exceptions. For example, the bricks that were shipped from Sevilla to the Caribbean so that the earliest Spaniards to arrive there could immediately construct the first churches, homes, and other buildings. But clay sources were quickly located, and these structural components could then be produced in the new American colonies.

The conveyance over long distances of earthenware was, at times, justified, when the artifact was used as a container for another product to be transported within it. This was the case with commercial storage receptacles such as oil, wine, vinegar, olive, raisin, and caper jars that were shipped aboard Spanish galleons to the Nordic countries and to the American territories.[9] This was equally the case for the large jugs that were used for the secure shipping of quality ceramics such as lusterware from Manises. Evidence of this manner of safeguarding fragile items has been found in shipwrecks in the sea near Arenys de Mar[10] and off of Sóller (Mallorca).[11]

Earthenware was sometimes transported great distances when the production costs were extraordinarily low in comparison to the quality achieved. An example of this would be some forms of containers and water coolers *(alcarrazas)* such as those manufactured in Andújar (Córdoba), which, in the eighteenth century, were sold very cheaply in Madrid. Stewpots and other cookware from Alcorcón (Toledo) supplied the region of Castilla; and *búcaros,* or fragrant, red-slipped, polished earthenware cups, from Estremoz (Portugal), were shipped during the seventeenth century to most of Spain and Latin America.

Finally, earthenware reached distant locations with groups of emigrants, who, accustomed to using certain objects in their native lands, would order them for their new places of residence. There are documented cases of objects found in Dutch cities where Jews from Portugal relocated and ordered customary household items from their birthplace.[12] This is a simple matter of continuing customs and practices associated with the homeland. For example, the need to cool water for drinking in cities with cooler climates, such as Amsterdam, Antwerp, or Bruges, was not as great as in Lisbon or in Mérida; but the use of water coolers constituted a distinctive emblem of a social class and formed part of the everyday domestic and dietary routines that these transplanted Iberians found difficult to leave behind. This was especially true in regard to ceramics that were intimately tied to traditional foods and their preparation (see chapter 2).

Mayólica

In the second category of procedural complexity would be mayólica or, as it is known in Spain, *loza tradicional.* (fig. 4.3). This pottery requires the use of silica and various mixed clays that were not widely distributed, because their considerable weight added to the difficulty of transportation, which greatly increased the price of the finished product. An interesting situation that occurred with some frequency in the past was the marketing of *bizcocho* (bisqued ware), ceramic objects that were fired once and then sent to nearby production centers for glazing and ornamentation; in some cases they were sent to their market destination, where the final production steps were completed. Except for lusterware, traditional loza was generally fired twice and at a higher temperature than other pottery, because of its lead- and tin-based enamel coatings.

4.3 *The Miracle of St. Hugo in the Refectory* Francisco de Zurburán, ca. 1633 Museo de Bellas Artes, Sevilla Photo by Pedro Feria Fernández This painting illustrates 17th century *loza tradicional*

One of the most frequent problems that potters of past centuries encountered was the increase in prices due to short supplies of materials. At times, supplies of lead—an element not only crucial to pottery glazing but also an indispensable component for the manufacture of munitions—were seized by the army. Fortunately, this metal was relatively abundant on the Iberian Peninsula. This was not the case for tin, which had to be brought in from distant areas. For example, the material used in the loza of Talavera came for the most part from Viseu, in Portugal. The independence of this kingdom in the middle of the seventeenth century brought about a curtailment in the supply of tin and the consequent darkening of Talavera ware enamels. In some periods, it was necessary to obtain tin from England, where it was abundant. Variation in the availability of this costly element resulted, at times, in higher prices for the final product. It also required the producers of ceramics to maintain a certain economic capacity that would allow them to import and stock this essential ingredient. Small workshops found this beyond their financial means. The problem of availability of raw materials also occurred in the nineteenth century for producers of industrial loza, when kaolin or other white clays were difficult to obtain.

The metallic oxides needed to produce the colors used in decoration were also subject to problems of supply that were not always easy to resolve if there were no mines in the vicinity. The operation of these mines always involved high financial risks. Prospecting for new sources, carried out by state technical experts, and in some cases by the ceramists themselves, required official permission from municipal or state authorities. However, the more common oxides employed in ceramic painting could normally be obtained in the vicinity. Copper, from which green pigments were produced, was obtained from cauldron makers. Iron was easily obtained from blacksmiths. Manganese, for purple and black tints, was brought from the nearest mines. Cobalt, for blues, was scarcer and was brought from Persia by Genoese merchants at the end of the Middle Ages. Because of the problems in obtaining raw materials, the centers that produced loza, although more numerous than generally is thought, were always fewer than the factories that manufactured common, everyday pottery.

Porcelain

We assign porcelain to the third major group (fig. 4.4). The secret of the fabrication of this sophisticated material was for many years a mystery that the Western world sought to appropriate from East Asia. One of the many reasons for this was to avoid the high cost of this expensive product as well as the cost of shipping it from what in those times was the other side of the planet. This art form was not successfully produced in Europe until the 1700s, in Meissen (Germany). The economic impact on eighteenth-century Europe of this accomplishment was due to the

4.4 *Porcelain Traders*
Aubusson tapestry,
18th century
Private collection

savings realized by no longer having to pay high transport costs from China and Japan.

Porcelain arrived in Europe from the Far East beginning in the fourteenth century. Initially this exotic and highly desirable pottery was transported across the vast stretches of Asia by caravans, but later two regular maritime routes were developed that ended at the Iberian Peninsula (see fig. 1.1). The first was the commercial trade circuit created by the Portuguese beginning in the early part of the sixteenth century. Portuguese ships navigated the length of Africa, rounded the Cape of Good Hope, and sailed across the Indian Ocean to ports in East Asia. They were the first to bring Chinese porcelain to the Iberian Peninsula. The other sea route was discovered by the Spaniards. Ships known as Manila galleons (1565–1815) crossed the Pacific Ocean between the Philippine Islands and Acapulco, where goods were then transported across Mexico to the port of Veracruz, to be reshipped to Cádiz and Sevilla.[13]

The next to bring porcelain to Europe were the Dutch, with the founding of the Dutch East India Company in the beginning of the seventeenth century. Later, French and English ships also transported these products on return journeys from the Far East. The extraordinary attractiveness of these porcelain objects, with their exquisite subtle finishes, provoked a continuous wellspring of imitations on the part of glassworkers and ceramists. Owners of these items gained a halo of social prestige, supported by both the indisputable aesthetic beauty of the objects and the exorbitant prices demanded for them in the marketplace.

Creation or Imitation: Counterfeit Loza

In each period there existed distinctive networks of distribution for each of these ceramic products. That invisible web is what we historians and archaeologists endeavor, with great pains, to discover. The resistance of ceramic materials to deterioration permits us, at times, to accomplish this reconstruction. The distribution of ceramics is a testimony to the commercial and cultural interchange among societies.

As part of this process, every place on the planet benefits from two classes of ceramic objects: those produced locally and those that have been imported. From the relation between these two groups arise conjunctions of objects peculiar to each center of production. For this reason, one should never forget the commercial and dynamic perspective that explains the characteristics of particular ceramic products not in terms of "originality" or "creation," but rather just the opposite. It is precisely the determination to "imitate" and even intentionally to "plagiarize," rather than the search for self-identifying styles, that have almost always acted as the catalyst for the creation of "styles" within the history of the art of ceramics. This matter is intimately linked to sales, demand, changes in fashion, and the general history of aesthetic tastes and preferences in which ceramics have at times played an essential role, not always sufficiently recognized.

As was suggested at the beginning of this essay, ceramic products have constituted an important sector of the economy of many towns. From its invention in Neolithic times, when people first founded cities and developed agriculture and animal husbandry, ceramics, whether locally manufactured or imported, have been put to many uses. Thus the fabrication of ceramics has been an important factor in the success of a community; as a center for trade and as a spur to the growth of communities in commercial contact. This has resulted in a phenomenon that one could only call paradoxical; ceramics began to move between peoples only when the producers became stationary and the first commercial routes were born.

The weight of ceramics has always been a negative aspect for ground transport. However, this factor had an opposite effect for maritime transfer, because these goods were usable as ballast in place of the traditional sacks of sand. Moreover, once the ship arrived at its destination, the ceramics could be sold for a good price, augmenting the profitability of the voyage.

Along with the ebb and flow of ceramics along these roads of communication, not only were the artistic works moving from place to place, but the artisans who produced them were also relocating. Due to a lack of documentation, we know very little of these migrations of specialists and, in general, of the diffusion of technologies between population centers. Fortunately, there is more information about ceramic items manufactured in one place that later appeared in another, that is, goods that were traded over a wide area.

When these new ceramics arrived at their destination, they were not simply used by the residents, but also became objects for imitation by local ceramists. The decorative elements were always the easiest to emulate. But attempting new techniques was much more complex, usually calling for the help of skilled artisans with the knowledge to develop the new methodologies. Copying products without a genuine knowledge of fabrication techniques only resulted in imitations of varying quality that focused on decorative features. These copies were made from locally accessible materials, using familiar methods.

The chronicle of these counterfeits, whether made with purposeful or casual intent to defraud the client, is almost the same as the history of mayólica, which from its beginnings was intended to supplant articles made of precious metals, glass, and, especially, fine oriental porcelain. In this attempt at imitation, at reproducing the ideal product seen and now demanded by consumers, in that uncertain terrain between what artisans had learned and what they were now forced to replicate, lay the possibility that new forms would arise. With this insight, we specialists in ceramics try, with varying degrees of success, to identify these pieces in order to determine their origins. In this sense, specialization in loza always involves some proof of authenticity, affixing an exact point that a piece should occupy in the endless chain of plagiarized articles. This problem of analysis relates equally to all periods, from the Asian-influenced ceramics of pre-Roman Spain to the transfer-printed mayólica of the nineteenth century and even the serigraphed imitations of Andalusian *alicatados* (tile mosaics) that are now fabricated in Castellón.

Fees and Taxes

Beginning in the Middle Ages, distinct levels of municipal, state, and royal administration were accustomed to obtaining remuneration from any traffic of manufactured goods or raw materials. The rates could be determined by either gross weight or by count of individual items (fig. 4.5). In the case of ceramics, fees for shipping basic fabrication materials, such as clays and metal oxides, had to be accounted for in the selling price.[14] We also should bear in mind that potters had to make a payment to their municipal governments each time they lit their ovens to fire their pots or tiles. In Sevilla around 1500, for example, potters paid the authorities an amount equal to the value of one jar for each oven in which more than 100 jars would be fired.[15] Once the ceramics were produced, the transport of the finished product generated additional costs, if the articles were not sold in the same locality. There was a type of exit fee for the objects even before they were put on the road toward their final destination. The level of fiscal pressure on producers was at times so intense that it dissuaded some craftsmen and merchants from taking up commercial ventures. In fact, one of the methods that nobles adopted to bolster and stimulate the economy of certain cities in their jurisdiction was simply to eliminate the payment of certain taxes from the production sectors they were interested in energizing. This occurred in Manises, for example, with the protective tactics of the Boil family (lords of Manises) and in Alcora, where artisans were afforded the opportunity to circulate their products freely, thanks to royal privileges granted to the count of Aranda. But such commercial protection was not common. When lead was purchased in the sixteenth century to be used in the glazing process, it was necessary to pay an import/export tax (*almojarifazgo*) of 5 percent and a sales tax (*alcabala*) of 10 percent.[16] Merchants had to pay an additional tax, known as the *avería* (an armed forces tax for military protection), to protect the merchandise loaded on ships until it reached its final destination.

We know now that during the eighteenth and nineteenth centuries, customs tariffs became a key factor in the creation and bankruptcy of many preindustrial and industrial factories of mayólica. In the 1700s, the monarchy became concerned that Spain was consuming enormous quantities of high-quality mayólica produced abroad, while local factories were not rising to challenge the foreign ceramics, in spite of the huge number of customers. One of the methods devised to encourage production was to impose heavy taxes on imports, which made domestically manufactured items more competitive. Of course, these levies had a negative effect on import businesses, who saw their interests and profits decline. They soon put pressure on the government to lower the duties. Balancing efforts by the authorities sometimes favored the potters, sometimes the merchants. This alternation in political leadership between liberals and conservatives was responsible for exaggerated fluctuations in prices and was an impediment to stability.

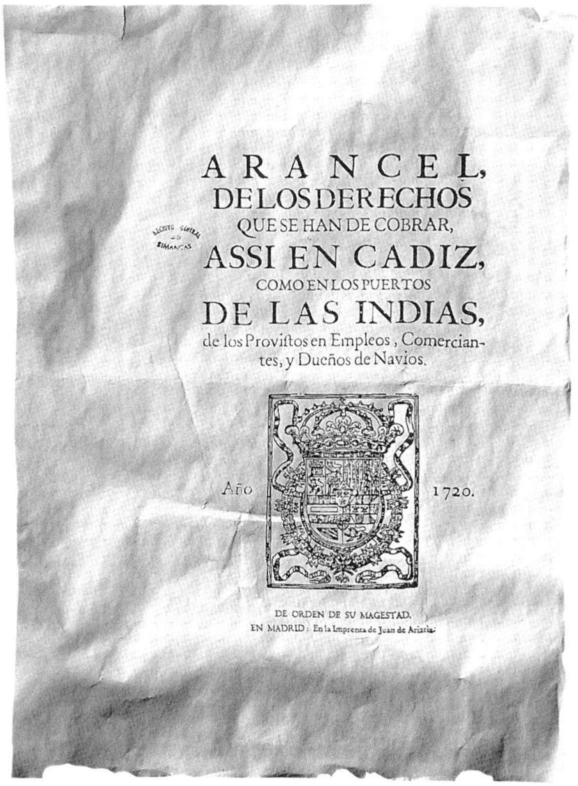
ARANCEL,
DE LOS DERECHOS
QUE SE HAN DE COBRAR,
ASSI EN CADIZ,
COMO EN LOS PUERTOS
DE LAS INDIAS,
de los Proviſtos en Empleos, Comerciantes, y Dueños de Navios.

Año 1720.

DE ORDEN DE SU MAGESTAD.
EN MADRID: En la Imprenta de Juan de Ariztia.

4.5 Book of *fees to be charged in Cádiz as well as at the Ports in the Indies*
Madrid, 1720
Archivo General de Simancas, Valladolid

Mule Drivers and Sailors

The larger centers of ceramic production were almost always strategically located at important hubs of transportation and communication. Factories in the interior of the country had the potential for satisfying the internal demand for products, but found it difficult to distribute their wares to distant marketplaces. In Spain, ceramic plants in Valladolid, Toledo, Talavera, Úbeda, Teruel, Muel, and Villafeliche played an important role as suppliers for the domestic market, but production centers located near the sea were the source for the majority of exported products. This is illustrated by the cities of Murcia and Málaga for medieval Islamic lusterware; Manises and Paterna for medieval Christian mayólica; Sevilla in the sixteenth and nineteenth centuries; Lisbon in the seventeenth century; Alcora and Valencia in the eighteenth century; and Castellón, Cartagena, and Sargadelos in the nineteenth century.

The rule functioned with an implacable commercial logic. A product from the interior would be hauled to a port city for shipment to foreign markets. In its price, besides the initial cost of fabrication, fees, and profits, it was necessary to include the cost of this transportation to the coast, which was sometimes a considerable amount. As a result, it was logical for the ceramists of the port city, if they had access to raw materials, to imitate these products and sell them at a more competitive price. This is what happened with Talaveran loza shipped from Sevilla. It was soon supplanted by imitations made by potters in Triana, who came to be called "painters of Talavera mayólica" in the same way that years before they had called themselves "painters of Pisa and Venice mayólica," when those were the best-selling products.[17] With equal audacity, in the 1600s they called themselves "painters of Chinese mayólica,"[18] and in the 1700s "Dutch-style painters."[19] Alongside these tolerated counterfeiters were found the true expert potters from Italy and Talavera who, viewing the potential of port cities for their trade, moved to coastal areas and from there continued directly on to the centers of foreign consumption. This was how the mayólica centers of Lisbon, Puebla de los Ángeles, and Lima came into existence.

4.6 *Loaded mules on the Camino de la India*
Mexico, 19th century
Anonymous lithograph

But land transportation systems also played an important distribution role within Spain and the Americas. Land routes were utilized in direct relation to the distances involved, the weight and volume of the objects, and the quality of roads to be traveled. When the routes consisted of *caminos de herradura* (roads suitable for shod horses), cargo could be loaded on carts, where the various fragile objects, whether mayólica or coarser wares, were packed with soft materials to avoid breakage during shipment. When the quality of the roads did not permit this method, it was necessary to turn to the use of mule or donkey trains, more adaptable to rugged terrain (fig. 4.6). The drivers who guided these pack animals were essential in the distribution of ceramics to the interior of the country. This system of transport made it possible for items such as the ceramics of Talavera to reach market areas such as the royal court. The mules carried packs woven from esparto grass or canvas, stretched over wooden frames and secured with wire. Wooden barrels, similar to those used for wine, were also used to protect pottery from the inevitable jolts of the journey. It is fascinating today to realize that a large quantity of Asian porcelains managed to arrive in Spain in the sixteenth and seventeenth centuries after crossing not only two oceans, but also the risky and tortuous Camino de la India, which traversed the high plateau of Mexico from the Pacific-coast port of Acapulco to Veracruz on the Atlantic.[20]

4.7 Cart loaded with pots
Portuguese *Alentejo*, 20th century
Photo from *La céramiqe populaire du Haut-Alentejo* (1968)

For shorter distances, ceramic products from some production centers in the interior were distributed by means of the so-called *caballerías menores*, animals of lesser strength and endurance than mules, but which cost less to maintain. These burros carried their cargo of pots and jars in panniers (*angarillas*) made of grass, wire, and canvas. This was the most frequently used means of transporting pottery to marketplaces in Spain up to the beginning of the twentieth century (fig. 4.7).

In the cities, humans took over the chore of hauling these objects. It was common to witness men or women loaded down with wicker or cane baskets or hampers (*serones*), suspended from a beam attached to a yoke, supported by the shoulders of these vendors, who sold their products in the streets, plazas, and local marketplaces.

When ceramics were destined for sale to more distant areas, it was necessary to transport them by sea. The lusterware of Málaga was shipped to Flanders and England; products from Manises reached the Italian coasts; and porcelain from China and Japan reached the tables of Europeans via maritime routes. The ceramics were placed in the cargo holds of caravels, carracks, naos, and galleons and packed in specific containers (fig. 4.8). Sometimes they were inserted into large clay containers listed in shipping documents by generic terms such as jugs (*vasos*) or urns (*jarras*). These were often large earthenware jars (*tinajas*), whose interiors were filled with plates, bowls, braziers, jars, and candleholders, among other items, packed with straw, aromatic herbs, and fibrous material (*hilaturas*) for protection. The containers were later sold at the point of delivery. Some documents cite the use of wooden boxes and barrels along with baskets of various plant fibers that proved to be light, durable, and

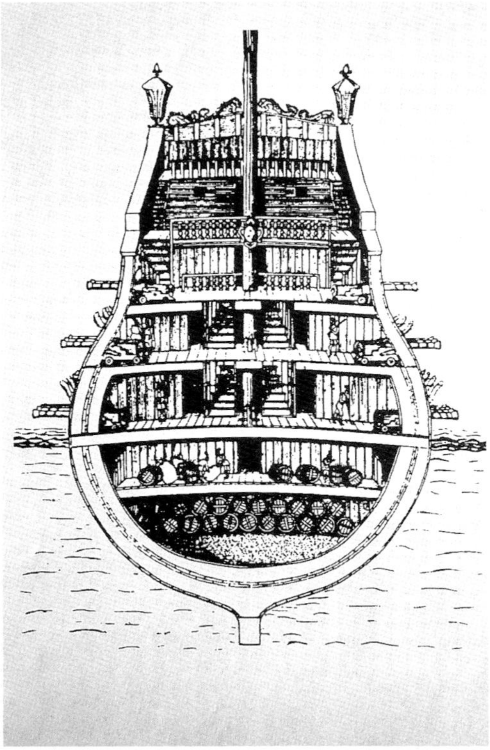

4.8 Section of the hold of a galleon

resistant to slipping and sliding when stacked one on top of another. Shipments of tiles were piled in handleless baskets (*seras*) or creels of intertwined esparto grass in a well-planned prismatic arrangement that allowed for the shapes of the tiles. We know through shipping lists that large basins (*lebrillos*) also eventually came to serve as receptacles for ceramic objects.

One specific problem involved with the ceramics business was posed by items destined to be containers for fluid products such as oil, wine, vinegar, rose water, honey, etc. In the Almohad Muslim world and in medieval Valencia, there were special containers that had been used for this purpose, just as there had been in ancient times. In the first years of the fleets that traveled to the Americas, simple domestic ceramics such as jugs (*tarros*), jars (jarras), pitchers (*cántaros*), and canteens (*cantimploras*) were used as containers for these liquids. But from the middle of the sixteenth century, the volume of such products exported called for the creation of specific containers. At this time arose the innumerable *botijas* for oil or wine that were loaded aboard vessels destined for ports in the Indies or the Atlantic seaboard of Europe. These globular jugs (popularly called "olive jars" in English) of various sizes were sheathed in woven esparto, a fragile material that has not survived in any of the thousands of examples that have been unearthed in archaeological excavations or salvaged from sunken ships (fig. 4.9). They were also covered with cork or plaster to assist in the preservation of their contents and were marked on their exteriors with symbols that served to identify the destination and the party responsible for delivery.[21] Spherical earthenware objects were expressly for use in transport; their round form and lack of handles facilitated rapid and inexpensive production. Their plant-fiber sheathing also allowed for them to be "timbered" or "shored" as cargo in the hold of ships without concern for dangerous shifts or displacement while at sea. The shape and size of their mouths also permitted easy handling during the loading and unloading process.

Some of the ceramics now being found in excavations in port areas and in wrecked ships still resting beneath the surface of the ocean, however, were not part of mercantile shipments but rather were items for the personal use of the

4.9 Olive Jar / *Botija*
Spain, 18th century
Lead-glazed earthenware
Gift of the Historical Society of New Mexico
Museum of International Folk Art (Museum of New Mexico), Santa Fe
Photo by Paul Smutko

crews of these ships or the personal possessions of travelers who had been aboard.

Shopkeepers, Storeowners, Street Peddlers

When a ceramist passed his qualifying examinations to be a *maestro* (master potter), he obtained with his certification permission from the guild to contract work in his own name, to train apprentices in his workshop, and to sell his products directly to the public. If the shop was small, it usually had little space for selling and storage. Frequently, though, pottery workshops that were situated in peripheral urban zones had more space available. Their organization was like that of a small factory, with different sections for production, storage for stock and supplies, and sales activities. At the beginning of the sixteenth century, a well-known Sevillian ceramist, Fernán Martínez Guijarro, maintained along with his workshop (*obrador*) lusterware stores (*las tiendas del dorado*),[22] where his products were sold. Given that ceramists' work was seasonal, artists and their families took advantage of production lulls to sell ceramics they had produced.

A certain percentage of the items made were not for sale to the public, since they served potters, on occasion, as payment to their suppliers of raw materials and also a means of paying rent for the facilities they occupied. These premises were frequently owned by private individuals, but more often the proprietors were religious institutions. Many of the pieces received as payment for rent or materials were not kept by those who received them but were resold. In Sevilla, for example, the convents of Santa Clara, San Clemente, and especially the Cartuja de las Cuevas Monastery held title to many pottery shops in Triana and did not charge rent in cash but rather purchased some of the finished products at very reduced prices. Some of these organizations were also owners of stores located on the *alcaicería de la loza*, a street set aside specifically for the sale of this product, situated next to the church of San Salvador, in Sevilla. Similar marketing practices took place in cities throughout Spain.

4.10 Ceramics Market on Feria Street
Postcard, Sevilla, ca. 1900
Private collection

Ceramists were not always the vendors of their own products. Often major mercantilists bought and stocked pots to sell wholesale to retailers. In this way the products acquired by the warehouses found outlets to the public through small shopkeepers and street vendors who set up kiosks in the temporary markets permitted by the municipalities (fig. 4.10). They also marketed their wares through itinerant salespeople, who sold items carried on the backs of their donkeys. However, the local authorities, pressured by manufacturing and shopkeepers' guilds, did not always consent to requests from merchants from other areas to set up sales operations. These restrictions aided in limiting the competition to local manufacturers and vendors who maintained permanent shops.

Tourists, Antique Dealers, and Collectors

Collectors and their commercial connections, although forming a small sector of the market, are of major importance to us today because of the record they have provided of the ceramics of the past. The collection of ceramics is not a long-established phenomenon. In the centuries of the modern era it was restricted to the affluent classes and basically centered on porcelain. Commonly known as china in Spanish as well as in English, it was displayed in pieces of furniture known as *chineros* or *escaparates* (china cabinets). Collecting at the time was not an exacting effort, but rather derived from a desire for possessing sumptuary objects that conferred on the proprietor a certain prestige. Such collectors often

4.11
Páramo's Collection
Oropesa (Toledo)
Photo from *La cerámica Antigua de Talavera* (1919)

4.12 Ruiz de Luna's Collection
Talavera de la Reina
Photo from *Historia de la cerámica de Talavera de la Reina y algunos datos sobre la de Puente de Arzobispo* (1943)

lacked a genuine interest in learning about the objects in their possession. In the nineteenth century, the revolution in transportation and communications permitted the middle classes as well to gain knowledge of exotic forms of ceramics imported from the colonies. But it was the trends in nationalism, and the consequent valuation of artisans whose work was in danger of extinction due to advances in the industrial world, that at the end of the 1800s provoked the formation of our first great collections of Spanish mayólica (fig. 4.11). With this shift, a new form of appreciation not attached to the functional character of the object, nor to its opulent nature, but to its historic and aesthetic value made its appearance, along with new marketing techniques for these articles. The lusterware of Manises awoke a sense of nostalgia for "Moorish Spain." The solid and strong mayólica of Talavera became important to those who reflected on "Imperial Spain" of the Golden Age (fig. 4.12), and collecting simple and austere earthenwares appeared to be essential to collectors of the great industrial cities, who viewed their disappearance as connected to that of a Spain of former eras that was less developed but also less dehumanized by modern urban centers founded on technology.

Everyone projects on cultural artifacts their anxieties, their hopes, their dreams, and their ambitions. Just as those Europeans of the fifteenth century who watched the fabrication of Spanish lusterware with astonishment and concluded that it was the result of a prodigious operation only explicable by secrets of the science of alchemy, we must not forget that in the end, this transformation of the earth into gold entails more than merely entrepreneurial activity. Part of the economic reward is the expansion of art and culture.

Notes

1. In the following pages I will not examine the economic aspects of work carried out in workshops, guilds, or factories. Neither will I delve into the circulation of ceramics or ceramists in Spain throughout history, since this subject is also treated in this publication. I will only approach the subject in very general terms and in its most basic aspects, regarding the interchange of ceramics between distinct groups of peoples. Other themes will be cited, such as the relationship between types of ceramics and their respective commercial networks, transportation channels traditionally used in this area, payment of tariffs, and customary marketing systems.
2. Julia Poole, *Plagiarism Personified? European Pottery and Porcelain Figures* (Oxford: Cambridge University Press, 1986).
3. Florence Lister and Robert Lister, "The Recycled Pots and Potsherds of Spain," *Historical Archaeology* 15:66–78; Fernando Amores and Nieves Chisvert, "Tipología de la cerámica común bajomedieval y moderna sevillana (ss. XV–XVI), I: La loza quebrada de relleno de bóvedas," *Spal* 2 (1993):269–325; Alfonso Pleguezuelo et al., "Loza quebrada procedente de la capilla del Colegio-Universidad de Santa María de Jesús (Sevilla)," *Spal* 8 (1999):263–92.
4. Fernando Amores, "La arqueología posmedieval en España: Panorama y perspectivas," in *Archeología postmedievale: L'experienza europea e d'Italia,* Conregno internazionale di studi (Sassari, 17–19 October 1994) a cura di marco milanese, pp. 51–67.
5. In the case of Spain, a vast number of studies of archaeological collections, most of which are unpublished and primarily centered on the medieval period, barely touch upon postmedieval materials and then only in the epilogues of their descriptions and analyses. Spanish research on this topic is scarce. Among those that stand out is Josep A. Cerdá Mellado and Albert Telese Compte, "Cerámica de procedencia italiana aparecida en Cataluña," *Laietana* (Estudis d'Historia i Arqueologia del Maresme) 9 (1994):293–353. Another very comprehensive and especially informative piece of work is Jaume Coll Conesa, "Mallorca, moviments i corrents comercials a través de la ceràmica," in *Mallorca i el comerç de la ceràmica a la Meditarrània* (Palma de Mallorca: Fundació "La Caixa," 1998), regarding the role of Mallorca as a fundamental enclave for the ceramic commerce in the western Mediterranean. There is still a lack of comprehensive studies of the central, northern, southern, and western peninsular zones. We have only some isolated documentary data on these areas; see José María Sánchez, *La cerámica exportada a América en el siglo XVI a través de la documentación del Archivo General de Indias (II): Ajuares domésticos y cerámica cultural y laboral.* Publicaciones de la Universidad de Sevilla, *Laboratorio de Arte,* Departamento de Historia del Arte, no. 11 (Sevilla: Universidad de Sevilla, 1998), pp.121–33. There is also some work on specific archaeological sites; see Alfonso Pleguezuelo, Rosario Huarte, and Pilar Somé, "Cerámicas de la Edad Moderna (1450–1632)," in *El Real Monasterio de San Clemente de Sevilla: Una propuesta arqueológica* (Sevilla: Universidad de Sevilla—Fundación El Monte, 1997), pp. 130–57; Alfonso Pleguezuelo, "Losas y vida monástica: Las vajillas de la cartuja de Jerez de la Frontera (Cádiz)," in *Las cartujas en Andalucía* (Sevilla: Universidad de Salzburgo, 1999), pp. 245-72; Pilar Somé and Rosario Huarte, "La cerámica moderna en el convento del Carmen (Sevilla)," *Arqueología Medieval* 6 (October 1999):160–71. In the

last few years, there have been some publications on the Canary Islands, a point of enormous interest, because they were a stopover port for ships that sailed the route to the Indies. Other relevant contributions have come from Portugal, a zone that must necessarily be included within a broad peninsular context. In spite of the few published facts, many archaeological collections await study. For some years, specialists have been gathering these ceramics as important testimony of the more recent past.

6. Christofer Gerrard, Alejandra Gutiérrez, and Alan Vince, eds., *Spanish Medieval Ceramics in Spain and the British Isles*, British Archaeological Reports International Series, no. 610 (Oxford: Archaeopress, 1995).
7. The major part of these later colonial materials in the Caribbean and Florida, the best-studied regions, remain unpublished and are therefore almost inaccessible to scholars. However, some excellent work done in the Atlantic zone, such as that concerning the southern part of England, as well as the Mediterranean, are immensely helpful in reconstructing the distinctive personality of Spanish ceramic mercantile history; see Alejandra Gutiérrez, *Mediterranean Pottery in Wessex Households (13th to 17th Centuries)* British Archeological Reports International Series, no. 306 (Oxford: Archaeopress, 2000); and Henric Amouric, Florence Richez, and Lucy Vallauri, "Le comerce de la céramique en Provence et Languedoc du Xe. au XIX siècle: Vingt mil pots sous les mers" *Musée d'Istres* (Aix en Provence) (May–November 1999).
8. Alfonso Pleguezuelo and José María Sánchez, "La exportación a América de cerámicas europeas (1492–1650)," *XV Jornades d'Estudis Històrics Locals, Transferències i comerç de ceràmica a l'Europa mediterrània (segles XIV–XVII)* (Palma: Institut d'Estudis Baleàrics, 1997), pp. 333–63.
9. The classic work on this subject is John Goggin, *The Spanish Olive Jar: An Introductory Study*, Yale University Publications in Anthropology, no. 72 (1968), pp. 163–203. A revision of the theme can be found in Mitchell W. Marken, *Pottery from Spanish Shipwrecks, 1500–1800* (Gainesville: University Press of Florida, 1994).
10. C. Ensenyat, "Colección de cerámica de Paterna en el Museo de Sóller, Mallorca," *Boletín de la Sociedad Arqueológica Luliana* 37 (1979):231–51.
11. Jaume Coll Conesa, "Contenedores cerámicos medievales en las costas de Mallorca," *IV Congreso de Arqueología Medieval Española* 3 (1993): 1073.
12. Jan Baart, "Terra sigilata from Estremoz, Portugal," in D. Gaimster and M. Redknap, eds., *Everyday and Exotic Pottery from Europe c. 650–1900: Studies in honour of John Hurst* (Oxford: Oxford University Press, 1992), pp.273–78.
13. We do not know which of these two routes was used by Felipe II to bring to the peninsula the porcelain articles that display his coat of arms. His emblem is found today in various Portuguese porcelain collections, and it is certain that these specially ordered items were imitated by the rest of his court.
14. José Gestoso y Pérez, *Historia de los barros vidriados sevillanos*, (Sevilla, 1904), pp. 99–100.
15. Ibid.
16. Ibid., p. 100.
17. Ibid., p. 238.
18. Diodoro Vaca and Juan Ruiz de Luna, *Historia de la cerámica de Talavera de la Reina y algunos datos de la de Puente del Arzobispo* (Madrid: Editora Nacional, 1943), p. 210.
19. Alfonso Pleguezuelo, *Cerámicas de Triana: Colección Carranza* (Sevilla: Colección Carranza—Fundación El Monte, 1996), p. 135.
20. Ramón María Serrera, "El camino de México a Acapulco," in *El Galeón de Manila*, ed. by Pilar Barraca de Ramos (Sevilla: Ministerio de Educación, Cultura y Deporte de España—Focus-Abengoa, 2000), pp. 39–49.
21. Alfonso Pleguezuelo and José María Sánchez, "Envases cerámicos comerciales en el tráfico con América en el siglo XVI: Síntesis de un panorama documental," *IV Congreso de Arqueología Medieval Española*, vol. 3 (Alicante, 1993), pp. 1091–98.
22. Gestoso y Pérez, *Historia de los barros vidriados sevillanos*, p. 164.

Detail, Fig. 5.6

5

Traditional Ceramics in Contemporary Sevilla

ANTONIO LIBRERO

IT IS NOT unusual to stroll through Sevilla and find one's eyes pausing to rest upon the ceramic ornamentation of this city's buildings. Striking colors, such as dazzling yellows, vivid greens, and particularly brilliant hues of blue, as well as a grand variety of designs and ornate schemes capture our attention. The majority of these works are not from the era their style appears to indicate. Almost all are in fact from the nineteenth century, the consequence of creative efforts during the revivalist period that we know as Regionalism, and it was this period that created the look that many people associate with Sevilla. In the nineteenth century, Sevilla was "reinvented" by architects such as Aníbal González and Juan Talavera; by decorators such as Manuel Cañas and Cayetano González; and by ceramic craftsmen such as Ramos Rejano, García Montalván, and many others. Special recognition must also be given to the work performed by historians and local scholars—José Gestoso Pérez, Luis Montoto Raustentrauch, Joaquín Guichot Parody, and Manuel Chaves Rey.

With regionalist architecture, an attempt was made to recover the grand artistic vitality of Spain, and especially Sevilla, of the sixteenth and seventeenth centuries, when this city became the center of the Spanish Empire and its American colonies. It was the golden age of Spanish art that would find rebirth within the tenets of the Regionalism movement, although changed social conditions would have an effect on the transformation. Consequently, during the last third of the nineteenth and the first part of the twentieth century, ceramists in Triana experienced a new impetus in creativity, stimulated by the expectations created by the Ibero-American Exposition of 1929. Because of this, they centered their production on designs from the Renaissance and Baroque periods.

Following a period of indisputable decline in the decades between the 1950s and 1980s, it appears that ceramic artisanship is presently gaining importance and interest, not only among the artists engaged in its revival, but also among the public and commercial entities. However, the growing appreciation for this popular Spanish artistic heritage still has not given it the recognition it deserves. The ceramic patrimony of Sevilla has not even warranted the establishment of a museum dedicated to its preservation—even though such museums exist in many other Spanish cities—and many pieces, especially tile dados, continue to be lost at an alarming rate.

There are many workshops dedicated to the production of ceramics in Sevilla, and in all these workplaces one can sense the same passionate enthusiasm for preserving the traditional models and techniques that are part of our iconographic past and present. At the same time, there is an interest in searching for new styles and manners of production that go beyond traditional forms, with the purpose of fully entering contemporary areas of custom-designed ceramics.

Background[1]

The traditional ceramic sector of Sevilla suffered a profound crisis in the first half of the nineteenth century. Its production was reduced to replicating already outmoded, although still basically popular, quickly fabricated models known as *de montería* (hunting scenes). Continuing with a system of hand production, due to the scarcity of innovations or acceptance of technological advances introduced into manufacturing, this period was one of small family-run workshops, whose market was confined to the city. It is not surprising that during this period there was an obvious decline in the production of Sevillian tilework. This was in stark contrast to the profuse production that existed in previous decades. One reason for this was the utilization of other materials considered to be more prestigious for architectural decoration, such as marble. Another was the intense competition of industrially manufactured products from the regions of Valencia and Castellón, which were available at much lower cost.

But at the end of the nineteenth century, the ceramic sector of Sevilla rejuvenated production, with a quality comparable to that of the artisans of the sixteenth and seventeenth centuries. This resurgence would reach its apex during the celebration of the Ibero-American Exposition in 1929, only to be temporarily stymied by the Civil War (1936–39). The end of the conflict would later give rise to a new period of creativity and appreciation in traditional ceramics.

The Commitment of Local Scholars: José Gestoso (1852–1917)

José Gestoso was one of the leading exponents of, and a driving force behind, the movement to revive traditional ceramic production at the end of the nineteenth century. A historian and archaeologist, his dedication to this art form was beyond that of simple participation and investigation. He provided models and inspiration for ceramists, who soon found themselves concerned with rescuing the themes and techniques of the past. His fascination gave rise to his most important work, *La historia de los barros vidriados sevillanos* (1904). This was the basis for subsequent papers that would awaken the interest of scholars of Sevillian art and archaeology who, stimulated by the insights of Gestoso, began the work of investigating the procedures and applications of traditional ceramic arts.

5.1 Tile Panel
ca. 1600.
Museo de Artes y Costumbres Populares, Sevilla
Photo from *Azulejo sevillano,* by Alfonso Pleguezuelo (1989)

The style that Gestoso attempted to recapture and to impose in the workshops of Triana was that of the sixteenth century, known as *imperio*. His efforts centered on the work of the Italian Francisco Niculoso, although the works of Cristóbal de Augusta from the seventeenth century serve as the principal models for tile as well as mayólica tableware. Consequently, the decorative repertoire reclaimed the Italo-Flamenco ornamental themes in ironwork, grotesques, candle holders, classic busts in medallion formats, etc., and the use of brilliant yellow backgrounds to emphasize the central theme of each piece (fig. 5.1).

The Importance of Art Collectors

The attention paid to ceramics in the nineteenth century was also supported by another important element, that of collections. Numerous collectors, Europeans as well as Americans, demonstrated a fondness toward tilework and ceramics produced in Sevilla, thereby restoring the trade routes established in earlier eras between this city and the Americas, which were interrupted by the War of Independence (1808–14). This commercial exchange grew during the first years of the twentieth century, indicating great enthusiasm for works from Andalucía.

It should be pointed out that in these same circles in Sevilla there was another focus of attention at this time, namely the discovery and transfer of mosaic works from Roman ruins in Italica to the home of the Countess of Lebrija. This event brought about a new way of thinking, marked by an eagerness to salvage and restore our most significant monuments. These restoration projects were almost always under the direction of José Gestoso, with the collaboration of the newly formed shops of Triana. Other countries had outstanding sponsors, such as Viollet-le-Duc in France and Ruskin in England, who also were advocates for this art form.

The Importance of Ceramics as Decorative Architectural Materials

The new demand for ceramics did not come about solely through the efforts of collectors. Architects at the end of the nineteenth and

5.2 The Crystal Palace Designed by Ricardo Velázquez Bosco, Madrid, 1887 Photo from *Cerámica aplicada en la arquitectura madrileña*, by Antonio Perla (1988)

5.3 Detail of the Crystal Palace Designed by Ricardo Velázquez Bosco, Madrid, 1887
Photo from *Cerámica aplicada en la arquitectura madrileña,* by Antonio Perla (1988)

the beginning of the twentieth century began to appreciate ceramic materials for their durability and vividness of color. The well-known architect and scholar Ricardo Velázquez Bosco demonstrated this with special enthusiasm in the prolific use of brilliantly colored glazed pieces in his projects (figs. 5.2, 5.3). To this could be added the desire to revitalize important architectural designs on a national scale, where deep-rooted historical models attained a new level of appreciation and became part of what would be categorized in the first thirty years of the twentieth century as Regionalist Architecture.

The architectural use of ceramics appeared early in our Sevilla, not only as an element of construction, in the form of bricks, but also as purely decorative pieces that have always been associated with color, particularly polychrome. Construction with brick reached its highest expression in Islamic Spain, but worthy heirs of traditional Mudéjar building forms carried on through the Baroque period and into what became Historical Regionalism. The last of these eras of traditional construction methods is slowly but surely being reclaimed as a visible and valuable component in many architectural structures.

Regionalism unified the diverse styles that made up the Neomudéjar: a synthesis of Mudéjar and Renaissance. This style conformed perfectly to the two basic pillars of our architecture: climate and history. Bright colors, characteristic of Sevillian architecture, had a practical application in the traditional ceramics produced in Triana. Along with the significance of climate, light played a special role in relation to these polychrome ceramics. It not only enhanced the architectural expression, but its consideration in the design of structures and how they would take advantage of its properties became a characteristic of the architecture of this period.

Industrialization: The Pickman Factory in La Cartuja

The resurgence of ceramic production in Sevilla at the end of the nineteenth century occurred in two phases: first, Triana pottery workshops saw their desires for experimentation and recovery of longstanding local methods realized through the historical research of José Gestoso. Second, the establishment of the Pickman Factory in 1841 brought industrial techniques and models from England. Although the focus here is on the first stage mentioned, we cannot deny the importance of the Pickman factory in the advancement of production technology and specialized training for the staff of workshops throughout Triana.

The most significant impediment to Spanish industrial development, as compared to other European countries, was, for the most part, Spanish colonization, which in turn led to the investment of capital and technology from western industrial countries and the installation of the first multinational corporations on Spanish soil. From 1880, Pickman also manufactured tiles based on British models. However, these models did not appeal to many local consumers, who preferred the replicas of native Hispano-Moresque, Mudéjar, and Renaissance art that were being produced in Triana workshops and whose colors were much more vivid and expressive. Although the technical innovations employed by Pickman (such as transfer printing) did not become established practices in the Triana workshops, other new ideas were accepted that considerably augmented production. This was especially true in the fabrication of tiles by the *arista* method (fig. 5.4). Other English innovations that were incorporated by local factories were the use of hydraulic presses for producing bisqueware and, later on, electric ovens.

5.4 *Arista* Tiles
Sevilla, 19th century
Museo de Artes y Costumbres Populares, Sevilla
Photo from *Azulejo sevillano,* by Alfonso Pleguezuelo (1989)

Ceramics at the 1929 Ibero-American Exposition in Sevilla

The great boom in construction between 1910 and 1917 was due to the works produced for the Ibero-American Exposition and to the application of industrial arts to architecture. The preference for a local typology, integrating basic, traditional elements of design along with the use of time-honored materials, made the work of Triana factories even more notable. The end result was increased research into ancient methods of manufacturing and decoration, at the same time that new avenues of technology were explored and novel designs based on historical motifs were tested.

The technical procedures for tile making utilized in the arista technique signified an important manufacturing precedent, since they offered a standardization paralleling industrial systems. And it was logical that the first designs created by the new factories commonly imitated original hand-painted art. In the twentieth century, production in Sevilla diversified, encompassing all types of ornamentation in tin-glazed ware, thereby recovering traditional styles that had been lost since the first half of the eighteenth century, when these types were most popular.

This broadening of production required the establishment of large, well-organized workshops. Triana industrial production was at its apogee in the last four years prior to the inauguration of the Ibero-American Exposition, when the majority of the pavilions for the event were being constructed. The number of workers in the principal factories had to be increased to meet the growing demand for ceramic products. Work assignments were organized to accomplish the greatest level of efficiency, and decorators were supervised by a master artist who was assisted by journeymen painters. Other tasks were performed by unskilled workers and apprentices.

At the beginning of the 1930s, before the Civil War broke out, the modernization of workshops leading to improved production was well under way. New equipment was introduced, such as friction presses and heat-resistant ovens designed for continuous production, known as *hornos de pasaje.* These new kilns were used for the firing of enameled pieces, while bisqueware continued to be fired in Arab-style ovens. Those factories that did not incorporate these new processes were not able to compete and slowly disappeared.

The decade of the 1930s was not a good time for the Triana pottery workshops. With the closure of the Ibero-American Exposition, the unparalleled construction activity in the city, which also affected the development of ceramic manufacturing, came to an end. When the Civil War erupted, in 1936, it had devastating consequences for Spanish society. It is not surprising that the sudden stoppage in construction should also affect subsidiary industries. But it would have seemed reasonable to expect that after the conflict came to an end, the ensuing reconstruction would have been an incentive for the recovery of the Triana pottery workshops. This was in fact true to a certain extent, but the reality was that the type of architecture advocated by the new regime did not always result in the utilization of traditional Sevillian tile, which was most appropriate for construction representing a folkloric, "nationalistic" Andalusian theme. Paradoxically, some tilework was used in towns populated by sympathizers of the Franco regime. On the other hand, buildings of minor importance were built following Baroque models of *lo blanco*, a style that called for walls to be plain and whitewashed, as were those of rural Andalucía, shunning the exuberance of vivid, multicolored, tin-glazed works.

Consequently, after the cessation of civil hostilities in 1939, the recovery of ceramic fabrication came very slowly. The hornos de pasaje (continuous fabrication kilns) had by then become common, and newer techniques and equipment were introduced: mechanical presses, grinding and crushing machines, and especially ovens heated by fuel oil. The decade of the 1950s, after the breakup of the international blockade that Spain had been submitted to because of its political affiliations, was an era of expansion. That meant an increase in exports to markets abroad, especially to the Americas. Adding to this regeneration was a revived internal demand for ceramics, with the initiation of the *Plan Nacional de la Vivienda*, whose objective was to reconstruct communities destroyed during the war years. Nevertheless, the commercial sector of Andalucía, and of course Sevilla, did not manage to take advantage of the new techniques. Factories chose not to reinvest their profits in the installation of equipment that would have given them a competitive edge in the marketplace. Italy now became the great producer of ceramics on the international level.

The period between 1960 and 1973 was a time of profound decline for the Triana tile factories. The majority of them continued producing their wares using the outmoded Arabic ovens, and only a few adopted the more modern, heat-resistant kilns. Consequently, by 1973 only four shops remained of the forty smaller shops that existed in Triana at the beginning of the 1970s. Some modernization had occurred in 1963, with the installation of the first two *hornos túneles* (tunnel kilns) in Spain, one at Betxi (Castellón) and the other at Santiponce (Sevilla). But while new deposits of clay continued to be mined in Castellón, which helped to keep production costs down in that area, in Sevilla the extraction of clay from the fertile plains of the Guadalquivir was abandoned, and potters in that zone had to order their materials from Castellón. The district still monopolizes the national market for ceramic materials. In spite of this, Sevilla maintains its deeply rooted artisan attitudes, while the region of the Levante is now dedicated to the industrial production of ceramics.

By the beginning of the 1970s, the use of automatic presses and tunnel kilns, fired by fuel oil, slowly but surely were having a positive effect on the recuperation of the ceramics industry. These kilns were utilized not only for the firing of bisqueware, but also for tin-glazed products. The more sophisticated methods resulted in an increase in the quantity and quality of pieces produced, which had a positive influence on the volume of pottery exported. But the 1973 crisis in the availability of petroleum products, due to the rise in prices of crude oil initiated by the member countries of O.P.E.C., made it imperative to search for alternative fuels to lower production costs and maintain competitive prices. Natural gas provided a solution to this problem; it was an inexpensive energy source, environmentally cleaner, and at the same time a new style of kiln appeared, known as the *horno monostrato a llama libre* (natural-gas kiln). In these ovens, the absence of sulfur and the potential for greater temperature control meant significant improvements in the firing process.

The Spanish ceramics industry, and workshops in Sevilla in particular, also had to face the competition presented by cheaper and more reliable materials used for decoration and construction—plastic and stainless steel.

It is obvious that the scientific search for long-lasting, reliable, and inexpensive materials has gradually lead to substitutions for that formerly heavily used and widespread natural element, clay. As a result, articles made with this material in Sevilla have shifted from utilitarian use to a decorative aesthetic purpose far removed from the standardization of industrial production. Therefore, the manufacture of ceramics in Sevilla is now very limited. The Levante zone of Spain currently controls more than 90 percent of commercial fabrication.

The Industry Today

The present condition of the ceramic sector in Sevilla is the result of the events just described; they were the catalyst for the recovery of workshops and the birth of the great Triana factories toward the end of the nineteenth century. Some of these factories continue to produce ceramic wares with the same enthusiasm and objectives as their ancestors, despite the fact that the majority have changed hands and their directors and proprietors do not belong to the families who originally founded and managed them.

In order to gain a comprehensive understanding of the origins of the present structure of the ceramic sector in Sevilla, we must look to its recent past. We have already touched upon the profound crisis that it went through from the 1940s to the 1970s. It not only affected the ceramists; the whole country lapsed into a general state of economic depression. This was especially true in regions of the south, such as

Andalucía and Extremadura, where the high rates of unemployment forced many Spaniards to emigrate to other regions within the country, as well as abroad.

This labor crisis in Sevilla was exacerbated by the collective ineffectiveness of the few productive sectors remaining in the city, ultimately creating a state of great poverty affecting numerous segments of the population. Natural catastrophes that came in the form of cyclical flooding of the Guadalquivir and other, smaller rivers, such as the Tagarete and the Tamarguillo, compounded an already grave situation. As a result of these events, in 1971, in an attempt to aid and employ victims of one of these floods, the government relocated them to an outlying neighborhood known as La Corchuela, where a ceramic training center was established. It later became a ceramics factory bearing the name of the community.

Between October 1971 and the summer of 1972, a course in ceramic techniques was developed by the Formación Profesional Obrera, the predecessor of the present Instituto Nacional de Empleo. This educational experiment, which had remarkably positive results, continued until 1976, functioning as a cooperative for ceramists. The training that was given in the school was quite inclusive, with emphasis on a hands-on approach that required little study in theory; the students' previous level of academic training made a highly theoretical curriculum impractical. The principal modules of training were the following: basic knowledge of creative drawing; preparation of plaster molds for the casting of slips; shaping ceramic pastes by hand and potter's wheel; tile design; and firing techniques. Numerous instructors and students passed through this training factory in La Corchuela, many of whom today have their own workshops.

The other center of training for ceramists in Sevilla, separate from the apprenticeships conducted in traditional Triana workshops or in the Escuela de Formación de Artesanos, was the School of Artisan Training "Della Robbia," located in Gelves. This facility had its origin in a consortium set up by the Employment Advisement Agency, the Technology Development Board of Andalucía, and the town council of the community of Gelves, in 1993. Their objective was three-fold: first, the revival of traditional trades such as ceramic production, that characterized Spanish culture; secondly, the search for a way to satisfy the demand for quality hand-crafted products that had become scarce in the face of an onslaught of industrially produced items of poor aesthetic quality; and lastly, the training of students to provide them the opportunity for personal creative development in an activity that would permit them to make a living.

The training was structured in two annual courses. In the first module, the fundamental techniques of ceramics were introduced. Later, in the second half of training, each student would decide, always under the guidance of an advisor, among the three specialties offered by the school:

5.5 *Plaza de España*
Designed by
Anibal González,
Sevilla, 1929
Photo by
Antonio Libero, 2001

pottery, design, and ceramic ornamentation. In this second phase of the training cycle, students acquired the skills essential for their area of expertise, through the reproduction of historical pieces. The school made use of a magnificent building, surrounded by gardens that incorporated six workshop-classrooms, an area for kilns, a room for the study of design, a classroom for basic technology, a classroom for sketching, two rooms for theory, a laboratory, a library, and an area for the exhibition of pieces, as well as offices and storage rooms.

The last training center in ceramic crafts sponsored by a public institution is the Escuela Taller Plaza de España. This training facility was founded in 1998 because of the pressing need for ceramic materials of the Sevillian style required for rebuilding the plaza (fig. 5.5), especially areas depicting bridges and benches illustrating the provinces of Spain; but it had the second objective of training young ceramists and giving them the necessary skills to enter the labor force. This initiative received the financial backing of the Instituto Nacional de Empleo as well as the Área de Economía del Ayuntamiento de Sevilla. After completing their training, some students went on to set up their own workshops.

The Escuela Taller Plaza de España is composed of three workshops organized in five modules, amounting to a total of sixty students. The most important workshop was that of painting and enamelwork, which took up three modules, leaving one unit for sculpture and modeling and one for pottery production. To accomplish the training objectives of the school, lessons focused primarily on the techniques of ceramic painting characteristic of the early twentieth-century: *pintura bajo baño, sobre baño, a la grasa,* and *cuerda seca.* At the same time, students were encouraged to experiment with enamels and personal designs.

Clay has also been the basis for the fabrication of artistic pieces of a much more modern character, although such pieces still employ traditional techniques in their manufacture. The most important institution responsible for the training of these artists is the Escuela de Artes y Oficios, with its Faculty of Fine Arts. Even such artists as express themselves in modernistic terms that deviate from the traditional ceramic models of Triana, however, are not avant-garde. Clear examples are found in works by Emilio García Ortiz, Enrique Ramos, Santiago del Campo, Carlos Lara, and others.

The Workshops

At present, a detailed analysis of the ceramic sector in Sevilla, without including those artists that employ ceramic materials only as a means of expression or as an alternative to other materials, allows us to distinguish three clearly differentiated types of enterprises. "Historical factories" are those founded since the middle of the nineteenth century, which reached their apogee during the celebration of the 1929 Ibero-American Exposition; although they are now under different management, they have preserved the same name and the same line of production. "New factories" are middle-sized entities that have at least fifteen employees and facilities sufficient for advanced fabrication media, although traditional methods are still utilized, mixed with industrial methods. "Small workshops" are the majority. They consist of two or three employees, but usually including just one ceramist who works on individual projects. This does not mean that the artisan is isolated from colleagues. Such ceramists usually hold membership in professional associations, in which a spirit of cooperation and solidarity predominates. It is only within this closed secular organization that a sharing of techniques and "secrets" of the profession takes place.

We can also distinguish three major categories with regard to types of production. We have to keep in mind that the diversity of sources and models that ceramists use today give them the ability to create a wide variety of pieces; the mixture of influences is such that from a historic-artistic point of view, it is sometimes difficult to clearly differentiate and define styles. The "traditional Sevilla production" category includes reproductions of a historical character, focused mainly on the imitation of Renaissance and Baroque wainscots, as well as pieces of Triana tableware of a decorative nature. To these we need to add traditional models, since they are designed by what we have previously called "historical factories." "Tourist production" is used to refer to a whole series of pieces clearly intended for sale to tourists, who are attracted to a group of stereotyped pieces quite different from traditional works. These are usually small pieces, such as ashtrays, coasters, etc., with typical Sevillian motifs such as the Giralda, the Plaza de Toros de la Maestranza, and the Torre del Oro. Sometimes tourists have shown an interest in objects of larger dimensions

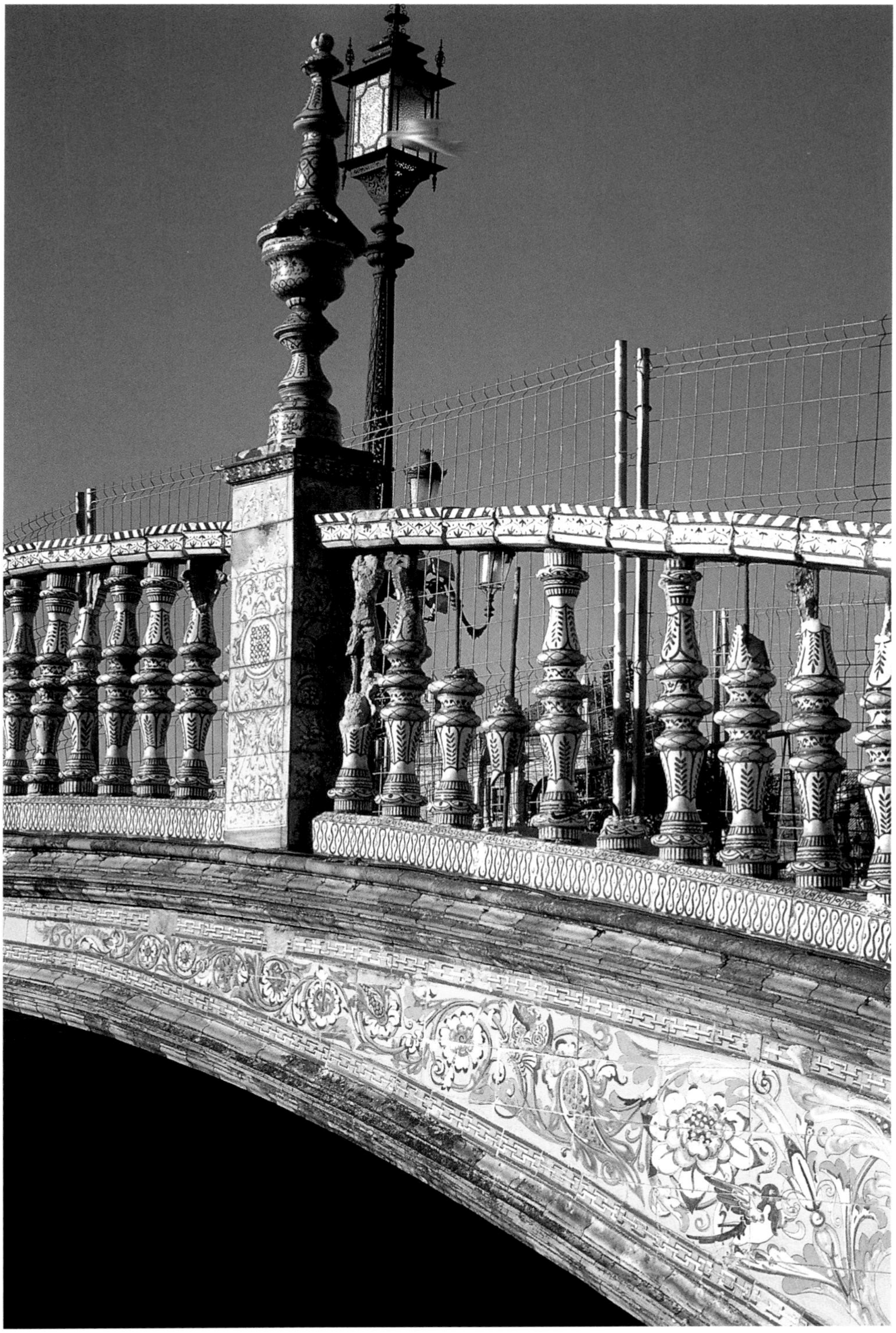

5.6 Balustrade, *Plaza de España*
Nuestra Señora de la O workshop (Montalbán family), Sevilla, 1927
Photo by Robin Farwell Gavin, 2002

made by the cuerda seca technique, displaying decorations of Arabic influence to which a mirror or a clock might be added. "Personal production" is different from the two former categories in the sense that although ceramists producing these works draw their inspiration from them, they add personal touches to each piece.

Let us now examine in detail a number of workshops producing works that correspond to each one of these groups. We have tried to select the best representatives of each group, but are fully aware that due to the large number of artisans now active, some may have been left out. (The following information was obtained by the author in a series of interviews with the potters conducted between 2 February and 23 May 2001.)

Historical factories

Montalván Ceramics is one of Sevilla's oldest ceramics factories, although the connection of the Montalván family with the production of ceramics ended in the eighteenth century. The layout of the factory as we know it today dates back to 1850. The most outstanding director was Manuel García-Montalván (1876–1943), who in 1895 inherited the factory from his father, Francisco García Montalván y Vera. García-Montalván Jr. gave the factory the name of Nuestra Señora de la O. At the time, the factory was quite well known even on an international level. In 1878 it was honored with the silver medal of the Universal Exposition of Paris.

Perhaps the most successful period for this factory was just before the 1929 Exposition, when it received numerous orders. Among them were *La fuente de las ranas* (the frog fountain), benches and pools for the Plaza de las Américas, Glorieta del Quijote, and balustrades for the estuary area of the Plaza de España (fig. 5.6). In the decades that followed, the factory went through the general period of decline, but at present it sustains good production levels. It is currently under the direction of José Manuel Canto, who took over the reins from his father, a close associate of Montalván for many years. The factory has kept its original name and the production standards that have made it famous for over 150 years. Its main focus is on tilework. It has preserved the early stencil drawings that have been imitated since the time they were first created. In order to safeguard the traditional craftsmanship of its pieces, the factory does not employ more than ten to fifteen workers. The only part of the production process that has not been retained is the manufacture of *biscocho* (bisqueware), which at present is obtained for the most part from the district of Castellón.

Recognition of the quality of the products of this factory is evidenced in the numerous orders it has received to renovate some of the unique buildings of the city. Some examples of these are the tin-glazed tiles for the cupola of the Iglesia de la Magdalena, in Sevilla, and the fountain for the Plaza del Ayuntamiento in Vejer (Cádiz), as well as works in other Andalusian localities. The demand for Montalván ceramics has also spread to other countries, such as Germany, where there are several hotels with decorations produced by this factory, and England, where they are seen in a chain of fast-food restaurants.

Santa Isabel Ceramics is currently owned by Francisco Ruiz Moreno. It belonged to his father, Joaquín Ruiz Gutiérrez, who in turn inherited it from his father, Sebastián Ruiz Jurado. Up until 1939, the factory belonged to the renowned ceramist Antonio Kiernam. In January of that same year, marking 150 years since its foundation, the factory was acquired by the present owner's grandfather. Up to that time, the workshop had been run by a partnership of three potters, from whom Ruiz Jurado purchased it with income acquired during the 1929 Exhibition. He established his residence in rooms above the shop.

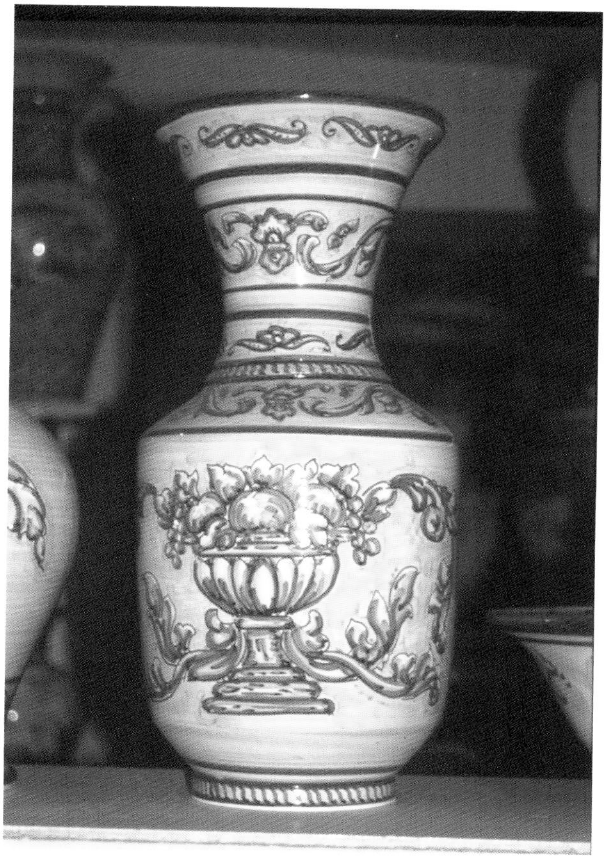

5.7 Jar / *Jarro*
Santa Isabel workshop, Sevilla
Photo by Antonio Libero, 2001

At present, the site is dedicated only to sales. The Santa Isabel Ceramics workshop is located close to Sevilla, in Palomares del Río. It has six employees and a workspace of around 500 square meters. The method of production continues to be completely traditional, except for the elaboration of rims (*cenefas*). Every order is painted by hand, except for custom orders or requests for large volumes of objects, in which case serigraphy is used. Unfortunately, the raw materials utilized—clay, pigments, glazes, etc.—are industrially fabricated, and the bisqueware is obtained as prefabricated pieces. Molds are employed solely to produce three-dimensional pieces with their own unique designs. Santa Isabel produces all types of ceramics, from very small pieces such as ashtrays to large jars, flower pots, fountains and tile dados.

This workshop has also maintained the feel for traditional designs, including those of Renaissance ceramic objects and pieces with the historically popular hunting themes, using the time-honored colors cobalt blue, light yellow, etc. (fig. 5.7). Catalogs with specific motifs are not used; the designs are passed on from instructors to their apprentices. Francisco Ruiz as a child used to play among his father's pots and gradually learned the intricacies of the art form at which he is so skilled today. He in turn teaches his employees, who come to him with very little experience or previous training. In this way he avoids certain "bad" habits acquired through approaches to teaching used in other media, such as painting on canvas.

Ceramics from the Santa Isabel Ceramics workshop are in great demand abroad; the factory has clients in the United States, Malaysia, and other foreign markets. However, it lacks any large-scale promotion for its products, and this is an impediment to growth in foreign sales.

Santa Ana Ceramics was founded around 1908 by Manuel Rodríguez y Pérez de Tudela, a distinguished painter and ceramist. After a rigorous apprenticeship at the factory of La Cartuja and the workshops of Mensaque and Soto (see chapter 1), he decided to establish his own factory. In 1939 he took over another factory, and the merger produced the Rodríguez Santa Ana Ceramics Co. This was the predecessor of the present Santa Ana Ceramics factory.

Among the many other excellent works the factory produced for the Ibero-American Exposition are a variety of dados on the facades of various buildings. Processional brotherhoods also placed numerous orders, which were completed by Manuel Rodríguez with products of high quality. José Macías (1879–1963) was another distinguished painter who worked for this factory; he was an expert in glaze-painting techniques. At present the factory continues to create traditional Triana pieces, mainly dados and ornamental pottery (*cacharrería*), which feature historical motifs dominated by hunting themes.

The last workshop of the historical group considered here is the Mensaque Rodríguez Company. The Mensaques were a family of industrialists, not ceramists, but they had the insight to see the commercial advantages that ceramic production could bring. As a consequence, they established one of the most important and successful ceramic companies. Their first factory was established in 1880, although Miguel Mensaque had been creating pieces since 1846. Production of artistic ceramics reached their high point toward the end of the nineteenth century, thanks to the work of some prestigious painters (fig. 5.8). In 1923, after several mergers, the present factory was created. In 1974, due to its tremendous growth, it was moved from Triana to Santiponce, a site in Sevilla.

The company's output has been geared toward heavy industrial fabrication, although works are still hand painted for special commissions. Production has focused principally on construction ceramics, particularly tiles, reproducing dados whose designs reflect the historical era of the factory.

5.8 *Arista* tile for a *remate* Mensaque Rodríguez y Cía, late 19th–early 20th century Collection of the Real Alcázar de Sevilla Photo from "Un depósito de azulejos históricos en los Reales Alcazares de Sevilla," by Alfonso Pleguezuelo, *Aparejadores*, journal of the Colegio Oficial de Aparejadores y Arquitectos Técnicos de Sevilla, 44 (1995).

5.9 Plates in the *cuerda seca* and lusterware techniques CEARCO, Sevilla Photo by Antonio Libero, 2001

New Factories

The factory known today as CEARCO was called Cerámica Artística Colón when it was founded in 1982. It maintained this name until 1994 and was located until recently in Triana. Initially, when its output was limited, it remained in a neighborhood of Triana, but the continued growth of the factory and its staff required new quarters, and it was relocated to an industrial complex situated on the outskirts of Gelves (Sevilla). The factory now occupies buildings with work and office space of about 2000 square meters and employs twenty-eight to thirty workers.

5.10 Painting *cuerda seca* in the workshop of CEARCO, Sevilla Photo by Antonio Libero, 2001

The interest in ceramics on the part of Joaquín García Colón and his wife, Concha Vidal Muñoz, was due to his father's work for the now inactive factory of Pedro Navia. Although the factory is predominantly craft oriented, the growth it has experienced and the great demand for its pieces have led to the industrialization of certain facets of the manufacturing process, especially since 99 percent of the production uses the cuerda seca method, which is conducive to standardization. For this reason, serigraphy is used to indicate the outlines of the designs that consist mainly of traditional Hispano-Moresque forms (figs. 5.9, 5.10).

CEARCO products are sold mainly in tourist shops. Hence its

repertoire consists for the most part of plates of various sizes, frames for mirrors and clocks, etc. The workshop has its own assembly area for the manufacture of wooden frames and stock rooms where mirrors and the clock mechanisms are set up and stored.

Antonio González Cerámica Artística was founded in 1981. González began his career in ceramics in Mairena del Alcor. The workshop at that site was successful, and as the business grew, he moved to a larger facility in the industrial center of El Viso del Alcor (Sevilla). Since 2000, the factory at the new location has had a staff of eighteen employees. There is also a shop in Triana, where products from this factory are marketed.

Antonio González received his training more than twenty-five years ago in Triana at the Montalván factory, where he had the opportunity to learn from distinguished ceramists of the caliber of José Escolar and Domingo the Potter. From the beginning, he was interested in the art of ceramic painting. He showed unusual talent and tried to imitate his much-admired mentor, Enrique Orce, an outstanding ceramist who produced many fine works during the golden era of the Triana workshops, at the beginning of the twentieth century. He furthered his education by taking some courses at the Escuela de Artes y Oficios. His principal goal was to improve his skills and recover the valuable ceramic artistry of the past. While he does not paint as much nowadays, he is busy imparting his knowledge of the craft to his children, who, following age-old traditions, work with him at the factory.

5.11 Tile panel Cerámica Artística Antonio González, Sevilla Photo by Antonio Libero, 2001

The models used by González are the traditionally popular motifs from Sevilla (fig. 5.11). He also draws on other Spanish styles, but he always places the greatest importance on the cultural and historical aspects of design. His production is centered above all on dados and panels depicting landscapes and country scenes. When he makes other pieces, such as finials or railings, he requires the help of an assistant. He uses a wide variety of colors for his compositions, which he obtains by mixing combinations of today's readily available industrial colors. However, he believes that the old methods of mixing paint, in which the ceramist actually fabricated the pigments himself, gave a better result. His advice to present-day ceramists is to try to imitate, to the best of their ability, the quality of the ancient pieces.

Small Workshops

The director of Cerámica Gran Poder is Rafael Abad. He had always been interested in the world of crafts, beginning with furniture restoration and woodcarving. About twenty-two years ago, he made the acquaintance of some recently graduated ceramists from La Corchuela factory, and together they decided to establish a workshop. He learned from them the skills of ceramic manufacture and seven years later decided to establish his own workshop. At the beginning, he specialized in various types of clay molding and gradually, as his technique developed, widened his repertoire and increased production (fig. 5.12).

Regarded as a self-taught artist, through hard work and experimentation, the quality of his products improved. When he decided to move his workshop from Trajano Street to a site close to the Basilica de Gran Poder, he adopted the name of the church for his workshop.

His production is exclusively crafts oriented; he never produces pieces in series. His designs are varied, but he always follows the authentic traditional repertoire of Sevilla,

5.12 Jar / *Orza*
Cerámica Gran Poder, Sevilla
Photo by Antonio Libero, 2001

5.13 Painting in the workshop of Cerámica Águilas, Sevilla
Photo by Antonio Libero, 2001

5.14 Ceramics from Cerámica Águilas, Sevilla
Photo by Antonio Libero, 2001

primarily those associated with religious and regionalist themes. He applies only traditional colors to his pieces, and consequently never uses red. He has created many works for processional brotherhoods in Sevilla, such as La Lanzada (Church of San Martín) and Las Aguas (Dos de Mayo Chapel).

Cerámica Águilas is one of the oldest in the city among the new, small workshops, established in 1979, under the direction of Cristóbal Rodríguez (fig. 5.13). At that time practically no one was working in ceramics in Sevilla, and the Triana workshops were filled with pieces from Valencia.

Cristóbal Rodríguez received his practical training from La Corchuela factory. Upon completing his education, he established his own workshop with the purpose of recovering traditional motifs that had gradually been disappearing, especially on items such as plates and tiles. The reputation of his workshop grew as he met the increasing demand for high-quality products. Today it is one of the most distinguished in the region.

The production of Rodríguez's workshop is diverse, ranging from tile panels of different styles and themes to all types of three-dimensional figures as well as plates, jars, and holy-water fonts (figs. 5.14, 5.15). The most common motifs portrayed on his pieces are traditional themes, using historical models as the basis for new creations. Although the demand for his products is mainly local, he has created some pieces for other areas, such as the one on display in the Iglesia del Rocío de San Pedro de Alcántara, in Málaga. But above all, his work is centered on the numerous panels made for the Sevillian brotherhoods.

5.15 Jar / *Tibor*
Cerámica Águilas, Sevilla
Photo by Antonio Libero, 2001

Cerámica Ruiz Gil follows a production line very similar to those of the previously mentioned workshops. Manuel Ruiz Gil, its founder and director, began production fifteen years ago. His initial training was in carving and sculpting, a background that is reflected in the smoothness and fluidity of his drawings (fig. 5.16). He studied at the Escuela de Artes y Oficios, where he became friends with one of his classmates, who noticed his talent for drawing and offered him the opportunity to work on ceramics. Once he was exposed to the wide range of applications that this art form encompassed, it became his life's work.

Soon thereafter, he established his own workshop and began working on tiles with *reflejo de cobre* (copper lusterware). His work in this area has been compared to the fine works produced by the other great manufacturer of reflejo, the Mensaque factory. Unfortunately, the industrial imitation of this technique in Castellón, though of a much poorer quality, has overshadowed the fabrication of these pieces in Sevilla.

Manuel Ruiz Gil's workshop turns out a wide variety of pieces, but he has a preference for painting. He draws special enjoyment from original compositions as well as emulations of historic paintings of the great masters such as Velázquez, Murillo, and Gonzalo Bilbao, among many others. Today Ruiz Gil is one of the few ceramists capable of creating great compositions in the style of historic pictures such as those on the benches of the Plaza de España.

5.16 Tile Panel
Cerámica Ruiz Gil, Sevilla
Photo by Antonio Libero, 2001

Because of his initial training as a carver and engraver, he is able to execute with exceptional fidelity the intricate Renaissance and Baroque decorative motifs such as *roleos* (volutes), putti, acanthus leaves, and shields. He reproduces these entirely from memory, without using models. He is continuously experimenting and never considers his work finished. Perfection for him does not exist, and he is always striving to reach more distant horizons and breakthroughs in the art of ceramic painting.

He has produced works for prominent world figures, such as the late King of Morocco, Hassan II. But if one were to decide which one of his works in Sevilla is most worthy of attention, it would have to be the magnificent tile altar that he designed and created for the church of San Nicolás del Puerto.

Cerámica Luchana is located in the

heart of downtown Sevilla and is under the direction of Juan Vela, who became interested in ceramics totally by chance (fig. 5.17). Ten years ago he was working for a car rental company when he was laid off and decided to try his hand at ceramics. He had always had an interest in handicrafts and had some experience working with papier maché. He began to work in a friend's workshop, where he learned the basic rudiments of ceramic fabrication. Later he decided to work independently and began to produce small clay pieces. His style and techniques have developed through trial and error, rather than through academic training.

5.17 Plate / *Plato*
Cerámica Luchana, Sevilla
Photo by Antonio Libero, 2001

At the beginning, Juan confides, he did not feel any interest for clay. Slowly, as he became more familiar with this material, he began to appreciate its plasticity, which allowed him to experience new creative sensations, to the extent that he now prefers modeling to painting. Following historic examples, he gradually imparts his own personal touch to each piece he creates. His work reflects a broad iconographic repertoire, and he combines motifs of different epochs to create the religious designs that are in greatest demand by the public.

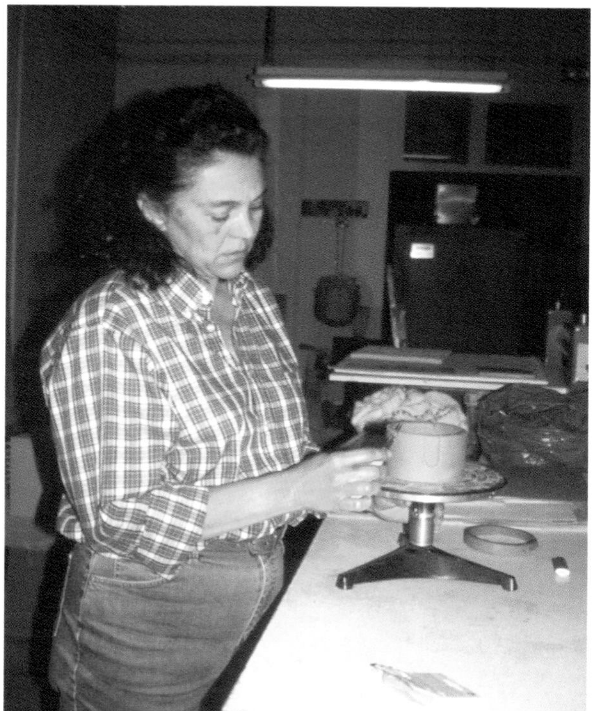

Perhaps the most outstanding characteristic of his work has been its predilection for "folk" Hispano-American designs, which he intends to continue producing. He takes pleasure in doing very small pieces, almost miniatures, filled with a child-like innocence and a graceful fluidity. There is no doubt that his prior experience with papier maché has carried over into his work with clay.

Mercedes Ferreyro began to work with ceramics on her own initiative (fig. 5.18). She was a teacher by profession, but always liked working with clay. Three years ago she

5.18 Ceramic workshop of Mercedes Ferreyro, Sevilla
Photo by Antonio Libero, 2001

5.19 Tiles / *Azulejos*
Mercedes Ferreyro, Sevilla
Photo by Antonio Librero, 2001

enrolled in the Escuela de Artes Aplicadas and upon completion of her studies, she decided to open her own workshop and sell her pieces.

The works she produces are based on traditional motifs, but she adds her own creative signature to every piece she makes. She works by commission, modifying her models according to her clients' wishes. Sometimes she follows samples available in catalogs or other publications. When she is not following historic models, her work is characterized by a sobriety of lines, simple designs, and an avoidance of pretentious patterns (5.19).

José María Campos came to be involved in ceramics after a less than agreeable previous work experience. After working in an unrelated field, he decided to begin training in artistic ceramics. Eventually, an outstanding painter of ceramics was born (fig. 5.20). After studying the fundamentals of design in the "Della Robbia" school in Gelves, he decided to establish his own workshop. He had always had an inclination toward painting, but his only experience had been with traditional materials such as canvas. He was happy to discover the wide range of possibilities open to a painter in the domain of ceramics. He has found a field that allows him to experiment and apply his sketching talents.

His historical reproductions are outstanding, especially those of the sixteenth and seventeenth centuries. He has ventured also into the reproduction of Hispano-Moresque and Turkish pieces. His work is not simple imitation; he has demonstrated his artistic ability by creating pieces sculpted in clay, for which he has received honors. This highly gifted artisan has also participated in important ceramic restoration work, such as that being carried out on the Pabellón de Telefónica, constructed for the 1929 Ibero-American Exposition.

Cerámica Artística Hera is operated by two ceramists; Antonia "Toñi" Azua and Cristina de Luis. It is located next to the famous Roman ruins in Santiponce, Sevilla. Their specialty is the reproduction

5.20 Plate / *Plato*
José María Campos, Sevilla
Photo by Antonio Libero, 2001

of Iberian ceramics that appeal to a discriminating clientele looking for rarer or unusual pieces. As a consequence, they have focused on historical reproductions, especially those of the eighteenth century (fig. 5.21), and on motifs that appear in places such as the Plaza de España and even on designs utilized on small utilitarian pieces such as necklaces, bracelets, and earrings.

Toñi stated in an interview that her training took place at the Escuela de Artes y Oficios. She furthered her education by taking several short courses, during which she met Cristina. They became friends and decided to establish the workshop they have been operating for the past three years. In addition to Iberian historic pieces of the sixteenth, seventeenth, and eighteenth centuries, they have produced some creative modern pieces; they have found, however, that the market for the latter is more limited, and for the time being they have discontinued their production.

Lucía Arriaga is another ceramist who comes from a totally

5.21 Tiles / *Azulejos*
Cerámica Artística Hera, Sevilla
Photo by Antonio Libero, 2001

different working environment (fig. 5.22). She was formerly employed in health care, but became enamored with traditional ceramics. She is almost completely self-taught, having taken only one short course on the basics of ceramics. She decided to open a workshop in her home, putting up with all the inconveniences that that entails. When she runs into areas beyond her expertise, she asks for help from her colleagues, for whom she has great respect.

In an interview she expressed the strong opinion that in small workshops consisting of one or two artisans, where there is simply no production of objects in series, the creative liberty that the ceramists enjoy allow them to become artists without any conscious thought about the transformation that occurs through performing the work.

5.22 Flower pot / *Maceta*
Lucía Arriaga, Sevilla
Photo by Antonio Libero, 2001

Unfortunately, as she herself comments, the need to sell one's products often causes the ceramist to feel "forced" to make historical pieces, since those are the most popular objects. In order to avoid this situation, Lucía Arriaga thought of continuing to make artistic pieces of a utilitarian nature, introducing into our "standardized" world an innovative touch in her work. To this end, her production has focused on utilitarian pieces such as accessories for the bathroom, designed with great originality. This does not mean, however, that her work is limited to this type of production. She has also done historic pieces, reproductions of Iberian art, and slip-decorated terra-cotta. She has a special interest in contemporary ceramics, to the extent that she has attended one of the summer courses offered in Sargadelos, where she had the opportunity to familiarize herself with the works of ceramists from all over the world.

Finally, Alfar 3 was founded by Teresa Vaya and Paula Felizón. Teresa studied ceramics at the "Della Robbia" school, in Gelves. Paula, originally a history student, took three courses in engraving at the Escuela de Artes y Oficios. Paula and Teresa went on to finish their art education with scholarships in France and Italy, respectively. Four years ago, they decided to open a small workshop, sharing the belief that it is better to start an enterprise step by step, gain some experience, and then begin to produce pieces in larger quantities and of superior quality.

They produce several kinds of pieces, especially painted pottery; but they also have employed other techniques, such as cuerda seca

5.23 Tile panel in *cuerda seca* technique
Alfar 3, Sevilla
Photo by
Antonio Libero, 2001

(fig. 5.23). Their production embraces a wide array of styles, but they are most enthusiastically involved in the reproduction of impressionist works, which they adapt to the most varied types of objects, such as plates, bottles, and tiles. They do not work much in traditional Triana ceramics, since they believe there are at present too many ceramists dedicated to these objects, so that the market is saturated with them. Therefore, they choose to look for other ceramic markets and areas of interest.

Addresses

Historical Factories

Cerámica Montalván; calle Alfarería, 21–23; Triana; 41010, Sevilla; Spain
Cerámica Santa Isabel; calle Alfarería, 12; Triana; 41010, Sevilla; Spain
Cerámica Santa Ana; calle San Jorge, 31; Triana; 41010, Sevilla; Spain
Mensaque Rodríguez y Cía.; avenida de Extremadura, 1; 41970, Santiponce, Sevilla; Spain

New Factories

CEARCO; Polígono Industrial Guadalquivir; calle Artesanía, 45–46; 41120, Gelves, Sevilla.

Cerámica Artística Antonio González. Factory: Polígono Industrial Santa Isabel, II Fase, Naves 13–14; 41520, El Viso del Alcor, Sevilla; Spain. Showroom: calle San Jorge, 17; Triana; 41010, Sevilla; Spain

Small Workshops

Cerámica Gran Poder; calle Menéndez Pelayo, 49; Sevilla; Spain

Cerámica Águilas; calle Águilas, 25; Sevilla; Spain

Cerámica Ruiz Gil; calle Cristo de la Sed, 25; Sevilla; Spain

Cerámica Luchana; calle Luchana, 2; 41004, Sevilla; Spain

Mercedes Ferreyro; Avenida de Cádiz, 25; 41004, Sevilla; Spain

José María Campos; calle Alfonso Chaves, 43; Castilleja de la Cuesta, Sevilla; Spain

Cerámica Artística Hera; avenida de Extremadura, 27; Santiponce, Sevilla; Spain

Lucía Arriaga; calle Enrique Granados, 1; Urbanización Mammpela; Palomares del Río, Sevilla; Spain

Alfar 3. Telephone numbers: 954-083-812 and 610-752-133. E-mail: alfartres@yahoo.es

Notes

1. This historical summary is based on the work of the following sources: Josep María Adell Argilés, Arquitectura de ladrillos del siglo XIX (1986); Juan Ainaud de Lasarte, Cerámica y vidrio (1952); Pablo Alzola, El arte industrial en España (1892); Antonio Bonet Correa, Historia de las artes aplicadas e industriales (1982); Alfonso Braojos Garrido, María Parias Sainz de Rozas and Leandro Alvarez Rey, Sevilla en el siglo XX (1990); José Cascales Muñoz, Las bellas artes plásticas en Sevilla (1929); Rafael Comenech Martínez, El azulejo sevillano (1988); Juan A. Fernández Laconva, Cerámica sevillana (1977); Guillermo García Ramos, La cerámica artistica y sus autores en la Sevilla actual (1997); José Gestoso y Pérez, Historía de los barros vidriados sevillanos desde sus orígenes hata nuestros días (1904); Antonio Librero Pajuelo, La cerámica en la Exposición Iberoamericana de Sevilla de 1929 (2000), El uso de la cerámica en la Exposición Iberoamericana de Sevilla de 1929 (2000); Alfonso Pleguezuelo Hernández, Cerámicas de Triana (1985), La cerámica arquitectónica en España (1987), Azulejo sevillana (1989), Sevilla y la técnica de cuerda seca (1991), Retratos históricos en azulejos sevillanos del siglo XVIII (1993), El barro, algo más que tierra y agua (1995), Cerámicas de Triana: Colección Carranza (1996), Cerámica de Sevilla (1997); Eduardo Rodríguez Bernal, Historia de la Exposición Ibero-Americana de Sevilla de 1929 (1994); and Alberto Villar Movellán, Arquitectura del Regionalismo en Sevilla (1979).

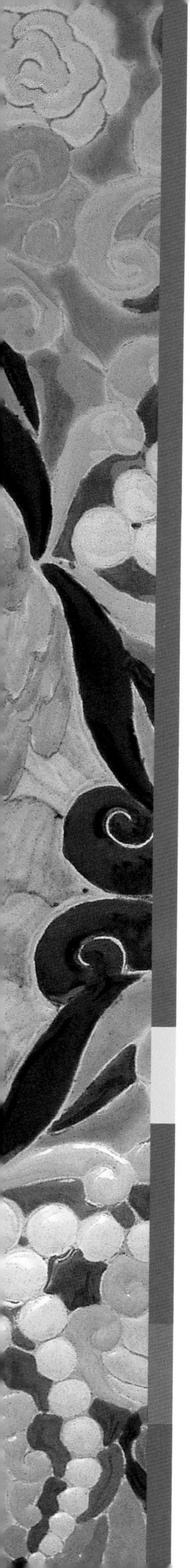

Detail, Fig. 6.9

6

Per Joan, Rosa i Joanito

Baroque to Neobaroque in Barcelona

ANNIE CARLANO

CERAMICS, WHETHER AS functional jars, tableware, tiles, and architectural ornaments, or as the nonfunctional "trick plates" of three-dimensional fake fruit, vegetables, nuts, and eggs, have been a part of the artistic expression of Catalonia since the Middle Ages. While the Romans occupied the region in ancient times, very little of their culture survived to compete with the Islamic world as the predominant source of peninsular ceramic design, as manifested in the lusterware of southern Spain. The ubiquitous drug jar (*albarelo*) is a salient example of the type of decorative art that migrated north both in form and decoration. Catalonia's geographic position, in the northeast of Spain, made it uniquely situated to receive not only influences from the Muslim world, but also from Europe. Gradually, synthesizing both styles and techniques, and exerting its own aesthetic sensibilities, regional styles developed in Girona, Terassa, Reus, Lérida, and other areas throughout the province. Like the Catalans themselves, these styles are straightforward, possessing an economy of means, *seny,* earthiness, and wit.[1] This chapter concerns the predominant technique of ceramics in Catalonia, tin-glazed earthenware, or mayólica, in the region's capital and predominant artistic center, Barcelona. Its intention is to connect the work of contemporary artists with the art of the past in ways both obvious and less obvious. Focused more on tiles than on pottery, representing the strength of a living tradition, it attempts to bring to light information about Catalan artists and their legacies heretofore unknown in English-language literature about mayólica and Catalan ceramics in general.

Early Ceramics

Barcelona has been a thriving metropolis, a hub of eastern Spain since the fourteenth century. While two-color tiles in the Arab style were made by small workshops in Barcelona at this time, the ruling sovereigns preferred to use tiles from Manises in grand architectural projects—typically wall, fountain, and patio designs. The medieval centuries were the period of major ecclesiastical building campaigns, which resulted in some of the most magnificent Spanish medieval church architecture. It was also at this time that the Catalan language, derived from the same root as Provençal, came into its own. In literature, troubadours flourished, writing passionate lyrical poetry rivaling that of the other side of the eastern Pyrenees. The *sardana,* a group dance, can be seen as an expression of the cooperative spirit of Catalans. As the culture took on a distinct personality in these arenas, so a type of mayólica evolved that was immediately identifiable as that of Barcelona.

6.1 Apothecary Jar / *Bote de farmacia*
Cataluña, 18th century
Gift of the Heard Foundation
Museum of International Folk Art (Museum of New Mexico), Santa Fe
Photo by Paul Smutko

By the late sixteenth century, Catalan potters were producing three types of mayólica: blue-and-white pottery, polychrome pottery, and tilework. Deceptively similar, the decorative borders of the blue-and-white plates and bowls are comprised of an elaborate vocabulary, based on abstracted plant and animal forms. Exhibiting the witty imagination of the Catalan artist and the close relationship between ceramic and textile design, a few patterns are named for fashion accessories, such as *carabata,* or cravat, a three-lobed motif that is a stylized version of men's lace neckwear of the period.[2] Sometimes characteristic orange lines appear as inner and outer borders.[3] Blue-and-white drug jars continued to be produced during this period (see figs. 6.1, 2.5), and, as we will see, remain a favorite today on the shelves of pharmacies of the region and in shipments of exports.

The polychrome mayólica of Barcelona displayed a baroque exuberance in its bright palette throughout most of the seventeenth and eighteenth centuries. The *serie floreada* pots and plates represent the high point of ceramic painting in both skill and composition. Fluidly drawn floral and animal compositions are colored with a rich, golden orange, highlighted in cool blues and greens (see fig. 1.9). Often actual scale is disregarded, with birds larger than figures and landscapes. Mastering the challenge of painting scenes in the round is a remarkable achievement. Both the animated, expressionistic brush strokes, the subject matter, and the occasional sense of whimsy seen in these wares reflect the influence of Italian *maiolica*, imported from Montelupo, near the central Tuscany coast. The influence of Montelupo wares cannot be overstated: it is probable that the importation of Montelupo ceramics led to the demise of lusterware in Barcelona.[4]

If the Catalan spirit was captured in the sober ebullience of the serie floreada as a painting style, it was released in the designs of the most original of their ceramic expressions, tilework. Tilework from the Middle Ages can be seen in the monasteries of Catalonia and in the superb collection of the Museo de Cerámica, Barcelona. Created as a part of architectural interiors, they form wall murals as well as ornate wainscoting, or dados. Their patterns follow the development of the pottery of the time, deriving chiefly from Islamic sources and illustrating coats of arms, fantastic birds, and elaborate geometric motifs. By the seventeenth century, some tilework was used as a vehicle for the same serie floreada motifs; rendered flat, the effect is even more lively and delightful (fig. 6.2). Sometimes tiles illustrated luscious fruit and vegetables (fig. 6.3).

Beyond the stunning botanical tilework produced in Barcelona, narrative scenes were produced with a typical palette and simple brush stroke. The earliest such documented tile narratives are now in the northern Catalan city of Narbonne, France, just over the Spanish

6.2 Tile Panel / *Plafón de azulejos*
Barcelona, 17th century
Museu de Ceràmica, Barcelona

6.3 Tile / *Azulejo*
Barcelona, 19th century
Collection of the International Folk Art Foundation
Museum of International Folk Art (Museum of New Mexico), Santa Fe
Photo by Paul Smutko

6.4 Mallorca Tapestry / *Tapiz de Mallorca*
Monastery of Pedralbes, Barcelona, early 17th century
Photo courtesy of the Museu de Ceràmica, Barcelona

border in the Languedoc-Rousillion. Dating to 1649, they depict a battle against Lérida. However, by far the most striking of these narratives are the famous extensive religious and genre scenes painted in 1710 for the Amat family "de la xocolada," now in the Museu de Ceràmica, Barcelona (see fig. 2.19). This highly evocative work is described at length in chapter two, above. Still in situ is the unusual landscape in the monastery of Pedralbes, purportedly representing the Island of Mallorca (fig. 6.4).[5] From this highly evocative repertoire of painted mayólica scenes evolved a more vernacular and popular subject for the artist, judging from numbers of extant pieces: individual panels depicting trades.

La Decadence

The period from the late sixteenth into the seventeenth century was a time when the artistic milieu in the city was waning—(known to Catalans as *La Decadence*); there were no great buildings going up as there were elsewhere in Spain or Italy, there were no painters such as El Greco or Velásquez on the scene. Nevertheless, ceramic and textile artists stand out as major innovators, although the most remarkable examples of mayólica tile work in Barcelona was that of a "foreigner" and of a foreign style. Archival records and excavations carried out in central Barcelona attest to the use of tableware from Deruta, Urbino, and Faenza. In 1596, Lorenzo de Madrid brought the Italian Renaissance aesthetic to Barcelona in his Saint George composition in the Sala del Consistorio Nuevo, Palacio de la Generalitat (see fig. 3.12). Ceramic paintings from the life of Saint George, patron saint of Barcelona, were the first scenes to appear. Surrounded by tiles of classical acanthus leaves and rosettes, they displayed even more emphatic Italian influence in the sense of perspective, in the use of chiaroscuro, and in the feeling of movement of horse and rider, a result of a more naturalistic, three-dimensional drawing style.[6]

Trades as a subject were a logical choice for Barcelona tiles, since the city has been renowned for its fine artisans and its business acumen since medieval times (fig. 6.5). Seny provided Barcelona workers with a rigorous and ethical business code, enabling them to make products of outstanding quality. From the Middle Ages until the industrial revolution of the nineteenth century, the highly efficient guild system was the structure in which artisans worked. Small workshops were typically run by one master and several apprentices. All ceramics workshops were in the same neighborhood, enabling artisans to share resources, and a general *esprit de quartier* obtained.

French influence, in the form of the very white and delicate Alcora wares designed by ceramic artists from the Provençal town of Moustiers, temporarily superimposed itself on mayólica fashion in Barcelona. Appearing even more like fancy porcelain than Catalan tin-glazed earthenware, it was all the rage throughout the region until the ceramics of the Neogothic style reasserted a romanticized view of an earlier Barcelona in the mid-nineteenth century.[7]

6.5 Trade Tile / *Azulejo de oficio*
Barcelona, 17th century
Museu de Ceràmica, Barcelona

The Neogothic

Mayólica objects, such as amphorae with medieval Andalusian Islamic decoration, from Espulges, were made for interiors designed by leading architects of the "neogòtic" in collaboration with their company's own group of artisans. This democratic approach to design echoes that of William Morris and the English Arts and Crafts movement, as well as ideology later taken up by the pan-European *Gesamtgewerk* of the art nouveau movement. Other functional objects made of mayólica, such as large planters and chargers, decorated entrance halls and reception areas, and a wide array of architectural elements such as floral studs and grotesques appeared on exterior surfaces. Tiles in imitation of earlier styles were produced to ornament architectural projects, often prominently, as on the facade of Josep Puig i Cadalfach's Casa Amatller (1898–1900), or in the details of interior elements such as the columns, walls, and ceilings of any number of buildings.[8]

Ubiquitous, tiles figured prominently in the creation of an entire new modern neighborhood in the enormous, gridded urban expansion of Barcelona, the Eixample. To this day controversial, the Eixample may be predictable in its cookie-cutter proportions of buildings and boulevards, but its architecture, street lamps, and street seating still turn heads. The same glazed earthenware tiles that formed the flooring of one of the main rooms of Casa Milà (known to Barcelonans as La Pedrera) were used unglazed for the pavement of the extension of the main commercial street of Barcelona's modern neighborhood, Passeig de Gracià. It was designed by Antoni Gaudí i Cornet (1852–1926), the influential architect whose imaginative and organic style represents the other strain of turn-of-the-century Barcelonese architecture, that of the "new" and of the "future". One of the most singular architects ever, his fantastic buildings have been revered as masterworks and dismissed as the expressions of a madman. While his extraordinary undulating designs impart an unprecedented organic "aliveness" to his buildings, it can be argued that his lampposts, objects, and tiles, are rooted in earlier medieval Barcelonese, Catalan, Spanish, and European styles and forms. In terms of ceramics, the use of shattered shards of mayólica tiles, called *trencadis* in Catalan, that are the hallmark of his mosaic work, is an adaptation of traditional Islamic and Persian techniques that, in their faceted composition yielding a sparkling surface, appealed to Gaudí's fundamental interests in both light and exoticism.[9] Chimneys and ventilators that appear to be palatial minarets atop Palacio Güell (1886–88) are early examples of the use of trencadis.[10] One can see a predilection for the clay, for the technique of laying tiled pavement, and for the composition of the pavement to be carried in part by individual tiles, none of which makes sense until places, like pieces of a puzzle, take their assigned position in the commotion (see fig. 3.17).

The tradition of drawing and painting on ceramics as architectural decoration culminated in Lluís Domènech i Montaner's (1849–1923) pièce de résistance of *el modernisme:* the decoration of the Palau de la Música Catalana (fig. 6.6). Representing the more Germanic, rational history-based approach to architecture and decorative arts, Domènech i Montaner is Gaudí's counterpart. For the 1888 Universal Exposition in Barcelona's Parc de la Ciutadella, he designed buildings that echoed medieval fortresses, with crenellated "towers" and escutcheons on facades, such as the exposition's Café-Restaurant. To produce the decorative arts for these building projects, Domènech i Montaner, along with another leading architect of the fin de siècle, Antoni Maria Gallissà,

6.6 Detail of the main balcony
Palau de la Música, Barcelona, 1908
Photo courtesy of the Museu de Ceràmica, Barcelona

created the Castell dels Tres Dragons workshop. Under their direction, a variety of artisans created objects that were sympathetic to the overall sensibilities of the interior architecture. In a composition of sculptures, pierced surfaces, glazed tiles, mosaics, stained glass, and light, the ebullience of this building radiates in all directions; the building sings. On the facade of the Music Hall is a trompe l'oeil scene, ostensibly inside the building, a lively allegorical composition that features a mixed choral group, Barcelona's own Orfeó Català. It is a wall mosaic, masterfully accomplished with broken pieces of tin-glazed earthenware tiles in a symbolist palette. Based on a drawing by Domènech i Montaner, the work was carried out by Lluís Bru, Mario Maragliano, and by two firms that worked often with the architect, Pujol i Baucis and Escofet i Cia.[11]

As these spectacular tile mural compositions adorned the walls of major public buildings, a parallel decorative movement continued on the inside and outside of less official buildings. Indeed, it seems that hardly a restaurant, pharmacy, café, or butcher shop survives without a tile facade or interior. Bustling with activity, the Boqueria, or central food market, dating to 1870, offers a plethora of simple plain industrial and hand-painted tiles on the back and side walls. Just down the block from the Boqueria, at a quiet corner of the Rambla (downtown Barcelona's main thoroughfare) is one of the oldest and most beloved Barcelonese pastry shops, chocolatiers, and cafés, Escribà (fig. 6.7), with its glistening and sensual curved facade decoration carried out in mayólica trencadis, dated 1903. Walking toward the Plaça de la Catalunya, a later art deco tile pattern adorns the doorframe of a pharmacy (fig. 6.8), and inside, the walls are covered with clean, white glazed terra cotta, virgin mayólica.

6.7 Façade of Escribà pastry shop
La Rambla, Barcelona, 1903
Photo by Annie Carlano, 2000

In the tiny bars cum restaurants of the harbor area and in the large family restaurants of the Barceloneta, an old-fashioned and newly fashionable neighborhood, one sees tilework on the interior walls as well as in friezes along the outer walls, both as advertisements and as decor.

A metro ride up the hill, in the Alta Zona residential neighborhoods of Sarrià and Tres Torres, one can see mosaic details on the large, early twentieth-century houses, many of which have been converted to business establishments. Farther up the hill, in Pedralbes, is the above-mentioned Güell house, the residence of Gaudí's patron.

6.8 Building façade with tilework
La Rambla, Barcelona, ca. 1920
Photo by Annie Carlano, 2000

Twentieth-Century Industrialization

The industrialization of the ceramics industry during the first decades of the twentieth century made available a large quantity of mass-produced, thin, strong and colorful dishes and plates for domestic consumption. No longer did consumers have to buy handmade mayólica, which was heavy and chipped easily, to get the colors and patterns they desired. Suddenly, traditional mayólica became old-fashioned, and for the most part, went out of use. Eventually, despite wars, revolutions, and xenophobic pretensions, foreign styles crept their way into the homes of upper- and middle-class Barcelonese, and in their mass-market versions, to anyone who wanted them. Italian, French, English, and Finnish dinnerware was replacing local handmade earthenware. Patterns, if present at all, were printed, on what is known as transferware, as opposed to painted.

Still, there were some prominent avant garde artists of the *noucentista* into the 1920s and 1930s who used the mayólica technique, or processes that yielded a similar surface quality, in their lyrical ceramic creations of the Neorenaissance style. Employing the Classical subject matter and figurative idiom of Italian Renaissance mayólica, particularly that of Urbino, the painter Josep Jordi Guardiola (1868–1950), who in 1923 visited Italy, made decorative plates and vessels depicting predominantly female subjects, such as Diana the Huntress (fig. 6.9).

6.9 *Diana*
Josep Jordi Guardiola (1868–1950), ca. 1925
Museu de Ceràmica, Barcelona

Traveling to Paris in 1922 and later exhibiting his works in the 1925 Expositions des Arts Décoratifs, one can see the influence of the colors of the Ballets Russes and of the art deco style in this and other works.[12] The second-generation noucentista artist Xavier Nogués (1873–1941) was a painter who occasionally worked in ceramics, with exquisite results. More modern and Catalonian in its subject, the attenuated form of this jar (see fig. 2.22), with its graceful curves, is the perfect "canvas" for its design. In a signature composition, Nogués depicts a young girl in generic Neoclassical dress looming over a Catalonian landscape against a clear sky in which swallows meander to and fro.

Barcelona's most egregiously famous artist, Joan Miró (1893–1983) exploited the propensities of glazed earthenware to express his colorful Surreal abstractions almost to the exclusion of painting from 1954 to 1959. So passionate was he about his clay work that he wrote the unpublished "De l'assassinat de la peinture à la céramique" ("From the assassination of painting to ceramics").[13] Charged with a primal lyricism and playfulness, his ceramic creations are an integral part of his oeuvre, in which he manifested the inherently enigmatic. Assisted in the technical aspects of these works of art by his close friend, the master potter Josep Llorens Artigas (1892–1980), his ceramics were exhibited at prestigious venues in Paris and New York. The fact that Miró was drawn to "the goodness of dirt, dust and mud" inherent in ceramics has as much to do with his Catalan belief that ancient art, Romanesque frescoes, and nature were the supreme art forms, as it does with any pervading fashion.[14] And it was certainly more than mere fashion that led Miró, when he received a commission from UNESCO, to choose to create two tile murals (*La Luna* and *El Sol*) rather than paintings or sculptures. Appreciated in terms of their brilliant colors, avant garde signs and symbols, as well as for the use of a humble material and handcrafted techniques, his revolutionary tilework can be found in the National Folklore Museum in Osaka, Japan; it also won him a coveted Solomon R. Guggenheim prize.[15]

The Revitalization of Mayólica

It was not until a different kind of revolution occurred in the world that mayólica in Barcelona began to flower again. The bucolic hippies' "back to the land" mantra spread across the Atlantic. During the 1960s, there was on the part of Catalans a renewed interest in the rural lifestyle and in the traditional folklore associated with that life. This was a result of a more general cultural interest in Catalonia's identity, an interest that has continued to resurface over time in ways less radical than those of the Basques. But the zeitgeist of the time was concerned with getting back to the basics, to love, to the land, and to the hand-made. Catalonian scholars of cultural and art history turned their attention to local archives and museum collections to learn about the material culture of the recent past.[16]

In the mid-1970s, a young man who was working at a furniture workshop in la Pobla de Claramunt, setting tiles of nontradtional design into furniture, noticed that the public seemed more interested in designs of the past. He decided that it was time to revive the local traditional patterns for use in ceramic work. With no formal art training, let alone in mayólica, Alejandro Jarandilla and two friends, Gegori Montagut and Xavier Font, formed a company, Montfont S.A. Capellades, a small industrial village known chiefly for its weaving industry and paper mills, was chosen as the firm's headquarters. Monfont's goal was to reproduce traditional mayólica as faithfully as possible, from the type of clay to the glaze recipes. They were fortunate that the clay used in the historic examples had been found in the hills near Barcelona and could be found there still. Relying on the knowledge and experience of a small workshop that had recently begun throwing pots with this clay, they immediately had a subcontractor for work done on the wheel. Discovering the secret formulae for the unique lead-silica-tin-based yellows and blues of the finest polychrome mayólica turned out to be more difficult.[17]

Around 1980, Alejandro Jarandilla approached Dolores Giral, then director of the Museu de Ceràmica in Barcelona, with a request to study the historic mayólica in the collection. Ms. Giral was extremely supportive of his efforts, and granted him permission to work with the museum in obtaining the glaze formulas he sought. In the process, they developed a collegiality and the idea to produce a line of reproductions of the most typical seventeenth-century masterworks from the museum: the woman at the well with two jugs (*cántaros*), birds, and single portraits of men and women in regional costume. In line with the internationally burgeoning museum-shop phenomenon, the plates and bowls would be sold in what had been the Museu de Ceràmica's bookstore. They are such perfect copies both in shape and in image, only a specialist would realize that they are not originals. In 1984, Alejandro Jarandilla went out on his own and opened the mayólica workshop Cerámica Camaró, in Capellades.[18]

His timing was impeccable. Barcelona had just become a "hot" tourist destination, and his wares were to be found in many of the small shops selling regional products that cluster around the cathedral. Since that time other small ceramic ateliers have sprung up, but none to date have been able to corner the market in the manner of Cerámica Camaró.[19]

What is it about the work of Cerámica Camaró that commands our attention? The painting; there is simply no better hand recreating historic designs in the round or on flat surfaces than that of Alejandro Jarandilla (fig. 6.10). Drawing first the contours with a brush dipped in black; he confidently fills in the colors with a characteristic swiftness of gesture and lightness of touch. With the vigilance of the best studio potters, Jarandilla is intimately involved in affecting every aspect of the pot, from the vibrancy of the color to the gloss of its patina and the old-master quality of the drawing. Superb elements combine to yield faithful reproductions. The result is a composition that to the uninitiated eye could indeed be a seventeenth-century Catalan original. Indeed, the depiction of the gallant young gentleman hunter and his horse is a testament to Alejandro Jarandilla's unparalleled skill.

6.10 Detail of Vase
Cerámica Camaró, Capellades (Barcelona), 1998
Collection of the International Folk Art Foundation
Museum of International Folk Art (Museum of New Mexico), Santa Fe
Photo by Paul Smutko

6.11 Alejandro Jarandilla painting a plate in his studio Capellades (Barcelona) Photo by Annie Carlano, 2000

6.12 Alejandro Jarandilla in his studio Capellades (Barcelona) Photo by Annie Carlano, 2000

Demonstrating the step-by-step process of painting a simple mayólica plate, Alejandro allowed us to document his technique (figs. 6.11, 6.12). From start to finish, this process took about ten minutes. After painting, the plate is set aside to dry on one of the many metal racks that fill most of the studio space, then returned to the other studio and kiln for a second firing. Finally, the finished mayólica works were packed and shipped to their local or foreign destination.

Today, the Cerámica Camaró company remains a small enterprise, with just four assistants in the painting atelier to help with backgrounds and to execute less-exacting patterns. An additional team, at a separate studio, throws the pots, and carries out the bisque and subsequent firings. They also make some pieces with the use of molds. Upon request, never to deliberately fool the eye, Cerámica Camaró will "antique" a work.[20] Today the wide array of domestic ceramics available include platters, plates, bowls, vinegar-and-oil sets, candy jars, old-fashioned washbasin-and-pitcher sets, pharmacy jars, and large planters on pedestals. But of all the works being created by Camaró, those that are part of living tradition, of life in Barcelona today, are his original designs for tile murals.

Traditional tilework mural scenes have been offered in the Cerámica Camaró brochure for some time.[21] Most types stocked are copies of seventeenth- through nineteenth-century genre scenes, Barcelona harbor and maritime subjects being a particular specialty. A few years ago, a friend of Alejandro's asked him to make a unique wall mural for his restaurant. Perhaps not coincidentally, Catalonia

6.13 Catalan Kitchen
Cerámica Camaró, Capellades (Barcelona)
Signed, "Alejandro Jarandilla, SPAIN," 2002
Collection of the International Folk Art Foundation
Museum of International Folk Art (Museum of New Mexico), Santa Fe
Photo by Paul Smutko

was at the time, and still is, in the midst of a culinary renaissance; the restaurants of the Empordà countryside are considered to be among the best in Europe. With this first commission, Cerámica Camaró entered its most significant artistic period. Producing compositions that are at once traditional and of our time, they reflect contemporary Barcelona. For example, a tile wall mural was recently commissioned by the Museum of International Folk Art for its *Cerámica y Cultura* exhibition (fig. 6.13). Depicted is a kitchen scene of a historic interior with regional details, yet in a presentation that is fresh and contemporary. The architecture of the space, the stoves, ovens, and furniture, and the earthenware ceramic storage jars, bowls, and platters are all seventeenth and eighteenth century in style, but these designs are being revived today for country houses, inns, and restaurants throughout Catalonia. Particularly alluring is the costume of the kitchen staff. The men carrying out food preparation, such as grinding herbs or nuts in a mortar and pestle or filleting fish, wear two distinct types of garb: the French white jacket and toque usually worn by restaurant professionals, and the Catalan bolero jacket, breeches, red sash, and *barratina* (red Phrygian cap), which is the signature dress of men throughout rural Catalonia. The only woman in the mural is wearing aristocratic seventeenth-century dress, but even she is familiar to Catalans from the ubiquitous historic reproductions of such a figure. In this formidable mural, Camaró captures the proud and industrious character of the Catalan, as well as the magnificence of the province's natural bounty. Fish, seafood, melons, game, and figs form a luscious frieze in the foreground of the composition.

American Artists in Barcelona

Ironically, while the traditionally based tilework of Cerámica Camaró serves primarily a foreign market (tile is the quintessential export ware of contemporary Catalan mayólica), it is the "neo-Neobaroque" trencadís ceramic work of several American artists that is the most visually exciting mayólica to be seen in Barcelona today. Beverly Pepper (b.1924), the American expatriate artist living in Todi, Italy, since 1972, began experimenting with Barcelona ceramist Joan Raventos, dividing her time between the two cities, to develop the tilework for Soli i Ombra park in Barcelona. Having created an earthworks exhibition in another park there in 1988, Pepper was on intimate terms with her adopted home. The collaboration yielded an exquisite watercolor effect in the finished environmental tilework, which was completed in time for the 1992 summer Olympics in Barcelona. Culturally specific, Pepper's *Soli i Ombra* is a continuation of Catalan ceramic tradition as manifested in the art and philosophy

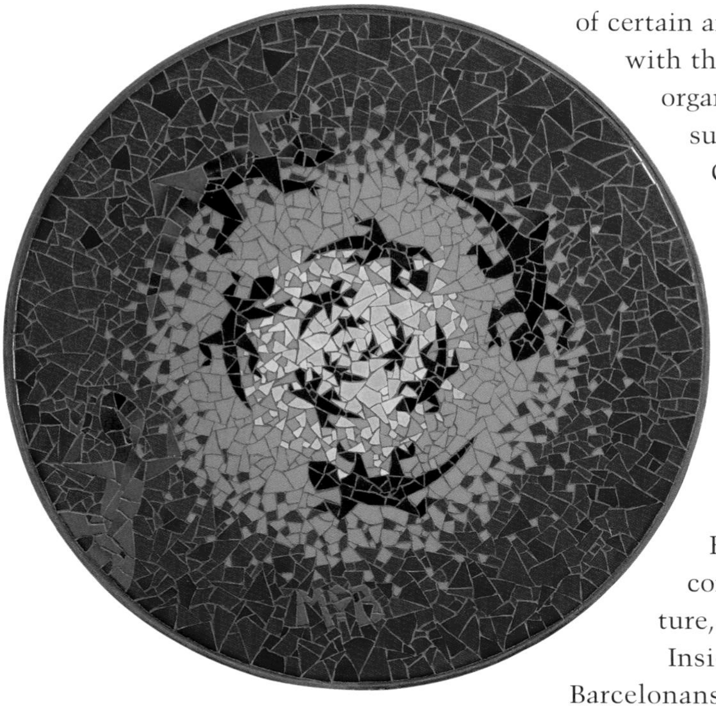

6.14 Lizard Table Top
Lisa McConnell,
Barcelona, 2000
Photo courtesy of
Lisa McConnell

of certain artists of the nuocentism and moderisme, with their emphasis on the natural world, its organic form, the broken tile, or trencadís, surface. Soli i Ombra is authentically Catalan.

Head of Barcelona, by American pop artist Roy Lichtenstein (b.1923), was also created for the Olympic games of 1992. An overt homage to trecandís and Gaudí, the siting of the work in the Ciutat Vella, the old maritime area that is now a bustling place for both tourists and locals alike, was a gesture on the part of the government of Barcelona to acknowledge the cultural content of Lichtenstein's mammoth sculpture, now one of the top ten icons of the city.

Inside the homes of middle-class Barcelonans, we are apt to find a table, chair, or other object with trencadís ornamentation by a less familiar American artist, Lisa McConnell (b.1965) (fig. 6.14). Raised in Alaska and New Mexico, she spent most of her adult life in Provence and recently moved to Barcelona. Mediterranean by choice, she uses "themes, tiles, and vibrant colors of the region" in her work. Why does she work only with mayólica tiles? Searching for the most sun-drenched colors for her designs, she found that only the low-fired glazed earthenware pieces carried the strong and varied hues she wanted. Why break the tiles? McConnell sees the mosaic technique as culturally charged with "the Mediterranean," recalling as it does the Romans, the *Gaudistas,* and the folk environments and memory jars of France.[22] Using a range of sizes, she carefully arranges the shards in swirling patterns that often incorporate slithering lizards, which immediately remind Catalans of Gaudí's large lurking lizards in the Parc Güell.

Mayólica Today

The story of mayólica ceramics in Barcelona is in some respects no different today from what it was one hundred or one thousand years ago. Since the late Middle Ages, foreign styles, at first in the form of Islamic tiles from the south, have been coveted and later modified and assimilated to reflect distinct Catalan tastes. Umbrian *istoriato* ware evolved into the figurative Baroque ware, which in its depictions of Catalonian personages, land- and seascapes became emblematic of

Barcelonese ceramics and the tradition that, more than three hundred years later, was revived in the Neobaroque pottery and tilework of Cerámica Camaró. As the world becomes a much smaller place, foreign influence, as in the case of the artists mentioned above, is more frequent and pervasive. Still, Catalan identity is encapsulated in the new mayólica by these artists, as we see through the artist's eyes that much of that identity—seny, wit, earthiness—is manifested in tilework, pottery, and trencadís.

Notes

1. *Seny* is a Catalan word, often used by Catalans themselves to describe their character. It means both wise and pragmatic and implies a certain sober manner. (Nonetheless, the Catalans are among the funniest people in Spain, known for their propensity for scatological humor.) For a thorough explanation of the term and a full description of the historical and contemporary comportment of Catalans, see Josep Ferrater Mora, *Les formes de la vida catalana, i altres assaigs* (Barcelona: n.p., 1980).
2. Artists who created designs for both textiles and ceramics often received the same academic training, such as that in flower painting. Workshops also retained drawings that were in many instances handed down from generation to generation. It is therefore nearly impossible to assign a specific artist to a textile or ceramics pattern of a nonnarrative composition.
3. For a thorough description, region by region, along with precise drawings of all known patterns, see Albert Telese Compte, *La vaixella blava catalana de 1570 a 1670* (Barcelona: Carrera Edició, 1991).
4. Anthony Ray, *Spanish Pottery 1248–1898* (London: V & A Publications, 2000), pp.202–3.
5. Joan Ainaud de Lasarte, "Cataluña," in *Cerámica Esmaltada Español* (Barcelona: Labor, 1981), p. 147.
6. V.V.A.A., *Cerámica Z* (Madrid: Espasa Calpe, S.A., 1997), pp.213–14; Maria Antonia Casanovas, "Cerámica architectónica catalana de época medieval y renacentista," in *La ruta de la cerámica* (Castellón: Ascer, 2000), pp.76–77.
7. The leading architects of late nineteenth-century Barcelona, Lluís Domenech i Montaner, Antoni M. Gallissà i Soqué, Bonaventura Bassegoda, and Josep Puig i Cadafalch, were conservative nationalists, "*catalanistes*," who looked to the magnificent Gothic architecture of Barcelona for inspiration. Following the ideas and theories of French architect Eugène Viollet-le-Duc, they most revered the great gothic cathedral as a paradigm for their work.
8. See Judith C. Rohrer, "Modernisme i neogòtic en l'archquitectura," in *El modernisme*, 2 vol. exhibition catalog, Museu d'Art Modern Parc de la Cituadella, Barcelona (Barcelona: Lunwerg Editores S.A., 1990–91), pp.323–34. I am indebted to Judy for the "tutorial" she provided me on *nuocentista* and *modernisme* architecture during my Mellon fellowship in Barcelona during the summer of 1992. It is also interesting to note that William Morris's first decorative arts for Morris & Co. were painted tiles that he decorated himself with floral motifs, before they were supplied by De Morgan to the firm. See J.W. Mackhail, *The Life of William Morris*, vol. 2 (London: Longmans, Green and Co., 1899), pp.42–43. That Gaudí and Morris believed in the supremacy of nature in art is another obvious parallel.
9. Juan Bassegoda Nonell, *Antonio Gaudí, Master Architect* (New York: Abbeville Press Publishers, 2000), pp.27–48. The Eastern influence on Gaudí is best discussed and illustrated in this book by a renowned professor of architectural history at the

Polytechnical University of Catalonia, in Barcelona. It should be pointed out that Gaudí was not unique in his interest in exoticism and orientalism, which were pervading trends throughout much of Europe. However, he was one of the few architects in Catalonia to follow this trend, influenced as he was at this time by the writings of John Ruskin and the English school. Japanese art and French art nouveau also figure in the mix of influences on Gaudí. Other Catalan architects were drawn more to German and other continental approaches to buildings and the decorative arts.

10. Ibid., illustrated pp.44–45.
11. The best source for information about the Palau de la Música Catalana in English is Josep Maria Carandell, Ricard Pia, and Pere Vivas, *The Palau Música Catalana* (Barcelona: Triangle Postals, 1996).
12. It is noteworthy that Guardiola abandoned painting for ceramics in 1918, finding the latter a more satisfying medium. His work was much appreciated by the French, and several pieces of his work on view at the 1925 Paris International Exposition of Decorative Arts were acquired by the National Museum of Ceramics, Sèvres.
13. Written in 1948, this text was intended to be a book. Now in the collection of the Fondation Zervos, Vezelay, France, an earlier version is in the collection of the Joan Miró Foundation, Barcelona. For more information about this poetic work, see Rosa Maria Malet, "From the Assassination of Painting to Ceramics," in *Miró: Playing with Fire* (Toronto: 2000), pp. 21–27.
14. It is striking that Picasso turned his attention to making ceramic vessels, plates, and sculptures about the same time as Miró. In the case of Picasso, his involvement began on a winter holiday in the Côte d'Azur town of Vallauris at the Madoura workshop, not in Catalonia. Miró was closer to Gaudí in artistic sensibility; nature was his primary motivating force.
15. Miró, Llorens Artigas and Joan Gardy Artigas collaborated on several other tile murals, most notably, those of the Aeropuerto de Barcelona and that of the Palacio de Congresos, Madrid.
16. J. Corredor-Matheos and Jordi Gumi, *Cerámica popular catalana* (Barcelona: Caixa d'Estalvis de Catalunya, 1978), p. 5. At this time in Catalonia, several ambitious books on folklore were published, the most comprehensive and sensitively written of which is, Xavier Fàbregas, *Tradicions, Mites,* vol. 1: *Creences dels Catalans* (Barcelona: Edicions62 S.A., 1979).
17. Jose Guerrero-Martin, *Alfares y Alfareros de España* (Madrid: Ministerio de Cultura, 1988), p. 184.
18. Cerámica Camaró is a wholesale place of business and is not open to the public. Most of the information about Alejandro and his company comes from an interview conducted in his studio on 27 October 2000. Toni Casanovas, curator of the Museu de Ceràmica, Barcelona, who accompanied me on the visit, served as translator. I deeply appreciate her every kindness, extended to me then and now. Her scholarship and our conversations have guided this essay.
19. It is not possible in this brief essay to discuss all the extant mayólica artists working today in Barcelona. The reader is advised to consult the Associaciò de Ceramistes de Catalunya and the F.A.D. (Formen Arts Decoratifs) as well as the Centre Catala d'Artesania, all in Barcelona, for more extensive information. The author is grateful to Judith Espinar Dillenberg, who first brought the work of Camaro to the United States, who first brought it to the attention of the Museum of International Folk Art before my tenure here, and whose business, The Clay Angel, has done much to enlighten the general public in the United States about mayólica.
20. The process is simple and impressive. As the firm is well respected for its ability to create an antique patina, I have given my word not to reveal the details.
21. It is not possible to assign a precise date here, as the corporate memory of the company is vague, and their brochures are not dated.
22. Interview with Lisa McConnell, Barcelona, 28 October 2000. There are stone and

broken-ceramic constructions throughout France, as there are throughout the world. For the most part, the artists who create such "yard art" use broken plates, for example, Sam Rodia's (c.1875–1965) *Watts Towers* in Los Angeles; Raymond Isidore's (1900–64) *Maison Picassiette*, in Chartres, France; Niki de Saint Phalle's (1930–2002) *Tarot Garden*, in Tuscany, Italy; or Nek Chand's (b.1924) *Rock Garden*, in Chandigarh, India. Both in France and in the United States, "memory jars" (vessels encrusted with pieces of broken plates, mementos such as jewelry, thimbles, and assorted bric-a-brac), are made and endowed with meaning.

A.
V
A

Detail, Fig. 7.2

7

Traditional Ceramic Production in Spain Today

JAUME COLL CONESA

THE STAGGERED AND irregular regional developments on the Iberian Peninsula throughout the centuries have been a key factor in the forging of its cultural and artistic diversity. For the field of ceramics, this has meant that creative and functional models and production techniques from a wide cross section of pottery-producing localities have been preserved. Workshops where *cazuelas a torneta* (casseroles and other vessels) were hand made, thrown on potter's wheels, and then fired in pit kilns were still in vigorous production well into the twentieth century. Communities such as Moveros (Zamora) held on to the typical family-run factories that used simple, long-established technology. These shops remained operating in the company of other, specialized shops that had developed methods for mass production. An example of this would be those factories that had the capacity for firing large volumes of *botijos* (drinking jugs) of calcareous clay (with salt added for increased porosity) in updraft kilns of three levels, with the capacity for as many as twenty thousand objects. We can still see evidence of some of these fabrication methods from the last stages of preindustrial ceramic production at the factory in Agost (Alicante).

The continued survival of these traditions in lingering, constantly receding forms, and their coexistence with industrial automation (such as in the *azulejerías*, or tile shops, of Castellón), makes Spain a true laboratory for analyzing the mechanisms for the establishment of new technologies and the persistence of the old. Numerous technical models still exist, with the same organization of labor that had its origins centuries ago; at times reduced to islands of traditions in remote places, they must confront the demands of modern industry. Their gradual disappearance constitutes one of the major disappointments for anthropologists and other researchers in the field of ceramic technology. The process is taking place at this very moment, while we are unable to implement procedures for sufficiently documenting or preserving this cultural heritage.

Unfortunately, the living Spanish laboratory is being exhausted, and a registry of the totality of its cultural and technological patrimony has still not been created. This has been due in part to the fact that the research focused on this topic has been carried out by people with different interests from those of contemporary society, people who have approached their studies with a somewhat naïve perspective, glossing over traditional values; the essence of life in the past, its immediate relation to nature, etc. In other instances, it has been due to a lack of knowledge of pottery or ceramic techniques, or even a clear vision of relevant aspects that have cut short anthropological analysis and registration. Fortunately, in the 1970s some ethnographic schools created precise methodologies for the description and systematic detailing of this art form and its products, which have been followed to some extent in a number of revealing works.[1]

The rapid transformation of society in the last thirty years has led to improvements in the quality of life, with changes in behavior and nutrition and the substitution of consumable goods for those of greater practicality, the latter generally produced with technology beyond the reach of traditional workshops. Popular ceramics, especially decorative pottery, has lost a lot in this process, since many of its age-old functions have had to be abandoned. The traditional shops have been overwhelmed by labor laws, tax systems, and regulations pertaining to health and safety. It is obvious that the pottery industry of today cannot continue hazardous labor practices in precarious work conditions, nor can it use dangerous materials.[2] But neither should the rigid production requirements and intense competition in today's modern marketplace

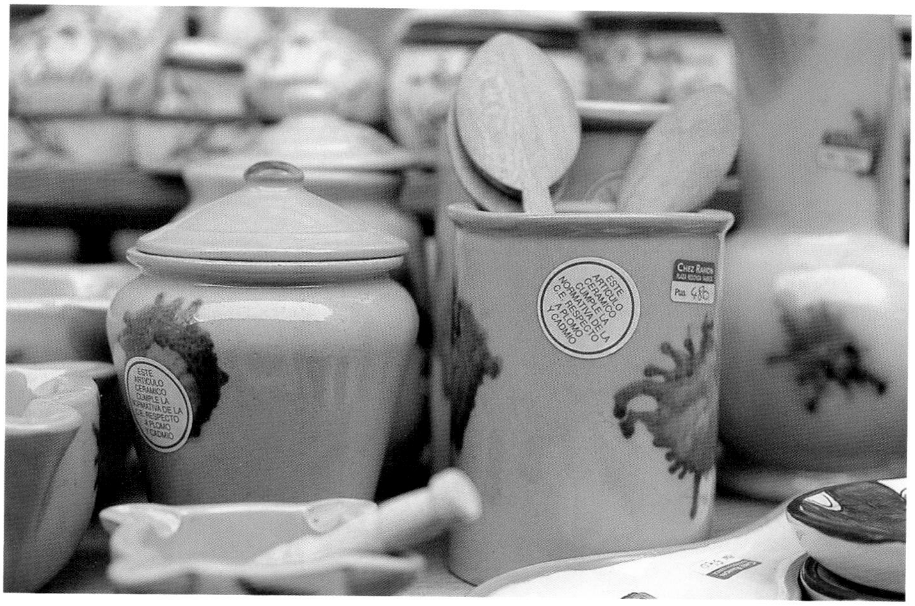

7.1 Utilitarian Earthenware/ *Loza utilitaria*
Manises, Spain, 2001
Photo by Jaume Coll
Traditional utilitarian *loza* made according to rules pertaining to lead and cadmium contents set by the European Common Market. The difference between this *loza* and that of years past is hardly noticeable.

engender the total collapse of traditional ceramic manufacture (fig. 7.1). There must be a thorough examination of what that would represent for our history and heritage. The present legal framework for cultural legacy allows tax incentives and other support that might save this indispensable art form. Special decrees granting protected-industry status can facilitate its continued existence while complying with the necessities of contemporary manufacturing.

The Transformation of Traditional Pottery Production and Decorative Ceramics in Spain

Ceramic manufacturing on the Iberian Peninsula has for the last ten centuries concentrated mainly on the fabrication of products for domestic use. However, the imaginative models and techniques noted in the recent ethnographic registry of utilitarian ceramics go beyond this context. Nowadays, the major economic emphasis of Spanish ceramics is architectural applications, which also have a long history in Spain, but which are less useful in the study of traditional ways of life.

In order to grasp how the production modes of ceramics for domestic use have developed in recent times, it is essential to summarize our present knowledge. This perspective is especially important in relation to the production of coarse wares and fine decorative ceramics. The first category includes those objects made with a utilitarian purpose: items for use in daily tasks in the kitchen and the pantry, or as tableware, etc. Fine decorative ceramics require a consideration of their special ornamental value, which marks them as more than just functional items.

Loza, coated with tin-based enamel and generally known as mayólica, would fall within this second group. Fine loza and porcelain have always required superior manufacturing technology and the highest level of expertise. Generally they have been allocated to limited market niches, due to their more expensive raw materials and restricted clientele. It is obvious that decorative ceramics have been intended to fulfill needs beyond common utilitarian use.

According to Natacha Seseña, the crisis for *alfarería popular de basto*, or rural everyday earthenware, began with the onset of the Stabilization Plan of 1959 and crystallized during the First and Second Development Plans (of 1967 and 1971).[3] Major emigrations of peasants and rural artisans shook daily urban habits anchored in time-honored routines. The destruction of the old rural way of life resulted in a decrease in demand for rural products such as pottery. Along with this shift came modern urban methods of manufacturing, a more urban lifestyle, and the introduction of such appliances as freezers, washers, televisions, and radios into outlying areas. Tourism was another part of this phenomenon.

The rural agrarian population of Spain consisted of a great mass of salaried manual laborers, among whom few were property owners. Even those with meager incomes from renting small landholdings had to survive on what they could produce themselves and the occasional salaried work that they could obtain. Except for industrialized areas such as the Basque region, Catalonia, Valencia, and a few other commercial centers, this description was valid for most of Spain. On the other hand, there did exist a diminishing rural affluent class of professionals or landowners, comparable to the urban middle class; but for the most part the proprietors of great estates resided permanently in the cities. This situation began to change in the nineteenth century, with the growth of urban industry and the demand for common labor that had been confined until then to rural environments. The rural stagnation in Spain began to change rapidly in the 1950s, however, as the country found itself part of the general European economic resurgence. This revival in trade and industry allowed for definite avenues of economic expansion, among which tourism was prominent. In these same years there was also a great demand for manual labor outside Spain, which triggered the most recent waves of emigration.

Decorative Loza

From medieval times, decorative loza has been distinct from utilitarian pottery. In the mid-fourteenth century, the distinction increased with the appearance of massive volumes of vessels produced for a rapidly expanding market: the golden loza (lusterware) of Manises and the loza produced in Talavera and Puente del Arzobispo, just to cite a few examples (fig. 7.2). These ceramic products became accessible to a broad spectrum of society, thanks to their low prices. Ceramic items superseded utensils and vessels made of wood and metal, relegating them to the rank of luxury items. The boom in the ceramics industry provided the iron and steel industries, especially, with the considerable supply of wood they required, as well as making timber available for use in other essential enterprises, such as shipbuilding.[4]

New ideas in politics, economics, and business that arose during the eighteenth-century Enlightenment encouraged new methods of research and experimentation with new materials. The days of empirical education were replaced by structured apprenticeships that were more academic in nature. Decorative ceramics were now sharply distinguished from those made previously, due to the evolving technologies and the continued search for economically optimal modes of operation.

In the words of Pérez Camps, the manufacturing evolution of the twentieth century in Manises was both cause and effect of the general rise in the standard of living. Great quantities of receptacles of all types were demanded, and this need was responsible for new technical and managerial procedures, the first steps toward full-blown industrialization. A white calcareous paste similar to that of loza was developed, and *moldes de colado* (straining molds) were widely used. Changes in ornamentation included the extensive application of creative edgings and the the use of airbrushes.[5] The change in the paste permitted modifications in the transparent coatings, which replaced the expensive traditional tin-based enamels. The firing process, however, remained unchanged, and this had a detrimental effect on the quality of the finished product. Naturally, the use of moldes de colado brought about the gradual disappearance of potter's wheel operators, who were replaced by modeling specialists. In contrast, the production

7.2 Ceramics from Talavera de la Reina and Manises in Valencia, Spain, 2001
Photo by Jaume Coll. Sample of low cost decorative *loza* production for sale today.

of luxury items entailed the abandonment of the serially applied decoration techniques such as *trepa* (stencil) or *calca* (transfer).

These changes came at a time when the increasing diversification of models in each factory also limited mechanization, because the variety of types and styles required a high investment in manual labor. This situation is still characteristic of manufacturing in Manises today. In the 1920s, the first auxiliary industries appeared in the vicinity of the major centers of production: plants in Onda and Manises specialized in varnishes, enamels, and pastes. Manises had thirty-two factories in operation in 1910. This grew to a total of fifty-two in 1932, which made it the foremost industrial decorative-ceramics center in Spain until the outbreak of the Civil War, in 1936. After the conflict ended, in 1939, the majority of factories reinitiated production, with lines of bathroom ceramics to supply reconstruction needs after the stagnation in the demand for ornamental objects.

Factories in Manises had always maintained traditional product lines, with less emphasis on technology and the use of a less-skilled labor force; on the other hand, they also followed the changing styles and fashions of the moment. Production today is compelled to respond to competition from Asian companies, who operate with the advantage of lower labor costs and access to raw materials of a higher quality.

Decorative ceramics are the basic products of Manises at present, although notable effort has been directed toward incorporating utilitarian products as well. Items such as table services, kitchen utensils, and other domestic ceramic products are being fabricated. Manises companies are now in the position of having to break away from strict ceramic technologies to incorporate quicker, cheaper decorating methods, such as *en frio* application of ornamentation. In order to compete with Asian products, in some cases ceramic objects and coatings have been supplanted by synthetic materials such as resins and polyurethane. This competitive process accelerated markedly through the 1990s, resulting in greater product diversification. Factories have begun to focus on areas such as historic ceramics (six businesses), innovative functional products (twenty producers), general earthenware manufacture (ten businesses), and the use of *tercer fuego* (a third, or decorative firing, after the bisque and enamel firings), with twenty enterprises generating products by this method. These twenty are subordinate to the Castellón tile industry, and their output is concentrated on items with historical designs. There is no regulation of prices, due to the wide variety of production, and for this reason each business tries to establish itself with competitive products. On the other hand, the sector has seen an explosion of a number of important auxiliary industries specializing in raw materials to supply the national market and who do not depend on the needs of local businesses.

The necessity for a skilled manual labor force and for training new workers in ceramic artisanship led to the creation in 1914 of La Escuela de Cerámica de Manises (the Manises Ceramics School). Officially recognized in 1916, its initial objectives involved ornamentation and not the technical aspects of the trade. In 1948, the school's curriculum was reorganized to provide training in both the artistic and technical areas of the craft; this orientation is still current. There remains today a tremendous need for formally trained workers with the skills needed to keep up with the demands of a growing market. As part of the process of adapting to new labor requirements, the industry has abandoned traditional gender roles (women applying decorations and men engaged in shaping and finishing products). Nowadays there is no distinction between the sexes in the performance of the various facets of fabrication. On the other hand, businesses are cognizant of the fact that formal training alone is not sufficient for efficient and profitable production. They have found that the core instructional methods must be supported with other initiatives, such as courses organized by the Asociación Valenciana de Empresas Cerámicas.

Actions undertaken by the Town Council of Manises to enhance educational development include the systematic coordination of opportunities for local industry in important trade shows. It is significant that the headquarters of Avec-Gremio was established in Manises; this organization has enabled numerous businesses to develop contacts and be exposed to a wide variety of products at the exhibits it has sponsored at trade shows. The ceramics sector has had to contend with the indifference of younger people with respect to its products, which only a short time before were recognized as an identifying part of the national heritage. This lack of interest is due to new habits of the consuming public, especially in large parts of the country where these products were never manufactured. In addition, Avec-Gremio has created a range of employment opportunities in order to nurture those positions that require certified training, at the same time that it has taught specialized classes and guided supporting businesses in applying for grants from the government. Along with this support it has provided labor advisement, fiscal management counseling, and training in safety, quality control, and environmental protection issues.[6]

The situation in Talavera and Puente del Arzobispo is similar, yet with unique characteristics. While Manises, with its many ceramic workshops, has enjoyed historical continuity, Talavera suffered serious setbacks in the nineteenth century. These were overcome, however, thanks to the quality of the products produced in the factories of La Menora and El Carmen. The latter incorporated potters from Manises, as well as such innovative artisans as Enrique Guijo and Juan Ruiz de Luna in the twentieth century.

Puente del Arzobispo found its renaissance in the nineteenth century, due to the initiative of Valencian ceramists such as Francisco Nebot and the appearance of pottery dynasties such as that of the De la Cal family.

Guijo and Ruiz de Luna created a product that achieved extraordinary success because of its authentic traditional character (see fig. 1.23). These products were stylistically tied to the golden age of Talavera and recalled the luxury enjoyed by the wealthy in that bygone era.[7] Their success led to the emergence of many new shops up until the 1940s, with a decline in production in the postwar years. Traditional manufacturing techniques included processing of raw materials within each shop and employing only basic technology, in an attempt to reclaim the artistic essence of the craft while attending to the most minute details.[8]

The industry had already begun to incorporate more modern methods in the 1950s, with the introduction of such innovations as electric and oil-fueled kilns and special commercially formulated enamels. By 1963, the ceramic workshop of La Menora, in Talavera, was one of the most advanced shops in the area, adopting a variety of innovative finishes along with new forms of technology. The new coatings ranged from a deep dull white to rich ochre hues. Slip-casting molds were also introduced into the production process in later years. Nevertheless, the decade of the 1970s was a period of crisis. After the closing of the Nuestra Señora del Prado factory, founded by Luna and Guijo, their former employees established a cooperative, which they called La Purísima. The El Carmen factory of Niveiro also became a cooperative. At that time there were five factories producing luxury wares in Talavera and thirteen in Puente del Arzobispo; by the 1980s these numbers had grown to eleven and thirty, respectively.

Among those interested in the survival of pure traditional forms was Pedro de la Cal, one of the most important figures in contemporary Puente del Arzobispo (fig. 7.3). He complained about the introduction of molds and transfers into local production methods. The electric potter's wheel coexisted with the traditional double wheel, the latter being necessary for the fabrication of large earthenware jars, because it provided greater control during shaping. Time-honored *hornos morunos* (two-chambered, updraft kilns), fueled with broom, thyme, and olive or oak branches, were used in parallel with electric or oil-burning kilns. In Talavera, one shop stood out for its use of technology: Artesanía Talaverana's tunnel kiln, using double conveyor belts, could simultaneously fire bisqueware and glazed objects, processing fourteen cubic meters daily.[9]

In a difficult economy, the ceramics industry of Talavera has shown remarkable progress. At present there are some thirty ceramic manufacturers in this city and another sixty in Puente del Arzobispo. Each averages between twenty and thirty employees. The majority of them are organized as small corporations, with 10 percent registered as individual artisans. Half of these companies produce local styles with traditional techniques. Slip-casting molds are increasingly used for shaping the pieces, but without mechanizing the process of pressing.

Through membership in the Asociación Provincial de Artesanía y Cerámica de Toledo (the Toledo Provincial Association of Crafts and

Ceramics), which in turn has been integrated into the Confederación Nacional del Vidrio y la Cerámica (National Glassware and Ceramics Federation), a system has been put into effect for maintaining quality in the traditional lines without disregarding the importance of decorative innovations. The main focus continues to be manufacturing imitations of loza from the Renaissance and Baroque periods. For that reason, the town council has promoted the use of the trademark and guarantee of excellence, "Talavera Cerámica," which testifies to the meticulous handcrafted character of the items produced.

7.3 Pedro de la Cal Rubio (ca.1907–2000) Owner, Santa Catalina Cerámica Regional Puente del Arzobispo, Spain Photo by Robin Farwell Gavin, 2000

There had not been changes in relation to manual labor except for the incorporation of specialists in slip-casting molds. These artisans have been highly trained at the Escuela de Artes y Oficios de Talavera. This technology demands imported materials; Manises provides the prepared pastes. This means that while pastes for general use are contributed by two recently established local factories, varnishes, enamels, and colorants are imported from Manises and Castellón. The training program is enhanced with classes provided by the Asociación Provincial de Artesanía, thanks to Forcem, the official institute of the Committee of Castilla–La Mancha for the provision of training for the ceramics industry.

Web pages have been constructed for wider market promotion, and videos are presented at various trade fairs. One result is the establishment of a market in Miami, Florida, at the same time that the local market is undergoing a clear decline. La Asociación Provincial de Artesanía and the organization Iniciativa para la Promoción Económica de Talavera (the Talavera Initiative for Economic Promotion) support these industries, both fiscally, by disseminating notices of grants and subsidies from the Assembly of Castilla–La Mancha, and technically.[10]

The organization of workshops and decorative ceramic plants throughout Spain has undergone major restructuring in recent years. With few exceptions, the survival of traditional systems of production and historical products has been due to the dedication and will of the potters. There is no doubt that in some cases the loss of the original function of the objects has mystified the previous clientele. Now tourists and collectors purchase the objects (fig. 7.4). In addition, the number of manufacturers has declined drastically, due to reductions in demand and the lack of new markets except for luxury items. This has

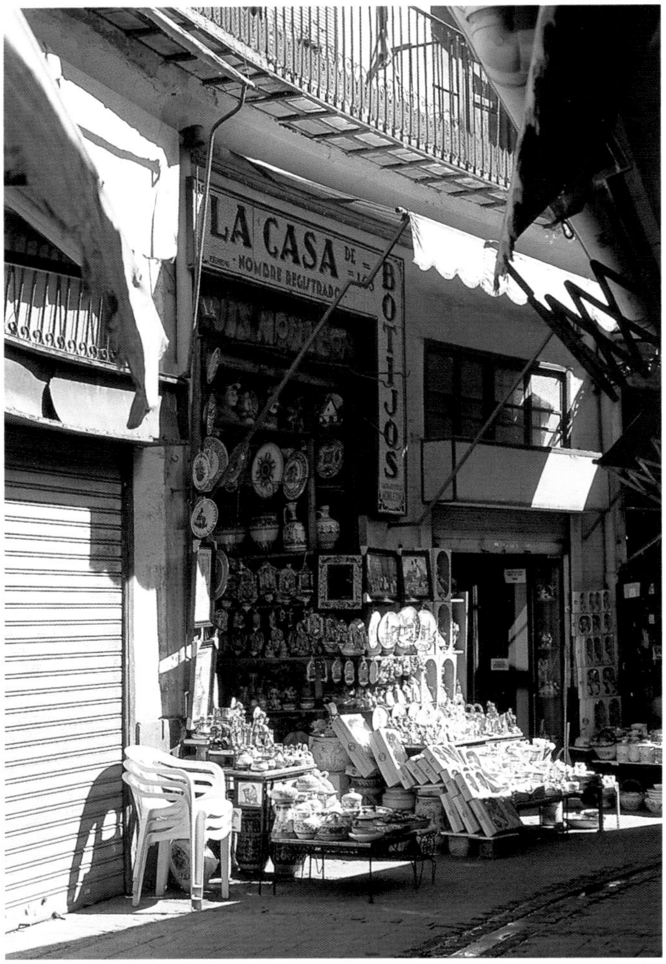

resulted, in some areas, in the survival of a single pottery shop.

In regard to decorative ceramics, since they must now be manufactured in immense shops with advanced technology in order to be competitive, the break with traditional production has become even more radical. The survival of the industry depends on strategies geared toward imitating products of the past while employing modern techniques. While innovation is central to the cultural dynamics of this art form, the technologies that in the past were an intimate part of our cultural traditions are now at risk of being lost; whether they be the "secret" methods involved in the production of medieval Valencian lusterware or the "confidential details" of the glazes produced in *hornos de reverbero* (glaze-frit kilns). This cultural heritage is in danger, but it is worth preserving, because it offers us important tools for interpreting our past. The lack of institutional support contributes to this unfortunate situation.

7.4 *Plaza Redonda*
Valencia, Spain, 2001
Photo by Jaume Coll
Traditional trade activities of decorative *loza* at the *Plaza Redonda.*

Training

Traditionally, training activities were accomplished in the workshop or the factory. From the most remote periods of antiquity, apprentices were ever-present figures who, at an early age, took part in the diverse tasks performed in the shop. They learned the trade while working in a variety of capacities, performing less-skilled jobs first and training by observation and hands-on experience. By a certain age, depending on ability and with formal instruction, and if the economic condition of the shop permitted, it was possible to assume the position of *maestro del oficio* (master artisan) following a career ladder outlined by the potter's guild.

The founding of the royal factory in Alcora during the Age of Enlightenment caused a break with the traditional system by establishing an academic training school within the factory itself. During the eighteenth century, guilds coexisted with these progressive initiatives in factory organization. Workshops and factories employed guild employees as well as technicians trained in royal academies and in the factory schools, breaking the old guild control. This situation was maintained throughout the nineteenth century, since technical training at the university level concentrated on chemistry or industrial engineering. On the other hand, artistic training was conducted in the royal academies, which in the case of Valencia became the Escuela de Bellas Artes de San Carlos (San Carlos School of Fine Arts). At least craft apprenticeships fell outside guild parameters, unless they involved practical instruction offered by collectives in industrial zones. Such training was intended to guide young workers toward specific local jobs.

However, the industry still required manual labor with technical training. To meet this demand, in July of 1877 two hectares of land in Moncloa were granted for the purpose of establishing the Escuela de Artes Cerámicas (School of Ceramic Arts) and a factory for the production of fine loza. This factory, administered by Eusebio Zuloaga and others, was established to continue the ancient tradition of porcelain production; the school did not begin to provide instruction until 1911, when Francisco Alcántara pushed for its inauguration. Only in 1914 did the school receive its first official subsidies, through a royal decree issued on the first of July, under the name of Escuela de Cerámica Artística. This institution was divided in 1982 into the present Escuela Oficial de Cerámica (Official School of Ceramics), and the Escuela Madrileña de Cerámica de la Moncloa (Madrid School of Moncloa Ceramics).[11]

In Manises in the nineteenth century, Rafael Valls David set in motion the recovery of the ceramics industry by advocating adequate training for workers. All of these concerns materialized in structured formal education oriented toward decorative production, as numerous programs were developed in the second decade of the twentieth century. In addition to the efforts of Francisco Alcántara in Madrid, in 1914 in Manises the Escuela General de Aprendizaje (General School of Apprenticeship) was created by the engineer and industrialist Vicente Vilar David and Vicente Mora Arenes, mayor of Manises and also a manufacturer. This institution evolved into the Escuela de Cerámica de Manises (Manises School of Ceramics) in 1916. In that same year, the workshop for the Escuela de Artes y Oficios de Valencia was organized. A few years later, pressures on the tile industry for similar instructional methods resulted in the Escuela Provincial de Cerámica de Onda (Onda Provincial School of Ceramics), established in 1925 but unfortunately abandoned during the Civil War.[12]

Concern for the improvement of education and the standard of living in rural areas caused the government of the Second Republic to initiate the project known as Misiones Pedagógicas (Educational Missions). Teachers and university professors, along with professionals, artists, and writers, traveled to towns where popular arts were thriving, to assist in upgrading production techniques so as to unite tradition with modernity. These initiatives continued after the Civil War, with actions taken by the Sección Femenina de la Falange Española (Women's Division of the Spanish Falange) (especially in the areas of needlework, the dance, and popular music) and the Obra Sindical de Artesanía (Union Artisanship) (in trades normally practiced by men). The latter was responsible for presenting the Carta de Artesano (Artisan's Letter) award to those who still worked in traditional crafts. Within these programs, it was necessary to enlist the assistance of numerous small provincial schools, such as the Escuela de San José, in Cuenca, which functioned essentially as a school for potters from 1954 to 1965.

There are ceramics schools in various production centers, where a range of professional degrees are conferred. Since the year 2000, the Escuela de Cerámica, in Manises, has been accredited, allowing it to grant degrees and certificates of higher education. The curriculum of these degree-granting institutions includes 25 percent elective courses, which allows the school to add courses to meet the ever-changing demands of the marketplace. The present curriculum of the school is centered on the instruction of tile technicians, since that sector has a greater capacity for absorbing newly trained workers. The placement of these students has helped to counteract the commercial stagnation still faced by the decorative ceramics sector. The few who finish the training supply the minimal demand for workers in small businesses and in local family-run workshops. The school also offers complementary informal training that consists of practical courses in creative subjects, computer science, business administration, and hands-on production techniques. The core program provides work opportunities in such areas as technical assistance in ceramics, creative self-employment, ceramic design, restoration of ceramic materials, research and analysis of materials, compliance with ISO standards, productive programming, environmental controls, the adaptation of businesses to the demands of the sector, and marketing.[13]

Madrid welcomed the Escuela Madrileña de Cerámica de la Moncloa and the Escuela Oficial de Cerámica, both founded in 1982, after the division of the school created by Francisco Alcántara. The first is under the sponsorship of the town council and is allowed to grant a degree with the title "ceramist," by agreement with Complutense University. The second follows the curriculum established by the Escuelas de Artes y Oficios (Schools of Arts and Crafts). Their programs of study include the teaching of midlevel courses in pottery and ceramic decoration and upper level courses in modeling, ceramic mold design, and artistic ceramics.[14]

In addition there are other institutions, such as the Escuela de Artes y Oficios Artísticos (School of Arts and Artistic Crafts), that offer specific training in ceramics. Examples of other instructional facilities are the Escuela de Artes de Talavera (School of Arts in Talavera) and the Valencia and Castellón schools of arts and crafts. The Talavera school was created in 1983; it has been providing instruction and granting degrees in ceramics specialties since 1992. Graduates receive a degree equivalent to Bachiller Superior Artístico (advanced bachelor's degree in art) in the specialties of decorative ceramics (midlevel) and artistic ceramics (upper level) At present, curriculum reorganization aims to reach the level of professional training, level IV. The majority of the students, who come from an area extending from the province of Cáceres to the region of Ávila, are trained for self-employment or to satisfy labor needs of the industry in Talavera. However, the best opportunities involve new businesses started by students from the school, who have conspicuously raised the technological level of local manufacturing.[15]

La Escuela de Céramica de la Bisbal (the Ceramics School in Bisbal Gerona) is a private degree-granting school in a traditional center of earthenware production. It is dedicated to improving practical knowledge (such as throwing, decorative techniques, and shaping), and for that reason it is a place of specialization for many students with formal theoretical training obtained elsewhere.

In Barcelona, ceramic training has been organized since 1915 by the Escola Superior dels Bells Oficis (Advanced School of Crafts), complemented since 1918 by the Escola Técnica d'Oficis d'Art (Technical School for Arts and Crafts), created by governmental action. These centers were closed in 1924 and reorganized as the Escola del Treball for specialization in ceramics, in 1928. This institution, in conjunction with the Escola Massana d' Art i Disseny and the Escuela de Artes y Oficios, is now the center of ceramics training in that city.[16]

Current programs in ceramics offer a wealth of technical information as well as encouraging creativity. Some problems in orientation still exist, however, due to the lack of well-defined curricula.[17]

One of the most important recent effects of this educational activity, however, is the growth in the number of craftspeople in the plastic arts who have chosen to use ceramic materials as a channel for their creative expression. Moreover, the contribution of artists engaged as professors in many of these centers has been a tremendous asset. This group includes artists of the stature of Josep Llorens Artigas, Alfons Blat, Angelina Alós, Arcadio Blasco, Elena Colmeiro, Luís Castaldo, Enrique Mestre, Ángel Garraza, Claudi Casasnovas, Juan Antonio Sangil, Alfonso D'Ors, and Xoan Manoel Viqueira. Their creations have been highly influential in the development of novel lines of decorative loza for a traditionally conservative market.

Finally, it should be noted that training in the permanent centers is complemented by a multitude of special courses offered in the majority of public and private schools and in centers such as the Seminario de Estudios Cerámicos de Sargadelos (Sargadelos Seminar in Ceramic Studies). This facility has attained international recognition for its innovative curriculum.

7.5
La Escuradeta
(the pottery washing)
Valencia, Spain, 1993
Photo by Jaume Coll

Final Remarks

Craft potters, previously often seen as involved in a difficult and miserable trade and on occasion subject to waves of professional maladies, have benefited from improved public perception in recent years. Social and legal protections are guaranteed, and occupational safety and health have improved. Nevertheless, concern for this cultural patrimony, although it exists, has not been sufficient to motivate more safeguards and stimulate commercial applications that may permit its survival. One way to ameliorate the situation would be to promote public knowledge of this traditional artistic endeavor and its association with parties, rituals, and ceremonies (fig. 7.5). Such a campaign would permit not only a continued valuable social role for ceramics but the retention of their purest artistic aspects as well. For instance, in traditional kitchens homeowners can demand the use of the *puchero* or the *cazuela*; or the *cántaro* can once again become popular through its use in parties and traditional events, as has been the case in Puertollano with the Fuente del Agua Agria (Fountain of the Bitter Water). We should not permit, as we enter the twenty-first century, any denial of the chance for survival of this rich and complex heritage from our past.

Notes

1. Rudiger Vossen,. *Töpferei in Spanien* (Hamburg: Hamburgisches Museum für Völkerkunde, 1972); Antonio Limón,. *Cerámica popular de Andalucía* (Madrid: Ministerio de Cultura, 1981); A. Carretero, M. Fernández, and C. Ortiz, "Alfarería popular de Andalucía occidental: Sur de Badajoz y Huelva," *Etnografía Española* 1 (1980):99–266.

2. A. Gómez, J. M. Clar, A. Rael, F. J. Rossello, and J. Sevilla, "Saturnismo de los alfareros de Mallorca," *Estudis Balearics* 22 (1986):45–52; Santiago Sánchez Ramos, "Intoxicaciones en la industria y laboratorios cerámicos," *Silicatos* (Escuela de Cerámica de Manises) 4 (1991): 38–41; and Santiago Sánchez Ramos and Pablo Botella Asunción, "Intoxicaciones en la industria y laboratorios cerámicos II, Tóxicos y su destino en el organismo: Efectos tóxicos de los silicatos," *Silicatos* (Escuela de Cerámica de Manises) 5 (1992):30–36.
3. Natacha Seseña, *Cacharrería popular: La alfarería de basto en España* (Madrid: Alianza Editorial, 1997).
4. Jaume Coll Conesa, "La ceràmica i canvi cultural a la València medieval . . .".
5. José Pérez Camps, "La cerámica valenciana en el siglo XX," in M. P. Soler and J. Pérez Camps, *Historia de la cerámica valenciana*, vol. 4 (Valencia: Vicent García Editores, 1992).
6. Josep Navarro, of Avec-Gremio in Manises, personal communication.
7. Natacha Seseña, *Barros y lozas de España* (Madrid: Ediciones Prensa Española, Magisterio Español, and Editora Nacional, 1996), p. 95.
8. Isabel Hurley Molina, *Talavera y los Ruiz de Luna* (Toledo: Instituto Provincial de Investigaciones y Estudios Toledanos, 1989), pp. 139–60.
9. José Guerrero Martín, *Alfares y alfareros de España* (Barcelona: Ediciones del Serbal, 1988): pp. 144–45.
10. Angel Núñez, President of the Confederación Nacional del Vidrio y la Cerámica, personal communication.
11. Foro Joven, "Dos escuelas distintas," *Boletín de la Sociedad Española de Cerámica y Vidrio* 33(6)(1994):361; María del Carmen Riu de Martín, "La Escuela de Cerámica de la Moncloa (Madrid)," *Revistart* 4 (1995):40–42; Francisco Royo Navarro, "La escuela madrileña de cerámica," *Revista d'informació ciutadana* (Manises) 18 (winter 1996):24; Fundación Universidad-Empresa, *Los Estudios de Cerámica*, (Monografias Profesionales 80) (Madrid: Fundación Universidad-Empresa, 1987).
12. Natacha Seseña, , *Cacharrería popular*, p. 23; Josep Pérez Camps, "La cerámica valenciana," pp. 166–67 and "Trajectòria del taller de ceràmica de l'Escola d'Arts i Oficis de València (1914–1999)," in *Ceramistes formats a l'Escola d'Arts i Oficis de València* (Valencia, 1999), pp. 20–28; Carmen García Portillo, "Escuela de cerámica de Manises," *Boletín de la Sociedad Española de Cerámica y Vidrio* 33(6) (1994): 355.
13. José Antonio Sanz de Miguel, Director of the Escuela de Cerámica de Manises, personal communication; María Roselló Verger and F. Costell Landete, "La Escuela de Cerámica de Manises ante las nuevas tecnologías, I," *Silicatos* (Manises) 5 (1992):22–24.
14. Escuela Oficial de Cerámica, "La Escuela Oficial de Cerámica (Madrid)," *Boletín de la Sociedad Española de Cerámica y Vidrio* 33(6) (1994):358–59; Escuela Madrileña de Cerámica, "Escuela Madrileña de Cerámica de la Moncloa," *Boletín de la Sociedad Española de Cerámica y Vidrio* 33(6) (1994): 359–60.
15. Jesús Engenios Martín, "Escuela de Artes de Talavera de la Reina: ¿Se puede enseñar cerámica?" *Boletín de la Sociedad Española de Cerámica y Vidrio* 33(6) (1994):356–57.
16. María del Carmen Riu de Martín, "La enseñanza de la cerámica en Cataluña durante el Novecentismo," *Cerámica* (Madrid) (45), (1995):39–41; "L'Escola Superior dels Bells Oficis i l'Escola Tècnica d'Oficis d'Art: L'especialitat de Ceràmica," *Finestrelles* (Sant Andreu de Palomar, Centre d'Estudis Ignasi Iglésias) 4 (1992):65–85; and "L'Escola del Treball: L'especialitat de Ceràmica," *Finestrelles* (Sant Andreu de Palomar, Centre d'Estudis Ignasi Iglésias) 5 (1993):173–223.
17. Enrique Mestre, "Enseñanza y cerámica," in *30 ceramistas—40 alfareros* (España en Salamanca'88) (Salamanca: Diputación de Salamanca, 1988) pp. 74–77.

Detail, Fig. 8.4

8

Mexican Ceramics in Spain

MARÍA CONCEPCIÓN GARCÍA SÁIZ

THE GREAT CERAMICS tradition of the Mesoamerican world was a magnificent basis for the introduction of European ceramic technology, especially that applied to the elaboration of clay vessels. But neither the novelty of the revolutionary potter's wheel nor the technique of tin–glazing that arrived directly from Spain in the sixteenth century were immediately successful in replacing local production practices. Historically, Mesoamerican earthenware had been modeled by hand, and brilliant sheens were achieved by manually polishing the fine clay slips applied to the objects. The new forms, adapted to the everyday habits and customs of the European culture that imposed them, enriched a typology that at the same time lost some of the beautiful models most directly linked to various expressions of indigenous religious beliefs; many were containers for offerings and occupied a place of the utmost social importance.

Ceramics manufacturing in the Americas in accordance with Western standards was centered on products for the secular world. These items were mostly used in kitchens and formed part of the diverse interior decor of homes constructed to conform to European styles. At the same time, these objects were only very slowly accepted by the native population, among whom more traditional ceramics survived. However, in some cases, for reasons that are still unclear today, new products from a particular locality would acquire an unexpected importance, and demand for them would reach high volumes. This was the beginning of the long road toward an unexpected future where deeply rooted local uses were reinforced. Such is the case for numerous vessels that came out of pottery workshops in the environs of the city of Guadalajara, in the Mexican state of Jalisco. Today we use the generic term *Tonalá* to identify these objects, derived from the name of a famous ceramic–producing Jalisco town.

The most unique feature of Tonalá ceramics is their glossy finish. This is obtained by a distinctive polishing technique that bears a strong relationship to Prehispanic Tonalteca pottery traditions. These earthenware traditions were further developed when the Spanish colonized the area. Along with their evangelical efforts, Spanish priests established workshops to train the local populace in various trades. They introduced processes utilized in their homeland that enhanced and perfected the age–old methods employed by the local inhabitants. This initial interaction gave rise to the fabrication of objects in which indigenous influences were still prominent but were adapted to satisfy the necessities of the new clientele. However, the diverse red, black, and polychrome ceramics that originated in this region were able to maintain their exceptional lustrous appearance with the continued use of traditional polishing techniques and the high–quality clays employed in the slip (fig. 8.1a and b). Consequently, a repertoire of great diversity and rich ornamentation was developed. Among these were very special forms that stood out for their obvious oriental influence; painted in red or blue, they were decorated with floral or animal scenes (fig. 8.2). Archaeologists have labeled this series "Tonalá Bruñida Ware," "Guadalajara Polychrome," or

8.1a Jar / *Jarro*
Tonalá (Jalisco), Mexico, 17th century
Red slipped earthenware
Museo de América, Madrid

"Polished Ornamental Ware."[1] These models have survived up to the present, although with obvious modifications and a notable loss of quality, due to the employment of inferior clays in their fabrication.[2]

A number of these pieces reached Europe throughout the seventeenth and eighteenth centuries. If we are to believe the testimony of chroniclers of that time, even the thousands of shards that resulted from the breakage of these vessels formed part of this unusual trade. Matías de la Mota Padilla reported that during the middle of the eighteenth century, "even the dust of the broken vessels was collected in pots and sold by the *arroba* [unit of approximately 25 pounds] in Jalapa, Veracruz and Acapulco."[3] These last two cities were the key ports for commerce between the West and Asia. The long voyages culminated with the transport of goods to the most affluent areas of the major cities and royal courts of Europe. Although the majority of these earthenware vessels, whole or fragmented, remained on the Iberian Peninsula, countries in the heart of Europe and Italy became the final destination for a substantial number. These objects were incorporated into collections of connoisseurs, who generally either had close blood ties with Spanish nobility or had traveled as ambassadors or special envoys for their monarchs and had become fascinated by exotic customs and artifacts. Hundreds of these Tonalá vessels were distributed throughout Spain and were exhibited along with the most refined oriental porcelains and high–quality Venetian glassware in the homes of the aristocracy. They even breached the cloistered walls of convents, in the hands of nuns who used them with great enthusiasm.

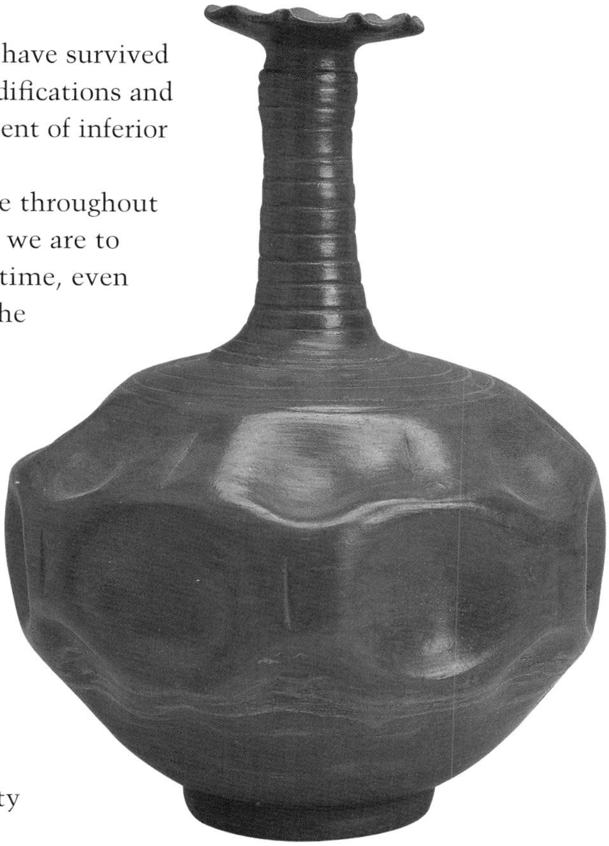

8.1b Bottle / *Botella*
Tonalá (Jalisco), Mexico, 17th century
Red slipped earthenware
Museo de América, Madrid

Why did these objects, even in the form of shards, acquire such a prominent status in settings so distant from where they were originally produced? Apparently the answer lies in organoleptic properties, that is, those related to the sense of taste and smell, derived from the type of clay used in their manufacture, something we cannot appreciate today because, with the passing of time, these characteristics have disappeared. In all likelihood, the consumption of a paste made from the pottery had an impact similar to that of certain hallucinogens, as revealed by the almost opium–like trance reported by those who enjoyed it as a delicacy.

If, in other occasions, a ceramic object was valued for the durability of the clay with which it was fabricated or for the delicacy of its designs and form, in this case it was appreciated for its ability to exude a pleasing aroma and impart a special taste to the water stored within it. This liquid was known as "fragrant water" (*agua de olor*). At the beginning of the seventeenth century, it was common throughout the Iberian Peninsula to use the term *búcaro* when referring to a globular vessel made with red clay (fig. 8.3). The main purpose of these vessels was to cool the water and provide women the pleasure of its consumption. The delight that women found in this odd delicacy led to a habit called *bucarofagia* (a penchant for eating *búcaros*). Their consumption became a common practice among Spanish women, reflecting a tradition that had been introduced throughout the Mediterranean by the Arabs. Búcaros were thought to have originated in Portugal.[4]

However, judging by the data we have, the production of Neohispanic búcaros was well established by the early seventeenth century. Toward the middle of the seventeenth century, they were clearly competing with and sometimes replacing the odoriferous clay vessels produced in peninsular centers. It appears that the extreme fragility of these items was sufficient reason for them not to appear in great quantities on the peninsula, as Mota Padilla records that "these very delicate objects can only be enjoyed in Guadalajara due to the difficulty in transporting them." Búcaros were so popular in Spain by the end of the sixteenth century that Talavera de la Reina pottery shops were producing similar vessels known as *brinquiños*. "The prime quality red clays are not only bright in color but have a pleasant aroma. . . *brinquiños* have been created for the ladies who enjoy drinking the water and eating the clay."[5]

8.2 Bowl / *Cuenco*
Tonalá (Jalisco), Mexico, 17th century
White slipped earthenware
Museo de América, Madrid

Proof of the importance of these fragile vessels in the export trade conducted from the viceroyalty is found in their presence in Spain and in several other countries in Europe, where they were utilized in many different ways and were highly valued. From early times, they are listed in official documents and found in still lifes and canvases illustrating the interiors of homes. There are also astonishing descriptions by chroniclers and travelers and deliberate references made to them in theatrical productions and in the literature of the era, ridiculing the capricious ladies who were so infatuated with them.

Several years after the Franciscan and Augustinian orders had initiated and promoted the activities of pottery workshops in Guadalajara and its surrounding areas, collections of vessels produced at those sites had already begun to be formed. The largest and best-known collection was owned by a Spanish noblewoman, Doña Catalina Vélez de Guevara, who was the niece and wife of Don Iñigo Vélez de Guevara, Count of Oñate and Viceroy in Naples from 1648 to 1653, under the reign of Felipe III, after having served as his ambassador in Rome. After Doña Catalina died, in 1684, a routine inventory of her possessions was carried out to place a value on each of her belongings, and numerous objects from various places of origin were detailed in the precise manner characteristic of the times. The personal effects of the countess illustrated the taste of those who, thanks to the commerce being carried out between the Far East, northern Africa, Europe, and America, adorned their homes and their bodies with all sorts of novelty items. When the appraisers Manuel de Villanueva and Gabriel Mayers performed the inventory of her collection, they recorded a total of five thousand pieces. Along with the Spanish pieces, Italian, Chinese, and Portuguese works and items from different places in the American viceroyalties were also noted. Some of the objects from the Americas were "embellished with silver," that is, mounted on silver supports. This was customary for articles incorporated into collections in Europe, and this fact reveals the high esteem in which these pieces were held.

When the appraisers inspected Doña Catalina's mansions, three china cabinets were found, which contained "a hundred and sixty-one clay pieces from Guadalaxara." The officials specifically mention, when referring to another "ninety and four" and "ninety and three," that these clay pieces were from "Guadalaxara de Yndias," in other words, the city of Guadalajara in the Viceroyalty of New Spain (now Mexico). These vessels were described as being red or black in color and were valued at five or six reales each. There were also others described as large jars, which were valued at up to twenty-four reales each, and which nowadays are known as *tibores*.

Two centuries after Doña Catalina's death, another member of her family, Doña Josefa de la Cerda y Palafox, Countess and widow of Oñate, donated her collection when she passed away. This countess

8.3 Globular Vessel / *Búcaro*
Tonalá (Jalisco),
Mexico, 17th century
Red slipped earthenware
Museo de América, Madrid

expressed in her will the desire to bequeath her extensive ceramics collection, consisting of 956 vases and 23 tibores of Mexican origin, to the Museo Arqueológico Nacional of Madrid. This collection included not only the red or black vessels specified in the old documents but also a significant number of polychrome ceramics that had not been mentioned before and that today we can also link directly to the Tonalá pottery shops.

Another figure from the inner circles of the Spanish court who demonstrated a predilection for these ceramic pieces is the well-known and influential Fernando de Valenzuela, who was called the "ghost of the palace," due to his close relationship with Queen Mariana de Austria, wife of Felipe IV. Valenzuela was born in Naples in 1636 and arrived in Madrid at the age of twenty-five, under the protection of the duke of the Infantado. His ties to the queen and his ambitious personality led him to the highest stations of power and distinction. In 1673, he was honored as a Caballero de Santiago (Knight of St. James). Three years later, he had become one of the most powerful dignitaries in Spain; however, within a year he was arrested, his goods were confiscated, and he was given the death penalty. Ultimately the death penalty was superseded by a sentence of exile, and the "ghost" moved to the Philippines, where he resided for ten years. Sometime later, he moved again, this time to New Spain, where he died in 1692. The eventful life of this ambitious personage permitted him to accumulate impressive personal holdings, known to us through the inventories carried out after his demise. His collection consisted of many objects of various origins, as well as the renowned vessels from Guadalajara de Indias.

Other wealthy Spaniards also showed an interest in red and black Guadalajara earthenware as well as in pieces from Chile and other areas of Hispanic America. The data offered by inventories of their belongings prove that these polished red–paste ceramic wares had achieved great prominence on the Iberian Peninsula, where they competed with, and were sometimes mistaken for, those fabricated in the Portuguese pottery shops of Estremoz and Lisbon. These are the same pieces that can be found in numerous convents, such as the Descalzas Reales, in Madrid. Despite the religious nature of these spiritual centers, an inclination for worldly goods seemed to reign, and shipments from America were often received from benefactors or relatives. Those nuns who were *criollas* (daughters of Spanish parents but born in the Americas) enjoyed keeping small objects of everyday use from their homelands among their personal effects.

Well into the eighteenth century, Spaniards continued to favor these vessels "of different sizes and shapes," such as the twenty–four pieces kept in 1717 by Isidoro Garma de La Puente, secretary to Felipe V. Don Prudencio Antonio de Palacios had in his possession several impressive tibores around the middle of the eighteenth century. These vessels were described in minute detail after his death, allowing us to relate them to models that are still preserved today: "two *tinaxas de barro de Yndia* . . . a little smaller than those previously mentioned and with distinctive forms. They have openings in the front and various figures with gilded wooden feet painted in flesh–tone (*encarnado*) can be seen in the interior."[6]

These documented facts are reinforced by images displayed in paintings of the times, especially still lifes, where it is easy to identify objects that are similar to those described in written records and which have survived until today. In some instances, these pieces appear as the focal point of the paintings. In other representations, they are not as obvious and appear with different food items and all sorts of other objects that make up the composition. Earthenware vessels from Manises (Valencia) and Triana (Sevilla), along with oriental porcelains and glass or silver objects, are usually depicted. In addition, the so–called *vanitas* (Allegories of Vanity) are embodied in these paintings to remind us of the ephemerality of life by depicting perishable goods that only serve to feed our senses and satisfy our ambitions. The ceramics of Guadalajara de Indias were also selected to form part of the great displays of exoticism popularly known as curiosity cabinets.

The painting of still lifes, or *bodegones*, reached its high point in Spain in the seventeenth century. It remained popular throughout this period, due to the magnificent works of Juan Sánchez Cotán and many other painters, who assured their fame and recognition by creating paintings for an increasingly flourishing market. Some of the bodegones were special-ordered, but the vast majority were painted and displayed with the hope that a customer would come by and purchase them. Since it was up to the artists to select the focal points of their compositions, the pictorial examples that follow demonstrate to us the familiarity of the artists with the ceramics in which we are interested, products found in the most diverse environments.

Juan Van der Hamen (1596–1631) was a painter from Madrid who cultivated his style in royal surroundings, putting himself at the head of those who developed still-life themes in the third decade of the seventeenth century. He was one of the first artists to introduce these red clay artifacts in his canvases. The object displayed in his painting *Bodegón con Dulces y Cerámica* (National Gallery of Art, Washington, DC), signed and dated in 1627, is a small vessel whose shape and texture link it directly to a variety of rose-colored ceramics made from the very fine paste that lent itself to the consumption so shocking to foreign visitors to Spain.[7] The fact that this vessel is exhibited in conjunction with candies and fruits gives rise to the conjecture that perhaps the intention of the painter was to make allusion to its condition of being a sweet rather than just a container for liquids.

The French countess D'Aulnoy lived in Spain between the years 1679 and 1680. During her residence there, she had the opportunity to visit numerous homes of the nobility and was able to satisfy her curiosity regarding the day-to-day habits of its members. While visiting with the countess of Monleón, who in one of her reports she calls "princess," the Frenchwoman was able to see for herself the yen that these aristocratic women demonstrated for this exquisite delicacy. On this and other occasions, she described them as eating *tierra sigilada*, a name given to the objects because of their similarity to ancient Roman ceramics of the same name. Surprised, she noted the effects: "They went into a trance. Their stomachs became distended and hard and their skin turned into a yellow color like that of a quince." As was to be expected, she was tempted to sample this highly praised dish: "I wanted to try this sweet delicacy so highly revered and yet almost irreverent." Afterwards, she declared, " I would have preferred to eat sandstone rather than this *tierra sigilada*." She did give credence to some of the numerous qualities attributed to it: "It cures certain illnesses and poison placed in the water of a *tierra sigilada* vessel will soon be detected." In spite of her rejection of such "delicacies," she appreciated the superior quality of the water kept in these vessels: "I myself have one that sours wine but enriches the taste of water. It almost seems to fizz when stirred or shaken. After not too long a time, the cup is empty. This happens because the clay is very porous and all that is left is a wonderful odor."[8] This delicious water was without doubt consumed at the wedding of one of the sons of the Count of Oñate, celebrated in Naples. All the guests commented about the exceptionally flavorful "clay water," as it was described to the Florentine scholar Lorenzo Magalotti, although in that particular reference the receptacles were probably larger vessels, such as tibores or *achibúcaros*.[9]

Another Spanish painter, Juan de Espinosa (active 1628–59), provided evidence in some of his still life works of the day–to–day association that the population of Spain had with these red ceramic vessels. They appear in such canvases as *Bodegón con Uvas, Vasija de Barro y Pájaro Muerto* (Prado), *Bodegón con Uvas, Manzanas y Ciruelas* (Prado), *Bodegón con Manzanas, Nuez Abierta y Cacharro de Barro* (private collection, Barcelona), and *Bodegón con Uvas, Frutas y Jarra de Barro*, signed and dated in 1646 (Naseiro collection).[10] In all these works, the size and color of the ceramics add a sense of equilibrium to the composition; they harmonize with the fruits, flowers, animals, and large shells that Espinosa portrayed again and again in his still lifes.

These same earthenware products attracted the attention of the clientele of Antonio de Pereda, an artist who was born in Valladolid in 1611 and died in Madrid in 1678. He is the creator of the interesting work *Bodegón con Dulces, Vasijas y Escritorio de Ebano* (the Hermitage, St. Petersburg) (see fig. 2.9). This remarkable canvas displays another object from the pottery workshops of the New World, an Olinalá bowl. As is true of many other still–life representations, this work focuses on *vanitas*. If this truly is the intention of the author, the choice of Guadalajara ceramics is a most appropriate illustration of the fleeting pleasures experienced through the senses of taste and smell.[11]

In many still lifes,objects produced in the New World are also seen in sets of dishes or bowls used to serve chocolate. In this particular painting, the set is positioned in the lower left corner of the composition. Chocolate, according to Bartolomeo Marradón (1618), was a very popular beverage, which in the opinion of doctors of the times produced "obstructions, trances and hydropsies" (see chapter 11, below).[12] Another painting by Pereda that has been extensively studied is his *Escena de Cocina*, also known as *Alegoría de la Virtud Perdida* (Penrhyn Castle).[13] This painting displays two small vessels resembling the Guadalajara pieces, placed in the center of a cluttered table. Such objects were always associated with an exotic distinctiveness that underscored their exceptional artistic character.

Francisco Barrera (1595–1658) created several paintings in series dedicated to fruits, landscapes, the four seasons, and the twelve months of the year. In his canvas *El Mes de Julio* (Slovak National Gallery, Bratislava), a small red clay container is shown set on a silver stand.[14] In his *Bodegón con Melocotones, Peces y Servicio de Chocolate* (private collection), an Olinalá vessel is exhibited along with the chocolate set.[15] The use of these special ceramics is again seen in the paintings of a little known *bodegonista*, Francisco Barranco, who was active between the years 1630 and 1640 in Sevilla, as demonstrated in his *Bodegón con Servicio de Chocolate y Pájaros Muertos* (Apelles Collection, London).[16] One of his contemporaries, Francisco Palacios (1622/25–52), also concentrated on still-life subject matter. His *Bodegón con Trenzas de Pan* displays a jar that is similar to those previously mentioned.[17]

Giuseppe Recco (1634–95) and Andrea Belvedere (circa 1652–1732) are two Neapolitan artists who were closely connected to the Spanish world. They both lived in Spain toward the end of the seventeenth century, where they painted their last still lifes. Giuseppe Recco's *Bodegón con Criado Negro* (Casa Ducal, Sevilla) is a remarkable painting, signed and dated in the year 1679. Here the polished red ceramics are displayed among a multitude of objects that include Venetian glassware.[18] Belvedere owes his fame in great part to his depictions of floral displays. In some of his works, the vessels that contain the flower arrangement are these same glossy red ceramics.[19]

All the foregoing examples belong to the seventeenth century and represent a splendid collection of samples of Guadalajara pieces. They were able to compete with other ceramics to the extent that in eighteenth century Spain they were recognized as originating in the "Indias," specifically Mexico. As time went by, they were identified as "a kind of jar made out of red clay from America." But perhaps the most remarkable representation of a piece from this repertoire may be one that is not significant in itself, but rather because of the identity of the painter and the work in which his unique talents are displayed. This is the small *bucarito* mounted on a silver stand that is being offered by an attentive María Angustia Sarmiento to one of the daughters of Felipe IV, the Infanta Margarita. The fact that this work is the masterpiece *Las Meninas*, painted by Diego Velázquez, adds a very special resonance to the utilization of an object from "Guadalajara de Indias," which is delicately and intricately portrayed in a common, everyday environment.[20]

It is apparent that the most elite elements of society of seventeenth-century Europe not only were aware of the existence of these objects, judging by their recurring presence in collections and personal possessions, but also that they were held in the highest esteem and were exhibited as cherished trophies, symbols of discriminating taste and refinement. Their aromatic qualities gave them a mesmerizing effect. This placed them in the same category as other items that at the end of the seventeenth century became widely popular subjects of attention. As a result, "everywhere, the curious, the erudite, the philosopher observed, studied, and wondered about them."

Lorenzo Magalotti, the Florentine scholar, reserved a special space for comments about Guadalajara ceramics among the topics in his invaluable correspondence directed to the Marquee Strozzi in 1695. He reported the interest people had in these pieces and described how carefully he handled them when he finally obtained his own samples in order to understand the value that was placed upon them. Through his descriptions, we know that from the moment he received the objects, he set about to construct what he considered to be the most satisfactory and secure containers for the vessels:

> The first thing I did was to perfume the little boxes by rubbing them for eight days with a little sponge impregnated with flower scents, especially aromatic water made out of thistles and carnations. Then I had them lined with pearl colored silk since this color is most suitable to reflect the color of the type of clay used in these pieces. I proceeded to dilute the tragacanth sap in the perfumed water of orange blossoms and their leaves, for as I recall having stated before, thistles and orange blossoms are flowers that best enhance the aroma of these lands. At the bottom of these little boxes I placed tiny cushions filled with perfumed cotton which was marinated for several days in a sachet with smoke of balsam. I took great care not to spoil its rich and delicate aroma. On top of these tiny cotton pads I placed the vessels in groups according to types, standing them straight up and burying the lower half in the treated cotton. Care was taken to let air flow freely among the vessels so that the cotton would absorb and retain the beneficial aroma emanating from them. Next I added a pinch of tiny pieces of amber skin and being aware that it is very important not to leave the boxes open since the outer air in the long run would draw off the oiliness that preserved the aroma, I carved an incision in each box before lining them. This slit was made in the thickest part of the rim on each side and since I did not have cedar or aloe, it was necessary to use on all of them the oiliest slat of cypress that I could find, placing on top of it a knot of ribbon that served as a kind of handle for raising the cover to avoid the risk of breaking one's nail every time it was opened and to facilitate taking out the vessels or re–inserting them into the little box.[21]

Some of the documented testimonies cited above remind us of the fact that the Guadalajara pieces were preserved throughout the eighteenth century, and their continued use was due to the high degree of care given to them, although shipments diminished, and these vessels were eventually replaced by other earthenware. As time went by, these pieces began disappearing, and it became prestigious to own them, to the extent that in the nineteenth century, it was still possible to find them in some Spanish homes: ". . . no more of them are made in America, so *bucaros* are beginning to become scarce, and in a few years' time they will be as hard to find, and as fabulous in price, as old Sèvres."[22] These are the words of Teófilo Gautier, who around 1840 clearly identified "the red clay pieces" with ". . . a sort of pot made of red American earth, rather like the kind of which the stems of Turkish pipes are made; they are of all shapes and sizes; some of them are picked out with gilded beadings and powdered with coarsely painted flowers."[23]

It is obvious that Gautier based his comments on the Spanish tradition itself. Furthermore, he did not hesitate to remind us that even up to 1840 the tradition continued: "Not content with inhaling the perfume and drinking the water, some people chew small fragments of *bucaros*, crunch them to a powder and end by swallowing them."[24] But this chronicler also described in minute detail their function as humidifiers and the role that these complex vessels played when they were stacked one on top of another and placed in the corners of rooms:

> When they want to use the *bucaros*, seven or eight of them are placed on marble–topped tables or brackets and filled with water, then the ladies go and sit on the sofa and wait for them to take effect, so as to enjoy this pleasure in a suitable state of repose. First the clay takes on a darker tinge; the water filters through its pores, and it is not long before the *bucaros* break into a perspiration, and diffuse an odour resembling the smell of wet plaster, or that of a damp cellar which has not been opened for a long time. The sweating of the *bucaros* is so profuse that by the time an hour has passed, half the water has evaporated; what remains in the jar is as cold as ice and has taken on a sickening flavour of well or cistern, which is considered exquisite by *aficionados*. Half a dozen *bucaros* would be enough to saturate the air of a boudoir with damp–enough to be noticeable as you enter; it is a sort of cold vapour bath.[25]

In the opinion of our French traveler, this method was one of the few ways that the inhabitants of Madrid had for weathering their severe summers: "This need for coolness has given rise to the fashion for *bucaros*, an odd, uncivilized taste which would not appeal to our French ladies who affect fashionable airs, but seems a most tasteful refinement to the fair Spaniards."[26]

These statements clearly attest to the continued existence of some of the uses of these objects shortly after their introduction into Spain, where they soon became deeply rooted in local traditions. The bucarofagia phenomenon probably came to the Iberian Peninsula from Asia Minor. The attraction to the aroma of fresh clay became the key element for the promotion and instigation of work in those pottery shops that utilized clays capable of transmitting these properties to the finished objects.

In spite of their continued popular use, these búcaros were eventually replaced in paintings of the eighteenth century by other models produced in the Tonalá workshops. The collection of the counts of Oñate, for example, grew in the nineteenth century to include an important number of high–quality polychrome pieces–bowls, drinking vessels, basins, and tibores of different shapes and sizes. Both the exteriors and interiors of these fragile pieces were painted with a slip that highlighted the magnificent finishes and contributed to the differentiation of their colors: cream, ochre, and red. There was great variety in their decoration and, although it was generally based on vegetable and geometric motifs, it was not unusual to encounter on many of these vessels (especially short, wide pots) a mixture of freely applied animal subject matter. Even representations of double–headed eagles and angel figures can be found. In some cases, these decorations were achieved as a result of the use of impressions on the clay body or with applications of *pastillaje*.[27]

These ceramics lack the references of those previously mentioned, and inventories do not even acknowledge their presence among the personal belongings of their proprietors. However, Magalotti counted them among his possessions. He valued their aromatic properties, but did not think they had decorative elements worthy of attention. He refers to their decoration as "quite coarse" and based on "certain black and red arabesque motifs," limited in some cases to "glazes in pinkish tones upon which milky white arabesques were applied."

Luis Meléndez (1716–80) had the ingenious idea to paint a repertoire that, in his own words, represented "the Four Seasons and above all the Four Elements in scenes depicting an amusing cabinet displaying all types of foods that are produced in the Spanish climate within those said four elements." These vignettes of small dimensions were painted over a period of years and, in fact, several became part of the royal collection, through patronage of the heir prince, the future Carlos V, and his wife, María Luisa de Parma, who became especially interested in them.[28] Several of these canvasses formed part of the interior decoration at the Casita de Abajo in El Escorial, the country home of the prince. Later on they were also displayed on the walls of the dining room of the royal palace of Aranjuez. Our interest in these paintings centers on the Tonalá pieces that some of them depict. For example, *Bodegón: Limas, Caja de Dulces y Otros Objetos* (Prado),[29] where these "objects" are placed on a silver tray that draws attention to each item, especially one small cup with a tiny handle, which can only be held "with the fingertips."[30] This was not the only time that Meléndez incorporated these pieces into his compositions, as seen in his typical placement of a bowl on a silver tray and in *Albaricoques, bollos y recipientes variados*

8.4 Jar / *Tinaja*
Tonalá (Jalisco), Mexico, 17th century
White slipped earthenware
Museo de América, Madrid

(Prado).[31] In the background of this painting, dated to around 1770, on top of the table behind the apricots and a honey vessel of the type fabricated in Manises, is a group of ceramics consisting of a polychrome bowl surrounded by a considerable number of red vessels on what look like silver stands. This is one of the few instances where the two types of ceramics related to Tonalá appear together.

Finally, it is necessary to recall another kind of Tonalá ceramics, one that is extraordinarily singular and impossible to confuse with other types of red earthenware from pottery workshops anywhere else. This assortment includes the remarkable *tinajas*, or *archibúcaros*, already known in the seventeenth century, which were frequently called tibores, alluding to their connection with themes of oriental inspiration (fig. 8.4). These large vessels, sometimes measuring more than a yard in height, were generally mounted on painted or gilded wooden bases. Their main function was to contain water, to which they would transmit the distinctive characteristics of aroma and taste that we have already made reference to. The Royal

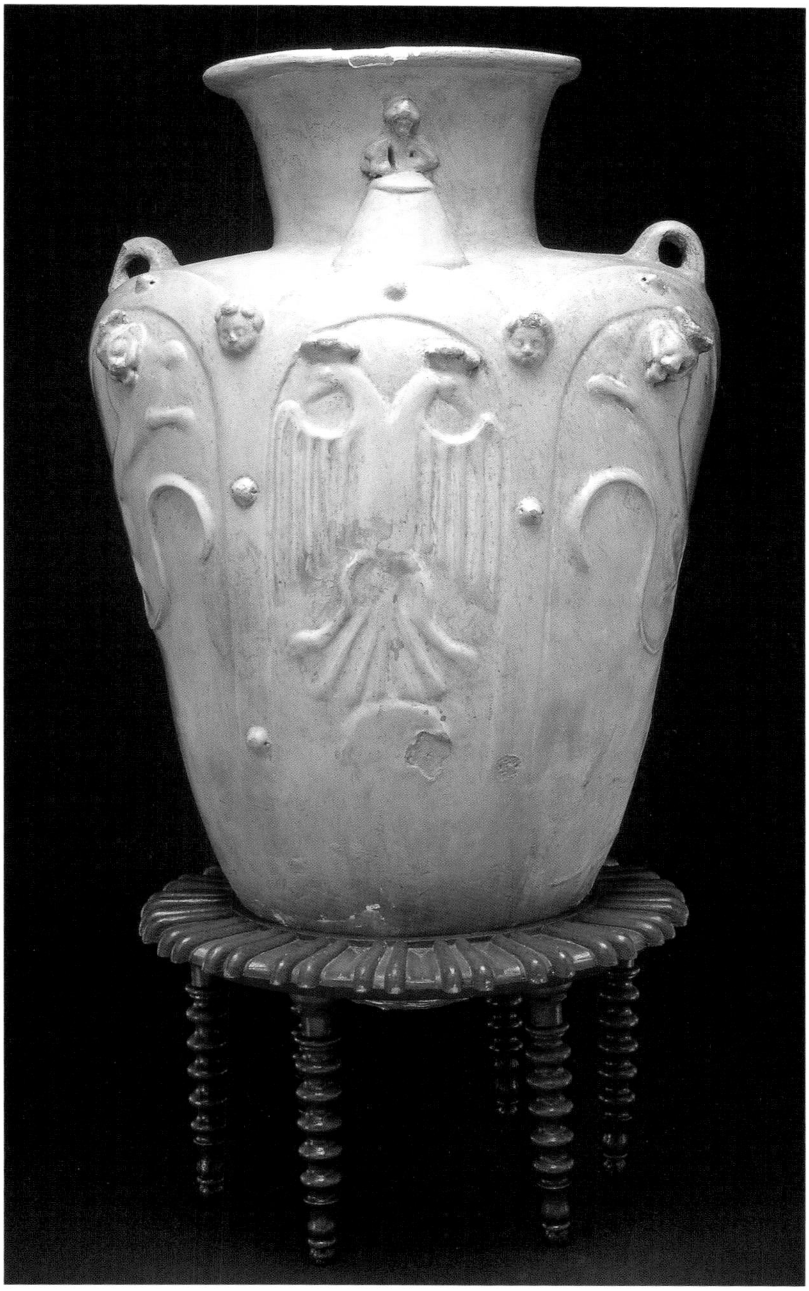

8.5 Jar / *Tinaja*
Tonalá (Jalisco), Mexico, 17th century
White slipped earthenware
Museo de América, Madrid

Palace of Turin, the Guinori in Florence, and the Quirinal at Rome have all had examples of these vessels. They have also been preserved in places like the Seo of Zaragoza, the Ecija church, and the Chapel of San Fermín in Pamplona.[32]

The tibores were also made in smaller sizes, sometimes less than 8 inches in height. Their decoration was distributed in two clearly differentiated facades. The one that could be considered more noticeable usually exhibited a two-headed eagle underneath arcades displaying cherubim heads flanked by raging wild lions. All these motifs were a mixture of painting and modeling, to form reliefs. The back was completely covered by animal and botanical motifs.

Some of these vessels have survived to modern times in an unfinished state, lacking the final ornamental applications. This has helped us to learn in greater detail the different phases of their fabrication. One example (4918, Museo de América) clearly displays the whitish slip that covers the whole piece, including the elements modeled in relief and the triple-arcade scheme with the two-headed eagle and the ferocious lions (fig. 8.5). In addition, on the neck of the vessel there is a feminine figure, dressed in the fashion popular prior to the occupation of the Spanish crown by the Bourbons. By viewing the completed objects (4915, Museo de América; fig. 8.4), we can observe how the polychrome completely conquered all space, emphasizing the shape of the form and calling attention to the figures that were hardly discernible in relief. Sometimes these tibores were gilded by their owners, who were eager to embellish them; in so doing, they caused them to lose most of their polychromatic features under the applications of purpurin or gold leaf.

Notes

1. Thomas H. Charlton, "Tonalá Bruñida Ware: Past and Present" *Archaeology* 32(1) (1979):45–53; Gonzalo López Cervantes, "En torno a la cerámica tonalteca del Museo Regional de Guadalajara," in *Tonalá: Sol de Barro* (Mexico: Banco Cremi, S.A.,1991), pp. 101–13; María Concepción García Sáiz and María Angeles Albert, "La cerámica de Tonalá en las colecciones europeas," in *Tonalá: Sol de Barro* (Mexico: Banco Cremi, S.A.,1991), pp. 47–97.
2. Gutierre Aceves and Rubén Páez, "Tonalá bruñida: Reseña de una técnica que perdura," in *Tonalá: Sol de barro* (Mexico: Banco de Cremi, S.A.,1991), pp. 37–45.
3. Matías de la Mota Padilla, *Historia del Reino de Nueva Galicia en la América* (Guadalajara: Septentrional, 1973; first published in 1742), p. 44.
4. Carolina M Vasconcellos, *Algunas palavras a respeito de pucaros de Portugal* (Coimbra: 1921) p. 334.
5. Natacha Seseña, "El búcaro de las Meninas," in *Velázquez y el arte de su tiempo* (Madrid: 1999) pp. 40–42.
6. María Concepción García Sáiz and José Luis Barrio Moya, "Presencia de cerámica colonial mexicana en España," *Anales del Instituto de Investigaciones Estéticas* (1987):103–10.

7. Peter Cherry, *Arte y naturaleza: El bodegón Español en el Siglo de Oro* (Madrid: 1991), illus. 105.
8. Condesa d'Aulnoy, *Viaje por España de 1670 a 1680* (Madrid: 1962), p. 84.
9. Teresa Poggi Salani and Francisca Perujo, "De los búcaros de las Indias Occidentales," *Boletín de Investigaciones Bibliográficas* 8 (1972):319–54.
10. Cherry, *Arte y naturaleza*, illus. 146, LIII; illus. 140, LV.
11. Cherry, *Arte y naturaleza*, p. 227.
12. de la Mota, *Historia*, p. 40.
13. Cherry, *Arte y naturaleza*, illus. 160.
14. Ibid., illus. XLVI, 1.
15. Ibid., illus. XLVII.
16. Ibid., illus. LXXXVII.
17. Pintura española de los siglos XVI a XVIII (1982): 92–93.
18. Pintura Napolitania (1985): 256–257.
19. Pintura Napolitania (1985) 84–87.
20. Seseña, "El búcaro," pp. 39–48.
21. Poggi Salani and Perujo, "De los búcaros," pp. 319–54.
22. Teófilo Gautier, *A Romantic in Spain*, trans. by Catherine Alison Phillips (Interlink Books, 2001), p. 93.
23. Ibid., p. 93.
24. Ibid., p. 94.
25. Ibid., pp. 93–94.
26. Ibid., p. 93.
27. García Sáiz and Albert, "La cerámica de Tonalá," pp. 47–97.
28. M. C. Espinosa Martín, "Aportes documentales a los bodegones de Luis Meléndez," *Boletín del Museo del Prado* (1989):67–77.
29. Luis Carlos Gutiérrez, Alonso, "Precisiones a la cerámica de los bodegones de Luis Egidio Meléndez," *Boletín del Museo del Prado* 12 (1983):162–66.
30. Poggi Salani and Perujo, "De los búcaros," p. 343.
31. *Luis Meléndez: Spanish Still Life Painter of the Eighteenth Century*, exhibition catalog (Dallas: Meadow's Museum, 1985), pp. 92–93;p. 82, no. 19.
32. José Tudela, "Tibores coloniales mejicanos en los palacios reales de Italia," *Revista de Indias* (1943):35–43; Carlota M. Mapelli, "Tibores de Jalisco en el Palacio del Quirinal," *Boletín del Instituto Nacional de Antropología e Historia* 39 (1970):30, and "Tibores de Jalisco en Turín," *Boletín del Instituto Nacional de Antropología e Historia* 21 (1978):58; García Sáiz and Albert, "La cerámica de Tonalá," pp. 47–97.

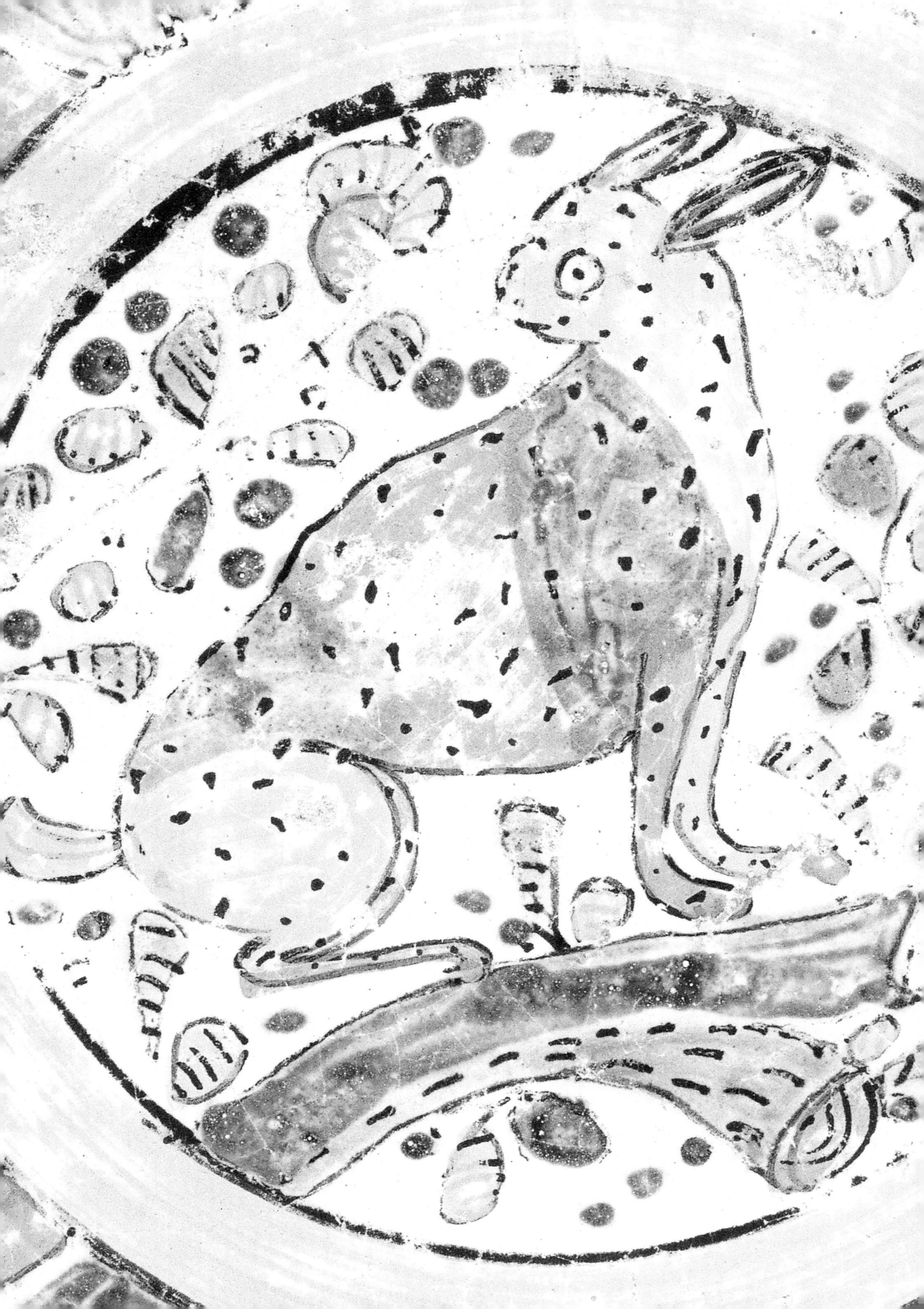

Detail, Fig. 9.3

9

The Emergence of a Mexican Tile Tradition

MARGARET E. CONNORS McQUADE

THE PRODUCTION OF tiles in Mexico has a long and rich history, involving the exchange of ideas, objects, and traditions across three continents. This essay traces the migration of tile production from its roots in Muslim Spain to the development of a uniquely Mexican tradition.

Decorative tilework was first employed in the ancient Middle and Near East, where it has enjoyed a long history of innovative styles and techniques. With the expansion of Islam, the tradition was introduced to Europe by way of the Iberian Peninsula in the twelfth century, by which time the production of mayólica had been well established.[1] The first tiles consisted of elaborate tile mosaics, known as *alicatados* in Spain, made with small polygonal glazed pieces (*aliceres*) to create brilliant geometric patterns of light and color on the walls and floors of patios, mosques, and churches, as well as in the homes of the noble and the very wealthy. Over time, the labor-intensive method by which this architectural decoration was produced was replaced by new techniques. Two distinct techniques were used to create designs by separating color oxides. One technique, known as *cuerda seca*, separates color by creating a resist with a mixture of manganese oxide and grease. The other, known as *cuenca* or *arista*, is achieved by using a stamp to create a negative mold. By the sixteenth century, however, polychrome designs were painted directly onto the flat surface of the tile bathed in tin glaze; this type is known as *pisano*.

The practice of decorating surfaces was not, however, a tradition unique to the Old World. In areas of Postclassic Mesoamerica (ca. a.d. 900–1521), wall surfaces of elite residences and ceremonial structures were painted with colorful patterns and figural images, and some exteriors were even embellished with mosaic stonework, cut and carved with elaborate geometric designs. Just as in Europe, architectural adornment was used to reflect prosperity and social status.

The long and impressive ceramic tradition of Mesoamerica dates back millennia before the Spanish arrived in the sixteenth century. Clay was used to build architectural structures as well as an array of vessel and sculptural forms. The use of tin- and lead-based glaze (mayólica), the potter's wheel, and the kiln, however, were techniques introduced by the Spanish, and may in fact be counted among the most important artistic traditions introduced to the New World at the time of the conquest. In time, this architectural treatment would define the distinctive Mexican style of Puebla de los Ángeles (also known as Puebla) and characterize some of the most impressive architecture of New Spain.

Spanish Tiles in the New World

By the first decade of the sixteenth century, Spanish fleets had begun traveling across the Atlantic, laden with supplies. Among the imported items were mayólica tiles, many of which came from the prolific potters of Triana, in Sevilla. Triana was the most important center for the production of ceramic tiles in Spain at the time, supplying ceramics and ceramists to colonies throughout the Americas.

Of the various types of tiles produced in Spain in the sixteenth century, the most important in the New World was the flat-surfaced pisano type. By the sixteenth century, these tiles had just begun to replace earlier Mudéjar styles and techniques. The term *pisano* is believed to have come from the Italian master ceramist Francisco Niculoso, presumably of Pisa, who arrived in Sevilla at the end of the fifteenth century. Among other Italians living in southern Spain, Niculoso is said to have brought the Italian technique for decorating tiles with a variety of color oxides unknown to the limited Spanish palette of the time.

Even though archaeologists have found only a limited number of Spanish tiles at Hispanic–American sites, historical documents indicate that Spanish tiles were shipped to the New World in large quantities. On the *Santa María Antigua*, sailing to Santo Domingo in the fleet of Diego Colón in 1509, for example, Diego Fernández de Morón sent forty wicker baskets filled with tiles, and the *San Juan* of the same fleet was reportedly carrying six baskets.[2] In Santo Domingo, both cuenca–and pisano tiles survive in situ at the cathedral, which dates from 1523 to 1540, and at the Hospital of San Nicolás, which was under construction between 1533 and 1552.[3]

Perhaps the best–known Spanish colonial interiors with Spanish tiles are those in the monasteries of Santo Domingo and San Francisco, in Lima, both dating to the first half of the seventeenth century. Many of these pisano tiles have been attributed to two distinct workshops in Sevilla: those of Fernando de Valladares, who had come from a family of potters in Triana, and Juan Martín Garrido, who by 1619 had moved from Sevilla to Lima to make over six thousand tiles for the monastery commissioned by the local Dominican procurator general. A contract from 1604 specifies that Valladares had been chosen to make eighty thousand tiles for the Dominican friar Francisco de Vega of the Order in Peru. In addition to the large and small square tiles and the narrow border tiles, there were 560 tiles to fill pilaster panels, as well as 550 tiles for the four altar frontals, "like those in the cloister of the Monastery of San Pablo in this city [Sevilla]."[4] Another contract, dated 23 September 1619, indicates that Martín Garrido had received an advance of two hundred *pesos de a ocho reales* for his work at the Monastery of Santo Domingo.[5] Impressed by the colorful decoration at Santo Domingo in Lima, Father Bernabé Cobo, a Jesuit historian residing in Lima, recorded the following in the first half of the seventeenth century: "The main cloister of Santo Domingo is the best decorated in all the kingdom; the walls and lower pillars for more than an *estado* and a half from the ground are covered with tiles of varied and careful workmanship, which were brought from Spain at great expense."[6] These early seventeenth–century tiled interiors in Lima may indicate how some other Spanish colonial interiors originally appeared, before extensive remodeling over the years drastically altered them.

Few early colonial interiors in Mexico survive intact, and many questions remain to be answered regarding their provenance. Extant Spanish tiles, which must have once emblazoned colonial buildings, are known in various museum collections in Mexico, such as the Franz Mayer Museum, in Mexico City, and the José Luis Bello y González

Museum, in Puebla. Of particular interest is the unit of one hundred and twenty Triana wall tiles that probably once embellished an early seventeenth-century church interior that is today found in the Bello Museum.[7]

Today there are only a few known colonial structures that still retain their original seventeenth-century Spanish tile decoration. Recent excavations at the former Monastery of San Francisco in Puebla have revealed that at least one of the interior rooms had been covered with tiles consistent with Spanish manufacture.[8] The construction of the monastery began in 1535, only four years after the founding of the city. It was the first monastery in Puebla and the twenty-first one in Mexico. The design and the color of these tiles are undoubtedly Sevillian, and may have come out of Valladares's workshop. Made in units of four tiles (fig. 9.1), together they create an irregular octofoil motif with radiating stylized leaves, deriving from textile designs, which seems to have been a favorite of Valladares. He used the motif at a number of locations, including the Convent of the Mother of God in Sevilla, founded in 1472 and tiled between 1550 and 1575 (today in the chapel of the University of Sevilla and the Museo de Bellas Artes in Sevilla); the Chapel of Álvaro Ponce de León in the Church of San Vicente (1602); and the Church of San Martín in Sevilla (1614).[9] The logical assumption, on the basis of style, color, and known documents, is that these tiles are Spanish; until precise documentation is found or until the clay bodies are analyzed, this must remain a hypothesis.

The crypt of the former Monastery of El Carmen in San Ángel (today southern Mexico City) is another interior space with similar tiles, as well as other tiles that Valladares had been producing in Sevilla at the time (fig. 9.2).[10] However, these tiles are known to have been imported to San Ángel in 1628. Perhaps Valladares's was the most

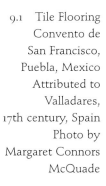

9.1 Tile Flooring Convento de San Francisco, Puebla, Mexico Attributed to Valladares, 17th century, Spain Photo by Margaret Connors McQuade

9.2 Altar / *Altar*
Attributed to Valladares, Spain, 17th century
Crypt of the former Convento del Carmen, Museo del Carmen, San Ángel, Mexico
Photo by Michel Zabé

important workshop to export tiles to the New World in the seventeenth century, before Puebla became a major center for the production of mayólica in the Americas.

Mayólica tiles were clearly not among the items needed by the first Spanish settlers in New World. Yet the Spanish began to ship tiles to the colonies at least a decade before Cortés embarked for present-day Mexico, in 1519. Why were Spanish tiles imported at the dawn of the conquest of the New World? Were they considered necessary to properly decorate colonial churches? Florence and Robert Lister discovered a document of particular interest regarding this matter.[11] In the document, dated Burgos

1512, King Ferdinand replied to a request for tiles, bricks, masons, carpenters, and cement workers to be sent to the island of Hispaniola (today the Dominican Republic and Haiti). The request was granted, but not without complaining that the items were unnecessary, as the island reportedly had substantial wood and clay resources as well as trained Spanish laborers. Nonetheless, the new colonists had not yet begun to produce the same quality mayólica to which they were accustomed.To the Spaniards, the church was a symbol of order and decency and was an essential part of the colonization; they must have felt it important to embellish the new colonial churches with the colorful tiles they had known in Spain. Churches were designed by lay brothers, who were masons as well as friars, and whose knowledge of architecture was largely based on European prints and the memory of structures back in their homeland; they were not necessarily ceramists. Spanish tiles were easy to ship and did not require the presence of such ceramists as Valladares. Those found in the New World are generally associated with some of the most important ecclesiastic structures, suggesting that they were valued greatly at the time.

Mexican Tiles

In the mid–sixteenth century, Mexico City, the viceregal capital of New Spain, was the center from which cultural and artistic standards radiated outward. No longer able to keep up with the demand for supplies in the New World, Sevilla ceased to be the unique source for fine manufactured goods and materials. Spanish potters living in New Spain established a ceramic industry of their own in the capital to meet the demands of the new colonizers. There, ceramic production retained its momentum through the sixteenth century, until a series of disasters, including flooding, epidemics, and famine, devastated the capital in the early–seventeenth century. Workshops in Mexico City continued producing ceramic ware for a local market throughout the colonial period (see chapter 10).

By the seventeenth century, however, the nearby city of Puebla had become the more important center for manufacturing mayólica in the New World. Founded in 1531, Puebla was the second city of New Spain and conceived by the first audiencias as a model for Spanish life. For ceramists, Puebla was an ideal location: the climate was mild, the soil fertile, and most importantly, there were extensive beds of suitable clay and sufficient deposits of the raw sodium essential for glaze preparation. The fact that the nearby city of Cholula had captured the market for quality ceramics before the Spanish arrived is surely not a coincidence. Native potters must also have played an important role in supporting the developing colonial industry.

According to the potter's ordinances published in 1653, only ceramists of pure Spanish heritage were permitted to rise to the title of master potter. Nevertheless, a number of mulatto and mestizo potters are mentioned in the documents; some of them, such as Francisco Martín, who worked from 1666 on the street of "Troje de la Santa Iglesia Catedral," did in fact become master potters.[12] Culturally speaking, however, the trade was designated as a European tradition from the start, which explains why the ware eventually became known as *talavera*, after the city of Talavera de la Reina, in central Spain, famed for its ceramic ware since the early sixteenth century.[13] Despite oral tradition suggesting that the production of mayólica in Mexico had been introduced exclusively by Dominican friars from the city of Talavera de la Reina, sent to decorate colonial monasteries with tiles, the notary archives of Puebla identify potters from a number of cities in Spain, Italy, and Portugal.

Little work has been done to identify the individual potters mentioned in colonial documents. Some names provide clues to their native land (or at least that of their family). Most seem to have been trained in Puebla, and a few learned the trade in Europe prior to their arrival. The master potter Francisco de Pezaro, who worked in Puebla at the turn of the seventeenth century, is one whose name can be traced back to Europe.[14] A relative of his, Tomaso da Pesaro, had come to Sevilla from Genoa, although his family had originated in Pesaro, Italy, as the name implies, and traveled to Venice before moving to Genoa. In Sevilla, the Pesaro family was known for work imitating the styles of both Venice and Talavera de la Reina.[15] Another master potter, Juan Pizón, was also from an Italian family of potters, although he had come to Puebla in the mid–seventeenth century directly from his home in Savona.[16]

One of the earliest documents regarding the production of mayólica in Puebla specifies a commission of tiles for the cathedral in Mexico City. Having moved from Mexico City to Puebla in 1580, to establish a workshop on Los Herreros Street dedicated to the production of tiles, the Spanish ceramist Gaspar de Encinas was chosen by Canon Francisco de la Paz to produce twelve hundred large tiles and six hundred narrow border tiles for the main altar and three hundred for one of the chapels, for which he was paid 186 *pos*.[17] The original structure, dated 1525, was still in use during the construction of a replacement begun in 1585. Additional adjustments were made to the church from 1601 and 1602. Excavations south of the cathedral in the early 1980s revealed parts of the original structure decorated with pisano–style tiles. Corresponding tiles were also recovered from the fill beneath the structure.[18] Could these be the tiles commissioned from Encinas? Or are they a product of the numerous tile shipments from Spain? Rosa de la Peña attributes these tiles to Encinas, whose commission corresponds to the modifications made to the interior between 1601 and 1602, when the choir stalls were removed.[19] Stylistically, the tiles are straight out of a Sevillian tradition, and must have been realized by a potter or potters trained in Sevilla. In fact, one particular set of polychrome tiles discovered appears patently similar to those attributed to the circle of Alonso García, who was making tiles in Triana in the early–seventeenth century.[20]

According to a manuscript written by Fray Hernando de Ojea, the second church of Santo Domingo in Mexico City had walls richly covered in tiles.[21] This construction dates to sometime between 1560 (when Cervantes de Salazar, official historian of New Spain, mentions the second construction) and 1607 (by which time the major structure had sunk nine feet below street level and had to be rebuilt).[22] Without having the original tiles to examine, we may never know if they were imported from Spain or were produced locally. According to a document discovered by Efraín Castro, however, master potter Diego Rodríguez of Puebla, who was in Mexico City until 1582, had been contracted in 1573 by Fray Hernando de Morales to make fifteen hundred tiles for the Monastery of Santo Domingo in Mexico City, which suggests that these tiles were of local manufacture.[23]

Enrique Cervantes, who wrote the first and only comprehensive monograph on Puebla pottery, in 1939, conjectures that the Puebla industry was initiated by some of the first settlers of the city and that production began sometime between 1550 and 1570.[24] Upon examining the documents published by Cervantes, Castro reports that the only potters recorded in Puebla prior to 1573 are Alejandro de Ojeda and Bartólome de Reina. Together, they established a partnership "to make earthenware of all varieties, including tiles."[25] Only a few of the contemporary documents that have been studied refer specifically to the production of tiles, which would imply that they were made side by side with vessel forms.

Cervantes lists a number of other potters working in Puebla between 1593 and 1599, although clearly it was not until the seventeenth century that Puebla would earn its reputation. In 1630, Father Cobo, who made a trip to New Spain from Lima between 1629 and 1642, wrote:

> Pottery so choice and so well glazed is made that that of Talavera [Spain] is not needed. In the past few years, they have begun to make imitations of [the pottery] of China, which looks very much like it, particularly that made at Puebla de los Angeles in New Spain and in this city of Lima. It is very good, prettily glazed and colored. Also produced are the most unusual tiles, which in the past were customarily brought from Spain, although those from around here do not appear to be of such fine colors.[26]

At the time Cobo put these thoughts to paper, he was residing in Mexico City, conducting research in archives and libraries. His criticism of "those [tiles] from around here" probably refers to the quality of the tiles produced at the capital not at Puebla. A certain amount of production, proficiency, and growth, nonetheless, must have preceded Cobo's remarks.

By mid–century, potters living in Puebla organized themselves and petitioned the viceroy to establish standards that would "determine the conditions, grievances, obligations and circumstances required for the benefit of the craft."[27] The potters' guild was officially founded in 1653, and its ordinances continued to be amended through the colonial period (1521–1820). It was modeled after Spanish guilds and used city ordinances to govern almost every aspect of the industry. Three different grades of ceramic ware were specified: cooking vessels (*loza amarilla*), common ware (*loza común*), and fine ware (*loza fina*).[28] A "refined" ware was added to the types, in an amendment published in 1682; in the same amendment, specifications for decoration were also outlined according to type.

The polychrome tiles with a balloon–like floral motif surrounding individual animals reflect the decoration reserved in the ordinances for fine ware, "in imitation of the [Spanish] Talavera with figures, foliage, and all five colors employed there" (fig. 9.3).[29] Archaeologists know this distinctive style as Abo Polychrome, after the mission in New Mexico, although based on the style and color, it appears to derive from the series known as *punteada*, which is based on a plant motif with

9.3 Tile / *Azulejo*
Puebla, 17th century
Abo Polychrome
Gift of Mr. and Mrs. John Holstius,
Houghton Sawyer Collection
Museum of International Folk Art,
(Museum of New Mexico), Santa Fe
Photo by Paul Smutko

9.4 Tiles / *Azulejos*
Puebla, 17th century
Puebla Polychrome
Museo Franz Mayer, Mexico City
Photo by Michel Zabé

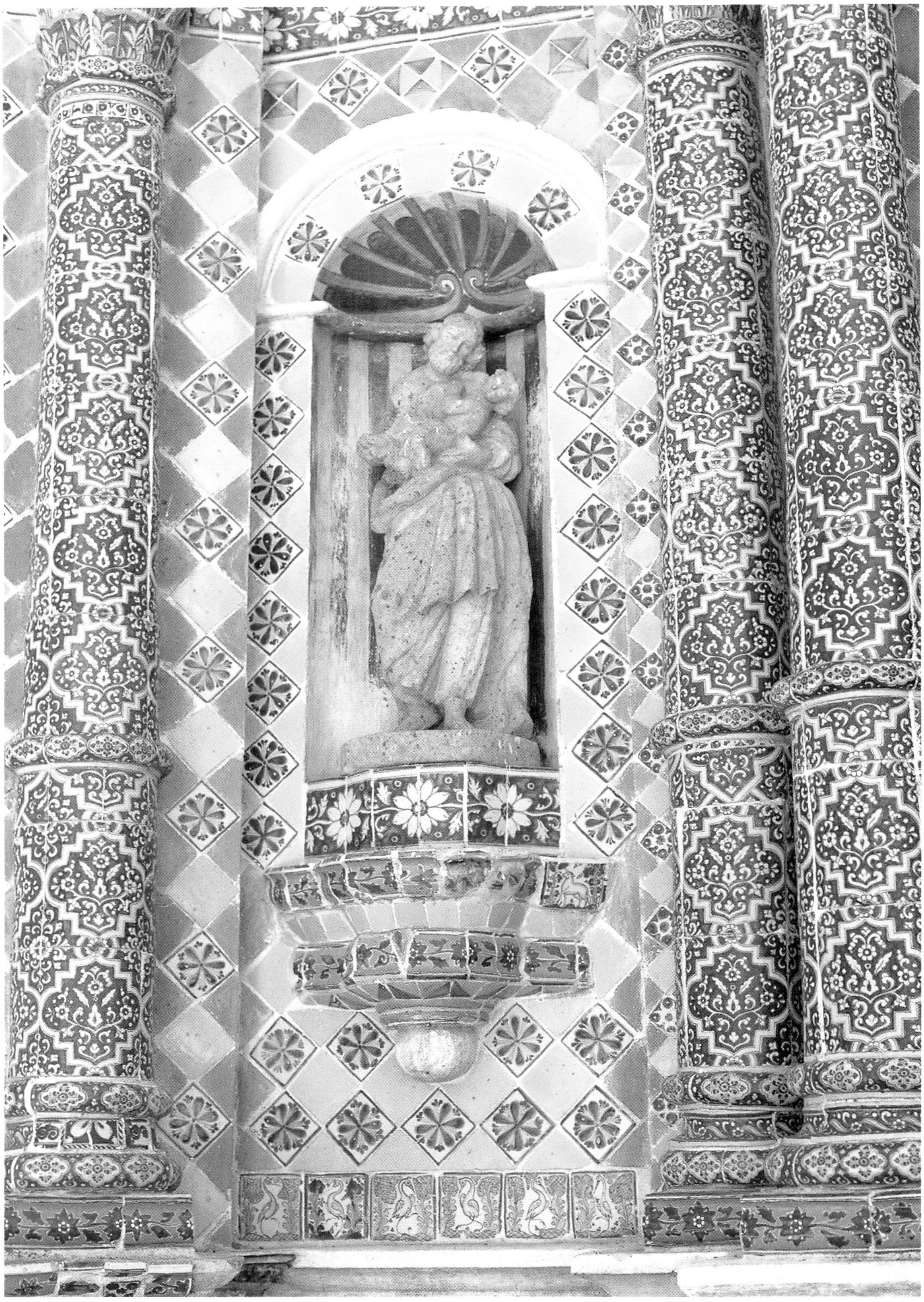

9.5 Façade of the Church of San Francisco
Acatepec (Puebla), 18th century
Photo by Barbara Mauldin

small leaves and dots in bright blue, yellow, and orange (see fig 1.6). But this was not the only style from Talavera de la Reina to have influenced Puebla potters. The pattern often referred to as Puebla Polychrome, characterized by its use of fine black lines and delicate textile decoration, derives from another Talavera type known as *encaje de bolillos* (bobbin lace). This motif must have been inspired by the cotton and metallic bobbin lace made in Talavera de la Reina during the seventeenth century, although it is also found on a series of seventeenth-century Portuguese tiles. Only a few examples of this motif remain intact, and even fewer are known in tile (fig. 9.4). In general, Puebla Polychrome tiles were used as borders or as framing devices for individual images.

From Islamic Spain, Puebla potters adapted the practice of decorating entire surfaces, often by using repeated dots to fill the space. The technique recalls the *horror vacui* (fear of empty space), referring to the Islamic penchant not to leave any areas undecorated so common in Spanish lusterware. One decorative treatment listed in the 1682 amendment to the potters' ordinances called for the use of such a dotting technique, or *aborronado,* which was more frequently used on vessel forms.[30]

While a variety of techniques and decorative motifs traveled across the Atlantic from Europe, another conduit of influences opened from the Pacific. With the settlement of the Philippines as a Spanish colony, in 1559, the Spanish Empire established a trade route that connected its territories across three continents. From 1565 to 1815, the ships known as the Manila galleons, or *naos de la China*, transported luxury goods, including highly prized Chinese porcelain, to the Mexican port of Acapulco for further shipment to other colonies and to Europe. Ming dynasty porcelain inspired a variety of patterns featured on individual figurative tiles, border tiles, and column tiles, such as those embellishing the church of San Francisco of Acatepec in Puebla (fig. 9.5). Certainly, the use of blue-and-white decoration so common on Puebla tiles reflects the love for Chinese porcelain, particularly the type known as *kraak*; although the Chinese style had come by way of Europe as well. Chinese-style lobed panels, pagodas, figures with queues (pony tails), animals, and flower and plant motifs all appear on Puebla tiles, but within a distinctive Puebla aesthetic (see Introduction).

It seems that few potters restricted themselves to the specifications of the ordinances. For example, despite the required use during firing of saggars (ceramic boxes used to separate individual pieces), potters preferred cockspurs (ceramic tripods used to stack pieces on top of one another). As a result, many of the tiles have three evenly spaced stilt pulls (or blemishes). The ordinances also stipulated the use of potter's marks for all fine-grade pieces, yet only a few bear such marks.

As in Spain, Puebla tiles were generally not signed or marked until the early twentieth century, when artists began to sign their names or used their initials to designate their work. Two types are among the very

(a)

(b)

(c)

9.6a, b, c Tiles / *Azulejos*
Puebla, 17th century
The Hispanic Society of America,
New York

few tiles that are marked: Abo Polychrome (fig. 9.3), and the series of blue-and-white trade tiles known in Spain as *artes y oficios*, influenced by a Dutch tradition (fig. 9.6a, b, c). Only three marks have been recognized on these tiles: "F," "X," and a figure of a bumblebee. The mark "F" is the most common of the three, and has been attributed to Miguel Fernández Palomino, who was master potter and inspector of the guild in 1685 (fig. 9.6c).[31] The curious bumblebee is believed to be associated with a decorator's name, although no such name has been documented to date (fig.9.6b).[32] Nonetheless, the bumblebee and the "X" mark may have been inventions of the artists or the workshop's adaptation as signatures of sorts, which makes one question whether other such marks also exist.

As we have seen, the production of tiles in New Spain consisted mostly of the flat-surfaced type. During the last quarter of the seventeenth century, however, a limited number of tiles were made in relief. Unlike the cuenca tiles of southern Spain, these tiles were not stamped but were made in a mold, causing the relief to project outward. Such tiles can be found in situ at the Rosary Chapel of the Church of Santo Domingo in Puebla, the construction of which began in 1632; it was finally consecrated in 1690.

Covering all three of the altars in the Rosary Chapel are white tiles in relief, which were originally finished in luster (referred to in the documents as *dorado*, or gilded), but they have since deteriorated significantly (fig.9.7). Gorospe's *Octava maravilla del Nuevo Mundo en la Gran Capilla del Rosario*, from 1690, highlights the superb quality of these lustered tiles: "The apse or the wall at the back of the crossing has an altar one *vara y media* [835mm] in height and a frontal of tiles (like that of the two on the sides) of such extraordinary craftsmanship and cost as they are so finely made and gilded without forgoing the luster for the sake of cost."[33] Both the texture and the repeated motifs on the panels evoke images of fine, embroidered cloths draping the altars. These tiles are similar to a rare type made in Sevilla, a series of which was used to decorate the walls of the National Palace in Sintra, Portugal. However, a number of documents contemporary with the construction of the chapel suggest that the tiles were made by a local potter producing "gilded" pottery at the time.[34] Lusterware had begun to pass out of fashion when Spaniards were first making their voyages to the New World; it continued to be made in Spain, supplying a domestic market instead of the international market it had benefited from in the past. This may be the main reason why the technique never took hold in the Spanish–American colonies.

9.7 Relief Tiles / *Azulejos en relieve*
Rosary Chapel, Church of Santo Domingo, Puebla, 1632–1690
Photo by Carlos Varillas, 2002

Notable among the few known tiles made in relief are those with polychrome cherub heads alternating with flat–surfaced tiles of the Dominican coat of arms, used to border the flat–surfaced polychrome tiles on the lower walls of the Rosary Chapel (fig. 9.8). In both Sevilla and Talavera de la Reina, tiles with cherub heads were often used to border elaborate panels, but none are known to have been made in relief. Nothing is known of the manufacture of these tiles, which seem to be unique to the chapel. Smaller versions of these heads appear again in a series of white tiles dressing the altar there, strongly suggesting that all the tiles in the chapel were produced by the same workshop.

9.8 Tiles / *Azulejos*
Rosary Chapel, Church of Santo Domingo, Puebla, 1632–1690
According to popular belief, the 365 heads, which wrap around the entire chapel, represent the rosary beads of the Virgin.
Photo by Robin Farwell Gavin

Together with the elaborate stuccowork and the remarkable painted panels, the church was celebrated locally as the "eighth marvel of the New World."

Clearly, the first tiles in Mexico, whether imported from Spain or of local manufacture, were destined for liturgical use. They embellished chapels, crypts, altars, and baptismal fonts. Together, series of individual tiles formed elaborate designs and representational images. Some panels were purely decorative, while others were also didactic.

The practical use of tiles as a washable surface also made them ideal for any kitchen. Certainly the most famous of the earliest existing tiled kitchens in Puebla is found in the former Convent of Santa Rosa, where unlike any other interior, the entire surface is covered in tile, including the ceiling (fig. 9.9). The exact date of this kitchen is unknown. Local tradition suggests that the original work was installed at the end of the seventeenth century, as a gesture of appreciation from Bishop Santa Cruz to the nuns, for creating the recipe for the thick chile and chocolate sauce popularly known as *mole poblano*. Numerous types of tiles are represented in the kitchen, dating from the seventeenth through the nineteenth centuries. Both the overall quality of the tiles and the manner in which they were mismatched throughout the kitchen, however, suggest that what we see is the art of recycling tiles that had previously been used in another area of the convent or in other buildings altogether.

By the eighteenth century, an important shift took place that brought decorative tilework to the exterior of both religious and secular structures. Exterior tiles were combined with unglazed terracotta or brick to create a variety of brilliant patterns with contrasting textures and reflections of light and color. This architectural treatment is not entirely unique to Puebla; it is found on Spanish structures dating back to the fourteenth century. Yet in Puebla, architects dressed these buildings in ways never seen before. Like the alicatado mosaics of Spain, tiles were used lavishly in a variety of geometric forms.

The concept of the tile mosaic was particularly important in the ornamentation of church domes (fig.9.10), the colors of which can be seen from great distances. Almost every church dome in Puebla is adorned with patterns of single monochrome tiles alternating in two or more colors. To complement the domes, adjacent towers are equally bejeweled in mayólica, with contrasting forms of carved stone.

Also at this time, ceramic workshops had begun to produce numerous large and small tile panels, known as *tableros* in Mexico, with figurative images. As in Spain, tableros had both decorative and didactic purposes. For religious institutions, they became particularly important for the display of clearly articulated and colorful images of saints. In the interior of churches, small tableros were commonly placed on altars and in areas where they would be most visible. Large examples, on the other hand, were destined to embellish facades, where they could be seen glistening

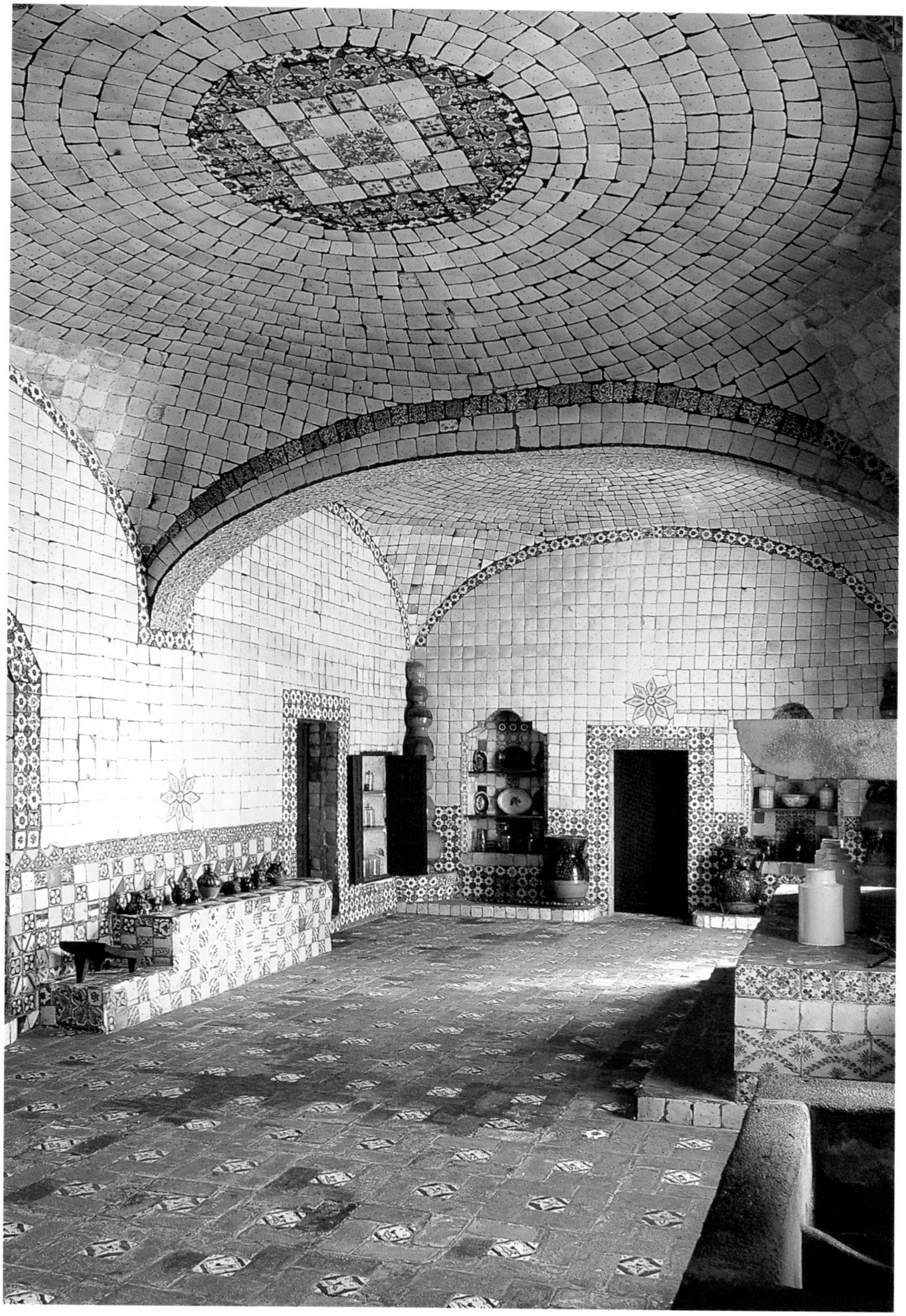

9.9 Kitchen of the Convento de Santa Rosa
Puebla, founded 1708
Photo by Carlos Varillas, 2002

in the sun from afar. Certainly, it is worth noting possible prototypes for their use on church facades. Perhaps the most notable is that of the Church of El Señor San Jorge (1647) of the Hospital of the Holy Charity in Sevilla (fig. 9.11).[35] In Puebla, however, tableros were combined with brick or unglazed terracotta, often alternating with simply decorated tiles, to create a distinct visual effect. This type of architectural ornamentation was most frequently designed for parish churches. In general, Puebla tiles were numbered on the unglazed reverse side, so that the pieces could be easily arranged, like a puzzle. In addition, the tiles were designed with deeply beveled edges, which allowed them to be mounted more closely together and secured by the plaster–fill binding. A striking tablero of the Virgin of the Immaculate Conception (fig.9.12) exemplifies the type found on a number of small church facades, including the parish church of San Marcos, dated 1797 (fig.9.13), which was the seat of the potters' guild during the eighteenth century.

Just ten kilometers outside of the city of Puebla is the church of San Francisco in Acatepec. Built at the end of the eighteenth century, the facade is unique among ultra Baroque colonial architecture (fig.9.14; see also fig. 9.5). It mimics the interior altar in all its splendor, with undulating and spiral columns pierced with brilliant colors. The variety of styles and textures work together to create an extraordinary work of art, while the rich colors give the appearance of precious gems sprinkled throughout. This effect is achieved by the uninhibited use of numerous patterns and styles; in fact, the effect is such that the sculptured figures and capitals are almost immediately lost to the exuberance of color, design, and reflections of the light against the glazed tilework.

The distinctive style of Puebla architecture was not limited to reli-

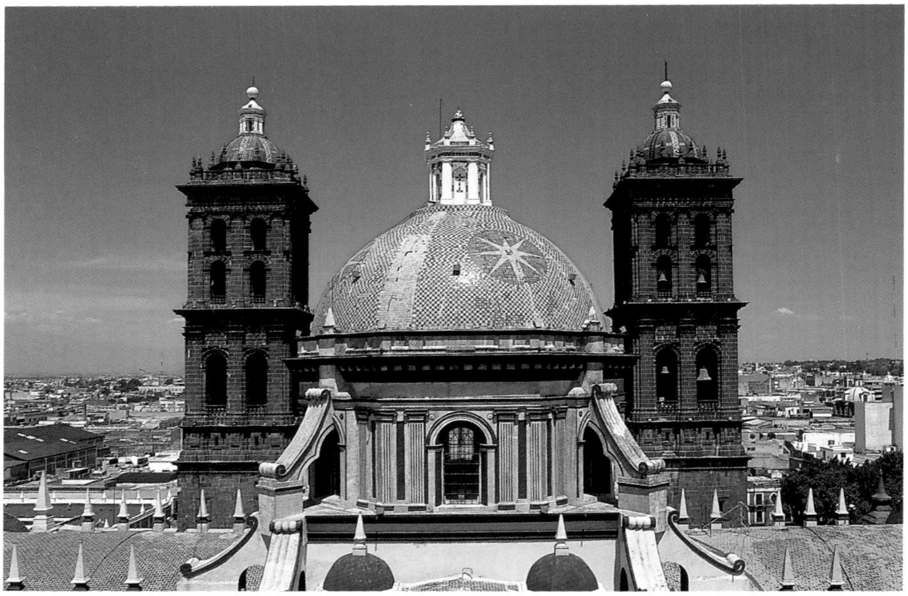

9.10 Dome / *Cúpula*
Cathedral, Puebla, 1575–1649
Designed by Pedro García Ferrar
Photo by Carlos Varillas, 2002

9.11 Hospital de la Santa Caridad
Sevilla, 17th century
Photo by Robin Farwell Gavin, 2002

gious structures. Throughout the historic section of the city, secular buildings equally dazzle the eyes of spectators. Unique among these is the House of the Figures, or *Casa de los Muñecos* (fig.9.15). Unlike most tableros, which are almost always rectangular, these panels take the form of the sixteen individual figures positioned between the windows on the second and third floors (giving the house its name). The house was built in 1792 by Agustín de Ovando y Villavicencio, town-council member from 1769 to 1773, and mayor in the years 1773 and 1791 to 1792. The figures alone recall eighteenth-century Portuguese "welcoming figures" made in tile. However, the Portuguese tiles depict men in contemporary clothing and were installed in interior spaces, primarily at entrance halls. Legend holds that against the orders of the city council, the owner not only intentionally built the house higher than the nearby town hall, but also satirized the council members by representing each of them as grotesques in tile on the facade of the house. Erwin Walter Palm offers an alternative interpretation, suggesting that the figures correspond to the mythological laborers of Hercules.[36] Until more research is conducted on Ovando's intentions, this fantastic and unique structure remains a mystery to us.

During the golden age of the ceramic industry (1650–1750), Puebla earned a reputation as the most important center for

9.12 *The Virgin of the Immaculate Conception*
Puebla, ca. 1780
The Hispanic Society of America, New York

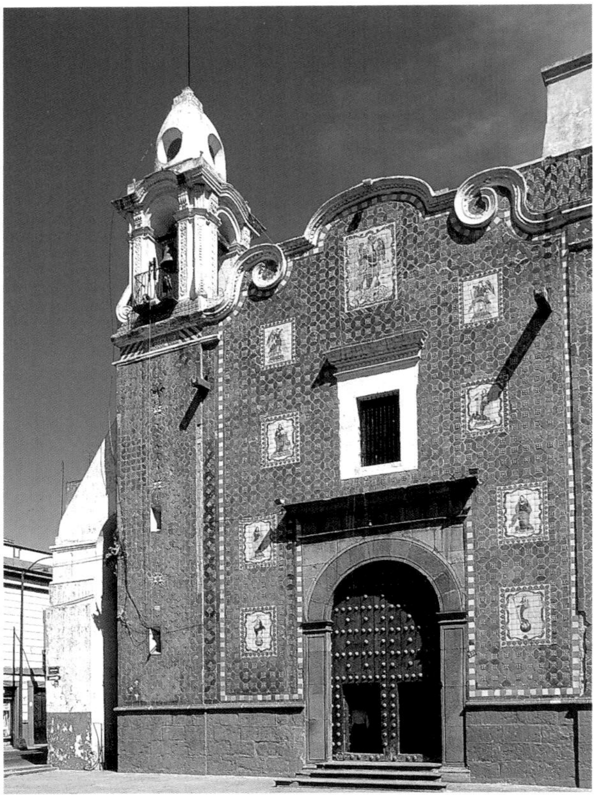

9.13 Iglesia de San Marcos
Puebla, 1797
Photo by Carlos Varillas, 2002

earthenware production in the New World. Famed for its products, the city enjoyed the widest distribution of any center of colonial ceramic ware, exporting throughout Mexico and the colonies in the Americas. By the end of the eighteenth century, however, a number other centers had sprung up to compete with it. For example, production at the capital continued into the eighteenth century, and Guanajuato also began to produce quality ware. As a result, it is often impossible to determine whether tiles were made in Mexico City, Guanajuato, or Puebla.

The nineteenth century witnessed a series of political and economic events that changed the direction of the ceramic industry in Puebla. A new constitution for the Spanish Empire, promulgated by an antimonarchical assembly at Cádiz, in 1812, eradicated the potters' guild and revoked its ordinances. Mexican ceramists were now free to create new styles of their own. Yet the opening of trade with France, England, Germany, and the United States meant that the fashionable tiles used in other parts of the world were also available to wealthy Mexicans.

By the end of the nineteenth century, the ceramic industry in Puebla was near collapse, when the fortuitous arrival of the artist Enrique Luis Ventosa of Barcelona, in 1897, is believed to have changed its direction. To help restore the industry, Ventosa gathered

9.14 Iglesia de San Francisco
Acatepec (Puebla), 18th century
Photo by Carlos Varillas, 2002

colonial works as well as information on their production and allied with Puebla ceramists and workshops to produce a variety of vessel forms and tiles (see chapter 12).

The Mexican Revolution of 1910 was particularly devastating to the ceramics industry in Puebla; many workshops were forced to close, and a number of the tiled buildings suffered considerable damage. Nonetheless, the industry eventually recovered, and production and popularity of this prized ceramic tradition began to thrive again into the twentieth century. Cervantes reports that from 1918 to 1928, the tile industry witnessed a substantial increase in demand and production for both local and foreign consumption.[37] In central Mexico, tiles were needed for the reconstruction of many buildings destroyed in the Revolution. It was also at this time that the United States began to experience a vogue for things "Mexican," which would eventually bring the tiles and colors of Puebla into the homes of millions of Americans.

Today, the distinct Puebla style can be found throughout Mexico, the United States, and Europe. Much more research is required before the final word is said about the production and use of tiles in Puebla. Certainly more information about the architects of the city's unique tiled structures and their relationship with the potters and workshops would shed light on the history and development of this most fascinating tradition. But clearly, Puebla ceramists and architects seized an opportunity to capture the Islamic love for color and design from the very beginning and carried it in new and exciting directions.

9.15 Casa de los Muñecos
Puebla, 1792
Photo by Carlos Varillas, 2002

Notes

1. Mayólica is defined here as tin-glazed earthenware. It is also known as majolica and faience. In Mexico it is popularly known as *talavera.*
2. Enrique Otte, "La fiota de Diego Colón, Españoles y genoreses en el comercio transatlántico de 1509," In *Revista de Indias*, vol. 97–98, año 24 (1964): 483, 486.
3. Diego Angulo Iñiguez, *El gótico y el renacimiento en las Antillas*, Escuela de Estudios Hispano-Americanos de Sevilla 36, no. 16 (1947):44–49 and figs. 62–72; see also John M. Goggin, *Majolica in the New World: Types of the Sixteenth to Eighteenth Century*, Yale University Publications in Anthropology, no. 72 (New Haven: Yale University Press, 1968), pp. 144–48.
4. Archivo de Protocolos Notariales de Sevilla, of. XXI, libro 2 de 1604, fol. 390–93; in Antonio Sancho Corbacho, "Los azulejos de sevillanos en Lima," *Arte en América y Filipinas*, 3(2) (1949):98–99.
5. Emilio Harth-Terré, "El azulejo criollo en la arquitectura limeña," *Revista del Archivo Nacional del Perú* 22(2) (1958):34; see also Alice Wilson Frothingham, *Tile Panels of Spain, 1500–1650*, Hispanic Notes & Monographs (New York: The Hispanic Society of America, 1969), p. 41.
6. Bernabé Cobo, *Historia de la fundación de Lima* (Lima: Imprenta Liberal, 1882), p. 261.
7. Illustrated in Enrique A. Cervantes, *Loza blanca y azulejos de Puebla*, 2 vols. (México: Privately printed, 1939) 1:163.
8. Like most convents and monasteries in Mexico at the time, the Monastery of San Francisco in Puebla was closed in 1861. It was transformed into a military hospital in 1867, at which time many of the interior rooms were reconstructed. Despite changes made to the original structure, enough evidence exists to support the presence of these pisano-style tiles in the original design of the interior structure. A few of these Spanish tiles were placed on the floor of the "bathtub" in the military quarters. In addition, the tiles are scattered in other locations of the former monastery, part of which is now a park; fragments are also among the archaeological material excavated there. I am grateful to Carlos Cedillo and Arnulfo Allende Carrera of the Instituto Nacional de Antropología e Historia, whose ongoing work on this impressive site continues to reveal important information.
9. Antonio Sancho Corbacho, "Los azulejos de Madre de Dios de Sevilla," *Archivo Español de arte* 22(87) (1949):235.
10. See Francisco Fernández del Castillo, *Apuntes para la historia de San Ángel (San Jacinto Tenanitla) y sus alrededores: Tradiciones, historia, leyendas* (México: Museo Nacional de Aqueología, Historia y Etnología, 1913), figs. 14–16; and Carlos Mijares Bracho, *San Ángel* (Editorial Clío, Libros y Videos, 1997), pp. 56–57.
11. Florence C. Lister and Robert H. Lister, *Andalusian Ceramics in Spain and New Spain: A Cultural Register from the Third Century b.c. to 1700* (Tucson: University of Arizona Press, 1987), p. 338, n. 59.
12. Cervantes, *Loza blanca* 2:218.
13. For a brief overview of the evolution of the term *talavera*, see Margaret Connors McQuade, *Talavera Poblana: Four Centuries of a Mexican Ceramic Tradition* (New York: Americas Society, 1999), pp. 14–16.
14. Cervantes, *Loza blanca* 2:223; Frothingham, *Tile Panels of Spain*, p. 35.
15. Frothingham, *Tile Panels of Spain*, p. 38.
16. Cervantes, *Loza blanca* 2: 223–24.
17. Ibid., p. 197, pp. 15–18.
18. Lister and Lister, *Andalusian Ceramics*, p. 231; Florence C. Lister and Robert H. Lister, *Sixteenth Century Maiolica Pottery in the Valley of Mexico*, Anthropological Papers of the University of Arizona, no. 39 (Tucson: University of Arizona Press, 1982), figs. 3–7.

19. Rosa Guadalupe. de la Peña V., "Azulejos encontrados en *situ*: Primer catedral de México," in *Ensayos de alfarería prehispánica e história de Mesoamérica: Homenaje a Eduardo Noguera Auza*, ed. by Mari Carmen Serra Puche and Carlos Navarrete Cáceres, Serie Antropológica 82 (México: Universidad Nacional Autónoma de México, 1988), pp. 437–38.
20. See Alfonso Pleguezuelo Hernández, *Azulejos sevillanos* (Sevilla: Padrilla Libros, 1989), fig. 223.
21. Hernando de Ojea, *Libro tercero de la historia religioso de la provincia de México de la orden de Sto. Domingo* (México: Museo Nacional de México, 1897), pp. 10–11.
22. Francisco Cervantes de Salazar, *Crónica de la Nueva España* (México, 1554), p. 318; George Kubler, *Mexican Architecture of the Sixteenth Century*, 2 vols. (New Haven: Yale University Press, 1948), 2:528–29.
23. Efraín Castro, "Five Centuries of Talavera," *Artes de México* 3 (spring 1989):104.
24. Cervantes, *Loza blanca* 1:18.
25. Castro, "Five Centuries," p. 104.
26. Bernabé Cobo, *Historia del Nuevo Mundo*, 4 vols. (Sevilla: Imprenta de E. Rasco, 1890), 1:243; translated in Frothingham, *Tile Panels of Spain*, p. 78.
27. Cervantes, *Loza blanca* 1: 20; translated in Castro, "Five Centuries," p. 105.
28. Cervantes, *Loza blanca* 1:23.
29. Ibid., pp. 28–29.
30. Ibid., p. 28. Editor's note: the definition of the seventeenth-century term "aborronado" varies among scholars. See Chapter 10, this volume, and Florence C. And Robert H. Lister, *A Descriptive Dictionary for 500 Years of Spanish-Tradition Ceramics* [thirteenth through the eighteenth centuries], Special Publication Series, no. 1, Society for Historical Archaeology (1976), p. 10.
31. Attribution made by Leonora Cortina in reference to the mark found on works in the Museo Franz Mayer collection, Mexico City. See Cervantes, *Loza blanca* 2:209.
32. Edwin Atlee Barber, *Mexican Maiolica in the Collection of The Hispanic Society of America* (New York: Hispanic Society of America, 1915), p. 47.
33. Fray Juan de Gorospe, *Octava maravilla del Nuevo Mundo en la Gran Capilla del Rosario* (Puebla, 1690), p. 39.
34. Castro, "Five Centuries," p. 106. In addition to the documents discovered by Castro, we learn from the archives published by Cervantes that Miguel de la Rosa was also an official *dorador* of fine ceramics in 1687; Cervantes, *Loza blanca* 2:227.
35. See Enrique Valdivieso, *A Guide for a cultural visit to the Church of El Señor San Jorge and the courtyards of La Santa Caridad Hospital in the city of Seville* (Hermandad de la Santa Caridad, 1998).
36. Erwin Walter Palm, "La fachada de la Casa de los Muñecos en Puebla: Un trabajo de Hércules en el Nuevo Mundo," *Actes du XLII Congrès International des Américanistes* 10 (1976):113–38.
37. Cervantes, *Loza blanca* 1: 290–91.

Detail, Fig. 10.4

10

The Forgotten Potters of Mexico City

ANA PAULINA GÁMEZ MARTÍNEZ

MAYÓLICA, OR *LOZA BLANCA,* as it was designated in the guild ordinances, was produced in great quantities and in all its various types in Mexico City throughout the colonial period. Then why is it that the capital of the Viceroyalty is not remembered as an important manufacturing center of this pottery? There are many reasons.

Perhaps the most important is that, at the end of the nineteenth century the ceramics industry in the few remaining factories in Puebla was being revived and invigorated by the Spaniard Enrique Ventosa, while Mexico City was converted into a manufacturer of industrial pottery. This has led to the erroneous idea that Puebla was the only producer of mayólica. Adding to the confusion are the type names assigned by North American archaeologists to mayólica, such as "Abo Polychrome" or "Puebla Blue on White," which did not designate the place of production but rather the name of the first site where these types were found, followed by a formal description.[1] Furthermore, documentation concerning the artisans is widely dispersed and difficult to track down. In addition, the subsoil of Mexico City rarely permits stratification studies or the examination of deposits that would help to define local production. It is only in recent years, owing to the constant reutilization of the land, that the discovery of kilns has been possible. Finally, the great quantity of bibliographic data dedicated principally to the study of Puebla ceramics, as opposed to the meager publication of works devoted to Mexico City production, has added to this misconception.

An Age-old Discussion

In 1939, the book *Loza blanca y azulejo de Puebla*, by Enrique A. Cervantes, appeared. The intent of the work was to make a systematic study of the production of tin-glazed earthenware in Puebla. However, it is worth pointing out the warning he gives in the introduction:

> The manufacture of earthenware and tiles of similar forms, with some variations, some radically different, that were produced in other places in New Spain will not be mentioned. For me suffice it to say that in Mexico City pottery fabrication was comparable and abundant, and . . . on a smaller scale, also in the population centers of Guanajuato, Guadalajara, Oaxaca, Aguascalientes, Atlixco, Pátzcuaro, and other well-known places[2]

From that moment on, the majority of researchers dedicated to this form of ceramics (archaeologists and art historians) attributed, almost automatically, the origin of any piece of mayólica to Puebla workshops, especially if they were referring to *loza fina,* in view of the fact that Cervantes had certified practically all of its styles as originating in the pottery studios of Puebla.

The controversy concerning the exclusivity of Puebla production dates back to 1922, when in the annals of the scientific association "Antonio Alzate," an article appeared written by professor Carlos Hoffman, entitled *Verdades y errores acerca de la talavera poblana.* As his final point, the author refutes the opinion of Edwin Atlee Barber, director of the Pennsylvania Museum and School of Industrial Arts, "that Puebla could have been the only locality during almost 300 years, not only in New Spain, but also in all of the American continent, in which mayólica would have been manufactured."[3] And he continues,

> Years ago I was already convinced that Barber's opinion was flawed in view of the great quantity of tiles, apart from those imported from Spain, that had been frequently found in convents and churches specifically in the Federal District [Mexico City], as in the case of the Convent of Carmen de San Ángel, in Churubusco and other places, and that they were in composition and configuration very different from the character of the Puebla tiles.[4]

As additional proof, he presents a written examination taken by master potter Joseph de Ortíz and prepared by the inspectors (*veedores*) of the potters' guild of Mexico City. He also mentions a kiln found in Tizapán, with "many remnants of tiles in its vicinity." Finally, he acknowledges the products from Oaxaca, Guanajuato, Sayula, and the Academia de San Carlos, in Mexico City.[5]

The year following the appearance of the essay by Professor Hoffman, a book by Manuel Romero de Terreros, *Las artes industriales de la Nueva España,* dedicated a chapter to ceramics.[6] The first paragraphs merely touch upon Prehispanic ceramics and the colonial production in Cuautitlán and Guadalajara, with the remaining text focusing on the mayólica of Puebla, without mentioning, even fleetingly, other ceramic centers.

It is surprising that Romero de Terreros, with his extraordinary erudition, did not at least mention the regulations for the potters of Mexico City that had been published two years earlier, in the "Compendio de ordenanzas de la muy noble, insigne y leal ciudad de México" by Francisco del Barrio Lorenzot and issued by the *Secretaría de Gobernación*, or even refer to the publication produced by Genaro Estrada in the year that followed.

Subsequent to the work of Cervantes is the book by Manuel Toussaint, *Arte Colonial en México*, published in 1948. Five chapters of twenty-five discuss the diverse aspects of the "minor arts;" ceramic topics are included in only three of these.

Although Toussaint draws on some of the ideas of Barber, Cervantes, and Hoffman, he also contributes new data that attest to the manufacture of mayólica in Mexico City. In chapter eight, he points out the existence of pottery products, the release of ordinances for the potters of Mexico City in 1677, and the names of some master potters from the eighteenth century, and he asserts that, "although few, these notices prove that a ceramic industry flourished also in the Capital of the Viceroyalty."[7]

In chapter thirteen, he speaks in detail about the ordinances of Mexico City as well as Puebla and describes very succinctly the evolution of this art during the seventeenth century. Finally, in chapter nineteen he addresses the ornamental tile produced in both Puebla and Mexico City during the eighteenth century and the architectural works of the two cities. Among those that especially stand out are the tiles in the house of the marquesa de Uluapan, attributed to the workshops of Mexico City. He concludes with a list of more than fifty master potters from the capital.

One year after the appearance of Toussaint's work, an American archaeologist, John Goggin, initiated his excavations in Fig Springs, Florida. Through his efforts there, he obtained, among other things, a great variety of mayólica shards of types unknown in former excavations of Spanish sites in the region. To classify their origin and effectively date them, Goggin undertook a lengthy study that would engage him until his death, fourteen years later.

During those years, Goggin studied both private and public collections in the United States (Hispanic Society of America, Metropolitan Museum of Art, Pennsylvania Museum, and the Art Institute of Chicago), the Caribbean, Venezuela, and Mexico (Museo Nacional de Historia, Museo Bello, and the collections of Carmen Vivanco, Franz Mayer, and Francisco Pérez de Salazar), and he would participate in excavations in various states of the United States (Florida, Georgia, Alabama, and New Mexico), the Caribbean (Cuba, Jamaica, Haiti, the Dominican Republic, Puerto Rico, Saint Croix, and Trinidad), Venezuela, Colombia, and Mexico (Mérida, Puebla, Huejotzingo, and Mexico City.)

The result of Goggin's investigations was a book, published posthumously in 1968, entitled *Spanish Majolica in the New World: Types of the Sixteenth to Eighteenth Centuries*.[8]

It instantly became a classic and indispensable work of consultation. It lists the different groups of mayólica encountered, describes them, and proposes ranges for dates as well as possible manufacturing sites. For some of the types traditionally attributed to Puebla, Goggin suggested the city only as a possibility and speaks of parallel production "elsewhere in Mexico."

In 1982, Robert and Florence Lister, researchers at the University of Arizona, published *Sixteenth Century Maiolica Pottery in the Valley of Mexico*.[9] In their report they described the types of mayólica found in the excavations of the Metropolitan Cathedral of Mexico City, as well as those discovered during construction for the Public Transportation System (*Metro*) and ascribed its manufacture to Mexico City.

Finally, in 1997, in an exposition organized by the *Museo de la Ciudad de México* entitled *La cerámica en la ciudad de México (1325–1917)*, the metropolis was regarded primarily as a consumer and a producer only of mayólica of a lower quality. In the catalog published for the occasion, two of the authors confirmed this statement. According to Carlos Aguirre Anaya, "And Mexico City, upon reaching its zenith in the Prehispanic period, became an avid and sophisticated center for the consumption of very diverse and useful ceramics that were initially handcrafted and later industrially manufactured. It remains so into the present."[10] Leonor Cortina de Pintado contends that, "The pottery produced in the City of Mexico was of an inferior quality to that of Puebla, with less tin oxide in the glaze and in a weaker blue. Above all, manufacturing was focused on tableware that was destined for local consumption."[11]

The Potters of Mexico City

Everything seems to indicate that loza blanca began to be manufactured in Mexico City about 1540.[12] The new ceramic technology introduced by the Spaniards (including the closed vault oven or kiln, the potter's wheel, and lead and tin-lead glazes) was recorded by some chroniclers as having an immediate impact on the local methods of manufacture.

Fray Bernardino de Sahagún, in his book *Historia general de las cosas de la Nueva España,* or the Florentine Codex, written about 1540, dealt with the production of the indigenous potter:

> The one who makes pottery, sells pots (*ollas*), large earthenware jars (*tinajas*), small pitchers (*cantaritos*), chamber pots, braziers, burnished hollowware, and all types of cups(*vasos*); scoops (*cucharras*), casseroles (*cazuelas*), and candle holders, some well-fired others not, some cracked in the firing process and others green because they are not well seasoned or fired, and then applies some superficial color or stains them with yellow.[13]

Interestingly, the chamber pots, casseroles, and candleholders are of Spanish origin; none of these were produced in Mexico before the conquest. Staining them with yellow is nothing more than applying a lead glaze.[14] Perhaps the Indians learned to make the glazed ceramics so rapidly that the missionary did not even realize that the technique was not indigenous.

Fray Gerónimo de Mendieta, in his work *Historia eclesiástica indiana,* written between 1571 and 1596, on addressing "the ingenuity and aptitude of the Indians for all of the trades," makes it clear that

> They were masters of pottery and clay hollowware for eating and drinking. Their crockery was finely painted and well made. And although they were not familiar with glazing, they learned this process later from the first master who arrived from Spain, despite the fact that he shied away from teaching them and guarded his methods.[15]

We can therefore conclusively affirm that there were Spanish artisans working with glazing in the decades immediately following the conquest. In addition, there are reports of a specialist in white pottery (*locero de lo blanco*) who emigrated from Talavera de la Reina to Mexico City around 1540.[16]

Ordinances for the potters of Mexico City were issued on 6 July 1677 and were confirmed by the viceroy of New Spain, Count de Paredes, Marqués de la Laguna, on 1 December 1681.[17] This time lag in establishing ordinances for potters is unusual when compared to the other trades, but on a par with that of their Puebla colleagues, who worked without official guidelines until 1653, even while other sixteenth-century artisans in New Spain, dedicated to other crafts, were governed by their respective ordinances. This phenomenon occurred also in the kingdoms of Castilla, where the potters of Talavera de la Reina did not have official guidelines until 1657, nor did they comprise a brotherhood or guild.[18] And there are no documents outlining regulations for the city of Sevilla.[19]

But why was it not until the middle of the seventeenth century that the potter's trade was regulated? Perhaps this relaxed attitude was due to the enormous volume of production, especially in Sevilla, and to the range of typologies and the variety of techniques that were utilized; but even more important would have been the excellent ceramic traditions that were conserved in the hands of Moriscos (Muslims who had accepted baptism into Catholicism) and the Mudéjares (Muslims who remained in Christian occupied territories) in Spain, and the Indians and mestizos of Mexico, who could not legally work as potters if the ordinances required them be of pure Spanish blood.[20]

The Mexico City regulations have twelve articles, of which eleven spell out operational statutes while one defines technical aspects. Although the operating rules are very similar to the ordinances of other guilds when it comes to the establishment of labor laws, instruction methods, the sale of articles, and types of examinations to obtain the rank of master, their late dissemination caused certain shortcomings.

In the first place, they established that "due to not having certified masters, the journeymen (*los oficiales*) would get together and choose two from among them who were of the status of acting masters, inspectors (*veedores*), and examiners (*examinadores*) to provide tests for the others."[21] This demonstrated the intention to structure the guild in a manner comparable to those of other occupations. Secondly, it was ordered that "on the seventh day of January of each year, the certified masters would meet at the parish of Santa Veracruz, where the brotherhood of Santa Justa and Santa Rufina was located, and would select two inspectors. One magistrate and representatives from two districts of the city would attend their election."[22]

To their advantage, the previous organization of a potters' brotherhood facilitated, in time, the formation of a guild, since they already had at their disposal a social structure and even their own chapel.[23] The chapel was located in a church of the pottery district, Santa María Cuepopán. Additionally, their devotion to Santa Justa and Santa Rufina might point to roots in the city of Sevilla for some of the potters.

In article four and articles six through twelve, it was established that only Spaniards and mestizos could be tested, as long as they had been apprenticed to a master, enabling them to learn the trade and therefore qualifying them to set up workshops and stores. This was not the case for blacks and mulattos, who could only work as journeymen. It also stipulated that twelve pesos would be charged for the examination and that the widows of masters would be provided for.[24]

Article eight indicates "that none shall pass the exam without proficiency in the potter's wheel and those that only perform painting will not be approved."[25] One thing immediately visible in the guidelines is the division of areas of expertise. On the one hand, there were the operators of the potter's wheel, who were in charge of forming clay pieces, subject to proficiency evaluations in order to qualify as candidates for the rank of master potter and as potential shopowners. On the other hand, there were painters, that is "those that are only skilled in paint," who were not accepted for the exam. This creates various questions. Why was there no test for painters? What status did they have within the labor structure of a workshop? Was a painter a member of the permanent staff or simply a temporary employee who floated from shop to shop as needed? Were women employed in this part of the art? And among them, were there both painters and decorators? We have no information in this regard, but we can infer that if they were not eligible for the exam and could not, thereby, become masters nor own their own shops, they must have worked solely as part of the general staff of a pottery workshop.

The stylistic uniformity within known pottery types leads us in fact to believe that there were itinerant painters who moved from one shop to another as they were needed, and they may well have been women, since this is a practice even today in some workshops in Spain and Puebla. Neither do we reject the likelihood of indigenous painters, especially in the sixteenth century, since early pieces have been found at the Colegio de Cristo with motifs very similar to those on ceramics identified as "Azteca III."[26]

Article nine goes on to say that, "Those who were proficient in all the trade (*oficio*) would be tested and approved, even if they came from some other region, and those that were familiar with working in white pottery would be evaluated in that specialty. Someone who had only worked in red would be examined just in that area of expertise."[27] What did to "work white pottery" mean? To operate a potter's wheel, or only to apply the enamel? To throw red work then turn it over to someone else to be bathed in enamel? How was the status of fashioning the unglazed pieces known as burnished ware? Article eleven specifies that, "No one may work nor sell pieces that have not been produced by masters of white, yellow, and red, and authenticated by their mark, under penalty of losing their work and an arbitrary fine."[28] It seems that not only did those who made loza blanca have to be certified but also those dedicated to other kinds of pottery as well. This raises another question: What happened to the indigenous pottery?

Regarding the technical aspects of the Mexico City document, the ordinances of Puebla originally issued in 1653 (and including four amendments in 1666) are unquestionably the model and precursor.[29] How is it that the potters of Mexico adopted, with only a few modifications, these technical guidelines? It is clear that pottery was being made in the same manner in both cities; proof is found in archaeological excavations and stylistic trends, such as the series called *encaje de bolillo* (bobbin lace) from Talavera de la Reina, later produced in Mexico and described in the Puebla and Mexico City ordinance.

10.1 Cup / *Jícara*
Mexico City or Puebla, Mexico, 17th century
San Juan (Fig Springs) Polychrome, restored
Museum of Indian Arts and Culture, Santa Fe
Photo by Paul Smutko.

Article five provides artisans with procedures for the manufacture of loza blanca. To make the vessels it was required that, "each straining must have ten basketloads (*guacales o chiquiguites*) of white clay and twelve of dark, so that the clay will be strong and will take colors well."[30] There is no difference in the preparation of the clay for the bisqueware according to the grade of the pottery. The grade was assigned by the three levels of glazing, which depended on the quantity of tin (the greater the quantity of tin, the thicker, whiter, and more opaque the glaze). The first level was that of common pottery (*loza común*), which required for its finish that in "each *arroba* (ca. twenty-five pounds) of lead, two pounds of tin should be mixed," and that "there should be painted in the center a small blue eggplant, so that it will be known for plain pottery; and in imitations the pottery must be carefully painted blue in the middle, and no other grade should be painted blue."[31] This type of decoration seems to correspond to three early series, one in blue ("Mexico City Blue on Cream") and two in blue-orange ("San Juan Polychrome" [fig. 10.1], and "Mexico City Polychrome").[32]

The second category of pottery (*loza entrefina*) was required by the ordinances to be finished with a glaze that had a composition of "one *arroba* of lead and four pounds of tin, painting the pottery only with interlacing or dots, and in types of colors which are superior and of great variety."[33] The ornamentation described appears to coincide

10.2 Basin / *Lebrillo*
Mexico City or Puebla,
Mexico, 1650–1700
Puebla Polychrome
The Metropolitan Museum of Art
Gift of Mrs. Robert W. de Forest,
1912 (12.3.1)
Photograph © 1990
The Metroolitan Museum of Art

with that of the series known as "Puebla Polychrome" (fig. 10.2), "Abó Polychrome" (fig. 10.3), "Aranama Polychrome" (fig. 10.4), and "Nopaltapec Polychrome" (fig. 10.5).[34]

The last type was *loza fina*, which necessitated for its glazing "one *arroba* of lead, six pounds of tin, and should be painted in blue and black." In addition it was indicated that, "The same should be done . . . keeping to the good colors that are required, rejecting the color green so that the said pottery should not be painted with it, since it is not permanent and exposes the pottery to the danger of crackling."[35] This description concurs with a series that is included within the category "Puebla Blue on White," which is called "San Elizario Polychrome" (fig. 10.6).[36] It also calls "for each Master to place his mark on each piece he produces to indicate the time of his quality check and to show the same on the certificate. The pottery generated in this manner would not be considered flawed and would indicate to its owners that it had been manufactured according to specifications."[37] In spite of all that, we almost never encounter marks on pieces of mayólica. And unlike the production of vessels, which was

10.3 Plate / *Plato*
Mexico City or Puebla, México, 1650–1750
Abó Polychrome
Museo José Luis Bello y González / INAH
Photo by Carlos Varillas, 2002

10.4 Plate / *Plato*
Mexico City or Puebla, Mexico, 18th century
Aranama Polychrome
Museo Franz Mayer, Mexico City
Photo by Michel Zabé

10.5 Plate / *Plato*
Mexico City or Puebla, Mexico, 18th century
Nopaltapec Polychrome
Museo Franz Mayer, Mexico City
Photo by Michel Zabé

regulated, the manufacture of glazed tiles is not even mentioned in the ordinances.

Other documents that prove the importance of the potters' guild in the capital city during the eighteenth century are the reports that inspectors submitted in 1727 regarding the petition of the Puebla potters to be allowed to discontinue using the color blue in loza común, due to its scarcity, and to be able to substitute green in its place. Their request was approved.[38]

Tangible Proof from Archaeology

The archaeological evidence confirming the production of mayólica in the Valley of Mexico, although scarce, has been known since the beginning of the twentieth century, the first notice of which is given to us by Hoffman: "Meanwhile, I received from Dr. Don Nicolás León the news that he had found in Tizapán the foundations of a kiln for talavera and many fragments of tiles in its vicinity."[39] In 1979, architectural elements and ceramics were found in the pottery district of Santa María

Cuepopán, indicating the existence of a pottery workshop from the colonial period.[40] The find was located to the north of Alameda Central, very close to the church of Santa Veracruz, beneath which the office of the Secretaría de Hacienda is located today. It appears that the site might form part of the cloisters of the Hospital of San Juan de Dios.

10.6 Plate / *Plato*
Mexico City or Puebla, Mexico, 18th century
San Elizario Polychrome
Museo Franz Mayer, Mexico City
Photo by Michel Zabé

The remains of a rectangular kiln, 2.50 meters by 3.80 meters, were discovered there. It was constructed of brick and basaltic rock. With it were found four small sinks for the decantation of clay, made of brick and stone, with a plaster of lime and sand. In the combustion chamber of the kiln, as well as in the neighboring areas, broken pieces of bisqueware were found. Glazed fragments, scorched by excessive temperatures, and cockspurs (*vícoles*) were also discovered. The glazed ceramic pieces included pots (*ollas*), jars (*jarras*), candleholders, chamber pots, and casseroles.

Among the pieces of mayólica were deep plates, some of which were stuck together, chamber pots, bowls, and cups, engraved with the mark of the hospital (H.d.S.J.d.D.d.M.), as well as both fragments and complete vessels of the types "Los Remedios Green on White" and "Puebla Blue on White"(fig. 10.7). The presence of pieces of the latter associated with the kiln proves that this was not a style exclusive to Puebla, but was manufactured in the capital as well. The fact that many pieces with the hospital's initials were found along with remains bearing other marks could indicate that the kiln was used not only to produce items for the hospital, but was also rented out to other potters, as was the practice in many places in Spain.

Between 1986 and 1988, the archaeologist Gilda Cano Salas carried out excavations within a colonial building known as "Casa Talavera" or "Casa del Marqués de Aguallo," located on the corner formed by the streets of República del Salvador and Calle de Talavera, in the southeast of the historic center of the city.[41] There they found a square structure measuring 1.50 meters on each side that could have been a ceramic kiln, along with the remains of ceramic materials such as clay, lead oxide and tin in different forms, and pigments. Cockspurs ,with three support struts used in the firing of loza común, and triangular pegs to hold the pieces of quality grade upright within saggars, were found mixed with fragments of bisqueware of different colors (pinkish, peach, white, gray, and brick red), with the characteristic ribs of pots thrown on a wheel. There were also glazed shards and fragments of

10.7 Bowls / *Tazones*
Mexico City or
Puebla, Mexico, 1700–1850
Huejotzingo Blue banded
and Puebla Blue-on-white
Museo Franz Mayer,
Mexico City
Photo by Michel Zabé

enameled plates stuck together due to excessive kiln temperatures. The forms that correspond to the fragments of this bisqueware are plates, soup bowls, small candlesticks, and the decorative series of matching plates of San Luis Blue on White; these last display the *aborronado* technique (a process of sketching a dark line around a figure [however, see note 30 in chapter 9]) which causes a thickness in the appearance as seen in the "Puebla Blue on White" series.

Other excavations that point to mayólica production in Mexico City are those made during the excavations for subway tunnels and those of the Capilla de San Antonio and of the Convento de Churubusco.[42]

Stylistic Evolution in Mexico City

Blue and Blue-Orange Series

Blue and blue-orange series originated between the second half of the sixteenth century and the first part of the seventeenth century. The first, or "Palm Series" (*serie de la palmeta*), has three variants, known as "Mexico City Blue on Cream," "Mexico City Polychrome," and "San Juan Polychrome" (see fig. 10.1). These all preserve a medieval style, which consists of quick and simple lines. The most important characteristic is the employment of a diluted blue used to paint a palm frond on the interior of the plates or bowls or on the walls of apothecary jars. These last two sometimes have touches of yellow or orange as well. The blue-orange series called "Tacuba Polychrome" stems from the first three and shares their decorative motifs, which, in this case, are framed by concentric circles.[43] The last blue-orange series, known as "La Traza Policrome,"is derived from the Talavera series with blue-orange dot designs and manganese (*serie punteada*), between the second half of the sixteenth and the first part of the seventeenth century.[44]

The next blue series is known as "San Luis Blue on White," developed from the Sevilla series of woodland designs, expressive of the last third of the seventeenth century, and from the talavera design, which depicts butterflies (*serie de la mariposa*) and ferns (*serie de helecho*), and which began in the middle of the sixteenth century (fig. 10.8).[45] The rim designs are based on semicircular bouquets in a radial composition that recall foliage and ferns or butterflies, from whose antennas originate rows of dots. The interiors of these pieces are decorated with variants of the same motifs. All the decorations are rendered in dark blue relief (aborronado) (see note 30, chapter 9).

There are two other series that developed from the foregoing; they are both categorized by archaeologists as belonging to "Puebla Blue on White." They keep the same rim-ornament structure, with the use of concentric circles of softer blues and a band of color, along with the bouquets created by quickly applied lines and distributed radially around the piece. We will call the first of these the "Floral Series" (*serie floral*). The background is ornamented with floral motifs that are also distributed in a radial scheme, either with three or four axes or with a single flower. This style is found in hollowwares as well as on tiles. The second group is denominated "San Elizario Policromo" (see fig. 10.6).[46] Its most important characteristic is the silhouette on the background of a heron or a phoenix in flight. This series also has polychrome variants, known as "Orangeline Polychrome" (fig. 10.9).[47]

The last blue series is called "Puebla Polychrome," and it originates from a talavera style known as "bobbin lace," which began in the last third of the seventeenth century and remained popular until the end of the eighteenth.[48] Its most important decorative elements are linear designs in black or brown, reminiscent of needle lace or bobbin lace, which often fill in spaces left between the blue, green, or yellow designs (figs. 10.2, 9.4).

10.8 Plate / *Plato*
Mexico City or Puebla, Mexico, 1600–1650
San Luis Blue-on-white
Museum of Indian Arts and Culture, Santa Fe

10.9 Plate / *Plato*
Mexico City or Puebla, Mexico, 18th century
Orangeline Polychrome
Museo Franz Mayer, Mexico City
Photo by Michel Zabé

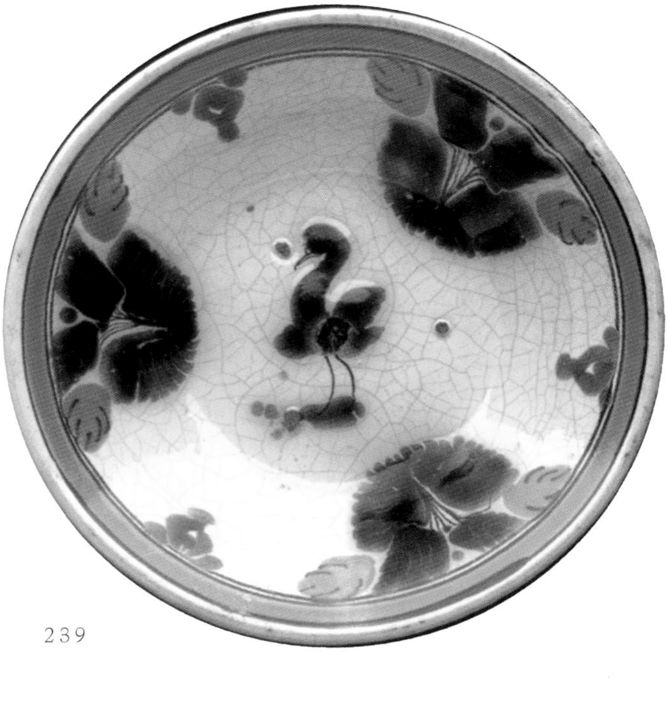

Green Series

The first three decorative varieties of this series can be dated to the first half of the seventeenth century.[49] The first of these series is known as "Mexico City Green on Cream."[50] Its designs are based on rapid, fluid strokes that form narrow striped patterns on the rim of the plates, very much like those of "Mexico City Blue on Cream," and include abstract motifs in the background. The two remaining series employed the colors green, red, orange, and black, the latter being used to sketch lines supporting the background composition and the motifs on the rims. It was also used to outline the concentric circles on the rim (one stripe), between the rim and the slope (one or two stripes), and between the slope and the bottom (three stripes). The first series is known as "San Luis Polychome" and derives from the "San Luis Blue on White" and "Tacuba Polychrome."[51] The last one is called "Santa María Polychrome."[52] It is characterized by radial compositions divided by black lines in the interior of the plates.

10.10a Cup / *Taza o jícara*
Mexico City or Puebla, Mexico, 1650–1750
Abó Polychrome
Museum of Indian
Arts and Culture, Santa Fe
Photo by Paul Smutko

10.10b Sugar Bowl / *Azucarero*
Mexico City or Puebla, Mexico, 1650–1750
Abó Polychrome
Museo José Luis Bello y González, INAH
Photo by Carlos Varillas

Emerging from the three previous series are two more; in both cases there are orange-brown bands on the border that are defined by one black line on the exterior and two on the interior. Likewise, the interior of the plates is separated from the slope by a similar band, framed by two black lines on both sides, reminiscent of the earlier series. The first of these series, known as "Nopaltapec Polychrome" (fig. 10.5), presents a composition in the cavetto based on radial symmetry worked in thirds. The interior is decorated with the same component in three separated sections, and it is surrounded by green dots and lines. The second of this series, called "Aranama Polychrome" (fig. 10.4), is differentiated by having a flower of six alternating yellow and green petals on the interior of the plates, which are outlined in black and have black lines to add volume. They radiate from a yellow circle, also outlined in black. In between the petals, a black line appears that ends in a yellow circle. The cavetto portrays eight peaks that rise from the central band and form a kind of star. The peaks are divided in two groups, one-half yellow and one-half green; they are delineated in black. In between them there is a bouquet with a green bud and two leaves, one green, the other brown, also delineated in black. This same structure has three variants.

Polychrome Series

The polychrome series known as "Abó Polychrome" uses the five colors of the Italian palette: blue, orange, green, yellow, and black; black is used to outline the figures (figs. 10.3, 10.10a, b). The outlining in black and the palette used both point to the previous series a possible precurser of "Abó Polychrome." The hollowware sometimes exhibits stripes on the rim. Compositions are based on zoomorphic or anthropomorphic representations, enclosed by small rings that may occasionally form a cluster of bouquets.

Conclusion

The archaeological record, along with historical documentation, provides sufficient data to affirm that Mexico City was an important center for the production of mayólica throughout the colonial period; nor was that production limited to common grade. The ordinances indicate, and archaeological discoveries confirm, that loza fina was produced as well.

Notes

1. John M. Goggin, *Spanish Majolica in the New World: Types of the Sixteenth to Eighteenth Century*, Yale University Publications in Anthropology, no. 72 (New Haven: Yale University Press, 1968).

2. Enrique A. Cervantes. *Loza blanca y azulejos de Puebla*, 2 vols. (México: Privately printed, 1939), p. xi.
3. Carlos Hoffman, "Verdades y errores acerca de la talavera poblana," *Boletín de la Sociedad Antonio Alzate* (Mexico, 1922), p. 626. He is referring to Edwin Atlee Barber, *The Maiolica of Mexico*, Art Handbook of the Pennsylvania Museum of School of Industrial Art (Philadelphia, 1908), p. 14.
4. Carlos Hoffman, "Verdades y errores acerca de la talavera poblana," p. 626.
5. Ibid., pp. 626–28.
6. Manuel Romero de Terreros, *Las artes industriales en la Nueva España* (México: Librería de Pedro Robledo, 1923).
7. Manuel Toussaint, *Arte colonial en México.* (México: Instituto de Investigaciones Estéticas/UNAM, 1974; originally published in 1948), p. 96.
8. Goggin, *Spanish Majolica.*
9. Florence C. Lister and Robert H. Lister, *Sixteenth Century Maiolica Pottery in the Valley of Mexico*, Anthropological Papers of the University of Arizona, no. 39 (Tucson: University of Arizona Press, 1982).
10. Carlos Aguirre Anaya. "La cerámica y la ciudad: Permanencias e innovaciones," in *La cerámica en la ciudad de México (1325–1917)*, ed. by Karina Simpson Hernández (México: Museo de la Ciudad de México, 1997), pp. 19–33.
11. Leonor Cortina de Pintado, "La cerámica: Usos e influencias," in *La cerámica en la ciudad de México (1325-1917)*, ed. by Karina Simpson Hernández, (México: Museo de la Ciudad de México, 1997), p. 85.
12. Lister and Lister, *Sixteenth Century Maiolica*, p. 13.
13. Fray Bernardino de Sahagún. *Historia general de las cosas de la Nueva España* (México: Editorial Porrúa, 1982; written ca. 1540), p. 571.
14. See article five of Puebla Ordinances, published by Enrique A. Cervantes in *Loza Blanca y Azulejo de Puebla* (Mexico, 1939), p. 23.This article states that "yellow includes pans and casseroles," which were necessarily always glazed.
15. Fray Gerónimo de Mendieta, *Historia eclesiástica indiana* (México: Editorial Porrúa, 1980; written between 1571 and 1596), p. 404.
16. Pastor Gómez, Toni Pasinki y Patricia Fournier. Transferencia tecnológica y filiación étnica: El caso de los loceros novohispános del siglo XVI. [Technology Transference and ethnic Affiliation. The case of the Novo Hispanic potters of the 16th century] in *Revista Amerística* (forthcoming).
17. Francisco del Barriot Lorenzot, *Ordenanzas de gremios de la Nueva España* (México: Secretaría de Gobernación, 1920), pp. 173–75.
18. Trinidad Sánchez Pacheco, "Cerámica de Talavera de la Reina y Puente de Arzobispo," in *Cerámica española*, vol. 42 of *Summa Artis: Historia general del arte*, ed. by Trinidad Sánchez Pacheco (Madrid: Espasa Calpe, 1997), p. 312.
19. See José María Sánchez Cortegana, *El oficio de olleros en Sevilla en el Siglo XVI* (Sevilla: Diputación Provincial de Sevilla, 1994).
20. Ibid., p. 28.
21. Francisco del Barriot Lorenzot, *Ordenanzas de gremios de la Nueva España*, p. 173.
22. Ibid.
23. Guild systems are corporations of artisans dedicated to line work. They are subject to ordinances in order to attain communal benefits. They contrast with brotherhoods, which are associations formed under the advocation of a patron saint, in order to promote that saint´s following, to participate in religious ceremonies, and to establish charitable organizations to benefit needy members of the confraternity.
24. Francisco del Barriot Lorenzot, *Ordenanzas de gremios de la Nueva España*, p. 174.
25. Ibid., p. 175.
26. I would like to thank archaeologist Gilda Cano for showing me these wares.
27. Fancisco del Barriot Lorenzot, *Ordenanzas de gremios de la Nueva España*, p. 175.
28. Ibid.

29. See Cervantes, *Loza blanca*, p. 22–25, 28–29.
30. Francisco del Barriot Lorenzot, *Ordenanzas de gremios de la Nueva España*, p. 174; *guacales* and *chiquihuites* are types of baskets of Prehispanic origin.
31. Ibid., p. 174.
32. Lister and Lister, *Sixteenth Century Maiolica*, p. 26; ibid., p. 14; Goggin, *Spanish Majolica*, p. 151, calls "San Juan Polychrome" "Fig Springs"; for "Mexico City Polychrome," see Lister and Lister, *Sixteenth Century Maiolica*, p. 28.
33. Francisco del Barriot Lorenzot, *Ordenanzas de gremios de la Nueva España*, p. 174.
34. Goggin, Spanish Majolica, p. 190; ibid., p.169; ibid., p. 196; Kathleen Degan, *Artifacts of Spanish Colonies of Florida and the Caribean, 1500–1800*, 2 vols. (Washington, DC: Smithsonian Institution Press, 1987, 2002), 1:88.
35. Francisco del Barriot Lorenzot, *Ordenanzas de gremios de la Nueva España*, pp. 174–75.
36. Goggin, *Spanish Majolica*, p. 169; Degan, *Artifacts*, p. 85.
37. Francisco del Barriot Lorenzot, *Ordenanzas de gremios de la Nueva España*, pp. 174–75.
38. Cervantes, *Loza blanca*, p. 34.
39. Hoffman, "Verdades y errores," p. 628.
40. See José Antonio López Palacios, María de la Luz Moreno Cabrera, and Araceli Peralta Flores, *La producción de loza novohispana en el barrio de Santa María Cuepopán de la ciudad de México*, in *Presencias y Encuentros: Investigaciones Arqueológicas de Salvamento*. pp. 177–87.
41. I would like to thank Gilda Cano for showing me this material.
42. Gilda Cano and María de la Luz Moreno Cabrera, personal communication.
43. Lister and Lister, *Sixteenth Century Maiolica*, p22.
44. Ibid., pp.18–22.
45. Ibid., p. 18; and Goggin, *Spanish Majolica*, p. 154.
46. Deagan, *Artifacts*, p. 85.
47. Ibid., p. 89.
48. Trinidad Sánchez Pacheco, "Cerámica de Talavera," p. 328.
49. Lister and Lister, *Sixteenth Century Maiolica*, p. 28.
50. Ibid.
51. Ibid.
52. Ibid.

11

Mayólica in the Daily Life of Colonial Mexico

DONNA PIERCE

IN DISCUSSING THE use of mayólica in the daily life of Mexico during the colonial period, it is useful to begin with the story of chocolate, since it illustrates the cultural exchange taking place during the era. Furthermore, the development of new vessel forms in this period is tied to the consumption of chocolate.

Chocolate: Its History and Incorporation into Daily Life

The ancient civilizations of Mesoamerica discovered, domesticated, and consumed cacao products, probably as early as 1000 B.C. among the Olmecs of the Mexican Gulf Coast lowlands.[1] Cacao beans are referred to as a sacred food in the *Popul Vuh*, the sacred book of the history of the Quiche Maya of the Guatemalan highlands, who

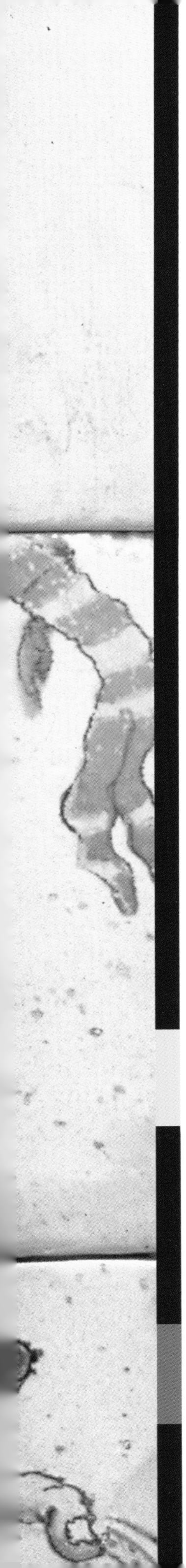

Detail, Fig. 11.7

flourished between A.D. 250 and 900. In other sources, Hunahpu, one of the twin gods of the Maya origin myth, is credited with inventing the processing of cacao. In other books and ceramic paintings of the Classic Maya, illustrations and hieroglyphic texts depict the God of Cacao. Cacao pods are described as a special offering to the gods, and the word for cacao has its own glyph.

In these same sources, the use of cacao in a drink among the elite Maya, and the special ceramics developed for its storage, preparation, and service, are also illustrated, and in some cases the ceramics survive. Tall cylindrical vessels of pottery were used as chocolate containers and employed in its preparation. The earliest illustration of the preparation of chocolate is found on a painted vase from the Late Classic Maya period (ca. A.D. 750), which shows a court scene with a standing woman pouring the liquid from one cylindrical vessel into another, a technique for creating foam, the most desirable part of the chocolate drink (fig. 11.1). We also know that they added numerous spices to it, including chile, and that they added chocolate to maize gruels of various recipes and thicknesses. The cacao beans were ground on a stone metate, often heated. Bishop Landa described the native use of cacao in the Yucatan, shortly after the conquest:

> They make of ground maize and cacao a kind of foaming drink which is very savory, and with which they celebrate their feasts. And they get from the cacao a grease which resembles butter, and from this and maize they make another beverage which is very savory and highly thought of. . . . They also parch the maize and grind it, and mix it with water, thus making a very refreshing drink, throwing in it a little Indian pepper or cacao.[2]

11.1 Maya woman pouring chocolate to raise foam
The Princeton Pot
Vase in Codex style, late classic Maya, Guatemala, ca. 750
Princeton University Art Museum
Museum purchase
Gift of the Hans A. Widenmann, class of 1918, and Dorothy Widenmann Foundation

These products can be identified as the traditional chocolate drink, cocoa butter, and the gruel drink called *pinol-atl* by the Aztecs, still used today and now known as *pinole*, still often seasoned with chocolate.

Although we do not know exactly when chocolate usage was introduced into central Mexico, we do have reason to believe that it was at least known and probably used in Teotihuacán during the Early Classic period. Certainly, in the Late Classic period, merchants from Maya areas were trading cacao from the hot coastal lowlands to the Valley of Mexico, via their trading post at Cacaxtla. By the Postclassic period, cacao and its chocolate products were so prized among the Aztecs that huge amounts were imported as trade or tribute (according to some sources the equivalent of 23 tons annually), and the royal households of Moctezuma and his relatives reportedly consumed over 11 million beans a year.[3] Chocolate consumption among the Aztecs appears to have been generally confined to the nobility, merchants, and soldiers, although servants and guards in the royal households apparently also partook of it daily.[4] Otherwise, consumption by the general populace seems to have been confined to certain religious ceremonies and festivals.

Among the Aztecs, the method of preparation was similar to that of the Maya, although the latter seem to have drunk the beverage hot, while the former drank it cool. The Aztec technique for making chocolate was described by one of the early conquerors:

> These seeds which are called almonds or cacao are ground and made into powder . . . [which] are put into certain basins . . . and then they put water on it and mix it with a spoon. And after having mixed it very well, they change it from one basin to another, so that a foam is raised which they put in a vessel made for the purpose. . . . and drinking it one must open one's mouth, because being foam one must give it room to subside, and go down bit by bit. This drink is the healthiest thing, and the greatest sustenance of anything you could drink in the world, because he who drinks a cup of this liquid, no matter how far he walks, can go a whole day without eating anything else.[5]

11.2 Aztec woman pouring chocolate to raise foam
Codex Tudela, late 16th century
Museo de América, Madrid

Similar to that on the Maya vase of eight centuries earlier, an illustration in the sixteenth-century Codex Tudela accurately depicts an Aztec woman raising the foam on chocolate by pouring the liquid in a standing position from one vessel to another (fig. 11.2). Here the preparation vessels used are deep-footed, open-necked bowls. According to various sources, the vessels used by the Aztecs for drinking chocolate were small, hemispherical bowls of polychromed pottery or painted and lacquered gourds, called *xicalli*, a word later Hispanicized as *jícara*. Like the Maya, the Aztecs flavored their chocolate with spices, including chiles, vanilla, honey, and various flowers. Among both groups, cacao beans were used as money or small currency, as they were throughout Mesoamerica during preconquest times, and such usage continued in the colonial period.

The first recorded European encounter with cacao occurred on Columbus's fourth and final voyage, in 1502. After weathering a hurricane, the fleet made land at the island of Guanaja, some 30 miles (50 km) off the north shore of Honduras, in what are now known as the Bay Islands. There they ran across one huge dugout canoe (possibly two) said to have been as long as a galley (between 141 and 164 feet long) and rowed by slaves. Now believed to have been a great Maya trading canoe from the Putún area of the Yucatán, the canoe had a structure "not unlike those of Venetian gondolas" that sheltered the women, children, and cargo.

After seizing the vessels, they examined the cargo, which included fine cotton garments, flat war clubs with razor-sharp stone blades along the edges (the formidable *macuauhuitl* or *macana* of the Aztec warriors), small copper axes and bells (the only worked metal, other than gold and silver, of preconquest America), and foodstuffs including items now identified as *pulque* ("resembling English beer") and cacao beans ("almonds"). About the latter, it was noted that, "They seemed to hold these almonds at great price; for when they were brought on board ship together with their goods, I observed that when any of these almonds fell, they all stooped to pick it up, as if an eye had fallen."[6] Columbus and his crew had no idea that these beans produced a beverage as esteemed in Mesoamerica as fine wine in Europe and that was eventually to invade the European palate as well; nor did they understand that they served as currency, much like the coveted gold and silver of the Old World.

Initially, many Europeans in the Americas did not appreciate the taste of chocolate, even if they recognized its stimulant qualities. As the Italian Girolamo Benzoni remarked in 1575, upon his return from the New World,

> It [chocolate] seemed more a drink for pigs, than a drink for humanity. I was in this country [Mexico] for more than a year, and never wanted to taste it. . . . But then, as there was a shortage of wine, so as not to be always drinking water, I did like the others. The taste is somewhat bitter, it satisfies and refreshes the body, but does not inebriate, and it is the best and most expensive merchandise, according to the Indians of that country.[7]

Within a short time, though, a hybridization between the two cultures began to take place on all levels, including in the kitchens of the New World.[8] As European foodstuffs were introduced, Native Americans began to incorporate some of these into their cuisine, at the same time that Europeans in the Americas adopted American products into their food culture. As we will see, some of these American and hybrid traditions eventually crossed the Atlantic as well. The new, creolized culture of the Americas combined elements from both cultures, and thus was different from either.

Women appear to have been the proponents of the food-culture exchange, both in the kitchens of the Americas and in the banquet halls of Europe. As early as 1538, an account by Bernal Díaz del Castillo, one of the original conquistadors, mentions Spanish women in Mexico drinking "chocolate with its foam" from gold and silver cups at a banquet hosted by Cortés and the first viceroy of Mexico, Antonio de Mendoza.[9] In 1590, the Jesuit José de Acosta commented on activities in the New World: "The main benefit of this cacao is a beverage which they make called Chocolate, which is a crazy thing valued in that country. It disgusts those who are not used to it, for it has a foam on top, or a scum-like bubbling. . . . And the Spanish men—and even more the Spanish women—are addicted to the black chocolate.[10]

The process of hybridization was already at work, and Spaniards in Mexico began to prefer the beverage hot rather than cold, a custom possibly adopted from the Yucatec Maya. They had also introduced sugarcane to Mexico, where it had rapidly become a cash crop on large estates, including that of Cortés himself; it became a staple ingredient in chocolate. Other spices popular in Europe, such as cinnamon, anise, and black pepper, were added to or replaced native enhancements for chocolate among the Spaniards. In producing the drink, the heated grinding stone, or metate, was retained from the native process, but the foaming technique of pouring from a height was replaced by the *molinillo*, a large wooden whisk, which was spun by rubbing the handle rapidly between the hands.

The English Dominican friar, Thomas Gage, traveled through Mexico and Guatemala between 1625 and 1637. He reported a scandal involving chocolate that occurred when he was in San Cristóbal de las Casas, in southern Mexico. Apparently the Spanish women there were so addicted to chocolate that they could not get through the long church services without it, and "(made) their maids bring to them to church in the middle of Mass or sermon a cup of chocolate, which could not be done to all, or most of them, without a great confusion and interrupting both Mass and sermon."[11] After the bishop forbade the practice and threatened to excommunicate the women, the controversy accelerated to the point that swords were drawn in the cathedral against the clergy. The Spanish women began to attend mass at convents and monasteries instead. The bishop responded by threatening the monks and nuns and by excommunicating the women. Shortly afterward, the bishop became ill and died, ironically, after drinking a cup of chocolate that had apparently been poisoned.

The Aztecs had used solid wafers of ready-ground chocolate to produce a type of instant chocolate for use during military campaigns. The Spanish continued the production of chocolate wafers or small bricks for storing and shipping. In this manner, consumption of chocolate spread throughout the Americas. Its use in Peru as well as in New Mexico, the northernmost frontier of New Spain, is documented by the early 1600s.[12] In an archived Inquisition document, a Pueblo Indian servant woman describes serving hot chocolate to the governor of New Mexico and his wife in the Palace of the Governors in 1660.[13] Don Diego de Vargas, captain general and governor of New Mexico (1691–1707), considered it a staple rather than a luxury for his troops (following Aztec tradition), repeatedly including it in his supply requisitions.[14] He also served it as a ceremonial drink to important figures, including local Indian leaders, as a form of formalizing a verbal agreement. While traveling or in the field on military campaigns, it was often the only sustenance served for breakfast and lunch, as a colonial equivalent to the freeze-dried foods or power bars of today. Chocolate was also imported by Franciscan friars for use in the missions and was a major commodity in the inventories of merchants active in New Mexico during the colonial period.[15]

During the course of the seventeenth and eighteenth centuries, chocolate consumption, generally restricted to the elite in Precolumbian times, spread to all classes in Mexico (fig. 11.3). By 1779, the viceroy of Mexico noted:

> In this country cacao is a primary food not only for persons of means as in other countries, but also among the poor people, especially servants both rustic and urban, who are given a ration of chocolate. It breaks your heart to hear the laments of the inhabitants of these vast regions, and particularly the poor male and female religious, whenever cacao hits an excessive price because of monopoly or poor harvest.[16]

No one knows when chocolate was first introduced to Spain. Cortés is often credited with its introduction, but there is no documentary evidence to substantiate this assertion. The first documented appearance of chocolate in Spain occurred in 1544, when a group of Dominican friars brought a delegation of Kekchi Mayan nobles to visit Prince Philip. Among the gifts the Mayan nobles presented to the prince were receptacles of beaten chocolate. Whether Philip tasted the beverage is unrecorded. The first officially documented shipment of cacao beans to Spain arrived in Sevilla in 1585. Of course, these documented occurrences may not have been the first, since many informal and unrecorded exchanges may have taken place previously.

Throughout the sixteenth century, chocolate, along with other American plant products, was studied by Renaissance medical experts, including the royal physician to Philip II of Spain, to determine their possible health benefits. By the end of the century, chocolate had been deemed beneficial, which aided its acceptance into Spanish and eventu-

11.3 *De Español y Negra, Mulato*
Anonymous,
Mexico, ca. 1750
Oil on canvas
Collection of Jan and Frederick R. Mayer
Photo by Denver Art Museum, 2002

ally other European cultures. Indeed, it is as a medicine that chocolate seems to have first entered most European countries. Its popular reputation as an aphrodisiac also helped.

During the early seventeenth century, chocolate became accepted at the Spanish court of the Hapsburg kings and from there eventually made its way to other noble tables of Baroque Europe. When Cosimo de Medici visited Spain in 1668–69, he was served chocolate in "huge cups" by Philip IV and quickly became one of the great chocoholics of all time. As in Mexico, women appear to have been instrumental in the acceptance of chocolate in Europe. Chocolate may have been introduced to the French court by the daughter of Philip III of Spain, Anne of Austria, in 1615, when she was married to Louis XIII. But certainly by the time Anne's son, the future Louis XIV of France, married Princess María Teresa, the daughter of Philip IV of Spain, in 1660, she and her court brought their tradition of chocolate drinking to Versailles. Ten years later, the noblewoman Marie de Rabutin-Chantal, Marquise de Sévigné, (clearly a Baroque chocoholic!) mentions chocolate frequently in letters to her family, including this 1671 passage to her daughter: "I took it day before yesterday to digest my dinner, to have a good meal, and I took it yesterday to nourish me so that I could fast until evening: it gave me all the effects I wanted. That's what I like about it: it acts according to my intention."[17]

The general recipe and method of production remained basically the same as that developed in the hybrid kitchens of sixteenth-century Mexico, with the optional addition of various European spices. By 1644, the chocolate recipes of the Spaniard Antonio Colmenero de Ledesma were published and widely distributed throughout Europe and England.[18] After midcentury, at about the same time that tea and coffee were being introduced to Europe from Asia and Africa, respectively, chocolate consumption spread to Italy, France, and England. Recipe books for chocolate with various additives and flavor enhancements, including perfumes, were published in these countries as well, in the second half of the seventeenth century.

Introduced to England after 1655, chocolate drinking eventually crossed the Atlantic again to the British colonies in North America.

11.4 *Alacena*
Antonio Pérez de Aguilar, Mexico, 1769
Oil on canvas, 125 x 98 cm
Museo Nacional de Arte / CNCA / INBA
Photo by Ernesto Peñaloza
Copper chocolate pot with *molinillo* and *jícara* on bottom shelf.

In 1697, Samuel Sewall, a judge at the famous Salem witch trials of 1692, recorded in his diary, "I wait upon the Lieut Governour at Dorchester, and there meet with Mr. Torry, breakfast together on Venison and Chockalatte; I said Massachusetts and Mexico met at his Honour's Table."[19]

New Vessel Forms

As we have seen, ceramics played a role in chocolate preparation and consumption from the preconquest period, with Maya and Aztec vessels for raising the foam and drinking the beverage. Ceramics continued to be involved in the chocolate ceremony during the colonial period, and several new vessels were developed. Those used by Europeans in Mexico and later in Europe for drinking chocolate were adapted from the traditional Aztec xicalli, or lacquered gourd cup (fig. 11.4). Indeed, these small ceramic or lacquered gourd bowls or cups continued to be manufactured by native artists in Mexico and used by Spaniards there, as well as being exported to Europe. The Michoacán area of Mexico specialized in lacquered furniture and utensils and continued to produce the brightly colored gourd jícaras throughout the colonial period. The Scottish wife of the Spanish ambassador to Mexico, Fanny Calderón de la Barca, described jícara production during a trip to Michoacán in the 1840s:

> Their dishes are still the xicalli, or, as they were called by the Spaniards, jícaras, made of a species of gourd . . . which they cut in two, each one furnishing two dishes. The inside is scooped out and a durable varnish given it by means of a mineral earth, of different bright colors, generally red. On the outside they paint flowers, and some of them are also gilded. They are extremely pretty, very durable and ingenious . . . . We

11.5 Chocolate Cups / *Jícaras*
Mexico City or Puebla, 17th century
Museum of Indian Arts and Culture, Santa Fe
Photo by Paul Smutko

11.6 Chocolate Saucer / *Mancerina*
Alcora (Valencia), 1748–1798
Museum of Spanish Colonial Art
Collections of the Spanish Colonial Arts Society, Inc., Santa Fe
Photo by Paul Smutko

also went to purchase jícaras, and to see the operation of making and painting them, which is very curious. The flowers are not painted, but inlaid. We were fortunate in procuring a good supply of the prettiest, which cannot be procured anywhere else.[20]

The indigenous jícaras were copied in mayólica in both Spain and Mexico, and eventually the rest of Europe as well (fig. 11.5). Similar in size and shape to Chinese porcelain handleless teacups, such vessels are still known today as jícaras.

In conjunction with these traditional cups, another New World form was invented for the chocolate service—the *mancerina* (fig. 11.6). Although undocumented, oral history maintains that its origin and name can be traced to Peru, where the viceroy from 1639 to 1648, Pedro de Toledo y Leyva, Marqués de Mancera, asked a silversmith in Lima to fashion a saucer or small plate with a fixed ring in the center to hold the jícara in place.[21] Soon manufactured in mayólica and porcelain, as well as metal, the mancerina (named after the viceroy), with its jícara, spread throughout the Americas and Europe, specifically for drinking chocolate (fig. 11.7). Another mayólica vessel, the *tibor* vase (similar to the Chinese ginger jar), was adapted to serve as a *chocolatero*, or storage jar for chocolate, by the addition of a locking iron lid, attesting to the value of chocolate in the Mexican colonial household (fig. 11.8; see also Introduction).

Although only occasionally manufactured in mayólica, at some point a specific vessel for preparing chocolate was developed (fig. 11.9). Possibly distantly related to the tall, cylindrical ceramic vessels used by the Maya, a tall, narrow vessel of copper evolved to heat and, along with the molinillo, to beat the beverage (fig. 11.10; see also figs. 11.3, 11.4). The pot had a curved or straight handle and usually a copper lid with a hole in the top, to accommodate the handle of the molinillo. Whether this form has any relationship to the smaller but similar Arabic or Turkish coffee pot has never been explored, but the eight-hundred-year occupation of Spain by Muslims makes this a connection worth considering. Although the French are usually credited with the invention of the silver *chocolatière*, or chocolate pot with the straight handle, in the 1680s (fig. 11.11), clearly there were predecessors made of copper and used in Spain and its colonies. Indeed, one is seen in a still-life painting dated 1652, by the Spanish painter Antonio de Pereda y Salgado (see fig. 2.9).

11.7 Woman carrying a *mancerina*
Alcora (Valencia), 18th century
Museu de Ceràmica, Barcelona

11.8 Chocolate Storage Jar / *Chocolatero*
Puebla, 17th century
Collection of Michael Haskell

11.9 Chocolate Pot / *Chocolatera*
Alcora (Valencia), 1735–1760
Museu de Ceràmica, Barcelona
Photo by Guillém Fernández

11.10 Copper Chocolate Pot / *Chocolatera de cobre*
Spain, 18th century
Museo Nacional de Antropología, Madrid

11.11 Silver Chocolate Pot / *Chocolatera de plata*
Peru, ca. 1730
Denver Art Museum
Gift to the Denver Art Museum by the Robert
Appleman Family (1980.316 a-b)
Photo by Denver Art Museum, 2002

The Hybrid Kitchens of Colonial Mexico

11.12 Mayólica tile depicting a nun making jam Valencia, early 19th century Museo Nacional de Cerámica y de Artes Suntuarias "González Martí," Valencia

As evidenced by the story of chocolate, the kitchens of the Americas served as loci of cultural exchange, with the vessels, ceramic and otherwise, literally mixing culinary customs together. Ceramics were imported from Europe both as containers for foodstuffs and as products themselves. In Mexican kitchens, they functioned side by side with Indian-produced earthenware pottery and, by the late sixteenth century, with mayólica produced in Mexico and porcelain from China.

Franciscan friars accompanied Cortés to begin the task of converting the Indians of the Americas to Christianity. By 1524, twelve more had arrived, soon to be followed by Dominicans and Augustinians and, by the late sixteenth century, many other orders.[22] The friars supervised Indian laborers in the construction of large mission establishments, which included churches, monasteries, and schools for Indian converts. Many of these compounds included large kitchens based on medieval models, but incorporating the latest in kitchen technology. A surviving example can be seen in the Franciscan establishment at Huejotzingo, completed in 1571, on the road between Puebla and Mexico City.[23] The self-sufficient food-preparation complex included a vegetable garden, orchard, cistern, aqueduct, cold room, kitchen, bakery, and refectory.

The kitchen at Huejotzingo had a large, open hearth fueled by logs, with cauldrons hanging from hooks above and a large clay and limestone oven for baking bread in the European manner. At the north (and therefore coolest) end of the kitchen, was a small passage leading to the cold room, a rectangular space approximately 3 by 4 meters, refrigerated by a system of clay pipes inside the walls, through which water circulated. Niches were carved into the walls for storing perishables, often in ceramic jars. Water came from an aqueduct and an underground cistern and was fed throughout the monastery by a system of stone-lined troughs and clay pipes. Staffed by monks and Indian servants, mission kitchens undoubtedly made use of a mixture of utensils from both cultures, such as the native grinding stone (metate) as well as the European mortar and pestle. Presumably mayólica imported from Spain was used alongside Indian-produced earthenware and eventually Mexican mayólica and some Chinese porcelain by the late sixteenth century.

By the seventeenth century, numerous convents had been founded in

11.13 Bowls / *Cuencos*
Convento de Santa Teresa
Puebla, 1750–1800
The Taylor Museum of the
Colorado Springs Fine Arts
Center, Colorado Springs

Mexico and Puebla. To some extent, all were known for their culinary prowess.[24] Many are credited with inventing the various hybrid recipes of the colonial period still known today in the distinctive cuisine of Mexico, such as *mole poblano*, the sauce made from chocolate, peanuts, chile (all New World products), sugar (African/European), and cinnamon (Asian), and used on turkey (New World) or chicken (European) dishes. Although in the sixteenth and seventeenth centuries some convents allowed nuns to maintain small kitchens, staffed by servants, in their own cells, by the eighteenth century most convents had developed large, communal kitchens. The raised kitchen range set against a wall, a technological innovation of the seventeenth century, was incorporated into these large kitchens and allowed for better and varied regulation of heat during the cooking process. (fig. 11.12; see fig. 9.9). In many convents, particularly in Puebla, these ranges, as well as much of the kitchen area, were covered with mayólica tiles. Floors were covered with clay bricks or glazed redware tiles. Copper, iron, and earthenware vessels were used for preparing and cooking the foods. Dishes and pots were usually washed in a nearby courtyard, with wells or running water from aqueduct systems.

In the convents, mayólica utensils were both communally and individually owned. Large numbers of extant mayólica dishes emblazoned with the names of various monasteries and convents demonstrate the quantity and variety of mayólica vessels made for communal use in these establishments (fig. 11.13). The estate inventories of nuns often record the private ownership of mayólica vessels as well as those of Michoacán lacquerware, silver, and Chinese porcelain. For example, when Sister Mariana de la Santísima Trinidad died, in 1686, in the Conceptionist convent of the

Encarnación in Mexico City, she had in her possession two plates of mayólica from Puebla and one of Chinese porcelain.[25]

The making, serving, and consuming of chocolate was an important part of convent life, both internally and when receiving visitors and dignitaries. From the mother superior down to the most recent novice, everyone took their turn at grinding the cacao beans with the chosen spices. Indeed, a proverb likens the preparation of chocolate to a religious act:

Oh, chocolate divino	Oh, divine chocolate
Arrodillado te muelen	Kneeling they grind thee
Manos plegadas te baten	Hands praying they beat thee
Y ojos al cielo te beben	Eyes to heaven they drink thee[26]

Although they did not include pieces of mayólica, the 1692 estate inventory possessions of Mother Catalina de San Juan, of the Conceptionist convent of Santa Inez in Mexico City, demonstrate the importance of chocolate to daily life in the nunneries.[27] She owned a small leather chest for storing chocolate, three plates and twelve small and large cups of Chinese porcelain, four coconut shells mounted with silver feet, and two painted and lacquered gourd jícaras from Michoacán—all objects used for the storing, serving, and drinking of chocolate.

11.14 *Birth of the Virgin*
Arellano (signed),
ca. 1710
Oil on canvas (detail)
Denver Art Museum,
Collection of the Jan and Frederick R. Mayer
(51.2000)
Photo by the Denver Art Museum, 2002

Although no secular kitchen has survived to the present from the colonial period, vague descriptions, eighteenth-century paintings, and nineteenth-century illustrations indicate that in upper- and middle-class homes, they were smaller versions of monastic kitchens; in lower-class homes they were more modest hearth areas. In a detail of a colonial painting of the Birth of the Virgin, an upper-class domestic kitchen is depicted with a raised cooking range and a large mayólica pitcher (fig. 11.14). The walls of colonial kitchens were usually fitted with cupboards and shelves, for storing ceramics and utensils. At times, these culinary vessels were hung from hooks in the walls or ceiling. A type of freestanding, open-shelf furniture, similar to a bookcase or hutch without doors, was also used to store ceramics and other food containers. These customs are depicted in colonial-period paintings, most notably in the *castas* paintings developed in the Americas to attempt to classify the various racial mixtures occurring there.[28] Assuming the ethnographic detail in castas paintings is reliable, if formulaic, we can observe the usage and storage of ceramics, including both mayólica and native redware, in middle- and lower-class kitchens of the eighteenth century in colonial Mexico (figs. 11.15, 11.16). Also seen in some of these paintings is the preparation of chocolate in middle- and lower-class homes, with the copper chocolate pot and wooden molinillo (see fig. 11.3), as well as jícaras and plates, or mancerinas, of mayólica.

Dining Rooms and other Domestic Usage

Although in most lower- and middle-class homes it was customary to eat in the kitchen, affluent homes had separate rooms for dining by the sev-

11.15 *De Chino y India, Genízara*
Francisco Clapera, Mexico, 18th century
Oil on canvas
Denver Art Museum, Collection of Jan and Frederick R. Mayer (190.1996.14)
Photo by Denver Art Museum, 2002

11.16 *De India y Cambujo, Tente en el Aire*
Anonymous,
Mexico, 18th century
Oil on canvas
Museo de América, Madrid

enteenth century. Although rare in the sixteenth century, one example was described as being "occupied by a great cedar table surrounded by benches; these come from Michoacán wood . . . or are made of white pine."[29] Such tables would have held vessels such as plates, bowls, sauce-boats, sugar bowls, and saltcellars, made of mayólica or silver from Spain or Mexico, and at times a few pieces of Chinese porcelain. Coordinated place settings as we know them were unknown until the nineteenth century. Indeed, a large variety of utensils, as opposed to matched sets, was desirable during the Baroque era and was considered a testament to the family's wealth and ability to acquire objects from various sources. Metal cutlery was generally confined to knives and spoons, although the latter were usually made of wood. The fork and napkin, both invented by Leonardo da Vinci, were only gradually being introduced into Europe at the end of the fifteenth century, but had become quite common in upper-class dining rooms by the eighteenth century. An example of a colonial Mexican dining room can be seen in an eighteenth-century painting of the Holy Family, where the table is set with mayólica plates and saltcellar, as well as cloth napkins (fig. 11.17).

11.17 *The Table Blessing*
José de Alcíbar (d. 1803),
Mexico, late 18th century
Oil on canvas,
223 x 237 cm
Museo Nacional de
Arte / CNCA / INBA
Photo by Arturo Piera

For those who could afford it, glassware was also available, either imported from Europe or made in the glass factories established in Puebla by 1542, when one was described as producing "white, crystal, green and blue [glassware] used by Spaniards and natives of these parts and as far away as Guatemala, and even further, arriving as far as Peru."[30] During the eighteenth century, the Puebla factories were still producing glass vessels, described as "if not quite able to compete with Venice, at least equal to that of France, double, strong, clean and clear, and of exquisite manufacture."[31]

Evidence of the use of mayólica in other areas of daily life in colonial Mexico can also be gleaned from paintings. For example, mayólica *floreros* can be seen in some casta paintings and occasionally in portraits, such as the one on the window sill in the portrait attributed to Fray Miguel de Herrera of María Josefa de Aldaco y Fagoaga as a young girl.[32] Religious paintings depicting the Birth of the Virgin painted in colonial Mexico are often set in an upper-class colonial bedroom and sometimes include a person serving St. Ann in bed with a mayólica blue-on-white plate and bowl (fig. 11.18).

11.18 *Birth of the Virgin*
Francisco de León, Mexico, 18th century
Oil on canvas
Denver Art Museum, Collection of Jan and Frederick R. Mayer (25.1993)
Photo by Denver Art Museum, 2002

Distribution of Mexican Mayólica

The mayólica of Mexico was locally appreciated at the time, as seen in various quotes from the colonial period. Speaking of Puebla in the late seventeenth century, Fray Agustín de Vetancurt chauvinistically claimed that "the glazed pottery is finer than that of Talavera, and can compete with that of China in its fineness."[33] As late as 1745, Fray Juan Villa Sánchez wrote, "The pottery, of which great quantities are made in Puebla, (is) so fine and beautiful that it equals or excels that of Talavera,...the ambition of the Puebla potters being to emulate and equal the beauty of the wares of China." Villa Sánchez went on to say, "There is a great demand for this product, especially for the most ordinary qualities which are most in demand throughout the Kingdom."[34]

This latter claim is certainly born out in the far northernmost reaches of New Spain, in the province of New Mexico. If we look at New Mexico as a case study, we see that a sizable amount of mayólica made the twelve-hundred-mile journey from central Mexico to the northern frontier (fig. 11.19).[35] Archaeological excavations at colonial sites, including Spanish homesites and mission convents, have yielded various types of seventeenth-century mayólica from both Puebla and Mexico City, including "Abo Polychrome," "Puebla Polychrome," "Puebla Blue on White," "Aranama Polychrome," "Castillo Polychrome," and "Puaray Polychrome." Eighteenth-century examples from New Mexican sites include later "Puebla Blue on White" types, "Huejotzingo Blue and Yellow Banded," and "Tumacácori Polychrome." Although rare in archaeological excavations in New Mexico, shards of Spanish mayólica

11.19 Mayólica Sherds
Mexico, 1600–1680
Excavated from the
Palace of the Governors, Santa Fe
Palace of the Governors
(Museum of New Mexico), Santa Fe

are occasionally found, including isolated examples of Hispano-Moresque lusterware, Teruel ware, and "Tallahassee Blue on White."

Throughout the seventeenth century, the missions of New Mexico were stocked at the expense of the king of Spain by a mission supply train that made the trek every three years. On the standard supply list was one box of "loza de Puebla," which was automatically sent to each mission every three years.[36] Friars at the missions also engaged in commercial activities, often earning enough money to make special orders, which occasionally included additional requests for mayólica vessels.

Although household inventories from the seventeenth century are extremely rare, Teresa Aguirre de Rocha de Mendizábal, wife of the governor of New Mexico, owned at least one "chocolate cup from Puebla" in 1662. Surviving wills and estate inventories from the eighteenth and early nineteenth centuries also list mayólica vessels, along with Chinese porcelain, in the households of colonial New Mexicans. Some examples include Luis García Noriega of Albuquerque, who owned an "olla from Puebla" when he died, in 1747, and Lugarda Quintana of Santa Cruz, who had "three small bowls, two fine and one ordinary," in 1749. In Santa Fe, Juan Montes Vigil had twenty mayólica jars in 1762; Juan Felipe Rivera owned seven cups, five bowls, and one pitcher "from Puebla" in 1770; and Juan Antonio Fernández had three cups "from Puebla" in Santa Fe in 1784. Juana Luján, who

11.20 Plate / *Plato*
Mexico City or Puebla, Mexico, 17th century
Puebla Polychrome
Museo Franz Mayer, Mexico City
Photo by Michel Zabé

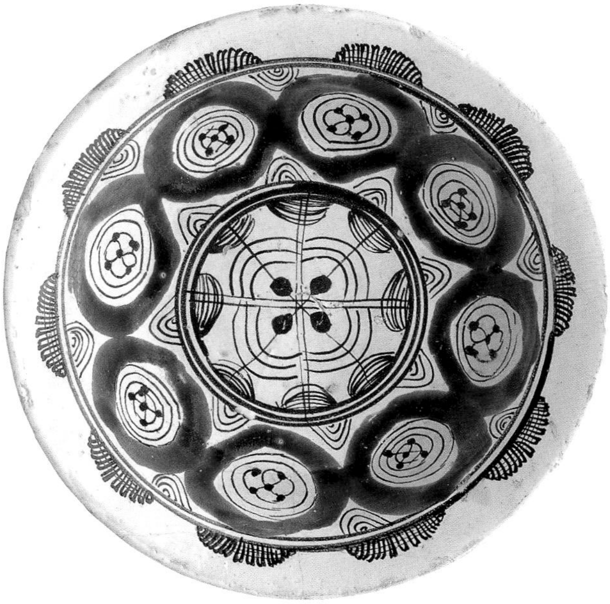

lived in a twenty-four-room house near present-day San Ildefonso Pueblo, had a mayólica saltcellar, three plates, and six cups "from Puebla," as well as two jars and two trays "from Guadalajara" (Tonalá), when she died, in 1762. In 1780, Manuel Vigil of Taos owned six plates, six cups, and three bowls "from Puebla," as well as ten olive jars and one "Guadalajara" jar.[37]

The Pueblo Indians of New Mexico continued their long tradition of making pottery after the Spanish came to the area. Within a matter of years, however, Pueblo potters began to imitate not only the shapes of mayólica vessels imported from Spain and Mexico, but also the decorative styles. Soup plates, footed cups, goblets, and candlesticks of locally made ceramics all became popular, while other vessels exhibited designs made in imitation of the Spanish bobbin lace design found on "Puebla Polychrome" mayólica from Mexico (figs. 11.20, 11.21). Although handled mugs had been made by several Indian groups in the Southwest prior to Spanish exploration and settlement, the manufacture of handled cups and jars expanded greatly after 1598.

During the colonial period, Spanish settlers used Indian ceramics in their homes alongside imported mayólica from Spain and Mexico, as well as some Chinese porcelain. The types of Indian-made ceramic wares found in excavations of eighteenth-century Spanish homesites include micaceous types from Picuris and Taos Pueblos, as well as that made by *genízaro* (Christianized Plains

11.21 Soup Plate / *Cuenco*
Cuyamungue, New Mexico
17th century
Tewa Polychrome
Museum of Indian Arts and Culture
(Museum of New Mexico), Santa Fe

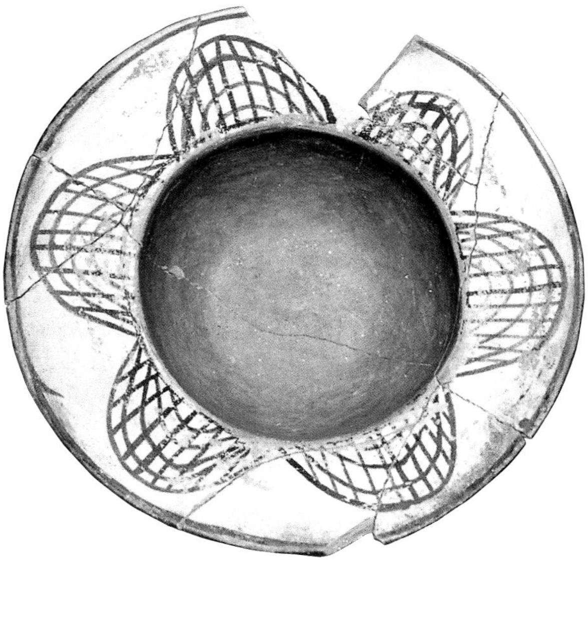

Indians) and Hispanic potters in several areas of New Mexico, such as Abiquiu and Albuquerque.[38] Other Indian-made ceramics found in Spanish homesites included "Ogapoge Polychrome" and "Powhoge Polychrome" pottery.

Mayólica was a part of the daily life of people not only in central Mexico, but also in the remote provinces, although probably in smaller quantities. As in the hybrid kitchens of central Mexico, mayólica was used alongside local Indian ceramics and Chinese porcelain in the households of New Mexico and may imply a similar usage in other provincial areas of the Spanish colonies.

Conclusion

As we have seen, the story of the New World product chocolate illustrates the acculturation occurring in the daily lives of people in both the Americas and to a lesser degree in Europe during the sixteenth through eighteenth centuries. Mayólica was rapidly incorporated into the preparation, serving, and drinking of chocolate, and new vessel forms soon emerged. All of the new forms—the jícara, mancerina, chocolate pot, and chocolate storage jar—seem originally to have developed in the Americas, with some influence from European and Chinese forms, and then spread to Europe. The jícara derived from the Aztec xicalli in Mexico in the early sixteenth century, although its shape eventually came to resemble the Chinese teacup. The copper chocolate pot, with its Spanish molinillo (probably related to the tall, cylindrical Prehispanic pots used for raising foam, as well as to the Arabic coffee pot), along with the locked chocolate storage jar (adapted from the Chinese ginger jar), both seem to have evolved in Mexico in the late sixteenth or early seventeenth century. The invention of the mancerina purportedly occurred in the mid-seventeenth century in Peru, with the concept credited to the viceroy but the actual production due to an anonymous Peruvian silversmith.

The new chocolate vessels were used in the multicultural kitchens and dining rooms of Mexico, along with other mayólica objects from Spain and Mexico, as well as Chinese porcelain and native redwares. Spanish and Mexican mayólica wares were shipped to many areas of the Americas, where they became a part of daily life; in the northern province of New Mexico, they were used, albeit in smaller quantities, alongside Chinese porcelain, Mexican redware, and local Pueblo Indian ceramics. In many colonial kitchens, particularly those of the nunneries of central Mexico, mayólica vessels served as containers for storing and combining ingredients from the Americas, Europe, Asia, and Africa, to create the distinctively hybrid cuisine of Mexico that we know today.

Notes

1. Sophie D. Coe and Michael D. Coe, *The True History of Chocolate* (London: Thames and Hudson, 1996). The Coes have amassed the most complete and comprehensive discussion in English of this topic; see also Ignacio H. de la Mota, *El libro del chocolate* (Madrid: Ediciones Pirámide, 1992). This section on chocolate is based on these two sources, unless otherwise indicated.
2. Alfred M. Tozzer, "Landa's *Relación de las cosas de Yucatán*," *Papers of the Peabody Museum of Archaeology and Ethnology* 18 (1941):90.
3. María Cristina Suárez y Farias, "Edificar un rito: De dioses, casas y cocinas mexicas," *Artes de Mexico* 36 (1997):8–17.
4. Bernal Díaz del Castillo, *The True History of the Conquest of New Spain*, as quoted in "Edificar una corte: La mesa de Moctezuma," *Artes de Mexico* 36 (1997):18–19.
5. Anonymous Conqueror, *Relatione di alcune cose della Nuova Spagna, e della gran città di Temestitan Messico* (Venice: Ramussio Giunti, 1556), p. 306a; Coe and Coe, *True History*, pp. 86–87; de la Mota, *El libro*, pp. 35–37.
6. Samuel E. Morison, *Journals and Other Documents on the Life and Voyages of Christopher Columbus* (New York: Heritage Press, 1963), p. 327; Coe and Coe, *True History*, pp. 105–8; de la Mota, *El libro*, pp. 61–64.
7. Girolamo Benzoni, *Storia del Mondo Nuovo*, facsimile of 1575 ed. (Graz: Akademische Druck- und Verlagsanstalt, 1962), pp. 103–4; Coe and Coe, *True History*, p. 109; de la Mota, *El libro*, p. 39.
8. María Stoopen, "Edificar una confluencia: Las simientes del mestizaje en el siglo XVI," *Artes de Mexico* 36 (1997):20–29.
9. Bernal Díaz del Castillo, *Historia verdadera de la conquista de la Nueva España* (Madrid: Instituto Gonzalo Fernández de Oviedo, 1982), pp. 607–11.
10. José de Acosta, *Historia natural y moral de las Indias* (Sevilla: Casa de Juan Léon, 1590), p. 251.
11. Thomas Gage, *Thomas Gage's Travels in the New World*, ed. with an introduction by J. Eric S. Thompson (Norman: University of Oklahoma Press, 1958), pp. 143–45.
12. George P. Hammond and Agapito Rey, *Don Juan de Oñate: Colonizer of New Mexico, 1595–1628*, 2 vols. (Albuquerque: University of New Mexico Press, 1953; France V. Scholes, "The Supply Service of the New Mexico Missions in the Seventeenth Century, I–III," *New Mexico Historical Review* (1930) 5: 93–115; 186–210; 386–404.
13. Inquisición 593, exp. 1, f. 60, Archivo General de la Nación, Mexico City.
14. John L. Kessell and Rick Hendricks, eds., *By Force of Arms: The Journals of Don Diego de Vargas, 1691–1693* (Albuquerque: University of New Mexico Press, 1992) and *Remote Beyond Compare: Letters of Don Diego de Vargas to His Family from New Spain and New Mexico, 1675–1706* (Albuquerque: University of New Mexico Press, 1989).
15. Scholes, "Supply Service," 1930; David H. Snow, "Purchased in Chihuahua for Feasts," *El Camino Real de Tierra Adentro*, comp. by Gabrielle G. Palmer, Cultural Resources Series, no. 11 (Santa Fe: U.S. Bureau of Land Management, 1993), pp. 133–46.
16. As quoted in Coe and Coe, *True History*, p. 181.
17. As quoted in Coe and Coe, *True History*, p. 159.
18. Antonio Colmenero de Ledesma, *Chocolata inda opusculum* (Nuremberg: Wolfgang Enderi, 1644).
19. Samuel Sewall, *The Diary of Samuel Sewall* (New York: Farrar, Straus & Giroux, 1973), p. 380.
20. Fanny Calderón de la Barca, *Life in Mexico: The Letters of Fanny Calderón de la Barca*, ed. and annotated by Howard T. and Marion Hall Fisher (New York: Doubleday, 1966), pp. 578–80.

21. The oral tradition is supported by the dictionaries of the Real Academia de la Lengua (Royal Academy of Language) of Madrid, which has attributed the mancerina to the viceroy since the seventeenth century; de la Mota, *El libro*, pp. 175–77. See also Coe and Coe, *True History*, pp. 137, 161. Other scholars insist that the form has either a Chinese or French origin; for recent expressions of these views, see Hector Rivero Borrell M., et al., *The Grandeur of Viceregal Mexico: Treasures from the Museo Franz Mayer* (Houston and México: Museum of Fine Arts and Museo Franz Mayer, 2002), pp. 29, 204, 280.
22. For information on the monastic orders and the missionary effort in Mexico, see Robert Ricard, *The Spiritual Conquest of Mexico: An Essay on the Apostolate and the Evangelizing Methods of the Mendicant Orders in New Spain, 1523–1572* (Berkeley: University of California Press, 1966). See also Samuel Y. Edgerton, *Theaters of Conversion: Religious Architecture and Indian Artisans in Colonial Mexico* (Albuquerque: University of New Mexico Press, 2001); and John McAndrew, *The Open-Air Churches of Sixteenth-Century Mexico: Atrios, Posas, Open Chapels and Other Studies* (Cambridge, MA: Harvard University Press, 1965).
23. Stoopen, "Edificar una confluencia," pp. 20–29. See also George Kubler, *Mexican Architecture of the Sixteenth Century*, 2 vols. (New Haven: Yale University Press, 1948).
24. Teresa Castelló Yturbide and Marita Josefa Martínez del Río de Redo, *Delicias de antaño: Historia y recetas de los conventos mexicanos* (México: Bancomer, 2000); María Cristina Suárez y Farias, "Edificar identidades: De ámbitos y sabores virreinales," *Artes de Mexico* 36 (1997):30–49.
25. Castelló Yturbide and del Río de Redo, *Delicias de antaño*, p. 48.
26. Although often cited as a Mexican colonial proverb, this ditty is sometimes credited to the Spaniard, Marco Antonio Orellana, a native of Valencia. See Coe & Coe, *True History*, p. 210.
27. Castelló Yturbide and del Río de Redo, *Delicias de antaño*, p. 53.
28. For more information on the *casta* paintings, see Ilona Katzew, *New World Orders: Casta Painting and Colonial Latin America* (New York: The Americas Society, 1996); and María Concepción García Sáiz, *Las castas mexicanas: Un género pictórico americano* (Milan: Olivetti, 1989).
29. Manuel Toussaint as quoted by Stoopen, "Edificar una confluencia," p. 24.
30. Letter written by the procurer of the city of Puebla, Gonzalo Díez de Vargas, to the king, as quoted by Manuel Romero de Terreros, *Artes industriales en la Nueva España* (México: Librería de Pedro Robredo, 1923), pp. 175—76; my translation.
31. Fray Juan Villa Sánchez, *Puebla sagrada y profana, informe dado a su ilustre Ayntamiento el año de 1746* (Puebla, 1746), as quoted by Romero de Terreros, *Artes industriales*, p. 176; my translation.
32. The portrait is reproduced in Manuel Toussaint, *Colonial Art in Mexico*, trans. And ed. by Elizabeth Wilder Weismann (Austin: University of Texas Press, 1967), fig. 231. For examples in casta paintings, see Katzew, *New World Orders*, pl. 23; p. 61, fig. 1; p. 62, fig. 3.
33. Fray Agustín de Vetancurt, *Teatro mexicano: Descripción breve de los sucessos [sic] exemplares de la Nueva-España en el nuevo mundo occidental de Las Indias*, vol. 2, *De los sucesos militares de las armas: Tratado de la ciudad de México; Tratado de la ciudad de Puebla* (Madrid: Colección Chimalistac, 1960), p. 305; my translation.
34. Fray Juan Villa Sánchez, *Puebla sagrada y profana*, as quoted in Edwin Atlee Barber, *The Majolica of Mexico*, Art Handbook of the Pennsylvania Museum and School of Industrial Art (Philadelphia: Pennsylvania Museum and School of Industrial Art, 1908), p. 17.
35. Donna Pierce and Cordelia T. Snow, "'A Harp for Playing': Domestic Goods Transported over the Camino Real," *El Camino Real de Tierra Adentro*, comp. by Gabrielle G. Palmer and Stephen L. Fosberg, Cultural Resource Series, no. 13 (Santa

Fe: U.S. Bureau of Land Management, 1999) 2:71–86. See also Cordelia Thomas Snow, "A Brief History of the Palace of the Governors and a Preliminary Report on the 1974 Excavation," *El Palacio* 80 (3) (October 1974):1–22; Florence Hawley Ellis, *San Gabriel del Yunque: Window on the Prespanish Indian World* (Santa Fe: Sunstone Press, 1988) and *When Cultures Meet: Remembering San Gabriel del Yunque Oweenge* (Santa Fe: Sunstone Press, 1970). Although little has been published on ceramics from colonial sites, personal communication with archaeologists as well as studies of unpublished field notes and public and private collections of excavated artifacts by the author has confirmed this information.

36. Scholes, "Supply Service."
37. Unpublished documents in the Spanish Archives of New Mexico (SANM), New Mexico State Records Center and Archives, Santa Fe, SANM I:489 (Mendizábal, 1662); SANM I:341, 342 (García, 1747); SANM I:968 (Quintana, 1749); SANM I:1055 (Montes Vigil, 1762); SANM II:105 (Luján, 1762); SANM I:793 (Rivera, 1770); SANM I:1060 (Vigil, 1780); and SANM I:280 (Fernández, 1784).
38. For information on Hispanic potters in the nineteenth century, see Charles M. Carrillo, *Hispanic New Mexican Pottery: Evidence of Craft Specialization, 1790–1890* (Albuquerque: LPD Press, 1997).

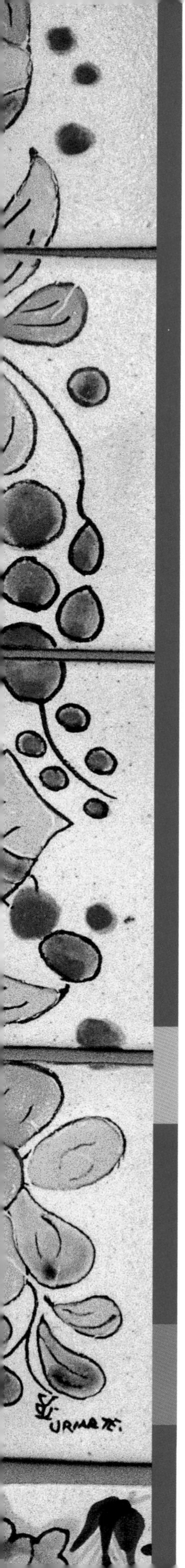

Detail, Fig. 12.28

12

The Revival of Puebla Mayólica in the Twentieth Century

BARBARA MAULDIN

DURING THE EARLY nineteenth century, many changes took place in the political and economic circumstances of Spain and Mexico, with dramatic effects on mayólica production in Puebla. The first of these occurred in 1812, when a new Spanish constitution led to the eradication of the pottery guilds and revoked the ordinances of the ceramic industry. Three years later, in 1815, another decree terminated the Manila galleons, ending the transportation of Chinese porcelain through Mexico. Meanwhile, an independence movement was taking place in Mexico that culminated in a final break from Spain, in 1821.[1]

In the wake of these changes, many of the mayólica workshops in Puebla closed or were sold to ceramists willing to carry on the colonial tradition under the new political regime. With no ordinances in place, the shops were freer to experiment with different styles of decoration and color combinations.[2] Some painters covered the surface of vessels with loosely rendered floral motifs, expressing a folk aesthetic that was breaking away from the more conservative European and Chinese models. This style often featured red, green, and white (the colors of the Mexican flag), along with accents of yellow, blue, and black, a lively palette that fit the mood of the Mexican people (fig. 12.1).

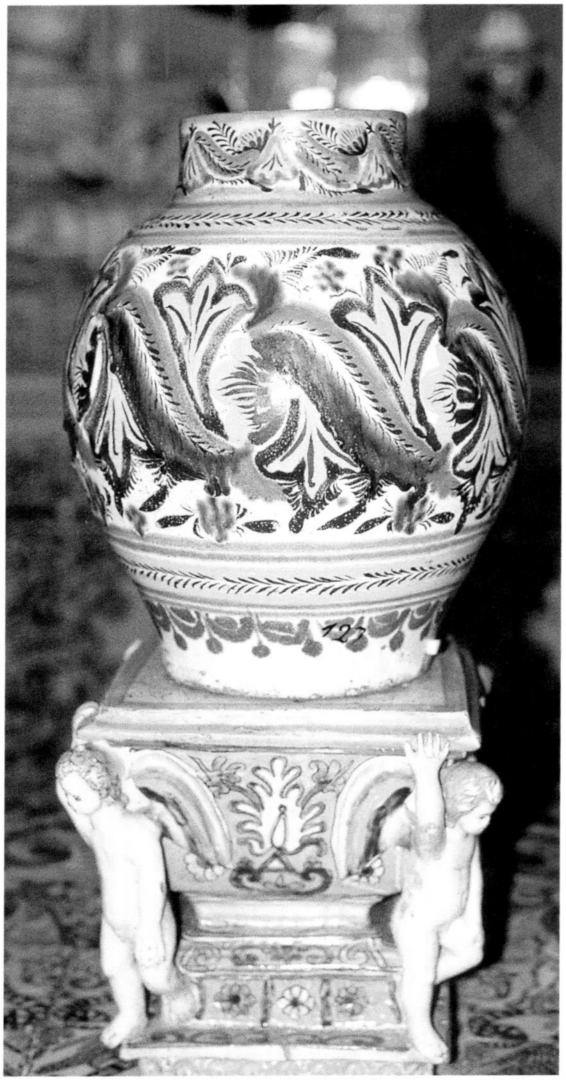

12.1 Jar / *Orza*
Anonymous Puebla workshop, mid-19th century
Museo José Luis Bello y González, Puebla
Photo by Barbara Mauldin

As the nineteenth century progressed, Mexico's political leaders developed a strong resentment against European institutions still operating within the country. This included the Catholic Church, and as part of the Reform Laws, all of the convents were closed. Property holdings and bank accounts of wealthy *criollo* citizens were broken up, and a move toward a new social order came into play.[3] The traditional buyers of the fine pottery and tiles produced by Puebla workshops were disappearing.

Only the more common wares, *loza común,* continued to find a place within the kitchens and dining rooms of the Mexican middle class.[4] Small, footed bowls with patterns on the exterior were still used for drinking *atole* (corn gruel), foamy chocolate, and other hot beverages. Larger bowls of this type were used for serving preserves and homemade candies, such as *cocadas.*[5] Flared bowls, called *platos,* with decoration on the interior, were used for eating such foods as chicken stew and turkey *mole* with rice (fig. 12.2).[6] Patterns and colors used to decorate loza común tended to be simple and loosely painted.

The Survival of Puebla Mayólica

By the end of the nineteenth century, the once-thriving ceramic industry in Puebla had

12.2 Common Ware / *Loza común*
Uriarte Talavera, Puebla, early 20th century
Collection of Uriarte Talavera
Photo by Carlos Varillas

almost collapsed, with only a handful of workshops in operation. One of these was owned by Dimas Uriarte, whose father, Ygnacio Uriarte, had begun the business in 1824, under the name of Fábrica de Loza de Talavera.[7] He was obviously making a reference to the famous mayólica ware from Talavera, Spain, but by the early twentieth century, the term *talavera* had become synonymous with all tin-glazed earthenware being made in Puebla.[8] Other notable shops producing Puebla talavera at this time included La Concepción, run by José Luis Guevara, Fábrica de Loza Blanca del País, owned by Antonio Espinosa and Martínez y Cía., operated by J. Miguel Martínez. As in the colonial era, all of these workshops were still located in the western quadrant of the old part of the city.[9]

In 1897, a Spanish artist named Enrique Ventosa arrived in Puebla and soon became very interested in tin-glazed earthenware. He made friends with a prominent art collector, José Mariano Bello y Acedo, who, along with his father, José Luis Bello y González, was in the process of assembling a large collection of Puebla mayólica. Ventosa studied the colonial examples and decided to try and help bring this important Puebla tradition back to life. He encouraged the talavera workshops to improve the quality of their techniques and reach out to new markets. Ventosa advised them to think of their painted ceramics as artwork, and he recommended they revive some of the historic styles, as well as introduce

12.3 Tile Panel / *Tablero de azulejos*
Enrique Ventosa and Uriarte Talavera, Puebla, 1919
Collection of Uriarte Talavera
Photo by Barbara Mauldin, 2001

modernist aesthetics.[10] This led to the creation of painted sculpture that could serve as decorative elements in hotels, offices, and wealthy homes.

In 1910, Dimas Uriarte brought electricity to his building, and with this came more efficient ways of producing ceramics. This workshop soon became the largest and best known in Puebla.[11] Enrique Ventosa began to design and paint some of Uriarte Talavera's pieces, including a large, tiled *tablero* that was installed on an upper wall in the courtyard of their building, in 1919 (fig. 12.3).[12] This composition featured peacocks, combined with colonial-style blue-on-white jars. In the 1920s, he collaborated with Isauro Uriarte, son of Dimas, who took over the business in 1918. Together they produced a series of vessels decorated with various types of patterns, including colonial Puebla, Spanish Mudéjar, Italian Renaissance, art nouveau, and even Mexican Precolumbian (figs. 12.4–12.6).[13]

In the meantime, Ventosa also worked in the shop owned by Antonio Espinosa. Like Uriarte, the Espinosa family had run their business since the early part of the

12.4 Plate decorated in Italian Renaissance style
Enrique Ventosa and Isauro Uriarte, Puebla, 1920s
Collection of Uriarte Talavera
Photo by Carlos Varillas, 2002

12.5 Plate decorated in *Art Nouveau* style
Enrique Ventosa and Isauro Uriarte,
Puebla, 1920s
Hispanic Society of America, New York

nineteenth century.[14] In 1895, two relatives, Felipe and Pedro Padierna Vallejo, began helping Espinosa, and they took over the workshop when he died, in 1917. Soon after that, the brothers oversaw the production of twenty-two oversize jars that were formed in a mold (fig. 12.7). Unfortunately, over half of the jars broke in the firing, but the remaining group was photographed in the courtyard of the shop, with the workers sitting in the foreground (fig. 12.8). Several of these *tibores* eventually went to Mexico City, where they were used as decorative elements in the National Palace, Chapúltepec Castle, and federal office buildings.[15] At least one also made its way to Los Angeles, California, where it was shown in a 1922 exhibition of Mexican popular art.[16]

Another shop that Ventosa worked closely with was Martínez y Cía. He was joined there by the Spanish artist Pedro Sánchez, who moved to Puebla in the early 1900s. With their help, the Martínez workshop came to specialize in tile suites that portrayed different types of subject matter, such as the Spanish Don Quixote and

12.6 Jar decorated in Mexican Precolumbian style
Enrique Ventosa and Isauro Uriarte, Puebla, 1920s
Collection of Uriarte Talavera
Photo by Carlos Varillas, 2002

12.7 Mold for creating large jars
Puebla, ca. 1917
Collection of José Miguel Padierna
Photo by Carlos Varillas, 2002

12.8 Historic photo showing the courtyard of Padierna workshop, with workers sitting in front of large jars / Puebla, 1917–1918
Collection of José Miguel Padierna
Photographer unknown, copy photo by Carlos Varillas, 2002

12.9 Tile panel with scene of Mexican woman holding tray
Pedro Sánchez, Puebla, 1926
Museo de Artesanías del Estado de Puebla, Puebla
Photo by Carlos Varillas, 2002

Mexican genre scenes (fig. 12.9).[17] Miguel Martínez also began decorating large plates with motifs taken from a range of stylistic traditions. In one example, he combined Renaissance floral motifs and Mexican Precolumbian stepped frets to form the border around a Chinese scene taken from late-nineteenth century English willow ware (fig. 12.10).[18]

12.10 Platter decorated with Renaissance, Mexican Precolumbian, and Oriental willow ware motifs
Miguel Martínez, Puebla, ca. 1920
San Antonio Museum of Art, San Antonio

The Revival of the Industry

The Mexican Revolution (1910–20) weakened the economy of the country, and the smaller mayólica shops in Puebla were forced to close, leaving the four larger ones mentioned above to carry on the work. Fortunately, in the aftermath of the war, there was a large demand for ceramic tiles to decorate the buildings being constructed to replace those damaged or destroyed during the war (fig. 12.11).[19] This use of tiles was part of a national aesthetic that developed in the post-revolutionary era, when artists and intellectuals began to view folk art as an important aspect of Mexican identity; the colorful talavera from Puebla fit perfectly in this scheme.[20]

This growing appreciation prompted city officials in Puebla to renovate the former Convent of Santa Rosa and turn it into the Museo de Cerámica, which opened in 1926 (fig. 12.12). Four of the most prominent ceramic painters, Enrique Ventosa, Isauro Uriarte, Miguel Martínez, and Pedro Sánchez, each created tile suites for the museum (fig.12.13; see fig. 12.9). These were installed in a room next to the famous convent kitchen, with its beautiful, tile-covered walls, dating to the late seventeenth and early eighteenth centuries (see fig. 9.9).[21]

By the 1920s, American tourists and collectors were also becoming aware of the colorful pottery and tiles being produced in Puebla. One of these was Frances Flynn Paine, who was born in Texas but spent many of her childhood years in Mexico, where she came to love handmade folk arts. In the mid-1920s, Paine began collecting pieces to be shown and sold at a special exhibit of Mexican folk art at the New York Art Center. Among the work she brought to the 1928 show was mayólica from contemporary shops in Puebla.

Abby Aldrich Rockefeller saw the exhibit and purchased a number of ceramic vessels and tile groups, which she used to decorate one of the Rockefeller houses on their Pocantico Hills estate, in upstate New York. She and her husband, John D. Rockefeller, Jr., continued to collect Puebla talavera over the next several years.[22]

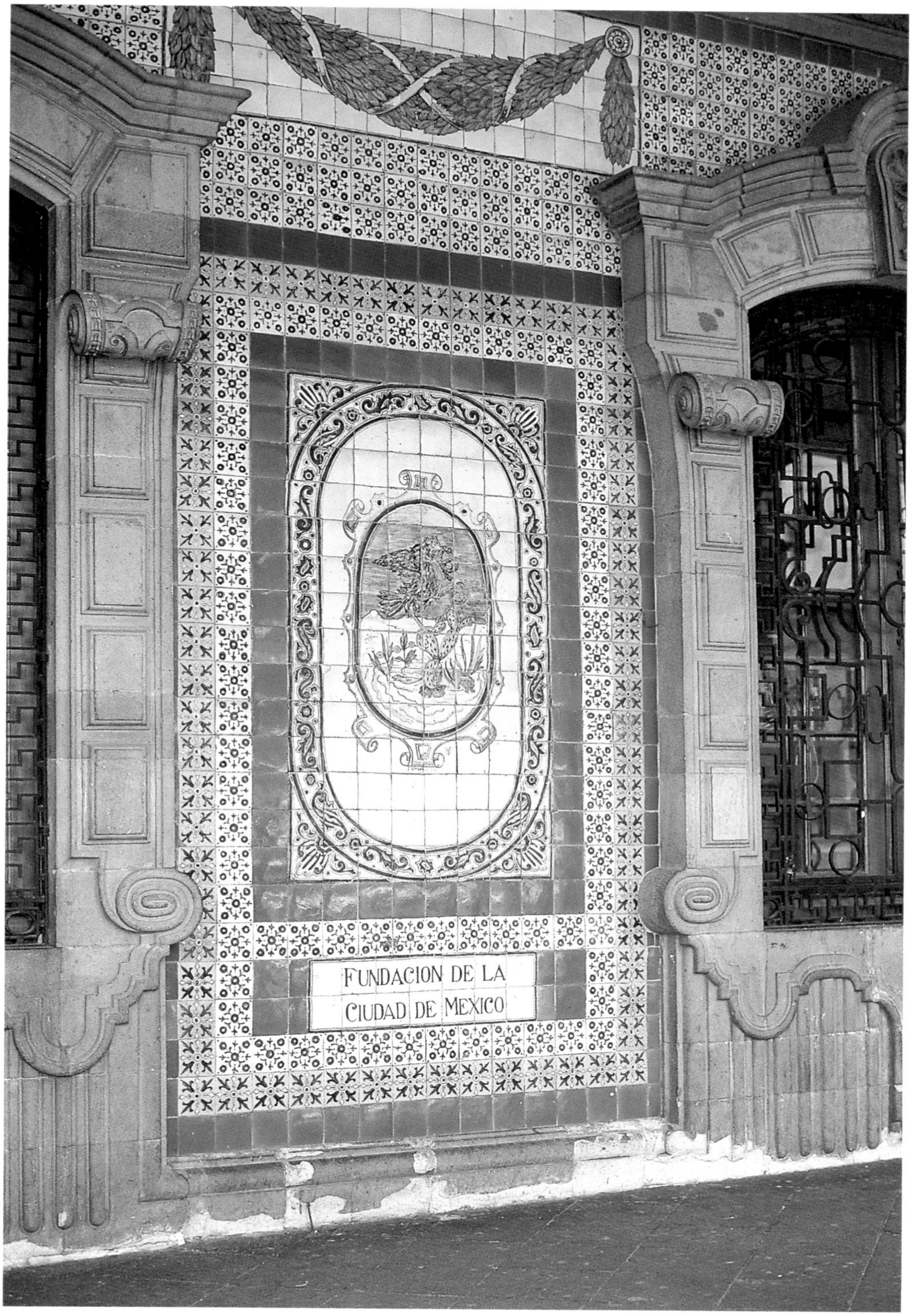

12.11 Tile panel with scene commemorating the founding of Mexico City
Uriarte Talavera, Puebla, ca. 1925
Located on the façade of City Hall, Mexico City
Photo by Barbara Mauldin, 2001

12.12 Sign commemorating the opening of the Museo de Cerámica in Puebla, 1926
Museo de Artesanías del Estado de Puebla, Puebla
Photo by Barbara Mauldin, 2001

In the meantime, prominent citizens of San Antonio, Texas, had begun using Puebla tiles to decorate their homes. One of these was Dr. Urrutia, who had been Porfirio Díaz's personal physician during the time he served as president of Mexico. After Díaz was forced to leave office, in 1911, Dr. Urrutia came to the United States and settled in San Antonio. He passed the medical exams and within a few years had successfully established himself within the community. In the 1920s, he built a home on a large estate north of San Antonio, called *Mira Flores*, and he commissioned Uriarte Talavera to produce a series of tile panels that were used to decorate the enormous entrance gate.[23]

In the late 1920s, Marion Koogler McNay, an oil heiress in San Antonio, was designing a home that was to be built at the north end of town. She loved ceramic tiles and worked closely with her architect to select pieces to use in various parts of the house.[24] One of the large tile suites installed on the wall of her courtyard was commissioned from Uriarte Talavera and closely followed the image painted by Enrique Ventosa on the large

12.13 Tile panel with floral decoration
Miguel Martínez, Puebla, 1926
Museo de Artesanías del Estado de Puebla, Puebla
Photo by Carlos Varillas, 2002

tablero in the Uriarte workshop in Puebla. Another tile panel in her home, from Martínez y Cía., portrays a scene from *Don Quixote*, painted by Pedro Sánchez (fig. 12.14).[25]

With the closing of the Martínez y Cía. workshop, in 1933, and the death of Enrique Ventosa, in 1935, Puebla lost two important forces in the mayólica movement.[26] However, the revival that had been set in motion continued to gain momentum, and several new workshops opened in the late 1930s. One of these was started by Hemeregildo Rugerio, who had been a potter in the Casa Padierna shop. His son Felipe had grown up in the workshop and was even included in the famous 1919 photograph, where he was seated in front of his father, wearing a white sailor's suit (see fig. 12.8). Together, Hemeregildo and Felipe knew all of the steps involved in producing talavera, and with the growing market, they decided to open their own shop in 1938, under the name Casa Rugerio.[27]

About the same time, another workshop was opened by

12.14 Tile panel with scene of *Don Quixote*
Pedro Sánchez, Puebla, late 1920s
Marion Koogler McNay Art Museum, San Antonio
Photo by Barbara Mauldin, 2001

12.15 Tile panels with geometric motifs installed on wall and planter
Uriarte Talavera, Puebla, ca. 1940
Collection of Uriarte Talavera
Photo by Barbara Mauldin, 2001

Concepción, Margarita, Ramona, and Liborio Guevara. Their family had run a mayólica shop in the eighteenth century, and in the 1930s, their father, Vicente Guevara, discovered some old family papers that contained recipes for mixing glazes and pigments. He experimented with these and began making talavera as a hobby. Soon his children were learning the techniques from him and producing their own pieces. In 1937, they decided to open a shop, called La Trinidad, and sell their work commercially. The three sisters had studied art at the Academy of San Carlos, in Mexico City, and were all very good painters. Their brother, Liborio, prepared the clay, formed the pottery and tiles, and oversaw the firing. Besides painting the ceramics, Concepción (Conchita) and Margarita ran the store, taking commissions and doing all of the marketing. La Trinidad soon gained a reputation for producing beautiful work.[28]

12.16 Tiles with Mexican genre scenes
Uriarte Talavera, Puebla, ca. 1930
Collection of Donna McMenamin, Tucson
Photo by Tim Fuller, 2002

12.17 Plate decorated with *mudéjar*-style patterns
Uriarte Talavera, Puebla, ca. 1940
Collection of Uriarte Talavera
Photo by Carlos Varillas, 2002

In 1938, Florentino Aguilar decided to open a mayólica workshop and employ his sons to carry out the work. One of them had worked in the Casa Padierno, and his daughter-in-law had worked for Uriarte Talavera, so they pooled their knowledge and were able to train the others in the various steps involved in the ceramic production. Over time, they perfected the process, and one of the sons, Agustín, became particularly skilled at painting. By 1950, they were in full operation in their workshop, Cerámica Artística de Puebla.[29]

Two other local residents, Pedro Torreblanca and his son-in-law Pedro Rodríguez, had never worked in the mayólica business, but in 1935 they decided to try their hand at this traditional Puebla craft. Without anyone to teach them the secrets of mixing the pigments and glazes or the other steps involved in the process, it took them many years to finally make pieces they could sell. Once they were producing mayólica for the commercial market, they called their workshop Fábrica Casa la Paz.[30]

The city of Puebla was growing in size and closing in around the section of town that had been the potters' quarters during the colonial era. Two of the oldest workshops, Uriarte Talavera and La Concepción, remained in their original buildings. However, some of the newer shops, such as La Trinidad and Casa Rugerio, set up their operations on the north end of town. Casa Padierna moved from the original building that had been used by Espinosa to a large tract of land farther north of the old city, where they found a good source of clay. The

12.18 Plate decorated with Chinese-style patterns
Uriarte Talavera, Puebla, ca. 1940
Collection of Uriarte Talavera
Photo by Carlos Varillas, 2002

Aguilars, with Cerámica Artística de Puebla, established their workshop on another tract of land near Casa Padierna, while Pedro Torreblanca and his son-in-law opened their Casa la Paz shop south of the city.[31]

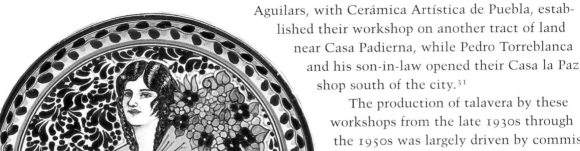

12.19 Plate decorated with Mexican genre scenes against colonial Puebla-style blue-on-white pattern Uriarte Talavera, Puebla, ca. 1940 Collection of Uriarte Talavera Photo by Carlos Varillas, 2002

The production of talavera by these workshops from the late 1930s through the 1950s was largely driven by commissions from consumers in Mexico and the United States. Tiles were an important part of this market, designed to be used in pictorial suites and as geometric elements combined into larger patterns (fig. 12.15). Mexican genre scenes painted on individual tiles also became popular during this period (fig. 12.16). Large and small jars continued to be in demand, along with new forms, such as flower pots. Large plates painted with patterns or pictorial scenes also maintained a prominent position in the production, primarily for use as wall ornaments (figs. 12.17–19). As in the early twentieth century, the patterns and images used on the various forms combined different artistic traditions: Mudéjar, Chinese, Italian Renaissance, French, and Mexican.

Puebla Mayólica after World War II

The demand for Puebla mayólica continued to grow during the second half of the twentieth century, as did the number of workshops producing these ceramics. One of the new shops was opened by César Torres Ramírez, whose grandfather, Bernardo Torres, had worked in a mayólica workshop in the nineteenth century and had written down instructions for carrying out all of the steps involved in making the pottery. César's father, Heliocloro, discovered these papers in 1963, and he and his son decided to try to produce some talavera themselves. It took them awhile to acquire all of the necessary materials, but they finally set up their workshop on the south side of the city. They experimented for two years before they were successful in making a decent piece, and three years later, in 1968, they started selling their work.[32]

Many of the other new businesses were opened by people who had been employed in mayólica workshops in Puebla and had learned enough of the process to branch out on their own. One of these was Pedro Tecayehuatl López, who had worked in the Aguilars' workshop. In the early 1970s, he taught his son, also named Pedro, what he knew, and together they experimented with the rest of the process to be able

12.20 José Miguel Padierna, Puebla
Photo by Carlos Varillas, 2002

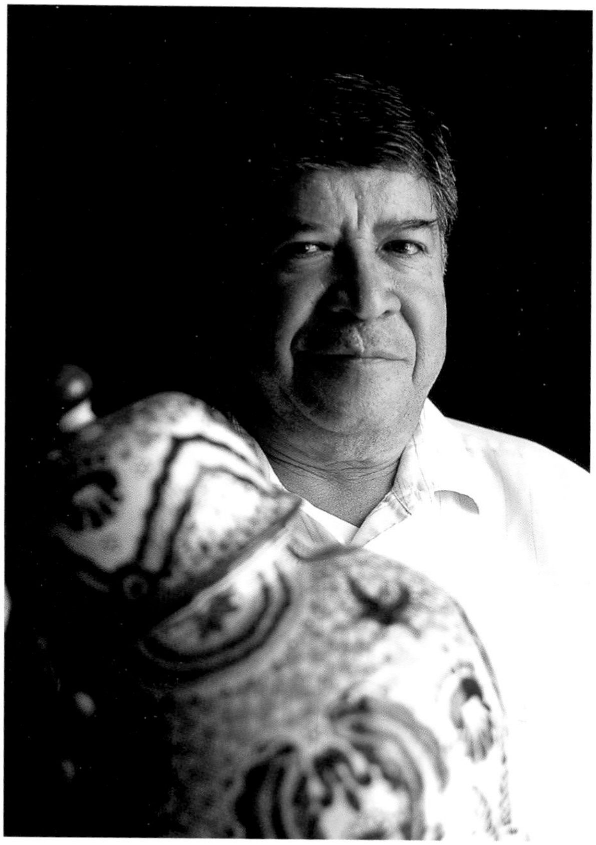

to successfully produce salable wares. They established their workshop near the Cerámica Artística de Puebla, on the north side of town, where it became known as Pedro Tecayehuatl.[33]

In the late 1970s, Cayetano Corona and his uncle Aurelio opened a workshop in San Pablo del Monte, a small town located north of Puebla, just over the border in the state of Tlaxcala. Cayetano had been throwing pots for Uriarte for about five years, and it took some time for him and Aurelio to determine the rest of the process. They called their shop La Corona, and as their business grew, many other members of their family got involved in the production. Over time, some of the family members and others who worked in the shop branched off and started producing mayólica out of their homes, in San Pablo.[34]

Due to deaths and illness in the family, Casa Rugerio closed in 1994, but all of the other talavera shops mentioned above have continued to operate.[35] Uriarte Talavera became a corporation in the mid-1990s, with Isauro Uriarte's son, also named Isauro, continuing to consult on the operation of the business. [36] The other workshops have been handed down through the families, with the younger generation carrying on the tradition. La Concepción is now being run by Guillermo Guevara, and Casa Padierna has been taken over by José Miguel Padierna (fig. 12.20). The work in La Trinidad is being carried on by Jorge Guevara (fig. 12.21), and Cerámica Artística de Puebla is managed by Teresa and Ernesto Aguilar. Their cousins have branched

12.21 Jorge Guevara, Puebla
Photo by Barbara Mauldin, 2001

12.22
César Torres Ramírez,
Puebla
Photo by
Barbara Mauldin,
2001

off and started other workshops, called Cerámica Artística Aguilar and Arte Cerámica. Casa la Paz is being run by Salvador Rodríguez, and Pedro Tecayehuatl is carrying on the shop he started with his father. César Torres Ramírez is also now running his workshop by himself, with the help of relatives (fig. 12.22). La Corona has been taken over by Israel Corona.[37]

During the last quarter of the twentieth century, more and more workshops continued to open on the outskirts of Puebla and in the neighboring towns of San Pablo, Amazoc, Tecali, and Cholula; they produce a wide range of work, of varying quality and price.[38] As in the past, many of them were started by people who had been associated with another shop and had learned enough techniques to branch off on their own. Other businesses were initiated by people with no experience in making mayólica, and who had to go through the difficult process of experimentation to learn the secrets of producing the tin-glazed ceramics.

Some of the new shops have been opened by women, such as that of María de los Ángeles Camacho Vaca. She is a medical doctor

12.23
Angélica Moreno
Rodríguez,
Puebla
Photo by
Barbara Mauldin, 2001

who started making mayólica as a hobby and eventually decided to sell her work commercially. In 1995, she set up a workshop in the northern part of Puebla and enlisted her husband and children to help with the production. She named her workshop Celia, in memory of her mother.[39]

A young woman, Angélica Moreno, has also created a very successful mayólica workshop, near the neighboring town of Cholula (fig. 12.23). In the late 1980s, Angélica decided she wanted to learn how to produce talavera, and she worked briefly for one of the shops in Puebla. After leaving there, she continued to experiment with the process and began building a small workshop on some property she owned near Cholula. She opened her business, called Talavera de la Reina, in 1990, and two years later she sold her first piece of pottery. By 1997, Angélica's business had grown enough that she could afford to construct the rest of the buildings for her work areas and showroom. She employed around twenty-five workers, and a younger cousin, Graciela, became the manager of staff and production. Angélica now handles

12.24 Jar / *Tibor*
Taller Talavera de la Reyna, Puebla
Photo by Barbara Mauldin, 2001

12.25 Table setting (*vajilla*) decorated with 19th-century Puebla-style pattern
Jorge Guevara, La Trinidad, Puebla, 2002
Collection of the International Folk Art Foundation
Museum of International Folk Art, (Museum of New Mexico), Santa Fe
Photo by Paul Smutko

12.26 Jar decorated with early 20th-century Puebla-style pattern
Fermin Contreras, 2000
Gift of Tom and Judy Dillenberg
Museum of International Folk Art, (Museum of New Mexico), Santa Fe
Photo by Paul Smutko

most of the marketing and sales, as well as developing new forms and patterns. Following a program and exhibition initiated by the art department of the University of the Americas, in Cholula, Angélica began inviting contemporary artists to paint their designs on the workshop's bisqueware and then glazing and firing them in the traditional mayólica technique (fig. 12.24).[40] As with Ventosa's art nouveau patterns in the early twentieth century, this was pushing the art form into the modernist ideas of the end of this century.

Over the past fifty years, demand for American-style dinnerware has grown among Mexicans as well as among buyers from the United States. The talavera workshops in Puebla have responded by producing place settings with different sized plates, bowls, cups, saucers, mugs, and serving dishes. The patterns used to decorate these pieces range from simple floral motifs, dating from the nineteenth century, to more complex combinations of designs, introduced in the first half of the twentieth century (fig. 12.25). Some of the workshops, such as Uriarte Talavera and

12.27 Jar decorated with serpentine handles and early 20th-century Puebla-style pattern
César Torres Ramírez, Puebla, 2000
Partial gift of the Clay Angel, Santa Fe
Collection of the International Folk Art Foundation
Museum of International Folk Art, (Museum of New Mexico), Santa Fe
Photo by Paul Smutko

12.28 Tile panel with 17th-century Puebla-style decorative scene
Magdalena Ayona Herrera, Uriarte Talavera, Puebla, 2001
Collection of the International Folk Art Foundation
Museum of International Folk Art, (Museum of New Mexico), Santa Fe
Photo by Paul Smutko

12.29 Basin (*lebrillo*) decorated with 18th-century Puebla-style pattern
Uriarte Talavera, Puebla, 2000
Collection of the International Folk Art Foundation
Museum of International Folk Art, (Museum of New Mexico), Santa Fe
Photo by Paul Smutko

12.30 Platter decorated with 17th-century Puebla-style pattern
Uriarte Talavera, Puebla, 2002
Collection of the International Folk Art Foundation
Museum of International Folk Art, (Museum of New Mexico), Santa Fe
Photo by Paul Smutko

12.31 Jar decorated with early 20th-century Puebla-style pattern
Uriarte Talavera, Puebla, 2001
Collection of the International Folk Art Foundation
Museum of International Folk Art, (Museum of New Mexico), Santa Fe
Photo by Paul Smutko

12.32 Basin (*lebrillo*) decorated with early 20th-century Puebla-style pattern
Talavera de la Reyna, Puebla, 2002
Collection of the International Folk Art Foundation
Museum of International Folk Art, (Museum of New Mexico), Santa Fe
Photo by Paul Smutko

Talavera de la Reina, have also developed lines that feature even more modern patterns.[41]

Other new forms, such as light switch plates, tissue-box covers, soap dishes, toothbrush holders, frames, clock faces, and wastepaper containers are also being made in many workshops. Alongside these objects, most of the shops continue to make decorative flowerpots, vases, and large jars (figs. 12.26, 12.27). Some tile suites are also still being produced (fig. 12.28), but most of the business in *azulejos* was lost to ceramic workshops in Dolores Hidalgo, Guanajuato, where machine-made tiles are sold at cheaper prices.[42]

Interestingly, the same workshops that are experimenting with contemporary patterns are also reviving some of the colonial forms. Uriarte Talavera, among others, has produced a series of collector's pieces such as *lebrillos, tibores, albarelos,* and *platos* directly copied from colonial examples (figs. 12.29, 12.30).[43] Uriarte and other workshops are also reviving some of the nineteenth and early twentieth-century Puebla styles (figs. 12.31–12.33).

12.33 Jar decorated with 19th-century Puebla-style pattern
Talavera de la Reyna, Puebla, 2002
Collection of the International Folk Art Foundation
Museum of International Folk Art, (Museum of New Mexico), Santa Fe
Photo by Paul Smutko

The Problem of Lead Glazes

Mexico has never enacted laws regarding the use of lead glazes on ceramics, but beginning in 1971, the United States Food and Drug Administration established safety standards to protect people from ingesting lead transferred into their food or drink from glazed pottery. The FDA began an inspection program for all dinnerware being commercially made in the United States, as well as that being brought into the country from foreign sources. In the mid-1980s, the percentage of lead allowed in the glaze was lowered even more, and since that time customs agents have become more stringent in testing ceramics for sale in the United States. If the pottery does not pass the tests, agents have been instructed to break it. To avoid this, some importers are having workshops paint the words "Not for Food Use" on the bottom of the pieces. However, dinnerware is in high demand, and if consumers cannot use the ceramics for food and drink, they may be unwilling to purchase them.[44]

As a result, several of the mayólica workshops in Puebla have been experimenting with new recipes for glazes and different firing techniques to reduce the lead content. To date, however, only a few shops have been successful in making this transition. The change is difficult, because the lead in the glaze is a key element in binding the pigments to the ceramics. The melted metal also creates a luster on the surface of the mayólica that reflects light in a beautiful way that is hard to duplicate with other materials.[45]

The Consejo Regulador de Talavera

With the large increase in the number of workshops producing mayólica, the inconsistencies in their training practices, and the push to change techniques to meet the United States standards, some of the Puebla shopowners became concerned that the integrity of talavera was being undermined. With the lack of a guild system and ordinances to insure the quality and authenticity of traditional mayólica, it was difficult for consumers to determine what they were actually buying.

In December 1998, some of the concerned parties formed an organization that came to be known as the Consejo Regulador de Talavera. The purpose was to establish quality control over the ceramics called talavera being made in the state of Puebla. They drew up a list of criteria to use in analyzing traditionally made mayólica, which would serve as the guide in granting certificates of authentication. Any workshop or individual artisan producing ceramics in the state of Puebla could apply and be reviewed by a committee of experts. If their work met the standards, they would be given the certificate and allowed to refer to their ceramics as talavera.

The organization proposed this certification system to the appropriate officials in the state and federal governments, and eventually the plan was approved and incorporated into regulatory ordinances. One of the ramifications of this development was that no mayólica workshop located outside of the state of Puebla, such as in Tlaxcala or Guanajuato, could use the term *talavera* in their name or in any reference to their product.

The first certificates of authentication were given out on 1 July 1999, to six of the Puebla workshops: Uriarte Talavera, Casa Padierna, La Concepción, La Trinidad, César Torres, and Talavera de la Reyna. By February of 2000, the number had increased to fourteen, and more workshops continue to apply. The office for the Consejo Regulador de Talavera is now located in the Museo de Artesanías del Estado de Puebla (the former Santa Rosa convent and Museo de la Cerámica), where they display talavera from the workshops that have been certified.[46] Federal enforcement of the ordinances has come into question, however, since the inauguration of a new Mexican president in the fall of 2000. Vicente Fox is a native of Guanajuato, and the mayólica workshop owners from that state have asked him to repeal the laws.[47]

The mayólica revival that began in Puebla a hundred years ago has been extremely successful; today there are over fifty workshops, large and small, actively involved in production. Much of this growth is due to the increasing number of buyers from the United States and other countries who appreciate the skill involved in creating the forms and artistic ability employed in decorating the pieces. For the most part, traditional mayólica techniques are still being used, although ceramists continue to experiment with new ways to satisfy the market. It will be exciting to follow the evolution of this Puebla art form as it moves into its fifth century of production.

Notes

1. Margaret Connors McQuade, *Talavera Poblana: Four Centuries of a Mexican Ceramic Tradition (*New York: The Americas Society, 1999), pp. 36, 47.
2. Ibid., pp. 47–48; Enrique A. Cervantes, *Loza blanca y azulejo de Puebla,* 2 vols. (México: Privately printed, 1939), 1:267, 290.
3. Michael C. Meyer and William L. Sherman, *The Course of Mexican History*, 5th ed. (New York: Oxford University Press, 1995), pp. 373–84; Josefina Muriel, *Conventos de Monjas en la Nueva Espana* (México: Editorial Santiago, 1946), pp. 507–17; Hugo Leicht, *Las Calles de Puebla Estudio Historia* (Puebla: Comisión Cultural del Gobierno del Estado de Puebla, 1967), pp. 426–27.
4. Edwin Atlee Barber, *The Catalog of Mexican Maiolica Belonging to Mrs. Robert W. de Forest* (New York: The Hispanic Society of America, 1911), p. 18; Patricia Eugenia Acuña, *Talavera de Puebla* (Puebla: Gobierno del Estado de Puebla, 1987), p. 16.
5. Daniel F. Rubin de la Borbolla, "Objects from Everyday Life," *in The Ephemeral and the Eternal of Mexican Folk Art*, 2 vols. (México: Fondo Editorial de la Plástica Mexicana, 1971), 1:126–27, pl. 60–63, p. 334 n.1.

6. Inteview with Gorky Gonzales, October 1999.
7. Interview with Isauro Uriarte, April 2001.
8. McQuade, *Talavera Poblana*, p. 15. Following the information provided by earlier historians, McQuade states that Dimas Uriarte founded the business in 1824. However, during my interview with Isauro Uriarte, in April 2001, he corrected that information and stated that it was begun and named by Ygnacio Uriarte in 1824 and later passed into the hands of his son, Dimas.
9. Donna McMenamin, *Popular Arts of Mexico 1850–1950* (Atglen, PA: Schiffer Publishing, 1996), pp. 119–121, 123.
10. Edwin Atlee Barber, *The Maiolica of Mexico* (Philadelphia: Pennsylvania Museum and School of Industrial Art, 1908), p. 33; McQuade, *Talavera Poblana*, pp.51, 55.
11. McQuade, *Talavera Poblana*, p. 55.
12. McMenamin, *Popular Arts of Mexico*, p. 125, fig. 49.
13. Interview with Isauro Uriarte, April 2001; Margaret Connors McQuade, "Talavera Poblana: The Renaissance of a Mexican Ceramic Tradition," *Antiques* 156 (1999):829–30.
14. Ibid., p. 828.
15. Interview with José Miguel Padierna, November 1999.
16. This photograph illustrated an essay by James Oles in *Casa Mañana: The Morrow Collection of Mexican Popular Arts*, ed. by Susan Danly (Albuquerque: University of New Mexico Press, 2002), p. 23. fig. 8.
17. Johanna Welty, "Talavera: An Overview of Viceregal Majolica," *Antiques West Newspaper* 12 (December 1992):18; McMenamin, *Popular Arts of Mexico*, p. 121; Cervantes, *Loza blanca*, 1:300–3.
18. Marion Oettinger, Jr., ed., *Folk Art of Spain and the Americas: El Alma del Pueblo* (New York: Abbeville Press, 1997), p. 155, pl. 73.
19. McQuade, *Talavera Poblana*, p. 830.
20. Victoria Novelo, ed., *Artesano, Artesanías y Arte Popular de México* (México: Consejo Nacional para la Cultura y las Artes, 1996), pp. 159–201.
21. McQuade, *Talavera Poblana*, p. 830.
22. Marion Oettinger, Jr., *Folk Treasures of Mexico: The Nelson A. Rockefeller Collection* (New York: Harry Abrams, 1990), pp. 38 and 102, plate 38; interview with Marion Oettinger, December 2000.
23. Interview with Marion Oettinger, December 2000. This tiled arch is now in the collection and on view at the San Antonio Museum of Art.
24. Interview with Heather Lammers, collections manager at the McNay Art Museum, January 2001. This home is now open to the public as the McNay Art Museum.
25. Personal examination of the tile suites and signatures of the artists, April 2000.
26. Cervantes, *Loza blanca*, 1:290, 300.
27. Interview with José Miguel Padierna, February 2001; he had spoken with Manuel Rugerio to confirm the facts.
28. Interview with Jorge Guevara, November 1999.
29. Interview with Teresa Aguilar, January 2001.
30. Interview with Salvador Rodríguez, January 2001.
31. Interviews with the office manager at Uriarte and Guillermo Guevara, February 1999; with José Miguel Padierna and Jorge Guevara, November 1999; and Teresa Aguilar and Salvador Rodríguez, January 2001.
32. Interview with César Torres Ramírez, November 1999.
33. Interview with Pedro Tecayehuatl, February 2001.
34. Interview with Israel Corona, November 1999.
35. Interview with José Miguel Padierna, Februray 2001.
36. Interview with Bibiana Yunes, director of sales at Uriarte, February 1999. In June 2001, the Uriarte corporation was sold to new owners, who began operating the business from San Antonio, Texas.

37. Interviews with Guillermo Guevara, February 1999; José Miguel Padierna and Jorge Guevara, November 1999. and Teresa Aguilar and Salvador Rodríguez, January 2001.
38. Interview with José Miguel Padierna, Februray 2001.
39. Interview with showroom manager of Celia, November 1999.
40. Interviews with Angélica Moreno, February and November 1999.
41. Fieldwork conducted in November 1994, November 1997, February 1999, and November 1999.
42. Ibid.
43. Fieldwork conducted in February and November 1999.
44. "Dinnerware—Safe or Toxic? *Consumer News* 7 (1977):2; Dale Blumenthal, "An Unwanted Souvenir: Lead in Ceramic Ware," *U.S. Food and Drug Administration Consumer Report* (12/1989–1/1990):1–4; interviews with Judy Espinar, a U.S. importer of Mexican ceramics and owner of the Clay Angel, Santa Fe, New Mexico, July 2000 and February 2001.
45. Interviews with Judy Espinar, July 2000 and February 2001.
46. Interview with José Miguel Padierna, director of Consejo Regulador de Talavera, Februray 2001.
47 Jorge Escalante, "Culpan a Fox por 'perder' talavera," *Mural* (16 May 2001):D-1.

Detail, Fig. 13.7

13

For Gorky González

The Mayólica of Guanajuato

PATRICIA FOURNIER

THE MAYÓLICA OF Guanajuato is best described in technical terms, because opposing opinions exist among local potters regarding glaze formulas.[1] To some it is the addition of tin oxide to the glaze that is characteristic, while to others it is the application of a single-color opaque glaze without regard to the ingredients. The methods of artistic elaboration and design and the technical processes utilized to create the objects have little bearing on its designation as mayólica.

Sources for a history of the mayólica of the present state of Guanajuato are found primarily in the census files of the late seventeenth and early eighteenth centuries, maintained in the National Archives, in Mexico City. They list *olleros*, who made smooth, polished terracotta pots and jars; *alfareros*, who manufactured lead-glazed ceramics; and *loceros*, who produced only white-enameled earthenware, or mayólica. The Guanajuato city census of 1791 records three alfareros (two from Spain and one indigenous), and the census of 1792 records a mestizo locero, Josef Albarado. Census data from Celaya and the Indian community of Acámbaro mention only olleros and alfareros. Unfortunately, we do not know if these potters were members of a guild or if they adhered to rules set down in ordinances such as those in force in Puebla and Mexico City since the seventeenth century. But the census data do provide conclusive evidence of the production of glazed ceramics in two towns, and glazed ceramics and mayólica in Guanajuato, starting at least in the last decade of the eighteenth century.

There is a popular belief that the tradition of polychrome mayólica in Guanajuato is due, in part, to Miguel Hidalgo y Costilla (hero of Mexico's independence movement) who, in the early 1800s, founded a pottery workshop in Dolores. According to the meager historical data available, Hidalgo was interested in experimenting with colored glazes and the creation of distinct forms on the potter's wheel and in wooden molds.[2] The Dolores workshop was equipped with vats to prepare the clay, a *padilla* kiln to prepare the glazes, a kiln for the first, or bisque, firing, and another for the final glaze firing, as well as storage areas. Apparently, Hidalgo's mayólica was distributed throughout Guanajuato, and it is said that its quality was not only comparable to the mayólica produced in Puebla, but even surpassed it. In reality, however, it is difficult to determine if the development of Guanjuato mayólica was due to the impact of Hidalgo's workshop or the result of the cumulative experience and contributions of numerous potters in the state.

What is clear, based on information from private and museum collec-

13.1 Pottery Sherds
Guanajuato,
19th century
Photo by
Patricia Fournier, 1994

13.2 Pottery Sherds
Guanajuato,
19th century
Photo by
Patricia Fournier, 1994

tions and limited archaeological data, is that Guanajuato became a potting center of importance, successfully establishing itself in the production of mayólica and other types of earthenware, perhaps in the final years of the eighteenth century and certainly throughout the nineteenth century (figs. 13.1, 13.2).[3]

The proliferation of mayólica in Guanajuato can be associated with the socioeconomic situation of the area. The local mining industry was flourishing, and the abundant exchange of metals raised the standard of living of the population. Workers and shareholders earned a lot and spent it lavishly, acquiring a wide variety of daily-use and luxury items. Merchants could barely keep up with the demand in a marketplace packed with avid consumers, hungry not only for local merchandise but for imported goods from Europe and the Far East as well. This commercial phenomenon, along with the fact that Guanajuato had ample sources of clay suitable for the manufacture of ceramics and abundant deposits of tin for glazes, probably promoted the surge in the manufacture of mayólica at the beginning of the nineteenth century.[4] The end result was the lucrative manufacture and sale of locally produced mayólica, which eliminated the need to rely on that made in Puebla and Mexico City, the most important production centers in the viceroyalty of New Spain since the end of the sixteenth century (see chapters 9 and 10).

In the nineteenth century, the mayólicas produced in Europe, Mexico, and Guatemala reflected their own regional stylistic contexts, as can be seen in archaeological collections and museums.[5] In Guanajuato, however, there was a move toward a fusion of multiple stylistic elements with roots in Europe, in China, and in the reworking of Italianate motifs. When compared with Puebla's designs, Guanajuato's are notably less elaborate in

13.3 Jar / *Orza*
Guanajuato, 1825–1900
Collection of the International Folk Art Foundation
Museum of International Folk Art
(Museum of New Mexico), Santa Fe
Photo by Paul Smutko

13.4 Plate / *Plato*
Guanajuato, 1825–1900
Collection of the International Folk Art Foundation
Museum of International Folk Art
(Museum of New Mexico), Santa Fe
Photo by Paul Smutko

their conception, with diminished attention to detailing and greater simplicity, but they exhibit a profusion of color: emerald green, orange, brown, burgundy, dark coffee, black, yellow, and blue. Blue was also employed by itself, when imitating the British flow-blue ceramics of the era.

The predominant patterns were wavy or straight bands, often concentric and alternating in distinct colors; chessboard designs and rectilinear geometric elements sometimes combined with dots; garlands, abstract petals, and leaves; and sparsely detailed small and large buds and flowers (fig. 13.3). In some cases, bright polychromes enlivened somber neoclassic elements, in a style reminiscent of the East India Company or heraldic porcelains produced in China (fig. 13.4). Some designs incorporated local personalities or popular themes, as can be seen in examples painted with images of Hidalgo or with Mexico's national emblem, an eagle with a serpent clenched in its beak, perched atop a prickly pear cactus. Animals such as rabbits, deer, cats, and birds were also popular ornamental subjects. Decorative elements appeared either exclusively on the rim and interior of plates, leaving ample areas unpainted, or, conversely, covered the better part of vessel surfaces.

The clay body of Guanajuato mayólica is compact and finely textured, with a pink or terracotta color, in contrast to that of Puebla, where the tonalities of the paste are usually light-colored, and the texture is grainier and less refined.[6] The majority of the hollowware was manufactured using a potter's wheel and included deep plates (see fig. 13.4), flat dishes, cups (*tazas*) with a lateral strap handle, globular bowls (*tazones*), mugs (*tarros*), spherical jugs (*jarros*), jars (*jarras*) with stubby necks and vertical strap handles (see fig. 13.3), pitchers (*cántaros*) with high cylindrical necks and round bodies, onion-shaped jars (*orzas*), high round-shouldered vases (*tibores*), barrels with lids, sugar bowls, pots (*ollas*), basins (*lebrillos*), cylindrical chamber pots with lateral handles, candleholders, flowerpots, apothecary jars, and miniatures. There were also oval and square platters, undoubtedly formed in molds.

Little is known of the traditional methods used in the production of mayólica in Guanajuato, although it is clear that the industry prospered and that sales were extensive in the northern areas of Mexico. Thousands of shards of Guanajuato mayólica have been found in archaeological excavations in León, Chihuahua, California, Arizona, and Texas. Findings in southern areas, such as Cuernavaca, Otumba, Mexico City, and the Tula region, however, have been sparse.[7]

In the nineteenth century, there were important mayólica factories in Guanajuato, in the districts of Mellado and San Luisito, where pieces of great beauty were produced and lavishly painted in vivid colors.[8] Some workshops remained active until the 1930s, when they began closing due to the lack of demand brought on by competitive glass and enameled metalware. It was not until the 1960s that new impetus was given to the manufacture of mayólica in Guanajuato.

13.5 Gorky González, owner, Alfarería Tradicional S.A., Guanajuato
Photo by Barbara Mauldin, 2001

The Traditional Pottery Workshop of Gorky González

The resurgence in the production of mayólica in Guanajuato is due to Gorky González, who rescued a forgotten tradition and brought it to a new level of interest and recognition, in the 1960s (fig. 13.5).

Gorky was born in Morelia, Michoacán, in 1939, and came to Guanajuato in his early childhood. His father, Rodolfo González, the celebrated sculptor, master of plastic arts and successful antique dealer, taught him to sculpt, smelt bronze, and appreciate historic ceramics. In 1963, Gorky set up a workshop in San Miguel de Allende, where, at the request of Jean Byron, an American painter living there, he began to delve into the use of molds to produce pottery on which she sketched designs. Later, he teamed up with Byron's husband, Dr. Fernández, to replicate vintage pieces of mayólica, while collaborating with Byron on terracotta creations such as stylized figures of women with a baby chick, doves, or roosters.

After moving back to Guanajuato, Gorky set up a ceramics workshop on Callejón del Búquero, near the university. Through his father's numerous contacts, an artisan was contracted to throw vessels, and it was through him that Gorky took a marked interest in the use of the potter's wheel, eventually achieving great expertise in shaping hollowware.

Gorky visited production centers in Dolores Hidalgo and Puebla, hoping to learn the fine points of colored glazes, but he found that artisans were very reluctant to share their knowledge with him. With the help of David Chowell, an assayer of metals and maker of ceramic crucibles, Gorky became familiar with the properties of the raw materials, and together they constructed an oven to test glaze colors based on formulas they found in books. Their inaugural efforts were unproductive. White glaze, produced with clay, silica, glass, tin, and lead oxide, was their first success, allowing them to reproduce beautiful mayólica vessels similar to those made in the mining district of Mellado, which in the 1960s were already considered collectors' items. The next triumph came with the achievement of glaze colors: blues, greens, and yellows.

At first, Gorky's plan was to manipulate the plasticity of clay and see what might be created, but gradually he began to interpret and master the numerous secrets of the art of mayólica production and to perfect various techniques. However, it turned out to be difficult to sell the pieces and, therefore, hard to maintain the workshop and pay the workers.

Fortunately, he received an important commission from Jorge Bellolli for sixty trumpet-shaped lamps for the restoration of the Marfil hacienda. This work, together with an exposition in Dolores Hidalgo, served to promote the workshop, and it began to capture attention and grow. Victor Manuel Villegas, a mayólica collector, made reference in his book on the handicrafts of Guanajuato, published in 1964, to the pioneering work of Gorky González, which was at that time just beginning to attain a certain measure of success.[9]

In this early period, Gorky exhibited works at the Institute of Technology in Monterrey, which were well received, and this was followed by the sale in Guanajuato and Mexico City of small objects with designs inspired by antique pieces. At an exhibit at the Museo de Arte Popular, he displayed several of the larger pieces that were not selling well, such as pots (ollas), the Chinese-influenced vases (tibores), and large deep dishes, as well as hanging plates for wall ecoration.

It was also at this time that Hisato Murayama, secretary to the cultural attaché of the Japanese embassy in Mexico City, with whom he had established a friendship, began urging him to expand his potential as a ceramic artist by studying in the Far East. Not without some difficulties, at the end of the 1960s, Gorky managed to obtain a two-year grant to study in Japan, under the direction of renowned masters such as Tsuji Seimei, Kei Fijiwara (a national living treasure), Kato Kobe, and Kioske Fujiwara. Under their tutelage, he learned traditional techniques associated with the production of high-fired ceramics and porcelain bodies, according to Japanese artistic standards. His work consisted of ceremonial tea vessels, flowerpots, and other ornate objects used since ancient times, and he received critical acclaim at exhibitions presented in Tokyo and Okayama, where he resided. It was in Japan that Gorky met Toshiko, whom he married and later brought to Mexico.

Once back in Guanajuato and in charge of his *Alfarería Tradicional* workshop, Gorky pursued his goal of reviving traditional mayólica (figs. 13.6, 13.7). His labors have continued and have gained him both national and international recognition. The shop has flourished, and its production has intensified. Gorky credits its success to the support that he has received and to the superb artisans of Guanajuato.

Gorky believes that the workshop is a team enterprise, not a factory, and that no single piece is exclusively the work of one individual. As a result, the potters sign no vessels; only the letters "A" and "T", the initials of the company, appear on the base.

The workshop uses black, yellow, red, and brown clays and limestone, extracted from the nearby Santa Rosa Mountains. These materials are pulverized and then placed in vats filled with water, to remove sand and organic matter. Later, they are mechanically mixed and placed

13.6 Flower Pot / *Macetón*
Alfarería Tradicional, S.A., Guanajuato
Photo by Paul Smutko, 2002

13.7 Show Room
Alfarería Tradicional, S.A.,
Guanajuato
Photo by
Feliza Medrano, 2001

in an electric press, to form cylinders of prepared paste. These are aged for one or two weeks before being used.

Only oval plates and square boxes are made in molds. All other vessels, regardless of size, are formed on a potter's wheel. Alfarería Traditional is one of the few mayólica manufacturers in Mexico that continues to use traditional throwing methods. In most workshops it is common to form all large pieces in molds.

Before 1986, Gorky used open updraft cylindrical kilns constructed of stone, with an arched opening for introducing the firewood; large ceramic fragments were used as a temporary cover. Sawdust was flung steadily into the firebox for seven hours, producing a very low flame that would not crack the ceramic vessels. After that, *pingüica* or live oak logs were added, first stacked horizontally and then positioned vertically, to allow the heat to reach all levels of the kiln. In total, the first firing lasted between twelve and fourteen hours, reaching between 650 and 700 degrees Celsius, and objects were judged to be ready by the color they acquired. The second firing lasted approximately ten hours, using firewood stacked end-on-end in the center of the firebox. In both firings, the kiln was allowed to cool for two to three hours before the vessels were removed, to avoid fractures. Today, Gorky uses gas-fired kilns; the maximum temperature is set at from 850 to 890 degrees Celsius, and digitized pyrometers control the firing process.

Fired pieces are submerged in metal vats containing the glaze solution—a mixture of silica, lead oxide, tin oxide, and water. A thick coat of glaze is needed to cover the reddish color of fired Guanajuato clays and, as a result, it may flake off in places following the second firing, an inevitable risk with the traditional techniques employed in the workshop. Once coated, vessels are left to dry before being decorated.

The workshop has a school for mayólica decorators. The training period lasts approximately one year, beginning with simple geometric motifs and continuing on to complex decorative essentials, as the artists attain the required dexterity. They use special brushes with high resin-content pine handles and horsehair or squirrel-tail bristles, affixed in such a way that, once dipped in glaze colors, the brush functions like a fountain pen.

The workshop does not use templates or stencils to mark out the design on vessel surfaces, although on certain pieces small dots or crosses are marked in pencil, to serve as reference points. This difficult, freehand application of colors made from metal oxides gives the quality and special appeal to Gorky's pieces (fig. 13.8).

Cockspurs, which tend to leave marks on vessel surfaces, are no longer used to separate pieces in the second firing. Instead, objects are set on special plaques in the kiln. The firing takes place at 970 degrees Celsius, to ensure, to the extent possible, that the glaze adheres to the vessels and that the toxic effect of the lead in the glaze is neutralized. Gorky considers it imperative to discover a glaze that would not contain lead oxide and that could still produce the same luster, thus making Guanajuato's mayólica acceptable for table use worldwide.

The vessels produced range from traditional pieces such as bowls (tazones), jars (jarros), plates, deep plates and platters, jars for preserves (*ollas conserveras*), vases (tibores), spice boxes, washbasins, chamber pots, and flowerpots, to objects derived from the mayólica of colonial Puebla, including religious images, candleholders, and boxes. There are also modern-day tableware pieces such as cups and saucers, sugar bowls, oil cruets, mugs (tarros), butter dishes, soup tureens, platters for roasts and other meats, vessels for cheese fondue, and teapots and coffeepots. Decorative pottery in a wide

13.8 Painting a plate
Alfarería Tradicional, S.A., Guanajuato
Photo by Patricia Fournier, 1994

13.9 Jar / *Orza*
Alfarería Tradicional, S.A., Guanajuato
Photo by Feliza Medrano, 2001

range of shapes and sizes includes flowerpots and large hanging platters, fine sculptures (such as Buddhist lions) with obvious oriental influence in their designs, umbrella stands, and lamp bases. In short, just about any type of ceramics imaginable.

The decorative schemes and colors of the nineteenth century, and even those of the colonial period, are evident in these works. Using cobalt blue, the artists recreate the Baroque designs produced in Puebla as well as Chinese designs with abundant foliage, flowers, graceful birds, and figures dressed in period costumes, appearing in successive paneled scenes. Rich polychrome pieces are painted in green, yellow, and orange, and sometimes with touches of blue. Copious garlands and delicate undulating geometric or rectilinear motifs often frame provincial scenes that recall vividly the mayólica of nineteenth-century Guanajuato. Some pieces display a faint blue or pale yellow background, reminiscent of old Puebla mayólica. Objects that attract the most attention are the beautifully shaped stark white or slightly cream-toned vessels on which the raising and lowering of artistic detailing, such as festooned rims, channel molding, and appliqués, create areas of light and dark (fig. 13.9).

Works produced in the shop of Gorky González have received broad acclaim in exhibitions in Mexico, Canada, the United States, Spain, and France. Moreover, they have received awards in Mexico and the United States.

The challenge taken up by Gorky and the staff of the Alfarería Tradicional to achieve perfect technical expertise in the recreation of the stylistic somberness, the bountiful chromatic richness, and the characteristic forms of nineteenth-century Guanajuato mayólica has been met. Through their persistence, vitality, and inspiration, they have given new life to the art and artistry of the mayólica of Guanajuato.

Capelo's Workshop

In the workshop of architect and ceramist Javier de Jesús Hernández, known as "Capelo," a remarkable display of creativity is on the rise. It is rooted in the artistic inheritance of traditional mayólica but has its own special aspects, attested to by the unique works produced under the stimulus of a strong visual aesthetic.

Hernández was born in León, in 1951, and has lived in the city of Guanajuato since he was seven years old. In 1979, after having familiarized himself thoroughly with the distinctive components of mayólica production, he established the Taller de Alfarería Mayólica de Guanajuato, also known as "Capelo" (fig. 13.10).

Observation, apprenticeship, and experimentation have been the defining elements in his quest to learn the secrets of this art, and illustrious potters, aficionados, have influenced him, as have artists such as Benigno Barrón, Jesús Macías, Fortino Guerrero, Jorge Wilmot, Luis Nishizawa, and Juan Ibáñez. In his youth, he researched various decorative formats and methods of sketching designs, constantly putting them into practice in his eagerness to learn the different stages of mayólica production. He has traveled to pottery centers within Mexico, as well as overseas, pursuing the goal of expanding his artistic and technological vision. Over time, he has become an expert in throwing techniques and the use of raw materials. In his effort to emulate the glazing process and the colors of the pieces that he has admired in private collections and museums, he has confronted the challenges involved in the construction and subsequent modification of wood-fired kilns and has learned the indispensable secrets of controlling firing temperatures and environments.

13.10 Javier de Jesús (Capelo) Hernández Taller de Alfarería Majolica de Guanajuato, "Capelo," Guanajuato Photo by Charlene Cerny, 1999

His aim has been to adhere strictly to what he considers authentic mayólica: the application of colors to a white glaze prepared with tin oxide. Among the first pieces he produced were small objects consigned to stores of the Fondo Nacional para el Fomento de las Artesanías, and as his prestige grew, he received a commission from the Office of the President of Mexico for a set of utilitarian mayólica pieces. However, from Capelo's perspective, repetitive work is not inspiring. Instead, he prefers to produce unique pieces, and he promotes this idea among his workers.

He feels that his work should be oriented more toward artistry than business, and he has presented numerous exhibitions in galleries and museums in Mexico and abroad (in Japan, Spain, Germany, and other countries), in search of one of his driving forces, artistic recognition.

Capelo's creativity lies in mayólica decoration, and he prefers to dedicate himself to this stage of the production process. Potters are left to work from rough sketches on which he has

13.11 Jar / *Tibor*
Taller de Alfarería Majolica de Guanajuato,
"Capelo," Javier de Jesús Hernández,
Guanajuato, 1996
Collection of Judy Espinar
Photo by Paul Smutko

marked weights and sizes, while he channels his imaginative efforts into the painting.

Initially, the designs he created closely adhered to traditional subject matter, but over time, he began to introduce variations and to search for his own color for the background glaze. He explored the use of a sulfurous yellow, an intense white, and various gray tones before settling on the slightly creamy hue, with an antique touch, that distinguishes the products of his workshop. He continually changes the color and form of the decorative elements as part of his creative adventure (fig. 13.11).

In ornamental terms, his sources of inspiration have passed from tendencies toward an austere somberness to an extreme Baroque character. While at present the predominant decorative styles are of Italian origin, the painters in the shop are free to choose compositions and colors. Capelo often suggests specific motifs, such as still-life themes, and then monitors how the painters are developing them. When he paints, he rarely produces more than three identical pieces; in his view, the imagination must be kept active, constantly creating new designs (13.12).

For Capelo, ceramics have a language and character that makes them different from other media. He seeks to interpret this language and articulate the uniqueness of mayólica. He believes that ceramics are born in volcanoes, and humans only step in to give them shapes; that mayólica is sustained through a deep-seated cultural tradition, in which errors must be avoided at all costs; and that production

13.12 Jar / *Orza*
Taller de Alfarería Majolica de Guanajuato,
"Capelo," Javier de Jesús Hernández,
Guanajuato, 1999
Collection of the International Folk Art Foundation
Museum of International Folk Art
(Museum of New Mexico), Santa Fe
Photo by Paul Smutko

13.13 Taller de Alfarería Majolica de Guanajuato, "Capelo," Javier de Jesús Hernández, Guanajuato
Photo from store booklet, n.d.

implies a large responsibility, if the potter's intent is to achieve high technical and aesthetic excellence in the finished product.

His work has been exhibited in the Museo de Alhóndiga de Granaditas, the Museo Franz Mayer and the Museo de Artes Decorativos in Mexico City. It has received enormous respect and acceptance within traditional arts-and-crafts circles. In the future, Capelo wants to produce works in other media, such as painting and sculpture, but at present, his activities are focused on two clearly distinguishable areas.

On a business level, in the shop managed by Capelo and his brother, Enrico, also an architect and artist, there is a move toward the manufacture of a variety of colorful pieces that are primarily reminiscent of Italian styles (fig. 13.13). Vases (tibores), spice holders,

13.14 Plate / *Plato*
Taller de Alfarería
Majolica de
Guanajuato, "Capelo,"
Javier de Jesús Hernández,
Guanajuato
Photo by
Patricia Fournier, 1994

plates, and platters are being painted with realistic designs conveying regional still-life and dynamic floral and geometric motifs, interlaced with angel figures. On occasion, tile murals are produced, demonstrating great detail in the drawing and careful painting.

On a personal level, he finds ceramics to be a wonderful means for expressing his pictographic restlessness, surpassing the known limits in the art of mayólica. He is creating abstract sculptures with volumes impacted by the contours and textures created by the covering silhouettes of fish, turtles, and frogs in high relief (fig. 13.14). Aquatic nature passes through a metamorphosis under his artistic inspiration, in an impressive series of platters in which he has resolved seemingly impossible technical problems: the employment of seldom-used mayólica glazes, the integration of petrous materials in the ornamentation, and the very size of these pieces.

This underscores an important and innovative tendency in Mexican plastic arts that began with the transformation of traditionalist Guanajuato ceramics, and that today includes excursions into the creation of pieces that are not for daily or casual-ornamental use, but destined to be collectors' items. It is precisely in Mexico that this artist has found an excellent response from collectors of ceramic objects as a nostalgic expression of the past and a connection to Mexico's roots. The works of Capelo have gone on to achieve international recognition as well, which can only bode well for his continuing success in the future.

The Aguilera Brothers' Workshop in Santa Rosa

The Santa Rosa workshop owned by Jaime Aguilera and operated in collaboration with his brothers is known as Alfarería Aguilera. Founded in 1987, it is one of the more recently established pottery workshops in Guanajuato. The work produced is based on experience in the field of ceramics acquired by Jaime Aguilera's father, beginning in 1963. This shop stands out among the pottery manufacturers of Guanajuato in its use of most of the old mayólica techniques, in marked contrast to factories that have adopted industrial processes.

Red and black clays, as well as clays that contain limestone, are extracted from the Santa Rosa Mountains. Foot-activated potter's wheels (see fig. 14.12) are used to shape the objects and, in the case of pieces of larger proportions, such as tibores, which can attain a height

13.15
Bisqueware / *Juaguete*
Alfarería Aguilera
Mayólica "Santa Rosa," Guanajuato
Foot-activated potter's wheels are used to shape objects. In the case of large pieces such as these *tibores*, two sections are thrown and later joined.
Photo by Patricia Fournier, 1994

13.16 Jar for Preserves / *Conservera*
Alfarería Aguilera
Mayólica "Santa Rosa,"
Guanajuato, 1999
Collection of the
International Folk
Art Foundation
Museum of International
Folk Art (Museum of
New Mexico), Santa Fe
Photo by Paul Smutko

of more than a meter, two sections are thrown and later joined (see fig. 13.15). Molds are used only for those objects whose contours are not circular, such as cofers (*cofres*), boxes, and oval soup tureens.

Once dried, the pieces are fired at 800 degrees Celsius, in gas kilns. The Aguilera brothers have found a substitute for lead oxide in glaze preparation, while maintaining the use of tin; occasionally they use industrial opacifying agents. Many of the colors in the Santa Rosa workshop are prepared with local minerals. Blue, green, and black predominate, but yellow and reddish orange are also used. Once the objects are painted, they are submitted to a second firing, at a temperature near 900 degrees.

They produce a wide variety of vessel forms that include tibores, platters, lebrillos, pitchers (*jarrones*) in various sizes, flowerpots of considerable dimensions, jarras, umbrella stands, cofres, oval jewelry boxes (*alhajeros ovales*) with faceted bodies, soap dishes, toothbrush holders, oil-lamp bases, lamps, candleholders of great originality, and tableware. The style of painting, even when the theme is similar to the mayólica patterns of Puebla and Guanajuato, has its own expressions: the brilliant coloring and the shading that is clearly the work of talented and skilled artists (fig. 13.16).

The inventory of designs is based on Chinese pieces, drawings taken from books and post cards, and the shop's own original works. Brightly colored polychromes display nature scenes of great quality and detail. Birds, fruits, and flowers are integrated into still-life scenes that include mayólica tibores or large platters. There are regional and folkloric designs depicting scenes of bullfights or rodeos, typical Mexican landscapes, or images of the Virgin of Guadalupe. Some pieces recreate the abstract geometric elements reminiscent of nineteenth-century Guanajuato mayólica. In addition, there is a great use of blue backgrounds with fine incising to emphasize the whiteness of the enamel, and the "tattooed" style embraced by mayólica potters from Puebla is frequently duplicated.

Since 1988, the pieces produced in Santa Rosa, particularly the highly decorated tibores and large platters, have won awards in national exhibitions and competitions, achieving recognition not only in the state of Guanajuato but also in Mexico City.

Notes

1. I would like to thank Gorky González, Capelo, and the Aguilera brothers for their help and hospitality, and for allowing me to interview them for this study. I would

also like to thank Carlos Castañeda, for granting us access to the archaeological collections of the historic sites in Guanajuato. Tony Pasinski edited the English version of this text. Most of the information presented in this chapter is derived from interviews with the master potters of Guanajuato and was collected in the field in 1994 and 1995 by the author.

2. Leonor Cortina, "La loceria del cura Hidalgo en Dolores," *Museo Franz Mayer, Boletín Trimestral* 15 (1986):2–5.
3. Anita G. Cohen-Williams, "Common Maiolica Types of Northern New Spain," *Historical Archaeology* 26(1) (1992):119–30; Donna J. Seifert, "Archaeological Majolicas of the Rural Teotihuacan Valley, Mexico" (Ph.D. diss., University of Iowa, 1977); Victor M. Villegas, *Arte popular de Guanajuato* (México: Banco Nacional de Fomento Cooperativo and Fondo de Fideicomiso para el Fomento de las Artesanías, 1964).
4. Alejandro de Humbolt, *Ensayo político sobre el Reino de la Nueva España* (México: Editorial Porrúa, 1978).
5. Martín Almagro Basch and Luis María Llubiá Munné, "Aragón-Muel," in *C.E.R.A.M.I.C.A.* (Barcelona: Talleres Gráficos de Hija de J. Ferrer, 1952), pp. 1–66; Henri Amouric, Florence Richez, and Lucy Vallauri, *Vingt mille pots sous les mers* (Aix-en-Provence: Édisud, 1999); Florence C. Lister and Robert H. Lister, "Majolica, Ceramic Link between Old World and New," *El Palacio* 76(2) (1969):1–15, "Non-Indian Ceramics from the Mexico City Subway," *El Palacio* 81(2) (1975):24–48, and "The Potter's Quarter of Colonial Puebla, Mexico," *Historical Archaeology* 18 (1984):87–102; María Teresa López Fernández, *Museo de Ávila: Catálogo de Cerámica* (Madrid: Ministerio de Cultura, Dirección General de Bellas Artes, Archivos y Bibliotecas, Subdirección General de Museos, Patronato Nacional de Museos, 1982); Luis Luján, *Historia de la mayólica en Guatemala* (Guatemala: Serviprensa Centroamericana, 1975); Carmen Nonell, *Cerámica y alfarería populares de España* (Madrid: Editorial Everest, 1978); Irena Pisútová, *Fajansa: L'udové umenie na Slovensku* (Bratislava: Tratan, 1981); Rafael Salinas Calado, *Faiança Portuguesa. Portuguese Faience* (Lisbon: Direction of Philatelic Services, Portuguese Post Office, 1992.
6. The main nonplastic components used for degreasing are feldspars, although there are also rhyolitic felsites, granite, carbonates, and quartz; Patricia Fournier G., "Mexican Ceramic Analysis," in *The Presidio and the River on the Borderlands*, 2 vols., ed. by Bradley J. Vierra and Richard C. Chapman (Albuquerque: University of New Mexico Office of Contract Archaeology, 1997) 1:199–256.
7. Cohen-Williams, "Common Maiolica Types"; Roy B. Brown, "Arqueología colonial en Chihuahua: El caso de El Carrizal," in *Memorias del Coloquio Internacional El Camino Real de Tierra Adentro*, ed. by J. C. Pacheco and J. P. Sánchez (México: Instituto Nacional de Antropología e Historia, 2000), pp. 49–62; Ronald V.May, An Evaluation of Mexican Majolica in Alta California," in *Mexican Majolica in Northern New Spain*, Pacific Coast Archaeological Society Occasional Papers, no. 2 (1972):25–50; Mark R.Barnes, "Majolica of the Santa Cruz Valley," in *Mexican Majolica in Northern New Spain*, Pacific Coast Archaeological Society Occasional Papers, no. 2 (1972):1–23; Fournier G., "Mexican Ceramic Analysis"; Rex E.Gerald, *Spanish Presidios in the Late Eighteenth Century in Northern New Spain* (Santa Fe: Museum of New Mexico Press, 1968); Thomas H. Charlton, "Loza Mayólica," in *Estudios de materiales arqueológicos del período histórico: El palacio de Cortés, Cuernavaca, Morelos*, by Thomas H. Charlton, Patricia Fournier G., Judith Hernández A. and Cynthia L. Otis Charlton (México: Archivo de la Coordinación Nacional de Arqueología, Instituto Nacional de Antropología e Historia, 1987), pp. 110–78; Seifert, "Archaeological Majolicas"; Lister and Lister, "Majolica."
8. Villegas, *Arte popular de Guanajuato.*
9. Ibid.

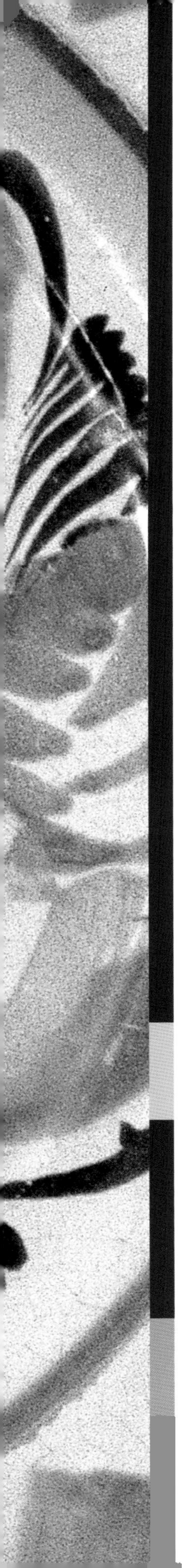

Detail, Fig. 14.6

14

In memory of
Maestro Juan Silva González,
master loza blanca potter
of El Caballo Blanco
(1910–99)

The *Loza Blanca* Tradition of Aguascalientes

GLORIA GIFFORDS AND JORGE OLVERA

Loza blanca, talavera, or mayólica (maiolica), tin-enameled soft-paste earthenware, was first introduced into Mexico at the time of the Spanish conquest and was produced in Mexico City soon afterward.[1] As early as the mid-sixteenth century, the industry was transferred to the city of Puebla, which became the largest production center of loza blanca in colonial Mexico, although by the beginning of the nineteenth century this type of pottery was also being made in several regions of north central Mexico. Researchers and collectors have directed most of their efforts toward central and southern Mexico, paying scant attention to the loza blanca tradition of the relatively obscure Bajío region in north central Mexico, and that of the city of Aguascalientes in particular, where the pottery was not produced until the early nineteenth century.

The present study developed from our discovery of the last functioning *alfar* (pottery workshop) to produce loza blanca in Aguascalientes, in the summer of 1979. We began research that August, locating the former loza blanca workshop sites in the city and interviewing potters or families of former owners of the workshops.

Two pottery sites were excavated in Aguascalientes: the then still-functioning alfar El Caballo Blanco, of Juan Silva González, at Calle Larreátegui 311, in 1979 (fig. 14.1), and the long-defunct alfar of Bernabé Hernández, just around the corner at Calle Libertad 415, a year later. Maestro Juan Silva González gave us permission to excavate between the rooms reserved for the throwing and drying of pottery and the *pilones* (clay tanks), where we were to find the oldest loza blanca shards in our initial surface collection, and in an area of the yard used by his father, Ruperto Silva. In 1980, the owner of the property, Roberto Hernández (b. 1922), directed us to a section of an overgrown back lot that he remembered as a child had been the general vicinity of the pottery kilns. While digging the foundations for his home, at the front of that property, he had uncovered part of a large kiln. In 1983, we incorporated our research and fieldwork into a larger project overseen by Professor Olvera and the Instituto Nacional de Antropología e Historia de México, to establish a museum of ceramics in Acámbaro (Guanajuato). We continued to visit and communicate with Maestro Silva until 1995, four years before his death.

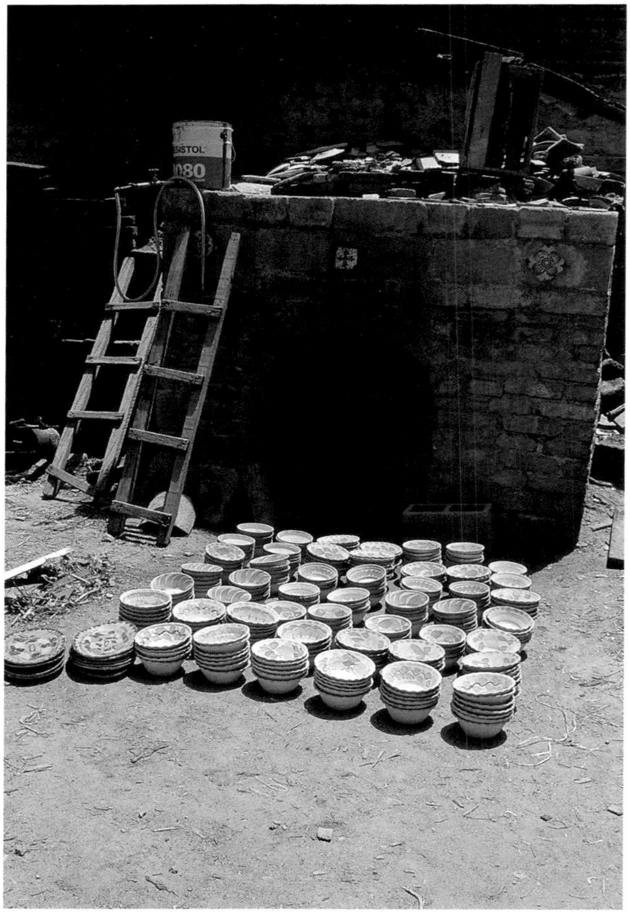

14.1 Bowls ready for firing, Alfar del Caballo Blanco, Aguascalientes Photo by Gloria Giffords, 1979

For lack of written records and because of conflicts among the many oral accounts, we were unable to determine the exact origins of the loza blanca tradition in Aguascalientes. Working with our fourteen consultants, however, we were able to piece together, from potters' recollections and from family traditions, a reasonable account of how loza blanca came to Aguascalientes, how it developed, and how it went into decline.

By describing the techniques and economics of loza blanca and by recalling the names of the patterns and various brush strokes used by some of the last loza

14.2 Jorge Olvera (left) and Maestro Juan Silva (right) Aguascalientes Photo by Gloria Giffords, 1979

blanca potters in Aguascalientes in the final decades of the twentieth century, our consultants (almost all in their seventies or eighties) provided us with valuable insights into the Mexican mayólica tradition and allowed us to more precisely date the material we excavated. Although all fourteen were generous with their time and their memories, Maestro Silva, as operator of the only functioning loza blanca pottery workshop in Aguascalientes, was especially helpful and informative, freely sharing with us his direct knowledge, thoughts, and reflections; we obtained most of our specific information on material, techniques, and marketing strategies from him (fig. 14.2).

The Origin of Aguascalientes Loza Blanca

During the colonial period, production of certain commodities was tightly controlled by Spain, to protect trade monopolies and to create tax revenues. Moreover, the politics of New Spain restricted certain professions, crafts, and industries—most notably for our purposes, pottery—to the Spanish-born, excluding Creoles (children of Spanish parents, born in Mexico) and mestizos (people of mixed blood, primarily Spanish and Indian).

The patriot priest Miguel Hidalgo y Costilla, a Creole himself, was captivated by the rationalism of the encyclopedist Diderot and by the spirit of freedom and independence embodied in the French Revolution. Virtually banished in 1802 to Dolores (later, Dolores Hidalgo, Guanajuato), a relatively unimportant little village, for his rebellious attitudes and unorthodox beliefs, Father Hidalgo introduced silk culture and wine production there as alternative livelihoods for the farmers in his area. Near his house, he established a leatherworking and saddle shop, a metal forge, a carpentry shop, a silk- and wool-weaving shop, and a pottery workshop. Although old maps of Dolores Hidalgo clearly locate the pottery workshop at Father Hidalgo's home and date its founding as 1804, the extent of his physical involvement or personal instruction in this and other enterprises is not as clear.

All our consultants were in agreement that Father Hidalgo had introduced the craft of loza blanca to Dolores Hidalgo. Other documents and earthenware (loza blanca as well as slip and glazed ware) from other sites strongly suggest that, rather than importing workers from Puebla or personally teaching local potters the craft himself, he may have gotten the idea and perhaps even the artisans from the nearby town of Guanajuato, which was already producing loza blanca (see chapter 13). Nevertheless, it was very likely thanks to Father Hidalgo's encouragement and influence that the craft spread to the surrounding towns of Venado (San Luis Potosí), Aguascalientes, and Sayula (Jalisco).

Most of the pottery produced in these locations was polychrome, instead of the traditional blue-on-white of the earlier Puebla loza blanca. The sites in the Bajío region would develop vessel shapes, decorative patterns, and techniques of applying the designs that were distinctive departures from those of Puebla. Moreover, the pottery of Guanajuato, Dolores Hidalgo, and Aguascalientes was virtually indistinguishable until the late twentieth century, suggesting the exchanges of ideas and techniques, possibly through itinerant artisans.

Early Aguascalientes Alfares

Aguascalientes appears to have been an important center for the production of pottery, beginning with *loza colorada* (unglazed or lead-glazed red earthenware), since at least the late eighteenth century.[2] That there were individuals skilled in the handling of clay may have been one of the important reasons for the establishment of loza blanca there in the early nineteenth century. Other factors helped spur its development: Mexico's independence from Spain in 1821, which generally favored the establishment and growth of new industries; the strategic location of Aguascalientes on principal trade routes to the north; and the availability of abundant supplies of high-quality clay, natural minerals for colors, and tin for the "enameling."

Although we were unable to determine the exact number of alfares producing loza blanca in Aguascalientes either by archival research or by personal interviews, it appears that five principal workshops operated from the late nineteenth century, and three to five minor ones from the mid-1920s, until around 1945. Most consultants agreed that all five of the principal alfares were family concerns; they consistently gave us the names of Araiza, Hernández, de Luna, Silva, and of a widow variously recalled as "Paz Martínez," "Martell," or "Becerra" as the owners and operators of the workshops, which were clustered in about a four-block area around Calle Libertad and Calle Larreátegui. All our informants agreed it was in this area, specifically on Calle Libertad, that the industry was established in Aguascalientes.

The nearby barrio of Guadalupe had been the location of alfares producing the ordinary, lead-glazed pottery (loza colorada). The geographic closeness of workshops producing two different types of pottery is consistent with the principles of Spanish colonial urban planning, which grouped similar crafts together, for convenience as well as for accessibility to raw materials, water, labor, and transportation.

The craft of loza blanca may have come to Aguascalientes as early as 1835, according to Maestro Silva, who claimed in 1984 to have the names of individuals from Dolores Hidalgo who were the earliest *loceros*. Other consultants stated that it arrived there with potters either from Dolores Hidalgo or Guanajuato who, most believed, had been personally taught by Father Hidalgo. Although it was impossible to pin down specific dates, members of the Araiza family, in their eighties in 1980, claimed that it was their great-grandfather Luis, from Guanajuato, who founded the tradition in Aguascalientes; they and other consultants established that his alfar had been at Calle Libertad 512.[3]

Maestro Silva, a third-generation potter (b. 1910), stated that the history of his family's business began when his grandfather Gumecindo Silva, already a skilled *tornero* (potter at the wheel), became the assistant to "Luis," the originator of loza blanca in Aguascalientes, whose last name Silva did not recall. Maestro Silva's father, Ruperto (1839–1925), was also a master tornero, who apparently passed his skill on to one of his three children by his first marriage, Valente (d. 1976), a potter in Venado. According to Maestro Silva, his half-brother was not only a good potter but knew how to make blue pigment without using cobalt.[4]

Although there are scant clues as to just how much loza blanca was produced from its introduction in Aguascalientes until the late nineteenth century, all consultants agreed that the high point of production was reached around 1880. At that time, according to de Luna, there were from ten to fifteen alfares making the loza blanca and about a hundred producing loza colorada. There was also an abundance of labor, perhaps even some with specific skills. The fathers and grandfathers of our consultants told them about a great pool of workers in the 1880s who used to wait on the corners in the mornings to be hired by owners or shop bosses in need of temporary, extra help. Most of the production was ordered in advance and shipped north by wagons or mule carts. Clients included vendors in the cities of Durango; Torreón (Coahuila); and Parral, Chihuahua, and Júarez (Chihuahua)."But," according to José de Luna, "not to Guadalajara, because they had their own [loza blanca]."

During the wet summer months, when it was difficult to fire the pottery, de Luna explained that the kilns were generally inactive. The alfar owners (his grandfather included) would set out in wagon trains of eighty to a hundred two- and four-wheeled carts to haul both types of loza northward, traveling together for protection against bandits and marauding Indians and for mutual assistance. The wagons were described as "rolling crates," with alternating layers of straw and pots laced together. Delivering orders to customers in the various towns and villages and taking new orders from merchants, the owners would remain together until the first had sold his wares. He would then return home, leaving the others to finish selling, and as each did, he, too, would return. His grandfather told him that the trip took about four months. The silver coins they received in payment were melted down into lumps and hidden in the wagons, to be resmelted and recoined at a mint in Zacatecas, for a fee, after their return.

Maestro Silva recalled his father telling him similar stories, especially about the wagoneers sleeping in the streets with their loaded wagons, ready to leave at three in the morning. According to Roberto Hernández, *arrieros* hauling sugarcane to Aguascalientes would typically backhaul pottery (presumably loza blanca) to their hometowns.

With the introduction of the railway through central Mexico, after 1882, the desire for pottery of a finer grade could be partially met by imported chinaware, especially by English soft-paste transferware. Indeed, one of the most important factors contributing to the decline of the loza blanca industry in Puebla in the nineteenth century was the flooding of the Mexican market with these imported wares, first from England and later from France. The isolated nature of north central Mexico served to protect it for a time, sustaining a limited local market for fine ware that allowed the alfares to eke out a living. Then, sometime in the 1920s, the Americans became interested in Mexican arts and crafts beyond curios, and the loza blanca pottery workshops of Aguascalientes started exporting directly to the United States, specifically to California and Texas, as Roberto Hernández and Maestro Silva recalled. In particular, dish sets and pitchers were in great demand.

Even as Mexicans turned away from traditional pottery and sought other kinds, demand remained high for clay tiles (azulejos), also produced by the loza blanca pottery workshops, to impart a "typical" Mexican decorative touch to the cupolas and walls of churches in Aguascalientes and elsewhere throughout Mexico, as well as to the

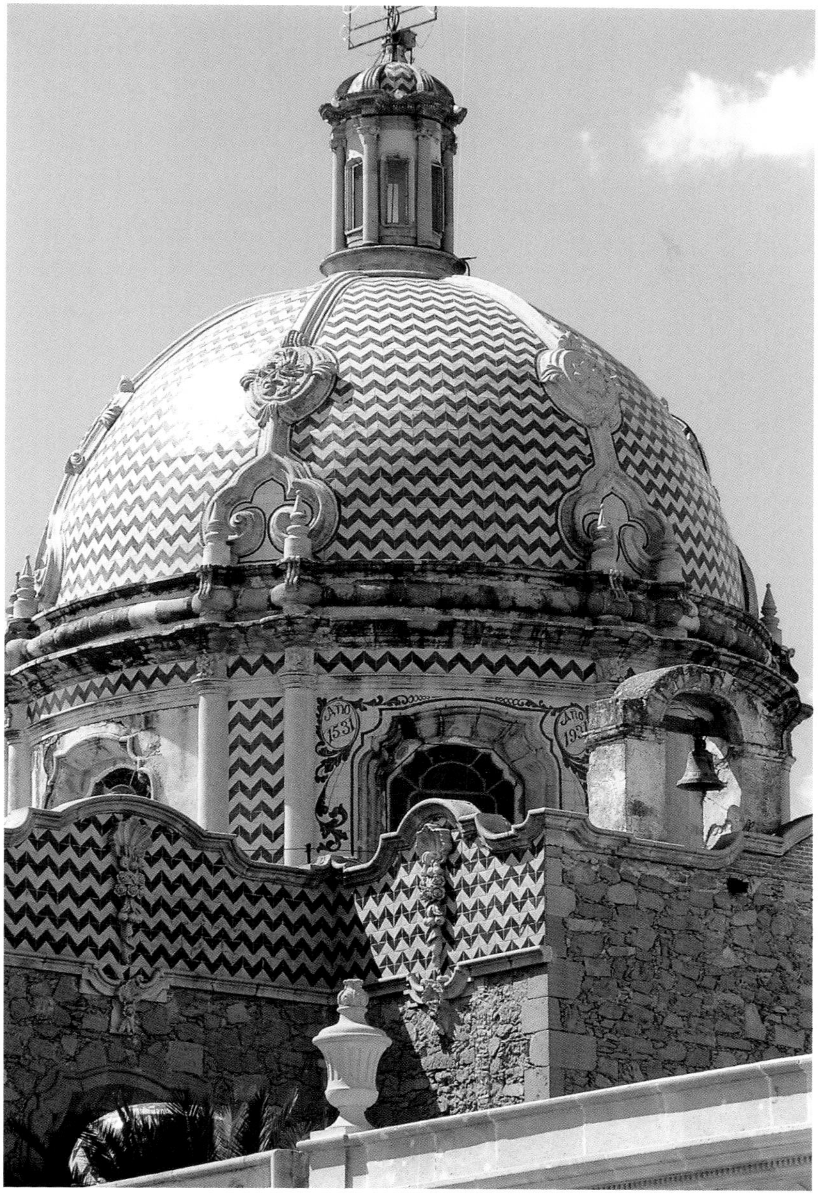

14.3 Dome / *Cúpula*
Iglesia de Nuestra Señora de Guadalupe, Aguascalientes
Photo by Gloria Giffords, 1979

walls of secular buildings. Maestro Silva recalled that, in 1928, his alfar produced tiles in the *laurel* pattern for the Centro Catalán Restaurant, in Mexico City, and, about the same time, for hotels in Acapulco.[5] Local buildings such as the cathedral of Aguascalientes and the parochial churches of San Diego, Nuestra Señora de Guadalupe, and San Marcos, also made use of tiles from Aguascalientes alfares during construction and repair. Francisco Araiza Rodríguez (former potter, son of Carlos Araiza, and great-grandson of legendary loza blanca originator, Luis Araiza) stated that both he and his brother Camarino made tiles for the parochial

14.4 Fountain / *Fuente*
Luis Fernández Ledesma
Aguascalientes, ca. 1940
Photo by
Gabriel Fernández Ledesma

churches of San Marcos (where they appear on the rear cupola), El Encino, and La Sagrada Corazón, as well as for the cathedral. Their father, Carlos, made them for the dome of the nearby parish church of Guadalupe (fig. 14.3). Shipped north to Chihuahua, their tiles were used on the cupola of a church in Gómez Palacio.

It is probably safe to say that during the 1920s, Silva's alfar, El Caballo Blanco, was the largest and best. Indeed, in 1926, the Spanish government honored it with a special award for handicrafts. Also during the 1920s, the Mexican artist and author Gabriel Fernández Ledesma returned from Mexico City to his hometown of Aguascalientes to work at El Caballo Blanco, helping to make tiles for the National Library of Periodicals, in Mexico City. His brother Luis, also working with him in the workshop, created a fountain for the plaza of San Marco, since destroyed (fig. 14.4).

The decline of loza blanca in Aguascalientes was gradual. World War II made materials hard to obtain, said the former owners, and it grew ever harder to maintain a foothold in a market made intensely competitive by the appearance of less-expensive, machine-produced, high-fired chinaware, both Mexican and imported, and then, of still cheaper plastic kitchenware. Moreover, Silva told us, after 1945, many workers decided to go into business for themselves, flooding the market with their wares and undermining prices for loza blanca, even as material costs soared. When the local market became saturated, the owners of the de Luna and Hernández alfares and a third workshop (the widow "Martínez" or "Martell" or "Becerra") decided to close their workshops altogether. The Araizas scaled back production, but kept their workshop going for another ten years. El Caballo Blanco, for its part, continued to export most of its wares through the 1950s, 1960s, and part of the 1970s to Santa Fe, Los Angeles, El Paso, and New York City.

Because of the high cost of materials and the weak market, the loza blanca produced from the 1960s until Maestro Silva's death, though it retained its traditional forms and patterns, became a pale reflection of what it had been eighty years before. Gone was the thick, opaque white paste, which was so thin the (now) red clay showed through; also gone were the once bright and distinctive colors. Seeking to produce for a largely export, art-pottery market had been a logical decision. But necessary economies in production had resulted in diminishing the aesthetic appeal of Maestro Silva's wares. Moreover, tastes, both foreign and domestic, had shifted. El Caballo Blanco would stay in business until Silva's death, but it would do so by the slimmest of margins.

14.5 Pitcher with *amapola* pattern
Aguascalientes, 1950
Private collection
Photo by Tim Fuller, 2002

Types of Aguascalientes Loza Blanca

Aguascalientes pottery was made in a wide variety of forms: *bacines* (chamber pots), *jarros* (pitchers; fig. 14.5), *platones* (fig. 14.6) and *charolas* (eating and serving plates), *tarros* (jars), from small cylinders for holding creams and salves to large, lidded vessels called *tibores*. *Ollas* (pots), sometimes holding up to a gallon, for preserve making or for serving other foods, were also made (figs. 14.7, 14.8a, b), along with *soperas* (soup tureens), mugs, and candlesticks. Among the bowl forms, however,

14.6 Platter / *Platón*
Aguascalientes, ca. 1935
Collection of the International Folk Art Foundation
Museum of International Folk Art
(Museum of New Mexico), Santa Fe
Photo by Paul Smutko

14.7 Large jar with *amapola* pattern
Aguascalientes, 1920
Private collection
Photo courtesy Tucson Museum of Art

the overwhelmingly most popular was a pint-sized, steep-sided bowl called a *posolero* (fig. 14.9)[6] By contrast, the *tazón*, more delicate and refined in shape and with about half the capacity of the posolero, was not nearly as popular (fig. 14.10).

Both white and grayish-white clays—(the combination was crucial because of the specific qualities each brought to the throwing and firing of the pottery) were obtained from local sources, until the end of the first decade of the twentieth century. Francisco Araiza remembered that the grayish-white clay was brought in from the hills, while the white came from around San Marcos, from an area near the railroad tracks, and from the "Gómez orchard." All our consultants agreed that at the beginning of the Aguascalientes tradition, the white clay was much finer and whiter.[7] As the city grew, however, houses and orchards gradually covered local sources, until around 1910, when it was no longer

14.8a Preserve Jar / *Conservera*
Aguascalientes, late 19th century
Private collection
Photo courtesy Tucson Museum of Art

14.8b Preserve jar with *rosa azul* pattern
Aguascalientes
Drawing by Juan Silva

14.9 Bowls / *Posoleros*
Aguascalientes, early 20th century
De la Luna Collection
Photo by Gloria Giffords

14.10 Three bowls (*tazones*) with patterns *pepitalla, avellana,* and *sombra*
Aguascalientes, 1920
Private collection
Photo by Tim Fuller, 2002

14.11 Mixing Tanks / *Pilas*
Alfar El Caballo Blanco,
Aguascalientes
Photo by Gloria Giffords,
1979

available locally, clays of darker color and coarser texture had to be brought in from elsewhere.

Both kinds of clays were mined as chunks, which were broken up and sifted through a screen, to remove pebbles and large rocks. A combination of the sifted clays was placed in a *pila* (or *pilón*) *de las mesclas* (mixing tank), a brick-lined mixing trough about 12 feet long, 6 feet wide, and 3 feet deep, where it was mixed thoroughly with water, with obvious debris removed. The clay mixture was further refined and separated from debris in a series of smaller pilas (fig. 14.11). Throughout this process, it was agitated from time to time, until the finest material had gone into suspension; this was then poured off into a *pila de recibir* (receiving tank), allowed to "rest," and later poured into a *landa*, a much shallower tank, to partially cure.

When it had dried out some, the clay was cut into squares and taken to the alfar, where it was either trod on or beaten with a wooden mallet or paddles, to remove trapped air, and covered with damp cloths, to keep it moist. Laid on a large slab (*sobador*) or a cement floor, it was kneaded by the potters, who used sand as fine as talcum (*desgrasante*), to keep it from sticking to their hands.

Vessels were thrown by means of a kick wheel (fig. 14.12). To produce consistent angles and uniform shapes, a wooden wedge (*casco*) was held against their inside and outside walls. Handles or spouts were then added to the vessels, which were allowed to dry until leather hard, when their bases could be trimmed and edges smoothed. Rims on the vessels were even, except those on posoleros and serving bowls, where potters created an undulating effect (*alechugado*) by pressing down with their thumbs. Tiles were made by rolling the clay out to the desired thickness on a smooth surface and then cutting it into appropriate-sized squares. When the tiles and vessels were dry to the touch, they were stacked on end on shelves in a kiln and the remaining moisture was driven off with a biscuit, or bisque, firing. Those broken in the firing were sold to builders for mixing with mortar or adobe for roofing material.

To obtain the creamy, opaque, enamel-like coating characteristic of loza blanca or loza colorada, the piece was dipped in a liquid tin-enamel or lead-oxide glazing solution, allowed to dry, and then decorated with colors applied with a *pincel de perro*, a brush made of dog's hair. Diaper patterns on tiles were created with a stencil. To apply overall coatings, skilled decorators developed techniques for spinning plates into tubs of glazing solution and quickly retrieving them before they sank. The final firing would bond the glaze or enameling to the piece and fuse the colors to the enamel, producing a surface with an appealingly smooth and lustrous quality. Depending on the amount added to the glazing solution, the tin used for loza blanca would create a thick, luscious glaze, from which the rich colors of the decoration would radiate.

Although in the 1980s Maestro Silva was buying powdered metal oxides and commercially produced substances for the colored decoration, he related that, during his youth, most of the colors and glazing materials had to be produced locally. In his yard was a small, donkey-powered *molino* (mill; fig. 14.13), no longer in use, which was used to grind lead and tin for glazes, as well as minerals for the colors; most of these were obtained not too far from Aguascalientes. Francisco Araiza recalled that their workshop ordered tin from Monterrey or bought it locally from an individual named Narcisco Lozano, who had a shoe store and a concession for tin and lead. To obtain colorants for green, scraps from old copper pots or wire were heated in the oven and then placed in water to oxidize. The oxidized film was then scraped off and mixed with silica: 20 grams (just under an ounce) of copper oxide to 1 kilo (just over 2 pounds) of silica. Red was made from *riñoncitos de hierro* (iron nodules) found locally, which were ground up and mixed with silica. Black came from manganese, found at a nearby site named "Picacho," where Maestro Silva and his family would pick it up from the ground. Yellow was made from antimony, most likely from local lead mines. Blue was made from cobalt imported from Germany,

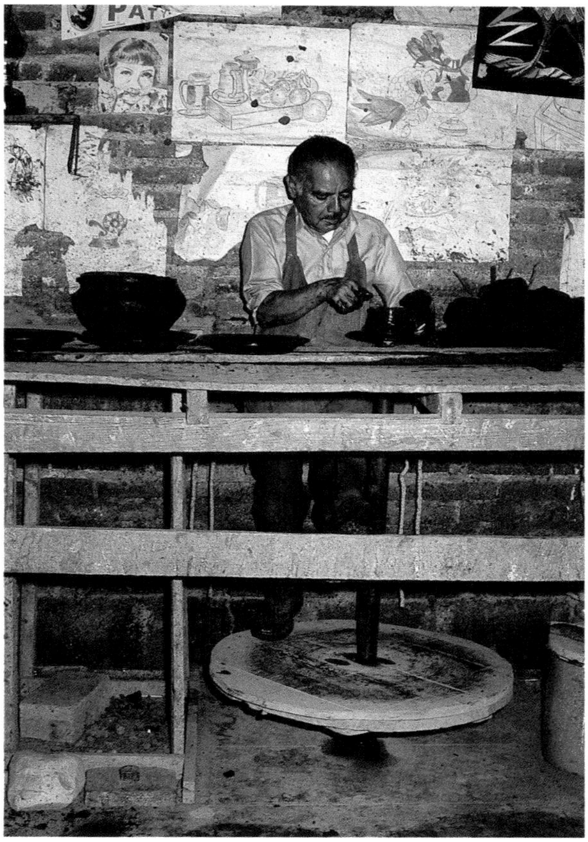

14.12 Maestro Silva at the kick wheel (*el torno*) Alfar El Caballo Blanco, Aguascalientes
Photo by Gloria Giffords, 1979

14.13 Mill / *Molino*
Alfar El Caballo Blanco, Aguascalientes
Photo by Gloria Giffords, 1979

while the background white came from the tin mined near San Luis Potosí.

The arrangement of pieces within the kiln was carefully thought out, for the most efficient use of both space and heat. Using flat slabs of previously fired, coarse pottery, the *maestro quemador* (kiln master) constructed a series of layers, *mesas* (tables), resting these on *peldaños* (heavy, unglazed clay tubes) capped with *tortas de barro cocido* (round, flat, unglazed clay disks). The peldaños not only served as supports for the next mesa, but tibores, bacines, and ollas were placed inside the tube for protection against smoke and from the accidental explosions of other pieces that would otherwise destroy these larger and more expensive pieces. The mesas were arranged so as to allow the heat to pass easily throughout the kiln. Whereas during a biscuit firing, pieces could touch and indeed might even be nestled next to each other, during a glaze firing, they had to be kept carefully apart. The plates and bowls were stacked on each other, separated in the glaze firing by *caballitos* (cockspurs, unglazed ceramic supports). The kiln door was sealed off with adobe blocks mortared together, with a *cota* (tube) as a peephole to check on the firing process. Because thermometers were not used, the skills and experience of the maestro quemador became critical. For the oxides and minerals to properly melt and fuse to the vessel and each other, there had to be just enough heat over just enough time. Too much heat or time and the glazes would run; too little and the colors and surface would be dull. Maestro Silva explained that, during the firing, a corncob stuck to an iron rod would be inserted through the peephole. The heat would ignite the cob, illuminating the nearby vessels, and if their surfaces looked as if they were covered with honey (transparent and ductile), the glazes had melted. By cutting off the fuel source, heat would then be steadily reduced over the next day or so; by opening the top of the kiln bit by bit, the vessels would be allowed to cool gradually.

When the kilns were in production, the largest alfares fired every fifteen days or so. In the earlier years, before fuel oil, they used different types of wood and, according to Maestro Silva, the results were better. "Manzanillo," "palo colorado," and pine were preferred, in that order, although mesquite could also be used. The flame from clean-burning wood made the surfaces of the vessels more brilliant, Maestro Silva maintained, whereas smoky wood could darken and dull them.

Each operation within the workshop was handled by a separate group of workers. Although all workers involved in making pottery were called alfareros, Maestro Silva preferred to call those working in loza blanca loceros. Most highly paid were the torneros, who received payment for each gross of pieces they produced. Next came the maestro quemador, the individual in charge of stacking and firing the kiln, who was paid per *carga de horno* (kiln load). The painters came next, paid for each gross of pieces they decorated. Wage workers included *tahoneros* (millers), in charge of grinding colors and preparing glazes; patio workers, who prepared the clay, took pieces out to dry, and charged the ovens; a *maestro cargador* (yard foreman), who oversaw the common laborers; and workers who supplied the kiln with chopped wood.

Youngsters at about the age of twelve were taught to handle the vessels and assist in the less-skilled tasks. Beginning as yardworkers, they would graduate to other positions as their ability or interests dictated. While certain individuals practiced only one part of the craft, the owner's sons were taught the entire operation; Maestro Silva recalled how, around 1922, his father began to teach him, before and after school and during school vacations, how to do simple things, such as prepare clays and throw *jarritos* (small pitchers).

All these different operations going on at the same time required a large amount of space. Roberto Hernández recalled that their yard was huge, stretching through to the street behind them, Calle Mesones; the doorways to the alfar were about 12 feet high and about 20 feet across. Of the yards and kilns remaining in 1980, only two were more or less intact: those at the Silva and the Araiza workshops. The Araiza yard was filling up with garbage, its kilns slowly crumbling away. But in spite of everything, the Araizas maintained the privy, whose interior they had decorated with loza blanca. Maestro Silva's yard contained the pilas, the throwing and drying rooms, the molino, and two kilns, now heated with fuel oil; however, it, too, was encroached upon by discarded autos, rubble, and the family's laundry.

Whereas Chinese pottery heavily influenced the form and decoration of Puebla loza blanca from the sixteenth century on, many of the forms, colors, and patterns of Aguascalientes loza blanca were inspired by nineteenth-century European pottery. In particular, the large jars and covered pots, with their pleated strap handles, have a much more globular form than those of the Chinese-inspired ginger jars of Puebla.

The most distinctive element of Aguascalientes loza blanca, though, is its decoration, and particularly the way it was applied. By far the greatest percentage of color combinations used red, orange, green, and yellow. Depending on the pattern, additional dashes of black were added. A small percentage of blue-and-white pieces were produced, perhaps in an attempt to imitate Puebla models. Although some have suggested that the paucity of blue in the earliest Aguascalientes pieces may have been the result of the expense of the imported cobalt, rather than a question of aesthetics, we must disagree, finding the later appearance of blue among the other colors to be a jarring departure from the tonal harmony of the earlier, more pleasing pieces.

As opposed to the tight and precious manner in which colors were applied to mayólica in Puebla, the decoration of Aguascalientes loza blanca exhibits a painterly quality and almost an expressionistic freedom in its brushstrokes. In the principal technique, different sizes of loaded brushes are pressed up against the walls of the vessel and then quickly pulled away, providing the diagnostic shape of the brushstrokes and inspiring the name of the technique, *jalón* (pull). There appear to have been few differences in the patterns, strokes, or color among alfares in Aguascalientes, most likely the result of the casual labor force and the circulation of skilled laborers from workshop to workshop.

Marking of Pieces by Alfares

In a system unique to the loza blanca tradition in Aguascalientes, the numbers 1 through 5 were placed on the inside bottom of the posoleros. Although it was generally agreed that each of the five principal alfares had its own number, to distinguish its output, there was little agreement as to which workshop had which number. Maestro Silva stated that his father, Ruperto, had invented the numbering system; others disagreed, saying that it was used before Ruperto or that their ancestors had come up with the idea. The number 1 was said to belong to the alfar owned by the widow "Martínez" (or "Martell" or "Becerra""). The number 2 indicated the Hernández alfar or the Araiza workshop, according to one Hernández we interviewed (and, indeed, we found many pieces of broken posoleros bearing this number scattered throughout the ruined Araiza kiln). The number 3 belonged to the alfar owned by Jacinto Becerra (husband to the widow also known by other names),

14.14 Bowls / *Cuencos y posoleros*
Decorated by Longina de la Rosa, Aguascalientes, ca. 1910
Private collection
Photo by Tim Fuller, 2002

according to Maestro Silva, or to the one owned by Luis Olivares, according to Roberto Hernández, or to that of Juan de Dios de Luna, according to his grandson José. The number 4 designated El Caballo Blanco, since at least the early 1920s (although the Araizas claimed that the number originally belonged to Carlos Araiza's alfar). And the number 5 belonged to the de Luna alfar, again according to Maestro Silva, who thought that part of the confusion may have arisen when other alfares took to pirating his number because the market recognized his pottery as the best. José de Luna, for his part, felt that when the workshops began to go out of business, the system broke down, and each one simply took whatever number it wanted.

One consultant told us that the Araizas used concentric circles on the inside bottom of their posoleros to distinguish their pieces. Francisco Araiza Rodríguez (b. 1900), the oldest living member of the Araiza clan, claimed that one of the best loza blanca painters, Longina de la Rosa (a man who worked in his grandfather's lifetime and whom he remembered from when he was a child), specialized in painting deer, rabbits, and birds in the plates' centers, in place of the number 4, which, according to Francisco, the Silva alfar later usurped (fig. 14.14).

Our impression was that the makers of

14.15 Plate with *jalón amarillo* pattern
Aguascalientes
Drawing by Juan Silva

(a)

(b)

(c)

(d)

14.16 Patterns / *Diseños*
The patterns include (a) *cúchila,* (b) *bocabajo,* (c) *mañana,* (d) *carlanga,* (e) *ambar de gotas,* (f) *cucaracha,* (g) *mariposa,* and (h) *perejil*
Drawings by Juan Silva, Aguascalientes

(e)

(f)

(g)

(h)

14.17 Plates / *Platos*
Aguascalientes, 1950
Two plates with patterns *rehileta* and *rosa*; the third contains blue pulls with green and yellow embracing strokes, eye-winker details, and the serrated, or crown, pattern on the edge.
Private collection
Photo by Tim Fuller, 2002

loza blanca considered themselves to be an elite. The trade had many secrets, and their close relationship, reinforced through extensive intermarriage, suggests an attempt by the families to keep their knowledge within a closed circle. That the Hernández progenitor might have learned enough to begin producing loza blanca simply by observing the processes as an outsider is highly unlikely; it is far more probable that he did so by marrying into a loza blanca potter's family.

Maestro Silva was asked to date and identify the patterns of some typical pieces from the first excavation. When, months later, he was asked to reidentify this material and other pieces from the excavation at the former Hernández alfar, he was consistent in his pattern names and dates, drawing and painting some of the popular patterns and pottery forms to help us in our identification of the pieces.

Some pattern names describe particular

14.18 Plate with *dos hermanas* pattern
Aguascalientes
Drawing by Juan Silva

flowers, fruits, or leaves; others describe animals. Some derive their names from the jalón technique (fig. 14.15). While names such as *quadritos* (little squares), a checkered band, are descriptive enough, others, such as *nada* (nothing), *mañana* (tomorrow), *bocabajo* (face-down), or *cúchila* (sic 'em!), defy interpretation (fig. 14.16a–h). Particular patterns were applied to vessels of particular shapes or shapes and sizes. For example, the patterns *carlanga* (tatters), *perejil* (parsley), *avellano* (hazelnut), *ambar de gotas* (amber beads), *mariposa* (butterfly), *tranquilo* (tranquil), *pepitilla* (pumpkinseed), and *sombra* (shadow) graced the insides of posoleros, although these same patterns might also be used on the outsides of tazones, because of their smaller size. *Rosas* (roses; fig. 14.17), *hermanas* (literally sisters, but actually clusters of roses; fig. 14.18), *fresas* (strawberries; fig. 14.19), *palomas* (doves), *jitomates* (tomatoes), and *amapolas* (poppies; see fig. 14.5) were painted on plates, pots, pitchers, and jars. *Coronas* (crowns), a serrated pattern, and *perfiles* (outlines), narrow bands of color, were painted along edges; *pestañas* (eye lashes), short, black dashes, and *tepocates* (tadpoles; fig. 14.20), narrow pulls of different colors, were tucked in and around the larger design elements.

The End of *Loza Blanca* in Aguascalientes

Although the loza blanca tradition is currently flourishing in Puebla, Dolores Hidalgo, and Guanajuato, it almost certainly will not continue in Aguascalientes, now that Maestro Silva has died. Although he had tried to persuade his son Juan Silva Muñoz to continue in the time-honored manner, Juan insists on making pottery of more contemporary design. Maestro Silva had been encouraged by the city of

14.19 Soup tureen with *fresa* pattern
Aguascalientes
Drawing by Juan Silva

14.20 Serving platter with *tepocate* pattern
Aguascalientes
Drawing by Juan Silva

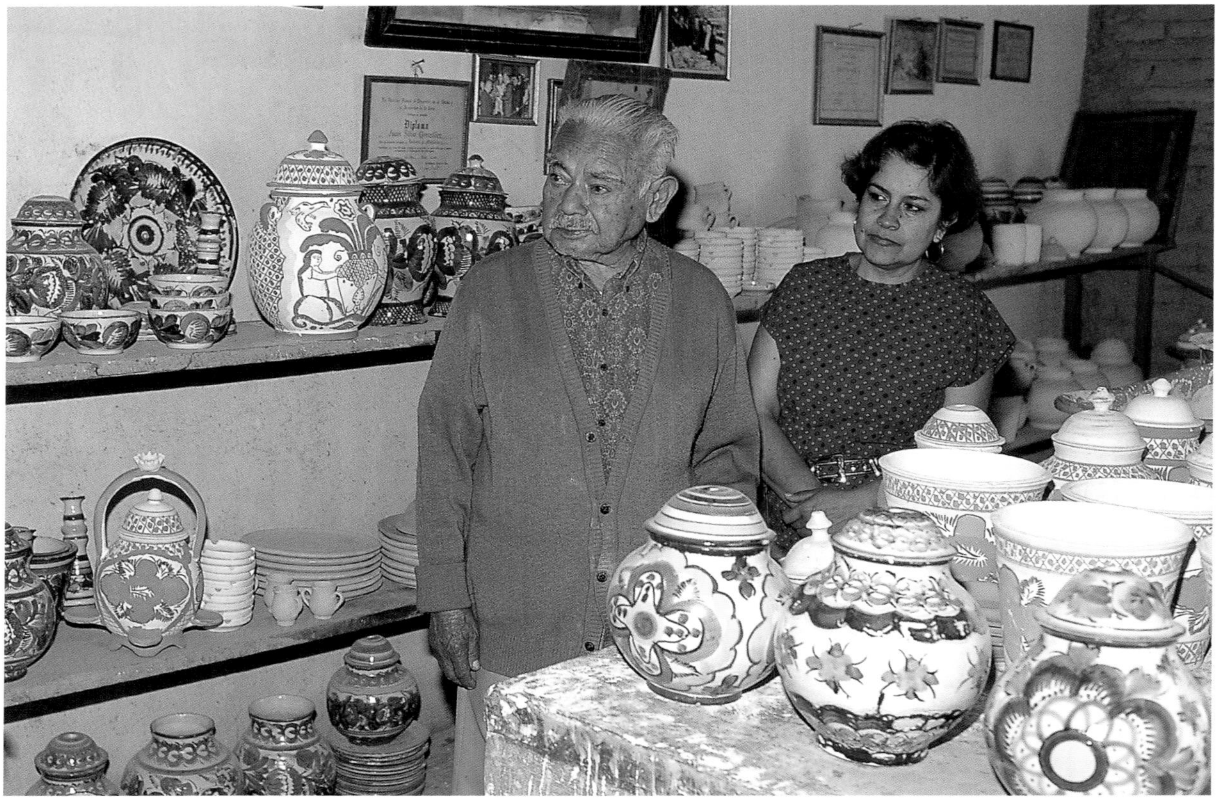

14.21 Maestro Juan Silva and Daughter Alfar El Caballo Blanco, Aguascalientes Photo by Gloria Giffords, 1994

Aguascalientes to teach his trade; one of his former students, Fernando Zertuche, had worked with him, trying to perfect the craft and revive the industry. Indeed, Fernando had married Silva's daughter María de Jesús, in 1988. But Zertuche's and Maestro Silva's efforts were apparently too little, too late. With its passing, the secrets and skills of the older generation are being swept away (fig. 14.21).

Notes

1. The term *loza blanca* as used in this article is derived from the Sevillian, and before that, Moslem tradition of using mostly white or blue-on-white tin glazes on pottery. See chapter 9, this volume, for production in Mexico City.
2. Archivo General de la Nación, Ramo de Padrones: Censo de 1792.
3. This Luis Araiza, who may well have been the "Luis" credited in popular tradition as the founder of the loza blanca industry in Aguascalientes, taught Maestro Silva's grandfather, Gumecindo. Luis's son Luis took over the business, although it is unclear whether he, in turn, passed the business to his son Carlos (d. 1932); Carlos had a different alfar number in his *posoleros* (see below). Be that as it may, one of Carlos's sons, Luis Araiza Rodríguez (1902–1979), owned and ran a workshop on a street north of Calle Larreátegui.

   Doña Victoria Araiza said that all three of her brothers, Luis, Francisco, and Camerino, were *alfareros*, as was Luis Araiza Rodríguez's son, Luis Araiza Aguilera, but of *loza gretada* (another variety of lead-glazed pottery). Doña Victoria is second cousin to Roberto Hernández and first cousin to Juan Jesús Hernández Araiza, whose bloodlines are linked to the de Lunas through Jermina de Luna, their maternal grandmother.

4. Maestro Silva's mother was Ruperto's second wife, Maria de Jesús González (1876–1938, daughter of Sotera Rubalcava). Upon Ruperto Silva's death, his widow, María de Jesús, successfully ran the alfar. During her management it grew, providing work for as many as thirty-five alfareros. Upon her death, in 1938, their son Juan took over. The Silva workshop's tradition continues with Maestro Silva's son Juan Silva Muñoz (b. 1955), a potter and teacher of pottery.

   Roberto Hernández stated that he had been told that the Silva alfar moved from Calle Libertad to around the corner on Calle Larreátegui in 1908 or 1909, whereas at least two other consultants told us that Ruperto did not work for his father, Gumecindo, but worked either for the de Luna family or for the Hernández family. According to Roberto, Ruperto Silva and his father, Quirino Hernández, were close friends; indeed, Quirino was Maestro Silva's godfather.

   Roberto Hernández told how his grandfather Bernabé Hernández (ca. 1835–1905) was originally an *arriero* (literally "mule driver," but more broadly, someone in the shipping business) who married a potter's daughter, Ramona Jiménez (d. ca. 1895), from León (Guanajuato). In traveling around San Luis Potosí, Dolores Hidalgo, Guanajuato, and San Felipe, Bernabé learned how to make loza blanca. According to Hernández family legends, Bernabé saw Aguascalientes, where no loza blanca was being produced, as a likely place to set up a workshop, and did so around 1855. It eventually included Quirino Hernández Jiménez (1853–1946); Ramona and Bernabé's son; Domililo and Juan Jesús Hernández Araiza, the sons of Quirino Hernández Jiménez and Quirino's first wife, Everando Araiza; and Rodolfo Hernández Guerra, the son of Quirino and his second wife, María Guerra. Roberto recalled his father telling him that loza blanca potters were originally brought to Aguascalientes from San Felipe (Guanajuato) and Venado (San Luis Potosí).

   José Raymundo Chávez de Luna Alvarado (nicknamed "El Largo" because of his long name), born the same year as Maestro Silva, stated that his grandfather Juan de Dios de Luna (d. 1908), came from Guadalajara in 1882 and established their alfar in Aguascalientes at that time. Taught the pottery business by his grandmother, Martina Alvarado (d. 1940), who was Juan Dios de Luna's second wife, José de Luna confirmed that women had also participated in the loza blanca industry; his best recollection was that it had been introduced into Aguascalientes by two potters, one from Guadalajara and the second, taught by Father Hidalgo (who in turn had learned pottery from the Spaniards), from Guanajuato.

5. The Centro Catalán is located on the second floor of the building next door to Sanborn's House of Tiles, on Calle Madero, and can be reached by elevator at the end of an arcade. The exterior walls of the restaurant are decorated with loza blanca tiles from El Caballo Blanco, as are many of the benches in the Parque del Reloj, in the Colonia Polanco, five miles to the west.

6. The *posoleros*, as the name suggests, were designed for eating *posole*, a distinctively north central Mexican stew of pork and hominy. The steep sides of the bowls helped eaters safely guide the stew to their mouths, with the aid of a folded or rolled tortilla, a common Mexican method of eating without forks or spoons.

7. The fineness and whiteness of the clay were, according to Maestro Silva, principal determinants for dating loza blanca shards.

Bibliography

A.A.V.V. *Cerámica esmaltada española.* Barcelona: Labor, 1981.
———. *Objets civiles domestiques.* París: Imprimerie Nationale, 1984.
———. *Le dressoir du Prince.* Service d'apparat à la Rennaissance. París: Réunion des Musées Nationaux, 1996.
———. *A table! Les arts de la table dans les collections du Musée Mandet de Riom.* París. Réunion du Musées Nationaux, 1997.
Aceves, Gutiérrez and Rubén Páez. "Tonalá bruñida: Reseña de una técnica que perdura." In *Tonalá. Sol de barro,* ed. De la Fuente Ediciones, S.A. México: Banca Cremi, 1991, pp. 37–45.
Acosta, José de. *Historia natural y moral de las Indias.* Seville, 1590.
Acuña, Patricia Eugenia. *Talavera de Puebla.* Puebla: Gobierno del Estado de Puebla,1987.
Adell Argilés, Josep María. *Arquitectura de ladrillos del siglo XIX. Técnica y forma.* Madrid: Fundación Universidad-Empresa, 1986.
Aguirre Anaya , Carlos. "La cerámica y la ciudad: Permanencias e Innovaciones" In *La Cerámica en la Ciudad de México (1325-1917).* Mexico: Museo de la Ciudad de México, 1997, pp. 19–33.
Ainaud de Lasarte, Juan. *Cerámica y vidrio. Ars Hispaniae: Historia Universal del Arte Hispánico.* Vol.X. Madrid: Plus Ultra, 1952.
———. "Cataluña." In *Cerámica Esmaltada Española.* Barcelona: Labor, 1981.
Albertos Solera, María Lourdes; Andrés Carretero Pérez; Matilde Fernández Montes. *Estudio etnográfico de la alfarería conquense.* Cuenca: Diputación Provincial, 1978.
Algarra Pardo, Víctor M. "Espacios de poder. Pavimentos cerámicos y escritura en el Real de Valencia en época de Alfonso el Magnánimo." In *Actas del XV Congreso de Historia de la Corona de Aragón* I: 271-289. Zaragoza: Diputación General de Aragón, 1996.
Almagro Basch, Martín y Luis Ma. Llubiá Munné. "Aragón-Muel." In *C.E.R.A.M.I.C.A.,* Barcelona: Talleres Gráficos de Hija de J. Ferrer, 1952. pp. 1-66.

Álvaro Zamora, María Isabel. "La cerámica en el mudéjar turolense." In *Teruel Mudéjar. Matrimonio de la Humanidad.* Zaragoza: Ibercaja, 1991, pp. 203–37.
———. *Cerámica aragonesa* (2 volumes). Zaragoza: Pórtico, 1976, 1978.
———. "Sobre los modos de irradiación de la cerámica ligúr y la presencia de ceramistas de esta procedencia en la Zaragoza del siglo XVII." *Revista Artigrama* 4, Departamento de Historia del Arte, Universidad de Zaragoza (1987), pp. 137–56.
———. "La cerámica aragonesa." In *Cerámica española. Summa Artis: Historia General del arte* XLII: 223–88. Trinidad Sánchez- Pacheco, ed. Madrid: Espasa Calpe, S.A. 1997.
Alzola, Pablo. *El Arte industrial en España.* Bilbao, 1892.
Amores, Fernando. "La arqueología posmedieval en España. Panorama y perspectivas." In *Archeología postmedievale: l'experienza europea e l'Italia.* Convegno internazionale di studi Sassari, 1994, pp. 51–67.
Amores, Fernando y Nieves Chisvert. "Tipología de la cerámica común bajomedieval y moderna Sevillana (ss. XV-XVI) I: la loza quebrada de relleno de bóvedas." *Spal* 2, 1993.
Amouric, Henri, Florence Richez and Lucy Vallauri. *Le commerce de la céramique en Provence et Languedoc du Xe au XIX siècle: Vingt Mille Pots sous les Mers.* Aix-en-Provence, France: Museé d'Istres, Édisud, 1999.
Andalucía: Alfares y cerámica. Los Palacios: Colegio Público Cervantes, 1986.
Angulo Iñiguez, Diego. "El gótico y el renacimiento en las Antillas." *Escuela de Estudios Hispano-Americanos de Sevilla* 36, no. 16 (Seville, 1947).
Aníbal, Cayetano and Carlos Cano. "La cerámica pintada de Úbeda. Avance de un estudio sistemático." *Revista de Arqueología* XX, no. 224, pp. 38–45.
Anonymous Conqueror, *Relatione di Alcune Cose della Nuova Spagna, e della gran citta di Temestitan Messico,* Venice: Ramussio Giunti, 1556.
Apraiz, Ángel de. *La cerámica de Busturia.* Valladolid, 1952.
Aragoneses, Manuel Jorge. *Artes industriales cartagenera: lozas del siglo XIX.* Murcia, 1982.
Archivo General de la Nación de México. Inquisición 593, exp. 1, f. 60.
———. *Ramo de Padrones: Censo de 1792.*
Artucio Urioste, Alejandro. *Azulejo en la arquitectura de Río de la Plata, Siglos XVIII–XX.* Montevideo: Intendencia Municipal de Montevideo y Junta de Andalucía, 1996.
Avery, George. "Pots as Packaging: The Spanish Olive Jar and Andalusian Transatlantic Comercial Activity, 16th–18th Centuries." PhD. Dissertation, University of Florida, 1997.
Baart, Jan. "Terra sigilata from Estremoz, Portugal." In *Every day and exotic pottery from Europe c. 650–1900.* Oxbow Monographs in Archaeology 23. Edited by David Gaimster. Studies in Honour of John Hurst. Oxford: David Brown Book Co., 1992, pp. 273–78.
Barber, Edwin Atlee. *The Maiolica of Mexico.* Art Handbook of the Pennsylvania Museum and School of Industrial Art. Philadelphia: The Pennsylvania Museum and School of Industrial Art, 1908.
———. *The Catalog of Mexican Maiolica Belonging to Mrs.Robert W. De Forest.* New York: The Hispanic Society of America, 1911.
———. *Mexican Maiolica in the Collection of The Hispanic Society of America* New York: The Hispanic Society of America, 1915.
———. *The Emily de Forest Collection of Mexican Maiolica.* New York: The Metropolitan Museum of Art, 1922.
Barnes, Mark R. "Majolica of the Santa Cruz Valley." In *Mexican Majolica in Northern New Spain.* Pacific Coast Archaeological Society Occasional Papers, No. 2 (1972), pp. 1–23.
Barrio Lorenzot, Francisco de. *Ordenanzas de Gremios de la Nueva España.* México: Secretaría de Gobernación., 1920.
Bello Piñeiro, Felipe. *Cerámica de Sargadelos.* La Coruña: Ediciones El Castro, 1972.
Beltrán de Heredia, Julia. *Terminologia i ús dels atuells ceràmics de cuina a la baixa Edat Mitjana. Del rebost a la taula.* Barcelona: Electa (1st edition), 1995.
Benzoni, Girolamo. *Storia del Mondo Nuovo.* Graz: Akademische Druck- u. Verlagsanstlat (Facsimile of 1575 edition), 1962.
Berti, Graziella and Liana Tongiorgi. *I bacini medievali delle chièse di Pisa.* Rome: Lérma di Bretschneider, 1981.
Berti, Graziella and Ezio Tongiorgi. *Ceramiche importate dalla Spagna nell'area pisana.* Florence, 1985.
Blumenthal, Dale. "An Unwanted Souvenir: LEAD in Ceramic Ware." *U.S. Food and Drug Administration Consumer Report,* December 1989–January 1990, pp. 1–4.
Bon, Philippe *Les premiers "bleus" de France.* Mehun-sur-Yèvre: Conseil Général du Cher, 1992.

Bonet Correa, Antonio. *Historia de las Artes aplicadas e industriales en España*. Manuales de Arte Cátedra. Madrid: Ediciones Cátedra, 1982.
Bordon Ferrer, María and María Paz Soler Ferrer. "Pavimentos valencianos de los siglos XIV y XVI." In *Actes du VI Congrès de La Céramique Médiéval en Méditerranée*. Aix-en-Provence: Narration Editions, 1997, 667-675.
Bottineau, Yves. *El arte cortesano en la España de Felipe V (1700-1746)*. Madrid: Fundación Universitaria Española (1st edition), 1986.
Braojos Garrido, Alfonso, María Parias Sainz de Rozas and Leandro Álvarez Rey. *Sevilla en el siglo XX*, No. 102 (2 volumes). Sevilla: Universidad de Sevilla, col. de Bolsillo, 1990.
Brown, Roy B. "Arqueología Colonial en Chihuahua: El Caso de El Carrizal." In *Memorias de Coloquio Internacional En Camino Real de Tierra Adentro*, edited by J.C. Pacheco and J.P. Sánchez. México: Instituto Nacional de Antropología e Historia, 2000, pp. 49–62.
Brown, Roy B. and Patricia Fournier. *Proyecto Arqueo-Histórico de la Frontera Norte: La Expansión del Dominio Español en Nuevo México y Nueva Vizcaya. Análisis de Materiales Arqueológicos*. México: Archivo de la Coordinación Nacional de Arqueología, Instituto Nacional de Antropología e Historia (Informe Inédito), 1998.
Buelga Marcos, *La fábrica de loza de San Claudio 1901-1966*. Oviedo,1994.
Cabezón, Miguel, Ana Castelló and Ramón Tirso. *La alfarería en Huesca. Descripción y localización*. Monografías del Instituto aragonés de antropología, 2. Zaragoza, 1984.
Caiger-Smith, Alan. *Tin-Glaze Pottery in Europe and the Islamic World: The Tradition of 1,000 Years in Maiolica, Faience and Delftware*. London: Faber and Faber, 1973.
Calderón de la Barca, Fanny. *Life in Mexico: The Letters of Fanny Calderon de la Barca*, edited and annotated by Howard T. and Marion Hall Fisher. New York: Doubleday, 1966.
Cantareros de Calanda. Videoproducción. Zaragoza: Asociación cultural Maderuela, 1996.
Carandell, Josep María, Ricard Pia and Pere Vivas. *The Palau Música Catalana*. Barcelona: Triangle Postals, 1996.
Carretero, Andrés, M. Fernández and C. Ortiz. "Alfarería popular de Andalucía Occidental: Sur de Badajoz y Huelva." *Etnografía Española* 1 (1980), pp. 99–266.
Casanovas, María Antonia. "Influencia de Alcora en otras manufacturas españolas." In *El Esplendor de Alcora*. Barcelona: Museu de Ceràmica, 1994.
———. "Alcora, Onda y Ribesalbes." In *Cerámica española. Summa Artis*, Vol. XLII. Edited by Trinidad Sánchez-Pacheco. Madrid, 1997, pp. 389–436.
———. "Cerámica arquitectónica catalana de época medieval y renacentista." In *La ruta de la cerámica*. Castellón: Ascer, 2000, pp. 76–77.
Casanovas, María Antonia and María Isabel Álvaro. *La manufactura de Alcora. Innovaciones técnicas y primicias artísticas*. Separata de *El conde de Aranda y su tiempo*. Zaragoza: Institución Fernando el Católico (CSIC), 2000.
Casanovas, María Antonia and María Isabel Álvaro. *Aranda industrial: La Real Manufactura de Loza y Porcelana de Alcora y su influencia en la cerámica aragonesa. La cerámica en la vida cotidiana del siglo XVIII*. El Conde de Aranda. Zaragoza: Diputación Provincial (1st edition), 1998.
Casanovas, María Antonia and María Isabel Álvaro. *Colección de botes y morteros farmacéuticos*. Barcelona: Laboratorios Novartis (1st edition), 2000.
Cascales Muñoz, José. *Las Bellas Artes Plásticas en Sevilla. La pintura, la escultura y la cerámica artística desde el siglo XIII hasta nuestros días. Apuntes históricos y biográficos* (2 volumes). Toledo: Imperial Colegio de Huérfanos María Cristina, 1929.
Castelló Yturbide, Teresa and Marita Josefa Martínez del Rio de Redo. *Delicias de antaño: Historia y recetas de los conventos mexicanos*. México: Bancomer, 2000.
Castro Morales, Efraín. "Puebla y la talavera a traves de los siglos." *Artes de México* 3 (Primavera, 1989), pp. 20–29 (English translation, pp. 77–81).
Cerdá Mellado, José A. and Albert Telese Compte. "Cerámica de procedencia italiana aparecida en Cataluña." *Laietana: Estudis d´Historia I Arqueología del Maresme* 9 (1994).
Cervantes, Enrique A. *Loza blanca y azulejo de Puebla* (2 volumes). México: Edición del autor, 1939.
Cervantes de Salazár, Francisco. *Crónica de la Nueva España*. México: 1554.
Charlton, Thomas H. "Tonalá Bruñida Ware. Past and Present" *Archaeology* 32 (1)1979, pp. 45–53.
———. "Loza Mayólica." In *Estudios de Materiales Arqueológicos del Período Histórico, El Palacio de Cortés, Cuernavaca, Morelos*. Edited by Thomas H. Charlton, Patricia Fournier, Judith Hernández and Cynthia L. Otis Charlton. México: Archivo de la Coordinación Nacional de Arqueología, Instituto Nacional de Antropología e Historia, 1987, pp. 110–78.
Cherry, Peter. *Arte y Naturaleza. El Bodegón Español en el Siglo de Oro*. Madrid, 1999.
Cobo, Bernabé. *Historia de la fundación de Lima*. Lima: Imprenta liberal, 1882.

———. *Historia del Nuevo Mundo* (4 volumes). Sevilla: Imprenta de E. Rasco, 1890.
Coe, Sophie D. and Michael D. Coe. *The True History of Chocolate.* London: Thames and Hudson, 1996.
Cohen-Williams, Anita G. "Common Maiolica Types of Northern New Spain." *Historical Archaeology* 26(1) 1992, pp.119–30.
Coll Conesa, Jaume. "Ceràmica i canvi cultural a la València medieval. L'impacte de la Conquesta." *Afers* 7 (1989), pp. 125–167.
———. "Contenedores cerámicos medievales en las costas de Mallorca." *IV CAME,* Vol. III, 1993.
———. "Comentarios acerca de la alfarería femenina Magrebí. Conservadurismo y transformación en el sistema doméstico de producción cerámica." *Forum Cerámico* 2, (Febrero 1994), pp. 33–35.
———. "Mallorca, moviments i corrents comercials a través de la ceràmica." In *Mallorca i el comerç de la ceràmica a la Mediterrània.* Palma de Mallorca, 1998.
———. "La ceràmica valenciana del segle XIII al XIX. Tècniques i processos de la producció. Visió diacrònica de conjunt". In *Ceràmica Medieval i postmedieval. Circuits productius i seqüències culturals.* Edited by J. I. Padilla and J. Vila. Barcelona, 1998, pp. 165–76.
Coll Conesa, Jaume and Josep Pérez Camps. "Aspectos de la técnica de fabricación en la cerámica de Manises (siglos XIV–XVI)". In *Actas del IV Congreso de Arqueología Medieval Española,* Vol. III. Alicante: Asociación Española de Arqueología Medieval, Diputación de Alicante, 1994, pp. 879–89.
Colmenero de Ledesma, Antonio. *Chocolata Inda Opusculum.* Nuremberg: Wolfgang Enderi, 1644.
Cooper, Emmanuel. *Ten Thousand Years of Pottery.* Philadelphia: University of Pennsylvania Press (4th edition), 2000.
Cortina, Leonor "La Locería del Cura Hidalgo en Dolores." *Museo Franz Mayer Boletín Trimestral* 15 (1986), pp. 2–5.
Cortina de Pintado, Leonor. "La Cerámica: Usos e Influencias." In *La cerámica en la Ciudad de México (1325–1917).* México: Museo de la Ciudad de México, 1997, pp. 65–95.
Corredor-Matheos, J. and Jordi Gumi. *Cerámica Popular Catalana.* Barcelona: Caixa d'Estalvis de Catalunya, 1978.
D'Aulnoy, Condesa. *Viaje por España de 1670 a 1680.* Madrid, 1962.
Deagan, Kathleen. *Artifacts of the Spanish Colonies of Florida and the Caribbean, 1500–1800. Volume I: Ceramics, Glassware, and Beads.* Washington, D. C: Smithsonian Institution Press, 1987.
Díaz del Castillo, Bernal. *Historia verdadera de la conquista de la Nueva Espana.* Madrid: Instituto Gonzalo Fernandez de Oviedo, 1982.
Díaz-Plaja, Fernando. *La vida cotidiana en la España de la Ilustración.* Crónicas de la Historia. Madrid: EDAF, 1997.
"Dinnerware - Safe or Toxic?" *Consumer News,* Vol. 7, 1977, p. 2.
Domenech Martínez, Rafael. *El azulejo sevillano.* Sevilla: Ed. Dialpa, 1988.
Edgerton, Samuel Y. *Theaters of Conversion: Religious Architecture and Indian Artisans in Colonial Mexico.* Albuquerque: University of New Mexico Press, 2001.
Ellis, Florence Hawley. *When Cultures Meet: Remembering San Gabriel del Yunque Oweenge.* Santa Fe: Sunstone Press, 1970.
———. *San Gabriel del Yunque: Window on the Prespanish Indian World.* Santa Fe: Sunstone Press, 1988.
Engenios Martín, Jesús. "Escuela de Artes de Talavera de la Reina. ¿Se puede enseñar cerámica?". *Boletín de la Sociedad Española de Cerámica y Vidrio* 33, 6 (noviembre–diciembre 1994), pp. 356–57.
Ensenyat, C. "Colección de cerámica de Paterna en el Museo de Soller, Mallorca." *Boletín de la Sociedad Arqueológica Luliana* 37, 1979.
Escalante, Jorge. "Culpan a Fox por 'perder' talavera." *Mural.* May 16, 2001, D-1.
Escribá de Romaní, Manuel, Conde de Casal. *Historia de la cerámica de Alcora,* Madrid, 1945.
Escuela Oficial de Cerámica. "La Escuela Oficial de Cerámica (Madrid)." *Boletín de la Sociedad Española de Cerámica y Vidrio* 33, 6 (noviembre–diciembre 1994), pp. 358–59.
Escuela Madrileña de Cerámica. "Escuela Madrileña de Cerámica de la Moncloa." *Boletín de la Sociedad Española de Cerámica y Vidrio* 33, 6 (noviembre–diciembre 1994), pp. 359–60.
Espagnet, François and Claire du Rusquec. "Regards sur Vallauris". In *Spécial Vallauris, La revue de la cèramique et du Verre* 29 (julliet/août, 1986).
Espinosa Martín, M. C. "Aportes documentales a los bodegones de Luis Meléndez." *Boletín del Museo del Prado* (1989), pp. 67–77.

Exposición Universal. *Exposición Universal de París de 1878: Catálogo de la sección española.* Madrid, 1878.
Fàbregas, Xavier. *Tradicions, Mites, I Creences dels Catalans.* Barcelona: Edicions 62 s/a, 1979.
Fernández del Castillo, Francisco. *Apuntes para la historia de San Angel (San Jacinto Tenanitla) y sus alrededores. Tradiciones, historia, leyendas.* México: Museo Nacional de Arqueología, Historia y Etnología, 1913.
Fernández Laconva, Juan A. *Cerámica sevillana.* Catálogo de la Exposición de la Caja de Ahorros Provincial San Fernando de Sevilla. Sevilla, 1977.
Filgueira Valverde, Xosé Santiago. *Sargadelos.* Santiago, 1951.
Flores Escobosa, Isabel. *Estudio preliminar sobre la loza azul y dorada nazarí de la Alhambra.* Madrid: Instituto Hispano-árabe de Cultura,1988.
Foro Joven. "Dos escuelas distintas." *Boletín de la Sociedad Española de Cerámica y Vidrio* 33, 6 (noviembre–diciembre 1994).
Fournier, Patricia. "Mexican Ceramic Analysis." In *The Presidio and the River on the Borderlands,* vol. I. Edited by Bradley J. Vierra and Richard C. Chapman. Albuquerque: Office of Contract Archaeology, University of New Mexico, 1997, pp. 199–256.
Frothingham, Alice Wilson. *Talavera Pottery, with a Catalogue of the Collection of the Hispanic Society of America.* New York: the Hispanic Society of America, 1944.
———. *Tile Panels of Spain, 1500–1650.* New York: The Hispanic Society of America, 1969.
Fundación Universidad-Empresa. *Los estudios de Cerámica.* Monografias profesionales 80. Madrid, Fundación Universidad-Empresa, 1987.
Gage, Thomas. *Thomas Gage's Travels in the New World.* Edited with an introduction by J. Eric S. Thompson. Norman: University of Oklahoma Press, 1958.
El Galeón de Manila (catalogue). Madrid: Aldeasa, Ministerio de Educación, Cultura y Deporte, 2000.
García Gómez, María Dolores. *Cuatro siglos de alfarería tinajera en Villarrobledo.* Albacete: Instituto de Estudios Albacetenses, 1993.
García Portillo, Carmen. "Escuela de cerámica de Manises." *Boletín de la Sociedad Española de Cerámica y Vidrio* 33, 6 (noviembre–diciembre 1994), pp. 355–56.
García Ramos, Guillermo. "La cerámica artística y sus autores en la Sevilla actual." Conferencia pronunciada el 24 de abril de 1997 en la Escuela de Formación de Artesanos "Della Robbia". Sevilla, 1997.
García Sáiz, María Concepción. *Las castas mexicanas: Un genero pictorico americano,* Milan: Olivetti, 1989.
García Sáiz, María Concepción. "Arte colonial mexicano en España." *Artes de México* 22 (1993–1994), pp. 26–39.
García Sáiz, María Concepción and Barrio Moya, José Luis: "Presencia de cerámica colonial mexicana en España." *Anales del Instituto de Investigaciones Estéticas* (1987), pp. 103–10.
García Sáiz, María Concepción and María Angeles Albert de León, "La cerámica de Tonalá en las colecciones europeas," in *Tonalá: sol de barro,* edited volume, De la Fuente Ediciones, S.C. México: Banca Cremi, S.A. 1991.
García Sánchez, E. "El consumo de aceite de oliva y otras grasas vegetales en Al Andalus." In La Mediterrània, área de convergència de sistemes alimentaris. Palma de Mallorca: Institut d'Estudis Balears, 1995.
Gautier, Teófilo. *Viaje por España 1840-1845.* Madrid, 1985.
———. *A Romantic in Spain.* Translated by Catherine Alison Phillips. Northampton, Mass.: Interlink books, 2001.
Gerald, Rex E. *Spanish Presidios in the Late Eighteenth Century in Northern New Spain.* Santa Fe: Museum of New Mexico Press, 1968.
Gerrard, Christopher, Alejandra Gutiérrez, J.Hurst and Alan Vince. "Guía sobre la cerámica medieval española en las islas británicas." In *Cerámica medieval española en España y en las Islas británicas,* by Christopher Gerrard, Alejandra Gutiérrez, and Alan Vince. British Archaeological Reports (*BAR*) International Series 610. Oxford: Archaeopress, 1995, pp. 281–97.
Gestoso y Pérez, José, *Historia de los barros vidriados sevillanos desde sus orígenes hasta nuestros dias.* Sevilla: Tipografía la Andalucía moderna (1st Edition), 1903.
Giral, María Dolores, María Antonia Casanovas and Joaquín Lara. *El reflejo de Manises: Cerámica hispano-morisca del Museo de Cluny de Paris.* Valencia: Institut de Cultura, Museu de Ceràmica, 1996.
Glassie, Henry. *The Potter's Art.* Bloomington and Indianapolis: Indiana University Press, 1999.
Goggin, John M. *The Spanish Olive Jar: An Introductory Study.* Yale University Publications in Anthropology. No.62. New Haven: Yale University, 1960.

———. *Spanish Majolica in the New World: Types of the Sixteenth to Eighteenth Centuries*. Yale University Publications in Anthropology, no. 72. New Haven: Yale University, 1968.
Gómez, A, J. M. Clar, A. Real, F. J. Rossello and J. Sevilla. "Saturnismo de los alfareros de Mallorca." *Estudis Baleàrics* 22. Palma de Mallorca, 1986, pp. 45–52.
Gómez, Pastor, Toni Pasinski, and Patricia Fournier. "Transferencia tecnológica y filiación étnica: el caso de los loceros novohispános del siglo XVI" *Ameristica* (in press).
Gómez Serafín, Susana and Enrique Fernández Dávila. "Cerámica novohispana del ex Convento de Santo Domingo." In *Historia del Arte de Oaxaca: colonial y siglo XIX* (2 volumes). Oaxaca: Gobierno del Estado de Oaxaca, Instituto Oaxaqueño de las Culturas, 1997, pp. 297–313.
Gomis Martí, Josep María. *Evolució Històrica del taulellet*. Castellón: Diputación de Castellón, 1990.
González Martí, Manuel. "Mancerinas." *Faenza*, 1956, pp. 23–25.
González Sevilla, Mª Emilia. *A la mesa con los reyes de España. Curiosidades y anécdotas de la cocina de palacio*. Madrid: Ediciones Temas de hoy, 1998.
Gourarier, Zeev. *Arts et manières de Table en Occident, des origines à nos jours*. Thionville: Edited by Gérard Klopp, 1994.
Gual, Elvira. *El sistema ornamental de la cerámica de Alcora. De la primera escuela de Fontanebleau y Francisco I a la primera época de Alcora y el Con de Aranda*. Castellón: Diputación de Castellón, 1998.
Guerra, Ramón. *La corte española del siglo XVIII*. Madrid: Anaya, 1991
Guerrero-Martin, José. *Alfares y Alfareros de Espana*. Madrid: Ministry of Culture, Ediciones del Serbal, 1988.
Gutiérrez, Alejandra. *Mediterranean pottery in Wessex Housholds (13th to 17th centuries)*. British Archaelogical Reports (B.A.R.) International Series 306. Oxford: Archaeopress, 2000.
Gutiérrez Alonso, Luis Carlos. "Precisiones a la cerámica de los bodegones de Luis Egidio Meléndez." *Boletín del Museo del Prado* 12 (1983), pp. 162–66.
Hammond, George P. and Agapito Rey. *Don Juan de Oñate: Colonizer of New Mexico, 1595–1628*, 2 vols. Albuquerque: University of New Mexico Press, 1953.
Harth-terré, Emilio. "El azulejo criollo en la arquitectura limeña." *Revista del Archivo Nacional del Perú* 22, entrega 2 (Lima, 1958).
Hoffman, Carlos. "Verdades y errores acerca de la talavera poblana." *Boletín de la sociedad Antonio Alzate*. México: Imprenta de la Secretaría de Gobernación, 1922, pp. 613–30.
Humboldt, Alexander von. *Ensayo político sobre el Reino de la Nueva España* (4 vols). México: Editorial Porrúa, S. A., 1978 (first edition 1869).
Hurley Molina, María Isabel. *Talavera y los Ruiz de Luna*. Toledo: Instituto Provincial de Investigaciones y Estudios Toledanos, 1989.
Katzew, Ilona. *New World Orders: Casta Painting and Colonial Latin America*. New York: The Americas Society, 1996.
Kessell, John L. and Rick Hendricks, eds. *Remote Beyond Compare: Letters of Don Diego de Vargas to His Family From New Spain and New Mexico, 1675–1706*. Albuquerque: University of New Mexico Press, 1989.
Kessell, John L. and Rick Hendricks, eds. *By Force of Arms: The Journals of Don Diego de Vargas, 1691–1693*. Albuquerque: University of New Mexico Press, 1992.
Köpke, Wulf. "Frauentöpferei in Spanien". *Baessler-Archiv*, Neue Folge, band XII. Berlin, 1974.
Kubler, George. *Mexican Architecture of the Sixteenth Century*, 2 vols. New Haven: Yale University Press, 1948.
La ruta de la cerámica (catálogo de la exposición). Castellón: Ascer, 2000.
Lafuente Ibáñez, Pilar, "La cerámica almohade en Sevilla." In *El último siglo de la Sevilla almohade (1147–1248)*, Magdalena Valor Piechotta, Editor. Sevilla: Universidad de Sevilla-Gerencia Municipal de Urbanismo, 1996, pp. 285–301.
Lajoix, Anne. *L'Age d'Or de Vallauris*. París: Les éditions de l'Amateur, 1995.
Laurioux, B. *Les livres de cuisines italiens à la fin de Xème et au début du XVIème siècle. La Mediterrània, àrea de convergència de sistemes alimentaris*. Palma de Mallorca: Institut d'Estudis Balears,1995.
Leicht, Hugo. *Las Calles de Puebla Estudio Historia*. Puebla: Comisión Cultural del Gobierno del Estado de Puebla, 1967.
Librero Pajuelo, Antonio. "La cerámica en la Exposición Iberoamericana de Sevilla de 1929: Aproximación documental." Trabajo de Investigación presentado en la Universidad de Sevilla, Sevilla, 2000 (unpublished).
———. "El uso de la cerámica en la Exposición Iberoamericana de Sevilla de 1929." *Actas del III Congreso Nacional de Historia de la Construcción*, Vol. II, pp.585–93. Sevilla, 2000.
Limón Delgado, Antonio. *Cerámica popular de Andalucía*. Madrid: Ministerio de Cultura, 1981.

Lister, Florence C. and Robert H. Lister. "Majolica: Ceramic Link between Old World and New." *El Palacio* 76, 2 (1969), pp. 1–15.
———. "Maiolica in Colonial Spanish America." *Historical Archaeology* 8 (1974), pp. 17–52.
———"Non-indian Ceramics from the Mexico City Subway." *El Palacio* 81, 2 (1975), pp. 24–48.
———. "The reclycled pots and potsherds of Spain." *Historical Archaeology* 15 (1981), pp. 66–78.
———. *Sixteenth Century Maiolica Pottery in the Valley of Mexico.* Anthropological Papers of the University of Arizona, No. 39. Tucson: The University of Arizona Press, 1982.
———. "The Potter's Quarter of Colonial Puebla, México." *Historical Archaeology* 18 (1984), pp. 87–102.
———. *Andalusian Ceramics in Spain and New Spain: A Cultural Register from the Third Century B.C. to 1700.* Tucson: The University of Arizona Press, 1987.
López Cervantes, Gonzalo. *Cerámica de Tonalá, Jalisco.* Mexico: Instituto Nacional de Antropología e Historia (INAH), 1990.
———. "En torno a la cerámica tonalteca del Museo Regional de Guadalajara." In *Tonalá. Sol de barro.* Ed. De la Fuente Ediciones, S.C. México: Banca Cremi, 1991, pp. 101–13.
López Fernández, María Teresa. *Museo de Avila. Catálogo de Cerámica.* Ministerio de Cultura, Dirección General de Bellas Artes, Archivos y Bibliotecas. Madrid: Subdirección General de Museos, Patronato Nacional de Museos, 1982.
López Palacios, José Antonio et. al. "La producción de loza novohispana en el Barrio de Santa María Cuepopán de la Ciudad de México." In *Presencias y Encuentros, Investigaciones Arqueológicas De Salvamento.* México: Dirección de Salvamento Arqueológico, Instituto Nacional de Antropología e Historia (INAH), 1995, pp. 177–185.
Luis Meléndez: Bodegonista español del siglo XVIII (catálogo de la exposición). Madrid: Ministerio de Cultura, Museo del Prado, 1983.
Luis Meléndez: Spanish Still-Life Painter of the Eighteenth Century. Dallas: Meadows Museum, 1985.
Luján, Luis. *Historia de la Mayólica en Guatemala.* Guatemala: Serviprensa Centroamericana, 1975.
Luna, Juan. J. "América en los bodegones de Luis Meléndez." *Congreso Nacional Madrid en el contexto de lo hispánico.* Madrid: Universidad Complutense, 1994, pp. 535–40.
Mackhail, J.W., *The Life of William Morris* (2 vols). London, New York & Bombay: Longmans, Green and Co., 1899.
Maestre de León, Beatriz. *La Cartuja de Sevilla: Fábrica de cerámica.* Sevilla, 1993.
Malet, Rosa Maria. "From the Assassination of Painting to Ceramics." In *Miró: Playing With Fire.* Toronto, Canada: 2000, pp. 21–27.
Mañueco Santurtún, Carmen. "La Real fábrica de porcelana del Buen Retiro a través de sus documentos (1760–1808)." In *Manufactura del Buen Retiro (1760–1808).* Edited by Carmen Mañueco Santurtún. Madrid: Ministerio de Educación y Cultura, Comunidad de Madrid y Museo Arqueológico Nacional, 1999, pp. 17–128.
Mapelli, Carlota M. "Tibores de Jalisco en el Palacio del Quirinal." *Boletín del Instituto Nacional de Antropología e Historia* (INAH) 39 (1970), p. 30.
———. "Tibores de Jalisco en Turín." *Boletín del Instituto Nacional de Antropología e Historia* (INAH) 21 (1978), p. 58.
Marken, Mitchell W. *Pottery from Spanish Shipwrecks 1500–1800.* Gainesville: University Press of Florida, 1994.
Maroto, Mariano. "Jarras y jarros toledanos de mediados del siglo XVI." *Quadrivium* (1999), pp. 27–36.
Martínez Caviró, Balbina. *Cerámica española en el Instituto Valencia de Don Juan.* Madrid: Instituto Valencia de Don Juan, 1987.
Martínez Caviró, Balbina. *Cerámica Hispanomusulmana.* Madrid: El Viso, 1991.
May, Ronald V. and Mark R. Barnes. "Majolica of the Santa Cruz Valley." In *Mexican Majolica in Northern New Spain,* Pacific Coast Archaeological Society Occasional Papers 2 (1972), pp. 1–23.
McAndrew, John. *The Open-Air Churches of Sixteenth-Century Mexico: Atrios, Posas, Open Chapels and Other Studies.* Cambridge, Mass.: Harvard University Press, 1965.
McCorquodale, Charles. *Historia de la Decoración.* Barcelona: Stylos, 1985.
McIlroy, Roger. *Tabaco y rapé. Técnicas de los grandes maestros de alfarería y cerámica.* Madrid: Herman Blume (2nd Edition), 1985.
McMenamin, Donna. *Popular Arts of Mexico1850-1950.* Atglen, Pennsylvania: Schiffer Publishing, 1996.
McMillen, V. Node. "Alfarería: Hispanic Ceramics in New Spain. Origins, Evolution and Social Significance." Ph. D. dissertation, Texas A&M University, 1983.

McQuade, Margaret Connors. *Talavera Poblana. Four Centuries of a Mexican Ceramic Tradition.* New York: The Americas Society, 1999.
———. "La Talavera Poblana: The Renaissance of a Mexican Ceramic Tradition." *The Magazine Antiques* 156:6 (1999), pp. 824–31.
Mendieta, Fray Jerónimo de. *Historia Eclesiástica Indiana.* México: Editorial Porrúa, 1980.
Mesquida García, Mercedes. "La cocción de cerámica en un horno medieval." En *Tecnología de la cocción cerámica desde la antigüedad a nuestros días.* Alicante: Asociación de Ceramología, 1992, pp. 121–40.
Mestre, Enrique. "Enseñanza y cerámica". In *30 Ceramistas-40 alfareros. "España en Salamanca"* 88. Salamanca: Diputación, 1988, pp. 74–77.
Meyer, Michael C. and William L. Sherman. *The Course of Mexican History.* New York: Oxford University Press (5th edition), 1995.
Morison, Samuel E. *Journals and Other Documents on the Life and Voyages of Christopher Columbus.* New York: Heritage Press, 1963.
Mota, Ignacio H. de la. *El libro del chocolate.* Madrid: Pirámide, 1992.
Mota Padilla, Matías de la. *Historia del Reino de Nueva Galicia en la América.* Guadalajara: Septentrional (reprint of 1742 edition), 1973.
Mudge, Jean McClure. *Chinese Export Porcelain for the American Trade, 1785–1835.* London: Associated University Presses, Inc. (2nd edition, revised), 1981.
Muriel, Josefina Muriel. *Conventos de Monjas en la Nueva España.* México: Editorial Santiago, 1946.
Navarro, Julio. "Murcia como centro productor de mayólica dorada." In *C.I.C.M.M.O.* 3 (1986).
Navarro Palazón, Julio and P. Jiménez. *Casas y palacios de Al Andalus. Siglos XII y XIII.* Barcelona: Lunwerg, 1995.
Navarro Reverter, Joaquín. *Del Turia al Danubio. Memorias de la Exposición Universal de Viena.* Valencia, 1875.
Nonell, Juan Bassegoda. *Antonio Gaudí Master Architect.* New York, London, Paris: Abbeville Press Publishers, 2000.
Novelo, Victoria, (editor). *Artesano, Artesanías y Arte Popular de México.* México: Consejo Nacional para la Cultura y las Artes, 1996.
Oettinger, Jr., Marion. *Folk Treasures of Mexico: The Nelson A. Rockefeller Collection.* New York: Harry Abrams Inc., 1990.
Oettinger, Jr., Marion, (editor). *Folk Art of Spain and the Americas: El Alma del Pueblo.* New York: Abbeville Press, 1997.
Ojea, Hernando de. *Libro tercero de la Historia religioso de la provincia de México de la orden de Santo Domingo.* Mexico, 1690.
Otte, Enrique. "La flota de Diego Colón: Españoles y genoveses en el comercio transatlántico de 1509." In *Revista de Indias* 97-98, año 24 (1964), pp. 483, 486.
Padilla Montoya, Carmen. "Las loceras de El Cercado." *Narria* 19 (septiembre 1980), pp. 22–25.
Palm, Erwin Walter. "La fachada de la Casa de los muñecos en Puebla: Un trabajo de Hércules en el nuevo mundo." In *Actes du XLII Congrès International des Américanistes,* vol. 10 (Congrès du centenaire, Paris, 2-9 September 1976), pp. 113–38.
Palmer, Gabrielle and Donna Pierce. *Cambios: The Spirit of Transformation in Spanish Colonial Art.* Santa Barbara: Santa Barbara Museum of Art, 1992.
Peña V., Rosa Guadalupe de la. "Azulejos encontrados en *situ*: primera catedral de México." In *Ensayos de alfareria prehispánica e história de Mesoamérica. Homenaje a Eduardo Noguera Auza,* edited by Mari Carmen Serra Puche and Carlos Navarrete Cáceres. Serie Antropológica 82. México: Universidad Nacional Autónoma de México, 1988, pp. 437–38.
Pérez Camps, Josep. "La cerámica valenciana en el siglo XX." In María Paz Soler and Josep Pérez Camps, *Historia de la cerámica valenciana,* IV. Valencia: Vicent García Editores. 1992.
———. "La producción tinajera de Villarobledo en 1959, según una recopilación de datos conservados en el archivo de Alfons Blat." In *Forum cerámico* 3 (1994), pp. 14–22.
———. "Trajectòria del taller de ceràmica de l'Escola d'Arts i Oficis de València (1914–1999)." *Ceramistes formats a l'Escola d'Arts i Oficis de València.* Valencia. 1999, pp. 20–28.
———. *La ceràmica de reflex metàlic de Manises 1850–1960.* Manises, 1997.
———. "Artesanía e industria cerámica en el país valenciano durante la primera mitad del siglo XX." In *Forum Cerámico* 1 (August, 1993).
Pérez Guillén, Inocencio V. "La azulejería valenciana en los siglos XVII, XVIII y XIX." In *La ruta de la cerámica.* Castellón: Ascer, 2000, pp. 112–22.
———. "Las exportaciones de azulejos valencianos a ultramar. Siglos XVII–XIX." In *La ruta de la cerámica.* Castellón: Ascer, 2000, pp. 123–25

Pérez Samper, M. Ángeles. *La integración de los productos americanos en los sistemas alimentarios mediterràneos. La Mediterrània, àrea de convergència de sistemes alimentaris.* Palma de Mallorca: Institut d'Estudis Balears, 1995.

Petrucci, Jean and Jean Claude Poteur. "La poterie traditionnelle de Vallauris. Le tournage des poteries culinaires." *Atti IX Convegno Internazionale della Ceramica.* Albisola, 1976, pp. 449–60.

Piera, Mónica and A. Mestres. *El moble català.* Barcelona: Angle, 1999.

Pierce, Donna. "Ceramics." In *Mexico: Splendors of Thirty Centuries.* Edited by Kathleen Howard. New York: Metropolitan Museum of Art, 1992.

Pierce, Donna and Cordelia T. Snow. "'A Harp for Playing': Domestic Goods Transported over the Camino Real." *El Camino Real de Tierra Adentro* 2. Santa Fe: Bureau of Land Management, 1999, pp. 71–86.

Pintura española de los siglos XVI al XVIII en colecciones centroeuropeas. Catálogo de la exposicion. Madrid: Ministerio de Cultura, Museo del Prado, 1982.

Pintura española de bodegones y floreros de 1600 a Goya. Catálogo de la exposición. Madrid: Ministerio de Cultura, Museo del Prado, 1983.

Pintura Napolitana: De Caravaggio a Giordano. Madrid: Ministerio de Cultura, 1985.

Pisútová, Irena. *Fajansa. L'udové umenie na Slovensku.* Tratan, Bratislava, 1981.

Pleguezuelo Hernández, Alfonso. "Cerámica de Triana (siglos XVI al XIX)" (Catálogo de la Exposición, Granada, Mayo-Junio 1985). *Colección Artistas Plásticos* 8, pp. 17–31. Granada: Caja General de Ahorros y Monte de Piedad de Granada, 1985.

———. "La cerámica arquitectónica en España." In *Manual-Guía de los revestimientos cerámicos y pavimentos cerámicos.* Castellón: Instituto de Tecnología Cerámica, Diputación de Castellón, 1987.

———. *Azulejos Sevillanos.* Sevilla: Padrilla Libros in collaboration with the Consejería de Cultura de la Junta de Andalucía, 1989.

———. "Sevilla y la técnica de cuerda seca: vajilla y azulejos (siglos XV-XVI)." In *Azulejo* no. 1 (1991), pp. 9–12.

———. "Retratos históricos en azulejos sevillanos del siglo XVIII." In *Archivo Español de Arte* 264 (1993), pp. 419–24.

———. "El barro, algo más que tierra y agua." In *Cerámica. Arte y Devoción,* Catálogo de la Exposición de la Colección Carranza (Daimiel, del 9 al 30 de abril de 1995).

———. *Cerámicas de Triana: Colección Carranza.* Sevilla: Fundación El Monte, 1996.

———. "Cerámica de Sevilla (1248-1841)." In *Cerámica Española. Summa Artis, historia general de arte* XLII. Edited by Trinidad Sánchez-Pacheco. Madrid: Espasa Calpe, 1997.

———. "Lozas y vida monástica: las vajillas de la Cartuja de Jerez de la Frontera (Cádiz)." *Los Cartujos en Andalucía.* Sevilla: Universidad de Salzburgo, 1999.

———. "Una breve historia de 100 años." In *Estampaciones para lozas de los siglos XIX y XX: La fábrica de San Juan de Aznalfarache, Sevilla (1854–1954).* Edited by Marcos Buelga. Oviedo: Museo de Bellas Artes de Asturias, 2000, pp. 11–24.

———. "Jan Floris (ca. 1520-1567), a Flemish Tile Maker in Spain." In *Majolica and Glass: From Italy to Antwerp and Beyond,* ed. By Johan Veekman. Antwerp, 2002.

Pleguezuelo, Alfonso and José María Sánchez. "Envases cerámicos comerciales en el tráfico con América en el siglo XVI: síntesis de un panorama documental." *IV Congreso de Arqueología Medieval Española* III (1993).

———. "La exportación hacia América de cerámicas europeas (1492-1650)." In *Transferències y Comerç de ceràmica a l'Europa mediterrània (segles XIV y XVII). XV Jornades d'Estudis Històrics Locals.* Edited by G. Rosselló Bordoy. Palma de Mallorca, 1996, pp. 333–66.

Pleguezuelo, Alfonso, Rosario Huarte, and Pilar Somé. "Cerámicas de la Edad Moderna (1450–1632)." *El Real Monasterio de San Clemente de Sevilla: una propuesta arqueológica.* Sevilla, 1997.

Pleguezuelo, Alfonso, Antonio Librero, María Espinosa and Pedro Mora. "Loza quebrada procedente de la capilla del Colegio-Universidad de Santa María de Jesús (Sevilla)." *Spal* (2001).

Poggi Salani, Francisca Teresa-Perujo. "De los búcaros de las Indias Occidentales." *Boletín de Investigaciones Bibliográficas* (1972) 8, pp. 319–54.

Poole, Julia. "From silver to ceramic." *Plagiarism Personified? European Pottery and Porcelain Figures.* Oxford: Cambridge University Press, 1986.

Portela Hernando, Domingo. "Apreciaciones sobre la evolución de 'las Talaveras,' Siglos XVI al XX." *Boletín de la Sociedad Española de Cerámica y Vídrio* 38/4 (July-August 1999), pp. 329–34.

Pradillo de la Santa, Juan Manuel. *Alfareros Toledanos* (2 volumes). Toledo: Centro de Promoción de la Artesanía, 1997.

Ray, Anthony. *Spanish Pottery 1248-1898 with a catalogue of the collection in the Victoria & Albert Museum.* London: Victoria and Albert Publications, 2000.

Ricard, Robert. *The Spiritual Conquest of Mexico: An Essay on the Apostolate and the Evangelizing Methods of the Mendicant Orders in New Spain, 1523–1572*. Berkeley: University of California, 1966.

Ríos, Amador de los. *Brocales de pozo árabes y mudéjares* (3 volumes). Madrid: Museo Español de Antigüedades, 1915.

Riu de Martín, Maria del Carmen. "L'Escola Superior dels Bells Oficis i l'Escola Técnica d'Oficis d'Art: l'especialitat de Cerámica." *Finestrelles* 4 (1992), pp. 65–85.

———. "L'Escola del treball: L'especialitat de Cerámica." *Finestrelles* 5 (1993), pp. 173–223.

———. "La Escuela de Cerámica de la Moncloa (Madrid)." *Revistart* 4 (1995), pp. 40–42.

———. "La enseñanza de la cerámica en Cataluña durante el Novecentismo." *Cerámica* 45 (1995), pp. 39–41.

Rodríguez Bernal, Eduardo. *Historia de la Exposición Ibero-Americana de Sevilla de 1929*. Sevilla: Servicio de Publicaciones del Ayuntamiento de Sevilla, 1994.

Rohrer, Judith C. "Modernisme i neogòtic en l'archquitectura." In *El Modernisme* (2 volumes). Sevilla, Barcelona: Lunwerg Editores S.A., 1990, pp. 323–34.

Romero, Alfonso and Santi Cabasa. *La tinajería tradicional en la cerámica española*. Barcelona: Ediciones Ceac, 1999.

Romero de Terreros, Manuel. *Artes Industriales en la Nueva España*. Mexico: Librería de Pedro Robredo, 1923.

Roselló Verger, María and F. Costell Landete. "La Escuela de Cerámica de Manises ante las nuevas tecnologias, I." *Silicatos* 5 (1992), pp. 22–24.

Royo Navarro, Francisco. "La escuela madrileña de cerámica." *Revista d'informació ciutadana* 18 (winter 1996).

Rubin de la Borbolla, Daniel F. "Objects from Everyday Life." In *The Ephemeral and the Eternal of Mexican Folk Art*, (2 volumes). Mexcio: Fondo Editorial de la Plástica Mexicana, 1971, pp. 126–27.

Sahagún, Fray Bernardino de. *Historia General de las Cosas de la Nueva España*. México: Editorial Porrúa, 1982.

Salinas Calado, Rafael. *Faiança Portuguesa. Portuguese Faience*. Portugal : Direction of Philatelic Services, Portuguese Post Office, 1992.

Sánchez-Cortegana, José María. *Arte Hispalense: El oficio de ollero en Sevilla en el siglo XVI*. Sevilla: Excelentísima Diputación Provincial de Sevilla, 1994.

Sánchez, José María. "La cerámica exportada a América en el siglo XVI a través de la documentación del Archivo General de Indias. Parte I: Materiales arquitectónicos y contenedores comerciales," Universidad de Sevilla, Departamento de Historia del Arte, *Laboratorio de Arte* 9 (1996), pp. 125–42.

———. "La cerámica exportada a América en el siglo XVI a través de la documentación del Archivo General de Indias. Parte II: Ajuares domésticos y cerámica cultural y laboral." Universidad de Sevilla, Departamento de Historia del Arte, *Laboratorio de Arte* 11 (1998), pp. 121–33.

Sánchez-Pacheco, Trinidad. "Cerámica valenciana," in *Musea Nostra: Museo de Cerámica, Palacio de Pedralbes Barcelona*. Barcelona: Ludion, 1993, pp. 17–32.

———. *Cerámica española*. Barcelona: Edi-Balmes, 1995.

Sánchez-Pacheco, Trinidad (editor). *Cerámica española. Summa Artis, historia general del arte* LII. Madrid: Espasa Calpe, 1997.

———. "Cerámica de Talavera de la Reina y Puente de Arzobispo." In *Cerámica española. Summa Artis, historia general del arte* XLII. Madrid: Espasa Calpe, 1997, pp. 305–42.

Sánchez Ramos, Santiago. "Intoxicaciones en la industria y laboratorios cerámicos." *Silicatos* 4 (1991), pp. 38–41.

Sánchez Ramos, Santiago and Pablo Botella Asunción. "Intoxicaciones en la industria y laboratorios cerámicos II. Tóxicos y su destino en el organismo. Efectos tóxicos de los silicatos." *Silicatos* 5 (1992), pp. 30–36.

Sancho Corbacho, Antonio. "Los azulejos de Madre de Dios de Sevilla." *Archivo Español de Arte* 22/87 (1949).

Scholes, France V. "The Supply Service of the New Mexico Missions in the Seventeenth Century, I–III," *New Mexico Historical Review* 5 (1930), pp. 93–115; 186–210; 386–404.

Schütz, Ilse. *Fang '92. La alfarería actual de Agost*. (Catálogo de la exposición). Agost: Centro Agost/Museo de Alfarería, 1992.

———. *La mujer en la alfarería española*. Agost: Centro Agost/Museo de Alfarería, 1993.

———. "Motivos y consecuencias de los cambios tecnológicos en la alfarería tradicional de Agost." *Visión global y acción local. IV Simposio Internacional de Investigación Cerámica y Alfareria* Agost: Centro Agost, 1995.

———. "En tiempos de los fundadores de la ermita de las santas Justa y Rufina." *Forum Cerámico* 4 (1995), pp. 24–37.

Seifert, Donna J. "Archaeological Majolicas of the Rural Teotihuacan Valley, Mexico." Ph.D. Dissertation, University of Iowa, 1977.

Seijo Alonso, Francisco. *Cerámica popular en la región valenciana*. Alicante, 1977.
Sempere y Gouriños, Don Juan. *Historia del luxo y de las leyes suntuarias en España* (2 volumes). Madrid: Atlas (facsímile), 1973.
Serrera, Ramón María. "El camino de México a Acapulco." In *El Galeón de Manila*. Sevilla: Aldeasa, Ministerio de Educación, Cultura y Deporte, 2000, pp. 39–49.
Seseña, Natacha. "Influencia del turismo en la evolución de la cerámica popular española." Comunicación al *Coloquio Internacional de estudios Etnográficos Rocha Peixoto*, Povoa de Varzim, Portugal, octubre 1966.
———. *La cerámica popular en Castilla La Nueva*. Madrid: Editora Nacional, 1975.
———. *Una clasificación de la cerámica popular española*. Cuadernos del Seminario de Estudios Cerámicos de Sargadelos 21. La Coruña: Ediciones del Castro, 1977.
———. *Las lozas de Talavera y Puente*. Madrid: Mercado Puerta de Toledo, S.A.. 1989.
———. "Doble mirada a las lozas de Talavera y Puente." In *Las lozas de Talavera Puente*. Madrid, 1989, pp. 19–35.
———. "El búcaro de las Meninas." In *Velázquez y el arte de su tiempo*. Madrid, 1991, pp. 39–48.
———. *Barros y lozas de España*. Madrid: Ediciones Prensa Española, Magisterio Español y Editora Nacional, 1996.
———. *Los disparates de la comisaria. La vida cotidiana en tiempos de Goya*. Madrid: Sociedad Estatal Goya, 1996.
———. *Cacharrería popular. La alfarería de basto en España*. Madrid: Alianza Editorial, 1997.
———. "Producción Popular en Talavera y Puente del Arzobispo." *Archivo Español de Arte* 161.
Sewall Samuel. *The Diary of Samuel Sewall*. New York: Farrar, Straus & Giroux, 1973.
Sierra Álvarez, José and Isabel Tuda Rodríguez. "Sureda y la renovación de la cerámica española durante el primer tercio del siglo XIX." In *Bartolomé Sureda (1679–1851): Arte e Industria en la Ilustración Tardía*. Madrid: Museo Municipal, 2000, pp. 89–158.
———. *Las lozas de Valdemorillo (1845–1915)*. Madrid, 1996.
Snow, Cordelia Thomas. "A Brief History of the Palace of the Governors and a Preliminary Report on the 1974 Excavation." *El Palacio* 80/3 (October 1974), pp. 1–22.
Snow, David H. "Purchased in Chihuahua for Feasts." In *El Camino Real de Tierra Adentro*, compiled by Gabrielle G. Palmer. Bureau of Land Management, Cultural Resources Series No. 11 (1993), pp. 133–46.
Soler, María Paz. *Historia de la cerámica valenciana* (4 volumes). Valencia: Vicente García, 1987, 1988.
Somé, Pilar and Rosario Huarte. "La Cerámica moderna en el convento del Carmen (Sevilla)." *Arqueología medieval* 6 (October 1999).
Spanish Archives of New Mexico (SANM), New Mexico State Records Center and Archives, Santa Fe.
Stoopen, María. "Edificar una confluencia: Las simientes del mestizaje en el siglo XVI." *Artes de Mexico* 36 (1997), pp. 20–29.
Spate, H.K. Oskar. *The Spanish Lake*. Minneapolis: University of Minnesota, 1979.
Suárez y Farias, María Cristina. "Edificar un rito: De dioses, casas y cocinas Mexicas." *Artes de Mexico*, 36 (1997), pp. 8–17.
———. "Edificar Identidades: De ambitos y sabores virreinales." *Artes de Mexico*, 36 (1997), pp. 30–49.
Subiás, María Pía. "La cerámica decorada en la época del Noucentisme." In *Cerámica Española. Summa Artis, historia general del arte* XLII, edited by Trinidad Sánchez-Pacheco. Madrid: Espasa Calpe, 1997, pp. 529–50.
Telese Compte, Albert. "Cataluña." In *Medi-terra-neum: Cerámica medieval en España e Italia*. Barcelona, 1992, pp. 92–102.
———. "Platos de cenefa punteada." *Galería Antiquaria* (1993).
———. *La vaixella blava catalana de 1570 a 1670*. Barcelona: Carrera Edició, 1991.
Toussaint, Manuel. *Arte Colonial en México*. México: Instituto de Investigaciones Estéticas/UNAM, 1974.
Tozzer, Alfred M. *Landa's Relacion de las Cosas de Yucatán*. Papers of the Peabody Museum of Archaeology and Ethnology, Harvard University, 18 (1941).
Tudela, José: "Tibores coloniales mejicanos en los palacios reales de Italia." *Revista de Indias* (1943), pp. 35–43.
Umbert, Marcelino. España en la Exposición Universal de París de 1878: la ciencia, las artes, la industria, el comercio y la producción de España y de sus colonias ante los jurados internacionales. Madrid, M. Minuesa, 1879.
Valdivieso, Enrique. *A Guide for a cultural visit to the Church of El Señor San Jorge and the courtyards of La Santa Caridad Hospital in the city of Seville*. Seville: Hermandad de la Santa Caridad, 1998.

Vaca González, Diodoro and Juan Ruiz de Luna. *Historia de la cerámica de Talavera de la Reina y algunos datos sobre la del Puente de Arzobispo.* Madrid: Editora Nacional, 1943.

Vasconcellos, Carolina M. *Algunas palavras a respeito de pucaros de Portugal.* Coimbra, 1921.

Vetancurt, Fray Agustin de. *Teatro Mexicano: Descripción breve de los sucessos exemplares de la Nueva-Espana en el nuevo mundo occidental de Las Indias* (2 volumes) [1698]. Madrid: Coleccion Chimalistac 9 (facsímile of 1698 edition), 1960.

Vicent Lerma, Joseph. *La mayólica gótico-mudéjar en la ciudad de Valencia.* Valencia: Ministerio de Cultura, 1992.

Vidal Castro, Francisco. *El agua en la arquitectura de Al Andalus.* Barcelona: Lunewerg, 1995.

Villa Sánchez, Fray Juan. *Puebla sagrada y profana, informe dado a su ilustre Ayuntamiento el año de 1746.* Puebla, 1746.

Villar Movellán, Alberto. *Arquitectura del Regionalismo en Sevilla (1900–1935).* Sevilla: Excma. Diputación Provincial de Sevilla, 1979.

Villegas, Victor M. *Arte Popular de Guanajuato.* México: Banco Nacional de Fomento Cooperativo, S.A. de C.V., Fondo de Fideicomiso para el Fomento de las Artesanías, 1964.

Viñamata, Águeda. *El Rococó.* Barcelona: Montesinos, 1987.

Vinyoles, María Teresa. *El memjar a la Barcelona gótica: necessitat, primacia i ritu social. Del rebost a la taula. Cuina i menjar a la Barcelona gótica.* Barcelona: Electa, 1995.

Vossen, Rudiger. *Töpferei in Spanien.* Hamburgo: Hamburguisches Museum für Volkerkunde, 1972.

Vossen, Rudiger, Natacha Seseña and Wulf Köpke. *Guia de los alfares de España.* Madrid: Editora Nacional, 1984.

Welty, Johanna. "Talavera: An Overview of Viceregal Majolica." *Antiques West Newspaper* 12/12 (1992), pp. 4, 8.

Index

Abó Polychrome style, **213**, 216, **235**, 241
aborronado technique, 215, 238, 239
Aguascalientes, 315–36
Aguilar, Florentino, 283
Alcázar, 85, 86
Alfar 3, 147
alfardones, 81
Alhambra, 4, **6**, 73, 79, **80**, 99
alicatados, 59, 205
aliceres, 78–79
altar screen, tile, **87**
amphoras, **43**
Andalusia, 3–4
Andries, Francisco, 86
apprentices, 12–13
Aranama Polychrome, 241
architecture: and interior decoration, 65; use of ceramics in, 77–101, 218, 220–23
arista technique, 82, 86, 90, 92, 93, 128, 129, 206
Art Deco style, 157, 160
Artigas, Josep Llorens, 160
Art Nouveau style, 73, 275
Augusta, Cristóbal de, 86, 126
Avec-Gremio, 177
Aztecs, 247, 249
baptismal fonts, 8, **28**, 51, **52**, 71
Barcelona, 151–69; American artists in, 165–66; ceramics training in, 183
Baroque style, 15–17, 33, 91–92, 306, 308
Barranco, Francisco, 196
Barrera, Francisco, 195
basins, **37**, **290**, **291**
Belvedere, Andrea, 196
Berain, Jean, 15, 71
beverages, 67; chocolate as, 195, 245–66
bisqueware, 136, **311**
bodegones, 193
Bosco, Ricardo Velázquez, 127
Böttger, Johann Friedrich, 15
bottles, **189**
bowls, **14**, **16**, **190**, **258**, **325**, **331**; Abó Polychrome, **240**; barber, **62**; Olinalá, 195–96; Puebla Blue-on-white, **238**; ready for firing, **316**; sugar, **240**; Tewa Polychrome, **265**
Bristol ware, 39
bucaritos, 196
búcaros, 190, 198–99
bumblebee mark, 216
Burgués, Marià, 45

cacao beans: as currency, 247
Cal, Pedro de la, 178, **179**
Cañas, Manuel, 123
cartabón, 93
Castellón: ceramics school in, 182
Castilla, 87
Catalan ceramics, 151–69
Catalan tilework, 91, 153, **158**, **159**
ceramics: in Aguascalientes, 315–36; architectural use of, 77–101, 127, 218, 220–23; and aromas, 189–90; as ballast in ships, 6, 111; in Catalonia, 151–69; collections, 117–19, 126, 179, 191–93, 273, 278; and commerce, 106; competition from plastic and stainless steel, 131; connection to other decorative materials, 104; consolidation of manufacturing centers, 33; counterfeit, 112; decorative, 176, 180; in dining areas, 66–68; distribution of, **26**, 114–17; in dressing rooms, 70; eating of, 189, 194, 198; and economic factors, 104; and glass and textile industries, 105; historical, 73; Indian-made, 265; Italian Renaissance influence on, 7, 60, 63; Italy as great producer of, 130; and kitchen utensils, 52–54; marketing of, 117, 119; and metalworking, 62–65; Mexican, 187–203; multiple uses of, 53, 54, 111; new forms, 291; organoleptic properties, 189; painting of, **20**, 72, **139**, 153; in paintings, 14, **57–58**, **108**, 193–96, 259, 262; and quality control, 292; and religion, 51–52, 71–72; reuse of, 105; shipped to colonies, 6; signing of, 82–83; styles in, 32–34; techniques introduced by Spanish to Mesoamerica, 206; and technology, 7, 172; Tonalá, 188–92, 199–201; used in towers, 79
ceramics production: competition requires break with traditional production, 180; historical factories, 136–38, 148; new factories, 139–40, 149; shift from coarse wares to decorative objects, 173; small workshops, 141–48, 149; workshop types, 134, 136
ceramists: and *arista* technique, 92; changes in, 83; cooperatives for, 132, 178; relocation of, 89; training for, 132–34, 179–83, 305
chamber pots, **18**
champlevé enamel, 80
chiaroscuro, 84, 155
La Chocolatada (tile panel), **69**, 97
chocolate, 68, 195, 245–66; addiction to, 249; as aphrodisiac, 251; Columbus and Benzoni on, 248; consumption of, 247; and foam, 247, 249; importance of, 250, 259; as medicine, 251; method of preparation, 247; new vessels developed for, 253; recipe books for, 252; and spices, 247, 249; in wafers, 249–50
cisterns, **53**
clay, 134, 144, 161, 172, 188, 189, 324; aroma of, 199; processing of, 326
clay water, 195
climate, 127
Cobo, Bernabé, 207, 212
colors, 28, 93, 98, 128, 137, 153, 159, 160, 207, 239–41, 272, 300, 302, 306, 312, 330; bright, 127; five traditional, 19; green substituted for blue, 236; increased range of, 94; industrial, 140; limited range of, 79; and metal oxides, 109; and Mudéjar ceramics, 5; sources for, 327; symbolism and, 51
Consejo Regulador de Talavera, 292, 293
containers: shipping, 6, 107, 115–16; storage, 52, 197
convents: closing of, 272; and kitchens, 258
cooperatives, 178
crypts, 208, **209**
Crystal Palace, **126**, **127**
cuerda seca, 147–48, 206; painting of, **139**
cup and saucer, **68**
cups, **234**; Abo Polychrome, **240**; chocolate, **253**
curiosity cabinets, 193

dados, 84–85, 89, 138, 153
David, Rafael Valls, 181
La Decadence, 154–55
"Della Robbia" school, 132–33, 145, 147
design, 41, 99; in flooring, 91; four-tile arrangement, 93; and imagery in Islamic art, 21 n.8; polychrome, 19; use of concentric circles, **331**; *See also* motifs; patterns
desornamentado, 86, 89
dining rooms, 260–63
dinnerware, 159, 288
Disdier, María, 96
Domènech i Montaner, Lluís, 156–57
domes, 218, **220**, **321**

earthenware, 2, 106–108, 159, **173**, 257; effect of changing lifestyles upon demand for, 174; Guadalajara, 193; and Juan Miró, 160; and Puebla, 221–22; red-slipped, 192; as street pavement, 156; as transport vessels, 116
Eixample neighborhood, 156
Encinas, Gaspar de, 211
Escaler, Lambert, 45
La Escuela de Cerámica de Manises, 176–77
Espinosa, Antonio, 274
Espinosa, Juan de, 195

factories: *See* workshops; *workshops in named locales*
fees and taxes, 112–13
Fernández, Juan, 85
Ferreyro, Mercedes, **144**

flooring, tile, **88**, **96**, **208**
Floris, Jan, 7, 31, 84
fragrant water, 190
functionality and ornamentation, 66

Gage, Thomas, 249
Gallissà, Antoni Maria, 156–57
Gaudí i Cornet, Antoni, 98, 156
Gautier, Teófilo, 198
Generation of '98, 19, 41–42
Gestoso, José, 125–26, 128
glassware, 262
glazes, 2, 7, 18–19, 39, 234, 302, 327; applying, **20**; lead and safety concerns, 292, 305, 312; new recipes for, 292
Goggin, John, 230
González, Aníbal, 123
González, Cayetano, 124
González, Gorky, **301**–306
González, Juan Silva, 316, **317**, 319–20, **327**, 334, **336**
gothic flooring, **81**
Guanajuato, 297–312
Guardiola, Josep Jordi, 159, 160
Guevara, Jorge, **285**
Guijarro, Fernán Martínez, 117
guilds, 13, 18, 50, 56, 155, 180, 213, 232, 236, 242 n.23; new Spanish constitution eliminates potter's, 271

Hernández, Javier de Jesús, 306, **307**
Hernández, Roque, 86
Hidalgo y Costilla, Miguel, 18, 298, 317
Hoffman, Carlos, 228–29, 236
hollowware, 16, 32, 68, 239, 241, 300
holy-water stoups, **34**, 71, 72
home decoration, 60–61
horror vacui, 5, 51, 215
House of the Figures, 221, **223**

Ibero-American Exposition of 1929, 124, 125, 129–31, 134, 138, 146
imperio style, 126
inkwells, **42**
interior decoration: and architecture, 65
inventories: chocolate vessels recorded in, 264; exported merchandise, 61; vessels of Catalina Véles de Guevara, 191
Islamic artisans, 10
istoriato style, 14, 59, 166

jalón technique, 330
Jarandilla, Alejandro, 161–65, **163**
jars, **2**, **41**, **44**, **62**, **73**, **137**, **141**, **142**, **272**, **275**, **287**, **290**, **291**, **300**, **306**, **308**, **312**; apothecary, **53**, **152**; chocolate storage, **255**; drug, 151, 152; honey, **58**; memory, 166, 169 n.22; oil, **39**; olive, 6, **116**; pharmacy, **54**; for preserves, **324**; Puebla-style, **288**; storage, **11**, **12**, **16**; Tonalá, **188**, **200**, **201**
jícaras, **68**, 247, 254, 259

kick wheels, 326
kilns, 7, **13**, 129, 130, 133, 236, 304–305; electric and oil fueled, 178; excavated, 237–38, 316; and firing process, 328–29; glaze-frit, 180; large capacity, 172; natural gas fueled, 101, 131, 312; updraft and tunnel, 130–31, 178; wood-fired, 307
kitchens, 52, 65, 218, **219**, 257–60; depiction on tile panel, **95**, **164**; mission, 257; secular, 259

Ledesma, Gabriel Frenández, **322**
Lichtenstein, Roy, 166
Lister, Robert and Florence, 230
loza amarilla, 13, 213
loza colorado, 318, 319
loza común, 13, 213, 234, 272, **273**
loza de pedernal, 36
loza dorada, 29
loza entrefina, 234
loza fina, 13, 213
loza tradicional, **108**
Luna, Juan Ruiz de, 19
lusterware, 5, 73, 119, 174, 217; appearance in paintings, 58; fonts of, 71; production of, 27–30; and table service, 55, 57

Madrid, Lorenzo de, 90, 91–92, 155
Magalotti, Lorenzo, 195, 196–97
Málaga, 28
Mallorca, 27
mancerinas, **68**, 254
Manila galleons, 9, 30, 110, 215, 271
Manises, 56, 174–76, 181, 193
Mansilla del Pino, Ignacio, 34
manual labor, 176, 181
mariposa, 32
Martín, Francisco, 211
Martín Garrido, Juan, 207
mayólica, 108–109, 174; in the Age of Enlightenment, 35–37; and archaeological excavations, 230; blue and blue-orange series, 238–39; Catalan revitalization of, 161; change in fabrication of, 30; and decals, 38; and decoration, 307; definition and synonymous terms, 1–2, 224 n.1; green series, 240–41; industrial, 37–38; markets for, 38; Mexican influence, 7–10; and Mudéjar, 27–30; origins of, 2–14; polychrome, 152–53; revivals of, 41–45, 278–84; as substitute for porcelain, 2–3; uses for, 262
mayólica production, 78, 302; in Aragón, 97; in Mexico, **8**, 227–41; and old manufacturing ways, 38–41; Puebla vs. Mexico City and other locales, 227–31; in Spain, **4**; women and, 12; *See also workshops in named locales*
McConnell, Lisa, 166
Meléndez, Luis, 199

Mendieta, Gerónimo, 231
Mexico City: evidence for early Spanish potters in, 231–32; excavations in, 238; ordinances for potters in, 232–34; and production of mayólica, 227–41
Miró, Jean, 160
Misiones Pedagógicas, 181
mixing tanks, **326**
molds, 80, **276**, 301, 304, 312
molinillos, 260
Moreno, Angélica, **286**, 287
Moriscos, 232
mortars, **53**
mosaic tile panels, **50**, **80**
motifs, 40–41, 59, 72, 81, 84, 91, 140, 201, 239, **278**, 306; abstract, 240; on altar tiles, 216; arabesque, 199; Asian, 71; asymmetrical, 64; bobbin lace, 215, 234, 239, **265**; in churches, 90–91; floral, 86, 272, 310; *florón principal*, 85; framed by concentric circles, 238; fruit, 95; geometric, 153, 199, 310; intermingling of, 86; irregular octofoil, 208; more varied, 94; on Puebla tiles, 215; recoving traditional, 142; *serie floreada*, 153; three-lobed, 152; vegetable, 199; *See also* design; patterns
Mudéjares, 5, 50, 232
Mudéjar styles, 206
Museo de Cerámica: sign, **279**

narrative painting, 7, 14
neogothic, 155–56
Neomudéjar style, 127
New Mexico: mayólica from Mexico City and Puebla found in, 263
Niculoso, Francisco, 7, 29, 83–84, 126, 206–207
Nogués, Xavier, **73**, 160
Nopaltepac Polychrome, 241
Novocentista movement, 74
numbering system, 330

olives, 74 n.4
Olvera, Jorge, **317**
ordinances for potters, 232
Ovando y Villavicencio, Agustín, 221

Padierna, José Miguel, **285**
Palacios, Francisco, 196
Palomino, Miguel Fernández, 216
Passoles, Lorenzo, 92
pastillaje, 199
El Patriarca, 89, 90
patterns, 88–89, 300, **332–33**, **335**; Aguascalientes, **325**; *cartabón*, 93; diamond, **90**; *helechos*, 32; *jalón amarillo*, **331**; *laurel*, 320–21; Talavera, 32; *See also* design; motifs
Peiró, 45
Pepper, Beverly, 165–66
Pereda, Antonio de, 195
Pezaro, Francisco de, 211
Philippines, 215
pisano technique, 206
pitchers, **34**, **323**
Pizón, Juan, 211
plates, **3**, **11**, **27**, **29**, 30, 32, 33, 40, **71**, **139**, **144**, **146**, **265**, **274**, 275, 283, **284**, 300, 310, 323, **334**; Abo Polychrome, **9**, **235**; Aranama Polychrome, **236**; with *jalón amarillo* pattern, **331**; lusterware, **55**, **56**; Nopaltepac Polychrome, **236**; Orangeline Polychrome, **239**; San Elizario Polychrome, **237**; San Luis Blue-on-white, **239**; trick, **67**
platters, **278**, **290**
Plaza de España, **133**, **135**
polychrome adornment, 62
polychrome finishes, 59
porcelain, 2, 5, 67, 109–10, 112, 181, 215
porringers, **27**, **54**
posoleros, 326, 330, 331
pots: for chocolate, **246**, **256**; for flowers, **147**
potter's marks, 215–16; absence of, 235
potters' quarters, 10
potter's wheel, 7
pottery, 323–24; exportation to United States, 320; importation into Mexico, 320; and Pueblo Indians, 265; types of, 13
pounce bags, 40
Puebla, 9, 206, 223, 229; as center for manufacturing mayólica, 210–13; and earthenware production, 221–22; and glass vessels, 262
Puebla Polychrome, **213**, 215, **235**, 239
La Purísima, 178

Ramírez, César Torres, **286**
Recco, Guiseppe, 196
redona style, 88
Regionalism, 123, 124, 127
Rejano, Manuel Ramos, 44
Rejano, Ramos, 124
Renaissance style, 91–92
Renart, Dionís, 45
Reyner, Francesc, 29
Rococo style, 15–17, 64, 67
Rodríguez, Diego, 212

Sahagún, Bernadino de, 231
saltcellars, 63, 64
San Elizario Polychrome, **235**, 239
San Jeronimo panel, **92**
San Jorge panel, **93**
San Juan Polychrome, **234**
San Luis Polychrome, 240
San Martin Tower, **79**
Santa María Polychrome, 240–41
Santiago, Herrando de, 89
saucers: chocolate, **254**
secularization, 56

serie floreada, 152–53
serigraphy, 139
Sevilla, 5, 86, 87; and ceramics production, 29; decline in tilework, 124; lack of ceramics museum, 124; mayólica workshops in, 6; reinvention of, 123
sherds, 156, 189, **264**, **298**, **299**
Simón, Antonio, 90
soup tureens, **36**
spice holders, **63**
stencils, 40
styles: austerity in, 72, 74, 90; imitative, 111; *See also styles by name*
supply shortages, 109
Sureda, Bartolomé, 36
symmetry, 64

tableros, 218, 220, 221, 274, 281
table settings, **287**
table top, **166**
tableware, 30–31, 54–55, 67, 96, 155, 173; and cost of production, 104–105; and new specialized wares, 64
talavera: commercial use of the word, 293
Talavera, Juan, 123
Talavera de la Reina, 7, 15, 86, 87, 177–78, 178; ceramics school in, 182; and color in ceramics, 33
tapestry, **65**
tibores, 191, 201, 254, 275
tile factories: division of labor in, 95–96
tile panels, **89**, **125**, **140**, **143**, **153**, **164**, **221**, **255**, **274**, **277**, **279**, **280**, **281**, **282**, **289**
tile production: and construction boom, 98; and Guanajuato, 222; more efficient methods of manufacture used, 98; and Valencia, 82; and workshops, 129
tiles, **6**, 31, **35**, 59, **60**, **90**, **145**, **146**, **153**, **155**, **216**; Abo polychrome, **213**; *Arista*, **128**, **138**; *artes y oficios*, 216; cherub heads, **217**; depicted in paintings, **81**, **257**; and depiction of scenes, 94; earliest date for, 78; as facade for buildings, 18; for flooring, 81–82; geometric, 18; for home decoration, 280; for liturgical use, 218; as medium for storytelling, 84; Mexican genre scenes, 282; in the Middle Ages, 78–80; in mosaic panels, **50**; narrative, 97; new uses found for, 94, 99; pictorial, 18; Puebla Polychrome, **213**, **235**; relief, 216, **217**; reuse of damaged, 105; signed or marked, 215–16; in Spanish colonial interiors, 207; as wall decorations, 65, 320–21
tilework: Catalan, 91, 153, **158**, **159**; on church domes, 218, **220**, **321**; on church facade, **214**; on fountain, **322**; mosaics, **80**; pictorial, 18
tin-enameling, 3–4; and health, 50, 98
tobacco, 69
Toledo, 85, 86, 87
tombstones, 72
tourism, 174, 179
Toussaint, Manuel, 229
trade, 3, 5, **8**, 27, 39, 110, 111, 126; and chocolate, 246–47; and independent registry, 36
trade shows, 177
trade tiles, **98**, 216
transferware, 159
trecandis, 166
trencadis, **100**, 156, 157, 166–67
Triana, 6, 10, 29, 129, 130, 193, 206; decline in tile factories, 130
trompe l'oeil, 65, 157

Uriarte, Dimas, 273–74
Uriarte, Isauro, 19

Valencia, 28–29, 56, **87**, 91; Baroque tiles in high demand, 97; ceramics school in, 182; first tile factories in, 95–96; and Gothic style, 88; importance as tile-producing center, 82
Valenzuela, Fernando de, 192
Valladares, Fernando de, 207–208
Van der Hamen, Juan, 194
Vélez de Guevara, Catalina, 191
Ventosa, Enrique Luis, 19, 222, 227, 273, 274, 280, 281
vessels, 189, 191, 193, 195, 223; drinking, **192**; earthenware, 193; effect on water stored in, 194, 201; Olinalá, 195
Vetancurt, Agustín de, 263
Vienna Sezession, 99
La Visitación (Pisano), 84

walls and benches, tiled, **86**
women: addiction to chocolate, 249; European acceptance of chocolate, 251; food-culture exchange and, 249; gender roles and, 177; kitchens and, 52; Mexican workshops and, 286–87; painting of kitchenware by, 72; production of mayólica and, 12; superstitions about, 12
workshops, 161–65, 207; in colonial period, 237; and division of labor, 329; effect of labor laws, taxes, and regulations on, 172; illumination in, 66; restructuring of, 179
workshops in Mexico (Aguascalientes), 318; Bernadé Hernández alfar (defunct), 316; El Caballo Blanco, 316, 322, 323, **336**
workshops in Mexico (Guanajuato): Alfarería Tradicional, **303**, **304**; Taller de Alfarería Mayólica de Guanajuato, 307–311
workshops in Mexico (Puebla): Arte Cerámica, 286; Casa la Paz, 283, 284, 286; Casa Padierna, 275, **276**, 283, 285, 293; Casa Rugerio, 281, 283;

Celia, 287; Cerámica Artística Aguilar, 286; Cerámica Artística de Puebla, 283, 284, 285; César Torres, 293; La Concepción, 283, 285, 293; La Corona, 285, 286; Fábrica de Loza de Talavera, 273; Martínez y Cía., 275, 281; Pedro Tecayehuatl, 285; Talavera de la Reina, 287, 293; La Trinidad, 282, 283, 285, 293; Uriarte Talavera, 273–74, 280–81, 283, 285, 288, 291, 293
workshops in Mexico (Santa Rosa): Alfarería Aguilera, 311–12
workshops in Spain, 37, 42–45, 134–49; (La) Menora, 44; addresses for, 148–49; Alcora, 35, 37, 66, 67, 70, 72, 96, 180; Alfar 3, 147–48; Antonio González Artistic Ceramics, 140; Buen Retiro, 36, 67, 72; El Carmen, 44, 177; La Cartuja, 42; CEARCO, 139–40; Cerámica Águilas, **141–42**; Cerámica Artística Hera, 146; Cerámica Gran Poder, 141–42; Cerámica Luchana, 143–44; Cerámica Ruiz Gil, 143; Ceràmicas Camaro, 161–62, 164–65, 167; La Ceramo, 42; La Corchuela, 132, 142; Fábrica de José Tova Villalba, 44; José María Campos, 145–46; Lucía Arriaga, 146–47; La Menora, 177, 178; Mensaque Rodríguez Company, 138; Mercedes Ferreyro, 144–45; La Moncloa, 36–37, 72; Montalván Ceramics, 136–37; Montfont S. A. Capellades, 161; Nuestra Señora de la O, 44, 136; Nuestra Señora del Prado, 44; Pasajes, 72; Pickman Factory, 100, 128; San Juan de Aznalfarache, 42; Santa Ana Ceramics, 44, 138; Santa Isabel Ceramics, 137–38; Soto and Company, 42
writing sets, **70**

xicalli, 247, 253

Zaragosa, 93